J.H. Andrews (1927–2019) was born in England and educated at the universities of Cambridge and London. He taught historical geography at Trinity College, Dublin, from 1954, where he became a Fellow of the College in 1969 and retired as associate professor in 1990. He was a member of the Royal Irish Academy and a past president of the Geographical Society of Ireland. Professor Andrews published many papers on historical geography and the history of cartography, and two books on the Ordnance Survey of Ireland, *History in the Ordnance Map* (1974) and *A Paper Landscape* (1975). He was also the author of *Shapes of Ireland: Maps and Their Makers* (1997) and *The Queen's Last Map-Maker: Richard Bartlett in Ireland, 1600–3* (2008). From 1971 to 1979 he was secretary to the editorial committee of the Atlas of Ireland published by the Royal Irish Academy, and was co-editor of the Academy's Irish Historic Towns Atlas from 1981 to 1992.

J.H. Andrews (1927–2019)
Image taken from F.H.A. Aalen and Kevin Whelan (eds),
*Dublin, City and County: From Prehistory to Present:
Studies in Honour of J.H. Andrews*
(Dublin: Geography Publications, 1992)
Courtesy of Prof. William Nolan

Plantation Acres

MAPPING IRELAND
The Irish land surveyor and his maps

In memory of
Paul Campbell
December Publications, Belfast
(1948–2021)

Cover images:
Theodolite, Rowland Houghton, *c.* 1735
(American Philosophical Society Museum)
Excerpt from Down Survey map of Co. Waterford *c.* 1665–70
(Bibliothèque Nationale de France)

Published in 2025
by Ulster Historical Foundation
www.ulsterhistoricalfoundation.com

Except as otherwise permitted under the Copyright, Designs and Patents Act 1988, this publication may only be reproduced, stored or transmitted in any form or by any means with the prior permission in writing of the publisher or, in the case of reprographic reproduction, in accordance with the terms of a licence issued by The Copyright Licensing Agency. Enquiries concerning reproduction outside those terms should be sent to the publisher.

© The estate of J.H. Andrews, Arnold Horner
and Ulster Historical Foundation

ISBN: 978-1-913993-76-4

DESIGN AND FORMATTING
December Publications
and FPM Publishing

COVER DESIGN
J.P. Morrison

PRINTED BY
Sprint Books

Contents

PREFACE	xi
PREFACE TO SECOND EDITION	xii
A NOTE ON J.H. ANDREWS AND THE MAKING OF *PLANTATION ACRES* by Arnold Horner	xiv
ACKNOWLEDGEMENTS 2025	xx
NOTE ON REFERENCES	xx

1	Surveying without maps	1
2	The only ground-work of our plantation	28
3	Controllers of the admeasurements	51
4	Public and private	81
5	Owners an tenants	110
6	Portraying the landscape	144

7	Remaking the landscape	187
8	Surveyors in society	222
9	Heads of their profession?	265
10	Tricks of the trade	295
11	Breaking into print	331
12	Taxes and tithes	363
13	Mapping without surveyors	387

APPENDICES

A	A surveyor's advice to farmers	406
B	Surveyors in dispute, 1743–1798	411
C	Peter Callan versus John Bell, 1753–1760	413
D	Books on land surveying published or advertised in Ireland	429
E	The cost of surveying	439

INDEXES

Personal names	445
Place names	455
Subjects	464

List of tables

1.	Land units in part of Co. Roscommon	9
2.	Some early Irish land measures	11
3.	A sample of medieval acreage figures	14
4.	Varieties of acre	16
5.	Varieties of perch	18
6.	Acreage figures in the survey of Offaly, 1550	20
7.	Scales of Irish farm and estate maps	167
8.	Surnames of Irish surveyors	223
9.	Territorial range of eighteenth-century surveyors	236
10.	Seasonal distribution of surveying	248
11.	Traverse surveys: chains and chaining	296
12.	Examples of Down Survey errors	299
13.	North points in a sample of farm and estate maps	304
14.	Acreage errors in a sample of estate maps	321
15.	Irish county maps	348

List of figures

1.	Examples of townland networks	7
2.	Part of the Bride and Blackwater valleys, 1589	37
3.	English and Scottish plantations, 1586–1625	53
4.	The pattern of estates in part of Co. Roscommon, 1852–3	111
5.	Eighteenth-century land measures in Munster	123
6.	Examples of surveyors' farm boundaries	205
7.	Distribution of parliamentary enclosure, 1800–29	207
8.	The re-arrangement of rundale holdings, 1918	213
9.	Geographical pattern of surveying activity, 1680–1839	233
10.	Certified surveyors, 1750–1810	235
11.	The Longfield maps	237
12.	Surveys by Henry Hewett, 1733–78	239
13.	Business addresses of Piers Patsull, 1760	241
14.	Patrons and maps of Jacob Neville	243
15.	Surveyors' addresses in the middle Nore and Barrow valleys, 1720–80	245
16.	Calculation of area by latitude and departure	317
17.	Printed town plans, 1700–1840	343

List of plates

Reproductions are by kind permission of the owners and custodians of the following collections: National Library of Ireland (Plates 1, 2, 3, 5, 6, 7, 10, 11, 15, 20, 21b, 25 and 27), Archbishop of Dublin's papers at Trinity College, Dublin (Plate 4), Devonshire Collections (Plate 9), Public Record Office of Northern Ireland (Plates 12 and 29), Public Record Office of Ireland (Plates 13, 14, 22b and 28), Library of Trinity College, Dublin (Plates 17, 18, 19 and 26), Cork Archives Institute (Plate 21a), Marsh's Library, Dublin (Plates 22a and 23), Royal Irish Academy (Plate 24). Some reproductions are reduced in size: scales of originals are given in Irish perches unless otherwise specified.

1.	Strafford Survey extract	61
2.	Down Survey extract	67
3.	Partition map by Garret Hogan	97
4.	Tenement map by Gabriel Stokes	117
5.	Surveys of small areas by John Wilson	134
6.	Demesne map by William Beauford	153
7.	Estate survey by Thomas Moland	157
8.	Manorial survey by John Rocque	163
9.	Town map by Bernard Scalé	165
10.	Estate survey by Sherrard and Brassington	169
11.	Farm map by Henry Hood	171
12.	Estate survey by Thomas Pattison	173
13.	Farm map by P. and C. McQuaid	175
14.	Enlargement of Ordnance Survey map by George Taylor	177
15.	Road map by Thomas Cuttle	195
16.	Bog map by Sherrard, Brassington and Greene	201
17.	Map of rundale farms, by C. P. Brassington	211
18.	Surveyors' newspaper advertisements	225
19.	Map of Dublin by Thomas Sherrard	279
20.	Title page by James Williamson	281
21.	Eighteenth-century surveying instruments	301
22.	Early surveyors' field notes	309
23.	Title page of Henry Osborne's *Exact Way*	319
24.	Printed estate map by Bernard Scalé	333
25.	Map of Queen's Co. by Oliver Sloane	339
26.	Map of Co. Armagh by John Rocque	341
27.	Map of Co. Wexford by Valentine Gill	351
28.	Tithe composition certificate map	374
29.	Map of barony of Orior, Co. Armagh, by William Armstrong	381

Preface

ANY STUDENT OF OLD MAPS must occasionally wish to know more about the people who made them, and there seems room for a book in which this curiosity is directed towards some of Ireland's earliest large-scale surveys, especially those produced by cartographers working wholly or partly outside the ambit of the state. It was before the advent of the Ordnance Survey that these men made their most distinctive contribution to Irish cartography, and I have therefore given most space to the two and a half centuries preceding the reign of Queen Victoria, with the narrative balanced on a fulcrum somewhere near 1750 and the developments of the post-1850 period compressed into a few concluding pages. Within this chronological framework there is a second, thematic, limitation. For many surveyors, map-making was only one facet of a career that also included such diverse activities as estate management, engineering, architecture and property valuation. My policy has been to identify these non-cartographic interests without deviating from the path of map history – and certainly without attempting the breadth and depth which F. M. L. Thompson brought to a whole profession in his *Chartered Surveyors*. Nor is the present book meant to take the place of a biographical directory. It does seek to illustrate the difficulties of such an enterprise by introducing a number of individual cases; but many notable figures have been deliberately left aside in the hope of one day seeing them all included in a new version of Peter Eden's *Dictionary of Land Surveyors and Local Cartographers of Great Britain and Ireland.*

My most informative single source has been some of the hundreds of large-scale maps in the National Library of Ireland. It is a pleasure to pay tribute to this congenial habitat, as well as to the other repositories that share in Ireland's cartographic heritage. What the libraries unfortunately cannot produce is any recognisable mass of written evidence that might help in analysing the maps and anatomising the cartographers. The records that do exist are too patchy and heterogeneous for a classified list of sources to make very much sense, and except for an appendix on early Irish surveying literature no such list has been provided. Secondary sources have in any case been itemised in Paul Ferguson's *Irish Map History, a Select Bibliography of Secondary Works* (1983). Primary sources are exemplified in the end-notes to the present book, but these derive from a series of sampling campaigns rather than the kind of exhaustive search that might be made by a Ph.D. student – or in this instance more probably a small army of such students. Most of the sampling has been done incidentally to other research, so freedom from bias cannot be guaranteed; but at least the results are abundant enough to spare the reader too much wearisome repetition of examples which Mr Ferguson's bibliography has made easily accessible.

In the citation of primary sources spelling has been modernised except where the old forms seem especially pertinent, and punctuation has sometimes been altered in the interest of clarity. Minor topographical names have been introduced more to identify maps than to denote the places themselves, and for this reason it has generally been thought best to preserve their original spelling. Personal names with variant spellings have been standardised, usually in the form most familiar to modern readers.

Apart from long service (not an unmixed blessing) and the occasional stroke of luck, my main asset in writing this book has been the help received from scholars, librarians and archivists. Among these I am especially indebted to Mr F. H. A. Aalen, Miss Ann Barry, Mr Charles Benson, Mr Nicholas Brannon, Dr R. H. Buchanan, Mr Michael Byrne, Miss Mary Clark, Mr Hugh Cobbe, Dr R. C. Cox, Dr Maurice Craig, Dr W. H. Crawford, Mrs Mary Davies, Dr D. J. Dickson, Dr P. J. Duffy, Dr Peter Eden, the late Mr N. W. English, Dr J. B. Harley, Professor J. P. Haughton, Professor G. L. Herries Davies, Ms Ailsa Holland, Mr R.

J. Hunter, Mr Ralph Hyde, Mr Edward Keane, the late Mrs Heather Lawrence, Mrs A. K. Leask, Mr Michael Long, Mr J. P. O'F. Lynam, Dr A. P. W. Malcomson, Mr James McCarthy, Mr Michael McCarthy Morrogh, Professor J. L. McCracken, Dr Edward McParland, Ms Joan Murphy, Mr Kenneth Nicholls, Dr William Nolan, Mr B. Ó Ciobhan, Dr Patrick O'Connor, Dr Patrick O'Flanagan, Professor T. P. O'Neill, Mr William O'Sullivan, Ms Mary Pollard, Mr Thomas Power, Dr Raymond Refaussé, Dr Anngret Simms, the late Dr J. G. Simms, Professor William J. Smyth, Miss Geraldine Tallon, Ms Avril Thomas, Mr G. L'E. Turner, the late Mr Alex Wallace, Mr Julian Walton and Dr Kevin Whelan.

A few more names must be singled out. Mr Richard Haworth's extensive bibliographical knowledge has been placed freely at my disposal for most of the gestation period of this book. My fellow worker in the field of Irish land surveying, the late Sean McMenamin, ungrudgingly approved my use of his index of Ulster surveyors and kept me informed of important new additions to it, a practice continued by the staff of the Public Record Office of Northern Ireland under the direction of Dr Brian Trainor. Dr Rolf Loeber's rare blend of erudition and generosity has brought me a number of out-of-the-way references, as well as a critical reading of the whole book in typescript. Dr Arnold Horner has likewise read the whole text and favoured me with many helpful comments. Members of the Ulster Historical Foundation have earned my gratitude in their capacity as publishers and editors: particular thanks must go to the Administrator, Dr Trainor, for much long-continued encouragement and support; and to Mr Trevor Parkhill for his tireless efficiency in guiding the book through the press. Generous material support has been received from the Provost's Fund of Trinity College, Dublin; the Institute of Irish Studies, Queen's University, Belfast; the Irish Society of Surveying and Photogrammetry; the Northern Ireland branch of the Royal Institution of Chartered Surveyors and the Society of Chartered Surveyors in the Republic of Ireland. Mrs Eileen Russell, Mrs Martha Lyons and Mr Terence Dunne have helped with typing, maps and photographs respectively. My wife made sure that I eventually did something more for the land surveyors than talk about them.

J.H.A.
August 1984

Preface to second edition

THIS REPRINT HAS BEEN PRODUCED by scanning the original text of 1985. A few errors have been corrected and a few references updated, but otherwise there have been no amendments apart from the following brief note.

Nearly all the records of the Irish Ordnance Survey, formerly kept at Phoenex Park, Dublin, are now held by the National Archives of Ireland, a repository which in this book still carries its original name of Public Record Office of Ireland. The archbishop of Dublin's estate maps (now fully listed in Raymond Refaussé and Mary Clark, *A Catalogue of the Maps of the Estates of the Archbishops of Dublin* (Dublin, 2000) have been transferred from Trinity College to the library of the Representative Church Body, Braemor Park, Dublin. The Down Survey maps preserved by the family of Sir William Petty have been acquired by the British Library.

Historical writings on surveying and local cartography in Ireland have appeared in a wide range of publications since 1985. Apart from a few regional studies, they have been mainly concerned with particular surveyors or with particular maps or collections of maps. A full list of individual contributions would include articles by Christine Casey on Joseph Ravell, J. S. Curl on estate maps in Co. Londonderry, Patrick Duffy on Thomas Raven and John Rocque, Peter Harbison on Henry

Pelham, Arnold Horner on Alexander Nimmo, A. Stuart Mason (with John Bensusan-Butt) on Bernard Scalé, Patrick O'Connor on Joshua Wight, Patrick Power on maps of County Wicklow, Jack Redmond on John Rocque, Emer Singleton on Charles Tarrant, Avril Thomas on Archibald Stewart, and W. A. Wallace on John White. The present author has written about David Aher, Josias Bateman, Brian Fitzwilliam, John Hampton, John Longfield and his associates, John Norden, John Thomas, James Williamson, and the cartography of Counties Laois, Offaly and Wexford. Full details of the foregoing publications are given by Paul Ferguson in a revised version of his *Irish Map History: A Select Bibliography of Secondary Works*. This may be seen in typescript in the Map Library of Trinity College, Dublin, and it is hoped shortly to make it available on the college website.

When *Plantation Acres* was first published there seemed to be little chance of placing its subject in an international context. Prospects for doing so have since been improved by the appearance in Britain of several important works, notably Sarah Bendall, *Maps, Land and Society* (1992); Sarah Bendall, *Dictionary of Land Surveyors and Local Map-Makers of Great Britain and Ireland 1530–1850* (two volumes, 1997); Roger J. P. Kain and Elizabeth Baigent, *The Cadastral Map in the Service of the Estate: A History of Property Mapping* (1992); and David H. Fletcher, *The Emergence of Estate Maps: Christ Church, Oxford, 1600 to 1840* (1995). Outside Britain and Ireland much remains to be done: that at least is the impression give in *Rural Images: Estate Maps in the Old and New Worlds*, edited by David Buisseret in 1996. For more recent literature reference should be made to the annual bibliographies by Francis Herbert, published in the international map-historical journal *Imago Mundi*.

J.H.A.
April 2003

A note on J.H. Andrews and the making of *Plantation Acres*

THE AUTHOR OF *PLANTATION ACRES*, John Harwood Andrews, was born at Streatham, London, in May 1927. He died at Chepstow, Wales, in November 2019. For most of his childhood and teenage years, he lived near Purley, on the edge of the North Downs, an area that he later acknowledged as being a stimulus in his developing an interest in landscape and maps. Following a scholarship, he studied Geography at Cambridge between 1944 and 1947 after which he completed his National Service and spent some time as a secondary-school teacher. From 1949 to 1954 he also undertook his PhD part-time at the University of London. In 1954, he was appointed as a lecturer in Geography at Trinity College Dublin, where his academic career extended over the following thirty-six years until his final retirement in 1990.[1]

After early research on a range of topics relating to English seaports and to the historical, economic and political geography of Ireland, John Andrews became increasingly focused on Irish maps, and especially the history of cartography in Ireland. A major stimulus to this developing interest was the 'Ireland in Maps' exhibition which was held in the great Long Room of Trinity College Library during the winter of 1961–2.

John was a central motivator and the effective curator of this initiative, for which he compiled the booklet, *Ireland in Maps*, containing an introductory commentary and catalogue. This experience demonstrated to him the potential for further research on the history of Irish cartography, a challenge which John explored across a broad front.

Several major strands of Irish cartographic history occupied John Andrews over subsequent decades. First, he engaged with the documentary treasure trove associated with the nineteenth-century activities of the Ordnance Survey of Ireland (founded in 1824). The outcome to this was a guide booklet *History in the Ordnance Map: An Introduction for Irish Readers* (1974) and *A Paper Landscape* (1975), a magisterial history of the OS organisation as it developed from its initial brief to create the great six-inches-to-one mile maps of Ireland to being 'a universal cartographic provider' offering a wide range of scales and map types. Second, he maintained an interest in the maps of much earlier periods, most notably those made during the late sixteenth-century as England sought to reassert and extend its control across Ireland. John had a particular fascination with the pioneer work undertaken during 1568–71 by the first major field mapper, Robert Lythe. But John wrote widely on the maps of the plantation period. As well as many articles, he produced one book, *The Queen's Last Map-Maker* (2009) which reviewed the maps of Robert Bartlett, the gifted mapper and illustrator of Ulster around 1600 who met an untimely end in Donegal when the inhabitants 'took off his head because they would not have their country discovered'.[2]

Other interests for John included studies of the maps made by the late eighteenth-century military engineer and antiquarian, Charles Vallancey, and a series of articles on the maps of Dublin city, which took in both the earliest map by John Speed (*c.* 1610) and a painstaking assessment (1973) of nearly twenty 'states' and editions of the 'six-inch' Ordnance Survey map sheet of the city made between 1837 and 1897. Yet another focus was to appraise how small-scale, single-sheet maps of Ireland developed between the mid-sixteenth and the mid-nineteenth centuries, i.e. from the time when Mercator made maps of Ireland to a period when the Ordnance Survey was increasingly influential. *Shapes of Ireland* (1997) selected a series of key maps and cartographers who successively refined the outline of Ireland and who progressively filled in topographic and other detail.

At the same time, John maintained a continuing concern with some more general aspects of Irish historical geography, contributing five chapters to the nine-volume *New History of Ireland* (ed. T.W. Moody, F.X. Martin *et al*, 1976–2005) and, in the 1980s and later. acting as editor and consultant editor to the Irish Historic Towns Atlas. During the 1970s he played a key role in the production of the *Atlas of Ireland*, published by the Royal Irish Academy in 1979. Throughout his career, John also maintained an interest in the history of cartography in general. He was chairman of the Tenth International Conference on the History of Cartography held in Dublin in 1983, and he wrote several articles on what can be broadly called the nature of maps. One of his final books was *Maps in Those Days*, (2009), published when he was aged 82. This was a wide-ranging study that embraced all stages of the mapping process, from conceptualisation through the technical aspects of production to the final presentation.

****

The diversity and sustained originality of John Andrews's scholarly work is quite breath-taking and has resulted in an output of some 250 publications, amongst which are nine books or large monographs and some one hundred articles and book chapters.[3] It is in this context that *Plantation Acres* is perhaps best appreciated. Yet another of John's early foci had been the maps in the National Library of Ireland. A particular attraction of this library, which has an estimated 150,000 maps in its collections, was that it could be easily visited, being on his regular walking route to his office in Trinity. As much as Trinity itself, the National Library was to be part of his staple research diet during John's years in Dublin. Quite apart from its maps, its great collection of early newspapers was a major attraction. To judge from his publications, John spent lengthy periods sampling early papers for advertisements and other references to maps and to surveyors.

One of John's first forays in the National Library was to investigate its unique manuscript collection of early nineteenth century road maps. The library has over 200 large strip-maps, many of them each over three metres in length. Compiled between 1805 and 1817, these maps were made to identify the roads that would be laid out or improved for the then relatively new mail coach services. In 1964, John used them, in conjunction with the legislative documents associated with the establishment of the earlier turnpike roads, to produce a definitive article on the theme of 'road planning in Ireland before the railway age'.[4]

But John's engagement with the estate and farm maps in the National Library proved to be much more wide-ranging and prolonged. In part, this was because of the sheer volume of these maps in the Library and elsewhere. Other reasons for John's long involvement with these maps included the delay that arose because during the 1970s the Library withdrew its map collection from public access for an extended period (over six years). Notwithstanding this obstacle, John's interest in local maps continued as he was committed to an ambitious project that sought to assemble, for Britain and Ireland, a directory (or, as the authors called it, dictionary) of land surveyors and local map-makers who had operated, at one time or another, over the long period starting around 1530 and ending about 1850. John undertook much of the Irish work for this greatly-drawn out project which ran for over thirty years and only ended in 1997.[5] Much of John's researches involved the meticulous identification of the activities of otherwise shadowy or unknown local surveyors from their maps in the National Library or from their advertisements embedded in contemporary eighteenth-century newspapers. A huge diversity of sources was involved, many of them with just fleeting references to a name, yet John decided he had the material to write a book on the history of the Irish land surveyor, the book which eventually became *Plantation Acres* and which first appeared in 1985.

Some particular landmark publications can be identified in John's researches into estate and farm maps. One such in *Irish Geography,* 1967, is especially significant as it offers an early insight to his understanding of the history of the Irish estate map. Entitled 'the French school of Dublin land surveyors', this article drew attention to the pivotal role of the celebrated John Rocque in estate map-making in Ireland. Rocque was, or was to be, the author of county maps of Surrey, Berkshire and Middlesex, and indeed was a maker of many other important printed maps. In Ireland, Rocque published a map of County Armagh as well as various maps of the city and county of Dublin. But John now highlighted how Rocque had also in the late 1750s compiled over 170 beautifully illustrated maps depicting the estates of the earl of Kildare. These maps, which set a new standard for estate mapping in Ireland, had been placed on sale in London in the early 1960s, and it was then that John 'discovered' them.

The 1985 book is, however, the main outcome of John's work into these types of local maps. Originally subtitled 'an historical study of the

Irish land surveyor', the somewhat enigmatic lead heading, *Plantation Acres*, is typical of the rather oblique titles favoured by him. Not only does it remind us that much of the work associated with the early land surveyors related to the consolidation of the sixteenth- and seventeenth-century landholding changes and settlement plantations that affected much of Ireland. It is also a reminder of the distinctive measurement system used by the Irish land surveyor. Whereas a five and a half yard (16.5 feet) rod or pole was used in England and became absorbed in statute measure, the Irish surveyor used a seven-yard (21 foot) measure, which resulted in the Irish, or plantation, acre which was 1.62 times the area of the English (statute) acre. Until the early nineteenth century, most land surveyors preferred to make their measures and present their area calculations, in plantation acres.

In his book John Andrews casts a wide net, going back to the sixteenth-century plantations and earlier, and also looking at such topics as those surveyors who broke into print by, for example, creating county and, occasionally, town or city maps. Indeed, this is a book that goes far beyond maps, to explore much about the evolution of land measures, surveying practices and surveying instruments, and also the attitudes and prejudices – often virulent – of the practitioners. Many of these topics had never really been systematically appraised before John Andrews. He patiently built his book over many years to create a remarkable synthesis from a diversity of fragmentary sources, including thousands of small advertisements from over a hundred years of general and local newspapers. The outcome is a really quite exceptional achievement: a far-reaching and highly original review of the social and economic significance of land surveying in Ireland during a 300-year period, 1550–1850. John Andrews produced so much of quality but this book must rank as a particularly virtuoso piece of scholarship: it is a distinctive view of Irish history, and there is no other source material like it.

In the four decades since, on the initiative of the Ulster Historical Foundation, *Plantation Acres* first appeared, knowledge on the land surveyor in Ireland in Ireland has been expanded as a result of new resources becoming available and with the appearance of new publications. For example, the accession to the Public Record Office of Northern Ireland of the Killarney-centred Kenmare estate papers, which include some 200 estate maps,[6] has introduced new information about the land surveyor in the south-west, as has the greater availability of material from the Bowood archive in Wiltshire.[7] Many local libraries and archives have also developed nascent collections of early maps. Such sources contain the work of names such as Henry Jones, Gerrot McElligott, Owen O'Sullivan and John Mangan – surveyors with strong local bases who appear to have been largely unknown to John Andrews. And a new book. *Land Surveying in Ireland 1690–1830* has also appeared, authored by Dr Finnian O Cionnaith (2022). As indicated by other more localised recent studies, including published reviews of the history of mapping in County Laois and in South Kerry, and a forthcoming book on County Cavan, research on the land surveyor in Ireland is an expanding and ongoing process. Yet it is also clear that *Plantation Acres* provides the main frame within which so much that is new is being, and will be, set. Its re-issue, with an expanded index, by the Ulster Historical Foundation is a welcome development which makes an exceptional work of all-Ireland significance once again available to a new generation of readers.

ARNOLD HORNER
August 2025

Notes

1. Greater biographical detail on the career of J.H. Andrews is available at Arnold Horner 'John Harwood Andrews, 1927–2019', *Irish Geography*, 53 (1), 2020, 189–96. Further perspectives of Andrews, including a list of his publications, 1950 to 2020, are offered in Sarah Gearty and Michael Potterton (eds), *Town & Country: Perspectives from the Irish Historic Towns Atlas* (Dublin, 2023).

2. Sir John Davies commenting in 1609. As quoted in J. H. Andrews, *The Queen's Last Map-Maker: Richard Bartlett in Ireland, 1600–3* (Dublin, 2009), p. 35.

3. Listed in Geary and Potterton, *Town & Country* ..., [*op.cit.*, note 1 above] pp 259–81.

4. J.H. Andrews, 'Road planning in Ireland before the railway age', *Irish Geography*, 5(1), 1964, pp 17–42.

5. Sarah Bendall (ed), *Dictionary of Land Surveyors and Local Map-Makers of Great Britain and Ireland 1530–1850*, 2nd edition, 2 vols., London, 1997.

6. Public Record Office of Northern Ireland (PRONI), D4151/S/1/A/1, D4151/S/1/D/1.

7. National Library of Ireland (NLI), MS L 508.

Acknowledgements 2025

Ulster Historical Foundation is pleased to thank and acknowledge the following individuals for their assistance in preparing this reprint. The late Paul Campbell of December Publications, Belfast, for undertaking the original capture and formatting of the text some 20 years ago. Also to Dr Arnold Horner, University College Dublin, for his personal, erudite and expansive background and new introduction to the work of J.H. Andrews. And to Dr Brian Lambkin, former Director of the Mellon Centre for Migration Studies, for compiling a greatly expanded and in-depth index to personal names, places and subjects. The Foundation is grateful to all three for their assistance.

Note on references

Places and dates of publication of printed books, and locations of manuscript-classes with recognisable titles, are given at first mention and subsequently omitted. Some journal titles are abbreviated: these may be found in T. W. Moody, *Rules for Contributors to Irish Historical Studies* (revised edition, Dublin, 1968) or in C. D. Harris and J. D. Fellmann, *International List of Geographical Serials* (3rd edition, Chicago, 1980). Major libraries and archival institutions are abbreviated as follows:

BL	British Library, London
Hist. MSS Com.	Historical Manuscripts Commission
Ir. MSS Com.	Irish Manuscripts Commission
NLI	National Library of Ireland, Dublin
OSO	Ordnance Survey Office, Dublin
PRO	Public Record Office, London
PROI	Public Record Office of Ireland, Dublin
PRONI	Public Record Office of Northern Ireland, Belfast
RD	Registry of Deeds, Dublin
RIA	Royal Irish Academy, Dublin
TCD	Trinity College, Dublin

1
Surveying without maps

CONSIDERING THE EXCITEMENT aroused by the land question among many generations of Irishmen, it is surprising how few members of this historically-minded nation have written about the early development of Irish land surveying. The first person known to have pronounced upon the subject (if it comes to that, he was almost the last) was a certain Eyre Evans in the middle of the eighteenth century, and the only motive for his or his lawyers' researches was a dispute about landed property in which he himself appeared as one of the principal parties. Confronted by his adversaries with some documents of 1576 and earlier relating to an estate near Dublin, Evans told the Irish House of Lords that 'he had now come to the knowledge of several records and evidences, from whence he charged, that the surveying and admeasurement of land was not then practised in Ireland.'[1] It was an agreeably downright act of historical judgement, but one that cannot be evaluated without first clarifying several points of terminology.

What Evans called the surveying and admeasurement of land, or what in later Irish usage was simply land surveying,[2] involves four distinct elements. First, it is not enough for a surveyor simply to look at the ground, or to sketch it, or to describe it in words, or to make it the subject of numerical estimates: his main task is to ascertain its exact shape and size with the aid of some more or less specialised measuring apparatus. Secondly, in this case a rather narrow meaning must be given to the adjectival noun 'land'. On the face of it, Evans's theory could be easily refuted by citing a number of good topographical and military maps made in several parts of Ireland at or before the time of his opponent's Elizabethan grants.[3] But what the land surveyor spends most of his time mapping is landed property, not just land in general. Admittedly many surveyors have also measured roads, commons and other public places to which the idea of proprietorship is not so obviously applicable, but their chief preoccupation has always been with estates and farms and their principal clients have always been drawn from the landowning class; what they have been selling, to put the matter in epigrammatic form, is a map whose subject has the same owner as itself. Besides placing the profession in its social and economic context, this proviso carries an important technical corollary, for the surveying of property, at least in well-populated countries like Ireland, implies that a relatively small area is being measured with a relatively high degree of precision; or in other (and more academic) words, that the land surveyor's interests are topographical rather than chorographical or geographical.

A third criterion relates to the degree of habitude and dedication implicit in Evans's word 'practised'. In land surveying the worker as well as the work must be open to contemporary identification: surveyors must form a recognisable occupational group. This in turn entails a certain complexity both in the land itself and in the measuring process. To find the length and breadth of a small rectangular parcel may not call for any unusual resources in the way of either skill or instruments, and it is possible to imagine an agrarian society whose farmers do all their own surveying without professional help. The Irish nation has not been such a society since the sixteenth century: hence the need for the present book.

The last and most question-begging of our four qualifications is the existence of maps and plans. This requirement, too, might reasonably be disputed on the ground that the exact sizes of quite irregular outlines can in theory be determined by field measurements without needing to be shown in graphic form. But at this juncture pragmatic sanction must be preferred to theoretical possibility. Most Irishmen who called themselves land surveyors simply happen to have given so much of their time to cartography that one of the best ways of proving their existence is to cite the maps they drew. In particular, map testimony seems essential if a firm decision is to be taken about the status and character of Irish land measurement in the evidential dark age that preceded the 1580s; and anyway it is maps that give the surveyor his historical interest for most modern readers and for at least one modern author.

Interpreted in this quadripartite form, Evans's disbelief in the existence of an early Elizabethan Irish surveying industry has yet to be challenged by historians. But proving a negative is seldom easy, and it would be helpful to know more about the unspecified 'evidences and records' on which he founded his conviction. Nobody in 1580 or earlier was propounding general truths about the presence or absence of land surveyors in the Irish countryside; it is a subject where even limited and partial statements are hard to come by. There are times, however, when the silence of contemporary witnesses itself becomes almost audible. One such moment was when Archbishop John Alen, in his register of the see of Dublin, decided in the late 1520s or early 1530s to rewrite a medieval boundary description in the nomenclature and terminology of his own time.

> It is a quadrangle [he noted], for our wood, supra, is on the south, the said vill on the north, the water of Dodir, supra, on the east, and the mountain or hill above-named on the west, where beyond it lies the great long, wide highway ... Take heed and never forget this and you will know for a fact where 'the Friars Wood' is, also the way from Kilmastam to Ballamor, riding on which on the right hand all the intervening land is that of the church of Dublin absolutely.[4]

Verbal boundary descriptions were common enough in Alen's time. It is the 'take heed and never forget' that brings matters a stage further by sharpening his self-portrait of an intelligent, responsible and powerful administrator who obviously needs maps and who is yet apparently unconscious of that need or who at least unquestioningly accepts his own inability to meet it.

If Alen's case seems trivial, a more significant though less personal example may be found a few decades later in the plan for an English settlement of the lands confiscated from the O'Mores, O'Connors and O'Dempsies.[5] By this time Ireland had already seen many transfers of land from conquered to conqueror, but the events of 1549 and afterwards in Leix and Offaly marked a new departure, different from medieval colonialism and similar to the settlements of the later Elizabethan period and the seventeenth century – or so at least historians unanimously suggest by applying the word 'plantation' to all these later schemes and none of the earlier ones. From the 1580s onwards, as will be shown in subsequent chapters, almost every British plantation in Ireland required the making of extensive admeasurements and maps. Such aids were as desirable in sixteenth-century Leix and Offaly as anywhere else, both to establish the amount of land given to each planter and to distinguish the limits of contiguous allotments. But the only maps surviving from this time and place are too small to count as land surveys;[6] and although contemporaries wrote of 'measuring' the planted area and dividing it into townships and farms, there are unlikely to have been any atlases among the 'books' in which these particulars were recorded;[7] the concept of the atlas or map-book was still so unfamiliar in the Ireland of c. 1560 that nobody would have lumped together script and map in such a casual fashion.

The same is true of all the many documents relating to the agrarian affairs of medieval Ireland — or at least of those that have been translated and printed by modern editors — up to and including the dissolution of the monasteries in 1539–40. These materials cover Crown, Church and private estates and they include charters, grants, extents, presentations and inquisitions, some of which might be called 'surveys' in a perfectly legitimate (if for present purposes rather misleading) sense of that term. What they do not include is maps or references to maps, even at points where such references would be commonplace in similar documents of seventeenth- or eighteenth-century date; and in Ireland this negative judgement applies not only to modern-style property maps but also to the kind of unscaled picture-map that survives for several localities in medieval England.[8]

So even if the history of Irish land surveying did begin before late Elizabethan times there is no adequate evidence from which to write it. But this does not mean that the whole of the preceding period can be ignored. On the contrary, when the true land surveyor comes into view his professional *mores* are found to be much influenced by the procedure for handling real property illustrated in medieval and pre-medieval sources. For Gaelic Ireland such sources comprise not only records of individual transactions but also law tracts and topographical literature, the latter including a poem which obligingly carries the whole subject to within ten generations of Adam.[9] On this indigenous ground-plan (which there is no obligation to regard as having been free from change at any period) were superimposed the agrarian practices of the Vikings and the Anglo-Normans. In some parts of Ireland, especially near Dublin, the Anglo-Normans remained open to influence from their ancestral homelands throughout the Middle Ages. Elsewhere the cross-channel links proved weaker, and twelfth-century Norman innovations were almost lost in the Gaelic renaissance of the fourteenth and fifteenth centuries. The result was a tangle which it is fortunately not the business of this book to unravel: all we need do is identify some of the main points of contact between medieval and modern.

Perhaps the chief feature common to both periods is the existence throughout Ireland of a network of small territories, like Alen's Kilmastam and Ballamor, whose names and boundaries were generally known to the resident population. Such 'denominations' originally represented lands held by individuals or communities and also served as a basis for calculating manpower resources and taxation levels.[10] One of the oldest ways of defining a large tract of land was not to describe its boundaries but simply to list the denominations contained within it. This procedure could be adapted to the local as well as to the regional scale by naming individual fields, where they existed, or even parcels within fields; and it was found equally convenient by natives and invaders, prevailing in Irish legal documents to the end of the plantation period and beyond. One quick-eared versifier, attending the Dublin Court of Claims at the start of the eighteenth century, took down the names of the lands, in addition to those of the lawyers dealing with them, when he placed the whole system in its solemn formal context of deeds, oaths, and seals:

> Give me the deed, says Worthington,
> Who then in ample form goes on,
> In sixteen hundred eighty-four,
> The lands are Knock and Derrymore,
> Dromonduffe and Ballyvarry,
> In Counties Ross and Tipperary;
> A thousand pounds the money lent,
> With interest after ten per cent;
> McCarty is the mortgaging party
> The seal is broke, but signed Clancarty.
> The witnesses are, Dermot Ryan,
> Murtagh Hogan, Teigue O'Brien.
> This deed, says White, with great submission,
> I own is found by inquisition.[11]

Nobody asked Mr Worthington to locate the lands any more precisely than by mentioning the larger territories of which they formed part, though without poetic licence he might have been expected to specify baronies and parishes as well as counties. The descendants of Knock, Derrymore and the rest are of course the townlands measured and mapped by the Ordnance Survey in the nineteenth century (Fig. 1). But many historical complexities lie hidden behind the authoritative simplicity of the Ordnance map. For one thing, before the final triumph of the word 'townland' a variety of generic terms was in use for minor territorial divisions, some of them puzzling in both etymology and geographical distribution, like the polls of Cavan and the tates of Fermanagh and Monaghan. Many regions had their own peculiar territorial hierarchies, the northern tate for instance forming a subdivision of the ballybetagh and the southern gneeve a subdivision of the ploughland; and it was not always the same tier of the hierarchical structure (supposing that equivalent levels can be recognised in different hierarchies) that was adopted by the Ordnance Survey for its townlands. This terminological complexity brought its own problems as the struggle for land grew sharper, but the problems solved themselves when many ancient territorial units fell out of use – a development which generally preceded or coincided with the arrival of the land surveyor (unfortunately for the writing of topographical history) and which indeed was part of the agrarian trend that the land surveyor himself personified. The following pages will swim with the tide of history by often loosely applying the word 'townland' to any recognised division smaller than a parish and larger than a field.

Before the nineteenth century there were many spreads of bog and mountain which lay outside the townland network and which were sometimes described as unprofitable, although most of them did a useful service by providing turf, timber or summer pasture for the surrounding farmers. The distinction between 'unprofitable' mountain and bog on the one hand, and profitable plains of arable and meadow on the other, is one of the most persistent features of Ireland's historical topography, and has always made considerable difficulty for the surveyor in every sense of that term. Some bogs and mountains were regarded as appurtenant to a nearby townland, without necessarily lying inside it. Other rough grazings belonged in common to a number of townlands. Since such uncultivated lands were often without visible boundaries, their proprietorial affiliations must sometimes have been hard to keep track of. But on good land the townland divisions were usually well marked and became both more numerous and more precise as properties were partitioned (a likely occurrence under the gavelkind system of inheritance)[12] and as wastes and forests were brought into cultivation. Nature provides some boundaries in the form of coastlines, rivers and the edges of reclaimable bogs. Man creates others by building walls, banks and roads; though such artifacts are more often a consequence of a legal boundary than a cause of it, and the same is true of certain pagan burial mounds[13] and Christian crosses,[14] both of which were used, in their time, to fix the ends of the imaginary straight-line boundaries known to the early Irish lawyer as 'eye-marks'.[15] Many boundaries incorporated several different kinds of line alternating in rapid succession, and one of the oldest ways of mastering their complexity was to 'tread' them. This process of perambulation might take place at regular intervals to prevent the line from being altered or forgotten, as with the triennial riding of the franchises of the city of Dublin, which included the delimitation of a maritime boundary by throwing a spear as far as possible into Dublin Bay.[16]

SURVEYING WITHOUT MAPS 7

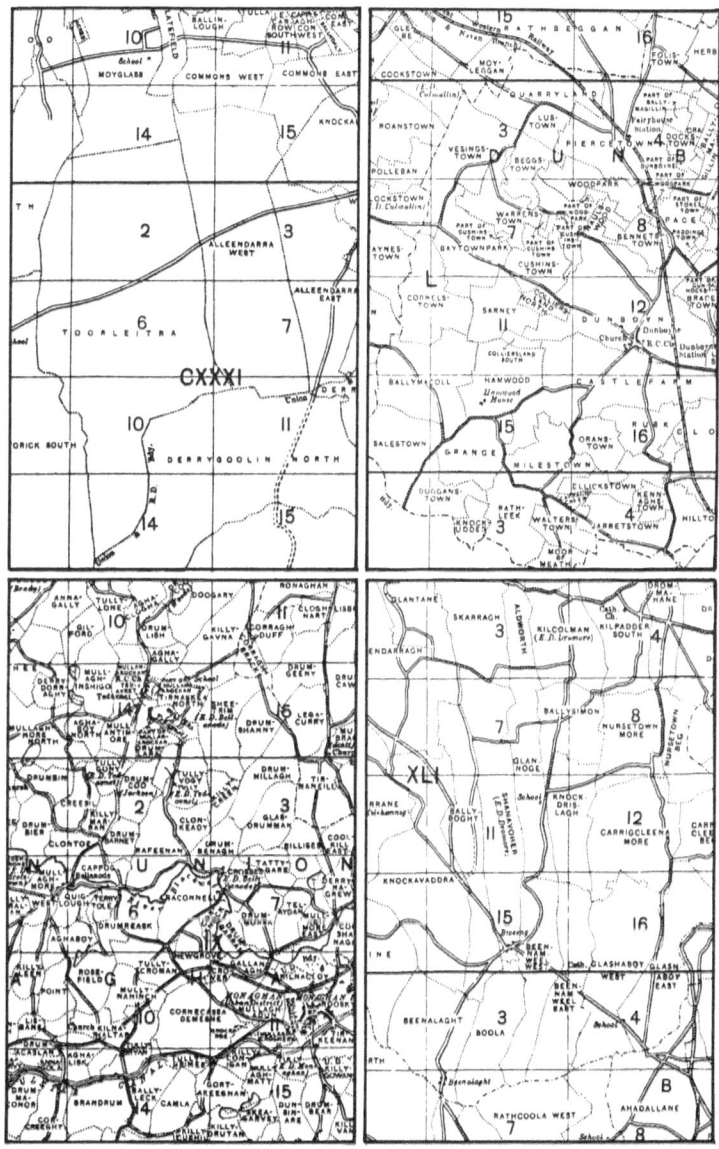

Figure 1. Examples of Irish Townland Networks from Co. Galway (upper left), Co. Meath (upper right), Co. Monaghan (lower left) and Co. Cork (lower right). Source: Ordnance Survey of Ireland, one inch to the mile townland index maps, by permission of the Government (Permit No. 4424). Scale about half the original. Sheets of the large-scale county Ordnance maps are represented by numbered rectangles.

Not all such survivals called for behaviour as self-consciously bizarre as spear-throwing; on the contrary, perambulation at frequent intenals was a routine activity on many seventeenth- and even eighteenth-century estates.[17] Alternatively an attempt might be made to settle an uncertain or disputed boundary once and for all, and from an early date commissions of perambulation were issued for this purpose by Irish courts of law.[18] The boundary was then determined by twelve 'good and lawful' men from the county through which it ran, though no doubt it was the residents on the spot, handing down their knowledge from father to son,[19] who provided the jury with the basis of its verdict. When the verdict was committed to paper or parchment, posterity could hope to learn of at least a few minor landmarks, perhaps even including particular rocks and trees, that would otherwise have no chance of being commemorated. Many such documents, among them the one by John Alen quoted above, attempt to recreate a putative primeval act of perambulation by using sequential phrases like 'thence to' or 'so to' as they proceed from one landmark to the next.[20] These progressions, some of which now seem bafflingly complicated, may be seen as ancestors of the true land surveyor's field book with its numerical distances and bearings, but the map drawn from such a field book did not altogether eliminate the use of non-cartographic descriptions, any more than the descriptions had eliminated the physical act of perambulation. Among these echoes of a pre-cartographic past are the boundary remark books and registers compiled by the Ordnance Survey of Ireland in the nineteenth century.[21]

Naming and bounding were only part of the business of medieval property description. An equally important task was to evaluate what lay inside the boundary. In some regions and at some periods, it was convenient and perhaps not wholly unrealistic to treat every denomination as equal, for there seem to have been obscure socio-economic influences, analogous to natural selection, that prevented the lands of a given community (whether a family, a kin-group, or simply an association of neighbours) from diverging very far from the mean in either size or wealth. Examples of this quasi-equality were the sessiagh or carucate, which supposedly contained enough land for one ploughteam; the knight's fee or the ballybetagh, which could support a specified number of fighting men; the ballybo, colp or martland, which could feed a specified number of livestock; and the gallon or pottle, which could ripen a certain quantity of seed corn. How much credence was ever given to these measures in daily life is uncertain. History yields no trace of either professional surveyors or ordinary countrymen actually verifying by deliberate experiment that a round number of cattle or ploughteams could be accommodated in any particular area. But where both ploughlands (say) and named territonal divisions were on record, there was usually a simple numerical relationship between them, sometimes a one-one relationship. As Table 1 illustrates, such equations were still perceptible in the 'county books' that continued to govern the levying of Irish local taxation until the advent of the Ordnance Survey.

TABLE 1

UNITS OF LAND RECKONING IN THE
PARISH OF TAUGHBOY, CO. ROSCOMMON, 1824

Denomination	Number of Units	
	Quarters	Cartrons
Carrowkeel	1	
Carowmore	1	
Lisnamanaugh	1	
Kilmavan	1	
Lissnamughah	1	
Cloonught	1	
Carrownarly		3
Killnokeery	¹/₂	
Carrowenlare	¹/₂	
Mullaghbidah	¹/₂	
Carrownlare	¹/₂	
Aghnapenpole	¹/₂	
Ballymahon		1
Cooltober	1	
Shanballyhiskey		1
Lissafoker		1
Turrock		4
Twepenbegg	¹/₂	
Turpenmore	¹/₂	
Ballyfornen	1	
Creghermore	¹/₂	
Taughboy	(No entry)	
Carreuentarue	" "	

SOURCE: *Report from the Select Committee Appointed to Consider the Best Mode of Apportioning More Equally the Local Burthens Collected in Ireland, and to Provide for a General Survey and Valuation of that Part of the United Kingdom*, p. 333, H.C. 1824 (445), viii.

But any simple relationship between name and number was liable to two kinds of disturbance. In the first place, territories inevitably showed some qualitative variation which in a market economy could be expected to assume a quantitative significance. Even if every townland happened to be the same size, not all of them could aspire to a castle, church, mill, mine, quarry, weir, harbour, fishery, orchard, wood or rabbit warren. (What the surveyor did have reason to expect, at least in peacetime, was a cluster or scatter of single-storey thatched dwelling houses in every townland, with the result that his report would probably allow such structures to go without saying.) Valuing such amenities might be difficult; recording them was a matter of using one's eyes and knowing how to write.

A more serious problem arose where denomination boundaries were deliberately changed to match the ebb and flow of settlement and ownership. Of the two possible kinds of change partition was evidently more common than amalgamation: the widespread occurrence in Irish land reckoning of numerical expressions – as with the number four in 'quarter', 'cartron' and 'carrow' – seems to express division much more often than multiplication. The result of such fragmentation was a scale or 'table' of numerically related measures, such as sixteen polls to a ballybetagh or six gneeves to a quarter, that seemed to parallel the hierarchy of denominations. Whether and to what extent the act of partition was accompanied by a professional admeasurement is a question that no Irish historian has answered. Not always, is the only verdict available at present: in the seventeenth century, at any rate, justice was often done by making the youngest heir effect the partition and then allowing the others to take their choice from his divisions in order of seniority.[22]

Few writers, ancient or modern, have felt able to discuss the ratios between different units of measurement without trying to combine them into one great series that runs from the province or kingdom at the top to the inch or barleycorn at the bottom (Table 2). In the present context interest attaches less to the relation between different versions of this table than to the way in which it seems at some point in the sequence to switch from subdivision to aggregation, with the lowest units formed not by breaking up some larger entity but by direct reference either to the human body – as with feet and inches – or to artifacts that suited man's physical capacity. Of the small units the most important for the surveyor was the rod, pole or perch, usually thought to have started its career as a goad for prodding the animals that drew the plough.[23]

TABLE 2

SOME EARLY IRISH LAND MEASURES

38,640 ploughlands	:	Ireland
120 acres	:	1 ploughland
4 x 40 perches	:	1 acre
21 feet	:	1 perch
12 inches	:	1 foot

SOURCE: *Calendar of the State Papers, relating to Ireland, 1598–9*, p. 431.

While cartrons, ploughlands and the rest served in practice mainly for bringing lists of territories to a rough and ready common denominator, the perch and its derivatives were part of actual mensuration in the familiar sense of repeatedly laying down a standard length across the surface being measured. This of course is how from time immemorial men have taken measurements of cloth, timber and building work as well as of small pieces of land – the crucial question in the case of land being the exact degree of smallness involved. A famous description of the humblest class of native farmers in an Irish county tells how:

> They will take upon them to be judges to an extreme nicety of the quality and quantity of each rood of ground; and, to make sure work, will bring their ropes to measure, as formally as a surveyor his chains.[24]

Although this passage was not written until 1682, it depicts a stratum of Irish agrarian society in which many ancient traditions are thought to have been kept alive. For Anglo-Norman as distinct from early Gaelic mensuration, the evidence is more demonstrably of the right period, with one typical thirteenth-century document, for example, describing land in Co. Louth as 'within the metes and devises aforenamed, as best and most fully measured and perambulated, whether more or less, within the said boundaries'.[25] Not long afterwards 'measurers' were distinguished from 'jurors' in Co. Tipperary.[26] Of course measurement need not always mean what it says, as has already been noted in the case of the Leix-Offaly plantation. But the legal escape-clause 'more or less' does at least seem to express a measurer's anxiety about having his results checked by someone else, for if the only way to find the area of a farm was by estimation such a proviso would be hardly worth including: nobody would expect two independent estimates to be exactly the same. Of course a measurement would carry more conviction if we knew who made it, but no one has been found to divulge this information until 1540, when fifty acres belonging to St Mary's Abbey in Dublin were measured by John Tasker of Dublin and John Tagen of Baldoyle.[27] Here at any rate the true land surveyor might seem to be finally making himself known: it is only the lack of maps that tilts the balance against Tasker and Tagen.

For the rest, the history of medieval mensuration in general, and of professional mensuration in particular, must be left to some future expert on the acre, the rood and the perch. What matters at present is the significance of these terms to the ordinary Irish countryman, who seems for centuries to have found it difficult to distinguish the units in question from the attribute that they were being used to express. Thus, where modern speech favours an abstract word like 'content', 'area' or 'size', a seventeenth- or eighteenth-century farmer would almost always prefer the phrase 'number of acres'. The acre was deeply rooted in rural consciousness among Irishmen and many other nations. One early philologist even placed it among 'the few words which have come down to us from the original language of man';[28] it was certainly old enough to have acquired a number of different meanings. One of these, as Eyre Evans pointed out when summarising his historical investigations, was simply a piece of land of more or less indeterminate size:

> Upon inquiry, he found that anciently the word Acre was used to express various and uncertain quantities, and was sometimes used to answer the Latin word AGER from which it was derived; so that the 18 acres mentioned in the old inquisitions ... might more probably mean 18 fields. [29]

The essentially unquantitative notion of a field has left a penumbra of vagueness around many acres, both medieval and early modern, that might otherwise be interpreted as uniform. The term 'conventional acre' is sometimes used to meet such cases, and makes linguistic sense in so far as it is more convenient to count up fields than to determine their exact dimensions. A different kind of uncertainty seems to vitiate a number of supposedly invariable acreage values – 60 to the ballybo, 120 to the ploughland, and so on – which by the sixteenth century had come to be associated with many kinds of Irish territorial division. Such 'fiscal' acreages were almost totally unrealistic:[30] that much is evident from their improbable constancy and 'roundness', and also from the disconcerting speed with which a given ratio could change its value, as when the tate was successively defined within the space of a few years as 24 acres, 30 acres and 50 acres.[31] However they originated, these equations form an almost impenetrable frontier-zone between medieval and modern ways of thought, a zone which in some parts of Ireland must be placed as late as the opening decades of the nineteenth century.

Despite the similarity of nomenclature, a distinction must surely be drawn between the sixtieth part of a ballybo on the one hand and what might be called the aggregative acre or what an early-modern source aptly describes as the 'perch acre' on the other.[32] Although the second variety was not precisely defined until the sixteenth century, some degree of exactitude had been apparent three hundred years earlier in the phenomenon of the acreable rent,[33] which was the sum that had to be multiplied by the number of acres in a farm to give the farmer's total rent. When writers defined this acre in terms of proximate smaller units (which unfortunately was not very often) the answer was always the same: every acre contained four roods or stangs, the rood being almost universal in modern Ireland, the stang more common in the Middle Ages – a terminological difference which itself suggests some kind of discontinuity not yet commented on by scholars. Each rood or stang contained forty square perches: that is how the twentieth-century arithmetic lesson would put it, but among surveyors the word 'perch' was applied without qualification to both areal and linear measure. More interestingly, the value of 160 perches to the acre was often stated by early writers in the specific form of forty perches by four perches,[34] the acre thus appearing not as any one of an indefinite range of equivalent figures but as a class of identically-shaped rectangles, a reminder of how the original acre-units must have been marked out by the farmer as visible strips of land. In Gaelic Ireland the acre has been defined as a bundle of spade ridges.[35] Elsewhere it has been equated with a day's ploughing, or with the selion formed by the furrows of a medieval open field.[36] If acres were actually identifiable in the landscape (whether or not as the 'fields' postulated by Eyre Evans) then much of a measurer's work could be done by counting rather than by the laying down of rods and lines, and the apparent absence of the professional land surveyor becomes easier to understand.

In meadows, pastures, and moors or bogs, the process of quantification was unassisted by either plough or spade, and in the absence of lines cut in the ground the observer would have to judge 'by eye' the number of equivalent areas that could be fitted into a given boundary. Whether or not the areas were still visualised as rectangular, such estimates surely mark a considerable advance in intellectual sophistication. In Ireland they were being made at least as early as the thirteenth century,[37] to judge from the indifference with which the acre was then applied to non-arable as well as arable land. Much later, though still just within the time-span of this chapter, a lake near Roscommon was 'measured' at eighty acres,[38] but it is hard to picture anyone carrying a chain along the edge of a not very valuable expanse of water for the sake of obtaining this not very useful piece of information, especially when the resultant number was such a round one. Most acreages from the same period and earlier are similarly approximate, with none of the odd roods and perches that the true measurer takes pride in exhibiting as proof of his attention to detail (Table 3). Another hint to the same effect is the kind of survey that simply collected its figures ready-made from a local jury: unpaid informants would hardly choose any but the least troublesome method of computing their acres.[39] And since estimation is subject to indefinitely varying degrees of roughness it could no doubt be accompanied by the use of arbitrary acres (of the sixty-to-the-ballybo variety) without much sense of incongruity.

In any system of non-arbitrary acreages the size of the acre depends on the length of the perch. In England the latter is known to have been highly variable, despite the fact that a value of $16^{1}/_{2}$ feet was given prominence as early as the thirteenth century and again in a statute of 1593.[40] In Ireland the position is not so clear. One suggestion for dispelling the fog is to calculate the sizes of medieval units by a comparison of the areas given in contemporary documents with the corresponding statute-acreages of modern times, the result of this comparison in the vicinity of Dublin being an Anglo-Norman acre of about $2^{1}/_{2}$ statute acres and a perch of about 26 feet.[41] The difficulty with such calculations is that they involve too many

TABLE 3

A SAMPLE OF MEDIEVAL ACREAGE FIGURES
(13TH CENTURY TO 1540)

Size of parcel	Smallest unit distinguished		
	Quarter-acre	Single acre	Ten acres
Less than 10 acres	57 references	115 references	—
10 or more acres	5 references	42 references	33 references

SOURCE: McNeill and Otway-Ruthven, *Dowdall Deeds*.

unknowns: not only (a) the size of the medieval units, but (b) the medieval boundaries of the territory under survey, and (c) the correctness of the old and new measurements or estimates. None of these variables can be determined without making assumptions about the others, and none of those assumptions can be conclusively proved from independent premises. Here is an unavoidable element of doubt affecting the histories of three different subjects: territorial boundaries, units of land measurement, and the accuracy of the measuring process. The problem of disentangling these variables will recur throughout the present essay, and theoretically seems capable of plaguing the historiography of survey methods at any period and in any part of the world. In medieval Ireland it may be more than theoretical – at least until someone can resolve all doubts as to whether the acreage of bog, wood and pasture within a medieval townland was necessarily included with the acreage of arable.

All things considered there is much to be said for avoiding calculations that draw their terms from more than one period, and for seeking explicit contemporary statements of equivalence, either between different kinds of acre or (better still) between the acre and some supposedly less inconstant unit such as the foot. While it is unfortunate that no such statements have been recorded from before the sixteenth century, when they do appear their effect is happily to make all earlier periods irrelevant. Whatever reasonable allowance is made for editorial mis-transcription, there is no escaping the fact that contemporaries recognised a number of different acres with a wide range of variation (Table 4). Early explanations of the differences are either ethnic or regional or both. Thus the seventeenth-century Irish historian Geoffrey Keating described the Irish acre as two or three times larger than that of the 'foreigners', in other words the English: the foreigners' acre, like their language, was thought to have been particularly associated with the Fingal district of north Co. Dublin.[42] Elsewhere the widespread expression 'country measure' was used not in antithesis to the 'burgage acre',[43] but to denote whatever territory the speaker had in mind, though little is known as yet about the pattern of territorial variation which seems to lie behind these words.[44] It may also be uncertain whether an acre was purely regional in significance or whether, like the English woodland acre, it referred to land of one particular type: a case in point is 'callowe measure which is the least in the country'.[45] To judge from the terms 'small measure' and 'great measure'[46] it was common for more than one acre to have currency in the same region.

TABLE 4

VARIETIES OF ACRE

Date	Location	Description	Definition	Source
1540	Co. Wicklow	Great acre	4 acres legal English measure	White, *Monastic Extents*, p. 126
1540	Co. Cork	Acre, greater measure	1½ acres, lesser measure	" " p. 142
1584	Small County, Co. Limerick	Acre	7 acres, great country measure	NAI, M.5039
1587	Co. Meath	Acre, great measure	15 acres small measure	Harris, *Ware*, 2, p. 224 (below, p. 25, n.42)
1587	Ireland	" "	4 acres, small measure	" "
1589	Co. Kildare	" "	3 acres, standard measure	" "
1595	Ireland	Acre, Irish measure	3 acres, small measure	Fiants, Elizabeth I, 5947, *16th Rept, Dep. Keeper Pub. Rec Ire.*, p. 272
1595	Ireland	Burgage acre	6/11 acres, Irish measure	" "
1642 Com.,	Ireland	Acre, Irish measure	3 English acres	Hist. MSS *Buccleuch & Queensberry*, 1, p. 304
1654	Clanwilliam, Co. Tipperary	Clanwilliam acre	4 plantation acres	Simington, *Civil Survey*, Tipperary, 2, pp 14, 44 (below, p. 26, n.46)

One observer despaired of reconciling all these different units 'unless the line be laid over every village, hamlet and parcel'. But then somebody would have to choose a length for the line. In Co. Limerick the 21-foot perch was given the name of 'Irish measure' as early as 1584, but only in a context that admitted the existence of a different standard within the same county.[47] If one Irish territory could establish itself as un-Irish in this respect, so could others; and there is a modicum of evidence that some of them did. Twenty-one feet might then be interpreted as the aboriginal standard from which particular localities had diverged, but that kind of evolution seems more likely to produce shorter regional standards than the generally longer examples listed in Table 5: if conditions were primitive enough, a long pole might lose some of its length simply by having a piece broken off it. And where in any case had the basic Irish standard come from? It was different from its geographically nearest British counterpart, the Cunningham perch of south-west Scotland – though (to complicate matters) the Cunningham perch is sometimes thought to have originated in Gaelic Ireland.[48] The only part of Britain where the Irish perch is known to have prevailed in the Middle Ages is Lancashire and Cheshire,[49] at first sight a likely enough source on geographical grounds, though in fact it was south-west rather than north-west England that provided medieval Ireland with most of its innovations and the 21-foot Lancashire perch may conceivably have crossed the Irish Sea from west to east. Historical speculation apart, it is clear that all the Irish perches are rather long as perches go (a point not without significance for immigrant Englishmen) and to suggest that in practice half-perch rods were more common in Ireland than whole-perch rods does little to explain this difference between the two countries.[50] One obvious comment is that any unit of more than twenty feet seems better suited to land than to buildings – especially Irish buildings – and that the perch is therefore not a problem that the agrarian historian can hand over to his architectural colleagues. Also worthy of note is that except for the 21-foot perch and its associated acre, none of the Irish units recorded in Tables 4 and 5 has ever been found on an Irish property-map – another sign of the gulf that separates the surveyor from the non-surveyor.

To summarise: many of the difficulties that confront the land surveyor were recognised in medieval and early sixteenth-century Ireland, and after a fashion most of them were under some sort of control. In relating different modes of control, both to each other and to later developments, one point of departure might seem to be the word 'surveyor'. This term did not reach the English language (from French) until relatively late, being uncommon in England before the fifteenth century and in Ireland before the sixteenth, though among Englishmen it was quick to assume a number of different connotations, some of them closer to overseeing or custodianship (the sixteenth-century Latin equivalent was 'supervisor') than to measurement and mapping. The historiography of land surveying has been bedevilled ever since by revenue surveyors, Post Office surveyors, highway surveyors, and surveyors of buildings and public works, to say nothing of certain

TABLE 5

VARIETIES OF PERCH

Date	Location	Length	Source
1511	Ireland	21 feet	Harris, *Ware*, 2, p. 225
1539	Co. Dublin	24 feet	White, *Monastic Extents*, p. 2
1571	Fingal, Co. Dublin	16½ feet	Harris, *Ware*, 2, p. 225
1572	Ireland	24 feet	Hill, p. 415
1584	Connello Co. Limerick	25 feet, 4 inches	NAI, M.5039
1584	Connaught	12 feet*	Harris, *Ware*, 2, p. 225
1586	Ireland	20.625 feet**	Hooker, p. 9
1586	Munster	21 feet 24 feet 27 feet 29 feet	Lambeth Palace, London, Carew MS 607, p. 125
1598	Ireland	21 feet	Table 2
1618	Co. Leitrim	18 feet	J. Lodge, *The Peerage of Ireland*, 2 (Dublin, 1789), p. 64
1621	Co. Down	24 feet	Harris, *Ware*, 2, p. 225

Hill: G. Hill, *An Historical Account of the Macdonnells of Antrim* (Belfast, 1873)
Hooker: John Hooker, *The Second Volume of Chronicles: Containing the Description, Conquest, Inhabitation, and Troublesome Estate of Ireland; First Collected by Raphaell Holinshed*, 2 (London, 1586)

* Probably a mistake for 21 feet
** Based on the statement that there were 320 Irish miles in 400 English miles and assuming an English perch of 16½ feet

customs officers who were known as 'land surveyors' to distinguish them from tide surveyors. Even within the vocabulary of land management the signification could vary between measuring and inspecting.

Whichever sense might be in question, in early Tudor Ireland surveying as such is mentioned in two kinds of administrative context. Courts or commissions of survey could be appointed to deal with particular situations;[51] or the surveyor might hold a permanent position, a descendant either of the native 'sergeant', rent-gatherer or bailiff whom English officials sometimes found on the estates they confiscated (without apparently learning how such men were described in the Irish language) or of the seneschal who administered the kind of manorial court familiar in medieval England.[52] In 1523 the first English textbook on surveying advised that every great estate should have an offficer who could 'extend, butt and bound and value', but although he described this person as a surveyor the author said almost nothing about techniques of measurement.[53] Instead he emphasised the quasi-legal questions of proprietorship and tenure that needed answering before the business of description could begin, and it was in keeping with this attitude that the first surveyors heard of in Ireland should be men of legal and administrative background. This was true of John and Thomas Alen, who in 1540 were jointly made constables of the castle, seneschals of the court and surveyors of the manor of Maynooth (not the last time this manor took the lead in matters of surveying);[54] and also of Walter Cowley, an ex-Solicitor-General of Ireland who was appointed eight years later to the new post of Irish Surveyor-General.

The full title of Cowley's office was surveyor, appraiser, valuer or esteemer and extensor general of all and singular the King's honours, manors, lordships, messuages, lands, tenements, woods, possessions, revenues and hereditaments whatsoever in Ireland.[55] As it turned out, the Surveyor-General was to be a less consequential figure in the history of Irish land surveying than these fine phrases would seem to portend, but he remained an officer of the court of Exchequer until well into the nineteenth century. While his salary varied from time to time (Cowley drew £100 a year, some of his successors only £60),[56] it was never large enough to support a staff of professional land measurers, and the department is unlikely to have comprised more than the Surveyor-General himself, a deputy, and one or two anonymous clerks. When major surveying operations became necessary, as they did in most of the plantation schemes, a special organisation had to be established to conduct them. In this connection there was an interesting foretaste of the future when surveys of rebel land were excluded from the new officer's jurisdiction and reserved to the King's own Deputy in Ireland.[57] Presumably the Deputy had some fairly quick second thoughts, for in the event it was Cowley who took care of the confiscated lands in Leix and Offaly, not by measuring but rather by viewing and estimating, his 'surveyor's' acreages proving to be just as approximate as any others of the same period or before (Table 6).

In England the usual explanation for the new importance of the land surveyor under Queen Elizabeth I is the greater emphasis placed on the monetary value of land in an increasingly commercial economy,[58] and it is therefore not surprising that the surveyor's first appearances in the sister kingdom were in the role of valuer. In 1547 Irish lands were said to be 'surveyed to' a certain sum of money[59] (later usage was generally 'surveyed at'),[60] and it was common for farms to be reported as on offer at favourable, easy or moderate surveys, in other words at low rents.[61] The valuation of land and buildings is a subject that will need its own historian. For the present purpose it is enough that sixteenth-century valuing was not necessarily preceded by measurement and mapping in the way that Victorian agriculturalists, for example, would have taken for granted. The two operations were in any case not necessarily conducted by the same person. The difference between them is that value has usually been a more subjective notion than size or shape or appearance. The 'real value' of a property – an alarmingly metaphysical phrase to find above a column of agricultural statistics – can hardly be given an intelligible definition except as what real buyers are willing to pay and real vendors willing to take.[62] If for any reason the valuer is unable to adopt this index, he can substitute the corresponding sum for some more 'normal' period (such as the last year before the outbreak of war or rebellion) or else a figure derived from some neighbouring estate thought to be of similar quality. Occasionally Irish valuers were specifically directed to pursue this kind of spatio-temporal extrapolation;[63] more often valuing was treated as something of a mystery, which like the choice between innocence and guilt belonged rather to a jury than to any single assessor, however expert. It was not until the nineteenth century that valuation emerged as an independent science, practised by calculating output and input, pricing them, and subtracting one from the other.

Among surveyors in England the shift of emphasis from inquisition and viewing to measurement and mapping is thought to have proceeded most rapidly in the 1570s,[64] and from an Irish standpoint it is notable

TABLE 6

ACREAGE FIGURES IN THE SURVEY OF OFFALY, 1550

Size of parcel	Extent of 'rounding': number of references			
	Units	Tens	Hundreds	Thousands
1-9 acres	32	—	—	—
10-99 acres	25	181	—	—
100-999 acres	0	20	79	—
1,000 or more acres	0	0	1	3

SOURCE: E. Curtis, 'The Survey of Offaly, 1550', *Hermathena*, 20 (1930), pp 312–53.

that this revolutionary period should interpose itself between the old-style plantation of Leix and Offaly and the advent of the true land surveyor with the Munster plantation of the 1580s. Events in Munster will occupy the next chapter. The point to stress here – it has been illustrated more than once already – is that earlier procedures did not immediately fall into disuse. On the contrary, what is perhaps the best summary ever given of pre-modern Irish surveying techniques comes not from the Leix-Offaly era but from a century later, in the orders issued by the commissioners for executing the Cromwellian Act of Satisfaction:

> You are forthwith, upon receipt of your commission, to meet in some convenient place within the said county, to take the oath prescribed in your said commission, for the due execution of the trust thereby committed unto you, and to consider in what barony or place you shall judge it most convenient to appoint the first court of survey to be kept, in order to the prosecution of your said commission, and accordingly to appoint time and place for that end. And for the more effectual performance of the said service, you are authorised to adjourn from time to time, and from place to place, in such manner as you shall judge to be most conducible to the speedy and effectual discharge of the said work …
> You are with all convenient speed to enter into and upon all and every the honours, baronies, manors, castles, messuages, and other the lands, tenements, and hereditaments whatsoever mentioned in your commission, lying within the said county … And by your oaths of good and lawful men, and by all other lawful ways and means, you are to inquire and find out the premises, and every of them, with their and every of their appurtenances. And you are to view and survey the same, or cause the same to be viewed and surveyed, so as the premises and every of them may (either by your own view, or by the view and testimony of good and lawful persons, upon oath) be certainly, distinctly, and entirely known from other lands, by their respective qualities, quantities, or number of acres by estimation (according to one and twenty foot to the perch, and one hundred and sixty perches to the acre), also by their names, situation, parish, or place where the same do lie, with their respective metes and bounds; the bogs, woods, and barren mountains, belonging to the respective premises, or any of them, being mentioned, and the quantity thereof estimated and distinguished from the profitable lands in the said survey. And for the better execution of your said commission, you are, as often as you see cause, to summon one or more juries, and to give them in charge to inquire and find out all and every the particulars of these instructions, and to cause such

juries, when and as often as you shall judge it necessary, to view and tread the metes and bounds of the premises, and to form all such other matters and things as are perfectly inquirable in courts of survey, as you shall give the same in charge unto them.

You are, by the like ways and means, to inquire of and find out the true yearly value of the premises, and of every of them, as the same were let for, or worth to be let, in the year 1640, or at any time before; and also what part of the premises are chargeable with any pious and charitable use or uses; and also to inquire of and survey, or cause to be surveyed, the buildings, houses, edifices, timber, woods, open quarries, or mines, upon the premises, and to make true and particular returns of the same in your books of survey.[65]

The instructions have more to say in the same vein, but this is enough to show that the spirit of the Middle Ages was still alive in 1654. The reference to the 21-foot perch might have puzzled a medieval time-traveller. Everything else was familiar: the emphasis on naming and bounding; the delegation of responsibility to juries; the dependence on estimation; the locational woolliness of the phrase 'belonging to' for bogs, woods and mountains; and the casual attitude to valuing expressed in the words 'let for, or worth to be let'. Most familiar of all was the absence of maps. But here the foregoing quotation is deceptive, for the Irish property map was well established by the 1650s, and the Cromwellian instructions went on to point out, by way of afterthought, that on this occasion maps were actually going to be made. Yet it is arguable that the only advantage of such maps was to close a narrow gap in an inquisitorial structure which otherwise remained as sound as ever, and that the content and character of Irish estate cartography reflect the subordinate role which was all that this structure had left room for. There may be some truth in this argument; but fortunately it is not the whole truth.

Notes

1. *Chancery of Ireland. Bellingham Boyle, Esq; – Appellant. Eyre Evans, Esq; and Others, Respondents. The Case of the Appellant* ([Dublin], 1759), p. 5. Other papers relating to this dispute, which concerned land in the manor of Portrane, Co. Dublin, are in NAI, IA. 36. 30. In denoting someone named Evans, as throughout this book, the term 'Irish' carries its broadest possible meaning.

2. Outside Ireland, the term land surveying is often used as correlative with hydrographic surveying, to include the mapping of any area, however large, on any scale, however small. The following Irish definition by Benjamin Noble is slightly too narrow for the present study, but would undoubtedly have won assent from most of Noble's pre-twentieth-century compatriots: 'Land surveying is an art that teacheth how to find how many times any customary measure is contained in a piece of ground, and to exhibit the true bounds of the same by a map' (*Geodaesia Hibernica or an Essay on Practical Surveying* (Dublin, 1768), p. 9).
3. Many of these are listed in R. Dunlop, 'Sixteenth-Century Maps of Ireland', *Eng. Hist. Rev.*, 20 (1905), pp 309–37.
4. C. McNeill (ed), *Calendar of Archbishop Alen's Register* (R. Soc. Ant. Ire., Dublin, 1950), p. 60.
5. R. Dunlop, 'The Plantation of Leix and Offaly', *Eng. Hist. Rev.*, 6 (1891),
pp 61–96; B. L. J. Rowan, *The Leix-Offaly Plantation*, M.A. thesis, University College, Dublin (1940); D. G. White, *The Tudor Plantations in Ireland before 1571*, PhD. thesis, TCD (1968).
6. Map of Leix and Offaly, TCD, MS 1209(9); BL, Cott. Aug. I, ii, 40. A third copy, without writing, is in the Dartmouth Maps, 33.
7. Instructions to the Earl of Sussex, 3 July 1562, PRO, S.P. 63/6/41.
8. P. D. A. Harvey, *The History of Topographical Maps: Symbols, Pictures and Surveys* (London, 1980), ch.5.
9. E.[O'] Curry (ed.), *Cath Mhuighe Leana or the Battle of Magh Leana* (Dublin, 1855), pp 106–09; J. Hogan, 'The Tricha Cet and Related Land-Measures', *Proc. R. Ir. Acad.*, 38C (1929), p. 170.
10. T. McErlean, ' The Irish Townland System of Landscape Organisation' in T. Reeves-Smyth and F. Hamond (eds.), *Landscape Archaeology in Ireland*, BAR British Series, 116 (1983), pp 315–39.
11. 'The Court of Claims, an Heroic Poem', NLI, MS 3870 (29).
12. K. Nicholls, *Gaelic and Gaelicised Ireland in the Middle Ages* (Dublin, 1972), pp 57–64.
13. T. M. Charles-Edwards, 'Boundaries in Irish Law' in P. H. Sawyer (ed.), *Medieval Settlement: Continuity and Change* (London, 1976), pp 83–7.
14. M. J. C. Buckley, 'Notes on Boundary Crosses', *Jour. R. Soc. Ant. Ire.*, 5th ser., 10 (1900), pp 247–52.
15. P. W. Joyce, *A Social History of Ancient Ireland* (2nd ed., Dublin, 1913), 2, p. 266.
16. Record of the riding of the franchises of Dublin, 1488, J. T. Gilbert (ed.), *Calendar of Ancient Records of Dublin* (Dublin, 1889–1944), 1, p. 493; P. Ferguson, ' The Custom of Riding the Franchises of the City of Dublin', *Sinsear*, 1 (1979), pp 69–79.
17. Provision for annual payment to persons making a perambulation appears in a lease of 1666 in NLI, Ainsworth Reports on Private Collections, 12, p. 2526 (no. 319, Meath papers). Other perambulation

covenants, from the early eighteenth century, are in the calendar of the Sarsfield Vesey papers in NAI.

18. An example from Meath in the reign of Edward VI is in NAI, M.3068. The process of perambulation is mentioned in a charter of 1288–9 quoted by M. Devitt in 'Old proprietors in Straffan and Irishtown', *Jour. Kildare Arch. Soc.*, 10 (1922–8), p. 278.
19. As for example in an inquisition of 10 May 1425 at Kiltiernan, Co. Dublin: *Calendar of Ancient Deeds and Muniments Preserved in the Pembroke Estate Office, Dublin* (Dublin, 1891), p. 40.
20. A good specimen of this form, combined with an account of the attendant field work, is the 'Perambulation of the Territory of Iveagh, Co. Down' in *Inquisitionum in Officio Rotulorum Cancellariae Hiberniae Asservatarum Repertorium*, 2 (Dublin, 1829), pp xli–xliv.
21. J. H. Andrews, *A Paper Landscape: the Ordnance Survey in Nineteenth Century Ireland* (Oxford, 1975), p. 57.
22. NAI, Chancery Bills, A/238 and T/86.
23. I. H. Adams, *Agrarian Landscape Terms: a Glossary for Historical Geography* (Inst. Brit. Geogr., Spec. Pub. 9, London, 1976), p. 2.
24. Henry Piers, 'A Chorographical Description of the County of West-Meath' in C. Vallancey (ed.), *Collectanea de Rebus Hibernicis*, 1 (Dublin, 1770), p. 116.
25. C. McNeill and A. J. Otway-Ruthven (eds.), *Dowdall Deeds* (Ir. MSS Com., Dublin, 1960), p. 4.
26. N. B. White (ed.), *The Red Book of Ormond* (Ir. MSS Com., Dublin, 1932), p. 62.
27. N. B. White (ed.), *Extents of Irish Monastic Possessions, 1540–1541* (Ir. MSS Com., Dublin, 1943), p. 2.
28. R. A. Armstrong, *A Gaelic Dictionary* (London, 1825), p. 4.
29. *Chancery of Ireland. Bellingham Boyle, Esq; – Appellant. Eyre Evans, Esq; and Others, Respondents. The Case of the Respondents Evans and Forster* ([Dublin], 1759), p. 2. Evans's suggestion is generally supported by those Irish townlands, most of them probably originating before the age of exact admeasurement, which bear names like Hundred Acres and Forty Acres. Very few of these names get within ten per cent of the truth on any known numerical definition of an acre.
30. For this use of 'conventional' and ' fiscal' see A. Jones, 'Land Measurement in England, 1150–1350', *Agr. Hist. Rev.*, 27 (1979), pp 10–12.
31. R. J. Hunter, 'Sir William Cole and Plantation Enniskillen, 1607–41', *Clogher Record*, 9 (1978), p. 339.
32. Roll of 19 & 20 Charles II, 6th part, Co. Antrim, Irish Record Commission, *15th Annual Report* (Dublin, 1825), p. 169.
33. In July 1285 the King ordered the Bishop of Waterford to value land by ascertaining the number of acres and 'how much each acre is yearly worth' (*Calendar of Documents, Relating to Ireland* (London, 1875–86),

1285–92, p. 40). There are late thirteenth-century and fourteenth-century examples in McNeill and Otway-Ruthven, *Dowdall Deeds*, pp 8, 9, 20.

34. 'A Briefe Note of Ireland', *Cal. S.P. Ire.*, 1598–9, p. 431.
35. I. Leister, *Peasant Openfield Farming and its Territorial Organisation in County Tipperary* (Marburger Geographische Schriften, Heft 69, Marburg, 1976), p. 44.
36. Adams, *Agrarian Landscape Terms*, p. 4. The 'day's ploughing' as a seventeenth-century unit of area appears in R. C. Simington (ed.), *Books of Survey and Distribution*, 4, Clare (Ir. MSS Com., Dublin, 1967), p. 230.
37. McNeill and Otway-Ruthven, *Dowdall Deeds*, p. 7. The acre had been a measure of meadow in pre-conquest England (T. Rowley (ed.), *The Origins of Open-Field Agriculture* (London, 1981), p. 45).
38. Fiants, Elizabeth I, 3134 (1 Nov. 1577), *Reports of the Deputy Keeper of Public Records in Ireland* (Dublin, 1869–), *13th Rept*, p. 52.
39. In 1623 surveyors were said often to value land 'proportionately to the number of acres returned in the office by the escheator or some such officer, who only returns but what the inquest or jury finds: and the jurors and country people number their acres only by common report, and according to the custom of those places where they reside' (G. O'Brien (ed.), *Advertisements for Ireland* (Dublin, 1923), p. 20).
40. 35 Eliz. I, c.6; P. Grierson, *English Linear Measures, an Essay in Origins* (Stenton Lectures, 5, University of Reading, Reading, 1972), pp 21, 27.
41. J. Mills, 'Notices of the Manor of St Sepulchre, Dublin, in the Fourteenth Century', *Jour. R. Soc. Ant. Ire.*, 4th ser., 9 (1889), p. 35.
42. J. O'Mahony (trans.), *The History of Ireland, from the Earliest Period to the English Invasion. By the Reverend Geoffrey Keating, D.D.* (New York, 1857), p. 93. W. Harris, *The Whole Works of Sir James Ware Concerning Ireland, Revised and Improved*, 2 (Dublin, 1765), p. 225. Acres of 'the measure of the English Pale' appear in *Cal. S.P. Ire.*, 1611–14, p. 296.
43. Particulars of the tenements, messuages and garden plots belonging to Piers Butler in the Burgagery of Callan, 1662, NAI, M.2835.
44. For the Tipperary acre see Leister, *Peasant Openfield Farming*, p. 41 *et seq.*, and W. F. T. Butler, *Gleanings from Irish History* (London, 1925), pp 298–300; for 'County of Ormond measure', NLI, D.4202 (1640); for the ' great measure of that lordship' (Arklow), NLI, D.4016 (1636); for the 'Carbre' acre, White, *Monastic Extents*, p. 311 (Co. Meath, 1540).
45. NAI, Chancery Bills, BB/96.
46. R. C. Simington (ed.), *The Civil Survey, A.D. 1654–1656* (Ir. MSS Com., Dublin, 1931–61), 6, pp 501–48 (Kilkenny). See also 'great acres, of great country measure' in NLI, D.4116 (1609).
47. Transcript of Desmond survey, NAI, 1A.53.36, f.25 d. For one attempt at reconciliation see White, *Tudor Plantations*, 2, pp 58–67.

48. F. Seebohm, *Customary Acres and their Historical Importance* (London, 1914), pp 110, 115, 264. The length of the Cunningham perch is 18 feet, 9 inches.
49. E. H. Smith, 'Lancashire Long Measure', *Trans. Hist. Soc. Lancs. & Ches.*, 60 (1959), pp 1–14. In 1592 Christopher Saxton used the 21 foot perch for a survey in the West Riding of Yorkshire (I. M. Evans and H. Lawrence, *Christopher Saxton, Elizabethan Map-Maker* (Wakefield, 1979), p. 90). Anglo-Irish metrological relations are further confused by an Irish reference in 1636 to 'English measure after the admeasurement of 21 feet to the pole' (NLI, D.4022).
50. Grierson, *English Linear Measures*, p. 20.
51. *Calendar of the Patent and Close Rolls of Chancery in Ireland, Henry VIII to Elizabeth* (Dublin, 1861), p. 152 (1547).
52. E. Lamond (ed.), *Walter of Henley's Husbandry together with an Anonymous Husbandry, Seneschaucie and Robert Grosseteste's Rules* (London, 1890), pp 84–9.
53. John Fitzherbert, *The Boke of Surveyeng and Improvementes* (Amsterdam and Norwood, New Jersey, 1974).
54. Fiants, Henry VIII, 160 (1 Oct. 1540), *Dep. Keeper Pub. Rec. Ire., 7th Rept*, p. 48.
55. R. Lascelles (ed.), *Liber Munerum Publicorum Hiberniae*, 1, ii (London, 1852), p. 55.
56. The Surveyor-General's annual salary was £80 in 1623 and 1629 (TCD, MS 808, ff. 66, 92) and £60 in 1669 (*A Third Collection of Scarce and Most Valuable Tracts* (Somers Tracts), 2 (London, 1751), p. 66). The latter figure was recorded at various times in the late seventeenth and early eighteenth centuries. After William Molesworth (appointed in 1714) had petitioned for an increase, it was augmented in 1729 by another £100 per year for his lifetime, and in the time of his successor Robert Rochfort this supplementary allowance was increased to £440 for the period between Molesworth's death and his own (Lascelles, *Liber Munerum*, 1, ii, pp 56–7). In 1811 the salary stood at £600 (Irish Record Commission, *2nd Rept*, app, p. 150).
57. Fiants, Edward VI, 219 (13 and 21 Sep. 1548), *Dep. Keeper Pub. Rec. Ire., 8th Rept*, p. 47.
58. H. C. Darby, 'The Agrarian Contribution to Surveying in England', *Geogr. Jour.*, 82 (1933), p. 529.
59. Fiants, Edward VI, 30 (20 June 1547), *Dep. Keeper Pub. Rec. Ire., 8th Rept*, p. 29.
60. Lord Chichester's answers to Recusants' complaints, 1613, *Cal. S.P. Ire.*, 1611–14, p. 379; A. B. Grosart (ed.), *The Lismore Papers*, 2nd ser., 2 (London, 1887), p. 130 (1618).
61. In 1560 the Lord Lieutenant of Ireland was instructed to have fresh surveys made when land was newly leased with the proviso that they would either be 'better' than the old or not worse (S.P. 63/2/18). For a much later use of the same criterion for judging surveys see King to Lord Lieutenant, 24 Mar. 1667, *Cal. S.P. Ire.*, 1666–9, pp 329–30.

62. In eighteenth-century surveys the 'real value' is often tabulated alongside the rent currently being charged. An example is Thomas Moland's valuation of the Earl of Malton's estate in Co. Wicklow in 1728 (NLI, 21.F.162).
63. Order of Commissioners for Affairs of Ireland on the valuation of lands in Co. Kilkenny, 21 Nov. 1653, NLI, MS 2499, p. 113.
64. S. Tyacke and J. Huddy, *Christopher Saxton and Tudor Map-Making* (British Library Series, no. 2, London, 1980), pp 18–19, 54–5.
65. Commission for surveying lands in Co. Westmeath, 2 June 1654, printed in T. A. Larcom (ed.), *The History of the Survey of Ireland, Commonly Called the Down Survey, by Doctor William Petty, A.D. 1655–6* (Dublin, 1851), pp 383–6, reprinted by R. C. Simington in each of his introductions to the Civil Survey.

2
The only ground-work of our plantation

'THERE IS NO MAN here skilful to make a map as it ought to be'[1] was the kind of comment that Queen Elizabeth's ministers often had to read in the voluminous bulletins of bad news that they regularly received from Ireland. At first sight this persistent and seemingly nationwide dearth of cartographic talent is hard to reconcile with all the town plans, fort plans, military sketches and topographical surveys of different parts of Ireland that survive from the later sixteenth century. Some of these might even be classed as 'estate' maps in the sense that they depict the topography of baronies or lordships assigned to individual grantees,[2] but not in any other sense: their authors were fast-working English soldiers and engineers who then moved on, probably with some relief, to other less unpleasant theatres of war or other less arduous branches of their profession. Similarly, no sustained effort went into the maps that came from amateur draughtsmen whose only qualification was a desire to propitiate the Queen's chief minister, Lord Burghley, by gratifying his interest in 'lineal descriptions'.[3] Even by these undemanding standards the period around 1582 (when the complaint quoted above was written by Warham St Leger, President of Munster) ranks rather low in quality and quantity of Irish maps. Several good cartographers had ceased work not long before, the most influential being Robert Lythe; others had not yet appeared.[4] By an unlucky coincidence the lull came when the country's need for cartographic skill was about to reach a level of urgency unknown to earlier generations.

St Leger was writing in the last stages of Elizabeth's war against the insurgent Earl of Desmond, which ended in 1583 when the Earl was finally caught and killed. To discourage further uprisings the government resolved to confiscate the rebels' lands and redistribute them among loyal colonists brought from the west of England. The forfeited properties lay mainly in the counties of Waterford, Cork, Kerry and Limerick. They were to be settled in large estates or 'seignories', each to be made the responsibility of a gentleman 'undertaker' supported by a carefully structured hierarchy of tenant farmers, craftsmen and labourers. The enterprise that drew them all to Ireland was the famous Munster plantation. Such colonies were not a new idea, but the attitude of the immigrants on this occasion was different from that of their predecessors, whether English, Norman or Scandinavian. Inspired by the recent progress of land surveying in England, their conception of an Irish estate was essentially quantitative. Unfortunately the domains of Desmond and his followers had never been measured except in the kind of vague and variable unit – in this case the ploughland – that contemporary Englishmen had come to regard as obsolete. Converting medieval to modern, ploughlands to acres, was the most revolutionary of the tasks laid on the commissioners appointed in June 1584 to take stock of the forfeited terrain. They also had to distinguish different qualities and uses of land, to establish the boundaries between unconfiscated and confiscated estates, and to make a description of the latter,[5] the description apparently being what Burghley's correspondent would have called 'lineal' as well as verbal. Such were the proceedings that one undertaker epitomised as 'the only ground-work' of the plantation.[6]

Inevitably the commission was made up of administrators rather than technicians. They included Sir Henry Wallop, Sir Valentine Browne, Thomas Jenison, Christopher Payton and Lancelot Alford – none of them names to conjure with in the history of Irish or any other maps, though the last did hold the office of Surveyor-General. But in August 1584 the government acknowledged the practical character of their task by appointing a non-establishment figure, one Arthur Robins, as an additional member.[7] A seventeenth-century historian called Robins 'a kind of surveyor'.[8] While the phrase is not necessarily derogatory (though Robins was to encounter plenty of criticism) it does imply a surveyor of a new breed, new to Ireland that is, who actually measured the land instead of just looking at it and who then expressed his measurements in graphic form. As an Englishman, with some knowledge of English surveying practice, Robins may have been invited to Munster especially for this purpose. His own ambitions were more than merely professional, and he later emerged as proprietor of a Co. Cork seignory known as Robins's Rock.[9] Seignoral status obviously marked Robins as a gentleman, but his daily earnings were only half those of his colleague Thomas Wiseman, who was added to the commission at the same time. Since Wiseman was employed in legal inquiries and not in measuring or drawing, this difference of salary provides an early indication that surveys such as Robins's ranked below the kind of investigation into titles, encumbrances, easements, etc., that was usually conducted by members of an older and more learned profession.

Robins, Wiseman and their fellow-commissioners were soon busy with a labour that lasted until the autumn of 1585.[10] They had no previous Irish experience and few precedents of any kind to guide them, and it is not surprising that they seldom if ever referred to earlier plantation schemes like those of Leix and Offaly. On the contrary, they seemed proud to dissociate themselves from the survey methods of the past. 'We do not resort to good towns and there take the report of the freeholders as the manner hath been to the great hindrance of Her Highness', one of them boasted after seven weeks' experience with all the superiority of the veteran fieldworker, 'our travel is in camping upon and near to any place where the lands lie'.[11] His air of confidence was misleading. It is true that by the spring of 1586 the government had been given an impressively accurate-looking total of 577,635 acres for the extent of the confiscated area.[12] Whether these were English or Irish acres (a question that nobody answered), they were more than Robins could possibly have measured by himself in the thirteen months he is known to have spent making 'plots', and there was no provision among his expenses for the employment of a subordinate field corps. So it seems likely that the main purpose of his survey was to identify the forfeited properties and to record their names, and that his acreages were not measurements but only estimates derived from local information. 'Plots' based on such estimates were probably simple location maps with boundaries sketched diagrammatically, like the map of east Co. Cork in the Public Record Office, London, which is endorsed with the date December 1585 and which may be an example (the only surviving example, it seems) of Robins's work at this early period.[13] In which case the government was right to express the opinion, in November of the same year, that the escheated lands 'be not so thoroughly surveyed as is requisite'.[14] By this time it was evident that a more detailed investigation would have to be made in the following spring and summer.

It is tempting to see these events of 1584–5 as the kind of false start that seems to have preceded almost every major national mapping operation in Irish history from the Ordnance Survey backwards. In retrospect such misadventures could usually be made to look like part of a carefully laid plan, and in Munster as elsewhere the tightness of the original deadline did much to make this comforting interpretation appear quite plausible.[15] The initial survey had to be done quickly enough to give intending undertakers early notice of the number of seignories available and their approximate size, and to establish proper links between each Irish county or part-county and the west-country catchment area from which its English settlers were to be drawn. In this scenario the detailed admeasurement and demarcation of individual seignories could appropriately be left until after the undertakers had been given the chance to start planning their journeys. Meanwhile the commission of 1584–5, whatever its shortcomings, had furnished the raw material for a long spell of indoor activity in London. The task of the office staff included fixing the sizes of the seignories (at either 4,000, 6,000, 8,000 or 12,000 acres), calculating the number of seignories on offer in each county, and deciding how many tenant farms each undertaker could be expected to find room for.

As part of these deliberations a possible disposition of demesne, tenant farms and manorial village was worked out in diagrammatic form, perhaps by Robins, who was retained on salary for nine months beginning in November 1585.[16] The seignory in the diagram was a square of just over four statute miles dimension, the government having by this time decided that the unit for measuring the new colony should be the English perch of $16^{1}/_{2}$ feet. At the centre was a village or hamlet comprising a church, a mill and thirty-two cottages. Small tracts of common pasture and open-field arable were to be provided near the village, but most of the seignory was to be made up of enclosed farms held in severalty. The farms were relatively small, ranging from 78 acres to 400 acres, compared with the undertaker's demesne of 1,000 acres. Farmhouses were laid out in clusters of from two to six, and each cluster was to be served by a road or lane, most of the bigger houses standing alongside the four main roads that quartered the seignory. With almost every farm a rectangle or triangle, the whole design was suffused with the kind of land surveyor's mentality that became familiar in the 'squaring' and 'striping' programmes of a later age. In particular, it carried the demand for professional expertise all the way down the socio-agricultural hierarchy from the landlord's broad acres to the garden of the lowliest cottager. Even the surveyor himself might have been surprised to find that in a seignory laid out to this specification there would have been well over a hundred miles of boundary line for him to measure or calculate.

At the cost of ignoring all physical variations on the ground, the creator of this ideal Munster estate showed a precocious ingenuity in reconciling optimum lay-outs for roads, farms and settlements; perhaps he was rather too ingenious, for the authorities gave little sign of understanding what he had to say. Nevertheless, by their adoption of an exact scale or table for farm-sizes they did seem to go some way towards guaranteeing the Irish land surveyor a future livelihood. The articles agreed between government and undertakers in June 1586 did not run to a diagram, but they were apparently based on the assumption that the landlord should keep 2,100 acres in his demesne, and that his tenants should include six farmers with 400 acres each, six freeholders with 300 acres each, and 42 copyholders with 100 acres each. Only the number of the smallest farms (50, 25 or 10 acres) was left unspecified, except that there were to be at least thirty-six of them.

None of this elegant theorising can have brought much comfort to the Munster undertakers. As European settlers were to find in other continents, the geometrical boundary has much to recommend it. But although the Elizabethan image of Ireland resembled that of North America in many respects, the old world was unlike the new in possessing a network of ancient land divisions which were considerably smaller than the Irish seignories on the governmental drawing board and which were too firmly grounded in popular consciousness to be ignored. To effect the translation, a multitude of confiscated ploughlands now had to be mapped and their contents measured. Once this was done, the English colonists of the sixteenth century would be just as willing to accept the native territorial structure as their Norman predecessors seem to have been. No Elizabethan undertaker really expected a square edge to his property; at any rate none of them complained about not getting one. But they did expect to get the property itself, and bitter recriminations followed when some of them found on arrival in Munster that they were still without official proof of the location of their seignory or even of its existence. Despite these complaints, it was not until after the best of the summer weather had been missed that a second survey commission began dividing and bounding the seignories on 21 September 1586. (No doubt there were a few more grumbles when the new commissioners chose to start with the lands of two rich and influential undertakers, Sir Walter Raleigh and Sir Christopher Hatton, who could have afforded to let some of their less affluent fellow-claimants take priority.)

For his new tour of duty in Munster Robins was supported by three measurers.[17] Two of them, John Lawson and Richard Whittaker (or Whiteacre), are otherwise unknown. The third, Francis Jobson, first mentioned by name in February 1587,[18] was one of the most prolific and idiosyncratic cartographers of his age. He had evidently been educated to a level that would have made many a later surveyor envious and may have been kinsman to an English knight of the same name,[19] but in Ireland his claim to gentility was insecure. It was 'Mr Robins and Jobson'. Since they were doing the same work, this looks like an early example of the social ambiguity which is said to be characteristic of the surveying profession. It was not Jobson's elevated status in his own world, but on the contrary his naggingly literate sense of being put upon, that eventually gave him a place in history. Like Robins he was an Englishman who needed an interpreter when collecting boundary information in Munster,[20] and although he seems to have lived in Ireland for some time before the plantation began (since c. 1579 if we take his rather rhetorical fragments of autobiography at their face value),[21] there was nothing Irish about his professional antecedents: the length of his measuring line was a multiple of the $16^{1}/_{2}$-foot perch;[22] and his jargon, for instance the phrase 'true proporsion and semitrie', was that of contemporary English textbook writers.[23] Why should one of nature's communicators have taken several years to make his presence known? It would be convenient to treat the years in question as a sign that Ireland had no need of land surveyors right up to the eve of the Munster settlement, but apart from a certain general plausibility this hypothesis seems to be straining the evidence (or rather lack of evidence) too far. One can only be grateful when Jobson does take the stage, in anonymous attendance on the 1586 commission.

The commissioners were soon bewailing the difficulty of their task 'by reason that the lands having been long waste are generally overgrown with deep grass, and in most places with heath, brambles and furze, whereby and by the extremity of rain and foul weather, ... we have been greatly hindered in our proceeding'. Nevertheless they kept their measurers at work until December, with the result that two of the four became incapacitated or at any rate sadly demoralised, causing the home government to be treated in February to a new variation on a familiar refrain: 'we have no other skilful measurers now in this land, but the said Mr Robins and Jobson'. The only exact record of the commission's progress is that 27,486 acres of west Waterford and east Cork had been measured in fifteen or sixteen days.[24] To a later surveyor such an output would have seemed almost too good to be true, but it still implied that two men would need approximately 650 more days to measure the rest of the forfeited area, not counting suitable allowances for travel-time between its constituent parts and for bad weather. Whether or not the government did any calculations of this kind, they soon realised that 'the survey cannot conveniently be performed this winter time ... in such an exact sort of working by the line as by the said commissioners hath been begun'. Instead, it was now decided, the measuring should proceed 'in a more speedy and superficial sort, by the eye or by the instrument, by persons skilful therein to be sent from hence'.[25]

It is unusual for English Privy Councillors to give technical advice on methods of land measurement. As often happens in such cases, the laymen were more explicit than the professionals, though the Council erred in opposing 'line' and 'instrument' as if these appliances were mutually exclusive. On the contrary: Robins's surveys were made 'both by line and instrument';[26] Lawson and Whittaker claimed expenses for 'two line bearers and a markman to keep and observe the stations of the instrument';[27] and Jobson's work was 'exactly measured ... with a wire line ... and justly by the said measure plotted upon the instrument'.[28] Like so many early surveyors, they all seemed reluctant to say what the instrument was, perhaps understandably when one remembers the outlandish names – holometer, polimetrum, theodelitus, etc. – that found favour with contemporary manufacturers. Jobson's 'plotted upon the instrument' suggests a plane table, but this was an essentially fair-weather technique and appears to have been little used by later Irish surveyors. It is also hard to reconcile with the emphasis that they all placed on linear measurement: in orthodox plane-tabling the chain is unnecessary except for the determination of a single base line, and to confine the table to the laying-off of angles between independently measured lines would be to sacrifice most of its advantages. At any rate the commissioners are unlikely to have been visualising a plane table when they ordered that Robins should 'leave off his plotting and that he and ... Jobson being returned into the said county of Cork should there proceed in measuring only'. Measuring and plotting were thus treated as two distinct operations, whereas the whole purpose of the plane table is to combine them. Unfortunately for this argument, it is not clear whether 'plotting' meant the laying down of measurements from field books (as in modern usage) or simply the making of fair copies from plane table drawings or field sketches. The 'plots' being drawn at the end of 1586 were evidently fair copies, done on the orders of Lord Burghley and his fellow councillors in England and not as an integral part of Robins's work for the plantation commissioners.[29]

In any case it is by no means a foregone conclusion that all four Munster measurers did their measuring in the same way. There is certainly no record of any common set of instructions. Jobson more than once took trouble to emphasise that he was speaking for himself, almost to the extent of hinting that there was something not quite right about the methods of his colleagues. Nor did any one surveyor necessarily apply the same technique to every occasion. The most that can be said is that speed, accuracy and simplicity could have been combined by treating each parcel as a polygon in which the length and bearing of every side was measured by line and instrument respectively. There are several ways of obtaining the angles in such a survey: they may be plotted graphically with alidade or sight-rule, observed from two readings on a graduated circle or semi-circle, or deduced from compass bearings. But in all cases the result is what the modern textbook calls a closed traverse. More will be said about this technique later; for the moment it may be briefly characterised as frontier surveying, a label well justified by its popularity in colonial America.[30]

The best alternative to the boundary traverse was some kind of triangulation, which could also be done either graphically or instrumentally, in both cases with linear measurement reduced to a single base line for each network of triangles. This may be what the Queen's councillors had in mind when they recommended using the instrument 'superficially', though since the change to superficial methods was never carried out it hardly seems to matter what they meant. The council itself was complaining in July 1587 that its advice had been disregarded,[31] and the surveyors' reports quoted above, referring as they do to both line and instrument, suggest that it was still being disregarded in the autumn. Jobson confirms this interpretation by treating the unsupported use of the instrument as a special case, attributable to the presence of thick woodland obstructing the passage of the line.[32]

For further light on the survey methods of the 1580s it is natural, though in the present state of scholarship not very rewarding, to turn to the maps themselves. Unfortunately most of the surviving Elizabethan maps of Munster are small-scale representations of the whole province or of complete counties, which even where they owe anything to the plantation surveys have been too much reduced in scale to be easily distinguishable from the ordinary topographical or geographical maps of the same period. The exceptions are two maps preserved in the National Maritime Museum at Greenwich.[33] Both show subdivisions of Sir Walter

Raleigh's seignories, one comprising Inchiquin and White's Island south of Youghal, the other a large tract of country near Tallow, Co. Waterford (Fig. 2). Both are dated 1589 and were probably associated with a special inquiry concerning the Raleigh estates in which Robins and Jobson are known to have participated.[34] Though not perhaps plantation records in the strictest sense, they may reasonably be taken to resemble the missing plantation surveys in style and content, and the caption to the Tallow map is worth quoting at length:

> All which do lie within known bounds in such manner as they are here described in true proportion and symmetry do contain of arable pasture wood and sortable land 22,719 acres whereof there is much barren and very bad grounds lying … upon the south side of the said lands adjoining to the great waste and general common called Slewvarise. And because time would not serve us to divide the same exactly from the good ground being a matter very intricate to be performed and scarce worth the travail, yet by due observation thereof as we passed along in measuring the extreme bounds, we have made a very near estimate of the quantity of the same to be generally considered of by the chief commissioners … The extreme bounds and circumference of Her Majesty's land described in this plat are distinguished by the carnation colour and the freehold land by the yellow colour. All which have been truly measured by lines of wire after sixteen foot and a half to the perch according to the best [?] use [?] of England and the contents of the letters patent in that behalf and exactly plotted by a scale of 40 perches to an inch and lastly reduced unto this scale of 80 to an inch for the more convenient use thereof.

As well as marking the first appearance in Ireland of the scale-ratio of forty perches to one inch, this passage fits the hypothesis of the closed traverse by its reference to passing along the 'extreme bounds' of the lands in question. Nothing is said about the possibility of estimating the area of barren land in the course of running lines across the middle of the territory as could be done in a triangulated survey. Both the Tallow and Inchiquin maps show the outer boundaries in detail. They also mark a number of rivers, several tracts of woodland, a few castles and churches, and one short stretch of main road. So they are not entirely confined to the boundaries. On the other hand they ignore farms and fences, unfortified houses, and minor roads. The most likely interpretation is that they were surveyed by boundary traverse together with some intersecting or sketching of interior points.

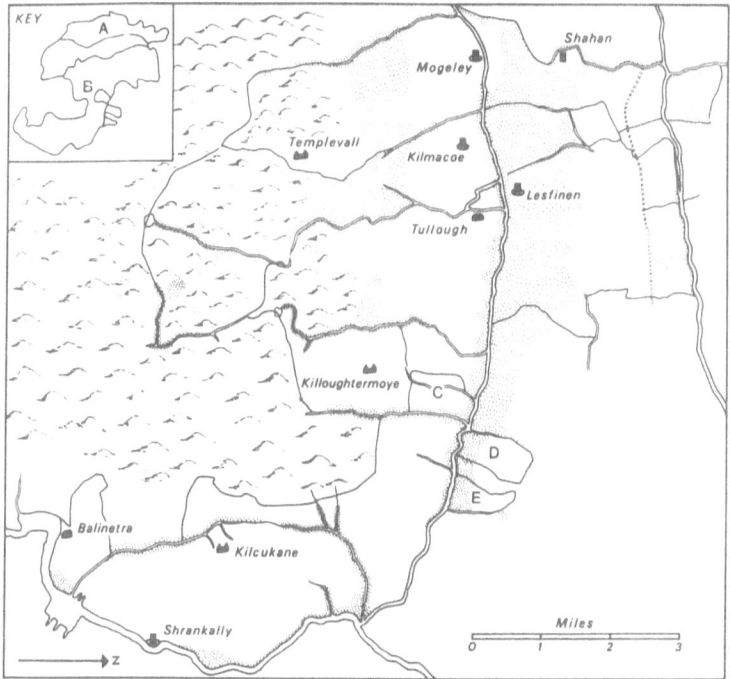

Figure 2. Part of the Bride and Blackwater Valleys, Cos Cork and Waterford, 1589. Redrawn from a photostat (NLI, 16.L.33(18)) and arbitrarily adjusted for distortion. The original, measuring about 41 inches by 46 inches, is in the Dartmouth maps, 29. The key in the upper left-hand corner replaces an inscription on the original (partly quoted on page 36) which lists the territories mapped. With Ordnance Survey spellings in brackets, these are Mogeley (Mogeely), Shahan (Shean), Lesfinen (Lisfinny), Tullough (Tallow), Kilbeg (Kilbeg), Kilmore (Kilmore), Kilwatermoy (Kilwatermoy), Tercullin (Tircullen), Balymachinell (unidentified), Kilnecarig (Kilnacarriga), Kilfentra (unidentified), Balinemadiagh (Ballymuddy), Balincty (Ballyneety), Balymucky (unidentified), Kilmackinchelon (Kilmanicholas), Baliphillip (Ballyphilip), Shrancally (Strancally), Balinetra (Ballynatray) and Culbeggin (Coolbeggan). The following notes summarise the territorial names and inscriptions within the survey area. Their locations are shown in the key.
A. Lands of Mogeley (Mogeely) and Shahan (Shean), 5,448 acres of 'sortable' land.
B. Lands of Lesfinen (Lisfinny), Shrancally (Strancally) etc., 16,419 acres of 'sortable' land.
C. Thomas FitzMoris FitzGibbon's ploughland.
D. Monetrin (Monatrim), half a ploughland.
E. Kilnacarig (Kilnacarriga), half a ploughland.
The modern names of the settlements represented on the map are Ballinatray, Kilcockan, Kilmacow, Kilwatermoy, Lisfinny, Mogeely, Shean, Strancally, Tallow and Templevally. Woods are stippled. The dotted line represents a road.

The Privy Councillors had been right to suggest that triangulation needs more skill than traversing. Whether it needed more skill than Robins and Jobson could command (which seems to be the implication) is a different matter. Even the most accomplished surveyor might think twice about the virtues of 'superficiality' where outer boundaries had to be carefully perambulated and where there was little of interest or value to be shown in the interior of an undeveloped or war-ravaged estate. What does seem clear is that the new measurers of February 1587, skilful or otherwise, never materialised. Evidently there was no one among the undertakers or their tenants who admitted to being a surveyor. Since Elizabethan surveying techniques appear to have been rather slowly diffused from metropolitan England through the provinces this deficiency may be a reflection of the immigrants' predominantly west-country origin. As for the problem of attracting measurers to Ireland in a purely professional capacity, this was posed by Robins himself in a short essay on 'The difference betwixt the surveying of lands here in England and the surveys to be made in Ireland'.

> Such as are entertained by noblemen and gentlemen here in England for the survey and extent of lands, for the plotting, measuring, description, and discovery thereof, have commonly the allowance of 10s by the day besides horsemeat and man's meat, travelling charges and all other charges whatsoever, and the servants of the said noblemen or gentlemen with the tenants of their several lordships or manors to attend upon them for measuring, setting up of marks, showing the mears and bounds or any other service appertaining thereunto at the direction of the said surveyors, besides this benefit, that their service is in a quiet country free from danger or other troubles, all care and charge for provision of things necessary depending upon them by whom they are entertained. And where they have not this allowance of 10s by the day they have commonly 3d for every acre, if it be but to deliver up the bare content, and 4d for every acre if they make description thereof.
>
> The service that I am appointed to do for Her Majesty, all the charges ordinary and extraordinary is to be borne by myself upon such entertainment as shall be allowed unto me in that behalf without any assistance of other men's men than my own, and without tenants of any manors nor others to instruct me in the mears and bounds thereof, but such as I shall be constrained to hire and maintain at great charges for that purpose, unless they be such as will do nothing else but misinform and seek to interrupt and hinder the service which also chiefly consisteth in a waste country, the people for the most part discontented with the

course to be observed, and therefore dangerous with the adventure of life by reason of the stratagems that may be laid by the evil disposed, and also extreme chargeable in respect of carriages of tents, bedding and other furniture, and for victuals and all manner of provisions for the field.[35]

Robins wrote in the emphatic vein of one who had been bombarded with rocks from an upper-storey window when approaching an Irish castle to ask for topographical guidance;[36] with enough emphasis, in fact, to get his application for a wage increase to ten shillings per day accepted.[37] But his homily appears to have been composed in September 1587, too late to influence the kind of recruiting campaign that the authorities might have considered launching among English surveyors six months earlier.

By this time the government had got used to accepting second-best. Already in the previous April it had authorised the 'esteeming' of such land as there was no longer time to measure.[38] The estimation was done by sampling. Robins reported in September 1587 that, when told by the commissioners to stop measuring, his response had been to 'computate the rest by that which I had already done'.[39] A different and more scientific method, suggested by the Munster commissioners at about the same time and approved by the London authorities as an experiment, was to treat the seignory as a sampling frame, measuring a few ploughlands in each one, calculating the area of an average ploughland, and then applying that average to the unmeasured ploughlands.[40] Measuring evidently continued in some form, for as late as October 1588 it was decided to continue Jobson rather than Robins in this duty, Robins having in effect priced himself out of the market.[41] But its incidence was apparently still very selective, for in the patents issued to undertakers in and after 1589, as well as during the previous two years, most of the acreages were said to have been determined 'by estimation'. It must be admitted that this formula was later to serve as a kind of legal fiction in cases where a proper admeasurement is known to have taken place; but in the Munster plantation estimating probably meant what it said, for it was often accompanied by a proviso that the rent would be adjusted if a further inquiry found the acreage in the patent to be incorrect.[42]

The failure of the Munster surveys – for failure it was – extended to almost every aspect of the work. One weakness was that not enough had been done to separate profitable land from unprofitable. The government at the outset had recognised geographical realities by agreeing to make an allowance for bog, heath and wasteland,[43] but there are at least two maps with inscriptions admitting that the author had not found time to measure the edge of every bog.[44] However, in a manner typical of Irish attitudes to land at this period and for long afterwards, it was total quantity of terrain, good or bad, that attracted most attention. One problem for the quantifier was to distinguish what had been measured from what had only been estimated. Jobson implied that there had been some deception on this point. 'I know by long experience and practice', he wrote, 'that these last surveys could not be exactly performed and accordingly plotted in so short a time as they were; and that I am ready to prove with any that shall go into the field with me. And to perform the like service let them bring what instrument or device they will thereto'.[45] It was the kind of challenge thrown out by many an Irish land surveyor in the years to come; the kind of challenge which (as on this occasion) the recipient almost always chooses to ignore.

In fact the accusations of inaccuracy embraced both measurement and estimation, and in both cases the validity of the criticism is, as always, by no means easy to assess. When an undertaker complained of short measure the reason might have been not an error in the survey, but the simple fact that there was insufficient forfeited land in the vicinity to constitute a full-sized seignory. Nor does the problem disappear when land is known to have been measured a second time. The seignory at Molahiffe in Kerry was counted as 6,560 acres in 1587 and as 3,280 acres in one of a series of surveys authorised in 1611;[46] on the face of it an enormous error, but without contemporary map evidence no one can say whether the same boundaries had been traced on both occasions. Even if maps had survived there might still be problems of identifying the streams, roads and ditches that defined the boundary; and it might also remain doubtful whether the balance of the profitable land in the survey and the unprofitable land left out of it had stayed the same from one admeasurement to the next, for judgements about profitability might well depend on the state of local agriculture at the time of a surveyor's visit.

Of the two possible kinds of error, giving a tenant more land than the surveyor said he had was more probable than giving him less. Such under-measurement (or over-granting) may have been due to technical factors, some of which will be considered in a later chapter: it was a common feature of Irish surveys made under a variety of tenurial and legal circumstances. Another reason for it, non-technical but far from unlikely, was put forward by the officers who in 1592 investigated an alleged case of this phenomenon in a survey made by Robins. Since the surveyor had been housed and fed by the undertakers at the time of the survey, they pointed out, it was not very probable that he would reward his hosts by unnecessarily inflating their liability for rent.[47] Similar suspicions were voiced by Robins's colleague. Without mentioning any names, Jobson claimed to know of land being given half or a third of its true area, and in one case only an eighth.[48] How far such gross discrepancies went beyond what was attributable to technical causes may be judged from the Inchiquin map of 1589. A comparison with present-day maps can be only approximate, partly because it is not clear whether the cartographer's return of 5,503 acres included the 'small underwoods and barren ground' referred to in his caption (barren ground is known to have been left out of the acreage recorded on its companion map of the same year), partly because post-Elizabethan coastal changes may have altered the real extent of the mapped area. All the same, it is interesting that the Inchiquin map appears to be in error not by the kind of huge margin cited by Jobson, but by something more like 15 per cent.

The extreme paucity of material for such comparisons points to another failure in the Munster plantation survey, and that is the lack of any adequate contemporary system for keeping a permanent record of the surveyors' work. Maps, as distinct from numerical lists, would have been useful not only as statements of location but as a means of calculating areas; in a boundary traverse, indeed, it was probably beyond the scope of Elizabethan mathematics to find the area of an irregular figure without first drawing a map. Yet with the two exceptions noted (both apparently special cases) no large-scale maps of Elizabethan Munster are known to exist. Such maps eluded, among others, that most pertinacious of Victorian cartographic scholars, W. H. Hardinge, who had hoped to treat the surveys of the 1580s as exhaustively as he treated those of the 1650s.[49] No copies are recorded in the eighteenth century, when other plantation maps, though not yet found historically interesting, were consulted for a variety of legal reasons. Even in the seventeenth century no one ever mentioned them. It is also significant that the Munster surveys had evidently been done with little reference to the Surveyor-General of the time (Lancelot Alford), who was surely the obvious person to be charged with maintaining a record of them. Whether the maps got lost at an early stage or whether they were never received into official custody is uncertain. Protractions on scales as large as forty perches to the inch, though at first sight harder to lose than small maps, often prove sadly vulnerable: because of the labour involved in copying them they tend not to be duplicated, so that a single mischance is enough to wipe the record clean.

As it happens, in this case some duplicates are known to have been made. Jobson drew 'fair plots out of the base he had made of those lands he first measured', and since he was paid for the time spent on them the 'fair plots' were evidently meant to remain in governmental charge.[50] Robins's experience was somewhat different. In February 1587, as already noted, the Munster commissioners told the Privy Council of 'plots he affirmeth unto us he draweth by your honours' appointment', a phrase which conveys a certain scepticism on the Irish side as to the wisdom of letting Robins stay indoors.[51] Burghley might have meant these maps to be kept in Dublin rather than under his own eye, for nothing of the kind is known in any of the repositories among which his personal map collection has been dispersed. If so, his wishes must have been in some way frustrated, for grants based on Robins's surveys were later to come under attack for 'not setting down either of whose possession the parcels were, neither what numbers of ploughlands they contain or where the same lieth';[52] from which it would seem that some of Robins's returns consisted simply of placenames and acreages with no maps.

But even without its maps the Munster plantation is full of interest for the light it throws, or rather the questions it provokes, on the state of cartography in contemporary Ireland and by implication in England. It undoubtedly gave new impetus to mapmaking and map-reading as a means of sharing spatial information;[53] but did Elizabethan Munster hold the seeds from which a distinctively Irish surveying profession grew to maturity in the seventeenth and eighteenth centuries? It may seem reasonable to think so, though safer to be content with the more modest inference that the plantation must have taught some contemporary Irish landowners the value of a measured survey. The undertakers may have been supplied with government maps of their seignories either as a matter of course or by special arrangement, the latter doubtless involving the payment of a fee. Some may have got their maps not officially but through unauthorised leakages of various kinds. Then, as has already been remarked, a further admeasurement within the seignories was implicit in the official policy for creating tenant farms of definite sizes. By the late 'eighties the details of this policy may well have been forgotten, and when Sir Hugh Cuff wrote that he had been unable to set out new farms for want of a measurer,[54] his report was probably seen as a convenient excuse for not recruiting tenants, though it did show that measurers could still be credibly represented as a scarce commodity. Another undertaker, Henry Billingsley, made the same point by proposing to import a surveyor from England to divide his lands at Rathkeale in Co. Limerick.[55] Raleigh actually did import one; at any rate the map of his farm at Mogeely, Co. Cork, that survives from 1598 is quite different from any earlier Irish maps and also from most later ones.[56] Was Mogeely mapped by Raleigh's famous Virginia associate John White? Several recent scholars have thought so, especially as White is known to have lived for a time in the same county, some thirty miles away.[57] But perhaps this question may be evaded under colour of irrelevance, for here is one Irish cartographer (whoever he was) who left no tradition behind him.

Of the plantation surveyors themselves, Lawson and Whittaker were never heard of again, and Robins died in about 1591 with no more maps to his credit except a mysterious 'plot' (now lost, and perhaps not a true map) of the White Knight's country in north Co. Cork.[58] Jobson by contrast not only survived but continued to give an impression of unceasing cartographic hyperactivity. Indirectly – directness was not a Jobsonian characteristic – the results have much to teach about Elizabethan mapmaking in general and the occupational frontiers of Irish land surveying in particular. To begin with, Jobson claimed to be in demand among the Munster undertakers to help lay out their farms, though none of the resulting maps, if there were any, have so far been produced by their descendants. Nor has either of the two private surveys on which he is known to have been employed in other parts of Ireland – one for the Earl of Ormond in Tipperary, the other for the Earl of Essex in Monaghan.[59] Here, it might seem, were two promising examples of cartographic diffusion outside the plantation environment. But Essex's lands were themselves a new plantation rather than an established estate and both he and Ormond were untypical by virtue of having been educated in England; in any case what they got from Jobson may have been throwbacks to the kind of small-scale barony map produced by the cartographers of the 1560s and 1570s rather than anything like the forty-perch protractions made for the government in Munster. To make matters worse, there seems to be no sign from the next two decades of any new influence on estate management in any of the other Irish provinces. The gentlemen of the Pale near Dublin, for example, continued in matters of surveying as in other ways to deserve their familiar appellation of 'old' English.[60]

It was not a long catalogue of private surveys for Jobson, yet there were times when he could claim to be too busy to go to England on government service, and when he could boast of earning 6s. 8d a day plus expenses in private employment.[61] Unfortunately the effect of these claims was weakened by Jobson's strenuous efforts to earn an official reputation for cartographic versatility and by his willingness on other occasions to take on government assignments for a daily wage as low as four shillings.[62] Travelling through Munster, he had made notes of places outside the confiscated area and put these together with reductions from his government surveys to produce two county maps, and a general map of Munster, which found their way into official keeping.[63] These are the most interesting of all his maps, for they show the land surveyor ranging freely along the scale-spectrum and supplying geographical needs from unlikely cadastral sources. In this respect Jobson belongs to a select company, for at most periods of Irish history large-scale and small-scale mapping have followed separate courses to the detriment of both.

Jobson's other enterprises included maps of Kinsale and Cork harbours[64] and a plan for fortifying Waterford harbour – the last done partly with the object of securing for himself the constableship of Duncannon fort.[65] Fortification was among the 'practices' and 'inventions' of which he claimed a mastery in the slightly hysterical letter that he wrote in 1589 at a time of more than average financial anxiety.[66] He also dedicated a manuscript book of fortification projects to the Queen.[67] After the main bulk of the Munster plantation survey was complete he went north to prepare a regional map of central and eastern Ulster, which he put to further use at the height of the Tyrone war in a plan for establishing new garrisons in the province.[68] Add to these an interesting map of Co. Monaghan[69] and a map of Connaught presented to Robert Cecil,[70] and the result amounts to a creditable life's work, especially as nearly all these maps were original creations (the map of Connaught, now lost, may have been an exception), made in circumstances as hazardous as anything that Robins had complained about in Munster. In the north of Ireland Jobson 'felt every hour in danger to lose my head' – by no means a fanciful prospect, as was shown by another cartographer who actually suffered this fate not long afterwards.[71]

Although he has had his detractors, Jobson's inadequate grasp of military science and admitted clumsiness with pen and brush were a small price to pay for the range, originality and general accuracy of his output.[72] Such variety and productivity must show a love of map-making for its own sake, a sentiment so rare that it might seem impossible to draw any general deductions from it. But two inferences seem fair enough. One is that in the 1590s, as in the 1580s, cartographers were still comparatively scarce in all parts of Ireland. Otherwise Jobson would hardly have turned up in so many different contexts. Two Lord Deputies bore witness to the continuing shortage of skilled manpower. 'Touching your pleasure for a plot of Ulster, there is not any here that can do it', Burghley was told in 1593, perhaps after having requested something more elaborate than Jobson's recent map.[73] Four years later, more explicitly: 'it is not in my power to send your lordship a topographical description of the places, none that I can meet being skilful in lines with pencil and by scale to describe them.'[74] In fact the only Anglo-Irish (or Welsh-Irish) cartographers of the time whose names are known were John Browne, who mapped Connaught to great effect in 1590,[75] and John Thomas, whose survey of Lough Erne was made in 1594.[76] Browne was a gentleman amateur, Thomas a soldier, neither a likely candidate for the surveying and dividing of estates. In the war which broke out in 1598 (and whose casualties, direct or indirect, included some of the fences on Raleigh's map of Mogeely)[77] a number of new and able military cartographers found employment in Ireland, but thoughts of land surveying were put aside, not to be revived until more than ten years later with the beginning of the Ulster plantation.

The second inference is that despite his apparent immunity from professional competition Jobson was unable to prosper outside the government service; a weakness that was rather cynically exploited by the authorities ('will be glad to be employed at far less charge than hitherto hath been bestowed' was the description applied to him in 1588) when they fixed his remuneration at only 3s. 4d per day.[78] In short, Elizabethan Ireland was not ready for the full-time private land surveyor. Yet Jobson had encountered and put on record many of the troubles that were to beset the profession and its patrons in the two and a half centuries that followed. There was the basic problem of finding competent practitioners and putting them to work. There were the physical dangers and discomforts, some of natural origin and others arising from the attitude of those whose homes were being surveyed. There was the difficulty of adjudging the time and skill involved in cartography and of deciding how much to pay for them. There was the threat of corruption among those surveyors who stood to benefit by doctoring their own results, and the impossibility of monitoring their work without doing it all again. There were technical questions concerning the choice of scales, units, instruments, and methods. There was the unavoidable dependence on hostile witnesses for facts beyond the reach of first-hand observation, such as names, boundaries and tenurial arrangements. There was the issue of professional status. All these problems had arisen in Jobson's Ireland and none of them had been solved. His own solution was simple. It was for some suitably qualified individual (such as himself) to 'attend upon the general surveyor or other commissions for Her Highness's lands and for to plat and measure such lands as often as occasion shall serve', receiving for his pains 'such standing stipend as shall be thought meet', that is to become a Surveyor-General in fact instead of in name.[79] But Jobson was never appointed to this post and neither was anyone else until 1824.

Notes

1. Warham St Leger to Lord Burghley, Cork, 20 Apr. 1582, S.P. 63/91/41.
2. See for instance the map described by P. O'Keeffe in 'A Map of Beare and Bantry, Co. Cork', *Jour. Cork Hist. & Arch. Soc.*, 63 (1958), pp 26–31, for which a date in the middle 1560s is suggested in J. H. Andrews, *Ir. Hist. St.*, 16 (1969), p. 374. Another example is the map of Idrone, Co. Carlow, dated to 1569–70 and attributed to Robert Lythe in J. H. Andrews, 'The Irish Surveys of Robert Lythe', *Imago Mundi*, 19 (1965), p. 31.
3. Sir Ralph Lane to Burghley, 4 Aug. 1597, *Cal. S.P. Ire.*, 1596–7, p. 368.
4. Andrews, *Imago Mundi*, 19 (1965), p. 28.
5. S.P. 63/110/71 and 72 (18 June 1584), printed in J. Lodge, *Desiderata Curiosa Hibernica*, 1 (Dublin, 1772), p. 73.
6. Valentine Browne, 28 Oct. 1586, *Cal. S. P. Ire.*, 1586–8, p. 186.
7. Fiants, Elizabeth I, 4514 (24 Aug. 1584), *Dep. Keeper Pub. Rec. Ire., 15th Rept*, p. 59.
8. Annals of Ireland, *sub.* 1590, S.P. 63/278.
9. Fiants, Elizabeth I, 5218, *Dep. Keeper Pub. Rec. Ire., 16th Rept*, p. 76.
10. The duties and salaries of Wiseman and Robins for a period of one year and 27 days ending on 30 Sep. 1585 are given in PRO, A.O. 1/285/1075.
11. Valentine Browne, 18 Oct. 1584, S.P. 63/112/18.
12. 'A brief note of the number of acres of escheated land …', 28 Apr. 1586, S.P. 63/123/56.
13. PRO, M.P.F. 299, not listed in Dunlop, *Eng. Hist. Rev.*, 20 (1905), pp 309–37.
14. Heads of instruction for Secretary [Geoffrey] Fenton, Nov. 1585, S.P. 63/121/28.
15. Except where otherwise stated, the following account is based on documents cited in R. Dunlop, 'The Plantation of Munster,

1584–1589', *Eng. Hist. Rev.*, 3 (1888), pp 250–69. For a broader view of the same events, see D. B. Quinn, 'The Munster Plantation: Problems and Opportunities', *Jour. Cork Hist. & Arch. Soc.*, 71 (1966), pp 19–40.

16. *Acts of the Privy Council*, 1586–7, p. 39. The diagram is M.P.F. 305, redrawn and reproduced by J. H. Andrews in N. Stephens and R. E. Glasscock (eds.), *Irish Geographical Studies in Honour of E. Estyn Evans* (Belfast, 1970), p. 187.
17. A.O. 1/285/1076.
18. Plantation commissioners, 16 Feb. 1587, *Cal. S.P. Ire.*, 1586–8, p. 261.
19. Sir Francis Jobson (d.1573) was Lieutenant of the Tower of London (*Dictionary of National Biography* (London, 1885–1901)).
20. Expense accounts of Robins and Jobson in A.O. 1/285/1077.
21. Jobson to Burghley, 30 May 1589, TCD, MS 1209 (36); Jobson to Essex [1598], S.P. 63/202/4/83.
22. Book of the parcels of land in Munster, measured by Francis Jobson from 15 Sep. 1586 to 10 Oct. 1587, S.P. 63/131/59.
23. Thomas Digges, *A Geometrical Practise, Named Pantometria* (London, 1571), ch.34.
24. Plantation commissioners' correspondence, 5 Oct. 1586, 16 Feb. 1587, *Cal. S.P. Ire.*, 1586–8, pp 168, 261.
25. Privy Council to Lord Deputy of Ireland, 28 Feb. 1587, *Cal. S. P. Ire.*, 1586–8, pp 272–3.
26. Robins's report of 17 Sep. 1587, S.P. 63/131/22.
27. A.O. 1/285/1076.
28. S.P. 63/131/59.
29. *Cal. S.P. Ire.*, 1586–8, p. 261.
30. S. S. Hughes, *Surveyors and Statesmen: Land Measuring in Colonial Virginia* (Richmond, 1979). This work reveals many similarities in surveying techniques between Ireland and colonial North America.
31. Privy Council to Lord Deputy, 14 July 1587, *Cal. S.P. Ire.*, 1586–8, p. 389.
32. S.P. 63/131/59.
33. Dartmouth maps, 29 (lands near Tullow, Co. Waterford) and 38 (Inchiquin, Co. Cork), both dated 28 Aug. 1589. The writing on these maps is thought to be that of the mathematician Thomas Hariot, who was himself a planter holding land nearby at Youghal, and Dartmouth 29 carries what has been described as a note in Hariot's cipher stating that the original was made by Arthur Robins (R. C. H. Tanner, 'The Ordered Regiment of the Minus Sign: Off-beat Mathematics in Hariot's Manuscripts', *Annals of Science*, 37 (1980), p. 155).
34. S.P. 63/131/59; Fiants, Elizabeth I, 5297 (8 Feb. 1589), *Dep. Keeper Pub. Rec. Ire., 16th Rept*, p. 92.
35. 'Robins the surveyor's bill' [11 Sep. 1587], S.P. 63/131/14.
36. Robins's report on his surveys, 17 Sep. 1587, S.P. 63/131/22.

37. Robins was paid retrospectively at this rate for the period from 15 July 1586 to 10 June 1588 (A.O. 1/285/1077; also in Bodleian Library, Oxford, Rawlinson MS 317).
38. Instructions for the survey and division of lands in Munster [26 Apr. 1587], *Cal. S.P. Ire.*, 1586–8, p. 309.
39. Robins's report of 17 Sep. 1587, S.P. 63/131/22.
40. Questions touching the surveys in Munster, S.P. 63/121/62. This document is undated. In *Cal. S.P. Ire.*, 1574–85, p. 590, it is assigned to Dec. 1585, but it seems to have been written about eighteen months later. For the documents that provide its most likely context see *Cal. S.P. Ire.*, 1586–8, pp 384–6.
41. Valentine Browne, 16 Oct. 1588, S.P. 63/137/21.
42. Patents for a large number of seignories, ranging in date from 1586 to 1593, are printed in Fiants, Elizabeth I, 5032–5782, *Dep. Keeper Pub. Rec. Ire., 16th Rept*, pp 35–220.
43. Dunlop, *Eng. Hist. Rev.*, 3 (1888), p. 258.
44. 'Note that there are diverse bogs and wastes within the body of the greatest continent in this plot besides those that are described which I have not in like sort made show of by exact lineament for the avoiding of too large an expense of time but have upon special view made very near and particular estimates thereof and subtracted the quantity out of the general content. And so the like in some of the smaller continents as the abruptness of time did urge the necessity thereof' (Map of the manor and abbey of Tralee, Sep. 1587, M.P.F. 309). See also Dartmouth maps, 29.
45. Jobson to Lord Deputy, 10 Mar. 1593, S.P. 63/168/67ii.
46. R. Dunlop, 'An Unpublished Survey of the Plantation of Munster in 1622', *Jour. R. Soc. Ant. Ire.*, 54 (1924), p. 138.
47. 21 Oct. 1592, *Cal. S.P. Ire.*, 1592–6, p. 6.
48. Jobson to Burghley, 23 June 1592, S.P. 63/165/17.
49. W. H. Hardinge, 'On Manuscript Mapped Townland Surveys in Ireland of a Public Character, from their Introduction to 23rd Oct., 1641', *Proc. R. Ir. Acad.*, 8 (1861), p. 46.
50. C. McNeill, 'Report on the Rawlinson Collection of Manuscripts Preserved in the Bodleian Library, Oxford', *Analecta Hibernica*, 1 (1930), p. 100.
51. 16 Feb. 1587, *Cal. S.P. Ire.*, 1586–8, p. 261.
52. Valentine Browne, 16 Oct. 1588, S.P. 63/137/21.
53. This trend is illustrated by several small-scale maps of Munster or parts of Munster which it is hard to account for except as by-products of the plantation. Some examples are cited below in relation to Jobson's career. Others are the undated maps of Kenry in Co. Limerick and of Muskerry in Co. Cork in the Dartmouth collection (23, 24).
54. Returns from undertakers [12 May 1589], S.P. 63/144/26.
55. Proceedings of Munster commissioners, 21 Oct. 1592, *Cal. S.P. Ire.*, 1592–6, p. 6.

56. NLI, MS 22028, reproduced in J. H. Andrews, *Irish Maps* (Dublin, 1978), 12.
57. D. B. Quinn (ed.), *The Roanoke Voyages, 1584–1590*, 2 (London, 1955), pp 715–16.
58. On 14 Nov. 1590 an order was addressed to Robins (Report on the manuscripts of the corporation of Kinsale, *Analecta Hibernica*, 15 (1944), p. 164), but on 14 Sep. he had been reported dangerously ill and by 31 May 1592 he was dead (*Cal. S.P. Ire.*, 1588–92, pp 363, 516). The survey of the White Knight's country was made by Thomas Danby (deputy to the Surveyor-General) in association with Robins under a warrant of 18 May 1590. It was described as 'a perfect view and survey together with a plot' but survives only in the form of a list (S.P. 63/153/45). See also A.O. 1/285/1077; *Cal. Pat. Rolls*, Elizabeth, p. 198; above, note 33.
59. Jobson to Lord Deputy, 10 Mar. 1593, S.P. 63/168/67ii, and to Earl of Essex [1598], S.P. 63/202/4/83. An unsigned 'imaginary plot or superficial description' of part of Co. Tipperary (M.P.F. 390) may be connected with Jobson's work for Ormond. His map of Farney and Clancarroll, giving quantities of land in acres, is M.P.F. 312A: Dunlop (*Eng. Hist. Rev.*, 20 (1905), no. 19) does not distinguish it from Jobson's small map of Ulster.
60. The largest of the old English landowners, the Earl of Kildare, complained at being obliged to have his lands surveyed in 1590, but his reference to survey 'commissioners' suggests that this was some kind of non-cartographic investigation (Marquess of Kildare, *The Earls of Kildare and their Ancestors: from 1057 to 1773* (Dublin, 1862), pp 290–91).
61. Jobson to Lord Deputy, 10 Mar. 1593, S.P. 63/168/67ii.
62. Expenses of Jobson's survey of Co. Monaghan, 1591, A. O. 1/286/1079.
63. Co. Limerick, 1587, two copies: M.P.F. 97 and TCD, MS 1209 (56). Co. Cork: TCD, MS 1209 (43), unsigned but attributed to Jobson in a near-contemporary endorsement. Munster, 1589, two copies: TCD, MS 1209 (36), with autograph letter to Lord Burghley, and Dartmouth maps, 22. A later version of Munster, probably by Jobson, exists in several copies, all unsigned: TCD, MS 1209 (37), Dartmouth maps, 18, 20, 27.
64. Described by Jobson in S.P. 63/131/59, the Cork map perhaps being the original of the one by Francis Candell in NLI, MS 2656, for which see G. A. Hayes-McCoy, *Ulster and Other Irish Maps, c. 1600* (Dublin, 1964),
p. 25, and J. H. Andrews in *Ir. Hist. St.*, 14 (1965), p. 270.
65. Jobson to Privy Council, [Dec. 1587], Hatfield House: Cecil papers, 13, p. 352; signed map of Waterford harbour in TCD, MS 1209 (64).
66. S.P. 63/143/11.
67. Cecil papers, 325. In Hist. MSS Com., *Salisbury*, 13, p. 152, this volume is attributed to Sir Francis Jobson, but it appears to be the work of the Anglo-Irish Francis.

68. Jobson received £50 for making this map (McNeill, *Analecta Hibernica*, 1 (1930), p. 100) and £8 17s 9d for carrying it to England (A.O. 1/286/1079). A signed copy of 1590 is in TCD, MS 1209 (15). There are copies of a small map showing the proposed garrisons in TCD, MS 1209 (16), in M.P.F. 312, and in Cotton MS Aug. 1, ii, 19.
69. Unsigned copies in TCD, MS 1209 (31), M.P.F. 76, and M.P.F. 79. This survey is noticed in E. P. Shirley, *The History of the County of Monaghan* (London, 1879), pp 88–9, 238–9.
70. Hatfield House, Cecil petitions, 363.
71. 'Ulster's unity', an essay by Jobson accompanying his small map of the province (S.P. 63/202/4/83); Hayes-McCoy, *Ulster Maps*, p. xii.
72. Jobson is criticised in Dunlop, *Eng. Hist. Rev.*, 20 (1905), pp 315–16, 319.
73. 20 July 1593, *Cal. S.P. Ire.*, 1592–6, p. 130.
74. Sep. 1597, *Cal. S.P. Ire.*, 1596–7, p. 393.
75. M. J. Blake, 'A Map of Part of the County of Mayo in 1584: with Notes thereon, and an Account of its Author, and his Descendants', *Jour. Galway Arch. & Hist. Soc.*, 5 (1907–08), pp 157–8.
76. Dartmouth maps, 21, with explanatory note by Thomas. He is better known for his battle-views (Harvey, *Topographical Maps*, pp 170–71).
77. Raleigh's tenant, Henry Pine, left Ireland at the time of the rebellion (E. W. Waters, 'The Castles in North-East Cork', *Jour. Cork Hist. & Arch. Soc.*, 22 (1916), p. 99); for the damage to his fences see Grosart, *Lismore Papers*, 2nd ser., 2 (1887), p. 38.
78. Valentine Browne, S.P. 63/137/21.
79. Jobson to Burghley, 23 June 1592, S.P. 63/165/17.

3
Controllers of the Admeasurements

THE MUNSTER PLANTATION was followed by a long series of further attempts to pacify Ireland through the seizure of native-owned estates and the introduction of British colonists. Most of the early projects were confined to particular regions (Fig. 3). Six counties of Ulster became escheated to the crown in 1609–10, after the flight of the Earls that marked the end of the Tyrone war. Inspired by its apparent success in this unpromising terrain, the government then sought to restore the Munster colony. It also revived an ancient royal title to a large part of north Wexford, for which a wholesale change of ownership was duly instituted in 1610. By the end of the next decade similar plans had been laid for Leitrim and Longford, and for a block of territory in Westmeath (O' Melaghlin's Country), King's Co. (Ely O'Carroll together with the countries of O'Molloy, McCoughlan and Fox) and O'Dunne's Country in Queen's Co. In the 'twenties a large part of the Ulster plantation area, in Co. Londonderry, became subject to further government activity as a result of reports received in 1622. Another royal title took effect in 1637–8, this time for O'Byrne's Country in Co. Wicklow, and in 1635–40 the most ambitious of all these regional schemes was attempted in Connaught along with Clare and adjoining parts of Tipperary and Limerick. Then all previous endeavours were dwarfed by the forfeiture of two and a half million acres (according to a contemporary estimate), scattered through every county of Ireland, in retaliation for the uprising of 1641. As modified by Cromwell, and later by Charles II, this was the most thoroughgoing change of ownership in modern Irish history. It precipitated a land 'fever' which spread not only down to the foreshore but over the horizon into hypothetical undiscovered Atlantic islands somewhere off the coast of Donegal.[1] Finally, and more realistically, after James II had lost the Battle of the Boyne there was another great confiscation involving about one million acres spread among twenty-eight counties.

None of these plantation schemes was wholly successful, and some were almost without practical effect. But there can be no disputing the early eighteenth century comment that 'the many revolutions that have happened in this kingdom have occasioned several surveys'[2] or that the surveys of the seventeenth century all entailed the making of either measurements or maps or both with the objects of identifying the estate to be taken over by each planter and of determining the rent payments or other obligations attached to it. That a general survey of the whole kingdom would save a great deal of trouble was an idea common to several observers. Theorists dwelt on this possibility with relish and in detail. Practical politicians, like Lord Deputy Viscount Falkland, dismissed it as a Utopian dream,[3] or at any rate as a long-term commitment that the present generation could cheerfully bequeath to its descendants. For most of the professionals who would have to carry it out, a nation-wide survey seems to have been simply inconceivable. Even William Petty — theorist, politician and professional surveyor rolled into one — never got far with his own plans for an all-Ireland cadastre.[4]

Since each of the plantations marks a new beginning, each plantation survey has a strong claim to individual notice. Some quickly became famous and have remained so ever since, like the Strafford Survey of Connaught in 1636–40 and the Down Survey of other forfeited lands in 1654–9. Some have never had much publicity. But in all cases the cartographic evidence is regrettably incomplete. Few of the plantation maps are available in their original form, and none of the field books, line plots or other survey documents. Nor do we have the financial accounts or correspondence of the survey authorities. At the higher levels of the public service, map-making in the post-Elizabethan period had lost its novelty for the statesman and the administrator. There were no seventeenth-century Lord Burghleys; the state papers and council proceedings of his successors cannot be expected to dwell on lines and instruments, exact and superficial views. In any case, only a certain amount of application can be taken for granted in the modern reader. To piece together all the evidence for the staffing and organisation of each survey would surely overstep that limit as well as trespassing upon areas of administrative history outside the scope of land surveying as understood by the great majority of its Irish practitioners. A more realistic policy for the historian is to curtail discussion by seeking common patterns among the various survey enterprises, which makes it natural to ask whether, beneath the seeming independence of each territorial settlement, there

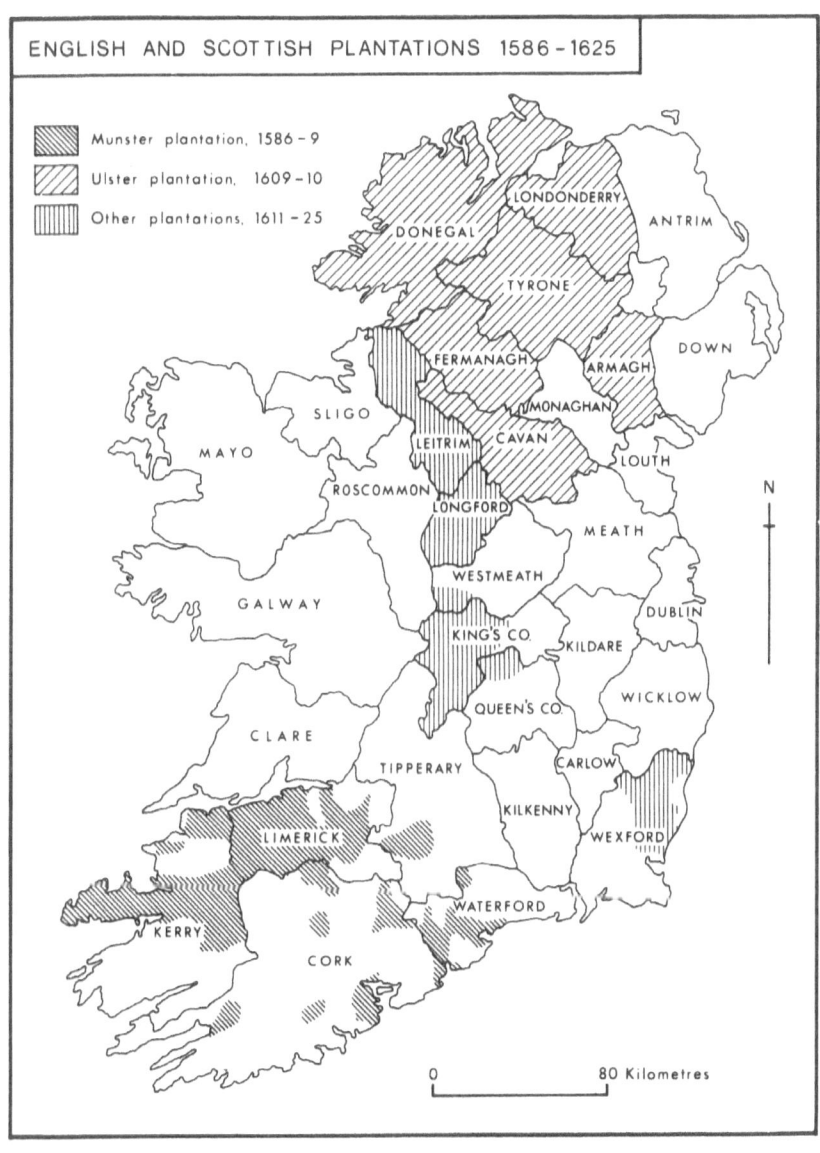

Figure 3. English and Scottish Plantations, 1586–1625. Sources: Map 2 (Tudor Plantations by K. W. Nicholls) and Map 6 (Plantations,1609–25, by A. Clarke) in T. W. Moody, F. X. Martin and F. J. Byrne (eds.), *A New History of Ireland*, 3 (Oxford, 1976).

runs some subterranean stream of cause and effect from which fructifying branches may have penetrated the wider arena of Irish estate and farm admeasurement. It is also permissible, of course, to picture unconnected groups of surveyors making the same response to the same stimulus with no awareness of each other's work. Certainly the quest for sources and influences can be overdone. A famous lecturer on the art of the novel once teased the historians among his audience by imagining the world's ancient and modern fiction-writers at work in the same room at the same time, all facing a single problem. In the historiography of land surveying there is something to be said for this approach.

Successive generations of surveyors might have been linked by a permanent official agency imposing uniform standards of technique and organisation on each new cohort of practitioners, but despite appearances to the contrary no such department existed. Although the office of Surveyor-General remained in being throughout the plantation period and for long afterwards, it was in no sense an executive organ comparable with the modern Ordnance Survey, and the Surveyor-General in the formative years from 1602 to 1641, William Parsons, was condemned by one critic as having 'never been trained up in the knowledge belonging to a surveyor'.[5] A Deputy Surveyor-General was recorded as far back as 1590,[6] but whatever attainments are attributable to individual holders of this office, outdoor skills were not in themselves a prerequisite for every aspirant. Under Charles I, the most that was expected from the deputy seems to have been 'viewing'[7] —a degree of leniency castigated on more than one occasion by the contemporary cartographer Thomas Raven, who also put in a convincing claim to a deputy's appointment on his own behalf.[8]

> ... His Majesty's lands have been so passed at random [wrote Raven] to the great hindrance of the revenues of the crown, for prevention whereof in time coming if His Majesty shall so think it fit, to appoint a sworn officer of his own sufficiently skilled and experienced in the art of survey and admeasurement of land, to be controller of the admeasurements in that kingdom, and that none of His Majesty's escheated or concealed lands shall be passed to any man whatsoever until such time as the said controller of the admeasurements, or his sufficient deputy or deputies such as he will answer for, have been upon the same, and made an exact and perfect survey thereof, setting forth in the said maps and plats as well the true quantity as quality of all the particular parts thereof signed under his hand as he will avouch the truth thereof, so as neither the King nor subject be wronged thereby, which plats so made up and

signed under the hand of the said controller, may be delivered into the office of the Surveyor-General there to remain upon record for His Majesty's use, the original plats and book of field notes to remain in the office of the said controller for his own discharge, and by this means shall neither the Surveyor-General nor his clerks enlarge or shorten the content of His Majesty's lands as have been too frequently done heretofore, neither will it be in the power of the said controller (if he would) to alter anything after his plats delivered ...

Plainly Raven's low opinion of the current Surveyor-General extended to the latter's shortcomings as an archivist. Parsons was nevertheless aware of his responsibilities in this respect. In 1613 he reported that no surveys of any moment had fallen into his hands except those of the Clandeboyes in Co. Down, of Leitrim, of the plantation of Ulster, and of lands in Co. Wexford.[9] This was by no means a discreditable tally, and Parsons had arrived too late to deserve any blame for its most obvious omission, that of the Elizabethan Munster surveys. But as a single-minded featherer of his own nest[10] he was perhaps even more likely than the average public servant of his time to treat departmental records as if they were private property, and it is hardly unexpected that no surveys from the period 1610–35 were later to be found among the contents of his office. Of course this does not exclude the possibility of one plantation survey being preserved for just long enough to influence the next without posterity becoming aware of the fact. But in practice each new survey director seems to have had to start afresh without an insider's knowledge of the government map archive. For Raven's advice was never taken: his expression 'controller of the admeasurements' serves here simply as a useful shorthand to cover a variety of cartographic trouble-shooters brought from outside the circle of officialdom and dismissed as soon as the current crisis was past.

These outsiders were recruited in two kinds of milieu, military and intellectual. The Ulster survey of 1609 was organised by Sir Josias Bodley, an engineer and fortification expert who had come to Ireland to serve in the Tyrone wars and who later went on, with more success apparently, to manage the survey of north Wexford.[11] The midland surveys were directed by two other military engineers, Captain Nicholas Pynner and Sir Thomas Rotherham.[12] Pynner did well enough to be put in charge of the Wicklow survey of 1637–8,[13] but after several decades of more or less uninterrupted peace in Ireland the soldiers were now beginning to make way for the men of science as a source of expert assistance. The Strafford Survey of Connaught was in the joint care of Dr William Gilbert and the

Revd John Johnson. Gilbert was a 'very able scholar and in particular a very good mathematician', who corresponded on astronomical subjects with the biblical chronologist, James Ussher,[14] while Johnson has been identified with a Fellow of the same name at Trinity College, Dublin.[15] The Cromwellian surveys were confided first to Benjamin Worsley (the only member of this group to be actually appointed Surveyor-General) and later to William Petty, both of whom were doctors of medicine.[16] Military and intellectual pursuits are not necessarily incompatible, and both found a place in the career of Sir Henry Sheres, director of the last plantation surveys in 1700–3, another authority on fortification whom one modern writer describes as 'something of a poet'.[17] About the only experience that all these admeasurers held in common was that none of them had ever earned his living as a professional land surveyor.

On the face of it, then, some variety of approach seems likely enough in the half-dozen or so plantation surveys that form the subject of this chapter. And the hypothesis of continuity receives an early shock in the first decade of the seventeenth century with Bodley's survey of the escheated lands in Ulster. His maps, which survive for four of the six counties involved, are diagrammatic sketches quite unlike the kind of 'plot' that Jobson may be assumed to have drawn in Munster, and certainly much inferior. The Ulster maps do not fit together along their barony boundaries. They have no scale-lines, the acreage of each parcel being calculated from an arbitrary formula which was soon shown to be producing figures absurdly short of the truth.[18] The same method seems to have been adopted in the earliest stages of the Wexford plantation, where the suspiciously round numbers of acres in the surveyors' initial returns were described as 'rather an apportioning by estimate than upon any due and exact measure', but here it was quickly superseded, perhaps as a result of rapidly growing doubts about the merits of the Ulster work as well as in response to complaints from on the spot.[19] By 1619 the mears and bounds of the confiscated area in Wexford had been 'set forth and trodden with the chain'.[20] Henceforth the laying-on of the chain was like a mystical rite, the agrarian equivalent of baptism or coming-of-age, which gave binding force (almost literally at the moment of survey; metaphorically forever) to the process of perambulation and which put the seal on one Irish townland after another as ready to be owned, occupied, and civilised.

Neither of the Wexford surveys can now be seen in its original form, but the reference to chaining, placed in juxtaposition with 'mears and bounds' (and thus ignoring the possibility of diagonal lines), is consistent with the idea of a boundary traverse. The fact that no angle-measuring appliance was mentioned does little harm to this interpretation: it was not unusual for either chain or 'instrument' to be ignored by early commentators in a context where the presence of both devices is beyond all doubt. A similar phrase – 'as the mears thereof were trodden with the chain' – was applied in 1620 to the recent survey of Co. Longford,[21] where a knowledge that chaining could not be done on the cheap found expression in a scheme for raising 'admeasurement money' from the owners of the measured land.[22] For this county a set of barony maps is providentially extant – not through the care of the Surveyor-General's office, but thanks to two contemporary scholars, Sir Robert Cotton and Sir James Ware.[23] Other maps surviving by accident from the same period cover parts of King's Co.[24] Although these midland maps appear to be only simplified reductions of the original surveyors' plots they are very different from the baronial diagrams previously returned for Ulster. They resemble the Ulster maps, it is true, in that the denominations are largely devoid of interior detail, but this was only to be expected from a boundary traverse. The difference lies in the more articulated and realistic appearance of the Leinster boundaries, and in the way they fit neatly together between baronies instead of contradicting each other. In Leitrim, Queen's Co. and Westmeath, it is only the barony statistics that remain on record, but it was taken for granted that each boundary had been traced with the chain and to judge from their numerical precision the measurements had been just as careful as in Longford.[25]

The importation of the chain to Wexford must have revived the problem of standard lengths in Irish land measurement. In the escheated counties Bodley had gone by the 'ordinary computation in the country', not saying what this meant except that it differed from the English statute measure that had been chosen for Munster in the previous reign.[26] After another interval, the perch of twenty-one feet was described in retrospect as 'the usual measure of the townland in our late plantation of Ulster'. Whether or not the Bodley team had actually worked to this degree of exactitude, by the second decade of the century the 21-foot perch was sufficiently widespread to figure in the official surveys of the north midlands as well as in a much smaller but equally official survey in Co. Limerick.[27] Thenceforth its use on such occasions went almost without saying everywhere in Ireland, and even outside the country it was soon established among textbook-writers (a notoriously conservative race) as 'the Irish perch'.[28] Nothing came of a mid-century plan to encourage a spatial equivalent of monetary inflation by re-adopting the smaller English units in order to disguise the scarcity of confiscated land.[29] Nevertheless, the 21-foot perch may have owed its victory to the circumstance that of all the best-known Irish perches it came nearest to the English standard. At all events it provided the plantation surveys with another common denominator: by the 1630s it had assumed the name of 'plantation measure'[30]—a status guaranteed by government policy, not unlike the French revolutionary calendar in its reference to particular historical events and free from any undesirable ethnic associations suggested by the older form, 'Irish measure'. (Though here, as in other departments of life, ethnicity was due for a revival: 'Irish plantation measure' was a standard nineteenth-century phrase and was far from unknown in the twentieth century.) The anomaly in all this was that as things turned out the plantation acre enjoyed least currency in the areas most affected by the plantation process, namely Ulster and parts of Munster.

Apart from the identity of units, another reason for postulating some similarity among plantation survey techniques (except in Bodley's Ulster) lies in the personnel employed. Of course only a small proportion of the work force was made up of engineers or scholars. The number of their subordinates was larger, and increased from one survey to the next. In Munster there had been four surveyors, in Ulster there were five, in King's Co. about six, in Longford eight or nine, in Connaught and Wicklow thirty-six.[31] This was no more than proportionate to what might be considered a natural rate of growth in the number of private surveyors at work in a developing country; and the early seventeenth century yields no positive evidence of surveyors being especially recruited from England or elsewhere to measure the confiscated lands, in the way that military engineers and other specialists were so often brought to Ireland at this period. By contrast there are at least a few cases of biographical, or at any rate genealogical, continuity from one plantation to another. The name Jobson appears on a map of part of King' s Co., and a Francis Jobson ('gent') is known to have been employed in Longford.[32] Was this the Jobson of Munster fame, gentility confirmed at last – though still earning little more than four shillings a day? Even if only a junior member of the same family, he may have learned the surveyor's craft from his Elizabethan namesake. The closest equivalent to Jobson in the seventeenth century was Thomas Raven: after making his debut in Bodley's Ulster survey of 1609, this gifted and energetic mapmaker appeared again in King's Co., in Londonderry, and finally, under Strafford, in Connaught.[33] Pynner also followed his stint in the midlands with an appearance in Connaught, this time in a subordinate position,[34] and the less well-known Henry Gee was employed in King's Co. and Wicklow as well as west of the Shannon.[35]

Subordinate or not, by the 1630s Raven and Pynner must have been too old to make willing pupils for Dr Gilbert or the Revd Johnson. How then did the two last-named gentlemen influence the course of the Strafford Survey? Perhaps they chose the scale at which the work should be plotted – forty 21-foot perches to the inch – as well as the smaller scales to which the plots should be reduced for easier handling. They may have decided the unit areas for which maps should be drawn at these different scales: parishes, baronies, counties, perhaps even the province of Connaught as a whole.[36] They may have produced a code of instructions for the surveyors. As later examples show, such codes are often more concerned with imposing checks on a familiar routine than with the enforcement of totally new methods. For instance the comparison of common boundaries was a matter likely to be neglected by different surveyors working independently. If the surviving maps are any guide, such comparisons had probably been done to a certain extent in Longford. In the Strafford Survey they are known to have been supervised by Gilbert in some detail.[37] Another hint on the subject of Strafford Survey instructions comes in a later reference to a denomination being 'measured by Thomas Kelly in 1637, and cast by the King's officer for measurement, Mr Carker'.[38] Carker could be a misreading of the Carter (or vice versa) who is known to have 'reduced' certain maps of Galway and Mayo.[39] While any map-maker could reduce his own maps, the separation of surveying from 'casting' (i.e. the calculation of area), either as a check on accuracy or as a contribution to economy, was a discipline more likely to come from a theorist than from a practical surveyor. It should be noted before leaving the Strafford Survey that the division of responsibility implied by any such set of rules was quite compatible with the use of traditional techniques; and the only surviving technical characterisation of this survey – 'surrounds made by the instrument' – is itself compatible with the method of the boundary traverse[40] (Plate 1).

These issues may be made clearer by turning from the admittedly feeble evidence reviewed above to the work of William Petty on the best known of all Irish plantation admeasurements, the Down Survey. After Petty had entered the surveying profession in December 1654 it took him approximately five years to become the most important map-maker in the history of Ireland. The Cromwellian surveys in which he made his name faced the government with a harder challenge than any previous Irish survey operation. Matters had begun promisingly enough in 1641 with a decision as to whose lands should be forfeited and with the determination of the confusingly named 'quit rents' which the new owners and their successors would pay to the government and its successors for ever more. The rent per acre was 3d in Leinster, 2¼d in Munster, 1½d in Connaught, and 1d in Ulster, a somewhat arbitrary assessment of regional variations in land quality, though no doubt accurate enough as an expression of relative degrees of development in the four provinces.[41] The land was destined for two kinds of government creditor. First there were the 'adventurers' who had invested money in the pacification of Ireland and who were mainly English merchants, guild-members, parliamentarians, and other town-dwellers. Then there were the officers and soldiers of the conquering army. As it turned out, the decision to divide the spoils between these two categories was followed by eleven more years of war in which surveying and valuation were at a standstill (and in which the unfortunate Henry Gee was probably not the only surveyor to lose his life by violence),[42] and even after peace had been restored the arrangements did not go very smoothly.

Some special surveys were ordered to meet particular cases,[43] but reliance was mostly placed on a preliminary investigation of the whole area set aside to satisfy the claims of both adventurers and soldiers. This, the so-called 'Gross Survey', soon had to be abandoned:[44] it was too gross to be useful, mixing estimates and admeasurements at the discretion of the local surveyor and blocking out the forfeited area in unsuitably large sections without regard to the *minutiae* of the forthcoming distribution. These faults were doubly unfortunate, for they distracted attention from some of the broader geographical aspirations of the Gross Survey, such as the mapping of parishes and baronies and the emphasis to be placed on harbours and river navigations.[45] The government decided to think again. Its solution was to divide the process of data-collection into two parts. First came a list of every piece of relevant information that could be obtained from local witnesses for the whole of Ireland, rebel and loyal, outside the area covered by the Strafford inquisition of the 1630s: this was the 'Civil Survey', whose terms of reference have been illustrated in an earlier chapter. Secondly – and here the provisions for the adventurers and the soldiers began to diverge – the admeasurers proper were set to work upon the forfeited land alone.

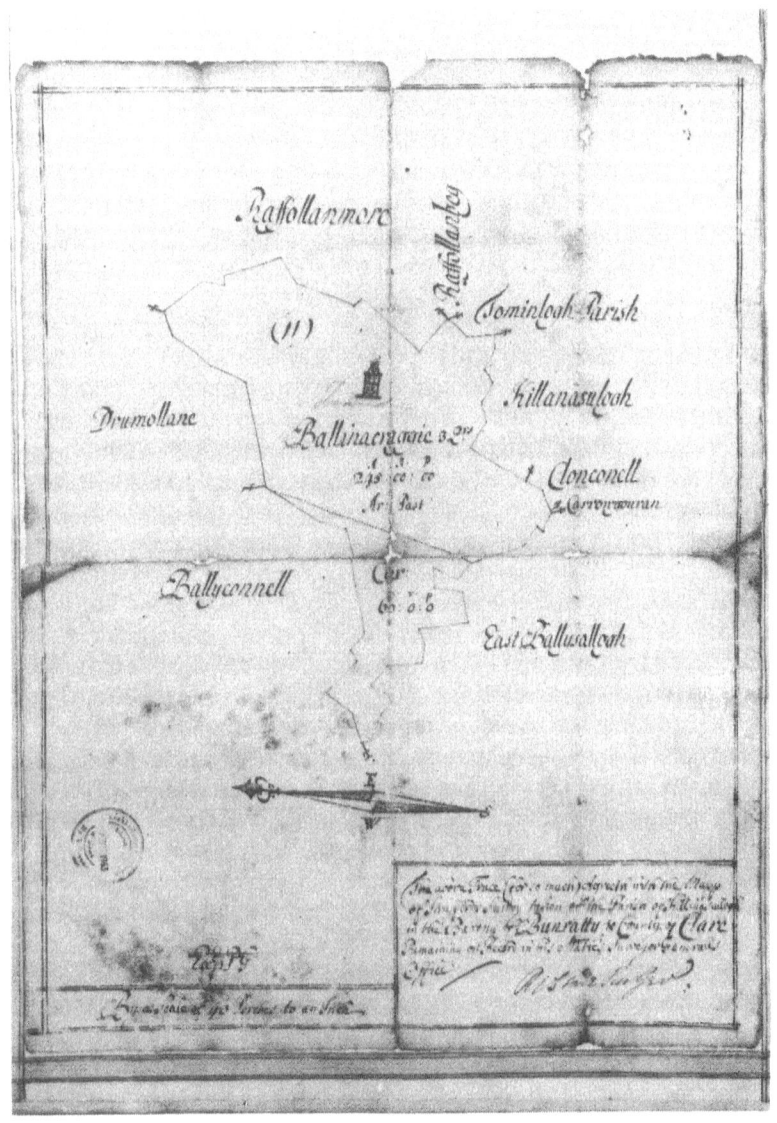

Plate 1. Strafford Survey transcript, Ballynacragga, Co. Clare. Scale of original 40 perches to one inch. From the O' Brien estate maps (see chapter 4, note 16). The units of measurement are 'quarters' (obsolescent by the time the survey was made in 1636–40) and acres with their modern subdivisions. The crosses represent boundary junctions. 'Cor' means corcass or low-lying pasture land. The signature is that of Richard Stone, Surveyor-General of Ireland from 1695 to 1714.

The adventurers were given the confiscated estates in ten counties to divide among themselves. It was later said that their lands 'were set out to them upon a gross survey and they sat down upon admeasurements and subdivisions of their own',[46] but this witness does not tell how they reconciled whatever differences were found between the Gross Survey acreages and those of their own surveyors. The latter were recruited by the adventurers and paid at the rate of £6 per 1,000 acres of profitable land and £1 per 1,000 acres of bog.[47] Some of them, like Robert Newcomen, had already been employed on the abortive Gross Survey;[48] others were newly brought from England. Very little is known of these 'private' surveys.[49] Their authors had the misfortune to be superseded by a rival whose writings constitute almost our only source of information about what they achieved.[50]

Outside the adventurers' reservation lay the counties assigned in lieu of arrears of pay to the Cromwellian officers and soldiers. Here were the lands that Benjamin Worsley began to measure in his capacity as newly-appointed Surveyor-General in 1653, and it was by casting doubt on Worsley's system that Petty managed to make his own formidable presence felt. To the student of technological continuity it is perhaps significant that these two fresh but strongly antagonistic minds did not disagree about the fundamentals of survey procedure. Their main differences were over organisation, deadlines and finance, with Petty promising to measure a closer network of territories than Worsley had thought practicable, and to do it more quickly and more cheaply. As much as anything else it was Petty's awesome self-confidence that got his plan and himself accepted under a degree of supervision from Worsley that both parties treated as a matter of form. His fee, a reasonable one by contemporary standards, was £7. 3s. 4d per 1,000 acres of profitable land and £3 per 1,000 acres of Crown land, Church land and unprofitable land. When Worsley was given joint responsibility with Petty for resurveying the lands of the adventurers in 1656 it might have looked like a partial turning of the tables; but it is Petty who gets most of the credit for this later achievement – not altogether unwarrantably, for Worsley left office in 1657 two years before the completion of their task, which seems in any case to have been done by the methods already devised by Petty for the soldiers' survey of 1654–6.

One accomplishment that distinguishes Petty from his contemporaries is that in addition to his gifts as planner and organiser he was far-sighted enough to produce a history of his own performance. In fact he wrote two histories: a short essay in 1656 and a whole book in 1659.[51] Neither was intended for early or extensive publication and Petty made no claims as a literary stylist. Even his term 'Down Survey', first recorded in 1654,[52] is idiosyncratic to a fault as well as grammatically maladroit, though thanks to its brevity this specimen of Cromwellian newspeak caught on surprisingly fast, and its echo in the title 'Lansdowne' was not felt as a disqualification when Petty's descendants were elevated to a marquessate.[53] It might seem perverse to argue that Petty showed more originality as a historian than as a surveyor, especially as he had so little to say (despite being given the run of the Surveyor-General's office) about his predecessors. But he did display some rare historiographical virtues. One was the importance he attached to primary sources. He quotes a large number of original records in their entirety, including the instructions he circulated to his staff in 1655;[54] and his treatment is less partisan than might be expected from his own involvement in what was at all times a highly controversial sequence of events. Not a few of the documents that he transcribes are bitterly hostile to himself, and sometimes disconcertingly effective in their criticism. The burden of these attacks, many of them inspired by the jealousy of professional surveyors towards the brilliant amateur, was that the Down Survey had been exploited by its director as a means of building up a personal estate. In one comment that he does not quote, Petty appears as

> He who had many acres got
> By measuring of land a spot,
> How that should be the art doth there lie,
> For some do say he measured fairly.[55]

Most modern commentators accept that Petty both measured and wrote fairly. A good example of his candour is the way he treats the events of the 1630s. The Strafford Survey had assumed a new importance under Cromwell as a means towards removing Catholic Irishmen across the Shannon,[56] and it is the only one of the earlier plantation surveys that Petty knew much about. No leader of the Strafford team can be shown to have remained in government service until the 1650s and Petty gives no sign of having interviewed any of them. His information came partly from the maps and reference books that they had left behind and partly from a report on the Strafford Survey made in June 1654 by Worsley and the mathematician Miles Symner to the effect that Gilbert, Johnson and the rest had done as well as any later surveyors could expect to do.

By accepting (and reproducing) this report, Petty implicitly approved the methods by which the admirable results of twenty years earlier had been obtained. Where his territory overlapped with that of the Strafford Survey, in parts of Munster, he was content to retain the older maps as a record of territorial boundaries, his own chief contribution being a review of the distinction between profitable and unprofitable land to allow for pasture that had subsequently deteriorated into bog.[57] In drawing on the work of his predecessors Petty was undeterred by the risk, of which he must soon have become ruefully aware, that his enemies (and some of his friends) would do their best to make this wise decision look like a culpable act of plagiarism;[58] and that he might even be accused of reproducing the Strafford Survey maps from one end of Ireland to the other without taking a single measurement himself.[59]

Petty's account of this affair demonstrates his freedom from the ordinary surveyor's habitual secrecy. As a distinguished natural philosopher, his own instinct was presumably to further the practice of free and open publication on which modern scientific progress depends. The brief list of his technical innovations which he submitted to the government in 1655 may therefore be taken as definitive. It stated that he 'had, by a more distinct, methodical, and comprehensive field book; by removing some entanglement in the card wherein the needle plays; by exterminating the use of triangles and intermixed multiplication in the casting up of the superficial content, much facilitated the whole practice of surveying'.[60] These happen to be among our earliest Irish references to field books and compass needles, though they are couched in terms that show both items to have been familiar already. The only point on which Petty enters into detail is the calculation of area, achieved in the Down Survey by plotting the field work on a grid of printed squares. In this case he is known to have done as he said, for a number of his grids survived long enough to be seen by a nineteenth-century historian.[61] But the squares were less novel than a non-graphical method of area calculation which Worsley had been considering in the spring of 1654 and which Petty ostentatiously neglects to mention.[62] Altogether his catalogue of improvements is not very exciting, and the critics of the Down Survey were seemingly justified in their claim that all he had done was instruct some new recruits in the 'ordinary and common method' of surveying.[63] As usual, there are few hints as to what that method was: the best of them, now apparently lost, is a tracing from a Down Survey plot in which the traverse stations are marked around the edge of a specimen townland.[64]

In subject matter, as distinct from method, Petty's title to originality is not so easily challenged. It is true that his instructions carried an echo from the Gross Survey, but taken as a whole the following extracts from them go beyond any code of Irish surveying practice previously recorded, combining cadastral and geographical specifications in a double burden that the hardiest map-maker would have found difficult to sustain.

> 8thly. You are carefully to describe the bounds of each surround you make, and the nature of the land surrounded, as first whether it be profitable or unprofitable, and then of what species or kind each of the said land is, as whether the profitable be arable, meadow, or pasture; and even of what sort or sorts the pasture land itself is, as whether it be boggy, heathy, furzy, rocky, woody, mountainous, and the like, etc. The same distinctions are to be likewise made in a very ample and exact manner, in all unprofitable lands especially, hereby to give the grounds and reasons of returning the same for unprofitable.
>
> 9thly. You are also to note the quality and difference of all your mears, as whether the same be a wall, ditch, bank, hedge, river, bogside, ridge, valley, etc., noting all the permanent and conspicuous objects, as churches, castles, houses, raths, trees, great stones, hedge corners, etc., that you shall meet with, in or near your said mears on either hand; that by them, together with the special marks which you are to make with the spade, the said mears may be the more easily trod over again; all which marks you are to gather into a list, as pertinent to the description of each surround.
>
> 10thly. In all common land, whether profitable or unprofitable, you are to mention the names of such places or persons as have commonage in the same, with the proportion belonging unto each of them.
>
> 11thly. You are by intersections to determine the true place of all towns, churches, castles, known houses, hills, raths, etc., within each respective surround, and to be frequent in making such observations, for the better examining and correcting your work.
>
> 12thly. You shall take good notice of all highways and rivers, noting their breadth and depths, together with the falls and islands in any of them.
>
> And where you come upon the sea, or navigable rivers, you are by intersection to observe the wideness of the harbour's mouth, bigness and distance of islands or rocks, the place of the bar in barred havens and you shall also inform yourself of the soundings, anchorage, course of channels, the place of sands and shelves in or about any of the aforesaid harbours or places.

13thly. You shall measure the height of all notorious high hills and mountains, describing their feet and manner of rising, together with their names and true places, as before directed.

Some of the objects in article 11 could have been fixed by the intersection of bearings taken from points near the territorial boundaries, as Petty suggests; but to reach places invisible from the boundary it would have been necessary to lay out laborious additional traverse lines or networks of triangles. Such interior detail had never been agreed upon between the director and his masters, and Petty dropped a hint to this effect when he drew the surveyors' attention to the 'most material and essential parts' of his instructions – leaving their familiarity with normal Irish survey practice to make clear to them which parts these were.[65] When it came to the point the typical Down Survey map looked very much like the typical Strafford Survey map. Its subject was a block of townlands, its scale either forty or eighty Irish perches to an inch. Townland boundaries were given prominence, profitable and unprofitable land were distinguished, and there were abbreviated captions for arable, meadow, bog, wood, mountain and several kinds of pasture, with acreage figures for each of these categories. Here, evidently, were the 'material and essential' features. Coverage of other subjects was uneven: sometimes blatantly so, as when a main road stopped in mid-townland or when a cartographer took it into his head to insert the kind of small object (like an individual tree, an inn-sign, or a gallows) that even Petty had been unwilling to ask for, sometimes more misleadingly, as with the inclusion of many dwelling houses and the omission of many others. Occasionally owners' names appeared *in situ*; more often they were separately tabulated as part of the 'terrier' accompanying the maps. The only surprise in all this is that the surveyors took so little notice of Petty's ninth rule, on the subject of boundary marks: although streams and roads were often shown running along a boundary, the maps make hardly any reference to those ditches, fences, walls, rocks, summits or ancient monuments that separated one townland from another (Plate 2).

The Down Survey style was in no way unique. As well as drawing inspiration from earlier Irish official maps, it had also been seen in English cartography when similar circumstances arose under the Commonwealth. The results are too bare and uninformative to have had much publicity from England's local historians (luxuriating as so many of them are in what their Irish colleagues would consider a wealth of alternative sources), but there is at least one modern reproduction – a map of Bestwood Park

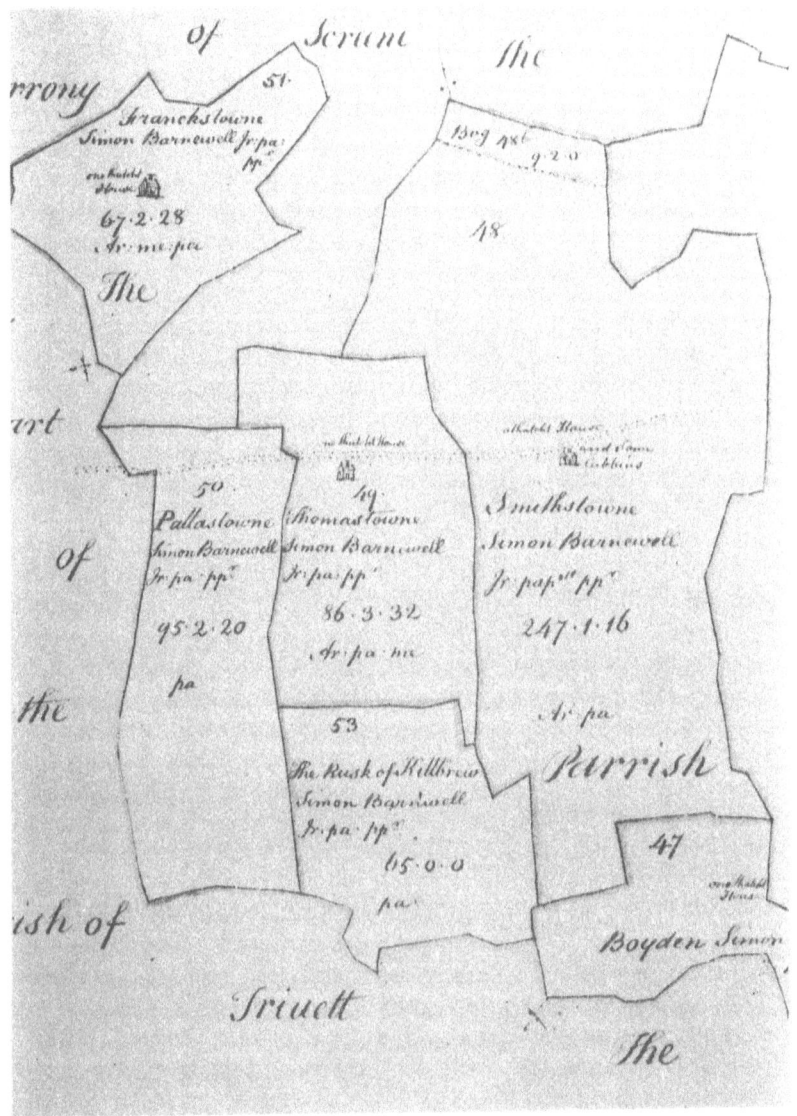

Plate 2. From the Down Survey parish map for Kilbrew, Co. Meath (NLI, MS 715), showing the lands held by the Irish papist proprietor Simon Barnewall in 1640 and confiscated under the Cromwellian settlement. Scale of original 40 perches to one inch. The cartographic conventions are similar to those of the Strafford Survey (Plate 1). This copy was made by Daniel O'Brien in 1787. The original of 1655 by William Farrand is lost.

in Nottinghamshire – that gives a fair idea of the genre.[66] Whatever its role in England, it was a style that did much to influence the history of the Irish estate map. But the department in which Petty felt most conscious of his own revolutionary status was that of personnel. It was always in the first person singular that he reminisced about chaining the equivalent of several times around the earth's equator (the exact number of times depended on the mood of the moment),[67] but on other occasions he saw himself 'rather a contriver of the way and method how many surveyors should work, than a surveyor myself'. In this context many meant approximately one thousand 'hands'. Not all these men could be called surveyors either – Petty sometimes gave the impression that none of them could. The point here was not the well-known fact that certain legal and inquisitorial accompaniments of the surveying process had been assigned to the conductors of the Civil Survey instead of to his own staff. What he had in mind was his new system of dividing cartography 'into its several parts, viz. [1,] field work, 2, protraction, 3, casting, 4, reducing; 5, ornaments of the maps; 6, writing fair books; 7, examination of all and every the premises'. Each of these tasks, he said, would be done not by all-round surveyors but by men chosen for their special aptitudes and remunerated by whatever method would most discourage fraud – for instance a fixed rate for each chain and angle, instead of for each acre as in his own contract with the government.[68]

For the field work of the Down Survey Cromwell's foot soldiers possessed the necessary qualifications of stamina, trustworthiness, physical mobility, and skill in self-defence. The protracting or plotting of the field books required 'another sort of men, especially such as had been of trades into which painting, drawing, or any other kind of designing is necessary'. The only process that needed much intelligence was examining, for which Petty was prepared to pay a salary of £100 a year and which involved reprotracting lines and angles from the field books, comparing common boundaries, recalculating areas, and checking the lands actually mapped against those that the Civil Survey had designated for mapping. Such narrow specialisation went beyond anything attempted in earlier official surveys. Its purpose was to do an unprecedentedly large amount of map-making as quickly as possible. A secondary motive, or at least an incidental bonus, was to deflate the pretensions of those professional land surveyors who had so much resented Petty's encroachment on their preserves: hence the relish with which he described his subordinates as 'workmen'.[69] Indeed to judge from Petty's statements of policy he succeeded in dispensing with the land surveyor altogether and in withdrawing the Down Survey from the ambit of this book. It was an objective which he was anxious to emphasise and which more than one historian has dutifully taken up.[70]

The truth was not so simple. In a staff of hundreds there must have been some chain of command, and according to one contemporary writer the Down Survey team included six 'conductors'[71] – an appointment that Petty's autobiographical essays mention only in passing, perhaps because he preferred to underline the extent of his personal control. Conductors were presumably not specialists but men with a good knowledge of how to make a complete survey. Below this level, different degrees of subordination seem implicit in a Down Survey map inscribed with the words, 'By William Brudenell and John Courtenay for John Humphreys';[72] and Brudenell at least was more than a mere workman, to judge from his subsequent reappearance in England as a freelance land surveyor.[73] Nor was it only the conductors who assumed responsibility for signing the final maps: the number of names to be seen on extant specimens is not six but more than seventy. Outdoor as well as indoor staff evidently took their share of signing, for on some maps the author's name follows the words 'admeasured by'. In any case 'workman' is hardly appropriate for signatories like the author of a surveying textbook (Henry Osborne) and the holder of a doctor's degree (Patrick Raggett). Elsewhere Petty himself distinguishes between an admeasurer and his chainmen, which if the word 'surveyor' is substituted for 'admeasurer' exactly corresponds with the distinction usually drawn in the kind of ordinary estate survey that he professed to be superseding.[74]

In short, Petty's fine division of labour was rather less watertight than a superficial reading of his historical commentaries would suggest. It is even arguable that he made no attempt to hide the gap between ideal and reality. The instructions admitted that a surveyor might plot his own work as long as this was done in the presence of two other sworn surveyors. More seriously, despite his attacks on the manner in which Worsley had started the survey Petty eventually felt compelled to hire a number of his rival's 'old surveyors' and to pay them on Worsley's allegedly discredited system of a fixed rate for every thousand acres. He also took on some veterans of even earlier vintage, perhaps including some of the Strafford surveyors. It might have been hard to make experienced all-rounders confine themselves to a single position on Petty's conveyor-belt, and he confessed that some of his staff were paid 'by the lump, for so many baronies', an arrangement that sounds just as free-and-easy as Worsley's or (worse still) as that of the adventurers' survey. Even within his own more rigid framework, a specialist could pick up a measure of general competence, as Petty himself revealed by deploring the ingratitude of those who left his employment as soon as he had taught them how to make a survey.[75]

However it was organised, the Down Survey did its job as a foundation for the Cromwellian and post-Cromwellian land settlements with surprisingly little argument except about money. No one objected to its somewhat sketchy representation of the Irish landscape. The only criticism that verged on the topographical was that, as with the Elizabethan surveys of Munster, the line between profitable and unprofitable land sometimes provoked dissent from grantees who found their estates disappointingly infertile, and especially from those who knew that the director was paid more for surveying profitable than for unprofitable land.[76] No doubt there were overtones of this feeling in the reference to Petty's

> ... having compassed the whole island,
> Surveying both the bogs, and dry land.[77]

In fact the charge of switching land from the low-paid to the high-paid category remains unproven. What Petty might have done more carefully was explain the difference to his surveyors, particularly to those who protested that his instructions had failed to anticipate the problem of classifying mountain lands in Kerry.[78] In theory land could be accounted unprofitable if the owner had no prospect of getting more from his tenants than he himself would have to pay in quit rent, but since in a period of economic abnormality there was no means of predicting future rent-levels Petty did well not to formulate this rule. On a commonsense judgement, good land must often have merged imperceptibly into bad, and the problem that he was evading – how to express the continuous by the discrete – was one that cartographers did little to solve until the invention of the isopleth.

As always, planimetric errors were harder to detect than alleged mistakes of land classification. Although Petty's enemies had strong enough motives for finding errors of any kind, not even Worsley was able to convict him of mismeasurement, and by April 1657, after forfeited land in ten counties had been surveyed, only three complaints had been brought against his acreage figures and none of these had been proved.[79] At least one objection he had laughed off, or at any rate shrugged off, by recommending that any proprietor claiming a deficiency of acres should find another proprietor who admitted a surplus, and that the owner of the surplus should be allowed to verify the existence of the deficiency before being compelled to make it good.[80] When at the end of the survey Petty, like so many of history's best amateur map-makers, moved briskly and irrevocably on to other avocations, his Down admeasurement stood 'stiff and staunch'.[81] He may have added a few more topographical features to the maps after 1659 as occasion arose.[82] He certainly did much to reduce and edit them for geographical use, partly in his manuscript barony collection 'Hibernia Regnum'[83] and partly in the epoch-making county atlas, *Hiberniae Delineatio*, which he finally published in 1685. He also remained a fertile source of new ideas for completing and maintaining a national survey, and for including in it such neglected subjects as cattle and corn output as well as a reformed vocabulary of Irish placenames.[84] But his career as a director of field operations was over.

With predictable shrewdness, Petty had set a time-limit on his financial liability for any errors in the Down Survey.[85] His triumphant emergence from this short period of vulnerability does not mean that the results were accurate in modern terms or even by the highest contemporary standards. Unfortunately, historians have done little to exploit their own immunity from Petty's deadline. In some ways the most authoritative statement on the matter is still that of the nineteenth-century surveyors, Sherrard, Brassington and Greene, who in most of their own acreage measurements recorded an increase of about one-sixth or one-fifth over the Down Survey.[86] It is interesting to see their judgement confirmed by a modern scholar, Y. M. Goblet, who found in a sample of thirteen townlands (with boundaries thought to have remained intact between the seventeenth and twentieth centuries) that Petty's area diverged from the truth by an average of about 15 per cent.[87] A more recent comparison of more than a hundred pairs of Down Survey and Ordnance Survey acreages suggests that the Down Survey's deficiencies are about seven times as numerous as its excesses and that the average deficiency is just over 11.5 per cent.[88] Nobody seems to know how this shortfall can have come about: it certainly exonerates Petty from any accusation of overcharging.

He himself would not have been very happy with these figures, for it had been agreed that in comparing the Down Survey with the adventurers' surveys the only differences to be disregarded should be those of less than three per cent.[89] However, the history of Petty's planimetric reputation in his own lifetime and for many years afterwards presents a number of familiar problems, not least the fact that what look like criticisms of Down Survey acreages often turn out to be judgements that the survey had been rendered obsolete by territorial boundary changes or by the reclamation of formerly unprofitable land. So far as seventeenth-century opinion is concerned the most significant fact in sight is that at the last major forfeiture of Irish history, following the Williamite wars, the authorities did not follow Petty's own example of simply copying the latest available official data. In most cases they made their own admeasurement, and were soon returning acreages greater than those of any previous survey.[90]

In the 'Trustees' Survey' of 1700–3 (named after the trustees for the forfeited estates) the Surveyor-General was bypassed – as usual – and a special organisation established. The rules of survey drawn up by its director, Sir Henry Sheres, no longer exist,[91] but the maps resembled those of the Down Survey, being mainly outlines of denomination boundaries at a scale of forty plantation perches to an inch.[92] (There were also some very large-scale Trustees' plans of urban house-plots of a type not represented in surviving Down Survey maps.)[93] The trustees evidently did not improve on Petty's method of finding areas, for some of their maps are drawn on grids of ready-printed squares. They were also subject to the same kind of criticism as the Down Survey. 'In some places', one writer protested, 'they have surveyed rivers, and in other places bogs, where they could not walk to lay their chains or fix their instruments'.[94] Of course a line could be surveyed through a bog by sinking poles along it and then intersecting the poles from stations off the line without getting one's instruments or chains wet; and there was nothing unreasonable about the trustees' policy of dividing the bogs among the upland properties that adjoined them.[95] What this critic meant by surveying bogs and rivers was classifying them as profitable land, a long-recurrent grievance from Down Survey times and earlier. But at least he makes clear that the basis of the Trustees' Survey was what we can now surely begin to regard as the traditional Irish mixture of chain and 'instrument'.

Most of what happened in 1700–3 may thus be seen as the application of time-tested methods. The very lack of documentation could be a sign of this. There is only one aspect of the work for which detailed records exist, and as it happens this is the aspect that Petty's narrative left obscure in the case of the Down Survey, namely the channel of command. The trustees employed a chief protractor or manager at £200 a year, four directors (perhaps one for each province) at £120 each, a number of protractors that varied from two to eight at £100 each, and about fifty surveyors.[96] 'Protractor' suggests that Petty's distinction between field and office work had been maintained – which makes it understandable that another of the trustees' officers should bear the comforting title of 'rectifier', responsible perhaps for closing the gaps in the protractors' lines. On the other hand a hundred pounds seems a lot to pay for simply laying down lines and angles. Perhaps the protractor exercised more general responsibilities analogous to those of a Down Survey examiner.

At any rate there is no sign that the division of labour was carried quite as far in the Trustees' Survey – to the extent of ' casting' or of 'ornaments', for example – as Petty had proposed to take it. The command structure of 1700 might be seen rather as the minimum needed to impose a check on ordinary surveyors using ordinary methods but freed from the kind of scrutiny (by a local landowner and his tenants) to which the independent surveyor must normally submit. Petty's system could then take its place not as a necessary condition of good surveying but as the best way to shoulder a workload which by normal peacetime standards, and even by the standards of the other plantations, had laid an exceptionally heavy burden on the available labour force; and we have seen that even Petty managed to get a lot done by ordinary surveyors when it came to the point. What this line of argument amounts to is that the difference between plantation surveys and non-plantation surveys may have been too baldly stated in previous writings on Irish map-history. Not only did the official surveyors have something to teach their brethren in the private sector, but much of their influence could be interpreted as 'feedback'. In many ways, after all, the Down and Strafford Surveys and the rest were not so very different from estate surveys. (On one authoritative definition, estate surveys are precisely what they were.)[97] Although the territory that they covered was very large, it all fell into comfortably small units which for the most part could be taken one at a time. Common boundaries admittedly called for special attention, but there was no attempt to lay down a preliminary trigonometrical or astronomical control, and there are no references to the invention of new instruments or new techniques; even the reduction of the surveys for small-scale geographical purposes, interesting though it is, seems usually to have been an afterthought. To this extent the term 'plantation survey' is a misnomer, at least in a professional and technological context; and the same may be true of the term 'plantation surveyor'.

Notes

1. *Cal. S.P. Ire.*, 1660–62, pp 10–11, 29; 1663–5, pp 444, 532.
2. William Nicolson, *The Irish Historical Library* (Dublin, 1724), p. 22.
3. Falkland to James Ussher, 15 Mar. 1626, Richard Parr, *Life of James Usher, Late Lord Archbishop of Armagh* (London, 1686), p. 379.
4. Marquess of Lansdowne, *The Petty Papers*, 1 (London, 1927), pp 83, 85, 108–09, 173.
5. C. L. Falkiner, 'Barnaby Rich's "Remembrances of the State of Ireland"', *Proc. R. Ir. Acad.*, 26C (1906), p. 134. For Parsons's appointment, see Fiants, Elizabeth I, 6739 (26 Dec. 1602), *Dep. Keeper Pub. Rec. Ire., 18th Rept*, p. 115; for his qualifications see Sir Geoffrey Fenton, 8 May 1603, *Cal. S.P. Ire.*, 1603–06, p. 49.
6. See above, ch.2, n.58. Robert Kennedy signed himself 'Dep. Supervisor Gen.' in 1617 (TCD, MUN/P/24/39).
7. King to Chancellor and Justices of Ireland, 10 Aug. 1629, TCD, MS 672.
8. Sheffield City Library, Strafford letter books, 14, nos. 319–20 (1634), NLI, mic. P.3586. See also *Cal. S.P. Ire.*, 1633–47, p. 104, and W. Knowler (ed.), *The Earl of Strafforde's Letters and Despatches*, 1 (London, 1739), pp 405–06. Raven had made a similar proposal in *c.* 1623 (S.P.63/237/62A). Parsons for his part paid tribute to Raven's reputation for 'sincerity and ability' (9 Aug. 1633, BL, Harleian MS 4297, f. 125).
9. Surveyor-General's answer to the complaints of the Recusants, *Cal. S.P. Ire.*, 1611–14, pp 379–80. The Clandeboyes survey mentioned by Parsons may be the one of 1605 printed in *Dep. Keeper Pub. Rec. Ire., 26th Rept*, app. 1, pp 43–51.
10. The humble remonstrance of the northern Catholics of Ireland now in arms [1641], quoted by G. Hill, *An Historical Account of the Plantation in Ulster at the Commencement of the Seventeenth Century, 1608–1620* (Belfast, 1877), p. 154.
11. R. Loeber, *A Biographical Dictionary of Architects in Ireland* (London, 1981), pp 21–5.
12. A brief certificate of the number of acres in Longford and Ely O'Carroll, as found by Sir Thomas Rotherham, William Parsons and Nicholas Pynner, 'by their own view and the labour of diverse measurers', 30 Nov. 1618, Carew MS 613, p. 87.
13. Hardinge, *Proc. R. Ir. Acad.*, 8(1861), p. 54. A similar document to the one printed by Hardinge, but containing more information, is in the possession of the Marquess of Bath at Longleat House, Wiltshire (NLI, mic. P.5894). For Pynner see Loeber, *Architects*, pp 85–7.
14. Sir George Radcliffe, 2 Dec. 1641, S.P.63/260/47; Parr, *Usher*, pp 492–4 (11 Dec. 1638).
15. Christopher Wandesford, 4 Oct. 1636, NLI, MS 2305, p. 121; T. C. Barnard, 'Miles Symner and the New Learning in Seventeenth-Century Ireland', *Jour. R. Soc. Ant. Ire.*, 102 (1972), p. 142; Loeber, *Architects*, pp 62–3.

16. Y. M. Goblet, *La Transformation de la Géographie Politique de l'Irlande au XVIIe Siècle dans les Cartes et Essais Anthropogéographiques de Sir William Petty*, 1 (Paris, 1930), p. 214.
17. *Dict. Nat. Biogr.* There is a love poem by Sheres in NLI, MS 3870.
18. J. H. Andrews, 'The Maps of the Escheated Counties of Ulster, 1609–10', *Proc. R. Ir. Acad.*, 74C (1974), pp 165–6.
19. *Cal. S.P. Ire.*, 1611–14, p. 134; 1615–25, p. 187; *Acts of the Privy Council*, 1616–17, pp 237, 243; A discourse of the intended plantation in the county of Wexford, Bodleian, MS Laud. misc. 611, f.50 (NLI, mic. P.3884).
20. King to Lord Deputy, 26 Mar. 1619, BL, Add. MS 4756, f. 138; *Cal. S.P. Ire.*, 1615–25, p. 305.
21. Commission for settling the plantation in Longford, 10 Apr. 1620, *Cal. S.P. Ire.*, 1615–25, pp 280–81.
22. Memorial of the natives of Longford, quoted by M. Hickson, *Ireland in the Seventeenth Century*, 2 (London, 1884), pp 293–99. There is a contemporary copy in TCD, MS 672.
23. Ware to Cotton, 24 Feb. 1630, *Analecta Hibernica*, 2 (1931), p. 296. The maps are in Cotton MSS Aug. 1, i, 47–48, and 1, ii, 24–6, 27. As Auditor-General of Ireland Ware also had a professional interest in the plantations.
24. M.P.F. 268(243–68) and S.P.46/91/211–12 are twenty-eight maps of various degrees of roughness and on different scales, apparently collected by Sir Matthew de Renzi in connection with his colony in McCoughlan's country in King's Co. (R. Loeber, ' Civilization through Plantation: the Projects of Sir Mathew de Renzi' in H. Murtagh (ed.), *Irish Midland Studies: Essays in Commemoration of N. W. English* (Athlone, 1980), pp 121–35). Some of them give the impression of being derived from the original plantation survey. Others are concerned with the delimitation of boundaries between individual planters. There are also several maps of the new town of Banagher and its environs, one of which is reproduced by Loeber, plate 23. Only one of the maps carries a date (1628) and an author's name (John Gwinn). On five others names appear alongside certain boundaries as if to distinguish the territories assigned to different surveyors. The names are Jobson, Moris, Gwinn, Raven, Stubs and Woodhouse, the last four of whom are also named as surveyors in a collection of documents relating to lands in King's Co. in 1633 (Harleian MS 4297, ff.119–65).
25. 'A brief certificate of the numbers of acres of land of several qualities in the county of Leitrim and the several territories within the Queen's County and Westmeath hereunder named', NLI, MS 8014(6). An explicit reference to methods of measurement, in the context of King's Co., was William Parsons's enunciation, on 9 Aug. 1633, of the 'essential rule and common right in the plantations that the mears made by the chain of all villages at the general measurement when the land was all in the king's hand should forever conclude the bounds thereof'. The plantation maps of Ely O'Carroll were still being consulted by Parsons at this time (Harleian MS 4297, ff.125, 132).
26. Josias Bodley, 24 Feb. 1610, *Cal. S.P. Ire.*, 1608–10, p. 393.

27. Lord Deputy and Council, 6 Feb. 1621, *Cal. S.P. Ire.*, 1615–25, p. 314; Survey of Ballahanaskadar, Co. Limerick, TCD, MUN/P/23/95.
28. John Eyre, *The Exact Surveyor or, the Whole Art of Surveying of Land* (London, 1654), pp 181–8.
29. Sir William Domvile to Lord Lieutenant, 10 Aug. 1664, *Cal. S.P. Ire.*, 1663–5, p. 417. Earlier, the converse policy had been contemplated as a means of overcoming the apathy of English investors: on 4 June 1642 W. Mountagu mentioned a parliamentary bill declaring that the 'measure of acres shall be Irish measure which is treble [*sic*] to ours' (Hist. MSS Com., *Buccleuch and Queensberry*, 1. pp 303–04). This is one of the few contemporary decisions bearing on the widespread modern belief (plausible enough on *a priori* grounds) that the choice of a large acre by the English in Ireland was prompted more by their own land-hunger than by respect for indigenous culture.
30. NLI, D.4121 (Co. Kilkenny, 20 Apr. 1639).
31. For Munster see above, ch. 2, p. 33; for Ulster, Andrews, *Proc. R. Ir. Acad.*, 74C (1974), pp 142–3; for Longford, Hickson, *Ireland in the Seventeenth Century*, 2, p. 294; for King's Co., above, n.24; for Connaught and Wicklow, Longleat MS (NLI, mic. P.5894), and Knowler, *Strafforde Letters*, 2, p. 76.
32. PRO, E.351/272.
33. Andrews, *Proc. R. Ir. Acad.*, 74C (1974), p. 143; D. A. Chart (ed.), *Londonderry and the London Companies, 1609–1629* (Belfast, 1928), p. 51; T. W. Moody, *The Londonderry Plantation, 1609–41* (Belfast, 1939), *passim*; Longleat MS (NLI, mic. P.5894); Hardinge, *Proc. R. Ir. Acad.*, 8 (1861), p. 54. See also above, n.8.
34. Longleat MS (NLI, mic. P.5894); W. P. Pakenham-Walsh, 'Captains Sir Thomas Rotherham, Knt., and Nicholas Pinnar, Directors-General of Fortifications in Ireland, 1617–1644', *Royal Engineers Jour.*, 10 (1909), pp 125–34.
35. Deposition by Henry Gee, 19 Apr. 1642, TCD, MS 810, f. 149. Gee also appears in several remeasurements made in King's Co. and Ely O'Carroll in *c*. 1633 (Harleian MS 4297, ff. 119, 132, 133).
36. A small-scale map in TCD, MS 1209(69), shows the areas involved in the Strafford Survey and is presumably a by-product of it (Andrews, *Irish Maps*, 6 and 7).
37. William Gilbert, 30 Sep. 1639, Add. MS 46923, f. 84.
38. Earl of Egmont, 10 July 1738, Add. MS 46989, f. 96. Egmont's authority was 'an old parchment map, with a paper of reference', apparently in his own possession.
39. Longleat MS (NLI, mic. P.5894).
40. Report by Benjamin Worsley and Miles Symner on the Strafford Survey of Co. Tipperary, June 1654, Larcom, *Down Survey*, p. 55.
41. 16 Charles I, c.33 (England).
42. Deposition by Gee's widow, Nov. 1642, TCD, MS 810, f. 149.

43. Survey (without maps) of the Countess of Ormond's lands in Co. Kilkenny, with related documents, 1653–4, NLI, MS 2499, ff.25–37.
44. R. Dunlop, *Ireland under the Commonwealth*, 2 (Manchester, 1913), p. 510; Larcom, *Down Survey*, p. 395; W. H. Hardinge, 'On Manuscript Mapped and Other Townland Surveys in Ireland of a Public Character, Embracing the Gross, Civil, and Down Surveys, from 1640 to 1688', *Trans. R. Ir. Acad.*, 24, Antiquities (1873), pp 9–12.
45. Instructions to the surveyor Nathan Pickles, 30 Nov. 1653, NLI, MS 11959, pp 341–5.
46. Sir William Domvile, 10 Aug. 1664, *Cal. S.P. Ire.*, 1663–5, p. 418.
47. Draft of adventurers' agreement for settling their lands, 1655, *Cal. S.P. Ire.*, Charles I (Addenda), p. 593.
48. *Cal. S.P. Ire.*, 1663–5, p. 620; Larcom, *Down Survey*, p. 19.
49. The several steps of proceedings from the present state of the adventurers unto the perfect settlement of them, *Cal. S.P. Ire.*, Commonwealth, p. 359.
50. Larcom, *Down Survey*, *passim*; *Cal. S.P. Ire.*, Commonwealth, pp 357–65.
51. Both printed in Larcom, *Down Survey*: (a) 'A Brief Account of the Most Material Passages Relating to the Survey Managed by Dr Petty in Ireland, Anno 1655 and 1656' (pp xiii–xvii); (b) 'History of the Survey of Ireland' (pp 1–307). These works, and the other documents printed by Larcom, are the source for the previous paragraph: see especially 'Order for the survey ... of the adventurers' lands and other lands', 3 Sep. 1656, pp 390–92.
52. Petty's recommendations 'as to a down survey' were mentioned on 31 Oct.: his proposal that the soldiers' lands should be 'surveyed down' had been noted on l6 Oct. (Larcom, *Down Survey*, pp 12, 14).
53. Lansdowne in Somerset is the source of the Marquesses' title, conferred in 1784, but this does not necessarily invalidate the pun imputed to Petty's descendants by modern Irish writers such as Alf MacLochlainn, *Irish Times*, 22 Mar. 1969. The family arms included a 'magnetick-needle, pointing at a pole star' (Lodge, *Peerage*, 2, p. 362), which is approximately where the needle did point in Ireland at the time of the Down Survey.
54. For the instructions see Larcom, *Down Survey*, pp 46–50, 123. For Petty's access to earlier records see Dunlop, *Commonwealth*, 2, p. 465, and Larcom, *Down Survey*, p. 32. Petty makes passing reference to a few of his predecessors in his *Political Anatomy of Ireland* (London, 1691), p. 58.
55. 'Itur Hibernicum or The Ramble, Being the Voyages and Adventures of Three Knights Errant. Also a Poem on the Double Bottom'd Ship built at Dublin', p. 144, BL, Sloane MS 360.
56. Dunlop, *Commonwealth*, 2, pp 513–14, 522, 526.
57. Larcom, *Down Survey*, pp 54–63.
58. Thomas Taylor, 3 Aug. 1681, Hist. MSS Com., *Ormonde*, new ser., 6, p. 119. For Petty's ' strict friendship' with Taylor see Lodge, *Peerage*, 3,

p. 173. See also Larcom, *Down Survey*, pp 259, 300. The general similarity in character between the Strafford and Down Surveys is acknowledged in a work thought to have been written by Petty, *The Case of the Kerry Quit-Rent* (n.p., 1681, p. 10).

59. This suggestion appears in some (otherwise fairly knowledgeable) notes on Irish cartographic history written in the 1830s and preserved at the Ordnance Survey Office, Dublin, among papers relating to the Survey's memoir on the parish of Templemore, Co. Londonderry.
60. Larcom, *Down Survey*, p. 17.
61. Hardinge, *Trans. R. Ir. Acad.*, 24, Antiquities (1873), p. 27; Larcom, *Down Survey*, p. 324.
62. Henry Osborne, *A More Exact Way to Delineate the Plot of Any Spacious Parcel of Land, as Baronies, Parishes, and Town-Lands, as also of Rivers, Harbours and Loughs etc. than is as yet in Practice. Also a Method or Form of Keeping the Field-Book, and How to Cast up the Superficial Content of a Plot most Exactly* (Dublin, 1654). See below, ch.10. There is room for inferring the use of more than one method of area-calculation in the Down Survey, however, for acreage values purporting to derive from the Survey differ from one source to another. These differences have been attributed to the fact that the survey was first plotted on a large scale and then reduced but it would probably have been thought bad practice, by all concerned, to have calculated areas on any scale but the largest available. Further study of the Down Survey and its derivatives will be necessary to resolve this problem. See G. Tallon, 'Books of Survey and Distribution, Co. Westmeath: a Comparative Survey, with Reference to their Administrative Context and Chronological Sequence', *Analecta Hibernica*, 28 (1978), pp 111–14.
63. 'The Humble Remonstrance of Several of the Surveyors lately Employed in the Service of the Commonwealth', Larcom, *Down Survey*, p. 18.
64. This tracing was discovered by Larcom (and described by him in NLI, MS 7760) and rediscovered by Mr T. P. O'Neill. The present writer dimly remembers seeing it in the late 1950s.
65. Larcom, *Down Survey*, pp 47–8, 51, 62.
66. S. J. Madge, *The Domesday of Crown Lands* (London, 1938), p. 336.
67. In Petty's 'Brief Account' of the survey (ostensibly relating only to the years 1655 and 1656) he says that he had measured a distance equivalent to 'near five times' round the earth (Larcom, *Down Survey*, p. xvii). In *Reflections upon Some Persons and Things in Ireland, by Letters to and from Dr Petty; with Sir Hierome Sankey's Speech in Parliament* (London, 1660) his figure is 'near four times'. In his treatise on Ireland (C. H. Hull (ed.), *The Economic Writings of Sir William Petty* (Cambridge, 1899), pp 614–15) it is eight times. In his letter of 31 July 1686 to Sir Robert Southwell (Marquess of Lansdowne (ed.), *The Petty-Southwell Correspondence, 1676–1687* (London, 1928), p. 223) it is 'near six times'. In the inscription he planned for his family monument it is 'above five times'(Lord Edmond Fitzmaurice, *The Life of Sir William Petty* (London, 1895), p. 314). No one has ever tried to discover which of these figures is nearest the truth.

68. Larcom, *Down Survey*, pp 17, 45, 51, 53, 294; *Reflections upon Some Persons and Things*, p. 106.
69. Larcom, *Down Survey*, pp xvi, xvii, 105, 110–11, 120, 123, 128; *Reflections upon Some Persons and Things*, p. 106.
70. John Aubrey, Bodl. MS Aubr. 6, fol. 14, quoted by G. Keynes, *A Bibliography of Sir William Petty* (Oxford, 1971), p. 87; Harris, *Works of Sir James Ware*, 2, p. 354; J. E. Portlock, *Memoir of the Life of Major-general Colby* (London, 1869), pp 223–5.
71. Anonymous 'libel', quoted in Larcom, *Down Survey*, p. 259.
72. Map of the territory of Ileagh, Co. Tipperary, NAI, Map Room, Drawer 67, no. 11.
73. P. Eden (ed.), *Dictionary of Land Surveyors and Local Cartographers of Great Britain and Ireland, 1550–1850* (Folkestone, 1975), p. 48.
74. Report on the distribution of forfeited lands, by William Petty and Miles Symner, 20 Dec. 1656, Oireachtas Library, Dublin, MS 3.G.12. Personnel employed on the Down Survey are listed in Hardinge, *Trans. R. Ir. Acad.*, 24, Antiquities (1873), pp 45–99.
75. Larcom, *Down Survey*, pp 49, 50–51, 122, 259.
76. Larcom, *Down Survey*, p. 125.
77. 'Itur Hibernicum', p. 145, Sloane MS 360. For the contrary view, that the soldiers and adventurers were deliberately favoured by 'throwing in', as allowances of bog, land that was really profitable, see P. J. McLaughlin, 'Surveys of Ireland in the Seventeenth Century', *Irish Ecclesiastical Record*, 73 (1950), p. 130.
78. 'The Narration of Lewis Smith Concerning Kerry', 30 June 1656, Larcom, *Down Survey*, p. 95. *The Case of the Kerry Quit-Rent* deals with the consequences of this problem.
79. Larcom, *Down Survey*, p. 176.
80. Petty-Symner report, 12 Mar. 1656[–7]; Larcom, *Down Survey*, pp 177, 189–90.
81. Larcom, *Down Survey*, p. 296. This was in spite of what Petty called 'the impugnation of some thousand diligent find-faults'.
82. For an example (the iron works at Kenmare, Co. Kerry) see Marquess of Lansdowne, *Glanerought and the Petty-Fitzmaurices* (London, 1937), p. 5.
83. Published in 1908 by the Ordnance Survey, Southampton, in photozincographic facsimiles from the originals in the Bibliothèque Nationale, Paris. See below, ch.4.
84. *Political Anatomy*, pp 108–09. See also above, n.4.
85. Article 19 of Petty's agreement with the Surveyor-General, 11 Dec. 1654, Larcom, *Down Survey*, p. 29.
86. Sherrard, Brassington and Greene, surveyors, report on lands in Co. Cavan, 3 July 1829, NAI, 2B.44.5. According to James Weale, one-sixth was the usual proportion by which Down Survey acreages were increased by early nineteenth-century surveyors (Report on lands in dispute between the Crown and the Primate of Ireland (1828), p. 1,

NLI, MS 864). Others favoured an increase of one-seventh (*First Report of the Commissioners of Municipal Corporations in Ireland*, appendix, pp 487, 663, 739–40, H.C. 1835, xxviii).
87. Goblet, *Transformation*, 1, pp 332–7.
88. See below, ch.10.
89. Declaration and petition of committee of adventurers, 17 Sep. 1658, Larcom, *Down Survey*, pp 241, 244, also known in a contemporary printed version entitled *Proposals to the Adventurers for Lands in Ireland*. Petty mentioned the proposal for a three per cent margin without objecting to it (*Cal. S.P. Ire.*, Commonwealth, p. 364).
90. Hardinge believed that the Trustees made use of such Down Survey maps as were available to them ('A Concluding Memoir on Manuscript Mapped and Other Townland Surveys in Ireland, from 1688 to 1864', *Trans. R. Ir. Acad.*, 24, Antiquities (1873), p. 281). But there are considerable differences between the Down Survey acreages and those of the Trustees' Survey listed in 'Abstracts of the Conveyances from the Trustees of the Forfeited Estates and Interests in Ireland, in 1688', Irish Record Commission, *15th Annual Report*, pp 348–96. The minutes of the Trustees (Annesley MSS, NLI, mic. P.259) include references to the resurveying of Down Survey boundaries, e.g. on 23 and 28 July 1702.
91. Sheres's 'scheme' for the survey and his instructions to the surveyors were approved by the Trustees on 16 July 1700 (Annesley MSS, NLI, mic. P.259). At least one contemporary critic wanted to see the 'rules of survey' published (*Some Remarks, upon a Late Scandalous Pamphlet, Entituled, an Address of Some Irish-Folks to the House of Commons* (n.p., 1702), pp 14–15).
92. Maps of forfeited lands in Co. Galway (Add. MS 13956) and in Cos. Leitrim, Mayo, and Sligo (Add. MS 14405).
93. Irish Record Commission, *8th Report*, supplement (Dublin, 1819), appendix iii (catalogue of maps preserved in the Auditor-General's office), pp 319, 343, 352. For an example see A. Barrington, *The Barringtons: a Family History* (Dublin, 1917), p. 131.
94. *Some Remarks upon a Late Scandalous Pamphlet*, p. 12. There is a similar argument in *Jus Regium: or, the King's Right to Grant Forfeitures, etc.* (London, 1701), p. 51.
95. *Considerations on Agriculture: Treating of the Several Methods Practised in Different Parts of the Kingdom of Ireland, with Remarks Thereon* (Dublin, 1730), pp 80–81.
96. Annesley MSS (NLI, mic. P.276), *passim*.
97. R. A. Skelton, reply to A. Gillies, 'What are Estate Plans?', *Cart. Jour.*, 4 (1967), pp 53, 140.

4
Public and private

FRANCIS JOBSON WAS NOT THE ONLY STATE SURVEYOR to spend part of his Irish career in private employment. In the early seventeenth century the same kind of transition was achieved by Thomas Raven, apparently to greater effect. Raven's spells with a succession of government authorities were separated by two periods spent partly or wholly outside the official sector, one on salary for the city of London,[1] the other surveying private estates such as those of Hamilton, Essex and Perceval.[2] Some of Petty's surveyors must originally have been trained as freelances, though Simon Garstin and Thomas Hunter, who worked respectively for the Earls of Thomond and Ormond, are the only ones who have so far been identified by name.[3] Conversely, Petty wrote of 'furnishing' manpower to individual landholders for their own use,[4] and several members of his staff appear later as estate or town surveyors, including John Humphreys, William Hunter, Robert Newcomen and John Young.[5] From the trustees' establishment the number of authenticated professional survivors is larger – about a dozen – perhaps because there was now more opportunity for private work but also, no doubt, because the documents are better for the eighteenth century than for the seventeenth.[6]

In the plantation surveys these men can hardly have failed to learn from each other and from their directors. But the cartographic effect of the plantations outlasted and outdistanced even the longest and busiest of individual working lives, for it was posthumously transmitted to successive generations through the medium of the maps themselves. For many people, map enthusiasts included, archival history is history at its dullest. Among Irishmen, however, the custody of the various government surveys has always been a subject of lively interest, stimulating more research and scholarly publication than any other topic discussed in the present essay –though it was a military engineer and not a scholar who best summed up the matter with his dictum that the records of a confiscated kingdom are more precious than gold, and that all official surveys should be secured in the strongest fortress of its capital city.[7] This is not what happened in Dublin. On the contrary, from the Elizabethan period onwards plantation maps were finding their way into the possession of many private landowners and private surveyors.

A Surveyor-General as sharp as William Parsons is not likely to have missed the chance of organising this traffic, and the entry 'to Mr Parsons for our map 20s' in the accounts of Trinity College, Dublin, for 1610 was probably a reference to Bodley's survey of some or all of the property which the College had been granted in Donegal and Armagh:[8] an innocent enough transaction among scholars and gentlemen no doubt, but such leakages may help to explain why so many of the early plantation maps are no longer in official custody, and perhaps why their departure so often went unrecorded. The processes by which such dealings were legitimised are unknown. It might be supposed that the financing of official maps with 'admeasurement money' collected from local landowners (as in Longford and elsewhere) would entail the giving of transcripts in return, but without extant copies in collections of estate papers this conjecture must remain unproven. Surveys, like medical reports, are not always considered suitable viewing for those who pay for them. At any rate it was not until Strafford's time that any Irish plantation survey became well known to the general public. Thereafter, Petty could explain the loss of certain Strafford reference books by supposing that they had come into the possession of army officers who hoped to receive land in Co. Tipperary under the Cromwellian settlement. For the historian, this dispersal of official records provides an interesting channel of cartographic influence. For the government of the day it was clearly regrettable. Again, Petty's remark that some of the Strafford measurers 'made great advantage by transcripts of their survey' conveys a fairly obvious hint of disapproval, though in this case the originals were presumably unaffected and the objection was to the government's loss of a promising source of revenue at monopoly prices.

Petty's own survey was by no means immune from wastage. He calculated that nineteen reams of paper had gone to make three reams of Down Survey maps, and not all the surplus material had been destroyed: he accused his critics of rescuing some of it from rubbish dumps and of seeking 'preparatory drafts' in a source inaccessible to posterity, namely 'under the bottom of tarts'. Meanwhile he himself had been attempting not so much to abolish the system of transcripts as to bring it under control. In the first place he agreed to supply a copy of the relevant section of the Down Survey to every new planter holding more than 1,000 acres: these are the first plantation maps known to have been made available to private individuals as a matter of government policy.[9] Of course Petty also had to provide maps for the state in the person of the Surveyor-General and it was not long before this officer began to furnish interested inquirers with particulars from the Down and Strafford Surveys and even with copies of the maps themselves. Some of the inquiries came from other official or semi-official bodies: in 1662 the Surveyor-General was allowed a sum of two hundred pounds by one group of trustees in lieu of fees for supplying duplicates.[10] But no special qualifications seem to have been needed by private persons to obtain such documents apart from the ability to pay for them. In 1702 they would have been charged 2s. 6d for a search and another 5s. 6d for the map of a denomination.[11] In 1718 the search fee was fixed at 5s and the map-fee left negotiable.[12] It must have seemed an unequal bargain when the Surveyor-General was the only source of supply: some clients were content with a brief certificate of acreage, perhaps accompanied by a written boundary description, rather than a complete map; and even an outstandingly conscientious cartographer, seeking complete Down Survey coverage for Co. Clare as a source for territorial boundaries, changed his mind when he found how much it was going to cost him.[13] The strength of the demand for the maps is suggested by the generally upward tendency of their price, but the expense arising in ordinary estate business seldom amounted to more than a pound or two on any given occasion, and in the late eighteenth century the Surveyor-General's deputy expressed some disappointment that his fees had been averaging only about fifty pounds per year.[14] Over a long period this represented an output that was far from negligible, and the number of surviving copies issued to private individuals is impressively large. They are usually uncoloured and unembellished, and carry the inscription: 'The above trace of ... agreeeth for so much with the Down Survey of the said lands [or simply 'the map of the said lands'] remaining on record in His Majesty's Surveyor-General's office', with the signature of the current Deputy Surveyor-General and sometimes the date.[15]

The Down Survey is much better represented in private collections than either the Strafford or the Trustees' Surveys. The difference is partly due to a serious fire which attacked the government offices in Essex Street, Dublin, on 15 April 1711. The Surveyor-General's copy of the Strafford Survey seems to have been the most serious casualty (so totally lost that

Dublin lawyers could later doubt whether the Strafford inquisition had ever included any maps), especially as it does not appear to have been duplicated in any other official collection.[16] The Trustees' Survey had been kept in the relative obscurity of the Auditor-General's office and so escaped destruction – for the time being. Of the Down Survey maps, eighteen out of thirty-one books survived.[17] Apart from fire damage, some maps were suspected of having been purloined in the subsequent confusion, and some that were not genuine official maps were thought to have been planted in the office when the surviving material was being rearranged.[18] In their different ways both accusations attest the connection between governmental and non-governmental cartography, but the system had clearly suffered a major setback. No one suggested doing the Down Survey all over again: the effect of the fire was rather to focus attention on surveys kept in other repositories as well as on maps drawn at smaller scales than might otherwise have been considered desirable.

Some of these additional copies had been kept by Petty himself. When taxed with retaining Down Survey records contrary to act of Parliament he did not deny the charge but insisted that the maps in question were only 'certain foul drafts of plot, signed by no man, confused, imperfect, hard to be understood'.[19] In that case why bother to keep them, was the obvious reply. Petty did not mention that even the neatest maps derive their authority from documents that contemporary parlance would class as 'foul' – or that he had also kept the most authentic of all Down Survey records, the surveyors' field books, as he admitted when making his will in 1685.[20] Later there were proposals for re-using the field books to construct a new set of maps of equal validity with the originals,[21] but this was never attempted. Nor have the books been made available by Petty's heirs; in fact the only Down Survey materials known to belong to his descendants are a set of relatively small-scale barony maps together with some even smaller maps of the counties and the provinces.[22] For Petty himself to have retained as much of the survey as possible was partly to show a disinterested (but largely frustrated) concern for future map-users, but he did not altogether forget the kind of down-to-earth motive that had brought him into cartography in the first place. In Petty's house, as in the Surveyor-General's office, a fee was charged for looking at the maps.[23]

Another collection deriving directly from Petty was the set of barony maps seized by a French privateer on their way from Dublin to London in 1707 and subsequently preserved in Paris.[24] Some sixty years later, these exotica were discovered by a British official in the Bibliothèque Royale. Having just lost Canada, the French might have been expected to stomach the surrender of the Down Survey; but when the time came to produce them the maps were found to be missing. (Rumour had it that they were being reduced into a new map of Ireland, for use if either side decided to restart the Seven Years War.)[25] They were safely in their place again, however, when interest in them was revived in 1786 at the instigation of the Irish antiquary and military cartographer, Charles Vallancey. This time the authorities in Paris agreed to the copying of the maps and Vallancey, perhaps not averse to the prospect of a Continental holiday, persuaded the Dublin government to let him direct the work.[26] There was talk of a conspiracy to leave the facsimiles in France and bring the originals home before anyone had a chance to notice the substitution.[27] One hopes that the authorities were suitably shocked by this nefarious scheme, but they showed themselves less grateful for Vallancey's efforts than he might have hoped. Although his copies stood up fairly well to a 'long and troublesome' comparison with the originals, a parliamentary bill confirming their legal validity was rejected by the Irish upper house, partly because they were not quite identical with the maps in the Surveyor-General's office, and partly because as barony maps their scale was too small (usually 320 perches to an inch or 1:80,640) to leave room for an adequate record of boundaries.[28] One surveyor gave additional strength to this impression by testifying that no Down Survey barony maps within his experience had ever been produced in court.[29] This did not prevent them from being consulted by the staff of the government's Quit-Rent Office, as indeed were the printed county maps of Petty's *Hiberniae Delineatio*.[30] But it was as historical records that the maps in the Bibliothèque eventually became most familiar, especially after they had been reproduced for public sale by the Ordnance Survey in 1908.

Yet another group of Down Survey maps was retained by Thomas Taylor, who had served as an examiner on the original survey and who later became one of the few practical surveyors known to have held the post of Deputy Surveyor-General.[31] By the middle eighteenth century this collection had been opened to inquirers at Headfort House, the Taylor family residence near Kells in Co. Meath, and was said to be of great use.[32] In 1837 the Headfort maps were sold to the government by one of Taylor's descendants.

By the time of the Headfort sale there was no longer any such person as the Irish Surveyor-General, but the reasons for his disappearance (to be considered later) had nothing to do with the value of the plantation maps, which were preserved by their subsequent custodians at least as carefully as ever before. From the Surveyor-General's charge, in Dublin Castle, they passed in 1832 to the Vice-Treasurer's office at the Custom House, and there, in combination with the records of the Office of Woods and Forests, they helped give birth to the Irish Landed Estates Record Office.[33] Surviving estate papers make clear that under all these regimes it remained possible, and was still often found desirable, to secure copies of the official surveys for private use. Indeed the first keeper of the Landed Estates Record Office, W. H. Hardinge, found that the maps were deteriorating as a result of being consulted so frequently, a problem he hoped to solve by taking photographs of them.[34]

With the foundation of the Irish Public Record Office in 1867 the surveys appeared at last to have found a permanent home in which they could be seen on the same terms as any other historical document.[35] But that was to reckon without the destruction of the Record Office as part of the Irish civil war of 1922. Losses included the Trustees' maps, all the Surveyor-General's authenticated copies of Down Survey parish maps, and the large barony maps with square grids from which Hardinge had deduced Petty's mode of calculating areas. Once more attention shifted to possible substitutes, though by now the principal motive for the search was historical curiosity rather than the needs of official business. A number of discoveries were made during this new phase. Firstly there were copies prepared on the authority of eighteenth-century Surveyors-General, not for meeting particular requests but in systematic anticipation of some more comprehensive future demand. One such volume of maps, of Co. Antrim, signed by William Molesworth (Surveyor-General from 1714 to 1770) assumed a special importance on account of its probable stylistic resemblance to the lost originals.[36] Another volume, for Wexford, was copied in 1777–8 by a land surveyor named Daniel O'Brien under the direction of the Deputy Surveyor-General, Matthew Handcock,[37] and in 1786–7 O'Brien produced a further set of volumes of the same kind.[38] His copies, especially those of the 1780s, are in a plain and neutered style which neither imitates seventeenth-century ornament nor substitutes the decorative conventions of his own time. Handcock described these volumes as tolerably accurate: those of the second series were subsequently acquired by the Surveyor-General's family, the Rochforts, and eventually found their way through a firm of Dublin solicitors (Messrs Reeves) into the National Library of Ireland and the Public Record Office of Northern Ireland.

Then from the Quit-Rent Office has come a large collection of copies and tracings done to meet specific departmental needs, some based on the Surveyor-General's or the Headfort maps, others on the Trustees' Survey, with an occasional oddity such as a modern estate map or a fragment of Bodley's Ulster survey. Most of these copies are of nineteenth-century date and do little to recall the style of the originals.[39] Reference must also be made to certain copies ordered for the Irish Record Commission of 1810[40] and to others drawn from time to time by the staff of the Ordnance Survey, including those made for the Irish Manuscripts Commission as recently as the 1960s.[41] Others were made by local government officials and by private individuals.[42]

All these collections badly need further study and collating. The object of the foregoing paragraphs is simply to show by how much the plantation surveys outlasted the plantations themselves. Their continuing influence was due to several causes. As many a private office and muniment room can testify, the Strafford and Down Surveys did some of the duty of the ordinary landowner's survey as discussed in the two following chapters: at least one seventeenth-century estate atlas consists partly of Down Survey copies and partly of original maps.[43] The same relationship appears in the frequency with which the government surveys were cited as authorities for names and acreages in documents concerning the transfer of private property, from formal deeds to humble newspaper advertisements, throughout the eighteenth century and well into the nineteenth.[44] The Strafford Survey won itself enough prestige to be mistakenly quoted as a source of information in a county where the survey had never taken place.[45]

Much of this prestige grew out of archival history. For anyone marshalling evidence on questions of landownership it was an advantage to secure confirmatory statements from outside his own possession. 'In my judgement there cannot be a directer rule to go by, than the private and public surveys since they so well agree', wrote one Co. Cork land agent in 1704.[46] But suppose they had disagreed? In another confrontation from the same county twelve years later, one party could reject the other's map because it was not 'out of the survey office',[47] his reason doubtless being that since the location of a Surveyor-General's map was known at every stage of its history it could not have been fabricated especially for service in the current dispute. It was thus in the lawyers' sense an ancient survey or survey of record.[48]

However, the acceptability of the Down Survey was more than just a matter of age and location. An author of 1697 described 'absolute acquiescence' in the Survey as a standing rule in Irish courts.[49] These were brave words for a subject as thorny as the law of evidence, but as late as 1850, after the whole of Ireland had been re-mapped by another government agency, the Down Survey could still be proclaimed by an Irish lawyer as evidence against all the world.[50] The source of its potency (which in areas with no Down Survey extended to the Strafford Survey) was the recognition accorded to it by the national parliament: this is what distinguished the two great seventeenth-century surveys from that of the Trustees, which has always been less well thought of in Ireland because its attendant legislation had been passed at Westminster and not in Dublin. Like most lawyers' pronouncements on cartography the statutes in question were not of a kind that cartographers themselves would find easily intelligible; but the fact of being mentioned at all was more important than the exact sense that Parliament had intended to convey. For what it is worth, the Act of Settlement of 1662, in authorising the distribution of confiscated land to the adventurers, had instructed the Lord High Treasurer of Ireland to 'cast up the whole debt and demand of the adventurers ... according to the survey commonly called Dr Petty's Down admeasurement'.[51] The survey made another appearance in the Act of Explanation of 1665, which accepted the claims of innocent Catholics to their former possessions, and which accordingly directed most of the soldiers and adventurers to surrender or 'retrench' some part of their recent acquisitions. The commissioners who executed the new act in 1666–9 were told to

> set out ... forfeited land ... in quantity of Irish profitable acres, to be computed by Irish measure according to the Down Survey or Down admeasurement, and not otherwise, where the Down Survey hath been taken, and where the Down Survey hath not been taken, by the survey taken in the Earl of Strafford's time, or by some other survey to be taken according to Irish measure, wherein the unprofitable land is to be cast in together with the profitable (according to the method of the said Down Survey) ...[52]

Although the law had a few more things to say about the Down Survey, none of them related to property rights as such, or to the boundaries between one estate and another. Yet surveys, of an unspecified character, had been recommended in a non-statutory context as evidence for ownership at an early stage of the Cromwellian settlement,[53] and in 1735 this procedure was justified by a court decision to the effect that the terriers or written pages which Petty had placed opposite his maps (and whose importance at the moment consisted in giving the proprietors' names) were just as much a part of the survey as any of its cartographic details. That writing needed special validation was a retrospective tribute to Petty the cartographer: unprecedentedly, lawyers had been preferring maps to words.

For the surveyor, a more interesting question was the proprietorial significance of the Down Survey boundaries. In theory a perversely minded executive could have obeyed the Act of Explanation, first by running totally new boundaries through the middle of Petty's denominations, and then (still in compliance with the law) by dividing his acreage value proportionately among the various new parcels so created, thus producing acreages that could be said to derive from Petty without having been mentioned anywhere in his survey. In practice, however, it had been accepted from the 1650s that the Down Survey boundaries should be observed as far as possible in the new distribution of land.[54] This principle was never put into any statute, but it seemed implicit in the dictum that the Down Survey gave valid evidence for boundaries between properties of the 'new interest' but not for those that separated the new interest from the old.[55] The old interest were the holders of titles that predated the Down Survey: if they were in quiet possession of their outer bounds it would be unjust for a subsequent survey of rebel land to stigmatise these bounds as in any sense incorrect. For the new interest, who took their titles from the mid-seventeenth-century settlement, the Down Survey evidence was deemed conclusive. In other words, if at any subsequent time their boundaries were found to differ from the Survey, the differences must be due to 'real' changes posterior to its completion – either a voluntary transfer of land (for which suitable documentary evidence could be expected) or else an unauthorised encroachment.

This legal continuity could survive any number of changes, whether due to purchase or inheritance, as long as the land in question retained its name and (presumably) its identity; and since in Ireland the historic territorial units did usually provide the framework for private land transactions the Down Survey was likely to preserve its evidential value long after it had been completed. Eventually, of course, its significance would begin to decline: seventeenth-century boundaries would be replaced by new lines agreed in the course of agricultural development; and all boundaries would end by being so well fenced as to convince any but the most captious observer of their credibility. But the Survey still held sway as an authentic boundary record at least until the nineteenth century, a common solution for a boundary dispute when brought before an Irish court being an order for Petty's lines to be traced out on the ground. The importance of this process is attested by the many surviving maps that show the modern boundary in one colour and the Down Survey boundary in another.[56] The making of such maps was a standard feature of the eighteenth-century surveyor's stock-in-trade. Instructions on the subject took a prominent place in the best of Ireland's surveying textbooks, published by Robert Gibson in 1752;[57] and 'lands traced from the Down Survey' were listed among their skills by surveyors advertising in Irish newspapers as late as the 1780s.[58]

To compare the Down Survey lines with the lines visible in the landscape was not always an easy task. Sometimes a simple inspection of the old and new maps was thought to be sufficient,[59] but a precise comparison entailed reconstructing the original field book by taking measurements from the Down Survey map and then using chain and instrument to lay down the appropriate distances and bearings on the ground. In brief, it meant repeating the Down Survey in reverse order. Before any measurements were made, at least one Down Survey landmark would have to be located in the field, though not necessarily more than one: in theory Petty's scale and meridian line would enable all the other points to be determined from the map. One objection to this somewhat idealistic procedure was that if old and new surveyors took their north points from the compass the two outlines could not be superimposed without allowing for any change in magnetic variation over the intervening period – a problem that the Irish natural philosopher William Molyneux considered worth bringing to the attention of the Royal Society of London in 1697.[60]

At least one well-known eighteenth-century surveyor can be found applying Molyneux's principles to a disputed boundary and he was Richard Frizell. With a local church as his origin ('I look upon a glebe and church to be the most permanent and invariable point taken notice of in any ancient survey'), Frizell first reoriented the Down Survey map by measuring the variation of the needle in his own time (1768) and then adjusted the Down Survey scale ratio by re-chaining the distance between two seventeenth-century landmarks that were still identifiable.[61] The Down Survey could then be superimposed on a modern map. But what if the result was to show that some equally permanent landmark in the same townland had moved to a new position? No cartographic sleight of hand could eliminate this kind of built-in error. Its consequences were not necessarily disastrous, however: with some problems the outcome may be the same whichever pair of points the surveyor chooses as the datum for his superimposition, a likely example being the question of whether a small parcel of land is wholly enclosed by a much larger one.[62] The difficulty arises when he has to commit himself to one particular boundary and therefore to one particular relationship between the two maps. On this subject the only available witness is Robert Gibson: 'when you have brought the greatest number of points in each to agree that is possible, the maps are then applied to the greatest advantage'.[63] There is no record of how Gibson's readers received such irritatingly brief advice, but it must have meant something to some of them, including the later mathematician who promised to correct 'a considerable error in the reigning method of tracing Sir William Petty's surveys'.[64] Unfortunately this writer seems never to have published his correction, or to have said what the reigning method was.

Gibson did not mention the case reported by his near-contemporary Gabriel Stokes, of a map which was too long in one direction and too short in another and which Stokes apparently hoped to rectify by making separate adjustments along two orthogonal axes.[65] Stokes was discussing a real map (of Rathcoursey in Co. Cork), but in practice the errors of the Down Survey were more likely to form a planless muddle in which Gibson's 'greatest number' of self-consistent points must often have been ominously small. Before the advent of twentieth-century mathematics such muddles were generally unravelled by the kind of ruthless and irregular adjustment known to surveyors as fudging, coaxing or humouring. For instance, a badly-fitting section of boundary could first be separately traced and then moved bodily across the map until by trial and error the lines had been made to 'jump something natural'. This last phrase comes from the Quaker surveyor-diarist Joshua Wight. His method of restoring a Down Survey map near Cork Harbour in 1710 is too full of incomprehensible detail to be quoted at length, but its reference to 'a little [piece of] cut paper' will be understood by any reader who has tried to push and pull an inaccurate early map into a better shape.[66] What remains obscure is how often, if at all, the errors of the Down Survey were, so to speak, put back into the landscape, thereby ceasing to be errors through a process of Orwellian historical revision.

All in all, there are times when one comes near to suspecting a conspiracy of silence about the faults of the Down Survey. This might seem the more curious when it is noticed that in certain contexts the law did recognise the possibility of survey error. The act of 1662 had ruled:

> that such of the said adventurers and soldiers as have taken surveys of their lands, do at or before the nine and twentieth day of September, 1662, bring in to you [the Lord High Treasurer] the said surveys or duplicates thereof, together with the field-books (if in their possession) the which you are carefully and exactly to compare with the surveys taken by order of the late pretended powers [i.e. the Down Survey]; and if you shall find any considerable difference between the said surveys you are to ascertain such adventurers' and soldiers' possessions by such of the surveys as shall appear most for our advantage, and furtherance of this service.

And according to the act of 1665:

> The Lord Lieutenant ... shall have power, upon information ... of any ... concealments by false admeasurement ... to cause a new survey to be made of the parcels and lots ... Where any new survey is ordered, the same shall be taken by two surveyors to be chosen for that purpose, one by the informer, the other by the defendants, and both surveyors shall be sworn.
>
> Where the books of distribution and the Down Survey agree in the satisfactions, which have been allotted to any ... persons, or do not differ more than in one tenth, there no resurvey shall be ordered, notwithstanding such information.
>
> What overplus soever shall appear upon the new survey, if the same exceed not one tenth part of what is due to the defendant ..., no retrenchment shall be made.[67]

There was much here that influenced or reflected national attitudes to the surveyor's role in land management. The emphasis on the comparison of surveys, the willingness to repeat them, the representation by surveyors of both parties to a dispute, the appeal to field books as well as to maps – all these are recurring themes in Irish agrarian history, though the limit of ten per cent, generous even by the standards of the previous decade, would have been rejected by most later practitioners as intolerably wide. But what did these provisions about comparing and repeating surveys do to help Ireland's new landowners? No adventurer would submit his survey for comparison with the government's if the government was already bent on adopting whichever of the two promised to yield the greater quit rent, especially as it must soon have become known, even if seldom noised abroad, that the Down Survey had favoured the landowner, rather than the Crown, by generally falling short of the truth.[68]

On the other hand surveyors still had plenty of scope to operate within the system, clearing up the details of the plantation settlement without attempting to overthrow its framework. One troublesome problem arose when the acreage to be granted or, later, to be retrenched, did not exactly coincide with the acreage of any particular townland or group of townlands in the appropriate district. Almost every aspect of this situation is shrouded in ignorance, notably how often it occurred, and when, by whom, and under what kind of technical instructions it was dealt with. Particularly disappointing is the lack of maps from the Cromwellian or early Restoration period that actually carve up the confiscated lands among the undertakers, the only example on record being a rough diagram outlining the division in a part of Co. Limerick.[69] In some townlands the surveyors who laid off the requisite acreages are known to have been appointed or instructed by the proprietors on the spot, as on one occasion in 1657 when incompatible boundaries were set out by rival surveyors employed by rival landowners.[70] Another case involved Petty himself by requiring him to give up some of his Kerry lands to the McGillycuddy of the Reeks. 'You will do well to be kind to Coner', wrote one of the McGillycuddy's advisers meaningfully in 1679, 'and get him well to consider how he runs the line before he cuts ground'.[71] (Coner or Connor was evidently a local surveyor, perhaps the Charles Connor who practised in the same area twenty years later.)[72] There were rules for laying out these lines, but no contemporary copy of them has been found. The main prerequisite was apparently straightness: several patents of the 1660s and 1670s specify lands to be cut off or separated by either north-south or east-west lines, and in one instance by a line from north-west to south-east;[73] and during a later controversy settled by William Hunter (formerly of the Down Survey) the line of division was found to have an angle in it and so to contravene the rules of retrenchment.[74]

As the Restoration land settlement gathered momentum, the government set up a new agency to collect the rents that had been decided upon in 1642. This was the Quit-Rent Office, which also assumed responsibility for two special categories of Crown property left over from the plantation. One was 'plus acres', which were scraps of forfeited land remaining in hand after each adventurer or soldier had received the exact area due to him. The other, known as 'undisposed lands', was made up of parcels that had been confiscated but not granted, usually because they were too barren for anyone to want them.[75] The Quit-Rent Office became involved in cartography on many occasions when doubts arose about the location of plus or undisposed lands or when the payment of quit rents was disputed or fell into arrear.

Much use was made of the Down Survey on these occasions, but many denominations had to be mapped afresh. In some grants and leases of forfeited land, the government stipulated that tenants should map the property at their own expense.[76] Where the responsibility for admeasurement lay on the office itself, a common expedient was for the local collector of revenue to be charged with finding suitable assistance in the neighbourhood of the lands concerned.[77] Only in especially difficult or controversial cases was a surveyor brought all the way from Dublin. Two recorded examples were in 1701 when Henry Pratt travelled to Kerry to survey the lands of Dunloe and Tooms in conjunction with the Mr Connor mentioned above,[78] and in 1710 when John Greene was sent to survey the plus and undisposed lands of Co. Longford after the local collector had admitted not knowing where they were.[79] Here was another route along which metropolitan influences could reach the provincial map-maker. Occasionally the impulse flowed in the opposite direction and a local private surveyor would report the existence of 'concealed' lands liable to quit rent in the hope of being rewarded for his discovery.[80] All this surveying, like most surveying, was done with a good deal of reluctance. When one official suggested obtaining a map of a certain property if there was any difficulty about getting information from other sources, his colleague replied brusquely that the department ought to undergo *much* difficulty before incurring the expense of maps.[81]

It was natural that the measures taken to secure the Crown's interest, such as they were, should also be invoked when purely private disputes were given a public character by being brought before the courts. Without any attempt to be exhaustive, a few specimens may be given of the circumstances in which a surveyor was likely to find himself in action as an instrument of the law. A commission of perambulation was one time-honoured device for settling boundary disputes, improved in the course of the seventeenth century by the recruitment of surveyors to record the referees' verdict. It could also be used to effect a partition of lands held 'together and undivided' by two or more proprietors.[82] A writ of dower might involve a surveyor in delimiting for a widow a third part of her late husband's land (Plate 3).[83] Some debts were settled by a court order for the sale of as much of the defendant's estate as would fetch a given sum of money.[84] Or a surveyor might help resolve a disagreement over tithes by determining how much of a given farm fell within a certain parish.[85] Among the duties attached to such cases were the tracing of boundaries shown by local witnesses, the superimposition of old and new maps, and the striking off of new division lines. The surveyors who performed them would often find themselves giving evidence in court; so might their chainmen and mearsmen.[86] In fact the law seemed generally to prefer the map-maker to the map; so much so that the death of a surveyor could deprive his work of its validity and necessitate a repetition of his survey.[87] Although the procedure for executing court decisions varied from one case to another, it is clear that outside the Quit-Rent Office, as inside, no permanent staff of government surveyors was available for such a purpose. To that extent the post-plantation adjustments resembled the plantations themselves. The act of 1662, a model for so much officially-managed surveying, rather unhelpfully directed the Treasurer to 'appoint' one or more surveyors in cases of dispute. Another possibility, envisaged in the Act of Explanation, was to let the principals choose their own surveyors, and the latter system seems to have prevailed wherever two opposing parties were distinguishable – which in Ireland meant much of the time.

Where the interest of the Crown was involved, or where one or both of the disputants refused to nominate a surveyor (another common occurrence), the choice fell to the government. In a late seventeenth-century review of the Surveyor-General's duties this responsibility ranked equal in importance to his archival function·

> He hath in his office all the surveys and inquisitions relating to the King's title for lands, houses etc., and if any controversy ariseth concerning the extent or boundaries of any lands or manors etc., he appoints surveyors to settle such mears and bounds, and the quantity of such estate, together with the yearly value thereof if requisite.[88]

In practice the two duties overlapped, for the new maps were kept by the Surveyor-General, and in some cases he insisted on taking possession of the surveyor's field book as well.[89] Recruiting surveyors was a task that went on in many parts of the country, largely unnoticed in the historical record, long after the appropriate plantation survey had been brought to an ostensible conclusion. One of the Surveyor-General's early nominees was Thomas Burgate, measuring a Co. Limerick ploughland in 1618.[90] Others were Henry Gee and the inevitable Thomas Raven, still tidying up the plantation of King's Co. as late as 1633.[91]

By the end of the century this right of patronage had grown to a respectable antiquity, and when it was threatened by the advent of the last of the plantation agencies in the shape of the Trustees' Survey the Surveyor-General did not hesitate to resist, formally applying to the courts of Chancery and Exchequer to be employed in all cases of partition and ascertainment of metes and bounds brought by petition in those courts.[92] Of course after the early 1700s there was nothing to fear from any *ad hoc* plantation authority, and the Surveyor-General continued to make his appointments at a fee of one pound a time.[93] Later W. H. Hardinge found two large books, extending into eighteen counties and ranging in date from 1704 to 1784, in which the maps made for successive Surveyors-General had been preserved.[94] Two volumes do not seem very much for eighty years work, and one wonders whether this collection was as carefully augmented and protected by its contemporary custodians as it should have been. They certainly failed to keep track of a book of extracts from the Down Survey which was copied in the middle eighteenth century by the Dublin mathematical teacher Robert Lewis and later offered by a private individual to the superintendent of the Irish Ordnance Survey.[95] Lewis's contemporaries have often been castigated for their lack of administrative zeal in all departments of official life, Irish and British; but as in similar cases at an earlier period, there was at least the possibility that archival migrations might help to diffuse the ideas embodied in official cartography.

Until the middle of the century nothing was said about how the courts, the Quit-Rent Office or the Surveyor-General made their choice of surveying personnel, except that the practitioners employed should be 'honest', 'known', or 'skilful'. For many years the obvious proof of skill would have been experience in a recent plantation survey. It was only when the last of the plantation surveyors were dying out that the problem of selection looked like becoming acute; and then it was not until an eminent practising surveyor, Gabriel Stokes, took office as Deputy Surveyor-General that anything positive was done. Stokes's appointment came soon after Irish surveyors had discovered new and more public ways of impugning each other's ability. Peter Callan of Drogheda was writing a book-length indictment of many of his colleagues,[96] and an exchange between William Thornton and John Noble in the *Dublin Journal* in

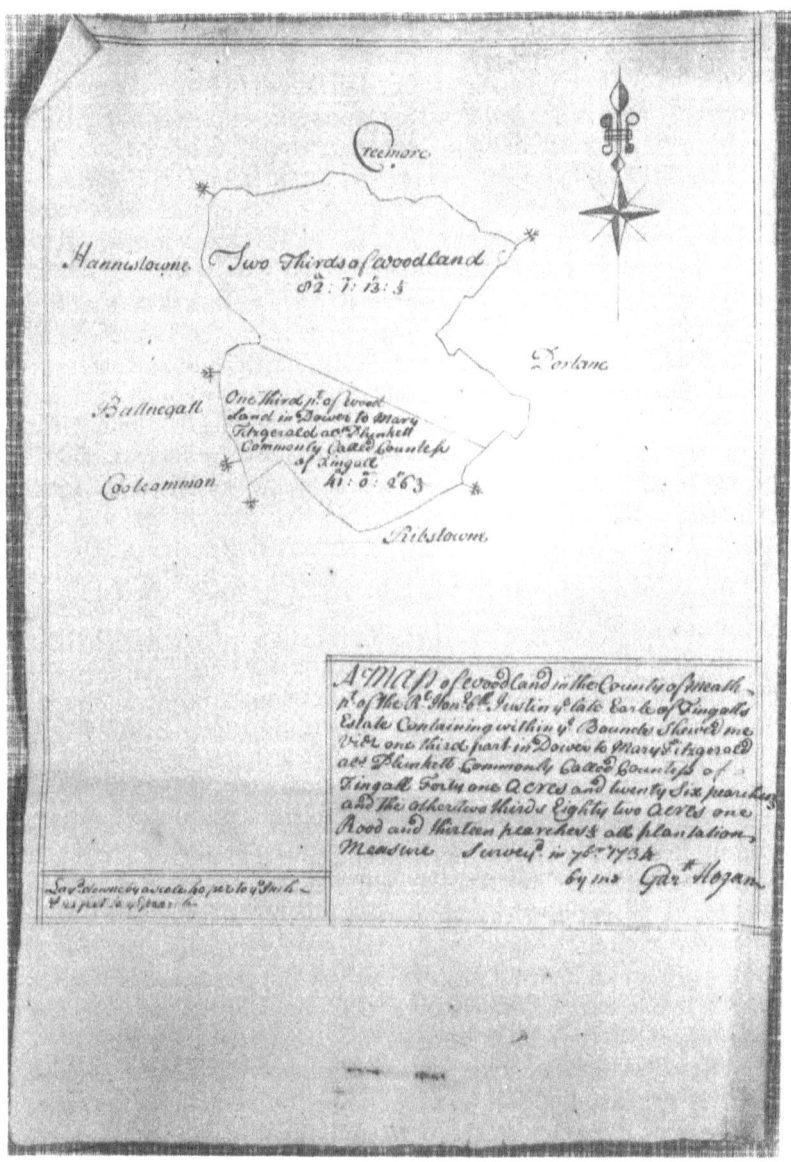

Plate 3. Copy of partition map by Garret Hogan, 1734. From the Fingall estate maps, Co. Meath (see chapter 4, note 83). Scale of original 40 perches to one inch. The townland of Woodland still exists, apparently with the same boundaries as are shown here, but Hogan's acreage is too small by about 5 per cent. His dividing line has left no trace in the modern landscape.

1749 showed that the practice of ventilating surveyors' professional disagreements had now begun to establish itself in the newspapers.[97]

Public confidence needed a tonic, and Stokes's prescription, on 20 January 1750, was as follows:

> Whereas by decretal orders from His Majesty's high court of Chancery, and court of Exchequer, the Surveyor-General is frequently directed to appoint skilful surveyors; and as the Surveyor-General knows not (for want of examining, as was in the original institution of this office) who are skilful, gentlemen would do well, for many other reasons, not to employ any surveyor, but such as have passed an examination, and obtained a certificate from the Surveyor-General's office, of their qualifications for the business of surveying of land, and of tracing Down Surveys.[98]

It looked as if, many years after the last of the Irish plantations, the Surveyor-General was about to come into his own. Stokes was already issuing certificates in the following May. The records of his office do not survive, but a total of some twenty such testimonials has been noticed in a sampling of contemporary newspapers. Thirteen of them follow Stokes's example by drawing attention to the problem of the Down Survey trace. A typical specimen, signed by the Deputy Surveyor-General, Matthew Handcock, in 1773, runs:

> I certify that I have caused Mr Thomas Kavanah, of Ballyroan in the Queen's Co., to be duly examined in the theory and practice of land-surveying, and find him perfectly skilled in that science, and very capable of performing any survey however complicated, and of tracing from the Down or any other survey, and of reducing and enlarging maps in any proportion, with exactness; and that he is well acquainted with everything in the art of surveying.[99]

Handcock is not known as a practical surveyor, though he did take an amateur's interest in the subject, and proved himself a good friend to cartography by allowing at least one map-maker to use the contents of his office free of charge.[100] He may have felt capable of conducting his own tests. Some of Stokes's other successors as deputy preferred to delegate their examining to a sub-deputy. Robert Gibson held this latter position from 1752 to 1760, followed in 1765 by his son George.[101] Nothing is known about the examination itself. A Sligo estate map of 1768 makes the incidental statement that 'a small trifle is allowed by the Surveyor-General', not saying how small,[102] and if this were a reference to the examination it would confirm the plausible suggestion that the candidate had to state the number of acres in a testing-ground that had already been expertly (and it is to be hoped, secretly) surveyed.

Much else about the certificate system is equally obscure, including the date and circumstances of its termination. Hardinge wrote in an offhand manner of the courts 'discontinuing the services' of the Surveyor-General, but contrary to his usual practice he gave neither date nor source for an event which both for himself and for later historians of his subject must surely be described as verging on the cataclysmic.[103] Nor does he say what services he meant. There might seem to be a clue in the terminal date of 1784 which he gives for the two volumes of post-plantation maps in the Surveyor-General's office, and it is true that the middle to late eighties show signs of being in some way significant for official Irish cartography, as witness the making of the Reeves and Vallancey copies of the Down Survey. But what exactly, if anything, happened in 1784 is impossible to say. Maps are not specified in the only legislation of that year which seems in any way relevant, namely the act making the national bank a place of safe keeping for documents submitted by suitors in the courts of Chancery and Exchequer.[104] In any case this act did nothing to prevent the deposit of duplicates in other public collections, and several maps not mentioned by Hardinge are known to have found their way into the Surveyor-General's office after 1790.[105] The office was still examining surveyors and pronouncing on their competence as late as 1789, but after that its certificates seem gradually to have fallen out of favour, and by 1807 the initials 'c.s.' could be used without fear of ambiguity to denote not the holder of one of them but the City Surveyor employed by the Corporation of Dublin.[106] Other practitioners went on claiming to be certified for some time after this, but most of them were old enough to have won the qualification in or before about 1790, and some may conceivably have inherited theirs from their fathers. The subject is further complicated by the mysterious and not very common expression 'registered surveyor', possibly a synonym for certified surveyor in the old sense but perhaps only a claim to authorship of one or more lease maps entered at the Registry of Deeds.[107]

When the law of Irish property transactions was finally exposed to the reforming ardour of the Victorians the idea of a proficiency certificate had been forgotten, and the apparently vague and subjective concept of a 'recognised' surveyor came back into favour.[108] In reality the recognised surveyor had been flourishing all along, and even before the 1780s it was only surveyors of the second rank who consented to submit themselves for examination. In 1771 an obscure and elderly practitioner was disparaged for lacking a certificate, but only as a courtroom trick.[109] The truth was that Ireland's most eminent surveyors had preferred to stand aloof from public commendation, like lecturers in an ancient university disdaining to take a doctor's degree, and the Corkman who styled himself 'P.L.S.' (practising land surveyor) may well have been making fun of formal qualifications.[110] By the end of the eighteenth century enough surveyors had gained enough recognition among enough employers for the cartographic business of both executive and judiciary to proceed without the benefit of quasi-academic labels. For the time being, the private land surveyor was agreeably self-sufficient.

Nothing conveys this state of affairs more clearly than the fate decreed for the Surveyor-General. Under an act of 1817 his office was not abolished there and then, but contemptuously allowed to wither away in company with various other sinecures, its final demise being delayed until such time as the current office-holder should happen to retire or die. To judge from contemporary directories, this event took place in 1829; the apparent absence of any more official publication of it may be accepted with composure.[111] The last act of the Surveyor-General's career, like so many of the earlier acts, was performed with the principal character offstage. It consisted of undoing the work of the plantations by selling off the property that his department had originally been appointed to administer. When in 1798 it was decided to dispose of almost all Ireland's remaining Crown lands the scheme foundered for the humiliating reason that the Crown had hardly any idea where its lands were.[112] Many of them lay among mountain tracts that had not been very well mapped by the Down Survey (though Petty's critics were wrong to accuse him of ignoring the mountains altogether) and although there had been plenty of time to survey them later it appeared that no one had done so. When the plan came up again in 1820 matters were arranged with more efficiency. Commissioners were duly appointed; a new act of Parliament was passed to regulate their proceedings; and a list of lands held from the Crown was compiled by Henry Hardinge and his son, the indefatigable W.H.[113]

It looked like the occasion for a miniature Down Survey. But as befitted a salute to the virtues of *laissez faire*, the new admeasurement was conducted with the maximum of private enterprise and the minimum of state control. Applications were sought from independent surveyors, five of whom received appointments. There was no question of paying a flat rate per man-day or per unit-area, as in previous official enterprises of the same kind; instead each surveyor submitted his own bill for each assignment. Nor was there any official director, examiner, or protractor, or any official code of instructions. Whether the new maps seemed to be consuming too much public money was left to the decision of another private surveyor, John Brownrigg, whose age and detached mode of life were thought (rightly, to judge from the entertainingly barbed reports he wrote) to qualify him for the task of referee.[114] By the 1820s it was too late for current modes of draughtsmanship to bear much resemblance to those of the plantation surveys. The Crown lands were depicted in a new manner brought into Ireland by the freelance cartographers of the eighteenth century, for in a stylistic sense as in other ways the private surveyors had now got possession of the public sector. It was a short-lived victory: they were soon to be beaten back by the advancing forces of the Ordnance Survey.

Notes

1. Moody, *Londonderry Plantation*, pp 112, 169, 194–5.
2. Raven's Hamilton maps of 1625 are in the North Down Heritage Centre, Bangor; some of them are reproduced in G. Camblin, *The Town in Ulster* (Belfast, 1951,plates 6–9). His Essex maps belong to the Marquess of Bath at Longleat and are mentioned in Shirley, *Monaghan*, p. 264; one of them is reproduced in Andrews, *Irish Maps*, 13. His surveys of 1631 for Sir Philip Perceval do not appear to survive; they are mentioned in Royal Irish Academy, MS 23.L.49, pp 175, 178, 183.
3. West Sussex Record Office, Chichester, Petworth papers, C.27.D (Garstin); NLI, D.4207 (Hunter).
4. Larcom, *Down Survey*, p. 173.
5. Newcomen's map of Drogheda and its environs (1657) is in the Corporation offices, Drogheda; it is noticed in T. Gogarty (ed.), *Council Book of the Corporation of Drogheda*, 1 (Drogheda, 1915), pp 22, 50,129. William Hunter's surveying activities appear in Glenstal Abbey, Co. Limerick, Cappercullen papers, 24 (1677). For Humphreys see below, n.89; for Young, ch.7, n.77.
6. Apart from surveyors discussed below in chapter 9, the best known examples were Garret Hogan (e.g. NLI, MS 5255), Abraham Carter (e.g. NLI, MS 2790(34)), and Peter Duff (e.g. NLI, 21.F.71(2)).
7. Charles Vallancey, Military Survey of the South of Ireland, 1796, p. 55, PRO, W.O. 30/63.

8. Andrews, *Proc. R. Ir. Acad.*, 74C (1974), p. 168.
9. Larcom, *Down Survey*, pp 14, 16, 26, 60, 263–4.
10. Commissioners for executing Act of Settlement to Vice-Treasurer of Ireland, 26 Nov. 1662, NLI, MS 816, p. 11.
11. Trustees of forfeited estates, minutes, 6 Nov. 1702, Annesley MS (NLI, mic. P.259).
12. *A List of the Fees of the Several Officers of the Four Courts*, reprinted from an edition of 1718 in H.C. 1821 (731), xi. The list had been republished at Dublin in 1734 and 1788, the Surveyor-General's fees being the same in all three cases.
13. *Report on Survey and Valuation*, 1824, p. 65, evidence of William Bald.
14. Manuscript autobiographical note by Matthew Handcock in Bernard Scalé, *Hibernian Atlas* (London, 1776), BL, Maps C.24.d.10. Handcock was Deputy Surveyor-General of Ireland from 1773 to 1798.
15. An early example is NLI, 21.F.80 (36), signed by Thomas Taylor, who died in 1682. Other copies, of various dates from 1709 to 1863, are listed in R. J. Hayes, *Manuscript Sources for the History of Irish Civilisation* (Boston, 1965). For a printed example see *Report from Select Committee on Petitions Relating to the Local Taxation of the City of Limerick*, p. 139, H.C. 1822 (617), vii.
16. Report of the sub-commissioners on the Surveyor-General's office, in Irish Record Commission, *3rd Annual Report* (Dublin, 1813), p. 541; J. P. Prendergast, *The Cromwellian Settlement of Ireland* (3rd ed., Dublin, 1922), pp x–xi; G. E. Howard, *A Treatise of the Exchequer and Revenue of Ireland*, 2 (Dublin, 1776), p. 117. Small extracts from the Strafford Survey appear in some collections of estate maps, e.g. NLI, 21.F.138(51), of part of the O'Brien estate. There are also facsimiles of larger extracts in Simington, *Books of Survey and Distribution*, 1, Roscommon, end-pocket and pp xlvii–li.
17. Surviving copies were noted by Handcock in BL, Maps C.24.d.10. More detailed lists, compiled in 1811, appear in Irish Record Commission, *3rd Annual Report*, pp 502–36, 541–3.
18. Weale, Report on disputed land, pp 23–5, NLI, MS 864.
19. Petty's reply to Sir Hierome Sankey, 21 Apr. 1658, Larcom, *Down Survey*, p. 300.
20. Hardinge, *Trans. R. Ir. Acad.*, 24, Antiquities (1873), pp 111–12. This statement by Petty was common knowledge long before Hardinge's time: the will had been published in full in the *Annual Register for 1761* (London, 1762), pp 16–21, and in the *Dublin Chronicle* for 28 July 1787.
21. This suggestion was reported (but rejected) in an undated eighteenth-century letter apparently written by the Surveyor-General or his deputy, Irish Record Commission, *3rd Annual Report*, p. 541.
22. Earl of Kerry, ' The Lansdowne Maps of the Down Survey', *Proc. R. Ir. Acad.*, 35C (1920), pp 393, 396–401. In the 1770s these maps were kept at the Earl of Shelburne's house in St Stephen's Green, Dublin (Report on the Down Survey, Irish Record Commission, *3rd Annual*

Report, pp 498–9). Their relation to the other surviving Down Survey maps is noted in *Dep. Keeper Pub. Rec. Ire., 53rd Rept*, pp 4–5.

23. Thomas Taylor, 3 Aug. 1681, Hist. MSS Com., *Ormonde*, new ser., 6, p. 119; John Russell, 2 Dec. 1715, NLI, unclassified Lismore papers.

24. Goblet's account of this collection (*Transformation*, 2, pp 21–73) is the best available, having been researched on his home ground in Paris.

25. Handcock's manuscript 'Memoire' on Vallancey's copy of the Down Survey, BL, Maps C.24.d.10, printed in Irish Record Commission, *3rd Annual Report*, pp 498–9.

26. Like so much of Vallancey's career, his work on the Down Survey is surprisingly well documented. His proposal to make the copy was reported by the Earl of Sydney on 22 Feb. 1786 (PRO, H.O. 100/18/97–8) and its progress was recorded in H.O. 100/19/302, 100/20/79, and 100/20/305. Other contemporary correspondence is in NLI, MS 1614, including Vallancey's account of his method of tracing. His own role seems to have been mainly supervisory. His subordinate, Alexander Taylor, told the committee on the Down Survey in 1813 that he (Taylor) had copied one volume and a French copyist the other (Irish Record Commission, *3rd Annual Report*, p. 497).

27. George Stone to Vallancey, 6 June 1787, NLI, MS 1614.

28. The Irish House of Lords accepted noncommittally that the Paris maps were authentic and Vallancey's copies accurate (*Journals of the House of Lords*, 6 (Dublin, 1792), pp 370, 375–6, 386–7, reported in more detail in *Dublin Chronicle*, 11 Mar., 6 Apr. 1790). The committee of 1813 on the Down Survey agreed that the copies should not be allowed to count as 'original records' (Irish Record Commission, *3rd Annual Report*, p. 496) but they were sometimes cited officially as a supplement to other sources of evidence, for example in *General Report of the Commissioners ... [on] ... the Title, Tenure, Extent and Value of all Lands, Houses, etc. Held under the Crown in Ireland on Determinable Leases*, appendix, p. 25, H.C. 1824 (458), xxi.

29. Report on the Down Survey, evidence of Mr [John] Brownrigg, Irish Record Commission, *3rd Annual Report*, p. 498.

30. The use of a 'book of Sir William Petty's maps', presumably the *Hiberniae Delineatio*, was mentioned in the Quit-Rent Office correspondence of 16 Nov. 1772 (NAI, 2B.42.119, p. 218). See also Howard, *Exchequer and Revenue*, 2, pp 123–4. Part of one of Petty's county maps was reproduced by lithography in connection with the survey of Crown lands made in 1821.

31. Lodge, *Peerage*, 3, p. 173; see above, n.15.

32. Robert Gibson, *A Treatise of Practical Surveying* (2nd ed., Dublin, 1763), p. 284. The Headfort maps are listed in Irish Record Commission, *8th Report*, appendix (1818), pp 15–19, 25–6, and noticed in *Dep. Keeper Pub. Rec. Ire.*, *56th Rept*, p. 306. The surviving maps are in NAI, V.20.59–60.

33. *Dep. Keeper Pub. Rec. Ire., 1st Rept*, p. 37, *2nd Rept*, p. 11; Hardinge, *Trans. R. Ir. Acad.*, 24, Antiquities (1873), pp 285–6.

34. Correspondence on the copying of the Down Survey and other early maps, OSO, files 2885 (1862), 3047 (1864).
35. Search fees for Down and Trustees' Survey maps (1s per map) and for making traces (2s. 6d for each surround, not exceeding 10s per parish) are quoted in *Dep. Keeper Pub. Rec. Ire., 1st Rept*, app 6, p. 40.
36. NLI, 16.K.11.
37. King's Inns Library, Dublin: 'Parishes in Wexford from Down Survey'.
38. These copies were noticed in Handcock's evidence to the committee on the Down Survey in 1813 (Irish Record Commission, *3rd Annual Report*, p. 499). Their later history is described by C. McNeill, 'Copies of Down Survey Maps in Private Keeping' and R. C. Simington, ' Origin of Copies of Down Survey Maps', *Analecta Hibernica*, 8 (1938), pp 419–30. The maps of Carlow, Cork, Dublin, Kilkenny, Leitrim, Leix, Limerick, Longford, Meath, Offaly, Tipperary, Waterford, Westmeath, Wexford and Wicklow are now NLI, MSS 712–26. Those of Antrim, Armagh, Donegal, Down, Londonderry and Tyrone are PRONI, D.597 (copies in NLI, 16.K. 11–15). See also S. O Domhnaill, 'The Maps of the Down Survey', *Ir. Hist. St.*, 3 (1943), pp 381–92.
39. *Dep. Keeper Pub. Rec. Ire., 56th Rept*, p. 305. The records are now arranged by counties and baronies in NAI, 2A.12.52–72. They appear never to have been described in print.
40. *Irish Record Commission, 2nd Report*, supplement, 1812, p. 414; *6th Annual Report*, 1816, p. 5; *8th Annual Report*, supplement, 1819, p. 51. It is not clear whether any of these copies were ever made. A later suggestion for reproducing the Down Survey came from the Incorporated Society of Solicitors and Attorneys (*Dep. Keeper Pub. Rec. Ire., 6th Rept*, p. 17).
41. The Quit-Rent Office's Ordnance Survey working sheets, annotated with Down Survey detail, are in NAI, V.20. Copies of the Co. Antrim Down Survey, drawn on a six-inch Ordnance Survey base by John O'Donovan, are in the Ordnance Survey Office, Dublin (J. H. Andrews, *History in the Ordnance Map* (Dublin, 1974), p. 60). Minute 3974 of the Irish Manuscripts Commission records that draughtsmen trained by the Ordnance Survey had made tracings of the Down Survey before 1922 for purposes connected with the 1903 land act. In 1947 the commission arranged for the Down Survey to be superimposed in colour on the six-inch Ordnance maps, and an ex-Ordnance Survey draughtsman was employed on this task from 1954 to 1966, by which time about one-fifth of the Down Survey had been completed. These superimpositions are now NLI, 20.D. See Irish Manuscripts Commission, *Catalogue of Publications, Issued and in Preparation* (Dublin, 1966), pp 43–4, and R. C. Simington, 'The Work of Robert Johnston', *Analecta Hibernica*, 25 (1967), pp ix–xi.
42. Copies of the Co. Sligo parish maps were made in the late nineteenth century at the instance of the Clerk of the Crown and Peace for the county and are now in the County Library (*Irish Library News*, 33 (1980), [p. 2]).
43. Adams rental, 1697, NLI, MS 391.

44. For the Down Survey see *Dublin Gazette*, 10 May 1709; for the Strafford Survey see RD, 28/442/18268 (1721). Because of the loss of the originals, citations of the Strafford Survey attracted attention from nineteenth-century writers such as W. S. Mason (*A Statistical Account, or Parochial Survey of Ireland*, 2 (Dublin, 1816), p. xvii) and T. A. Larcom (*Down Survey*, p. 325).
45. Advertisement for lands in Kerry, *Dickson's News Letter*, 23 Sep. 1727.
46. Perceval letters, 26 Sep. 1704, Add. MS 46964A, f. 56.
47. Thomas Pearce, 2 Apr. 1716, Brown of Clonboy papers, *Analecta Hibernica*, 15 (1944), p. 88.
48. For an eighteenth-century Irish use of this term see E. MacLysaght (ed.), *The Kenmare Manuscripts* (Ir. MSS Com., Dublin, 1942), p. 443. See also the Lord Chancellor's opinion in Archbishop of Dublin vs Coote and Lord Trimlestown, *Irish Equity Reports*, 12 (1850), p. 266, apparently citing S. M. Phillipps, *A Treatise on the Law of Evidence* (London, 1815), p. 303 ; and M. O'Donnell and F. Brady, *A Treatise on the Law of all Actions and Suits within the Jurisdiction of the Civil Bill Court* (Dublin, 1844), p. 282.
49. W. Molyneux, 'A Demonstration of an Error Committed by Common Surveyors in Comparing of Surveys Taken at Long Intervals of Time Arising from the Variation of the Magnetick Needle', *Phil. Trans. R. Soc.*, 19 (1697), p. 631. For the same opinion, see *Chancery of Ireland. Sir William Barker, Appellant. Viscount Ikerrin and Phanniel Cook, Respondents. The Appellant's Case* ([Dublin,] 1732).
50. Argument for plaintiff in Archbishop of Dublin vs Coote and Lord Trimlestown, *Irish Equity Reports*, 12 (1850), p. 257.
51. 14 & 15 Charles II, c.2, Instructions to Lord High Treasurer, sec. 2.
52. 17 & 18 Charles II, c.2, sec.5. Rules based on the act were separately printed and are reprinted in *Cal. S.P. Ire.*, 1666–9, pp 35–9.
53. Lord Deputy and Council, 1 Aug. 1655, Dunlop, *Commonwealth*, 2, p. 535.
54. Petty-Symner report, 13 Mar. 1657, Oireachtas Library, MS 3. G. 12.
55. Howard, *Exchequer and Revenue*, 2, pp 114–15.
56. For example an early eighteenth-century map of Mealiff, Co. Tipperary, NAI, M.2033. Among the most sophisticated of these superimpositions are the detailed topographical maps of certain townlands in Co. Donegal made by George Knox in 1816 (TCD, MUN/ME/15).
57. Gibson, *Practical Surveying*, p. 284. Gibson's treatment of the Down Survey was singled out for special mention in advertisements for the first edition of his book (*Faulkner's Dublin Journal*, 9 May 1752).
58. *Dublin Evening Post*, 3 Apr. 1781.
59. A case where a look at the map was enough to show the boundaries agreeing in 'the most minute particulars' is mentioned in a report of *c*. 1821 on quit-rent arrears in the Trim district, NAI, 2A.11.59.
60. Molyneux, *Phil. Trans. R. Soc.*, 19 (1697), pp 625–31.

61. Report on lands of Courelicky and Cappagh, Co. Cork, 1768, Cork Archives Institute, U.137/-/51.
62. Superimposed modern and Down Survey boundaries on a mid-eighteenth-century map of Kilbarron, Co. Tipperary, Minchin estate maps, NLI, mic. P.5701. A contemporary note states that the Down Survey 'being laid down on the private map from any two points shows the land in dispute to be part of Kilbarron'.
63. Gibson, *Practical Surveying*, p. 287.
64. Advertisement by John Donovan of Cork, *New Cork Evening Post*, 10 Nov. 1794.
65. Gabriel Stokes, 6 Aug. 1737, TCD, MUN/P/23/1440.
66. Kearney estate maps, NLI, mic. P.5306.
67. 17 & 18 Charles II, c.2, sec.23. The 'Books of Distribution' were the Books of Survey and Distribution in which the grantees and acreages of estates involved in the Restoration land settlement were recorded. They include no maps, and their acreage figures are derived from the Strafford and Down Surveys. Some of them have been reprinted by the Irish Manuscripts Commission with a commentary by R. C. Simington: see above, n.16.
68. As early as *c.* 1662 an honest grantee in Co. Louth was reporting that one of his townlands was 21 per cent larger than the Down Survey had stated and asking what he ought to do about it (Dowdall and Peppard deeds, NLI, D.16196). There is no evidence that anybody told him.
69. 'A Character of the Dividing of the Barony of Connello', May 1658, in Prendergast, *Cromwellian Settlement* (2nd ed., London, 1870), p. 240. Retrenchment had analogous implications to the order of 1628 allowing Ulster planters to let one-third of their land to Irish tenants: there are no relevant records from that period either.
70. Petty-Symner report, 29 Apr. 1657, Oireachtas library, MS 3.G.12.
71. W. M. Brady, *The McGillycuddy Papers* (London, 1867), p. 135.
72. Quit-Rent Office letters, NAI, 2B.39.89, f.96.
73. Irish Record Commission, *15th Annual Report* (1825), p. 223 (1670) and *passim*.
74. Report by William Hunter, 29 Sep. 1677, Cappercullen papers, 24. In the original plans for the subdivision of the soldiers' lands, according to Petty, the 'subdivisional lines' were to be 'all streight' (Larcom, *Down Survey*, p. 42).
75. Undated account of the public revenue of Ireland, Add. MS 18022.
76. *Report on Lands Held Under the Crown*, 1824, p. 57.
77. Clerk of quit rents to local collector (Westmeath), 28 Aug. 1693, NAI, 1A.41.88, p. 49; commissioners of quit rent to local collector (Athlone), 24 July 1705, NAI, 2B.39.89, f.126.
78. J. H. Andrews, 'Henry Pratt, Surveyor of Kerry Estates', *Jour. Kerry Arch. & Hist. Soc.*, 13 (1980), pp 6–7.

79. Commissioners of quit rent to local collector, 7 Sep. 1710, NAI, 2B.39.89, f.148.
80. Petition by Timothy O' Driscoll, surveyor, on his 'discovery' of lands in Co. Cork, 1793, NAI, 2A.11.2. Memorial of Denis Ahern, Cork, 7 Nov. 1833, NLI, MS 982.
81. Notes by Samuel Bradshaw and William Bower, Apr.–May 1806, NAI, 2A.12.42.
82. G. E. Howard, *A Treatise on the Rule and Practice of the Equity Side of the Exchequer in Ireland* (Dublin, 1760), pp 693–701. Also, 'Rules of the Chancery Side of the Court of Exchequer in Ireland', NLI, MS 5784, pp 45–6; *Dep. Keeper Pub. Rec. Ire., 1st Rept*, p. 58. For a map of 1782 accompanying a writ of perambulation of Banemore alias Rathanane, Co. Cork, see Land Commission Office, Dublin, Box 634, sch. C.l, no.1147 (a copy of 1891).
83. Examples are maps by Garret Hogan of property in Co. Meath allocating a one-third share to the Countess of Fingall (NLI, MS 8030) and by Owen Flanagan of land in Co. Roscommon, 1797 (NAI, M.3010). In a map of 1765 by John O'Brien, among the Gormanston estate papers, third-shares are delimited in each of five townlands by straight lines (NLI, 21.F.145(4)).
84. T. J. Beasley, *A Synopsis of Proceedings in the Master's Office, under the New Rules; With an Historical Account and List of the Masters in Chancery* (Dublin, 1837), pp 114, 125, and *General Precedents in the Master's Office, Approved of by Her Majesty's High Court of Chancery in Ireland* (Dublin, 1838), pp 152–3.
85. *John Buckworth, Esq; Appellant. Barnaby Phelan, Respondent. The Respondent's Case* [Dublin, 1758], p. 2 (parish of Gale, Co. Tipperary).
86. Depositions by a chainman on a survey of the Dunleer estate, Co. Louth, 1739 (Add. MS 19858, ff.16–21) and by Maurice Kinsella of Stradbally, Co. Leix, Oct. 1764, TCD, Hartpole papers, MS 1499(347).
87. In legal proceedings of 1837 relating to lands near Garristown, Co. Dublin, a survey had to be repeated as a result of the surveyor's death (NAI, 2A.11.43).
88. 'The Constitution of the Exchequer in Ireland', 1693, NLI, MS 11969, p. 12. The same passage occurs in a similar essay in NLI, MS 46, ff.6–7.
89. Commission from Deputy Surveyor-General to John Humfrey and John Jackson, 23 Sep. 1680, Ainsworth reports, 12, p. 2532 (no. 319, Meath papers).
90. Survey of Ballahanaskadan, Co. Limerick, TCD, MUN/P/23/95.
91. Harleian MS 4297, f. 118 *et seq.*
92. Hardinge, *Trans. R. Ir. Acad.*, 24, Antiquities (1873), p. 285.
93. *A List of the Fees of the Several Officers of the Four Courts* (1734), p. 134.
94. Hardinge, *Trans. R. Ir. Acad.*, 24, Antiquities (1873), p. 285.
95. Michael Hickie, bookseller, 26 Apr. 1890, OSO, file 8277. What seems to be the volume referred to by Hickie is now in the Dublin City

Library (Gilbert MS 226); it includes copies of originals in the Surveyor-General's office, the Headfort collection, and the Quit-Rent Office.

96. *A Dissertation on the Practice of Land Surveying in Ireland, and an Essay Towards a General Regulation Therein* (Drogheda, 1758). This book had been first published as a whole in 1752 and part of it had appeared in 1750. It seems likely to have been the first book ever printed in Drogheda (E. R. McC. Dix, *List of Books, Pamphlets and Newspapers Printed in Drogheda from the Earliest Period to the End of the Eighteenth Century* (Dundalk, 1911), pp 15–16).
97. *Dublin Journal*, 16 Dec. 1749.
98. *Dublin Journal*, 27 Jan. 1750. 'Down' is printed with a small 'd', but the meaning is obvious. On 1 May 1750 the same newspaper published one of Stokes's certificates.
99. *Leinster Journal*, 14 Aug. 1773.
100. D. A. Beaufort, *Memoir of a Map of Ireland* (Dublin, 1792), p. vi. Handcock's notes in BL, Maps C.24.d.10, include information about units of measurement and magnetic variation as well as some arithmetical exercises germane to surveying.
101. *Dublin Journal*, 25 July 1752, 19 Mar. 1765.
102. Quoted by A. K. Longfield in 'A County Sligo Estate Map of 1768', *Bull. Ir. Georgian Soc.*, 20 (1977), p. 67. Conceivably this was a reference to the act of 1665 (see above, n.67), though, as already suggested, differences of ten per cent are hardly likely to have been accepted in the 1760s.
103. Hardinge, *Trans. R. Ir. Acad.*, 24, Antiquities (1873), p. 285.
104. 23 & 24 George III, c.22. The supplement to the *Second Report* of the Irish Record Commission includes a long list compiled by the acting deputy usher of the court of Chancery enumerating the deeds, papers, securities and other effects of suitors in the court delivered to the bank in June 1784. Only one map, dated 1771, appears in this list (p. 99).
105. Handcock's notes in BL, Maps C.24.d.10, list surveys in his office of various dates up to 1792.
106. Map of the Earl of Clonmell's property in Harcourt Street, Dublin, by A. R. Neville, 1807, Representative Church Body Library, Dublin, Archbishop of Dublin's maps, no. 58; map of Haroldstown parish, Co. Louth, n.d., NAI, TAB 3/18.
107. The term 'registered surveyor' appears as early as 1770 (James Miller of Mountrath, Co. Leix: *Leinster Journal*, 20 June) and, in the form 'R.L.S.', as late as 1842 (Michael and Peter O'Loghlin, Co. Clare, NLI, 21.F.75(1)). A total of about ten occurrences of it has been noticed, most of them from the period 1805–27. Pat McLoughlin called himself a certified surveyor on various occasions between 1826 and 1842 (NLI, 16.M.14(4, 6, 8, 38, 41)). An overlap between certification and registration is suggested by Joseph Lanigan's assumption of the title registered land surveyor not more than two years after receiving a certificate (*Leinster Journal*, 22 May 1784, 19 Apr. 1786).

108. *Report from the Select Committee on Court of Chancery (Ireland) Bills*, q.2897 (evidence of S. F. Adair, solicitor), H.C. 1856 (311), x.
109. Evidence of Daniel Moore, land surveyor, Oct. 1771, TCD, MS 1933 (415).
110. Advertisements by Matthew Healy, *Volunteer Journal*, 10 Nov. 1783, *Cork Evening Post*, 4 June 1787.
111. 57 George III, c.62 (7 July 1817); *Watson's or the Gentleman's and Citizen's Almanack* (Dublin, annual).
112. Hardinge, *Trans. R. Ir. Acad.*, 24, Antiquities (1873), pp 287–8.
113. 3 George IV, c.63 (15 July 1822); *Report on Lands Held under the Crown, 1824*.
114. Brownrigg's reports are in *NAI, 2B.44.61*.

5
Owners and tenants

MOST OF THE LAND that the Irish surveyor got his livelihood from measuring belonged to a small class of powerful proprietors.[1] Some of them were the descendants of seventeenth-century planters, Protestant in religion, loyalist in politics and English in culture, perhaps to the extent of spending all or most of their time in England. Other landlords came from Gaelic or medieval English families who had managed to retain their estates by embracing the new religion and much of the outlook that went with it. Meanwhile the number of Catholic landlords had dropped to a small minority, a few of them in the English Pale round Dublin, others west of the Shannon where Cromwell had sought to create a Catholic reservation. Estates of around 50,000 statute acres were by no means uncommon in all these categories, many of them comprising a few blocks of land in fairly close proximity, sometimes only a single block. With the 'Ascendancy' class of landowners should be grouped the great institutional proprietors, such as Trinity College in large areas of Ulster and Munster, and the city of London in Co. Londonderry. Smaller estates included those of the lesser gentry and also of the Church (enormous in total but much divided in geographical distribution and mode of administration), of certain schools, and of the municipalities (Fig. 4).

Provided that he paid his taxes and quit or Crown rents and obeyed the criminal law, the typical Protestant Irish landlord of the eighteenth century was free from all but family-imposed restraints on what he did with his estate. The results naturally varied a good deal, but the one thing that the resident owner seldom attempted was to stock and cultivate all his land himself. He might maintain a small home-farm of one or two hundred acres and he would almost certainly create an ornamental park or garden as a setting for his mansion house. But most of the typical estate was let to tenants, usually in units of one or more townlands, on leases

Figure 4: The pattern of estates in part of Co. Roscommon, 1852–3. Source: NLI, 21.F.103(8). Proprietors' names are spelt as in the original map.

that ran for twenty years or longer. Some tenants worked their holdings as single enterprises as large as a landlord's home-farm or larger, the most extensive being on land that was especially good for beef cattle or sheep. Others, the much maligned class of middlemen, subdivided and sublet to undertenants, many of them family farmers with little capital of their own who held from year to year rather than by lease. Since the size of tenements within the landlord's or middleman's estate depended partly on the presence of non-agricultural wealth, it is no surprise that many of the smallest farms were either in the north, where the linen industry was well established from the late seventeenth century onwards, or in the neighbourhood of fishing settlements along the coast. Elsewhere the worst effects of individual poverty might be mitigated by co-operation, with farmers holding land in partnership and making communal arrangements for the exploitation of pasture and turf bogs. Many of these uncultivated tracts had never been partitioned among individual tenants, perhaps not even among individual head landlords.

Finally there were those Irishmen who held no more than a cabin and a small garden with a patch of potato ground rented from one season to the next. The more affluent members of this lowest class laboured on the landlord's demesne and lived in a village outside his gates; the less fortunate found work with the larger tenant farmers. What made the whole system unstable, and in the end intolerable, was the speed at which Ireland's rural population began to increase at some time between the Restoration and the Famine, especially as it was the lower social classes that experienced the steepest rate of growth. The additional numbers were accommodated partly by the subdivision of existing farms and partly by the reclamation of new land from the waste either with the support and encouragement of their landlord or else, on the less closely supervised estates, by squatting.

There was an active land market in pre-Famine Ireland, but large estates were more likely to be broken up than sold intact. Units of selling and letting were often of comparable extent, and the surveys made for these two kinds of transaction may appropriately be treated together. The size in question could range from 20,000 acres of mountain land down to a single house and yard, but it was generally between 100 and 500 statute acres. What might be called the advertisement or sales-particulars map is at least as old as 1634, when the Earl of Arundel is known to have been given the plan of a site in Wexford that he contemplated buying.[2] This map was probably no different in appearance from several other kinds of farm or estate survey, and apart from such stray documentary references the only trace left by the sale-map as such is the kind of printed property advertisement that did not become common until the eighteenth century.[3] Even then it is only a minority of such advertisements that call on cartographic support. Others, with typically Irish dependence on word-of-mouth communication, simply state that the premises are too well known to need describing, or else refer the inquirer to some local resident who will 'show the lands'. But as newspapers grew larger and more numerous, maps were increasingly announced as available for consultation in the offices of lawyers and agents (sometimes in London as well as at an Irish address), at local inns, in the house of a nearby tenant farmer, or in the possession of the surveyor who had drawn them and who was perhaps taking the first steps in the agency business. If a map's custodian lived on the spot, the visiting client might be given the opportunity to compare it with the ground. Maps of urban property were often displayed in a mayor's or town clerk's office or some other place of public resort: in Dublin the coffee room of the Royal Exchange was a favourite cartographic exhibition gallery for the wide streets commission and various other official bodies as well as for the corporation, and there were similar coffee rooms in eighteenth-century Cork and Belfast.

Several copies might be made of a single advertisement map – one vendor offered half a dozen – and with town sites it was not unknown for them to be engraved. An example is the map of the North Lots in Dublin as first set out in 1717;[4] another, no doubt, was the map of Aston's Quay of which all inquirers were promised a free copy in 1762,[5] a pleasant change from being expected to pay for the map as well as the property. But whether printed or manuscript, early advertisement maps were seldom carefully preserved, and it is only when they began to be reproduced by lithography, from the 1820s onwards,[6] that it becomes possible to generalise with confidence about what they looked like. Cheap printing also created a new cartographic form in the small-scale 'geographical' advertisement map showing the relation of an estate to the towns, roads and railways of the surrounding area.[7]

One advertisement of 1776 solicitously gave notice of 'a survey now taking for the inspection of proposers'[8] but most advertisement maps were probably by-products of surveys made to form part of the bargain between owner and client. Such surveys did not necessarily achieve cartographic expression: most large collections of estate records include a number of scraps of paper in the form of surveyors' 'returns' comprising a single denomination-name and a single acreage figure. But the sale or lease map was sufficiently common for lawyers to popularise (if only among themselves) the term 'terre chart' or 'ter chart' as a description of it.[9] Whether such maps counted as part of a lease or conveyance for purposes of stamp duty was a moot point;[10] so was the question of what happened when the map appeared to contradict the wording of the deed that went with it. But whatever their exact legal status, many maps were deliberately given the character of a legal document. They were drawn on parchment or good-quality paper (one landlord was kept waiting for his lease maps in 1750 because of a local shortage of 'strong or royal paper')[11] and they sometimes appeared on the back of a lease or as an inset, or carried a slit through which they could be attached to other documents. The location of the premises by townland, parish, barony and county was commonly spelt out in the title, while many maps were signed on oath by their makers and precisely dated (often in words rather than figures) as well as being witnessed by observers present at the survey, endorsed by the parties to the agreement, and occasionally even annotated with the names of the men who held the chain.[12]

Leases based on *ad hoc* mapping probably came in with the English settlements of the late sixteenth and early seventeenth centuries, and owed much of their popularity to the example of the official surveys through which the planters had acquired their estates. In fact there may well be a general coincidence between regions of Tudor and Stuart plantation and regions of early estate cartography. Already in 1588 Sir Walter Raleigh was ready to increase a farm by adding a measured acreage taken from the next ploughland;[13] and in the same county Raleigh's successor, the Earl of Cork, wrote of land in lease to Sir John Leake that was 'measured to be 2,242 acres' – too many to be seen in the same light as the dubious 'measurements' recorded in the Middle Ages.[14] Not far to the north, on the Ormond and Perceval estates, tenants took land according to surveys made in or about 1640; in both cases there was a link with plantation cartography.[15] Later it may have been the Cromwellian admeasurements, with their officially-sanctioned distribution of survey data to the new owners, that inspired the notion of physically attaching maps to leases. The lack of early seventeenth-century evidence makes this a difficult hypothesis to test (some of the evidence was destroyed in the rebellion of 1641) but the records of certain well-documented public bodies are suggestive. No map appears among Dublin's pre-Cromwellian muniments, for example, but a spirit of change is seen in several disputes over the dimensions and boundaries of city property that came to a head in the 1650s. Cartography played an important part in the letting of large blocks of land in Oxmantown Green and St Stephen's Green in the following decade, and the use of maps was thenceforth taken for granted in most of the leases and property-petitions preserved in the city archives.[16] Another east-coast town with good records is Drogheda, where the use of maps begins in 1657 with a detailed survey of the corporation estate by Robert Newcomen and Thomas Cockayne.[17]

By the Cromwellian period, perhaps for the first time in history, the English Pale could be expected to act as a focus of cartographic innovation. Elsewhere progress was probably slower. And nowhere did the stimulus to cartography come from Ireland's greatly increased population of lawyers, whose indifference to maps, later notorious, became apparent when the Irish Registry of Deeds was opened in 1708. Although the act establishing this repository gave detailed rules to Ireland's legal draughtsmen about the kinds of territorial division that should be specified in a lease ('counties, baronies, cities, towns corporate, parishes, townships, hamlets, villages, precincts') it did nothing to provide for the use or preservation of lease maps.[18] As it happened, one of the earliest deeds entered in the registry (the twenty-sixth) made reference to a property map, again in Dublin,[19] but outside the city cartographic diffusion after 1700 was not much faster than before. The eighteenth century was more than half over when maps were urged on landlords in a surveying textbook as an aid that could evidently not yet be taken for granted,[20] and the landlords themselves gave many signs of treating them as a novelty even when they had good reasons for knowing better. Thus when in 1711 the Earl of Thomond decided to insert acreages in his leases instead of ploughlands and quarters, he did not mention the fact that proper admeasurements had been carried out on his estate nearly eighty years earlier.[21] And although at about the same time Sir John Perceval expressed a desire to accompany each lease with its own survey, he later claimed to have found a way of doing without such expensive appendages (an achievement nowhere explained in his voluminous correspondence), returning with some reluctance in 1738 to an advocacy of maps, this time in triplicate.[22] Municipalities made equally good resolutions on the same subject and were equally bad at keeping them. In 1724 a by-law at Kilkenny required surveys to be made of all the town's lands before they were let or sold, with a map or terrier to be affixed to leases and conveyances, but the corporation later had to admit that its by-laws were not always observed.[23] In 1735 the Earl of Orrery, annoyed at having to settle his tenants' boundaries in Kerry by the drastic expedient of a personal visit, resolved in future to annex maps to all new leases.[24] Lord Castlecomer made the same decision in 1746[25] and Lord Shelburne in 1775, though the latter felt obliged to repeat his order after his agents had been given twenty years in which to obey it.[26] By that time even the lawyers showed signs of capitulation: in 1795 the Society of King's Inns persuaded itself to commission a map when conveying some of its own property.[27]

The surveys associated with Irish land transactions served one or both of two basic purposes, the delimitation of boundaries and the calculation of areas. The boundaries are usually those of townlands or other recognised denominations. They are shown by continuous lines, often tinted with a band of colour; some deeds made specific reference to these coloured edgings,[28] despite the lawyers' objection to colour as more likely to fade than black ink.[29] The names of adjoining townlands, and sometimes of their owners or occupiers, are written in position outside the boundary, and the junction of three properties is shown by a characteristic symbol, usually some variant of the cross (Plate 4). It seems significant that these junction-symbols, placed where the consequences of a territorial dispute would be most serious, were much the commonest map convention employed by Irish estate cartographers. The belief that they perpetuate the ancient tradition of the boundary cross does not appear particularly probable; but neither is there any proof that they represent the pole, surmounted by some kind of marker, towards which a surveyor would direct his instrumental observations. Rivers and roads that followed the leasehold boundary were shown with considerable care, but non-linear boundary marks such as trees and raths are almost as uncommon on early lease maps as they are on the Down Survey, though (as with the Down Survey) their significance was well enough understood by the more enlightened contemporary experts.[30] Where no boundary was visible on the ground, as in certain tracts of bog and mountain, the map might state the bearing and length of the line in words and numbers as well as drawing it,[31] but this practice too is not as common as perhaps it should have been. Most of Ireland's estate surveyors were put to shame by the detailed official boundary sketch-maps produced at the time of the Ordnance Survey.[32]

But like the men of the Ordnance the private surveyor obtained most of his boundary information from local residents chosen for their age and reliability and usually paid a small gratuity for their services.[33] A punctilious cartographer would put the names of these 'mearsmen' on his map – a logical practice, as their existence was his only justification

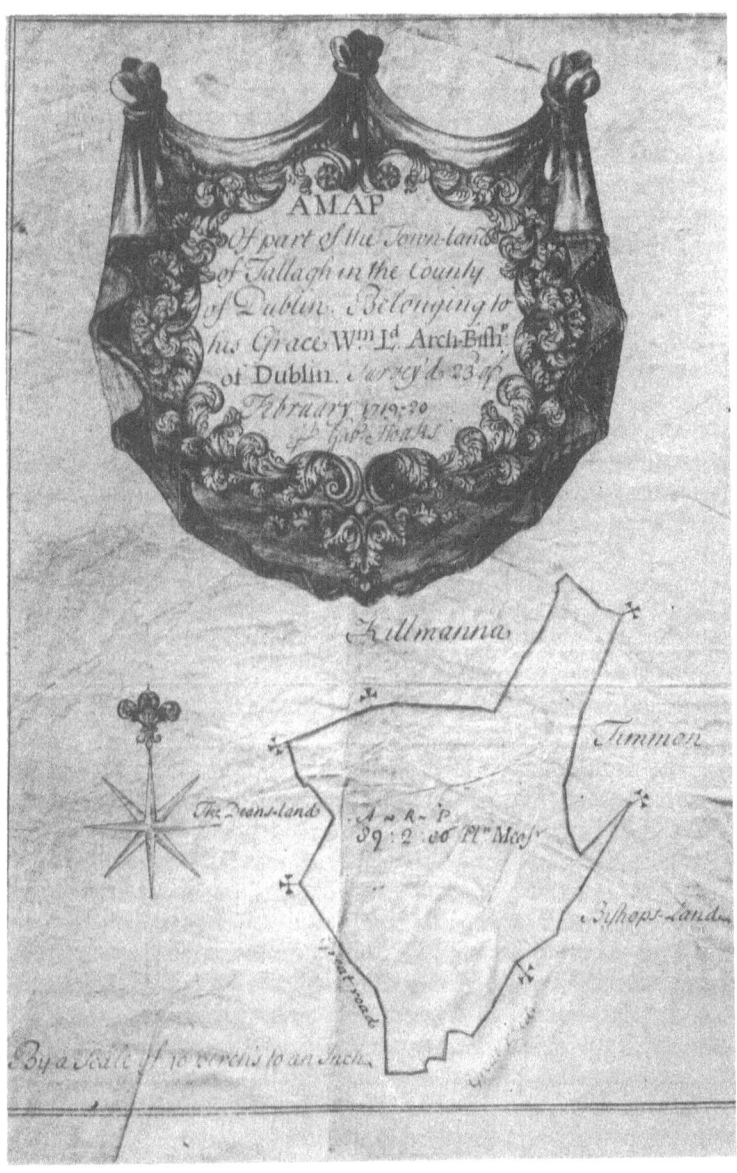

Plate 4. Lands near Tallaght, Co. Dublin, by Gabriel Stokes, 1720 (TCD, Archbishop of Dublin's maps, 132(27)). Scale of original 40 perches to one inch. The use of printed 'compartments' in an otherwise hand-drawn farm map is common in early eighteenth-century Ireland. So are the prominent boundary crosses and the lack of interior topographical detail.

for omitting so many landmarks. Where mearsmen disagreed, a special investigation might be called for, eventuating first in an *ad hoc* map showing the rival lines (and probably little else) and later, it was to be hoped, in an agreement between the adjoining proprietors. Where no knowledgeable mearsmen were forthcoming, it might be necessary to reconstruct the boundary shown on the Down Survey or another old map;[34] or even to extract a more or less credible boundary from some wholly non-cartographic document. Here was ample scope for dispute, because the features mentioned in earlier records, even if correctly described there, might well have been subsequently obliterated or (worse still) moved. Surveyors sometimes heard of boundary stones being secretly buried, or trees cut down at night, to cover up an encroachment.[35] Not even Dublin's famous Long Stone was above suspicion; though, as one archaeologically-minded surveyor pointed out, after standing immovable since pre-Christian times it was not likely to have gone astray during the term of the Restoration lease that cited it as a landmark.[36] At the other extreme from Dublin, on rough land where boundaries were both undefined and unrecognised, the surveyor might find himself cast in a more creative role, as when William Starrat mapped the line where 'the water would most naturally run, which in cases of this kind is commonly taken for the mearing'.[37] Another ancient maxim for use on such occasions was that to him that hath shall be given: this enabled a boundary bog to be divided in proportion to the length of each proprietor's frontage on its margin.[38]

Surveyors were also aware that even an apparently unambiguous boundary like a hedge or ditch will appear on the ground as a strip of measurable width, so that they had to decide which line within this strip to treat as the strict mathematical limit of the property – a decision that could make a difference of several units per cent to the size of a small enclosure. Few maps record their authors' policy on this point (as in their omission of boundary landmarks, cartographers were easily seduced by the simplicity of the single line) and modern historians of the enclosure movement are equally uncommunicative. Yet there was a definite conflict between those who favoured putting the whole bank and ditch in one property on the principle that this would make the fence easier to keep in repair, and those who wanted the boundary to follow the centre of the barrier or the roots of the trees and bushes in a quick-set hedge. The former practice was recommended in Peter Callan's book of 1750 on Irish land surveying, which claimed it to be common in most parts of

Ireland except the north.[39] It can certainly be authenticated from estate maps in the east midlands.[40] Meanwhile, in Cork, Perceval had committed himself to the centre line as what surveyors 'always do' (admitting in the next breath that it may not have been done by the particular surveyor he was finding fault with),[41] and was later supported in this preference by his fellow Corkman Joshua Wight.[42]

By the end of the eighteenth century it was not uncommon for surveyors to distinguish the gross or outside area (with ditches) from the net or inside area (without ditches) of each field. The practice of giving separate areas for roads had become widespread a good deal earlier. It did not imply any general intention to exempt the roads from rent. On the contrary, except in conacre lettings[43] the usual custom was for the acreage of a farm to include the whole width of any road inside it and half the width of any road along its edge, the process of bisection being shown in map form, logically enough, by sandwiching the denomination boundary between the two edges of the road. The subordination of topography to proprietorship in such cases was betrayed by the use of 'pops' or broken lines for the verges visible on the ground. 'Popping the lines of a map ... is generally done to represent where there are roads. Nowhere else', as one surveyor put it rather too sweepingly in 1764.[44] As Irish farms got smaller through repeated subdivision, the counting-in of roads came to seem oppressive, especially to very poor farmers who might have as much as one-eighth of their acreage in this unproductive category and who, to add insult to injury, could be fined if their cattle were found on the highway that they were paying rent for. (They might nevertheless have a right to the dirt swept off the road.) From about 1820 landlords began to relent, and exemption was increasingly given for roads recently built, for roads near towns, and for mailcoach-roads, while on progressive estates the roads were omitted from the calculation altogether. A new road thus meant a new survey, not just for engineering reasons but to ascertain the area it covered. The same principles applied to the practice of charging rent for half the width of boundary streams, and for lakes in the middle of farms.[45] On the coast the usual farm boundary was high water mark, and Irish surveyors are not known to have got involved in rival claims to beds of seaweed or other offshore resources.

However carefully drawn, a boundary line was incomplete without the name of the area enclosed by it; the ideal course of action for the surveyor, as was crisply remarked in 1661, being to name each parcel that was nameable.[46] Irish land surveyors would have agreed with the famous

Anglo-French cartographer John Rocque that custom is the best guide to the spelling of names,[47] and they gave no sign of anticipating the laborious methods adopted by the Ordnance Survey to make the townland names of Ireland in some objective sense 'correct'. Only one case has been noted, at Banefune, Co. Cork, in 1767, of any preference being felt for surveyors conversant with the Irish language,[48] though the most anglicised of mapmakers might profitably check the local pronunciation of placenames against the spelling in the Down Survey, or get a name of Gaelic derivation translated to throw light on the durability of a mearing.[49] Nor did surveyors generally follow certain contemporary lawyers in providing long lists of aliases and variant spellings to ensure the validity of an agreement: no doubt they were influenced by the cartographer's natural dislike of spoiling his visual effect with a large admixture of script. Special attention would be needed, however, where names were nonexistent or uncertain, or particularly liable to be forgotten – especially as the boundaries of many such areas were exceptionally vulnerable to defacement. Here location had to be expressed not just by boundary and name but by establishing a relationship with some external object or objects. One way to prevent a small parcel from getting lost, suggested in Petty's instructions for the Down Survey, was to measure and map a 'tie-line' of known length and direction, connecting named and unnamed parcels. Another was simply to write on the map the bearing and distance between some point on the boundary and a nearby landmark such as a church tower.[50]

A stranger to Ireland might be surprised to find that it was in the towns that the 'townland' system was least satisfactory as a guide to location, but the typical townland was too large to be of much use for this purpose in a closely built-up area. Where scattered urban properties were under survey, confusion could best be avoided by mapping the edges and names of the streets connecting them. If the whole town belonged to one owner, the solution was to make a complete map of it and then identify the individual sites by numbers or letters in default of names. At Londonderry and Coleraine the plot-numbers cited in leases and advertisements appear to denote locations on the surveys made of these towns and of their environs by Archibald Stewart in the early eighteenth century.[51] A similar problem arose for the purchaser of scattered strips in one of the former Anglo-Norman open-field villages of the English Pale. Here, the historian might argue, a renaissance colonist's frontier-style surveying technique had spread eastwards and in a sense backwards (reversing the ordinary course of geographical diffusion) to encounter the complexity of a medieval landscape, with results which seldom looked convincing until the later eighteenth century and which went on causing trouble even then. Thus at Rathmore, Co. Kildare, in 1817, John Longfield made a separate survey of the local road system with the sole object of trying to pin down the *disjecta membra* recorded by an earlier surveyor for a previous owner of the same estate. He never managed to find them.[52] With hindsight and the appropriate Ordnance Survey sheets the modern historical geographer may have more success. Among the medieval-type strip fields on which he can experiment are those shown in early surveys of Newcastle Lyons, Dalkey, Crumlin, Rathcoole, Swords, Ballymore Eustace, Fethard (Co. Tipperary) and Dungarvan.[53]

Farmscapes of the Rathmore type were mercifully rare in post-medieval Ireland. None of them could have been known to the learned judge who pronounced in 1850 that metes and bounds, by which he meant non-cartographic boundary descriptions, were 'at least as good as a map'.[54] But it was not only irregular field patterns that made metes and bounds a difficult medium to interpret. In one eighteenth-century lease a farm was said to be bounded on both the north-west and the south-west by the same straight line.[55] Such anomalies are enough to make the non-lawyer look coldly on all purely verbal modes of communicating topographic data, but the identification of seventeenth- and eighteenth-century attitudes on this point is complicated by the close relationship between the two main objectives common to sale and lease cartography. If the cartographer's only concern was with boundaries, it would seem fair to accept a modicum of planimetric inaccuracy – partly because no one is perfect, but also because a sketch may be sufficient to locate the appropriate features without ambiguity provided that the boundary has some known relationship to what can be seen on the ground. Nevertheless, it may be noted in passing, farm sketch-maps are not particularly common in Ireland, and most of them can be interpreted as casual *aides-mémoires* derived from more accurate surveys. Most of them are also historically rather late: the Irish estate is unproductive terrain for any theory of cartographic evolution that proceeds from the pictorial to the planimetric.[56]

More interestingly, the antithesis of sketch-map and true map raises some curious, if over-theoretical, questions about the nature of a boundary. Outside Ireland it has been ruled that 'pegs are paramount to plans' and that 'marks come before measurements'.[57] This doctrine ignores the almost metaphysical respect for pure space that has so often invested the Irishman's agrarian activities. Monuments can be relocated even in defiance of holy writ ('cursed be he that removeth his neighbour's landmark'), as also can natural features such as streams; but a line in the abstract Euclidean sense retains its geometric position for all eternity. Some such feeling may lie behind the Irish estate cartographer's adherence to the single-line convention for boundaries, and could even explain his otherwise inexplicable half-heartedness about mapping visible boundary markers. On the same principle the acreage of a parcel can be seen as one of its essential attributes. If the acres were mis-stated on a map it was in the nature of the case impossible for that map to show the edges of the parcel correctly: they would necessarily be displaced either inwards or outwards. The recording of boundaries and the measurement of area thus become logically inseparable. Of course no one ever actually stated this argument; on the contrary, some lawyers rather spoilt it by insisting that the quality of the land, as well as its quantity, was essential to the process of identification.[58]

The measurement of area, and therefore by necessity of distance, was in any event a major preoccupation of the Irish land surveyor. His basic unit of reckoning was the perch, which made it natural for map scales to be expressed in linear perches to the inch. One justification for what an Irish estate atlas described in 1695 as 'the common scale of 40 perches in an inch'[59] was that forty perches are equal to ten chains, so that it took no more than the shift of a decimal point to derive the number of inches needed on the map from the number of chains recorded in the surveyor's field book. Here the chain as a unit of reckoning must be distinguished from the chain as a physical object. In English usage the two were identical, but most Irish surveyors preferred a measuring chain whose length was two rather than four perches – or, in one sense, a chain that was half a chain, though these were perches of seven yards and not five and a half. The foregoing explanation thus points towards a non-Irish origin for the forty-perch map scale, but it is not necessarily any the less probable for that.

Another complication is that the 'Irish' perch was only one of three such measures widely used in post-plantation Ireland, the others being the English perch just referred to and the Cunningham perch of eighteen feet nine inches. Broadly speaking, the regional distribution of different perches (and therefore of different acres) reflected the history of colonisation and settlement in the sixteenth and seventeenth centuries. The prevalence of the English acre in east Co. Cork and west Co. Waterford evidently stemmed from the Munster plantation (Fig. 5), and in Ulster the distribution of statute and Cunningham acres matched the

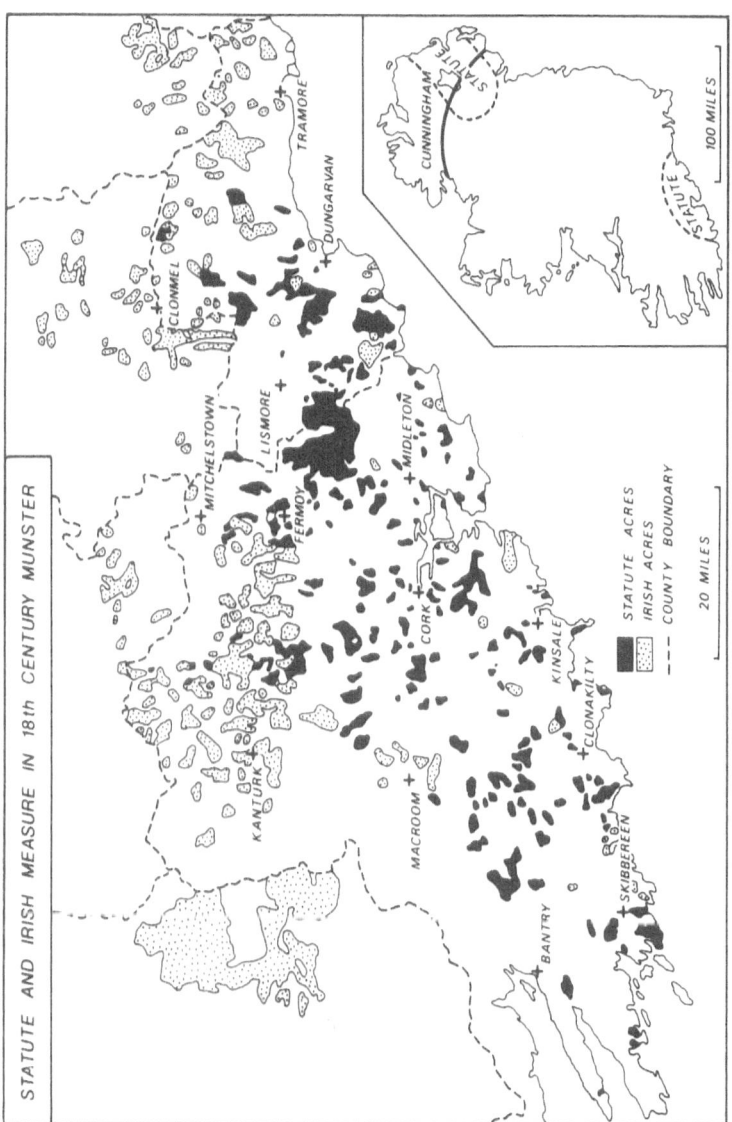

Figure 5: Eighteenth-century land measures in Cos. Cork and Waterford and parts of Cos. Kerry, Limerick, Tipperary and Kilkenny. Sources: a sample of contemporary maps, newspapers and deeds. Inset: approximate limits of statute and Cunningham acres in the 1840s, from P. M. Austin Bourke, 'Notes on some Agricultural Units of Measurement in Use in Pre-Famine Ireland', *Ir. Hist. St.*, 14 (1965), p. 241.

pattern of English and Scottish influence respectively.[60] The exact details of these distributions were highly complex. In the Glenavy district of Antrim in 1816 the Cunningham acre was used by the Countess of Longford and the statute acre by all her neighbours;[61] but the differences were more than a matter of landownership: on the Abercorn estate there were both Cunningham and Irish acres, with the Earl sometimes at a loss to know which was which.[62] Nor did the pattern ever quite settle into stability, even long after the plantations were over. In another part of early nineteenth-century Antrim the Cunningham acre was said to have encroached on the Irish acre, presumably in living memory.[63] Not long afterwards, in 1824, Parliament sought to reduce the whole of Ireland to statute acres.[64] On some estates compliance with the new law consisted simply of altering the phrase 'Irish measure' to 'late Irish measure', but it soon became common for surveyors to specify statute acres as well as the local variety.

Whatever the acres, roods and perches actually signified, they were an essential part of any lease map, written either inside the appropriate parcel or else in a marginal table or 'reference'. For urban building plots, acreage was replaced by length and breadth in feet and inches (sometimes half-inches), these also being written in position on the face of the map. The importance of acreages or footages was that rents were often agreed at a fixed sum per unit of space, and until well into the nineteenth century there were many maps that drew no qualitative distinction between one such unit and another: in words that had not yet become entirely metaphorical, rough was taken with smooth. The only important exception was the difference between bog and non-bog. Sometimes the former was mapped in a brown colour or flecked with a pattern of short pen or brush strokes; sometimes it was simply separated from the 'upland' by a broken line and given its own caption and its own acreage figure.

The comparative emptiness of the maps through which the Irish landlord dealt with his tenants was explained by the Co. Cork surveyor Daniel McCarthy in 1759:

> In the maps fixed to leases it is not required to describe the qualities, in as much as they are only intended to protect the outbounds from encroachments, and gentlemen are not desirous to make others as wise as themselves, I mean, to enable others by describing the qualities in the maps fixed to the leases to judge by the surveys the value of the land as well as the landlord or his agent can.[65]

The less the tenants know, McCarthy seems to be saying, the more rent they will be prepared to pay. Convincingly or not, he had acknowledged an aspect of Irish cartography which has already made more than one appearance in the present essay and which is due to appear again. The practical reason for mapping 'quality' would be its influence on the letting value of a farm. But many Irish rents were fixed not by valuation but by a process of competitive bidding in which the landlord accepted the highest rent he could get. In these circumstances the intrinsic character of the land and its buildings was irrelevant, especially as Irish tenants did not expect their landlord to provide them with a house or other amenities. But if quality was to be left off the kind of 'anti-map' that McCarthy had conjured up, why not omit the quantity as well? An excessively logical question, perhaps, though as it happened this inference had already been drawn by another surveyor, William Starrat of Strabane, who objected to writing in the contents of each farm for the reason that it 'gives everyone an opportunity to know the acres that sees the map, which the owner of an estate is often unwilling they should'.[66] Starrat was fighting a battle which in many parts of Ireland had already been lost, but there was indeed an alternative to the acreable rent and that was to let land 'by denomination', 'by bulk', ' in the lump', 'in the gross', or (in some mountain areas) 'by the side'.[67] In other words, a total rent would be agreed for a whole denomination without regard to its precise acreage. Although the various units applied to such denominations are well known, no historian appears to have traced the extent of their survival in private land dealings at any given period. On a superficial view of the evidence, the longevity of traditional measures other than the acre would appear to be associated with two variables: firstly distance from Dublin, and secondly the proportion of uncultivated to cultivated land in the district concerned. In the middle eighteenth century, for example, leases were still quoting ploughlands in Kerry and west Cork, polls in Cavan, tates in Fermanagh, and quarters in much of Connaught together with Donegal.[68] Units indicative only of cattle capacity remained common in the far west for many decades longer: even in the period of the Ordnance Survey a witness from Kerry could admit that his local community knew little about modern systems of mensuration.[69]

'A grant by acres presupposeth a survey', it had been sagely observed in 1622, when the notion of accurate land surveys had still not yet spread very far.[70] In practice this rule was often broken; so was its converse, that a bulk rent implied the absence of a survey. Measured acreages were sometimes converted into bulk rents on Starrat's principle that a tenant would be unable to dispute his landlord's survey if he did not know what was in it. At the same time many acreage figures were not measured but guessed at, or deduced from some standard ratio between the acre and the denomination. Such practices were partly a heritage from the prehistory of Irish land surveying, partly due to a belief that strict exactitude was not always necessary. Thus when one estimate was challenged the acres were said in reply to have been given 'by way of description of the land, and not as a measure of rent'.[71] The fact that this challenge had been put in a court of law was itself a pointer to the dangers of treating 'rounded' acreages as the numerical equivalent of a sketch-map, notwithstanding that some eighteenth-century farmers, estate employees and (for that matter) surveyors had developed a genuine ability to estimate acres fairly well by walking or riding over them.

On the other hand no acreage figure, whatever its origin, can be guaranteed perfectly accurate, and a number of devices were invented to protect such figures from hostile criticism. They included self-deprecatory phrases like 'by estimation', 'by computation' (which in pre-Ordnance Survey times meant estimation and not calculation as in modern usage), 'or thereabouts', 'more or less', or simply 'about'. Such formulae can be deceptive. The words 'containing by estimation 82 acres according to Mr Moland's survey'[72] did not mean that Ireland's leading land surveyor was incapable of taking measurements. The retention of approximative phrases for land that had in fact been properly surveyed was due in part to lawyers' conservatism but also to a care for preserving the effectiveness of an agreement even if a second survey should slightly contradict the first. The same kind of caution might also justify quoting round figures where more correct values are known to have been available.[73]

These precautions were not always successful. In particular, much uncertainty arose from the centuries-old stipulation 'greater or less'. Thomas Raven had taken umbrage at this phrase long before Moland's time, apparently regarding it as a slur on the profession they both adorned.[74] A more serious problem was whether it meant that rent would be increased or decreased according as the notional acreage might subsequently be corrected, or contrariwise that the real acreage might prove to be more or less than the notional figure *without* altering the tenant's liability. One lessor attempted to cover every eventuality with the formula 'containing by computation about 900 acres, be the same more or less'; but this did not stop the lessee from taking him to the House of Lords; nor did it prevent their lordships from nullifying the whole transaction when the land was found to measure only 874½ acres.[75] As John Perceval had already concluded some years earlier, the remedy was to omit the provisoes altogether and revert to the simple unembellished acreage,[76] but many lawyers were unwilling to abandon the bad old phraseology. It is strange that none of them devised a form of words to suit what must have been a common occurrence.

Land once surveyed might reasonably be expected to remain surveyed. This at least has been the view taken by non-Irish commentators like the historian who found that the activity of English land surveyors in one century had the effect of reducing the demand for the surveyor's services in the next century.[77] More generally, it was an English philosopher who hoped with the aid of a map to give rest and quiet to all the world.[78] Not quite all: in Ireland the making of a new map was often immediately followed by the need for an even newer one. Admittedly some of the reasons for a second survey would have been convincing enough in any country. They were expressed in Petty's dismal picture of the troubles that would follow 'when the mearers were fled, the surveyors dead, the marks on the land worn out, the rats had eaten the original plots, and a new interest risen up, for showing different mears ... from what were shown at the first admeasurement'.[79] But given a good map to start with, these difficulties could be avoided simply by keeping out the rats, which is why lease and conveyance maps were usually preserved with greater care than say advertisement maps or engineering plans. They were often kept as long as the property itself, and then transferred with it to the new owner and later in turn to his successor.[80] If lost, strenuous efforts were made to recover them, sometimes from commercial dealers many years after their disappearance.[81] Much land was advertised, sold or let on the explicit basis of surveys described as ancient or as having been done many decades earlier,[82] and the copying of old surveys, with only the style of decoration changed, was a skill given prominence in many surveyors' advertisements – though none of these advertisers said how he proposed to allow for whatever shrinkage or stretching the early map may have suffered since it was drawn.[83] For posterity, the copy and the resurvey were not always easy to distinguish, but the surreptitious copyist could sometimes be detected by the methods of textual criticism. In 1814 John Longfield found the same small error in the work of Abraham Carter (1704), Thomas Cave (1729), Thomas Reading (1751–2) and Samuel Byron (1781).[84] The culprits were all highly respected surveyors, and in the right circumstances the copying of old estate maps was no more reprehensible than the copying of the Down Survey and served much the same purpose, albeit at a less authoritative level. Another intermediate case was the old map that the surveyor took into the field and revised by drawing in new lines. This is what the Ordnance Survey did with some of its printed sheets in the middle nineteenth century; when applied to a manuscript map, as on the Abercorn estate in 1804, the method clearly has its pitfalls for the historian.[85]

Despite the longevity of individual maps, there were several reasons for replacing them that Petty did not mention. One was to mark a new relationship between landlord and tenant; another was to interrupt an existing relationship. There was also a multiplier effect whereby any two conflicting surveys could be expected to generate a third. To begin with, before a lease expired a landlord might wish to know whether the tenant had complied with its conditions, or with the law in general. For instance under an act of 1763 the penalty for burning land, a practice that sacrificed long-term fertility in favour of immediate gain, was a fine proportional to the number of burnt acres as determined by an admeasurement paid for by the defendant. Or the tenant might have signed covenants forbidding him to plough more than a certain number of acres, or to sublet more than a certain number, again with the penalty of an acreable fine.[86] Although such rules might be difficult to enforce, they seem to have provided the local surveyor with commissions that were remuneratively numerous even if individually very small.

Another motive for resurveying was to take account of improvement rather than deterioration, as when a tenant could earn an acreable premium by enriching his land with limestone-gravel.[87] For the landlord the most noteworthy of such improvements was the conversion of non-rented bog or mountain into profitable tillage, meadow or pasture. Before being made cultivable, rough land had often been 'thrown in' to a lease, according to the precedent of the early plantation schemes, without being measured or bounded and without being paid for.[88] The amount of it reclaimed in the century that followed the Battle of the Boyne was put at one million acres.[89] Where a farm had been thus improved or extended its owners would naturally feel justified in raising the total rent even if the acreable rent remained the same. Where reclamation was the work of squatters he would hope for rent where none had been paid before. The value of a survey in this context can be seen by comparing the Duke of Devonshire's rentals for the manor of Lismore before and after the manor was surveyed by Bernard Scalé in 1773; a large number of tenants suddenly appeared on the flanks of the Knockmealdown hills.[90] Without a survey such squatters might try to claim a freehold interest in their farms on the strength of twenty years' undisputed possession.[91]

The tenant's attitude to resurveying showed less enthusiasm, as its most probable effect was to increase his financial obligations. The resultant anxiety emerges clearly from the following dialogue on the subject of improvement, recorded by the Devon Commission in 1844:

> The land adjoining this is all let to tenants-at-will, without lease, and they dread improving, for they consider that the chain would be laid at a future day upon this land that was improved, and consequently it remains in its original state.
> Do you mean that if the land was improved it would be measured into their farms?
> Yes, and they would be charged for it.
> Has anything of that kind occurred in your neighbourhood which has been a check to improvement?
> I have seen that land has been taken into the survey.[92]

This was a popular line of argument in the early nineteenth century, even if it did leave readers wondering how any land ever came to be improved.

Irrespective of what had happened during the period of the previous lease, a landlord might decide on its expiry to divide a farm into two or more new ones. Such decisions were common during the period of population growth that was also the golden age of the Irish land surveyor, and it was the progress of subdivision, as much as anything else, that helped to make it his golden age. A particular motive for the creation of new farms was to increase support for a politically ambitious landowner by setting land to 'forty-shilling freeholders' eligible to vote in parliamentary elections. (It was taken for granted that a tenant would cast his vote on the right side.) Of one townland near Mallow, the owner, Denham Jephson, was advised:

> If you have not, you ought to have a survey of every field in it; to each field you may give a name now and inform your steward and others of the christening without telling them your reasons and from time to time their memories ought to be kept up. Out of each field, by its name, you may spring and form a freeholder.[93]

Jephson's farms were evidently assumed to be laid out in fields already. Elsewhere, the partition of irregular outlines into equal or other prescribed proportions, as foreshadowed in the 'divisional' lines of the Cromwellian and Restoration settlements, was a prominent motif in surveyors' advertising throughout the later eighteenth century. Not every surveyor could claim complete success in this exacting branch of his profession. When John Smith of Charleville divided the townland of Ballygrace by a network of straight lines, the resulting parcels varied from 38a. 2r. 24p. to 39a. 3r. 26p.[94] Such results, though creditable in their way as well as commendably honest, would not have satisfied the planimetric perfectionism of Smith's successors. In 1760 James Morphett announced a textbook that would explain the first true method of dividing ever known, but since the book failed to appear it is impossible to describe the method.[95] The same applies to the technique which one Mr Cowell in 1780 was offering to teach his pupils and for which he claimed an accuracy of one perch in 100 acres or one part in 16,000;[96] an unlikely story to say the least, but one that shows how much enthusiasm the whole subject had generated. The kind of straight fence still sometimes seen running across a whole townland can no doubt be attributed to this process of dividing by professional surveyors. Where they separate different kinds of fieldscape such lines are likely to be of early or middle eighteenth-century date.

Perhaps the most interesting reason for a resurvey was not to take account of landscape changes, past or future, but to achieve the higher levels of accuracy made possible by technical improvements in the surveyor's art. This is not a matter on which early Irish surveyors had much to say: they would criticise an individual, especially one whom they knew personally, but seldom a whole generation, and as pre-Victorians they showed little sign of anticipating the Victorian belief in progress. As late as the 1820s John Brownrigg could assume that surveys made (by other surveyors) at the beginning of his long career were as good as those made at the end.[97] Earlier, Peter Callan appears to have attributed the 'great increase of land found by late surveys' to the single circumstance that the older surveyors' chains were from four to eight inches too long.[98] This would make a difference in area values of little more than $2^{1}/_{2}$ per cent, not enough to explain the magnitude of the 'great increase'. But Callan had put his finger on the point that mattered. Explicable or not, the increase was genuine, and it meant that a resurvey would probably add to a landlord's acreage and therefore (potentially) to his rent without any alteration in either his acreable charges or his boundaries. The resulting increment might be small, but it could still leave a worthwhile surplus even after paying for a new survey. For instance given a hundred-acre farm, a rent of eight shillings per acre, and a surveyor's fee of twopence per acre (all reasonable assumptions for the Callan era) any increase in acreage of more than about two per cent would yield a profit for the landlord in the first year after the survey. It was a notable contrast to those underdeveloped countries of the twentieth century where the cost of a survey may be more than the land is worth. If anything Ireland's troubles were those of overdevelopment or at any rate overpopulation.

The effects of reclamation and of increased accuracy together explain contemporary references to landlords having their estates surveyed as a means of reducing indebtedness or of 'squeezing out a few perches' more from them.[99] They also help to account for the popular hostility towards new surveys which coloured Irish history from the sixteenth century to the nineteenth. It was widely thought that tenants had the right to deny a surveyor admittance unless their leases expressly provided otherwise. Many of them certainly acted on this assumption.

But the surveyor's benefactions were not altogether one-sided. If a new survey returned more acres than the former tenant had paid for, it could at least help to ensure that the incoming lessee would actually get those acres. An old map might be too inaccurate to be depended on; it might predate encroachments made from other farms; it might even be a fake. At a new admeasurement the tenant could see that all was in order by accompanying the surveyor along the boundaries. Accordingly some advertisements and some leases offered him the chance to request a survey, or promised one – perhaps even two, with landlord and tenant each nominating his own cartographic champion.[100] At least one advertisement, less intelligibly, offered 'benefit of survey'.[101] Perhaps this meant that whatever a future survey might reveal the tenant should not be made to suffer any financial disadvantage as a result. Perhaps it just meant that some kind of survey had recently been carried out, for after all the most reasonable course on these occasions was to measure the land before completing the agreement and then to embody in the lease a statement that the results were to be accepted as conclusive.[102] Liability for the cost of such a survey seems to have been a matter of bargaining power, with the expense sometimes being equally divided between the two parties.[103] Another possibility was for the tenant to submit his own survey, or at least his own map, along with his initial offer or proposal for the lands; in Co. Limerick Sir Vere Hunt even drew a specimen map to show his intending tenants the signs and symbols expected from them.[104] For his part the proposer might give explicit instructions as to where the chain should be laid along the edges of the farm he was bidding for,[105] or if he was applying for a new lease, he might seek to impress the landlord by producing a map of improvements to be made at his own expense.[106]

Of course no proprietor would object to a tenantry who took his word for how many acres they were getting – or better still who accepted the land in bulk without any mention of acres. The tenant unpopular with every landlord was the one who first signed the lease and then commissioned a survey of his own. If this new survey showed more acres (or more feet of frontage) than were in the lease, nothing further would be said. If it showed fewer, the tenant might refuse to pay for the alleged excess, or even claim a refund of what he had paid in previous years; or he might prefer to store up his survey in secret, as a grievance to be ventilated when he got into arrears or otherwise fell foul of his landlord. A possible counterploy was for the owner to insist on a new valuation to go with the new survey (on the assumption that the new acreable value would be high enough to wipe out the deficiency of acres), followed by a new lease and a higher total rent.[107]

This kind of landlord-tenant cartographic battle was being fought on the Perceval estate as early as 1639, when certain lettings were denounced as resting on survey errors of 25 per cent or more.[108] As surveyors grew more proficient, windfalls of that magnitude became less likely, but tenants fond of disputation continued to make their 'clandestine' or 'private' surveys.[109] Such incidents were not unknown on the other side of the Irish Sea, as at least one English surveying textbook makes clear,[110] but men with experience in both countries seem to have regarded them as characteristically Hibernian: 'In England a bargain's a bargain' was Perceval's nostalgic comment on one of many such mishaps that had befallen him in Co. Cork.[111]

For one reason or another, then, there was no diminution in the Irish agrarian community's need for measurers and maps, and this seems to have been as true of the nineteenth century as of the eighteenth. Any impression to the contrary is probably due to a change in the surveyor's public image that had little to do with his employability. Much of the most accessible documentation on surveys and counter-surveys comes from the disagreements that seem to have been constantly breaking out among the surveyors concerned. After about 1800 there was a falling off in professional controversy (perhaps surveyors were now so skilful that their differences had become too small to be worth arguing about), but surely not in professional activity. In the aftermath of the Napoleonic wars, it is true, the granting of leases appears to have become less common,[112] and with fewer leases there must have been fewer lease maps. But the concomitant decline in the middleman system meant that landlords, most of them now thoroughly habituated to surveys and surveyors, were having to deal directly with a population of undertenants that far outnumbered the old leaseholders; and under the tenancies-at-will that were the Irish alternative to the lease, the landlord-tenant agreement was renewable annually instead of once every twenty years or more. That suggests more surveying rather than less, even if some allowance is made for the little-known surveys done for the former middlemen and their clients. The difference was that, as population pressure mounted, the individual tenant farmer was becoming too poor and weak to get much publicity for any trouble that he managed to make for his landlord.

A possible flaw in this somewhat hypothetical line of argument is that many of the new farms were too small for measuring them to call for any particular skill. How many tithe proctors, it had been asked back in 1787 of a class of people usually regarded as distinct from land surveyors, 'are so ignorant as not to know how to step out, as they call it, an acre of ground, potato ridges lying in right lines, and the whole garden being, without exception, almost either a square or parallelogram, can be measured by the most ignorant almost to the greatest degree of exactness'.[113] Squares and parallelograms were certainly coming into fashion at this period, and even on holdings of well over an acre it could be maintained that if measurement were done entirely with the chain, instead of partly with an 'instrument', every farmer could become an expert surveyor after only a few hours practice.[114] Another possibility, canvassed many years earlier, was for the amateur to pace the sides of rectangles and the perpendiculars of triangles and lay off his right angles with a home-made wooden cross.[115] In reality the surveyor was not so easily dispensed with, even on very small farms. Plans drawn of Kerry potato-gardens in the 1730s were professional enough to be shown to Lord Orrery (who doubtless concealed his impatience at their insignificant territorial extent),[116] and the measurement of highly valued conacre ground was a normal feature of the country surveyor's routine, often in assignments that could yield him a fee of only three or four shillings a time. The minute partitioning of bogs among the adjacent tenantry was another product of rural population pressure, sometimes requiring a separate survey of the irregular face or 'breast' dividing cut from uncut turf.[117]

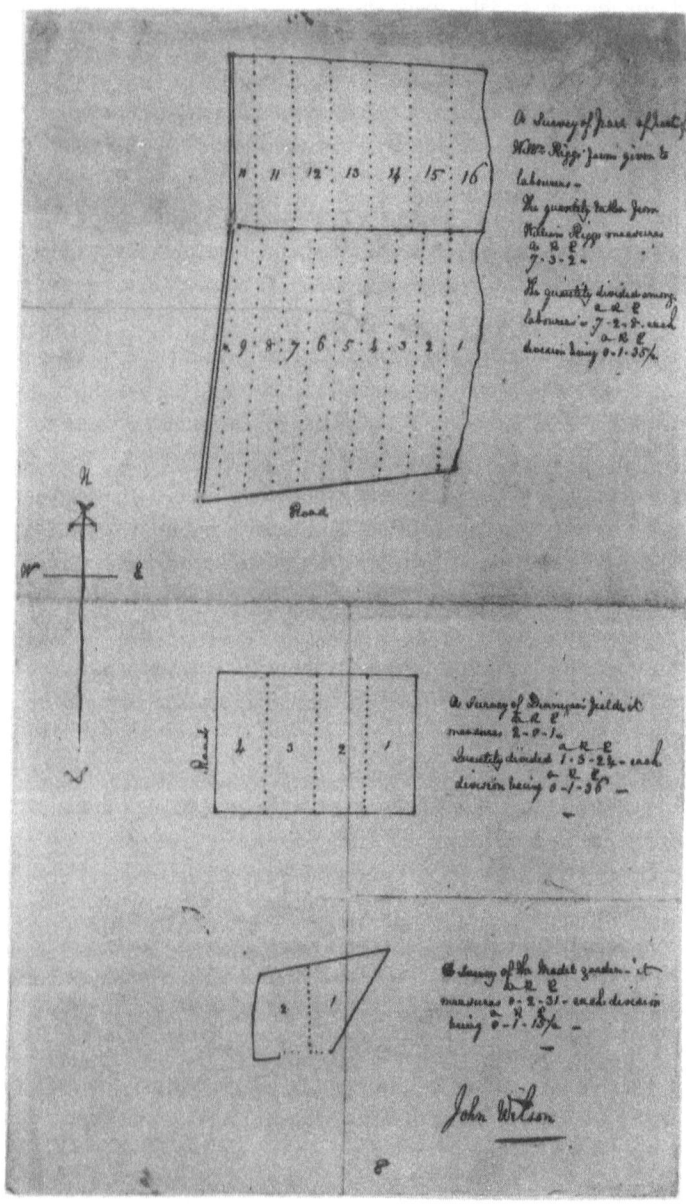

Plate 5. Survey and division of labourers' plots in Co. Westmeath by John Wilson (NLI, 21.F.80(8)). Scale of original about 10 perches to one inch. The maps are undated, but there are others by Wilson dating from 1840. Nothing else is known about him and the precise location of these surveys cannot be identified.

In any case it was not the technical difficulty of measurement, but the argumentativeness of its beneficiaries and the consequent need for impartial adjudication, that brought the demand for the surveyor's services down to the level of the smallholding (Plate 5). As long as he had a rent to pay, the countryman never lost his obsession with the simple reckoning of area. By the 1830s this feeling had assumed a new intensity, well seen in the close watch kept by small farmers on the inclusion or exclusion of roads when reckoning their rent, a question so vigorously put to a royal commission on the occupation of land in 1844–5 that they felt obliged to make it the subject of a special proposal.[118] Still later, and on a still lower social plane, a like concern was felt in England by those migratory piece-working Irish harvesters who used the new Ordnance map to justify their latest wage claim.[119] It probably never occurred to English observers of this strange phenomenon that the art of land surveying had been taken to Ireland by men of their own nation; or that these mathematically-minded labourers deserved a welcome as a native race which had now outdone its colonial masters and grown more English than the English.

Notes

1. No single work does justice to this theme. Some of the literature is reviewed in A. A. Horner, 'The Scope and Limitations of the Landlord Contribution to Changing the Irish Landscape', Permanent European Conference for the Study of the Rural Landscape, *Collected Papers, Denmark Session 1979* (Copenhagen, 1981), pp 71–7.
2. Grosart, *Lismore Papers*, 1st ser., 4, p. 41.
3. In 1725 Sir John Perceval described the printing of advertisements for farms as common in Ireland though still unusual in England (Add. MS 46976, f. 73).
4. Reproduced in *Cal. Anc. Rec. Dub.*, 7. What may be the original of this map is in Add. MS 29881. The printed version enjoyed a long life. It was frequently cited in leases (e.g. RD, 119/392/82944–5 (1746), 142/193/95170 (1750), 490/322/314636 (1789)), and two new features were subsequently added to the plate, first the Royal Canal and later, in 1847, the Dublin-Drogheda railway.
5. *Dublin Journal*, 26 June 1762. For another example see *Cal. Anc. Rec. Dub.*, 12, pp 256–7 (1773).
6. An early example is J. Cooke's plan of property in Kingstown (Dun Laoghaire), Co. Dublin, as laid out for building in 1823, NAI, 1A.38.48.

7. Such small-scale maps are common in the records of the Landed Estates Court (below. ch. 13). Those produced for the court by private surveyors are especially interesting; the Ordnance Survey generally used its own one-inch map when supplying the court with this kind of information.
8. *Leinster Journal*, 28 Feb. 1776.
9. Examples from 1759–60 are in RD, 206/17/134677 and 206/108/135358. For 'terrier-chart' see W. Tighe, *Statistical Survey of Kilkenny* (Dublin, 1802), p. 420. See also below, ch. 12.
10. G. Crawford and E. S. Dix, *Abridged Notes of Cases Argued and Determined in the Several Courts of Law and Equity in Ireland*, 1 (Dublin, 1839), pp 5–6. Some surviving lease maps have stamps affixed to them.
11. Perceval letters, 19 Apr. 1750, Add. MS 47002B, f. 140.
12. Examples are Bernard Scalé's atlas of the Hutchinson estate in Co. Tipperary, 1771 (NLI, MS 2735) and James Goggins's map of a townland on the Blake estate in Co. Mayo, 1796 (NLI, 21.F.74(17)).
13. J. Pope Hennessy, *Sir Walter Ralegh in Ireland* (London, 1883), p. 234; Ainsworth reports, 8, p. 1975 (no. 194, Stephenson papers).
14. Grosart, *Lismore Papers*, 1st ser., 1, p. 252 (June 1620).
15. For the Ormond lands, which had been scheduled for plantation, see NLI, D.4207 (8 Oct. 1640). For a connection between Sir Philip Perceval and the Strafford Survey team see Earl of Egmont, 10 July 1738, Add. MS 46989, f. 96; also Sir Philip Perceval to William Gilbert, 27 Sep. 1639 and reply, 30 Sep., Hist. MSS Com., *Egmont*, 1, i (1905), pp 110–11.
16. Most of the early references to surveying in *Cal. Anc. Rec. Dub.* are complaints of inaccuracy or uncertainty (e.g. 4, pp 12 (1651), 85 (1656), 134 (1658), 149 (1658)). The survey of St Stephen's Green by Robert Newcomen is mentioned in 4, pp 272, 297, 317 (1663–4) and a map of Oxmantown Green in 4, pp 323–4 (1665). J. P. Prendergast seems to suggest (in C. Haliday, *The Scandinavian Kingdom of Dublin* (2nd ed., Dublin, 1884), pp xxi–xxii) that city leases had maps attached to them as early as 1662, but such maps are not referred to in the *Calendar* until the middle 1670s, and do not survive among the city muniments until the 1680s.
17. Gogarty, *Council Book of Drogheda*, 1, pp 22, 47, 50. For a reference to a map in a Drogheda lease of 1699 see D. McIomhair, 'Some Drogheda documents', *Co. Louth Arch. & Hist. Soc. Jour.*, 18 (1973), p. 2.
18. 6 Anne, c.2, sec. 7.
19. RD,1/47/26 (31 May 1708). By the middle eighteenth century such references are very common among the memorials. Some of them even include miniature maps (e.g. 392/14/257730).
20. Gibson, *Practical Surveying*, pp 285–6.
21. J. Ainsworth (ed.), *The Inchiquin Manuscripts* (Ir. MSS Com., Dublin, 1961), p. 556.
22. Sir John Perceval, 16 Apr. 1715, Add. MS 46966, f. 51: 14 Mar. 1738, Add MS 46989, f.41.

23. *First Report of the Commissioners of Municipal Corporations in Ireland*, appendix, p. 548.
24. Knight of Glin, 'Lord Orrery's Travels in Kerry, 1735', *Jour. Kerry Arch. & Hist. Soc.*, 5 (1972), p. 51.
25. W. Nolan, *Fassadinin: Land, Settlement and Society in South-East Ireland, 1600–1850* (Dublin, 1979), p. 102.
26. Marquess of Lansdowne, *Glanerought*, pp 70, 81. A later advocate of the pre-lease survey was John Perkins, agent on the Gore estate in Co. Sligo in 1806–07 (TCD, MS 7588(36, 46, 53)).
27. *Dublin Journal*, 1 Aug. 1795. The Society of King's Inns had acquired a number of maps from the engineer-surveyor George Semple at a much earlier period, but the purpose of these is unknown (King's Inns, Library, 'Admission of Benchers Commencing in Hillary Term 1741', entries for 6 May and 13 June 1758; a reference kindly supplied by Dr E. McParland).
28. RD, 119/490/83341 (6 May 1746); 495/2/320751 (11 Sep. 1793); 657/420–21/451730 (1 Nov. 1810). Colouring the whole of each tenement became more common in the nineteenth century.
29. J. Stewart, *The Practice of Conveyancing* (London, 1827), p. 44.
30. For example James Irwin, *A Treatise on Gunnery ... to which is Subjoined an Appendix, Containing some Useful Remarks, etc. on Surveying* (Limerick, 1787), pp 135–6. Irwin recommended the mapping of 'all remarkable houses, barns, mills, also kilns, quarries, gravel-pits, water-cuts, hills, hollow-ways, land-marks, bridges, roads, remarkable old trees or old buildings' as a means of preventing boundary disputes.
31. For example a map by Patrick Fogarty in 1826 of a bog on the Trant estate in Co. Tipperary (NLI, 21.F.24(25)).
32. Andrews, *History in the Ordnance Map*, pp 12–13.
33. Note on the boundary of Ballynagran in Sherrard, Brassington and Greene, atlas of Lynch Blosse estate, Co. Mayo, 1811, NLI, MS 2713(6).
34. For the use of a fifty-year old survey in the absence of mearsmen on the Gore estate in Co. Sligo in 1807 see TCD, MS 7588(55).
35. Trustees of forfeited estates, minutes of discoveries, 21 Feb. 1700[–1], pp 55–6 (NLI, mic. P.259).
36. *Report of Roger Kendrick, City Surveyor, Concerning Ground in Fleet Street etc., against the Opinion of Messrs Gibson and Stokes* (1753). For the Long Stone see Haliday, *Scandinavian Kingdom of Dublin*, pp 151–4.
37. Survey of the manors of Craigtown and Castle-Craig, Cos. Leitrim and Cavan, 1732, NLI, MS 3252, p. 4. For a comparable view of 'the fall of the drop' of rain, see E. Wakefield, *An Account of Ireland, Statistical and Political*, 1 (London, 1812), p. 399.
38. Note on Down Survey tracing, 1812, TCD, MUN/ME/30.
39. Callan, *Dissertation*, pp 8, 23.
40. For example, 21.F.37(171) (Celbridge, Co. Kildare, 1838). This kind of boundary was discussed in OSO, file 2708 (1861).

41. 22 Mar. 1739, Add. MS 46990, f. 36.
42. Diary of Joshua Wight, 2 May 1754, Society of Friends Historical Library, Dublin, Room 4, Shelf P, No. 3.
43. Con acre or corn acre grounds were prepared at the owner's expense and let to labourers or other smallholders at high rents on eleven-month tenures. According to one surveyor, to survey in the manner of corn acres meant 'taking no more into measure, than what is fit for tillage, rejecting all ditches, roads, shrubberies, trees, and wastes – and all but what is fit for plough, spade or scythe to work on' (John Dolan, Feb. 1808, TCD, MS 7330(7)).
44. Nicholas Moran, 1764 (Co. Offaly), NLI, 21.F.79(6).
45. From the mid-eighteenth century onwards there are references to the exclusion of roads and ditches from farm-acreages (e.g. from the 1740s, NLI, 16.H.19(14)), but the foregoing sentences are based mainly on the very large number of statements regarding past and present practice on this subject in two sources: (a) *First Report from His Majesty's Commissioners for Inquiring into the Condition of the Poorer Classes in Ireland*, H.C. 1836, xxxii; (b) *Report of Her Majesty's Commissioners of Inquiry into the State of the Law and Practice in Respect to the Occupation of Land in Ireland*, H.C. 1845 [605], [606], xix; [616], xx; [657], xxi; [672], [673], xxii (henceforth cited as *Devon Report*). There are few early references to boundaries passing through large bodies of water. An unusual case of the explicit representation of low water mark is Joshua Wight's map of Red Island, Co. Cork, in 1723 (NLI, 21.F.73(5)). A boundary of 1736 runs through a lake in NLI, 21.F.80(9).
46. W. J. Smith (ed.), *Herbert Correspondence* (Ir. MSS Com., Cardiff and Dublin, 1963), p. 172.
47. J. Rocque, *Alphabetical Index of the Streets ... in the Plan of the Cities of London and Westminster* (London, 1747), p. vii.
48. Dean Chinnery to Lady Midleton, 17 Mar. 1767, PRONI, T.2862/4/4.
49. Sherrard, Brassington and Greene, report on Curracombera and Curracanderry, Co. Cavan, 3 July 1829, NAI, 2B.44.5.
50. James Purcell's map of glebe lands at Killenaule, Co. Tipperary, 1752, NLI, MS 2790(46); Richard Steile's map of lands in the liberty of Kilkenny, 1770, NLI, 16.H.17(21).
51. *Historical Narrative of the Origin and Constitution of ... The Irish Society* (London, 1865), pp 64, 66. Copies of Archibald Stewart's maps of 1738 are in PRONI, T.2116/1 (Londonderry, mentioned in 1746 in RD, 119/538/83603) and PRONI, T.837 (Coleraine, mentioned in 1757 in RD, 206/32/134741). Leases mentioning local town plans are also cited at Strabane in 1775 (Public Record Office of Northern Ireland, *Sources for the Study of Local History in Northern Ireland* (Belfast, 1968), pp 60–61) and at Kildare in 1798 (RD, 1849/17/173; NLI, MS 22004).
52. Report to Dean of Raphoe, 6 Feb. 1817, NLI, MS 861 (269).
53. For examples from Newcastle, Ballymore Eustace and Dalkey, with references, see F. H. A. Aalen, *Man and the Landscape in Ireland* (London, 1978), p. 172. For Rathcoole see J. Harvey, *Dublin: a Study*

in Environment (London, 1949), p. 65 and R. A. Butlin, 'Agriculture in County Dublin in the Late Eighteenth Century', *Studia Hibernica*, 9 (1969), p. 105; for Fethard, I. Leister, *Das Werden der Agrarlandschaft in der Grafschaft Tipperary (Irland)*, Marburger Geographische Schriften, 18 (1963), pp 138–9. Some unpublished strip maps are listed in M. Hollwey, *Medieval Field Systems and Rural Settlement in South-West County Dublin*, B.A. Dissertation, Department of Geography, TCD, 1980, pp 96–9. Others are in NLI, MSS 2789–90.

54. *Irish Jurist*, 9 (1857), p. 388.
55. Correspondence and lawyer's opinion on a boundary in the estate of James Franck Rolleston, June–July 1784, NLI, MS 13797. Roger Kendrick had noted a ninety-degree difference between the directions in a lease and those of the appended map (*Report Concerning Ground in Fleet Street* (1753)).
56. Sketch maps are mentioned by E. McCourt, 'The Management of the Farnham Estates during the Nineteenth Century', *Breifne*, 4 (1975), p. 536, and by W. A. Maguire, *The Downshire Estates in Ireland, 1801–1845* (Oxford, 1972), p. 110; but it is not always easy to distinguish (a) maps drawn from field sketches, and (b) hasty and inaccurate copies of ordinary farm or estate maps. The special case of the tithe 'certificate maps' is discussed below in ch. 12.
57. P. F. Dale, *Cadastral Surveys: an Analysis of the Efficacy of Certain Types of Cadastral Survey; with Special Reference to Countries in the Commonwealth* (Council for National Academic Awards, London, Ph.D. thesis, 1976), p. 28.
58. '... the close and content of acres and place where it lay, not sufficient without the quality of the land' (Reports of Irish law cases, Add. MS 19854, f. 31(1730)). There is a related comment in Add. MS 19855, f. 146 (1737).
59. Map of Irishtown, Co. Westmeath (NLI, MS 391), reproduced in P. Walsh, 'The Adams Rental', *Analecta Hibernica*, 10 (1941), following p. 286.
60. The only modern account of the distribution of these units is that of P. M. Austin Bourke, based on evidence from the 1830s and 1840s ('Notes on Some Agricultural Units of Measurement in Use in Pre-Famine Ireland', *Ir. Hist. St.*, 14 (1965), pp 237–41). For the use of statute measure in plantation Munster see above, ch. 2. Any study of the Cunningham acre in Ireland would have to begin at least as early as 1625, when the 'Scotch perch' was mentioned in Thomas Raven's atlas of the Hamilton estate in Co. Down. A fourth unit, the woodland perch of 18 feet, appears in maps of the Adair estate near Ballymena, Co. Antrim, in 1789 (PRONI, T.1310/3) but has not been found in any other Irish maps.
61. Mason, *Statistical Account*, 2 (1816), p. 263. For another example, see John MacCloskey, *Statistical Reports of Six Derry Parishes, 1821* (ed. D. O'Kane, Ballinascreen Hist. Soc., 1983), pp 33–4.
62. PRONI, T.2541/IA1/5/92 (25 May 1759), T.2541/IK8/1(49) (24 Jan. 1766).

63. Mason, *Statistical Account*, 1 (1814), p. 266.
64. 5 George IV, c.74.
65. Letter to Lord Midleton, 7 July 1759, Surrey County Record Office, Guildford, 1248/20/136.
66. Survey of the Brooke estate, Co. Fermanagh, 1722, PRONI, D.998/21/1. The same opinion was held by Perceval's agent, who took care to keep acreages out of his advertisements (6 Oct. 1726, Add. MS 46977, f. 41). It also appears several times in the *Devon Report* (e.g. 1, pp 655, 957; 2, p. 810).
67. Bulk rents are mentioned in the Dublin Society's *Statistical Surveys* (e.g. Leitrim (1802), p. 46, Armagh (1804), p. 219, and Clare (1808), p. 135), in Wakefield, *Ireland*, 1, pp 280, 309, and in the *Devon Report*.
68. This statement is based on a sample of memorials of leases in the Registry of Deeds, Dublin.
69. *Devon Report*, 1, p. 784 (Donegal); 2, pp 905, 958 (Kerry).
70. Journal of the proceedings of the plantation commissioners, 4 May 1622, NLI, MS 8014(iii).
71. [House of Lords], *Sir Richard Meade, Bart. Appellant. Daniel Webb Esq; Respondent, The Appellant's Case. Sir Richard Meade, Bart. Appellant. Daniel Webb, Esq; Respondent. The Respondent's Case* ([Dublin], 1744). For a similar phrase, see notes on lands in Co. Clare, *c.* 1721, in NLI, MS 1600.
72. RD, 119/121/81823 (Knocknadozen, Co. Wicklow, 26 July 1745). For a somewhat similar formula of 1781, citing '[John] Barker's survey', see Northern Ireland Record Office, *Sources for Local History*, p. 76.
73. Sometimes the approximation was very rough indeed. On the Duke of Leinster's estate, the two townlands of Maganey and Levitstown were advertised at about 550 acres (*Dublin Evening Post*, 17 Aug. 1786) instead of the 720 acres returned in John Rocque's authoritative map of 1760.
74. Raven wrote that 'the words sive plus sive minus ... are not fit to be used when lands are passed by number of measured acres' (S.P. 63/237/62A).
75. [House of Lords], *Meade vs Webb*.
76. Perceval letters, 25 Aug. 1726, Add. MS 46977, f. 34; 30 Jan. 1728, Add. MS 46979, f. 19; 14 Feb. 1737, Add. MS 46988, f. 19.
77. F. M. L. Thompson, *Chartered Surveyors, the Growth of a Profession* (London, 1968), p. 23.
78. 'Outline of a Plan of a General Register of Real Property', 1831, in J. Bowring (ed.), *The Works of Jeremy Bentham*, 5 (Edinburgh, 1843), p. 430.
79. Larcom, *Down Survey*, p. 42.
80. The map of Mogeely in the Lismore papers, for example, presumably passed from Raleigh or Raleigh's tenant to the Earl of Cork, and through the Earl's heirs to the Dukes of Devonshire. Similarly, a map

by Maurice Downer of Viscount Jocelyn's property in 1768 travelled through the Carden family to the Trant family (NLI, 21.F.24(14)).

81. This was the history of Roger Kendrick's map-book of 1754 in Marsh's Library, Dublin (MS Z.2.1.14). Other examples are mentioned in D. R. M. Weatherup, 'The Armagh Public Library, 1771–1971', *Irish Booklore*, 2 (1976), p. 291.

82. For instance 'by an old survey' (*Saunders's News-letter*, 28 May 1784) and 'by ancient survey' (*Cork Mercantile Chronicle*, 4 Sep. 1812). A survey of 1747 was cited in the *Northern Star* of 10 Aug. 1795, and a survey of 1735 in a memorial of 27 Oct. 1795 (RD, 491/144/317385).

83. This problem was encountered by William Montgomery on the Abercorn estate in 1837 when he tested a survey made by John Hood more than half a century earlier (PRONI, D.623/391/3).

84. John Longfield, report on the lands of Ash Park, 9 June 1820, NLI, MS 861(265). Longfield's maps of the same area are in NLI, MS 2790(34, 37).

85. Henry Hood, 28 Mar. 1804, PRONI, T.2541/IA3/4/10A. A more glaring example is the neatly drawn railway that appears on a map of 1791 by John Brownrigg (NLI, 16.H.15(17)).

86. 3 George III, c.29. Penalties for burning are recorded in *Dublin Chronicle*, 19 Aug. 1788. There is a summons for pernicious burning in NLI, MS 8526 (18 June 1801). Threats to survey burnt ground as a means of extracting a bribe appear in *Devon Report*, 3, p. 619. For retaliation against a surveyor conducting such a survey see *Report from the Select Committee on the State of Ireland*, qq. 6681–3, H.C. 1831–2 (677), xvi. R. L. Edgeworth imposed acreable fines for subletting (*Memoirs*, 2 (London, 1820), p. 21). *Finn's Leinster Journal* of 13 May 1775 reported on the use of surveys to prove unauthorised ploughing in Co. Kilkenny. A lease of 1813 with a penalty for ploughing ancient meadow is printed in J. Fitzsimons, *The Parish of Kilbeg* [Co. Meath] (n.p., 1974), p. 225.

87. Return of land surveyed by John Bannan, 28 Mar. 1811, Rolleston papers, NLI, MS 13794. Other returns in the same bundle relate to the survey of burnt land and of land taken for new roads.

88. Examples of leases in which no charge was made for bog are in RD, 120/250/82505 (Co. Louth, 1745) and in *Universal Advertiser*, 7 Nov. 1758 (Co. Meath). Legal opinions on the matter appear in Add. MS 19856 (notes on cases in the court of Exchequer, 1738) and in House of Lords, *Meade vs Webb, Respondent's Case*, p. 2.

89. *Saunders's News-letter*, 31 Dec. 1791. A near-contemporary estimate puts the reclaimed area at 400,000 acres 'in the course of a century' (*Dublin Chronicle*, 24 Apr. 1792).

90. NLI, MSS 6643–7.

91. J. C. Alcock, *Registry Cases Reserved for Consideration and Decided by the Twelve Judges of Ireland, from November 1832, to June 1837* (Dublin, 1837), p. 38. An example, on Ardfert commons, is described in T.

Radcliff, *A Report of the Agriculture and Live Stock of the County of Kerry* (Dublin, 1814), p. 213.

92. *Devon Report*, 3, p. 309 (lands near New Birmingham, Co. Tipperary).
93. 22 Apr. 1783, M. D. Jephson, *An Anglo-Irish Miscellany, Some Records of the Jephsons of Mallow* (Dublin, 1964), p. 111.
94. John Smith's survey and division of Ballygrace, Co. Cork, Mar. 1715, Add. MS 46966, f.42.
95. *Belfast News-letter*, 1 Mar. 1760.
96. *Dublin Journal*, 13 Jan. 1780. The normal method of dividing was described in Gibson's *Practical Surveying*, p. 317, but Irwin (*Treatise on Gunnery*, p. 143) felt that the subject had been neglected.
97. John Brownrigg, report on surveys of Lackendarragh, Co. Cork, 10 Apr. 1826, NAI, 2B.44.61.
98. Callan, *Dissertation*, p. 24.
99. *Dublin Evening Post*, 3 June 1784, comparing Irish landlords unfavourably with their English counterparts.
100. *Limerick Chronicle*, 5 Jan. 1778, has an advertisement providing that land might be surveyed at the desire of either landlord or tenant. Articles of agreement authorising a 'joint survey' of land in Co. Tipperary in 1745 appear in RD, 118/389/81219. A Co. Leitrim agreement of 1759 provided that two named surveyors should resurvey a parcel to resolve the difference between their previous surveys and that a third named surveyor should be brought in if they continued to disagree (RD, 200/192–3/132696).
101. *Pue's Occurrences*, 2 Mar. 1742.
102. A formula used in 1720 ran: 'as by a map ... hereunto annexed may more fully and at large appear with which said map and survey the parties hereunto are contented and satisfied without any further or other survey' (NAI, D.5363/26).
103. Equal division of surveying charges between two parties was agreed in Co. Cork in 1695 (Bowen papers, *Analecta Hibernica*, 15 (1944), p. 13). A Co. Wexford sale in which the purchaser was expected to pay for the survey was advertised in *Morning Register*, 21 Nov. 1832. On the Annesley estate in Co. Down it was proposed in 1778 to make the tenants pay for the surveying of disputed lands, but the agent reported that they were too poor to do so (W. H. Crawford (ed.), *Letters from an Ulster Land Agent* (PRONI, Belfast, 1976), p. 22). One tenant on the Perceval estate was willing to pay for the survey that he expected to prove Perceval's acreage incorrect (Add. MS 46968, f. 26 (5 Apr. 1717); Add. MS 46969, f. 7 (18 Feb. 1718)). Perceval himself thought that when a tenant requested a new survey the tenant should pay for it if it showed no difference from the landlord's previous survey (Add. MS 46971, f. 69 (20 Aug. 1720)).
104. Letters of Sir Vere Hunt, 26 Nov. 1817, Limerick City Library (NLI, mic. P.5527).

105. Tenants' proposals for lands on the Rolleston estate, Co. Offaly, 1823–4, NLI, MS 13794 (7).
106. Fitzwilliam estate correspondence, 6 Sep. 1807, NLI, MS 8814.
107. Lord Abercorn made this suggestion in 1761 (PRONI, T.2541/IK/7/37).
108. Philip Perceval to William Gilbert, 27 Sep. 1639, Add. MS 46923, f. 82. Perceval did not positively state that the whole error was due to mismeasurement (as distinct from faulty valuation) but this is the general tendency of his complaint.
109. A tenant of Blayney Townley Balfour claimed a sum of £13 as accumulated compensation for an overmeasure of less than five per cent made twenty years earlier (NAI, M. 1474a (1 Nov. 1765)).
110. George Atwell, *The Faithful Surveyour* (Cambridge, 1662), p. 4.
111. 17 Aug. 1728, Add. MS 46979, f. 80.
112. M. Longfield, 'The Tenure of Land in Ireland' in *Systems of Land Tenure in Various Countries, a Series of Essays Published under the Sanction of the Cobden Club* (London, 1870), pp 5–6. For confirmation from recent research, see Maguire, *Downshire Estates*, pp 129–35, and J. S. Donnelly, *The Land and People of Nineteenth Century Cork: the Rural Economy and the Land Question* (London, 1975), pp 63–6.
113. *Strictures on a Pamphlet Signed Theophilus: Explaining the Real Causes of the Discontents in Every Part of this Kingdom, Respecting Tithes* (Dublin, 1787), p. 15.
114. William McMenamy, 'A New Method of Calculating the Area of a Survey, Universally', *Trans. Dub. Soc.*, 1, ii (1800), p. 5.
115. *Letter from an Old Proctor to a Young One, Containing Serious Advice for the Conscientious and Prudent Discharge of his Duty ...* (Dublin, 1733), pp 17–18.
116. Knight of Glin, *Jour. Kerry Arch. & Hist. Soc.*, 5 (1972), p. 58.
117. Map of part of Trant estate, Co. Tipperary, by James Miller, 1812, NLI, 21.F.24(23), map of Barbawn Bog, Co. Kildare, by James Morrin, 1847, NLI, 16.H.15(11).
118. *Devon Report*, 1, p. 25.
119. *Report of the Progress of the Ordnance Survey and Topographical Depot to the 31st December 1864*, p. 3, H.C. 1865 [3467], xxxii.

6
Portraying the landscape

EVERY MAP-CLASSIFICATION runs into trouble sooner or later, and there is only a certain amount to be said for dividing Irish property maps into the two classes of farm survey and estate survey – the most predictable difficulty being that no one will remember to reserve the word 'estate' for maps that show a whole property and not just a part of it.[1] It might also be objected that mere territorial extent gives no adequate basis for definition and that there are as many ways of mapping a property as there are of mapping a country or a continent. However, the difference between part and whole is often enough to produce a distinct change of format, making the two categories recognisable either by their scale (which necessarily affects both style and content) or more often by their physique, with the estate appearing as an atlas, a wall-map, or a roll, instead of as a single flat sheet.[2]

More interestingly, the dualism of estate and farm has the merit of extending the kind of territorial hierarchy, from national down to local, that was given cartographic expression by some of the government's surveyors. Petty's printed and manuscript atlases between them proceeded from the kingdom through the province and the county to the barony. To these geographical divisions can now be added the topographical entities of the property and the tenement, the whole sequence a reassuring picture, in map form, of a country parcelled among successively smaller units each in the care of an appropriate authority. It was a view implicitly put by Robert Southwell when he asked Petty for the Down Survey maps that took in the Southwell estates;[3] and again, this time explicitly, in the advice that Southwell gave the young John Perceval: 'You are born to acres sufficient in that country, and ... you must have drafts for your bounds and denominations of each part ... Besides the drafts of the estate you must have maps of the county, of the province, and of the kingdom, to know how all are bounded, and see in general how the parts of Ireland bear to England and Scotland.'[4] From his frequent appearances in the present work it will be clear that Perceval paid heed to this advice, though he soon grew disillusioned about the technical competence that Southwell apparently took for granted among contemporary map-makers.

But to picture cartographic inspiration spreading downwards through the pyramid of scales is to overlook a number of cases where the farm map has preceded the estate map in both a logical and a chronological sense. And although it might be admitted that distinctive map-categories were necessary to illustrate the descent from Crown to landlord and from landlord to tenant, the first of these relationships had to all appearances been taken care of in the plantation surveys, thus providing the landowner of the 'new interest' with a ready-made memorial of his outer boundaries. It was only at the next level downwards, where the estate was partitioned among a large number of tenants, that the private individual had to make his own cartographic arrangements. In support of this view it may be recollected that the earliest known Irish 'estate' map, apart from certain geographical or regional maps of complete baronies, is a representation of a single leasehold; and that the first great improving landowner of post-medieval Ireland, the Earl of Cork, made a large number of surveys of particular farms without apparently ever commissioning a map of his whole estate.[5] And after several more bouts of plantation surveying to set the landlord class an example, one of its members was told that if he and all other gentlemen had such a thing as a survey of their lands they would 'find their accounts in it', suggesting that in Jonathan Swift's time (it was his advice) the complete estate survey could still be considered a novelty.[6] Without an authoritative census of farm and estate maps the best one can offer by way of hypothesis-testing on this subject is the thought that, if the lease had been a necessary condition of the map, land held in fee would have been left as cartographic *terra incognita*, and that while much of this land was the kind of bog and mountain that mapmakers of any brand were prone to ignore, it also included several more valuable categories such as woods, home-farms and parks. Sure enough, as late as 1780 Arthur Young often had only approximations to offer when tabulating the acreages of demesnes, and it was unlike him to be content with round figures if he could have given exact ones.[7] Perhaps his informants had no comprehensive record that took in both rented and unrented land.

Another comment unfavourable to the 'devolutionary' hypothesis is that the Irish estate map seems to take most of its character from contemporary farm maps and not vice versa. In particular, it falls into denominations of just the kind that appear in farm maps, often with each denomination on a separate page of an atlas or album. 'A book of maps with a townland on each leaf' was the specification given to one surveyor in Co. Armagh in 1831,[8] by now a rather superfluous piece of advice, one might think, for most cartographers had been choosing this form since the early seventeenth century. It was an arrangement well suited to the kind of large property that prevailed in Ireland, and it could be adapted to the manorial system by giving each manor its own volume or its own title-page within the estate volume. (There are no other reasons in Ireland for treating the 'manorial map' as a different cartographic entity from the estate map.) At the same time it would be hard to find an album with its page-rectangles filled up to their edges in the manner of a multi-sheet Ordnance Survey map; indeed the Ordnance Survey's first response to Irish conditions was to abandon its rectangular system in favour of separate maps showing particular territorial units.[9] And while the Survey's scale was set at six inches to the mile, the scale of the private atlas would often vary from page to page according to the sizes of the denominations. Such variations make it all the harder to apply the concept of the single estate map, except to the small-scale index diagram that prefaced many of these volumes. In any case what looked like a composite estate map in atlas form may have been put together from maps intended as separate tenement surveys, like the book in which the Dublin City Surveyor of 1766 was told to bind up all his past and future output.[10] Outside Dublin, too, some surviving albums were 'atlas factices' in which there was nothing new except the title page.[11] Others, like those so unflaggingly turned out by the Frizell family of surveyors, are no more than reductions from large-scale farm maps done by the same cartographer at the same time or earlier.[12]

If the estate map resembles the farm map in origin, authorship and appearance it may be presumed to resemble it in purpose as well, and some proprietors doubtless did hope to use a general survey as what Perceval called the rule and standard for letting lands.[13] A landlord about to let his whole estate on new leases would naturally have it all surveyed, as did the Drapers' Company in these circumstances with its proportion of Co. Londonderry in 1817.[14] A difficulty here was that many Irish farms were let 'for lives', implying that the lease expired on the death of the last survivor among a group of named individuals. This yielded the political bonus that a tenant for lives ranked for electoral purposes as a freeholder and could thus be mobilised in support of his landlord's parliamentary career, but it also meant that different leases might expire at different times according to the choice of lives and that the need for new surveys would therefore arise sporadically instead of all at once. Some proprietors tried to overcome this problem by keeping farms untenanted in expectation of a general rearrangement and a general survey,[15] but such a strategy might entail a long and expensive delay, and in any event the 'staggering' of leases was not always considered harmful. On the contrary it was a favourite maxim of estate administration that a large area should not fall out of lease at the same time, the point being that a steady flow of lettings would spread the managerial load, reduce the loss of income incurred in any one year through waiting for suitable tenants to present themselves, and protect the owner from combinations of tenants in quest of lower rents.[16]

In short, a comprehensive survey was not necessarily an ideal vehicle for leasing. At the most elementary level, the agent on the estate might find it difficult to extract a valuable book of maps from an absentee employer, or to persuade him to have it duplicated.[17] Where the book did remain accessible, it might cause confusion by disagreeing with recent farm surveys; and then if it was itself successfully challenged at any point the landlord would face a demand from other tenants holding under the same survey to have their lands remeasured. On the Perceval estate there were few years in the 1720s and 1730s without at least one new farm survey, even though the farms in question had been mapped as recently as 1702.[18] Another objection was against concentrating the outlay on surveys into one or two years instead of distributing it over a longer period in small instalments. Surveyors might solicit the chance of tackling an entire estate, but not many of them would go to the length of mapping it at their own expense simply in the hope of future patronage, which is what John Greene offered to do as part of his bid for the post of Dublin City Surveyor.[19] They were more likely to ask a three-figure fee. To resurvey the whole of the Abercorn estate in 1803, for instance, would have cost £500: Lord Abercorn decided to seek a cheaper solution for his cartographic problems by having the previous survey revised.[20] As standards of accuracy rose, a revision must have become increasingly preferable to a resurvey, though references to this subject are not very common.[21] Another compromise, on the Pembroke estate, was to confine the new survey to land where the leases had either fallen in or were due to expire within a specified period.[22]

All of which not only blurs the simplicity of farm versus estate but also raises the question of why an estate should ever be surveyed as a unit at all. It was a question with several answers, most of them obvious enough but some more easily felt than stated. The way Petty's friend Sir Richard Cox dealt with it in 1687 was: 'the best view of an estate is a patent or settlement and the next is a rent roll, yet it must be allowed me that the map and topography of it is neither unpleasant nor unprofitable'.[23] This is a hopeful basis for discussion, though in evaluating both pleasure and profit a difference must be observed between two phases, roughly before and after the arrival in Ireland of the Anglo-French cartographer John Rocque. At both periods, men who wished to seem businesslike were ready to follow Cox's precept. 'If there comes a new agent ... there will be a survey; they are anxious to make some show off', a royal commission was told in 1844.[24] It was a point on which many landlords agreed with their employees. An owner's imminent coming-of-age prompted surveys of the Perceval estate in 1702[25] and the Earl of Cork's estate in 1716–17.[26] The Earl of Kerry surveyed the Listowel district in 1697 apparently to celebrate taking possession of it,[27] and the death of Viscount Kenmare in 1720 was immediately followed by an admeasurement of the Kenmare lands around Killarney.[28] On a somewhat lower social level the same thing happened to the Kildare estate of Mr Pole Cosby in 1728.[29] There were new maps when the Earl of Antrim inherited his title in 1734;[30] and when the provost of Trinity College acquired an *ex officio* estate in 1759.[31] The third Marquess of Downshire began with a fresh survey in 1803.[32] One could almost propose the 'succession map' as a cartographic category in its own right.

For purchaser or inheritor, what gave the estate its unity was that all parts of it were equally unknown. According to an anonymous *Address* to the noblemen and gentlemen of Ireland, one use of the surveyor was to 'search out lands that are your right, though you have never known them'. Once again maps were being visualised as a book rather than as a collection of sheets or rolls: 'to have the maps of thousands of acres reduced to a portable volume, is the best and most valuable agent, unless a faithful one is to be found!'[33] This was rather hard on agents, plenty of whom were faithful enough to point out that it would take a 'general directory' (as one agent called the extensive survey he was recommending),[34] and not just a sheaf of farm maps produced at different times by different individuals, to inform the landlord of concealments and protect him from encroachments. Cartography can be both aggressive and defensive, and poring enviously over the maps of a neighbour's estate might not be quite as futile as a famous Irish novelist made out.[35] The neighbour must have found it an unpleasant experience to open a newspaper and see parts of his own property being offered for sale or rent by somebody else.[36]

Here were some good enough reasons for taking inventory; for identifying zones of potential dispute before they broke into life; and for leaving a few blank pages at the end of an atlas to accommodate any townlands that might be conquered or reconquered in the future.[37] In fact the representation of lands 'in controversy' is one way of distinguishing the estate map from the lease map – as long as the estate cartographer had not been intimidated by the locals into ignoring one of the disputed boundaries in favour of the other. The need to stand back and see each threatened parcel in its spatial context was implicit in the kind of surveyor's advertisement that undertook to 'unite' the surveys of different tenements, thus creating another intermediate category between the smallest survey and the largest.[38] The same need gave proprietors a particular interest in the survey of peripheral denominations, especially where one of their tenants also happened to be the owner of an adjacent property.[39] But if a whole estate needed 'rounding out' by the elimination of bays and salients, enclaves and exclaves, there was evidently no substitute for the single comprehensive view.

It was in this connection that the estate index could be expected to transcend its original function, as has so often happened with other kinds of index map. Indexes were sometimes drawn on separate sheets, in which case they are likely to be lost (always a sign of usefulness rather than the reverse), as happened to the general map that went with Thomas Raven's atlas of the Essex estate in Monaghan. Or they might appear as cartographic prefaces, an early example being Thomas Taylor's remarkable map of the lands held by Edward Roberts in 1659, which gets three of Ireland's four provinces on one not very large sheet and so qualifies as the earliest surviving attempt to show the results of the Down Survey at the kind of scale that would have been found in a general atlas.[40] Normally something like one inch to one mile was found adequate for estate indexes. That was approximately the scale chosen for Lord Chichester's map of the Inishowen peninsula in 1661[41] and later for indexes to the Egmont,[42] Southwell[43] and Herbert[44] estates, all of which owed much in style as well as scale to the kind of barony map drawn by the plantation surveyors. Each of these last four examples was engraved, and the first two did enough service for their errors to be put right on subsequent states of the plate. The enlightened spirit seen in some indexes could spread into a kind of estate cartography that was almost purely geographical, like the 'Diagram or map of the spacious and fine Logh Lean' done for Lord Kenmare in 1721.[45] Rare enough at the best of times, in the later eighteenth century such *jeux d'esprit* are even less to be expected, for small-scale geographical information was now available in an increasing number of printed county maps, which on large estates were sometimes copied, or adopted as they stood, and then converted into indexes by annotating them with tenurial data.[46] Elsewhere the estate index became standardised as a kind of miniature political map showing a mesh of townland divisions in different colours on a base-skeleton of local roads, perhaps with circles to mark the distances from some centrally-placed town or village.[47]

Most of the maps reviewed above satisfy Cox's criterion of not being unpleasant. Of course a landlord might sometimes be put off by maps that were too elegant to work on: he might even make a point of requesting a 'foul' (i.e. unfinished or undecorated) map, as did Lord Abercorn in 1769.[48] But even the most philistine proprietor would be likely to welcome some artistic outlet for his sense of ownership. The map of a man's lands met the same psychological need as a picture of his house or a portrait of his wife and children. It deserved the dignity of being hung in a frame, or of being bound into a book with expensive covers and lettering. It might even enter the realm of literature, and perhaps get into print, by illustrating a historical essay on the family or the estate.[49]

It seems to be only in fiction that an Irish gentleman can actually be caught enjoying his estate maps.[50] But their aesthetic appeal is easily revived by opening a typical early eighteenth-century atlas. It is especially eloquent in the title pages with their coats of arms, trophies and allegorical figures, sometimes accompanied by improving verses or by an obsequious comment on the age and distinction of the proprietor's family.[51] The margins of subsequent pages would be treated in the same spirit. Thus many maps are framed in broad bands of colour (yellow being the favourite) or in patterns of repeated circles, pellets and spirals. Other designs embody a professional allusion: some borders are checkered, as if to mark the divisions of a graticule or reference-grid; some feature the kind of heavily stylised leaf pattern which was engraved on the brass surfaces of many contemporary drawing and surveying instruments.[52] Inside the border, north is represented by a fleur-de-lys surmounting a colourful compass rose (often replaced in the eighteenth century by an almost equally eye-catching eight-point star with no outer circle), again in simulation of contemporary instruments. Title panels, and sometimes scale bars and reference tables, also attracted a penumbra of decoration.

Views and prospects of houses and scenery are comparatively rare;[53] so are pictures of the author and his instruments, though at least when he does appear he is always wearing his best clothes. More often the artist is simply following current styles of decoration in drapery, furniture or monumental masonry.

In his handling of decoration the average Irish land surveyor might arguably be described as naive. Some draughtsmen certainly failed to notice that their more ambitious efforts had not quite come off; that symbolic human figures, for example, should not appear to be convulsed with disrespectful laughter when pointing across the page towards the title of a nobleman's estate.[54] The best artists were those who not only understood their own limitations but also managed to exploit them, as in the lively self-caricatures seen on a Sligo estate map of 1768.[55] And if they avoided some of the more delicate motifs in the map-maker's repertoire – such as the daintily embroidered flower arrangements found in some English cartographic title pieces – that may have been for reasons of taste quite unconnected with technical facility.

The real naiveté appears not so much in execution as in design, and especially in the emphasising of marginal features as a means of trying to show the importance of what they enclosed. Some Irish north points in particular are almost ludicrously large as well as distractingly colourful.[56] A more complex failure of judgement was the use of engraved ornament for printing or pasting onto a manuscript map. North-points and scales were often applied in this form – at least one artist also had his own stamps for house-symbols – but the practice was most common with title panels. The usual engraver's cartouche was a baroque surround sometimes incorporating a printed impression of the surveyor's name, with a blank interior in which the individual title could be inserted by hand.[57] It was a device that seems to have been introduced in the late seventeenth century and to have remained current for nearly a hundred years: 'compartments for surveyors' were still being advertised by one Dublin engraver in 1784.[58] There is no need to despise the engraved compartment: it was accepted by at least one impeccably orthodox textbook-writer as an alternative to hand drawing,[59] and it sorted well with the contemporary aspiration that the whole estate map should be neat enough (in the words of Joshua Wight) to 'pass for a copper plate'.[60] It is true that the longevity of the ready-made cartouche tended to put a brake on stylistic change, but that is not necessarily a cause for regret. What jars on a modern reader is the incongruity of so plain a map in so pretentious a frame, with the compartments standing out like overdressed late arrivals at a not very exciting party.

For in its topographical content the typical early eighteenth-century estate map showed little advance on run-of-the-mill lease maps of the same period, or for that matter on the kind of plantation map from which they both have the air of being derived. Specific resemblances to the Down or Trustees' Survey are revealingly numerous in both leases and albums: the phrase 'laid down by' prefacing a scale statement (the nearby scale bar was often inaccurate or nonsensical, a mere allusion to the possibility of using a ruler); the scale ratio itself, forty plantation perches to an inch except where the denomination was too large or too small for the page; the boundary junction symbols, emphasised and elaborated by many private surveyors but still almost always featuring some kind of cross; the informal and often rather untidy script used for names as well as other kinds of writing; the lay-out of the reference panel with arable and pasture combined in a single total; and the sparing use of colour in the body of the map, 'run finely along the boundaries', as Gibson put it, and applied as uniformly as possible with the colours changing abruptly where different tenements were shown on the same page. All these traits were still observable in Gibson's time, the first conspicuous eighteenth-century innovation being an increased admixture of bold roman script.[61]

As for the landscape itself, one seventeenth-century cartographer was requested simply to distinguish bogs, woods, mountains, lakes and rivers,[62] and another seemed content with profitable and unprofitable land, supplemented by highways and bridges.[63] Gibson went further with a recommendation for 'all the roads, rivulets, rivers, bridges, bogs, loughs, houses, castles, churches, beacons (or whatever else may be remarkable on the ground)'. But even he says nothing of woods, tillage, meadow, pasture, gardens, walls, hedges, paths, mills, kilns, bleach greens, quarries or cabins. His list is in fact a good deal shorter than the one that Petty had seemed so pleased with. Where it resembled Petty's was in not being taken seriously enough by its readers. For the student of roads and houses, in particular, the Irish estate map of the Gibson era will come as a disappointment. Such sparsely appointed interiors owe little to the estate cartography of other countries. In England, for instance, the best map-makers offered a complete tableau of rural life: a village set among orchards, meadows and fishponds; comfortable houses nestling around a massively constructed inn and church; the whole scene brought to life by cheerful law-abiding ploughmen and milkmaids.[64]

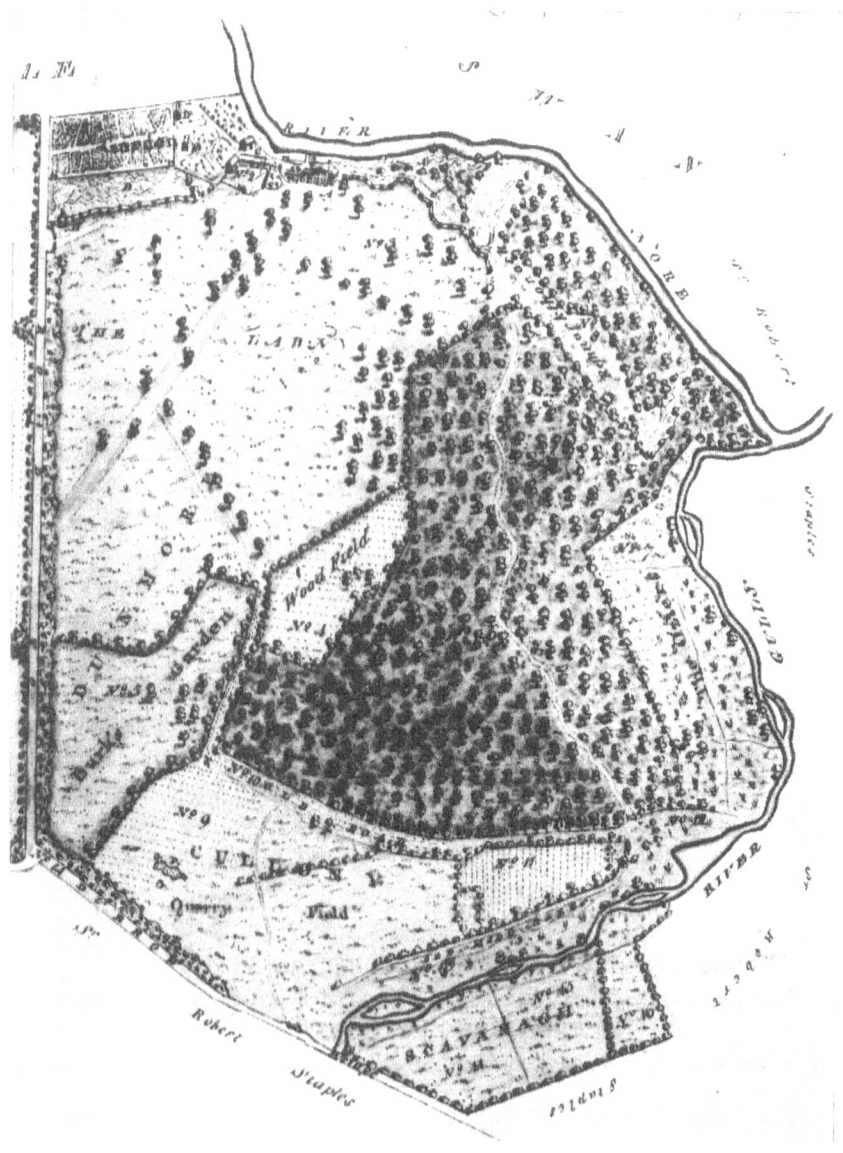

Plate 6. Part of the demesne at Dunmore, Co. Leix, by the antiquary and topographical draughtsman William Beauford, 1772 (see chapter 6, note 70). Scale of original 24 perches to one inch. Magnetic north is on the left. Except for the house, most of the man-made features shown here had disappeared by the time of the first Ordnance Survey map (1841).

In Ireland the main exceptions to the prevailing blankness were features of personal concern to a landlord. An early and obvious example was the mansion house, as minutely depicted by Thomas Raven at Killyleagh in 1625 and at Carrickmacross about ten years later.[65] Gentlemen's parks were too simple to need the same amount of attention at this early period, but if an enclosure contained no mappable improvements the cartographer could at least identify its outer fence by a distinctive paling symbol, like the line of sharpened stakes with which William Sapperton defined the Earl of Thomond's park at Bunratty in 1637.[66] A bolder draughtsman, such as John Cooley at Thomastown in 1682, might venture a portrait of the deer inside.[67] When formal avenues, vistas, canals and other ornamental features became fashionable in the late seventeenth century, they had the advantage of being easier to draw than animals. It took little more than straight lines and a standardised tree symbol to show the lay-out of a park like Carton, in Co. Kildare, before it was remodelled in the 1750s; the interiors of its various rectangles and triangles could be dealt with in marginal inscriptions such as 'a cherry garden walled' or 'a garden for sparragrass'.[68]

Both park and garden continued to receive special favour from land surveyors until far into the nineteenth century. On a general estate map, if the outlying townlands appeared without colour, the demesne might stand out in a succulent green;[69] if the townlands had farms, the demesne might go one better with fields; if a farm included fields, the demesne might still upstage it by adding the names of the fields. The same difference often appeared in estate atlases, where it became traditional to honour the demesne with the first map after the index. And Arthur Young's apparent ignorance of demesne-acreages is balanced, outside the pages of his *Tour*, by a number of excellent demesne maps, often surviving now in isolation and seemingly not part of any larger survey, some of them drawn by artists more gifted than those available for the mapping of ordinary tenements (Plate 6).[70] Such a map would make an attractive wall-decoration, and an enterprising surveyor might offer to frame and glaze it as part of his service.[71]

The other creations in which the Irish landowner could take special pleasure were his villages and towns. Here economic promise blended with military and social motives, for the planting of defensible civic communities had figured in many plantation schemes and remained an issue at least until the late seventeenth century. The connection appears in a number of separate plans of Londonderry, Coleraine, Omagh and

Bandon, and of the villages on the Londoners' estates and on the Hamilton estate of east Co. Down, many of them by Thomas Raven.[72] But the skeletal style of the plantation maps could invade the work of estate surveyors in town as well as country, with results that were scathingly described in Perceval's criticism of his local surveyor John Smith:

> I expected Mr Smith would have been so exact as to have laid out the street and lanes of Kanturk and situation of the houses with their due extent in length and breadth as Mr Southwell has caused Kinsale to be done and Downpatrick and as all other towns are done that ever I saw. There wants even a scale of acres and feet, so that I must say the gentleman has very little edified me with his survey and is not likely to be employed by me again.[73]

Though Perceval was perhaps letting other town cartographers off rather too lightly, he was right about Mr Southwell. The plans of Downpatrick not only showed the built-up area and its division into Scotch, English and Irish quarters, but also made use of such modern devices as block-plan symbols and 'concentric' waterlines, and in 1729 Southwell took a leaf out of Perceval's book by having them engraved.[74]

Mr Smith's neglect of houses was common enough in rural areas outside demesnes, as Perceval could have discovered from the survey of his own estate made by Thomas Moland in 1702.[75] While Moland and his contemporaries did indeed offer profile or half-profile views of numerous houses, some of them grouped into recognisable clusters or clachans, he nevertheless omitted (for example) the small cabins mentioned in his own non-cartographic remarks on Perceval's townland of Caherbane; and at Ballygiblin he failed to include a stone-walled house big enough to have its own stable, garden and orchard. It was not only houses that escaped attention. The same set of maps yields no trace of the 'several handsome enclosures ... and quickset hedges' recorded in the reference at Knocktemple; or of the enclosed parks that were a great convenience at Ballybrittig; or of the handsome avenue to the house at Killivarig.

As in many Irish estate maps of their period, Moland's buildings catch the eye like tiny islands in an otherwise empty ocean of parchment which does little to recall those earlier and more famous Irish artifacts (such as the Boyne passage graves and the sculptured crosses) that made a point of crowding every available space with detail (Plate 7). Of course the gap between ancient and modern makes this comparison rather far-fetched, especially as there seems to be no such thing as a medieval Irish large-scale map.⁷⁶ Moland's clients must have been familiar with closely patterned maps of various kinds from their own time, even supposing that he was not. Why then did they not encourage him to take more trouble? To see in his empty spaces the nakedness of the contemporary Irish landscape is an oversimplification: that much is clear from the Perceval townlands of 1702 discussed above, though admittedly the bleak and open appearance of rural Ireland in the early plantation era may have helped to inspire the preconceptions that Moland was heir to, just as the official maps of that period had done more than a little to influence his cartographic style. Nor could his reticence be put down to artistic timidity. There may be much in Ireland's soft and misty landscape that is more easily caught in words than images, but this hardly applies to houses and field boundaries, and in any case Moland was a good enough draughtsman to take such details in his stride. A more interesting theory is that here, as in other respects, the estate map was taking its tone from the rather uninformative kind of tenement map which (it will be remembered) the Cork surveyor Daniel McCarthy felt to be appropriate, on what may be called security grounds, for the normal Irish lease. But whatever the need to block the tenant's curiosity, within the walls of the big house self-censorship seems hard to justify, unless by fear of semi-literate spies or burglars who might find maps more comprehensible than the remarks that went with them. As with most failures in cartographic initiative, force of habit provides a better explanation than considered policy-making.

In the end, as will be seen, the estate survey was to make its own response to the development of landlord-tenant relations, though as it happens no leases were concerned in the incident that perhaps best exemplifies the shortcomings of the Moland style. This case involved another eminent Dublin surveyor, Gabriel Stokes, and its interest lies in the bisection of a townland between two owners.⁷⁷ Stokes gave the impression of broaching a new subject when he stressed the relevance of quality as well as quantity on such occasions: the fact that the Down Survey showed a castle on one half of the land but not on the other he took to imply a difference of value, not because the castle was worth much in itself but because 'the ancient Irish (who were never given to much industry) always chose the best part of the land to sit down on'. Though Stokes came from a later generation than Moland, his cartography was no more advanced; despite his interest in castles he had not bothered to show the one at Finglas on a map he drew for the Archbishop of Dublin a few years earlier.⁷⁸

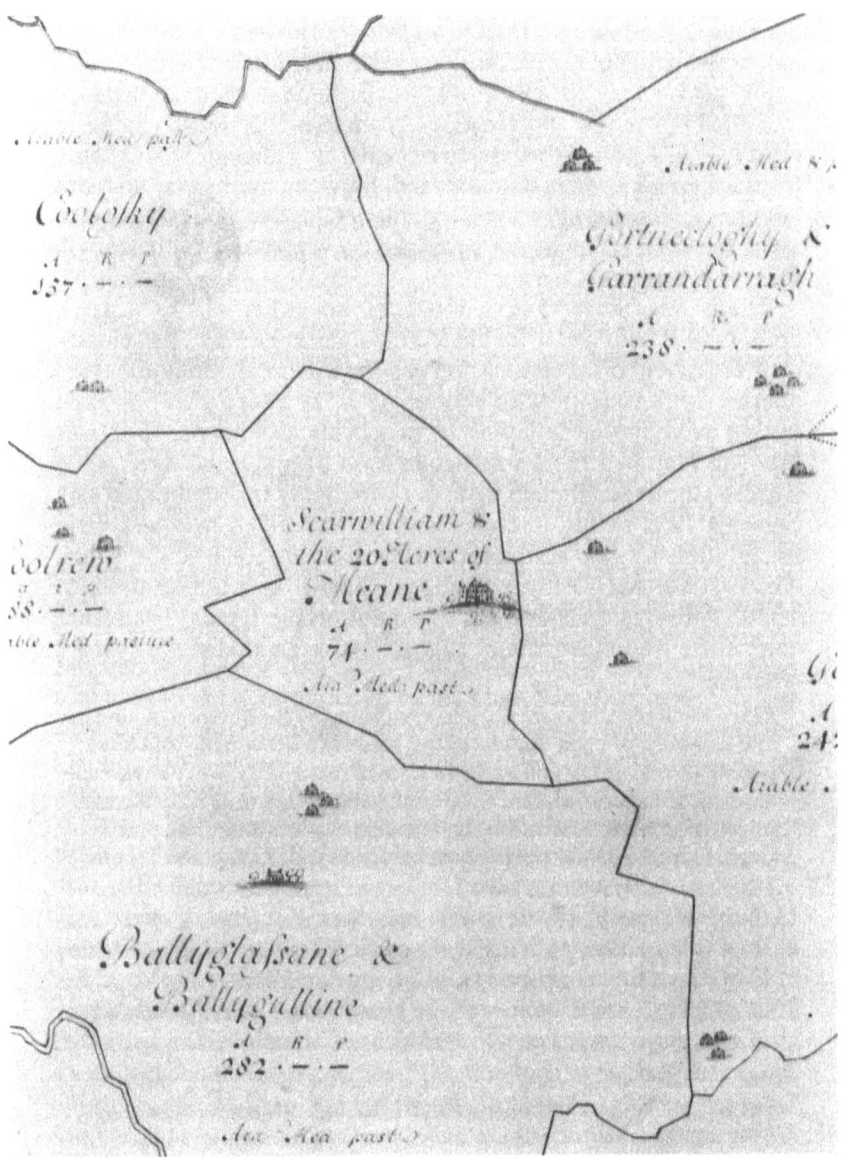

Plate 7. From Thomas Moland's atlas of the Courtenay estate, Co. Limerick, 1709 (NLI, 16.F.2). Scale of original 40 perches to one inch. The complete survey comprises twenty-three maps, each accompanied by a terrier or written description on a facing page. The terrier for Scarwilliam records the recent discovery of 'a considerable quantity of very good lead ore'.

There was more than a touch of absurdity about Stokes's comment. If land had to be judged in monetary terms, then clearly archaeological observations and unsympathetic theories about the ancient Irish were not the way to do it. A lessor who preferred letting by valuation to letting by proposals was bound, sooner or later, to favour a more instructive kind of map; and even while Stokes still lived (though now in retirement) this additional link between land tenure and cartography was given new and vivid recognition by two commentators writing in consecutive years. The first was McCarthy, soliciting custom from Lord Midleton in 1759. After his discouraging comment on the typical Irish lease map came a complementary suggestion for an alternative system, whereby

> Many denominations are put into a map, and by the different qualities and quantity of each quality in the lands are described, which will enable your lordship and lordship's posterity to judge, when a lease is expired, whether a fair rent be offered, and besides, your lordship will have the satisfaction of seeing how your lordship's estate lies, and distinguishing the good from the bad, in regard your lordship will (I may say) have a geography thereof.[79]

McCarthy's point about a fair rent was developed by a non-cartographic visitor to Ireland, Lord Chief Baron Willes. Writing in 1760, he noted the gap separating the comfortable Irish middleman with his lease from the tenant-at-will who actually worked the land and who could expect to find himself homeless if he improved it too energetically:

> For it is not here as in England that it is thought unfair to take a tenant over another man's head but the course is if the landlord thinks he can make more of a farm which he certainly may if 'tis improved he gives notice that he is ready to receive proposals for such land and if you ask him what rent he expects he fixes none but asks you what you propose to give him and so receives proposals from all that have a mind to bid for it and consequently takes the highest bidder. In England when you are treating with one man 'tis thought unfair to offer it to another but in Ireland 'tis set up to the best bidder ... Lord Kildare who is one of the greatest improvers in Ireland is sensible of the injustice of these kind of leases and therefore he has at an expense of some hundred pounds had his estate surveyed and curious maps made of his lands at Carton, Maynooth and that part of the kingdom and proposes as the leases and lives drop in to set his lands at a reasonable rate to each tenants [sic] as in England and to divide it into farms from 80 to 200 acres except odd pieces which may serve for labourers and cottagers.[80]

There were several issues here for the Irish estate cartographer to think about. At first sight Lord Kildare's good intentions meant putting less emphasis on the outer boundaries of a medium-sized middleman tenement and more on the small subdivisions inside it. Questions of format would then arise in densely populated areas where the undertenant had too little land to be given his own individual map at any of the accepted scales or sheet-sizes. The remedy was a mosaic showing several farms: many late eighteenth-century map makers favoured this arrangement (undeterred by problems of classification as between tenement map and estate map), and by the 1800s it must have seemed unconvincing for an experienced Ulster surveyor to assume a show of surprise when told to map the boundaries of farms as well as townlands.[81] What should have surprised him was the apparent indestructibility of the townland unit in the face of declining middleman influence. Once again, tradition was having more effect than logic.

Meanwhile Lord Kildare's preference for valuing over competitive bidding as a basis for rents would have its own effect on the distinction between farm maps and estate maps. Valuing farms, like marking examination papers, is easier with large samples than with single specimens. Compared with admeasurement, valuation thus provided another motive for assessing each property as a whole and so for mapping it as a whole, with obvious repercussions in the output of estate atlases and other composite maps. It is another difficult theory to test: the nineteenth century has more surviving atlases than the eighteenth, but then it has more of most things.

To return to the passages quoted above from 1759–60, exactly what McCarthy meant by 'qualities' may be hard to visualise. What Willes meant by 'curious' presents no problem. By a stroke of luck the maps that caught his eye remain extant: they are in eight large volumes produced for Lord Kildare in 1755–60 by John Rocque and they inaugurated a widely-copied style of Irish manuscript cartography and a widely-envied school of land surveyors that was dominated for many years by Rocque's Dublin pupil Bernard Scalé.[82] Both surveyors sought to increase the yeomanry of Ireland, as Scalé put it, by mapping every subdivision of the landscape, however small.[83] At this point a word of caution is necessary, however. Aware that not every farmer was a yeoman and not every landlord an improver, the Rocque school also offered an older style of mapping –surveys 'in farms', as they expressed it, instead of 'in fields' – and since the new style cost considerably more than the old (Appendix E) the magnificent maps shortly to be discussed may well have been in the minority. The simpler 'in-farms' surveys, though disappointing to the modern historical geographer, did help to show both clients and competitors a widened range of cartographic possibilities, for Rocque was an innovator in manner as well as in matter, achieving without apparent effort a poise and sophistication that makes it almost cruel to put his maps on the same table as those of any previous Irish cartographer.

Among the Rocque-Scalé hallmarks was a flowing, asymmetrical style of marginal decoration, in which natural features and abstract rococo motifs formed improbable but harmonious combinations, and in which the artist's skill and freedom with the brush had displaced the previous ideal of the counterfeit engraving – Gibson's sober advice about fine lines and neat compartments having been made obsolete within three years of its appearance. For all its aesthetic vitality the new style was far from being unrelated to practical considerations: much of its point would have been missed by clients who took their surveys 'in farms' – especially the fact that Rocque's and Scalé's marginalia were meant not to distract attention from the emptiness within but rather to provide an unobtrusive framework for a central mass of complex utilitarian detail and colour. To this end the most flamboyant decoration was concentrated at the front of the volume, while on the maps themselves borders were simplified into plain black lines and scale-bars into modest but easily legible grey-and-white checkers. Later, rococo shellwork dwindled away from the map titles, and the cartouche came to look like what it was, a piece of paper, given due prominence by a *trompe l'oeil* effect of casting a shadow over the page on which it seemed to rest as a torn fragment. Eventually it disappeared altogether. Where marginal designs survived, their effect was not to engross the reader's attention but to complement the map-interior or to supplement its realism with views of local houses and scenery. In many of the new maps there was only a single overtly frivolous embellishment (on the same principle that there was just one decorative window to relieve the severity of a Georgian house-front) and that was the Scalé north-point, a kind of visual pun in which the meridian line might be transported through the air in a bird's beak or help a cherubic acrobat keep his balance on a tightrope; and even the north-points often feature serious representations of local industries or agricultural implements, though the main emphasis in these conceits is on variety, a reminder that Scalé's maps were meant to be bound as atlases and not observed in isolation.[84]

The attraction of the Rocque-Scalé style was more than functional and more than artistic. It was also intellectual, one might almost say academic, drawing the estate survey into the wider field of map-making as a whole. Of course the connection between geographical maps and cadastral maps had never quite been broken: it was symbolised throughout the seventeenth and eighteenth centuries by a strong similarity in the design of scales, cartouches and north-points. But although the Irish land surveyor must have known something of contemporary small-scale maps, his knowledge was more a reader's than an author's. Petty was the last map-maker in Ireland for nearly a hundred years to treat the land survey as part of a cartographic continuum. Even when his successors happened to draw maps of more than one kind they kept them in separate categories, the only noticeable overlap being in the small-scale estate index. Thus one good post-Petty map of Ireland came from the work-room of a land surveyor, Henry Pratt, in 1708. It was an enterprising and progressive piece of geography; yet the estate maps drawn by Pratt a few years earlier for the Earl of Kerry were dispiritingly conservative, almost more like the Down Survey than the Down Survey itself.[85]

Rocque brought unity back into Irish map-making, and on a level that Petty had never aspired to. In England he had begun as a designer or draughtsman of parks and gardens, but by the time he reached Dublin in 1754 his main interests were topography and geography.[86] A prolific advertiser, his publicity campaigns were usually built round printed maps of towns and counties: he seems never to have canvassed for estate work, and if he really took no more than a hundred pounds for the Kildare manors he could claim to have been doing Lord Kildare a favour. Paradoxically, then, the most influential of Irish estate surveyors was a man to whom estate surveying was only a sideline.

In taking this wider view Rocque differed from every previous Irish land surveyor and also from his own Irish pupils. A unique status in the world of non-estate maps was asserted by his imposing title 'Topographer to the Prince of Wales' and it was with the word 'topography' that he liked to characterise his personal style. The same word had been used more broadly by earlier writers (including Ireland's Richard Cox) to mean any map or other description of a place or small area; now it assumed something more like its present-day cartographic meaning, so that when two of Rocque's pupils, Samuel Andrews and John Powell, went into business on their own account in 1760, they too announced themselves as 'topographers' and promised topographical drawings of estates and demesnes, complete with roads, walls, pales, hedges, heaths, rocks, mountains, valleys, bridges, rivers, wells, ponds, woods, loughs, bogs, commons, parks, churches, houses, gardens etc. – exactly the kind of verbal bombardment that Rocque had mounted to advertise his county maps.[87] It was only Andrews and Powell's further promise to include 'the true contents of each division' that recalled their readers to the world of the traditional Irish land survey. Powell was still describing himself as a topographer when he drew his last recorded Irish estate map in 1764.[88] Meanwhile Scalé had been undertaking to survey gentlemen's estates 'topographically, after the manner of Mr John Rocque', a specification expanded in his later boast that 'at one view is seen the topographical appearance of the whole'.[89] To the English reader such language might have seemed unadventurously reminiscent of John Norden's *Surveyor's Dialogue* a century and a half earlier. In Ireland it struck an original note.

By this time the essence of the topographical manner will be fairly obvious (Plate 8). Its underlying philosophy was a dislike of written explanations, its symbolism being either self-evidently realistic or easily interpreted on the basis of circumstantial evidence. The main innovation was to show relief by hachures drawn with pen or brush in brown or grey. (Scalé did his by intensifying the colours chosen to indicate land-use.) Water is greenish blue, often darkened along the edge. Each wall is a single fine ink line, each earthen bank a row of green herringbone symbols, each tree a vivid green profile drawing. Field boundaries are shown planimetrically and not in the kind of conventional diagram seen on Rocque's county maps. Meadow and pasture are green, with dark streaks and tussock-like blobs to mark patches of coarser vegetation. Where rough grazing merged gradually into bog the transition is achieved by making these darker patches more numerous and by colouring some of them brown instead of green. In fact an aversion to hard-edged colours was one of the most revolutionary features of the Rocque style.

By 'arable' Rocque seems to have meant land recently ploughed and not just land capable of being ploughed as in many other Irish surveys. (It was not until later that Irish estate cartographers made much play with the word 'tillage'.) His symbol for arable depicts furrows or cultivation ridges on a background of brown, grey or mauve, and this is where the principle of self-evidence breaks down: nobody knows whether there is any point to the colour variations in his arable fields (the reference tables throw no light on the matter) or whether his ridges are meant to depict the actual courses of these features on the ground. Lack of guidance on

PORTRAYING THE LANDSCAPE 163

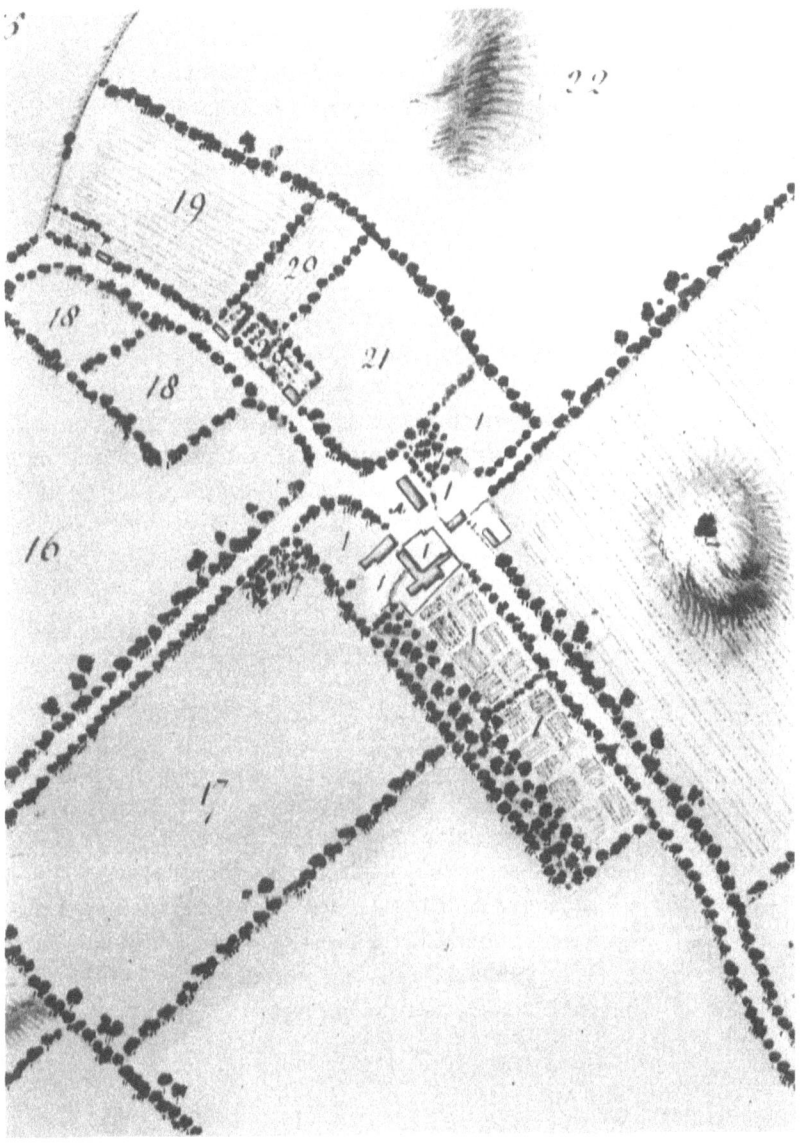

Plate 8. From John Rocque's atlas of the manor of Kildare, 1757 (TD, MS 10434). Scale of original 16 perches to one inch. Part of an extensive survey made for the Earl of Kildare, which appears to be the earliest Irish example of Rocque's 'topographical' method.

this matter may help to explain why some of his successors, even Scalé in his later work, carried the colour distinction to unpleasantly garish lengths while saying no more than Rocque did about its significance. Although Rocque made no explicit claims for his ridges they do look fairly realistic, whereas Scalé sometimes makes the plough cut a series of diagonals across a rectangular field and on one occasion can be found flaunting a highly implausible whirlpool effect. At this point attention should be drawn to the simplified versions of the 'in-fields' maps that the topographers sometimes supplied as working duplicates of a fully-coloured set,[90] for while fences and land-use categories appeared on the duplicates there was no representation of either arable-colours or ridges. Were these features an example of aesthetic pleasure taking precedence over agrarian profit? The map historian must take Rocque's foibles as he finds them: to adapt a twentieth-century writer's comment on a different art form, there are times when the poor interpretative hack must show proper respect for the true creative artist.

In gardens the furrow symbol of the topographical school is miniaturised, with lines of green bushes between one ridge and the next. Lime-kilns are marked by red circles, quarries and outcrops by simulated rocks. Milestones are in profile, turnpike gates in plan. Scalé sometimes shows churches isometrically, but his houses in general are planiform, coloured carmine and darkened on two sides. (Here too a map-maker's dogma had overridden the needs of utility: however offensive to later cartographic prejudice, a variety of profile symbols for different kinds of building would have helped the contemporary estate manager as well as the modern historian.) In contrast to maps of the Down Survey type, there is no suspicion that any of these features are less accurately located than the rest. It seems quite natural to find a Scalé estate map being quoted in legal evidence on the position of a gap in a fishery weir.[91]

All this required a larger scale than had hitherto been sufficient for the mapping of an Irish townland. Twenty perches to an inch was now becoming more common than forty (Table 7), and another favourite post-Rocque scale was sixteen perches, perhaps a sign of renewed cross-channel influence as it was the nearest Irish equivalent to a scale of twenty statute perches to an inch. For town plans a common scale was eight or ten perches to an inch; plots within towns were generally mapped at some simple multiple of twenty feet to an inch depending on their size. The kind of proprietor who patronised the Rocque school might well possess one or more complete towns of his own, or a large enough

PORTRAYING THE LANDSCAPE 165

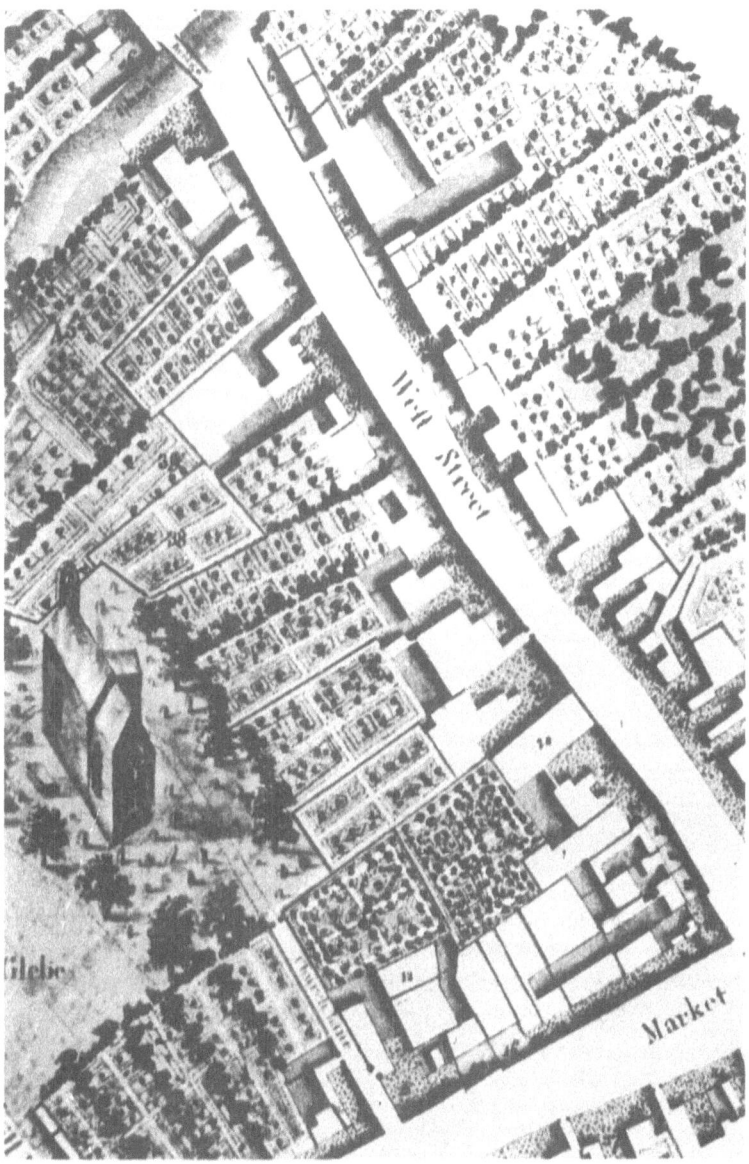

Plate 9. From Bernard Scalé's plan of Tallow, Co. Waterford, 1774 (Devonshire collections, Chatsworth House). Scale of original 8 perches to one inch. An urban version of Rocque's topographical style. Part of a survey of the Duke of Devonshire's Irish estates which also included town plans of Bandon, Lismore, Youghal and part of Dungarvan.

share of one to make the other landowners' plots seem worth including in his maps (Plate 9).

Other things being equal, larger scales meant larger maps. Rocque's measured about 36 inches by 24 inches, perhaps a record for Irish estate maps drawn on unbroken sheets of paper up to and including the 1750s. Of course, small sheets had been joined together to make large ones from a much earlier date, but until the middle of the eighteenth century the largest of Ireland's estate maps had been generally drawn on vellum or parchment. Apart from not always being easy to obtain, these materials were a less appropriate medium for the subtly varied colours of the topographical draughtsman, and their use was henceforth increasingly restricted to maps made for expressly legal purposes. Rocque patronised the Dutch papermaker Honig; later members of his school drew their maps on paper from the famous Kentish mill of James Whatman.

Altogether the only obvious resemblance between the 'topographical' artist and the earlier Irish estate cartographer lies in their common emphasis on townland boundaries, which Rocque recognised partly by a finely drawn variation (featuring three trios of dots) on the old boundary cross and partly by the indirect method of not colouring in the outlines of the small selection of objects that he chose to show outside the denomination boundary. The precedent of one page per townland was thus faithfully observed, which meant that Rocque shared with his predecessors a certain ambivalence as between farm maps and estate maps. On the whole he helped to reinforce the distinction. It is true that many later single-sheet maps were drawn in a style derived from his, and that with the shift in landlord-tenant relations, from competitive bidding towards valuation, 'topographical' data were becoming as relevant in a lease survey as anywhere else. Nevertheless the new cartography went beyond the needs of any single tenurial bargain. Its initial appearance in the albums of a large estate was no accident, for the importation of ideas from other cartographic media must have seemed more natural in maps of considerable tracts than in maps of single farms. In any case, delicate hachures and subtle land-use shading were too expensive to squander on maps handed out to tenant farmers or shut away in lawyers' offices.

The last point was acknowledged in the 'outline' duplicates made as lease maps by Scalé and his successors.[92] These inherited from an earlier tradition the one feature that Rocque's Kildare maps had made a point of omitting, namely the pink or yellow tint along the edge of the tenement under lease. The omission might be seen as proof of a topographer's

TABLE 7

SCALE OF IRISH FARM AND ESTATE MAPS

Scales in perches to an inch	Percentage of sample			
	1680–1719	1720–59	1760–99	1800–39
<16	—	3.6	5.8	18.0
16	2.5	3.2	3.9	14.8
20	30.4	28.1	55.9	54.7
20–40	—	3.6	3.0	2.5
40	63.3	53.4	27.0	8.7
>40	3.8	8.1	4.4	1.3
Number of maps in sample	79	221	363	311

Index maps, and maps on scales larger than 10 perches to an inch, are excluded. The difference in Irish, statute and Cunningham perches has been ignored, partly because the cartographers ignored it themselves and partly because it is in any case unlikely to have influenced their choice of scale.

distaste for invisible boundaries, but the tenements may have been omitted by request, especially if Lord Kildare was contemplating the kind of wholesale reorganisation attributed to him by Willes; or they may have been shown on an extra set of Kildare maps not now extant.[93] The omission of tenements, whatever the reason for it, was a step towards a later system of cartography, in which various kinds of thematic 'foreground' can be independently superimposed on a uniform base map showing more permanent features. Printing had to get cheaper, however, before this possibility could be fully exploited.

Rocque and Scalé had made a remarkable synthesis of the profitable and the pleasant. A landowner seeing a neighbour's Scalé atlas (and such treasures must often have been displayed in library or drawing room) would surely want one for himself, thus opening up another channel of cartographic influence in addition to those already traced. On the supply side of the market, the third generation of Rocque's professional descendants was still being known in his honour as the 'French school' as late as the 1820s. Its members included Thomas Sherrard, John Brownrigg, James Asser, John Longfield, Richard Brassington and Henry Walker.[94] The early nineteenth-century partnership of Sherrard, Brassington and Greene was especially productive, though with them the essence of the 'French' style suffered a good deal of dilution: no new artistic inspiration was vouchsafed, and several marks of distinction became simplified and coarsened (Plate 10). A 'French style' of colouring was being recommended as late as the 1830s,[95] but eventually — in the work of Brassington and Gale, for example — Frenchness got lost in the mainstream of Victorian large-scale cartography, preserving a separate existence just long enough for a few of its trademarks, such as the nine-dot boundary junction symbol, to penetrate the drawing office of the Irish Ordnance Survey department.[96]

Meanwhile similar ideas were surfacing in the minds of local cartographers not known to have received them by direct instruction. In Co. Wicklow, the language of Scalé's and Sherrard's advertisements was echoed by Jacob Neville.[97] Another practitioner not too far from Dublin influences was Benjamin Noble of Ballinakill in Queen's Co. He said nothing about map styles in the book on surveying which he published in 1768,[98] but five years later was announcing 'finished drawings and expressive maps of estates, distinguishing the different kinds of ground, as arable and pasture land, mountain, moor, bogs, woods, roads, rivers, and everything worthy of notice', a formula repeated almost verbatim in the following year by Edward Connor in Athy.[99] From Cork, Patrick Aher ('land surveyor and topographer') is later found advertising 'lands exhibited at a view and so natural a representation that gentlemen may behold their estates as if on the spot': one remembers that two of Rocque's ex-employees had settled in Cork.[100] Traced over a longer period, mere words can carry less conviction as a basis for 'cartogenealogical' inference: when Peter Blake called himself a topographer in a Ballinasloe newspaper of 1828 it was too late to deduce where his ideas had come from; only that by now even Ireland's most backward province had been invaded by the spirit of modernity.[101]

With other cartographers, more satisfyingly, it was the maps and not their attendant publicity that charted the course of change. Jonathan Barker had been trained by Thomas Cave, a Dublin surveyor of *c.* 1720 vintage, but his master would have been astonished at the topographical treatment which Barker gave to the field and settlement patterns on the Pembroke estate near Dublin in the 1760s.[102] Some topographers of the next generation were less lifelike in their mimicry. Another Dubliner, Michael Kenny, professed to record the 'natural' soil of every farm;[103] Richard Frizell added the topographical method to his repertoire after migrating from Wexford to Dublin;[104] John Travers made the same leap into the future without leaving his home county of Roscommon.[105] Many surveyors are honourably deficient in artistic flair and there is no

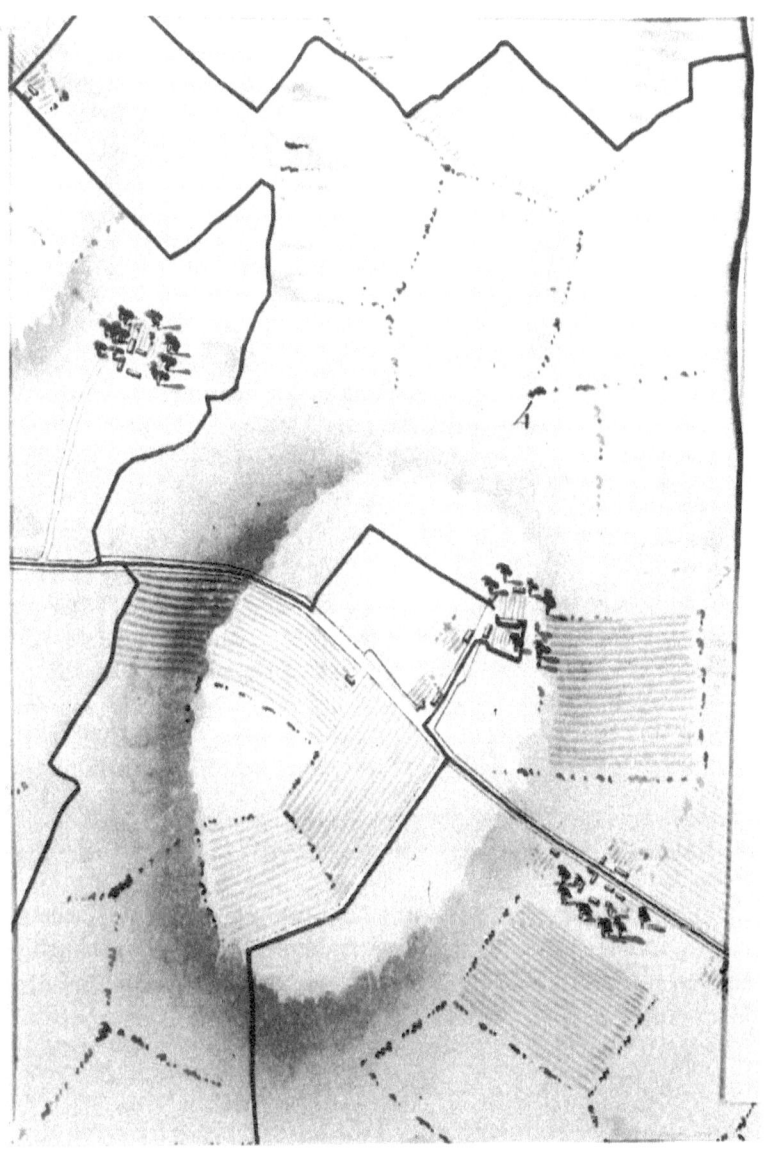

Plate 10. From Sherrard and Brassington's survey of Lord Spencer Stanley Chichester's estate, Dunbrody, Co. Wexford, 1803 (see chapter 9, note 82). Scale of original 20 perches to one inch. In this late version of the French or topographical style it is not immediately obvious whether every field or parcel of land is intended to be shown planimetrically.

need to blame these men of the 1770s for painting their townlands with improbably coloured streaks and flecks more reminiscent of a clown's make-up than of any known Irish vegetation cover. What matters is whether they got the symbolism right. The answer is, not always: their maps and reference tables are sometimes in conflict over the question of arable versus pasture, and their field boundaries often suggest a military sketch survey rather than a true admeasurement.[106] Some of Rocque's coinage had been debased in these successive remintings.

Rich in style and substance, the 'French' maps carry the viewer into realms of cartography beyond the limits of agricultural profit and loss. Scenic beauty is not often a rural preoccupation, and Rocque saw Ireland through the eyes of a Londoner. To some landlords, the maps he inspired must have seemed so vivid as to eliminate the need for first-hand knowledge, a kind of absentees' charter declaring that all the grass was green, all the houses freshly painted, all the roads smooth, all the water blue, and all the rentpayers happy. Coming back to earth, as guides to land valuation even the best of the topographers were not without their faults. Landscape maps, like the landscape approach in twentieth-century geographical studies, can be faulted for their preoccupation with appearances and for their unwillingness to penetrate metaphorically (or literally, if it comes to that) beneath the surface. To express the productive powers of the soil, an Irish surveyor might be better served by his nation's well-known facility with words, written either within the body of the map or in the accompanying reference. (Especially as several of the words in question, like 'esker', 'corcass', 'callow' and 'curragh', had been imported from his ancestral tongue.) This verbalistic philosophy, so different from the one attributed here to Rocque, found expression well before Rocque's time in the exceptionally long and variously informative commentaries accompanying the maps of the Strabane surveyor William Starrat.[107] Seven kinds of land appeared in Starrat's classification – arable, green pasture, wood and shrub, mountain, bog, curragh, and moor – and each kind was further divisible into excellent, very good, good, pretty good, ordinary or bad. As one of the earliest resident surveyors recorded in the north-west Starrat has claims to rank as a father figure – he is known to have kept a school – and there may be a hint of his influence in the use of the rather uncartographic term 'ordinary' by his successors in the Strabane area, John and Henry Hood. The complexity and qualitative refinement of the Hoods' land classifications may also be linked with the brief presence

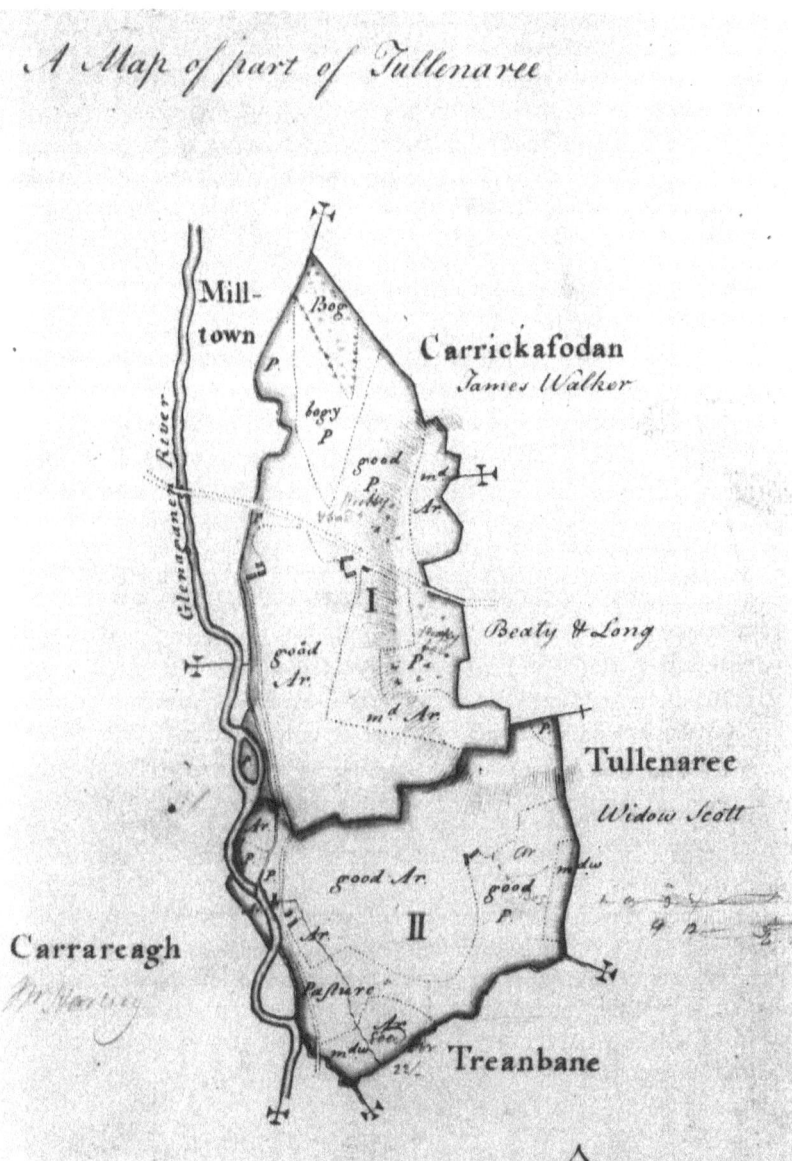

Plate 11. A farm near Carndonagh, Co. Donegal, by Henry Hood, 1790 (NLI, MS 5023). Scale of original 32 perches to one inch. A style independent of Rocque and Scalé but typical of the late eighteenth century in its use of block plans for buildings and hachures for relief.

in the same district of the London surveyor James Crow, and with the lifelong Ulster career of Crow's Derry pupil David McCool.[108]

Whatever its immediate origins, the Hood-McCool style is not very much like Scalé's (Plate 11). It includes a seemingly complete representation of roads, houses (in plan), and major relief forms (by hachures); also, and more conspicuously, a profusion of irregular dotted lines separating various qualities of arable and pasture. Neatness and austerity prevail, and colour is absent except for the tinting of farm boundaries. The impression is of an 'open-field' terrain in which both tillage and pasture played a part, though the reader is left to decide whether the fences were really absent from the landscape or whether they had just been crowded off the map by a profusion of contour-like 'natural' boundaries. An English visitor at work in Co. Londonderry in 1837 dropped an interesting hint on this subject when he described the local surveyors as 'unaccustomed to the English method of surveying and plotting in fields but using only the distinctions on their maps of imaginary lines bounding imaginary qualities'.[109]

But with the Ordnance Survey at work in Ireland the time for facile generalisations about 'schools' of cartography was running out: more education, more travel, and more professionalism brought elements from what had once been distinctive assemblages into new combinations whose provenance is impossible to trace without a great deal more research than anyone has yet done. To take a single example, from about 1820 onwards it was in the part of Ireland ostensibly most immune from 'French' influence, namely north-east Ulster, that the furrow symbol for arable land received most attention, notably from William Greig, Thomas and Robert Pattison, and Alexander Richmond, the first of whom claimed to map the course of each individual ridge in its correct position. Whether Greig brought his furrows from Scotland or found them in Ireland is at present unknown.[110] This group of surveyors also resembled their Dublin counterparts in choosing planiform symbols for both settlement and relief, but such a preference was now so widespread in maps of every kind that nothing cartogenealogical can be made of it. At all events the resulting mixture looked quite different from what Sherrard, Brassington and Greene were doing further south. The east Ulster maps made less effective compositions, and were relatively unsophisticated in decor; where they excelled was in sharpness and neatness of detail, and they were also better – arguably the best Irish maps ever – at combining tenurial and physical features without confusion into a single all-purpose cartographic statement (Plate 12).[111] Thus in map-making as in other respects Ulster had been transformed from

PORTRAYING THE LANDSCAPE 173

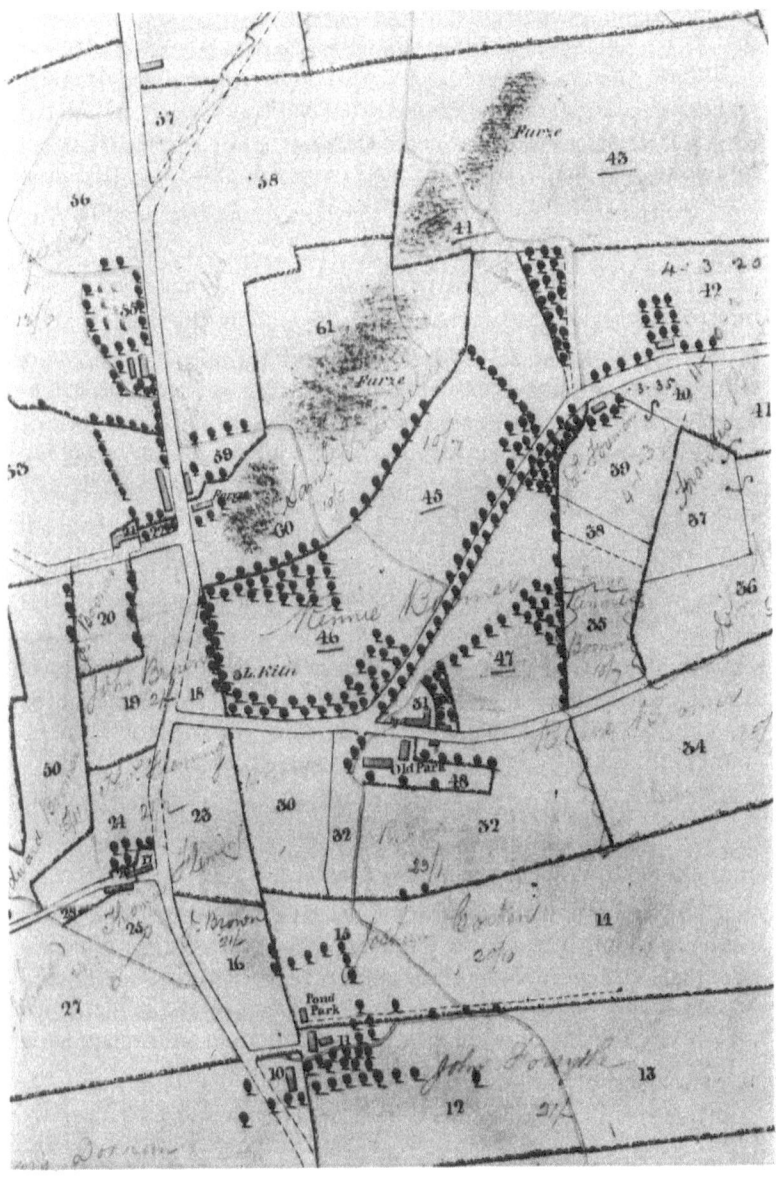

Plate 12. From Thomas Pattison's survey of the Earl of Hertford's estate, Co. Antrim, 1833 (see chapter 6, note 111). Scale of original 20 Irish perches to one inch. A fuller portrayal of the landscape than that of the earliest Irish six-inch Ordnance Survey sheets published in the same year.

the most retarded Irish province into the most forward, while nineteenth-century Dublin (as in other respects) was doing little to outgrow its past.

But on the whole the main cartographic differences in early nineteenth-century Ireland were not so much between regions as between the professional equivalents of social classes, or at any rate between progressive and conservative mentalities. Survivals from an earlier epoch among the latter included buildings shown in profile instead of in plan; ornamented or coloured borders instead of plain black lines; formal cartouches, often reduced to narrow oval or circular bands of decoration but still an anachronism even in that form; and north-indicators made up of stars and circles, both of which were now giving way among more fashionable cartographers to simple lines or crosses with less conspicuous embellishments and smaller arrowheads or fleurs-de-lys. A more subtle hint of primitivism – perhaps vestigial of the obsolete engraved cartouche – was seen in the unnecessary prominence still given by some cartographers to the preliminary words 'A MAP': surely the modern reader could tell what he was looking at without such heavy-handed assistance. In the first thirty years or so of the new century these archaisms were increasingly linked with a certain roughness and ineptitude in the treatment of letters, colours, and even line-work – faults which had always been present among Ireland's cartographic lumpenproletariat and which naturally outlived every change of fashion (Plate 13).[112]

Sophistication by contrast came from sources beyond the artist's immediate environment. Some nineteenth-century intrusions, especially in lettering styles and title-pages, affected many of Europe's visual arts and therefore need no comment – provocative and domineering though they were. Others, such as pen once more taking priority over brush, and line over colour, betrayed the influence of the printed map, especially after the 1820s when many estate surveys were themselves reproduced by lithography. The last trend may also owe something to the rise of the engineering profession and to the art-form appropriately known as 'mechanical drawing'. It expressed an unsentimental conception of cartography appropriate to the new industrial era. Lines were hard, edges sharp, textures uniform; black clashed belligerently with white, and even the decoration had the soulless look of a ruling machine.[113] Matters of taste aside, however, in a purely technical sense the best Irish estate maps of the period could more than hold their own (Plate 14). When an employee of the Ordnance Survey found a private admeasurement in progress on Lord Hertford's Ulster estate in 1834 he said he had never seen maps so neatly

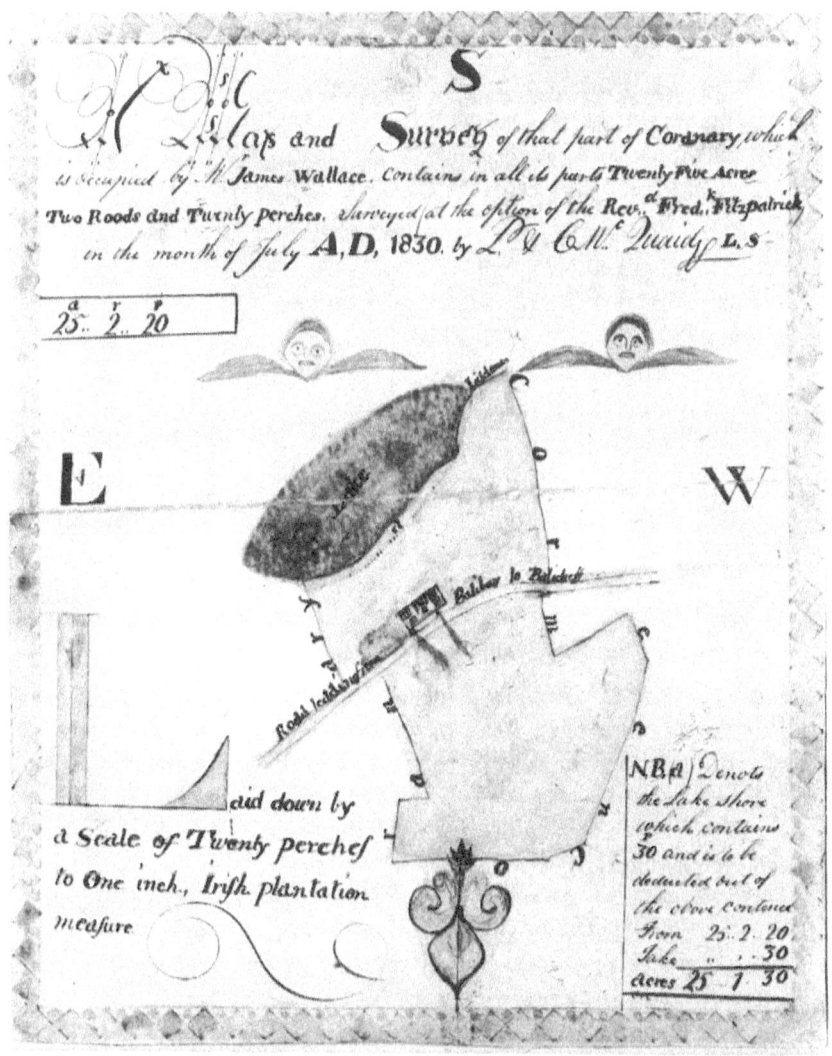

Plate 13. A farm near Corraneary, Co. Cavan, by Patrick and Charles McQuaid (see chapter 6, note 112). Scale of original 20 perches to one inch. Magnetic north is at the bottom. Despite the crudity of presentation, every angle in the farm boundary is identifiable on the six-inch Ordnance Survey map of 1880.

executed. 'Our own fair plans are only middling in comparison to them', he told the officer responsible for editing the plans in question.[114]

Finally, and this is true of any period, after the scholar has filled his last pigeonhole some individuality will always remain. The ninety-ninth in a succession of estate maps may look boringly similar to all its predecessors; then the hundredth springs a surprise. And when one considers that by the 1800s almost the whole of Ireland had been covered by such maps (or so it was widely thought)[115] a fair number of surprises may be assumed to lie in wait. Some of them are trivial enough; but it was a nice touch to honour a recent balloon ascent with a suitably inflated north-indicator, and to find an excuse for incorporating the words 'Protestant interest' in the plan of a town which had a reputation for bigotry – the next stage being to decorate an ordinary estate map with a fully-fledged political cartoon. One also sympathises with the surveyor who spent an idle moment drawing and labelling a 'fat triangle' and a 'thin triangle'. And who would not remember seeing an atlas overrun in its final pages by drawings of the unpleasant winged insects which its author had first introduced as an occasional inconspicuous embellishment?

For the more serious student, almost every topic of social concern or scholarly research may turn up on the hundredth map. Religion is acknowledged not only in churches and chapels but in altars, penitential stations and holy wells; literature in dedicatory verses; language in a variety of otherwise unrecorded placenames, occasionally with a distinction between English and Irish forms. Antiquity appears in Danish forts and giants' graves; physical geography in evidence for altered stream courses or coastlines, as well as in Ireland's 'best and strongest spring'. For historians, not even an estate survey could lend much novelty to yet another tradition about Oliver Cromwell or William III, but it might be worth knowing which particular field, now empty, had once contained the seat of an ancient local family. The more modern vogue for hedge history was foreshadowed by the surveyor who tried to date a ditch from the many old whitethorn trees growing in it. The same happened with urban morphogenesis when an 'insignificant back lane' was described as 'formerly the main street'; and unlike most other authors of town plans, the estate surveyor might pay as much attention to the backs of houses as to the fronts, noting a privy, a dust-hole, a dairy yard, a cock pit or a dog kennel before reaching the fragment of medieval fortification that provided many an urban house-plot with its rear boundary. There were similar rarities in the map of economic life: one cartographer, at work

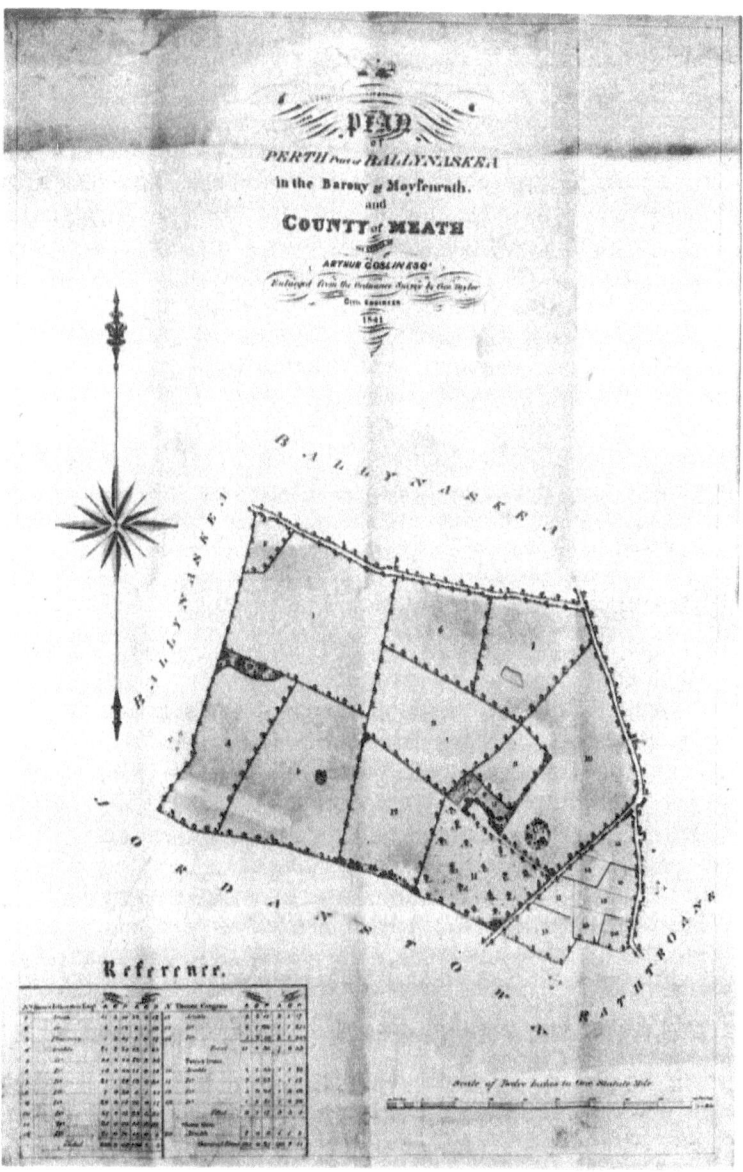

Plate 14. A farm in Co. Meath by George Taylor, 1841 (NAI, M.3007). Scale of original 12 inches to one mile. By graphical enlargement from the Ordnance map the areas of individual fields could be measured to a generally acceptable degree of accuracy, though this practice was not approved by the Ordnance Survey authorities.

near the seaside, took note of a Dutch trading vessel; another not only measured his fields but counted the livestock grazing in them; another showed the local copper mines with engine-houses drawn in profile and simulated holes in the ground. Recreation has given us a maypole and rackets court; early welfare measures, a Georgian poorhouse; crime, the site of a recent murder; punishment, a gallows in use. There was even a cartographic place for medical treatment and its aftermath when a hospital appeared complete with fever ward, operating theatre, 'dead house' and dissecting room.

Notes

1. Little has been written about the classification of property maps since an unsuccessful attempt was made to reserve the term 'estate map' for maps of land in the process of being sold. See Gillies, *Cart. Jour.*, 4 (1967), p. 53 (with reply by R. A. Skelton, p. 140), and the same author's paper on 'Surrey Estate Plans' read at a conference on the history of cartography, London, 1967.
2. With property maps, as with small-scale printed maps, it seems likely that atlases have enjoyed a higher survival rate than single sheets, but the historian's views on this point may reflect the accessions-policies pursued by individual librarians and archivists.
3. Marquess of Lansdowne, *Petty-Southwell Correspondence*, p. 141 (25 Aug. 1685).
4. Southwell to Perceval, Sep. 1702, Hist. MSS Com., *Egmont*, 2, pp 208–09.
5. This seems a reasonable inference from Grosart, *Lismore Papers*, which contains many references to surveys of individual farms, and from T. O. Ranger, 'Richard Boyle and the Making of an Irish Fortune, 1588–1614', *Ir. Hist. St.*, 10 (1957), pp 257–97.
6. H. Williams (ed.), *The Correspondence of Jonathan Swift*, 1 (Oxford, 1963), p. 53 (15 June 1706). The question asked a few years earlier by another literary man, John Dunton, as to why 'many of great estates can hardly make their minds or thoughts stretch to a geometrical measuring of their own lands', seems not to have been specifically directed to Ireland, though it appeared in Dunton's Irish travel book, *The Dublin Scuffle* (London, 1699, p. 3).
7. Arthur Young, *A Tour in Ireland, 1776–1779*, ed. A. W. Hutton, 2 (London, 1892), pp 149–50.
8. William Warren to John McArthur, 6 May 1831, PRONI, D.1606/5/1/88.

9. Andrews, *Paper Landscape*, pp 66–7. Part of the Pembroke estate in the outer suburbs of Dublin was mapped in 1851 at the scale of 1:1584 as a block of connecting sheets, a decision obviously influenced by the fact that large-scale Ordnance Survey coverage in this style was now available for the inner-suburban portion of the estate.

10. *Cal. Anc. Rec. Dub.*, 11, pp 326–7; 12, pp 114–15; F. Morgan, *Rental of the Estates of the Right Honourable the Lord Mayor, Aldermen and Burgesses of Dublin* (Dublin, 1868), p. v.

11. An example is the atlas of the estates of the Dean and Chapter of Christ Church cathedral, Dublin, by Brownrigg, Longfield and Murray in NLI, MS 2789, though in this case the maps were copies, not originals.

12. Charles and Richard Frizell's small atlas of the Earl of Kerry's estate in 1762–3 (Add. MS 17507) was matched by larger single-sheet maps of several of the same townlands done at about the same time (NAI, M. 3305–8).

13. 18 June 1717, Add. MS 46968, f.47.

14. *Reports of Deputations, who in Pursuance of Resolutions of the Court of Assistants of the Drapers Company of the 23rd January 1817, 3rd August 1818, 2nd August 1819, 7th August 1820, and 7th April 1827, Visited the Estates of the Company in the County of Londonderry in Ireland, in Those Years, and Which were Ordered by the Court to be Printed for the Use of its Members* (London, 1829), p. 53.

15. This policy was pursued on the Bath estate in Co. Monaghan before it was mapped by Bernard Scalé in 1777 (L. Ó Mearain, 'The Bath Estate, 1777–1800', *Clogher Record*, 6 (1968), pp 558–9).

16. Wakefield, *Ireland*, 1, p. 305; William Greig, *General Report on the Gosford Estates in County Armagh 1821* (ed. F. M. L. Thompson and D. Tierney, Belfast, 1976), p. 143; James Weale, *Report ... [on] Proposed Improvements of the Lands of Pobble O'Keefe, Co. Cork*, p. 14, H.C. 1831–2 (355), xlv.

17. Between 1804 and 1808 John Perkins, on the Gore estate in Mayo, made five requests for 'the book of maps', when writing to his employer in Dublin (TCD, MS 7588(14, 15, 17, 57, 68)).

18. Add. MSS 46964A–47003, *passim*. For the survey of 1702–03 see below, ch. 9.

19. *Cal. Anc. Rec. Dub.*, 5, p. 184 (30 Oct. 1679).

20. PRONI, T. 2541/IA2/12/2,6. The old survey had been made at various times between 1774 and 1781 (J. H. Gebbie (ed.), *An Introduction to the Abercorn Letters (as Relating to Ireland, 1736–1816)* (Omagh, 1972), pp 250–51, 333).

21. An example is John Wiggins's revision, in 1835, of a survey of the Grocers' Company estate in Co. Londonderry made fifteen years earlier (Guildhall Library, London, MS 7317/3, f.576).

22. Sherrard, Brassington and Gale, 'Survey and valuation of those parts of the Hon. Sidney Herbert's estates in Ireland out of lease or the leases of which will expire within fifteen years from the date of valuation ...',

1831, Pembroke Estate Office, Dublin. Parts of the Hill of Howth that were out of lease were surveyed in *c.* 1803 (*Dublin Evening Post*, 28 May 1803).
23. Quoted in R. Day (ed.), 'Regnum Corcagiense', *Jour. Cork Hist. & Arch. Soc.*, 8 (1902), p. 67. The second 'is' has been substituted for the 'in' that appears in Day's text.
24. *Devon Report*, 1, p. 827.
25. Add. MS 47043; *Dict. Nat. Biogr.*
26. Josias Bateman, *A Just and True Relation of J. Bateman's Concern, under the Right Hon. Richard Earl of Burlington, ever since the Year 1713* (n.p., n.d., *c.* 1734).
27. Andrews, *Jour. Kerry Arch. & Hist. Soc.*, 13 (1980), p. 5.
28. MacLysaght, *Kenmare Manuscripts*, pp 455, 471.
29. 'Autobiography of Pole Cosby, of Stradbally, Queen's County, 1703–1737(?)', *Jour. Kildare Arch. Soc.*, 5 (1906–08), p. 177.
30. J. Frey, ' A Catalogue of the Eighteenth and Early Nineteenth Century Estate Maps in the Antrim Estate Office, Glenarm, Co. Antrim', *Ulster Jour. Arch.*, 16 (1953), p. 93.
31. Samuel Evans, survey of the Provost's estate, 1759–60, TCD, MUN/ME/30.
32. Maguire, *Downshire Estates*, p. 30.
33. *An Address to the Noblemen and Other the Landed Proprietors of Ireland by a Gentleman* (Dublin, n.d.), pp 65–6. The second and fifth editions of this work (both of which contain the passage quoted) are in volume 332 of the Haliday pamphlets in the Royal Irish Academy, Dublin, under the year 1766.
34. John Moore to Arthur Annesley, 17 Sep. 1781, in Crawford, *Ulster Land Agent*, p. 33.
35. Maria Edgeworth, *Tales and Novels*, 9 (London, 1893), p. 308 (from *Ormond*, first published in 1817). The maps in question could have been 'leaked' by their author: in 1790 the Londonderry surveyor David McCool copied his own map of the Skinners' Company's estate for the benefit of a correspondent whom he was advising to take a lease of this property (PRONI, D.2433/A/2).
36. For examples of this situation see *Universal Advertiser*, 19 Aug. 1755, and *Cork Evening Post*, 4, 8 June 1787.
37. Samuel Evans, survey of the Provost's estate, 1759–60, TCD, MUN/ME/30.
38. Advertisement by William Jordan of Downpatrick, *Belfast News-letter*, 5 Oct. 1764.
39. A map is described in MacLysaght, *Kenmare Manuscripts*, p. 241, as 'the more necessary as the tenant's own estate is contiguous to it and some of our land lies even in the midst of his'.
40. '3 provinces of Ireland described, in which is included the estate of Ed: Roberts Esq., representing each particular pcell of the estate and

how it is scituated in its Bar^s & Parish^s w^h a description of all ye most eminent cities towns loughs etc. in the said pvinces collected from admeasurement in l659 by Tho Taylor', Harleian MS 4784, discussed by Goblet, *Transformation*, 1, pp 313–19.

41. J. H. Andrews, 'An Early Map of Inishowen', *Long Room* (Bulletin of the Friends of the Library of Trinity College, Dublin), 7 (1973), pp 19–25.

42. Six copies in Add. MS 47049; others in Add. MS 47050A and 46974, in NLI, 15.B.13(7b) and in TCD, MS 7109 . On 20 July 1716 Perceval undertook to send his agent a copy of 'the new impression', asking for the old one to be burned 'because of its faultiness' (Add. MS 46967, f. 79).

43. 'The mannor of Downpatrick 1710', Linen Hall Library, Belfast.

44. Map of Castle Island seignory, Co. Kerry, by Garret Hogan, 1729, NLI, 16.H.8(18).

45. Photocopy, NLI, MS 2770. See MacLysaght, *Kenmare Manuscripts*, pp 270, 455. Another example is Josias Bateman's index map of the Burlington estate in Co. Cork at two inches to a mile, made in 1717 (NLI, MS 6148).

46. J. H. Fryer and J. B. Knight, valuing the Marquess of Antrim's estate in 1813, promised 'maps of the Co. of Antrim as the estate is now divided' (NLI, MS 8215(4)). A manuscript copy of part of Valentine Gill's map of Co. Wexford appears as an index in an atlas of the Hughes estate in 1821–2 by Sherrard, Brassington and Greene, in the possession of Messrs Kirwan and Kirwan, solicitors, Wexford. G. V. Sampson's map of Londonderry was the source of *A Map Shewing the Manor of Lizard in the County of Londonderry Ireland the Estate of the Worshipful Company of Ironmongers* (London, 1830).

47. An example is the index to Bernard Scalé's survey of the manor of Lismore (1773) at Chatsworth House, Derbyshire.

48. PRONI, T.2541/1K/2/77.

49. The 1702 map of the Perceval estate appears in at least one copy of J. Anderson, *A Genealogical History of the House of Ivery* (London, 1742). Maria Edgeworth tells how her grandfather wrote the history of his estate 'giving copies of the Down Survey and other old maps of the lands' (NAI, M.2320, p. 1).

50. For an example see Charles Lever, *Luttrell of Arran* (London, 1865), p. 77.

51. There are introductory verses in Francis Plunkett and Francis McDermott's survey of the estate of Garet Moore in 1721 (NLI, MS 2707 (photocopy)).

52. This kind of border appeared in the late 1740s and remained popular for about thirty years. It was favoured by Thomas Reading, Robert Lewis and Michael Kenny (Dublin), John Mooney (Co. Kildare), William Steile (Co. Kilkenny), Robert Livingston (Co. Armagh) and James McClatchey (Co. Down). Instruments featuring the same style are in the Science Museum, London, and in the Egestorff collection, Wellington Place, Dublin.

53. The drawing of views and prospects was nevertheless recommended as a 'very necessary qualification' for land surveyors in 1744 (*Dublin Journal*, 20 Nov. 1744).
54. Kenmare estate maps, NLI, MS 2770(15).
55. Longfield, *Bull. Ir. Georgian Soc.*, 20 (1977), p. 66.
56. A good example is in John Baker's map of lands in Co. Kilkenny in 1739, NLI, 21.F.157(6).
57. Andrews, *Irish Maps*, 16, 17 (Richard and Charles Frizell). For earlier examples see Andrews, *Jour. Kerry Arch. & Hist. Soc.*, 13 (1980), pp 7, 16–17. Some engraved cartouches made reference to particular places and authors, like those of John Carty in Cork, later used by Dennis Carty (NLI, 21.F.152(2, 5); Cork Archives Institute, U. 137/Box 30). Perhaps the most prolific user of these aids was the Dublin City Surveyor of the 1740s and 1750s, Roger Kendrick, represented in the maps of St Patrick's Cathedral as well as in NLI, NAI and TCD, but none of Kendrick's plates could match the elegant portrayal of surveying instruments (signed G. Bertrand) seen on the maps of his successor Thomas Matthews (Dublin city muniments, C1/S1/80; NLI, 16.G.16(38)). A different medium, the wood block, seems to have printed the compass roses in NLI, MS 19848.
58. Advertisement of Pat Fitzpatrick, engraver and copperplate printer, *Volunteer Evening Post*, 24 June 1784. The engraved stick-on scale bars used by Josias Bateman on his Burlington estate maps of 1716–17 (NLI, MS 6148) appeared again in a Co. Waterford map of 1761 by John Brien (NLI, 16.J.6(4)).
59. Gibson, *Practical Surveying*, p. 318.
60. Wight's diary, 25 Sep. 1752.
61. *The Roman Print, both Capital and Small Letters, Necessary to be Taught in Mathematical, Drawing and Writing Schools*, by William Williams, writing-master, accomptant, and surveyor of land, in Drogheda (Dublin, 1751).
62. Extracts from the books of the Mercers' Company, 11 Mar. 1659, quoted in E. Freshfield and E. Freshfield junior, *A Statement of Facts Deduced from Ancient Records and Other Authentic Sources Relating to the Irish Estates of the City of London Companies in Ulster* (London, 1898), p. 228.
63. T. Knox, A survey of the lands of Termond Magragh, 1682, NLI, MS 19786, p. 2.
64. For examples see E. Lynam, *British Maps and Map-Makers* (London, 1944), p. 21, and *The Mapmaker's Art* (London, 1953), pp 17, 19; Essex Record Office, *The Art of the Map-Maker in Essex* (Chelmsford, 1947); F. Hull, *Catalogue of Estate Maps 1590–1840 in the Kent County Archives Office* (Maidstone, 1973).
65. Hamilton estate maps, 1625; Essex estate maps, 1635.
66. Thomond estate maps, Petworth papers, C.27/G.

67. 'A description of Thomastowne Deere Park, Decoy, and part of Rossnegrally belonging to the Honble George Mathew', in private possession.
68. 'A Resemblance of the Improvem^{ts} of Carretowne', reproduced in A. Horner, 'Carton, Co. Kildare: A Case Study of the Making of an Irish Demesne', *Bull. Ir. Georgian Soc.*, 18 (1975), Fig. 1.
69. Map of the manor of Lyons, Co. Dublin, 1801, by John Roe, NLI, 21. F.50(25), reproduced and discussed in National Library of Ireland, *Ireland from Maps* (Dublin, 1980), no. 10.
70. Such was William Beauford, whose map of Dunmore demesne, Queen's Co., is in NLI, 16.H.19(11). Demesnes were sometimes mapped by army officers, perhaps for their own diversion while staying as guests of the family. An example is the map of Ladistown, Co. Westmeath, in 1823, by 'H.S.S., Lt 29th Regiment' (NLI, 21.F.80(21)), presumably Henry Sykes Stephens, who is not otherwise known as a cartographer.
71. L. Price(ed.), *An Eighteenth Century Antiquary: the Sketches, Notes and Diaries of Austin Cooper (1759–1830)* (Dublin, 1942), p. 54, recording a visit to Brenanstown, Co. Dublin, in 1780; advertisement by James Williamson, *Belfast Newsletter*, 6 Nov. 1801.
72. Camblin, *Town in Ulster*, plates 4–13.
73. 27 Oct. 1724, Add. MS 46975, f.81.
74. Copies in Linen Hall Library, Belfast and in Add. MS 21131, reproduced in E. Parkinson, *The City of Downe from its Earliest Days* (Belfast, 1928, pp 85–6, 145. The map is attributed to James Maguire in *Downpatrick Civic Week: Catalogue of an Exhibition of Documents Illustrating the History of Downpatrick* (Public Record Office of Northern Ireland, Belfast, 1966), no. 8.
75. Add. MS 47043. Moland was also guilty on occasion of omitting houses in towns, notably in his map of Jamestown, Co. Leitrim, drawn in 1730 (Mountrath estate maps, TCD, Armytage deposit). His practice contrasts with that of Archibald Stuart and Philip Jackson in mapping the demesne lands of the manor of Pellipar, Co. Londonderry, in 1740 (wall map in Stationers' Hall, London). Alongside their house symbols Stuart and Jackson inserted roman figures to denote 'the number of houses or cabins standing together'. This could be interpreted as acknowledging that a correct enumeration of houses was not to be taken for granted in Irish estate maps. Perhaps significantly, Jackson was a London surveyor not otherwise recorded in Ireland.
76. Harvey, *Topographical Maps*, passim.
77. Correspondence on Rathcoursey, Co. Cork, 1737, TCD, MUN/P/23/1440.
78. TCD, Archbishop of Dublin's estate maps, 132 (33).
79. 7 July 1759, Surrey County Record Office, 1248/20/136.
80. 'Miscellaneous observations on Ireland', PRONI, T.2855/1, p. 13, from an original formerly in the Warwickshire County Record Office, Warwick. See also Marquess of Kildare, *Earls of Kildare*, p. 296.
81. Henry Hood, 28 Mar. 1804, PRONI, T.2541/IA3/4/10A.

82. J. H. Andrews, 'The French School of Dublin Land Surveyors', *Ir. Geogr.*, 5 (1967), pp 275–92.
83. *Freeman's Journal*, 13 Jan. 1770.
84. Scalé north-points are reproduced in G. C. Duggan, 'An Old Irish Estate Map', *Geogr. Mag.*, 27 (1954–5), pp 359–63 and in *Bull. Ir. Georgian Soc.*, 17 (1974), *passim*.
85. Andrews, *Jour. Kerry Arch. & Hist. Soc.*, 13 (1980), p. 31.
86. J. Varley, 'John Rocque: Engraver, Surveyor, Cartographer and Map-Seller', *Imago Mundi*, 5 (1948), pp 83–91; H. Phillips, 'John Rocque's Career', *London Topographical Record*, 20 (1952), pp 9–25.
87. *Cork Evening Post*, 5 June 1760.
88. Marquess of Lansdowne, *Glanerought*, pp 59–60.
89. *Sleater's Public Gazetteer*, 23 Sep. 1758; Bernard Scalé, *Tables for the Easy Valuing of Estates* (Dublin, 1771).
90. NLI, MS 22502 is a signed but roughly drawn and evidently much used version of Rocque's survey of the manor of Maynooth, in which colour is applied only to water, road fillings, houses, and boundary-edgings. Scalé followed the same system in his maps of the Devonshire estate in Cos. Cork and Waterford (1773–5). Three 'outline' volumes are NLI, MSS 7216–18 (21.F.131–3) and four 'fully coloured' volumes are at Chatsworth.
91. *Report from the Select Committee on Fisheries (Ireland)*, qq.5344–50, H.C. 1849 (536), xiii.
92. Scalé's outline lease maps are well represented in the Drogheda deeds (e.g. NLI, D.20741–20900), Sherrard's in the Domville papers (NLI, MSS 11840–51).
93. A. Horner ('New Maps of Co. Kildare Interest in the National Library of Ireland', *Jour. Kildare Arch. Soc.*, 15 (1975–6), pp 475–6) points out that farm boundaries appear on a preliminary map of one townland which Rocque may have submitted as a specimen before being appointed to map the rest. The lack of farm boundaries on some of Scalé's maps may explain a comment of 1773 in Co. Meath that 'Scalé's survey looks best on paper' but that a survey by the less eminent James Boyle would be better for setting farms (PRONI, T.3465/17).
94. Henry Walker of Islandbridge, Co. Dublin (RD,491/294/318116 (1795)), whose surviving estate maps belong to the period 1806–09, was presumably the Henry Walker referred to as an apprentice of John Brownrigg in 1794 (*Commons Journals, Ireland*, 15, ii, pp dcxx–dcxxi); see also R. Heard, *Public Works in Ireland, 1800–1831*, M. Litt. thesis, TCD (1977), p. 199. For other members of the French school see Andrews, *Ir. Geogr.*, 5 (1967), pp 83–92.
95. Advertisement by Mr Shine, drawing and writing master of Carlow, *Kilkenny Moderator*, 6 Feb. 1836.
96. This feature appears on the manuscript 'fair plans' of the original six-inch Ordnance Survey and on the printed one-inch townland indexes of the twentieth century, both described in Andrews, *History in the Ordnance Map*, pp 14, 46.

97. *Hibernian Journal*, 9 Apr. 1773. Jacob's extant estate maps are few and unrevealing. Those of A. R. Neville (presumed to be his son) certainly reflected French influence.
98. Benjamin Noble, *Geodaesia Hibernica*.
99. *Leinster Journal*, 18 Dec. 1773, 8 Jan. 1774.
100. *Hibernian Chronicle*, 2 Jan. 1783. Patrick may have been related to David Aher, who later claimed to have been brought up under his father in 'the French school of Rocque' (*Report on Survey and Valuation*, 1824, p. 108), but Patrick's surviving maps are not in the Rocque style.
101. *Western Argus and Ballinasloe Independent*, 30 Apr. 1828.
102. *Dublin Journal*, 27 May 1749. Barker's plans of 1762, showing both suburban and rural properties, are in the Pembroke Estate Office, Dublin. His plan of Merrion Square is reproduced in J. Harvey, *Dublin*, plate 135. On one occasion Barker was accused of assigning property to the wrong owner (PRONI, D.562/7632), but several Irish newspapers obituarised him as 'the greatest land surveyor in this kingdom' (e.g. *Leinster Journal*, 11 Nov. 1767). He is not to be confused with John Barker of Belfast, for whom some particulars are given in D. G. Lockhart, 'The Land Surveyor in Northern Ireland before the Coming of the Ordnance Survey *c.* 1840', *Ir. Geogr.*, 11 (1978), pp 103–04.
103. *Dublin Journal*, 2 Jan. 1772. An early (1773) map by Kenny in this style, of part of the Domville estate in Co. Meath, is in NLI, 21.F.103(4).
104. Richard Frizell's first use of this style seems to be in his maps of the Trinity College estates in 1775, one of which is reproduced in F. H. A. Aalen and R. J. Hunter, 'The Estate Maps of Trinity College', *Hermathena*, 98 (1964), pp 90–91.
105. John Travers, survey of Mountrath estate in Cos. Roscommon, Leitrim and Westmeath, 1770, NLI, MS 2793.
106. Richard Frizell, atlas of Trinity College estates, 1775, TCD, MUN/ME/4. A later example of diagrammatic-looking field boundaries is Richard Manning's atlas of the Shuldham estate, Co. Cork in 1801–03, NLI, MS 3025, illustrated and discussed in National Library of Ireland, *Ireland from Maps*, no. 11.
107. J. B. Cunningham, 'William Starrat Surveyor-Philomath', *Clogher Record*, 11 (1983), pp 214–25.
108. Starrat and the Hoods practised in the same area of west Tyrone and east Donegal (Gebbie, *Abercorn Letters*, pp 250–1). An early (1755) map by John Hood shows buildings in profile instead of in plan (NLI, 21.F.66(43–54)). His and his son's mature style is represented in PRONI, D.623/391/3; NAI, M.5862; NLI, MSS 5023, 5585. Crow's Irish maps date from the middle and late 1760s; see below, ch.8.
109. Guildhall Library, London, MS 7317(3), f.578.
110. Greig, *Gosford Estates*, pp x, 71, the former reproducing an advertisement by Greig and his partner John Hill printed in 1819. James Williamson had claimed to show individual ridges on his maps in *Belfast News-letter*, 6 Nov. 1801.

111. A fine example is Thomas Pattison's survey of the Hertford estate in Co. Antrim in 1833 (PRONI, D.427/8).
112. The 'naive' style was well exemplified by Patrick and Charles McQuaid and by John and James Niblock, all practising in Co. Cavan in *c.* 1830 (NAI, M.6178); and by Jeremiah O'Leary of Enniskean, Co. Cork, as late as 1899–1900 (Cork Archives Institute, U. 137/–/71, 72).
113. A good example of 'mechanical' decoration was the compass star in which each point consists of closely spaced parallel lines. The star was originally meant to give a grey effect when seen at a distance, and was used in this fashion in a map by Sherrard, Brassington and Greene of the manor of Clontarf in 1823 (Irish Society for Archives, Dublin), but by the 1840s, when the device was near the peak of its popularity, the individual lines had become unpleasantly obtrusive.
114. M. O'Flanagan (ed.), *Letters Containing Information Relative to the Antiquities of the County of Down Collected During the Progress of the Ordnance Survey in 1834* (Bray, 1928), p. 9.
115. *State of Ireland Considered with an Enquiry into the History and Operation of Tithe: and a Plan for Modifying that System, and Providing an Adequate Maintenance for the Catholic and Presbyterian Clergy* (2nd ed., Dublin, 1810), p. 86.

7
Remaking the landscape

IT WAS AS A GUARDIAN OF PROPERTY RIGHTS that the Irish land surveyor made his best-known contribution to the nation's life. Compared with this solemn duty his other functions must have seemed uninterestingly technical and arcane, at any rate to most of his contemporaries. Modern historical geographers have reacted more variously: many would attach less importance to the proprietorial than to the physical condition of the land, with crops, fields, houses and roads all claiming precedence over the forces that have placed them in position. These forces are sometimes called 'landlord activity', a convenient dismissal of numerous specialised occupations that might otherwise prove difficult to separate.

On the level of finance and decision-making, the Anglo-Irish landlord did indeed become more active as builder, planter and drainer in the later stages of the Ascendancy era. In mapping the future, as in mapping the present, he naturally began with his own house and its immediate vicinity. Outside the demesne wall he was slower to commit himself. Throughout the eighteenth century, his interference with tenanted land was usually confined to the partitioning of large farms, a process often implicit in the making of new lease maps and dealt with under that heading in an earlier chapter. The internal features of the head tenant's farm – and *a fortiori* the external boundaries of undertenant farms – were largely left alone. On most of the estate the landlord's interest was focused rather on the provision of communal infrastructures such as roads, streets, bridges, canals, drains, harbours and public buildings, some of it at his own expense, some through the medium of corporate bodies (which were usually composed of local landlords) such as grand juries, turnpike trusts and navigation boards. It was only after the Napoleonic wars that landlords seem to have done much rearranging of entire rural landscapes.

Any review of the surveyor's part in landscape-making must inevitably become an exercise in job demarcation. His co-workers were the engineer, the architect, the agriculturalist, the agent, the steward, the bailiff, and on occasion the landlord in person, all of whom could be involved in mapping improvements as well as in designing them. While some of these people had learned to make plans as part of their vocational training, others had simply found it a useful art to teach themselves, so that men seeking employment as stewards, for example, would often advertise their competence in land surveying.[1] Even for the proprietor himself, the drudgery of the map might be relieved by the pleasure of depicting the products of his own imagination. Barnaby Carroll in King's Co. was only one example of a landlord who drew a plan for improving his estate, complete with avenues, groves, orchards, and a new village; though happy for the village to be called Carrollstown, he refused to sign the plan with more than his initials, perhaps not wanting to be mistaken for a professional man.[2] In fact, and it is an unfortunate fact for the student of occupational categories, many such maps are without signatures of any kind, perhaps because they had none of the quasi-legal, witness-bearing character that belonged to the normal farm or estate map. For the same reason, mortality among planners' maps is discouragingly high. Apart from their lack of legal authority, they seldom displayed the polish and artistic merit of the best estate atlases, and were more likely than other surveys to suffer wear and tear in the field. These circumstances may explain why so few contemporary maps have been reproduced in the hundreds of pages written by Irish historians on the subject of landscape planning.

Even if a signed map survives, the business of putting a label on its author is by no means over. One problem is whether he should be classed as a land surveyor or not; this will be mentioned again in a later chapter. Another is that to make a drawing is not the same thing as to devise a plan: the surveyor may be no more than a recorder, not in this case of a real landscape but of the contents of someone else's mind; perhaps simply a copyist of someone else's sketch. The only way of recognising these possibilities at present is first to record a general impression of the whole subject, and then to illustrate the kind of evidence available to future researchers engaged in verifying or correcting that impression. The burden of the following pages, then, is that with one exception the part played by the Irish land surveyor in the design of new landscapes was relatively small. The exception is the remodelling of farms, so at least this hypothesis keeps the surveyor in the mainstream of his country's life.

Although maps and building-plans are often grouped together by librarians, in practice the distinction between them is usually quite sharp, except that the need to visualise a building in its context created an area of overlap when the candidates in an architectural competition were supplied with a map of the site[3] or (more rarely) when an architect gave a client a small-scale map showing the extent of the view from his new house.[4] A more important overlap took place in demesnes and parks, which from the seventeenth century onwards witnessed some of the most intensive planning in the history of rural Ireland. Much of the planner's work was destructive – farms extinguished, fields amalgamated, streams dammed or diverted, houses demolished, placenames consigned to oblivion. From the time of the plantations, however, the kind of pattern that replaced these lost landscapes must often have been laid out in map form, an early instance being the park created for Lord Conway in 1628.[5] Responsibility for such maps would have depended on fashions in parkmaking. As long as gardens were small and symmetrical, that is up to the late seventeenth century, they could be set out by the owner himself or by whichever of his employees did the actual planting. An unusually elaborate design might be the work of a professional architect, and indeed the enclosed and rigidly patterned gardens of the seventeenth century have often been likened to the floors and walls of a house rather than to any other kind of exterior. Even in the early Georgian period the walks through Phoenix Park were created by the architect William Dodson[6] and the gardens at Powerscourt by the architect Richard Castle.

As gardens grew more extensive, with paths and vistas stretching further from the house and at a greater variety of angles, so the task of drawing them became less like architecture and more like normal cartography. Ireland's earliest surviving garden design, an 'Ichnographia' of Dromoland, Co. Clare, in c. 1740, is a map in every sense of the word.[7] The affinity between map drawing and park design was further strengthened with the advent of the informal or naturalistic mode of landscaping pioneered by Mary Delany at Delville near Dublin in the 1730s, for in this style the walls, streams, verges and avenues were allowed to twist and turn in the manner of ordinary geographical features. It might seem that a deliberately 'negligent' park would hardly need to be set out on paper in advance. In fact the change in fashion simply brought a shift of cartographic emphasis from the artificial to the natural, for houses, tree-plantations and man-made (though accidental looking) lakes all had to be placed in sympathetic relations to the fall of the land.

Support for this interpretation comes from a map of Carton park in which, as early as 1744, two not very well known surveyors (Charles Baylie and John Mooney) produced something remarkably similar to contour lines.⁸ While their map is seemingly unique, would-be gardeners continued throughout the eighteenth century to claim skill in surveying as well as in the designing of rural improvements.⁹ In a demesne the size of Carton such skill was indispensable. Of James Donnell, who worked in the even larger Phoenix Park, it was deduced from his map that although he had been a gardener to Lady Massereene he must also have some knowledge of surveying; but that did not make Donnell a surveyor, and in his own publicity he confined himself to 'improving and decorating ... domains and conducting buildings of every denomination'.¹⁰ Gardening, like so many occupations that overlapped with surveying, required talents less common than the ability to measure and draw. In his public face, too, the gardener differed from the typical surveyor: one difference was his habit of advertising anonymously and of failing to sign his plans; another was his tendency to claim experience in England, a boast unusual among early Irish land surveyors unless they professed to be agricultural improvers as well. Contrariwise, it was rare for established land surveyors to undertake the laying out of parks and gardens, and the subject is never mentioned in Irish surveying literature. To assert proficiency in both occupations may have been a sign of second-rateness, as with the Mr Weldon, 'a limner, a projector of gardens, and a land surveyor', whose only claim on public attention was to be accused of stealing a horse.¹¹

Outside the park gates stood the estate town, its straight wide streets leading to the carefully chosen sites of courthouse and Protestant church. The practice of drawing new towns before they were built is one of the few kinds of Irish cartography that pre-date the first recorded plantation surveys and the first recorded professional land surveyors. The plan of a proposed new building at Mullingar was sent to London as early as 1567,¹² and in July 1581 Sir Nicholas Malby submitted a 'plot of the house at Roscommon and of the new town, which God willing I will finish in performance of my promise.'¹³ He never did finish it, which perhaps was not surprising in a project that included no less than five new streets. Malby's streets were parallel straight lines; another common urban lay-out was the checkered grid, as in the 'pattern to make the town by' which appears in a map of Derry from *c.* 1600. The Derry map features an early Irish example of pecked lines to show developments not yet executed, but this useful convention was slow to take root and some seventeenth-century cartographers drew real and imaginary houses in much the same style and with equal enthusiasm.¹⁴ Since most of these early plans were drawn by government employees they have a fair chance of being mentioned in extant records. Unfortunately Thomas Raven was the last (maybe also the first) man who claimed an official title as comprehensive as surveyor of lands, fortifications and buildings.[15] It is true that the fortifications of Dublin were mapped by the land surveyor Robert Newcomen in the 1660s,[16] but by that time town planning had become a matter of mainly civil and private concern and correspondingly elusive in the historical record.

This is all the more frustrating when one considers how many new towns, villages, suburbs and streets were planned in Ireland during and after the late seventeenth century. The first generation included Charleville, Lisburn, Blessington, Newtown Forbes, Lanesborough and Kilrush, as well as Oxmantown Green and St Stephen's Green in Dublin, but even the minutest research has yielded no more than a single advance plan relating to this whole group of projects – an outline of King Street, Bennet Street, James Street and Queen Street in the town of Portarlington, dated 1678, which qualifies for inclusion here by distinguishing certain sites as 'built' and so implying that others would be similarly treated at some future date.[17] The eighteenth and nineteenth centuries are not much better off. On the ground, of course, numerous square, linear, cruciform and T-shaped lay-outs, and a few crescents, still proclaim the influence of the planner-draughtsman, and some of them have attracted close attention from modern architects and topographers, notably Westport, Maynooth, Slane, Fermoy and Mitchelstown. While early plans survive for a number of these places, there are few that can be shown to pre-date the buildings they depict, even where the relevant estate maps have been carefully catalogued, as at Hillsborough in Co. Down.[18] In one admirable survey of early maps of Northern Ireland it is only at Cookstown (1736) that a main street is said to have been mapped in advance of its construction.[19] The problem is even worse with schemes that were never brought to fruition, like Ballymote with its four seventy-foot-wide streets and its central octagon of 180 feet diameter.[20]

Even where we have a map its sources are usually obscure. Jonathan Barker did not necessarily design the prototype of Fitzwilliam Street that appears on one of his Dublin estate maps. It is true that he had taken part in the laying-out of Merrion Square a few years earlier (an occasion marked by drinks all round) but only in company with a 'projector' known unhelpfully as John Smith.[21] Nor should John Rocque be held responsible for the intended new street shown on his map of Newry. Even to name the surveyor as a maker of improvements may not quieten the sceptics.

Thus when Arthur Richards Neville received the freedom of Monaghan in gratitude for improving the town, the effect was spoiled by nominating someone else (Lieutenant General Robert Cunningham) as 'director' of the works in question.[22]

Not surprisingly, it is in Dublin that the creators of Irish Georgian urbanism are most richly documented. The City Surveyor for instance can be seen to have done much more than measure land, for his duties as laid down in 1674 included looking after sewers and watercourses and setting out the foundations of houses. Eighteenth-century holders of his office are found taking levels for pavements and pipes, staking out new streets, and recommending new lots for building.[23] New thoroughfares were also the business of another Dublin body with its own surveyor, the wide streets commissioners established in 1757.[24] Exposed to the glare of metropolitan publicity, town surveyors met two kinds of rivalry from outside their own profession. On the one hand stood the enthusiastic amateur. With the aid of a good base map, such as Rocque's *Exact Survey* of the city published in 1756, any Dubliner with pencil and ruler could easily open up a few building blocks in his imagination, in one instance by running a continuation of Moore Street across the Liffey to a point between Trinity College and the Parliament House.[25] This kind of table-top street-making soon became popular enough to draw satirical comment from a member of the House of Lords, who found something 'very ludicrous' about the idea of the wide streets commission gathered over a map of Dublin with each commissioner cutting and carving out his own favourite frontages and intersections.[26] In 1785 the commission was said to have been drawn into many errors and put to much expense by ignorant and incapable projectors.[27]

As it happened, the wide streets commissioners found an exceptionally versatile land surveyor to advise them on a variety of topics (he gets more attention in a later chapter), but that was only rather late in the day. Parliament Street, the successful enterprise that had given birth to the wide-streets idea, was the creation of a man who had no reputation in ordinary surveying but who could be variously described as an inventor, projector, architect and engineer, namely George Semple.[28] Such jacks-of-all-trades could also be found in the provinces: Michael Priestley, designer of extensions to the town of Strabane for the Earl of Abercorn, was only one of a number of small-town characters who appear to have been cast in the Semple mould and who shared Semple's lack of commitment to routine cartography.[29]

In the meantime the higher branches of the architectural and engineering professions were beginning to diverge, but without either of them vacating the expansive field of urban design. It was an architect, Thomas Ivory, who laid out new building plots at Oxmantown in *c.* 1776;[30] and a canal engineer, Colonel Charles Tarrant, whom the wide streets commission appointed to advise it nine years later.[31] Outside Dublin the same kind of work-sharing is recorded in several nineteenth-century sources. An engineer assisted Lord Midleton in the setting out of Midleton and Cove (Cobh),[32] while the architects W. J. Booth and William Tite helped in choosing new streets for the towns and villages of the London Companies' estates at the other end of the country.[33] Plans of mines and factories form another 'grey area' involving professional men of more than one kind, and although in a country like Ireland industrial maps are hardly an important issue, it would still be interesting to know who drew certain plans of the underground coal workings at Ballycastle, Co. Antrim, that were said to date from 1725.[34]

Away from the towns, the most active planning of new landscape features in the eighteenth century was in the field of communications. The grand jury act of 1727 required that 'able, knowing and skilful' persons should be made surveyors or directors of new county road projects.[35] Surveying in this context may have meant simply overseeing rather than exercising the skills of the trained measurer, though genuine land surveyors were often used by contemporary landlords in laying out estate roads (or conversely in dividing unwanted roads among the adjacent farms)[36] as well as in illustrating schemes that the same landlords had prepared for submission to the grand jury as possible county roads; and eventually the grand juries themselves became an important if badly-documented source of professional employment.[37] Whoever was responsible for them, Ireland's early eighteenth-century highways show little evidence of an eye for country. Many of them appear to have been planned by erecting poles in straight lines from town to town or from one landmark to another in the manner of the Romans, who in a classically-minded era were sometimes held up as models to the Irish roadmaker. In this way hills were often disregarded; or, in extreme cases, avoided by semi-circular deviations as rigid in their geometry as the remainder of the road. The importance attached to minimising horizontal distance appears in the frequency with which the early eighteenth-century land surveyor is found simply measuring the length of a road, or of an intended road, rather than exhibiting its relationship to physical or human geography.[38]

However, taking measurements itself becomes a modification of the landscape when the surveyor marks its progress with a line of milestones. Irish road mileages remained in a state of disarray well into the eighteenth century. A good deal of legislation embodied distance limits of one kind or another, but often without properly specifying any particular unit.[39] According to one such law of 1719, a chapel of ease could be built in any parish where there were members of the Protestant faith living more than six miles from the parish church. But were they to be 'measured' miles (whatever that might mean in this context) or 'country' miles? And were there two measured miles to every country mile, or one and a half?[40] It was in the 1730s that such uncertainties began to be dispelled by actual measurement. It was at this time, too, that mileages began to assume a more explicitly financial significance – for example in postal charges, in fares for public transport, and in the granting of state bounties on the carriage of corn. At first the surveyor's role was as much to complain about the inaccuracy of the milestones set up by masons or quarrymen as to provide more exact replacements of his own.[41] Such accusations could involve something worse than incompetence: more than one inn-keeper was charged with deliberately causing stones to be too widely spaced in the hope of enticing travellers towards his establishment under the erroneous impression that it would shorten their journey. In this way the land surveyor's traditional quarrels about acreage could be translated into equally acrimonious one-dimensional terms (though nobody has yet found a milestone signed by a land surveyor and countersigned by a witness), with standards of accuracy that were correspondingly sharp.[42] In two independent measurements of the route from Dublin via Ashbourne to Drogheda (another road whose milestones were said to have been clandestinely uprooted and relocated) the difference in controversy was only $4^{1}/_{4}$ perches in about 22 Irish miles.[43] That was in the 1820s; not long afterwards the Ordnance Survey began gradually to bring an end to such disputes, often by answering letters from correspondents who were unwilling to take their own measurements from the Survey's published six-inch map.

If the eighteenth-century surveyor's task was simply to prove one route shorter than another, his road map need show little more than two lines and a few placenames – if a road was to be made dead straight the map had only to mark the old line and leave the clients to insert the new one, though usually the cartographer would do that himself (Plate 15). From the middle of the century such maps are represented in a number of

REMAKING THE LANDSCAPE 195

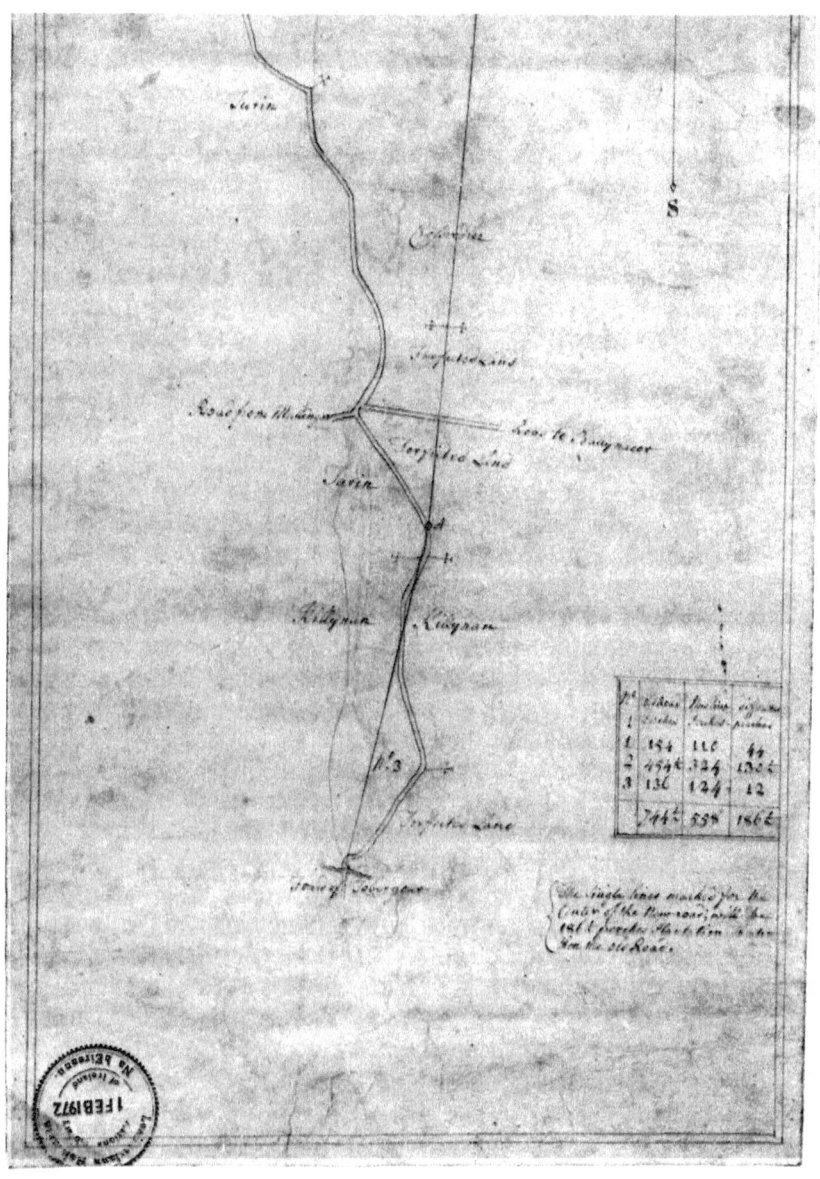

Plate 15. From Thomas Cuttle's survey of roads in the parish of Rathconnell, Co. Westmeath, 1752 (see chapter 7, note 36). Scale of original approximately 32 perches to one inch. Cuttle's proposal appears never to have been carried out, but many other Irish roads were straightened in the eighteenth century as a result of surveys like this.

estate collections, the traditional 'reference' table of acres giving way to a prominently placed subtraction-sum whose answer was the difference in perches between the old and new lines. However, the main emphasis in eighteenth-century road cartography fell on networks rather than individual lines, with so many new roads being projected that there was an inescapable need for large county maps on which the rival schemes could be pencilled in. These maps will be discussed in detail later. They began to be made in the 1730s and 1740s and were supported by Parliament from 1774. Fifty years later every grand jury had its county map and some had two. Their effect was to help revolutionise the single-road or strip map by showing that the local road planner needed considerably more topographical knowledge of his chosen area than he could hope to get from a general county map.

Significantly, the first single-line road maps requested by Parliament, in 1751, had been those that would show a connection between mines and navigable waterways.[44] The exploitation and transportation of largely non-existent minerals presented a serious if delusory problem to eighteenth-century Irish opinion, and gave a powerful stimulus to the development of canals as well as roads. The first canal proposals, contained in an act of 1715, bear all the marks of the armchair geographer and the surveys on which they purported to depend were probably done by travelling at speed across the country with no more cartographic endeavour than looking at a small-scale atlas map.[45] Of the first detailed scheme, for a canal between Newry and Lough Neagh, it was said that an illiterate man had been employed to take the levels and an ignorant man to make the survey (each working independently of the other), while a third had exhibited a 'senseless, useless though beautiful nothing'. The writer did not say which of these three men was Francis Neville, the only surveyor to be mentioned by name in other references to the Newry canal.[46]

But the competence of Neville's co-workers is not much of an issue in the present context. Many an Irish canal-maker has been named by modern industrial historians, but very few are known to have flourished as land surveyors.[47] On the other hand at least one simple surveyor of canals (the one the Grand Canal Company was trying to recruit in 1773) has remained ignominiously nameless, if indeed he ever existed, as well as being kept subordinate to the company's engineer.[48] In the 'eighties, it is true, the occasional land surveyor can be found offering inland navigations as part of his service,[49] and one of Scalé's pupils, John Brownrigg, did achieve considerable eminence in both fields.[50] But most canal-minded estate surveyors either failed to rise from obscurity – like Thomas Cuttle, whose route from Lough Allen to Sligo is still unfinished – or else preferred to play safe with straightforward mapping operations under the command of a proper engineer, as when Thomas Williams and John Cooley mapped the northern line of the Grand Canal for Thomas Omer in 1756.[51]

The one concomitant of a canal survey that would not often occur in ordinary estate work was levelling, and it may have been experience with canal levels that helped, from the 1760s onwards, to popularise a new and more relief-conscious theory of road design. Another influence, this time from within the field of cartography itself, was that of the military sketch surveys done by army officers like Charles Vallancey, which put much emphasis on the representation of hills and which sometimes contributed directly to the planning of new military roads.[52] Perhaps more important was the need for gentler gradients to accommodate Ireland's increasingly heavy road traffic, notably in corn, and also its increasing number of fast passenger vehicles. The results were seen in turnpike legislation providing that new roads should run not just in more direct lines, as previously required, but in lines that were as far as possible both flatter and straighter. To begin with, flatness was treated in an essentially qualitative spirit. When Hugh O'Neill hired surveyors to prove that travellers would not lengthen their journey by patronising his horse and chaise hire service at Balbriggan, he published the relative distances correct to the nearest yard (in fact the Balbriggan route was slightly longer) and then concluded rather lamely that the difference in gradient was obvious to everybody. Such imprecision was still typical of the 1770s.[53] What brought quantitative gradients into fashion was the law providing for mailcoach roads to be laid out by the Post Office, whose surveyors were first told simply to avoid the hills and precipices and later (in 1805) to aim at gradients less than 1 in 35.[54] Two of these late eighteenth-century influences came together when a military engineer, Major Alexander Taylor, was appointed 'inspector of designs and surveys of post roads'.[55] As can be seen from the many loops and re-entrants on his own military road through the Wicklow Mountains, the inspector took his orographic responsibilities seriously: 'I confess it appeared somewhat ludicrous', wrote one observer in reference to the best-known member of Taylor's staff, 'to behold Mr Larkin's clerks employing mathematical instruments and exhibiting all the parade of scientific measurement, to show, what every quick eye could have seen just as well without them – where a coach might run with least interruption from hills.'[56]

Whether or not travellers really derived much direct benefit from them, the mailcoach road maps were magnificent specimens of cartographic art,[57] and can hardly have failed to influence the surveying and building of county, turnpike and private roads. The following clause, in an act relating to the first of these three categories, was clearly framed by a close student of Taylor's work:

> Whenever any such application shall be for the making any new road or line of road, whatever the proposed length of such road shall be, or for the widening any old road, or for the lowering any hill, or for the filling up of any hollow in any line of road, the map or plan accompanying the estimate on such application shall be drawn up on a scale not less than that of 20 perches to an inch; and such map or plan shall correctly exhibit the ground plan of every such proposed road, and also of every adjoining public road or highway with which it may be necessary or desirable to compare it, in order to determine on the expediency of complying with such application; and such map or plan shall also be shaded in such manner as to represent and exhibit the situation of all hills occurring on the line of any such proposed or existing road, and also shall exhibit all streams of water which may run or flow across any such proposed or existing road, and all bogs or marshes through which any such proposed or existing road may pass, and the boundaries and denominations of all such townlands as any such road shall traverse, so far as they are respectively intersected by the said road, and all houses standing or being within ten perches of any such proposed or existing road respectively, and the names of the occupying tenants thereof respectively, and every such map or plan shall be accompanied by a perpendicular section of every such proposed and existing road, and in the case of a new road by a cross section likewise of the same, showing the intended form of the said new road, and the depth and position of the materials to be employed thereon; the scale of which section or sections shall be in such proportion to the ground plan of such proposed and existing roads, as shall be convenient for the due comparison of such sections and ground plans with each other, and every such map and perpendicular section shall show in every part of all such proposed or existing roads, and of all such hills and hollows as shall be delineated in such map, the degree of rise or fall and inclination or declination (expressed in feet and inches) of every part of the surface of such roads, hills, and hollows respectively, and the height (expressed in feet and inches) of every part of such surface above the base line thereof.[58]

This formidable mixture of lawyer's and cartographer's prose may well be unique in the annals of Parliament. In minuteness of detail it went beyond any specification ever imposed on the Irish Ordnance Survey, and although sectional drawings now became common it is improbable that even the Post Office's own surveyors managed to comply with every single requirement of the act. Contemporary opinion on this point is hard to find; but in 1828, after a mailcoach road in Co. Armagh had been approved by the grand jury, the survey describing it was publicly branded by three independent practitioners as 'grossly erroneous', with a horizontal error of some 22 per cent in about eleven miles and altitudinal errors of up to 80 feet. The critics fought their battle with weapons reminiscent of the previous generation and its quarrels over farm-size: they offered to pay the professional fee of any third party who could prove them wrong, or alternatively to accept the arbitration of an acknowledged expert.[59] The expert of their choice was an eminent engineer, but at least one of the complainants, Joseph James Byrne, had been better known for some time as a land surveyor and valuator. There were also a number of other good Irish land surveyors who made a speciality of high-quality road work. One of them, William Greig, wrote his own book on the subject;[60] some, like Greig and Mr Larkin's anonymous 'clerks', had actually worked for the Post Office. But on the whole the effect of the new interest in gradients was to take Ireland's longer and more important roads beyond the reach of the ordinary local land measurer and into the jurisdiction of the civil engineer. In the planning of railways the engineer's supremacy can obviously go without saying, though at least one land surveyor is known to have worked on the Dublin-Drogheda railway.[61]

Much the same seems to have happened in the case of land drainage. The surveyor's contribution to this subject was somewhat optimistically taken for granted in a famous essay by Archbishop William King.[62] In reality, to judge from an incident on the Perceval estate, the beginning of the eighteenth century found Ireland's bogs and marshes in a technological as well as an ecological no-man's land. At some time before 1701 a local land surveyor, Thomas Smith, had produced a map showing nearly seven miles of river between Annagh and Buttevant, identifying rock obstructions, measuring the head of water (28 feet), and showing how the adjacent grounds could be made productive if the river was lowered, widened and cleansed. When the subject came up again twenty years later, however, the new local surveyor (Smith's son) found himself ignored, not just because he was in disgrace for recently having made a bad farm survey but because the bog was now to be inspected and surveyed by no less an authority than Captain John Perry, famous for his work on the River Thames at Dagenham. Perry happened to be in Dublin at the time (in 1725 he was to make a plan of its harbour) and Perceval thought it worth offering him twenty guineas to report on Annagh bog. In the end, however, the task fell to a local resident who was neither a surveyor nor a professional engineer but simply a 'man of judgement'. To round off the story, when it came to the point Smith's map was found to be of little value.[63] Another twenty years later, a similar decision was taken on the Fitzwilliam estate in Co. Wicklow when a threatened incursion of the sea was to be met by seeking help from England or Holland rather than from any of the estate's usual surveyors.[64] The same must have applied to taking the offensive outwards across a coastline. The Londonderry land surveyor David McCool was able in 1795 to 'divide' the waters of Sheephaven and Dunfanaghy Bay by the same methods that he would have used for dividing a townland; but few people can have expected him to change the water into land, and two hundred years later the bays remain unreclaimed.[65]

One of the resemblances between the landed property and the sovereign state is that a natural watercourse can provide both parties with a good reason for transcending legal boundaries. Flood control and river navigation were among the few subjects capable of inspiring three or more proprietors to collaborate in the sponsorship of a single survey.[66] But the multipartite estate map remains among the rarest of cartographic phenomena, and vast areas of Ireland were still more or less waterlogged at the beginning of the nineteenth century. The only solution was an appeal to super-proprietorial authority, and in the reforming period after the creation of the United Kingdom, when farm prices had been raised by the Napoleonic wars, the government accordingly appointed commissioners to inquire into the nature and extent of the bogs of Ireland and the practicability of draining and cultivating them.[67] In 1809 the commissioners chose a number of engineers, each of whom was given the responsibility of finding his own subordinate surveyors. They were to make maps at a scale of four inches to a mile, showing the limits of all bogs of more than 500 acres in extent, the nature of the contiguous soil, the courses of rivers, roads and canals whether existing or proposed, and the drains and other works that they believed necessary to convert wet land into dry. Heights would be given in relation to a datum on the base of the Nelson Pillar (then newly erected in Dublin) and lines of levelling would be so arranged as to 'cross and correct each other'. Permanent marks were to be left at the extremities of

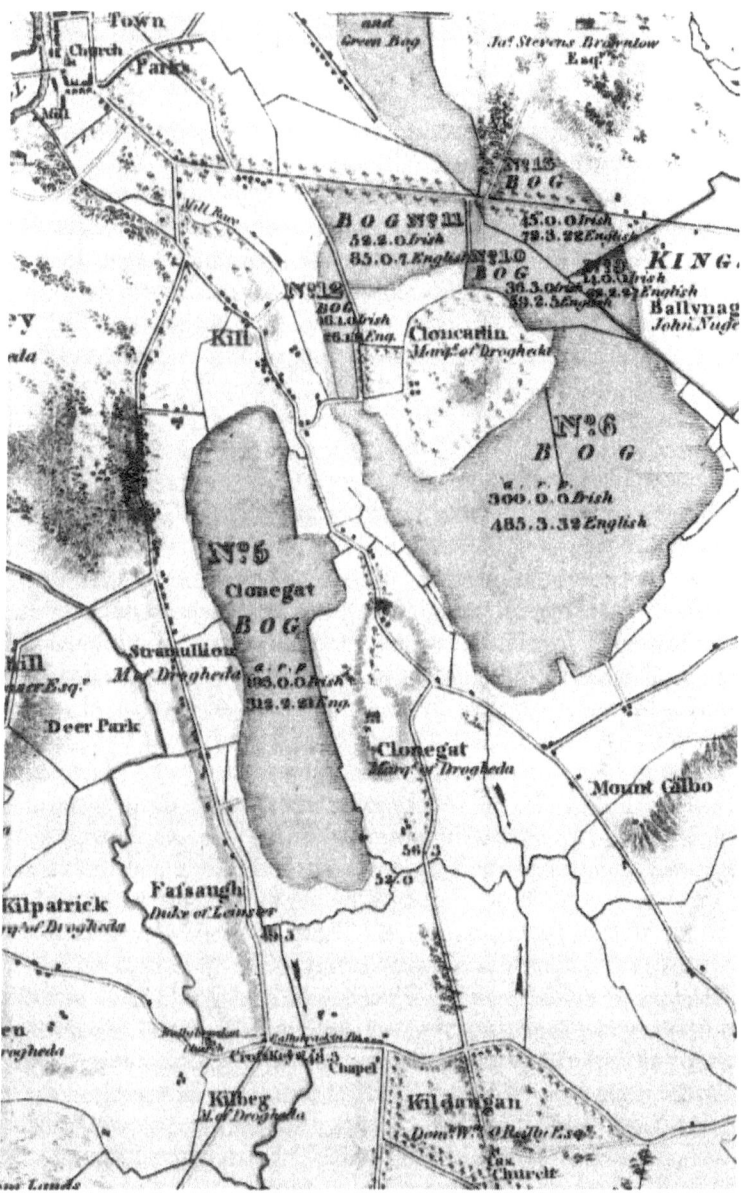

Plate 16. Bogs near Monasterevan, Co. Kildare, surveyed for the bogs commission by Sherrard, Brassington and Greene, engraved by James Basire, with bogs hand-coloured, and published in 1814 (see chapter 7, note 67). Scale of original 160 perches to one inch. Most of the maps made for the bogs commission were produced by civil engineers rather than by land surveying firms like Sherrard's.

these lines, while towers, raths and hilltops were to appear on the maps as a means of facilitating subsequent trigonometrical operations. In their emphasis on altitude and slope, the results bore a family resemblance to the Post Office road maps made at about the same time.

The bogs commissioners were discriminating in their choice of personnel. A known canal engineer was sure of a welcome; ordinary land surveyors found themselves unceremoniously passed over. The final selection yielded a unique assemblage of talent, including names that were to become nationally famous in several areas of Irish public life. Only two of the commission's 'engineers' came from the world of farm and estate surveying, and it was natural that they should betray occasional signs of an inferiority complex. John Longfield was over-anxious to emphasise the trigonometrical basis of his bog surveys. Richard Brassington preferred to anticipate his critics by striking the first blow, in the form of some sharp comments on the base map of Co. Kildare (a derivative of Alexander Taylor's map of 1783) supplied by his employers. He then showed off his estate-surveyor's knowledge by augmenting the same map with a mesh of townland boundaries, perhaps in oblique allusion to the fact that his less experienced engineer-colleague, Richard Griffith, at work in a neighbouring district, had failed to elicit the relevant estate survey from its custodian (Plate 16). None of this by-play disguised the success with which the engineers had come to dominate another important area of medium-scale surveying and cartography.[68]

Thus wherever he turned in the field of landscape planning the surveyor's fate was to meet someone more expert than himself. Even on the farm he found a rival in the kind of 'agriculturalist' personified by Arthur Young. But here if nowhere else he managed to hold his own, at any rate until even straightforward map-making began to fall victim to the engineers of the Ordnance Survey department in the 1830s. At first the surveyor's main chance to influence the landscape of the ordinary tenant farm was through exhortation, perhaps in the remarks column on the reference page of an estate atlas, perhaps in a special introduction or appendix. Such prescriptions have a long history – Raven, Moland and Starrat were all notable exponents – but it is as manifestoes of the agricultural revolution that they make most of a showing; and in manifesto-writing no one excelled the Frizell family of Co. Wexford who never tired of advising the client to improve his fences or rotate his crops, and who rivalled Young himself in the precision of their recipes for spreading fertiliser and for mixing seed. The difference is that while

Young is the best known agriculturalist in Irish history the Frizells are still waiting to be rescued from oblivion (Appendix A).

If exhortations failed (as it seems most of them did) then maybe money would succeed. As noted in an earlier chapter, some landlords inserted covenants about building, fencing and planting in their leases and then gave a rent rebate if the provisions of these covenants were met. From the 1740s this policy was institutionalised by the Dublin Society. The Society's system of premiums was inspired by Dr Samuel Madden (consequently nicknamed Premium Madden) and among its beneficiaries were farmers who manured unusually large amounts of land with marl, lime, limestone-gravel, or sand, as well as those who could extract a record wheat yield from a measured acre of ground. Premiums for planting were also reckoned by the acre, or by the perch when the trees followed the edge of an old fort, mound, rath, mote or churchyard.[69] Claims for premiums had to be supported by a surveyor's affidavit sworn before a Justice of the Peace. A famous case in point was the unprecedentedly heavy wheat crop grown on a rectangle of ten by sixteen perches marked out by the Co. Tipperary surveyor James Purcell in 1742.[70] A number of similar schemes were promoted by local farming societies and also by the Irish Linen Board which employed land surveyors to certify the acreage devoted to flax.[71]

Calculating inputs and yields in the manner of the Dublin Society gave an advantage to orderly farm lay-outs in which the area of each field could be easily determined. Straight lines meeting at right angles were obviously best: it was a lone voice that held straightness to be unsuited to the irregularity of Ireland's relief and the density of its stream network.[72] Theorists proposed ideal farm shapes[73] and surveyors had the chance to create them, combining their traditional concern for boundaries with a newer and more positive role. Although it was planning on a humble scale, with sufficient ingenuity the imposition of a new fieldscape could be made to look difficult enough. In Co. Kilkenny in 1802, for instance, a Mr Barton divided his fields:

> in acres by means of trees; the field is first accurately surveyed, and at the intersection of each acre, he plants either a horse chestnut, timber sallow, birch, or Scotch fir; this may be done though the fences are irregular: one ditch being taken as the base; the fractional parts will be marked on the map, as well as the complete acres, and all equally known by the trees; the angle of every acre at the fence, has also its tree, which must differ from those in the hedge-rows.[74]

Outside the home farms of progressive landlords, the surveyor could either design new holdings or remodel old ones (Fig. 6). The large amount of waste land believed by experts to be potentially useful in a country beset by poverty and overpopulation was a subject of much debate in eighteenth- and nineteenth-century Ireland, and there was a growing literature on the best way of reclaiming it. Landlords were often advised to bear some of the initial costs of reclamation by drainage works, fences and farm roads, as well as by gravelling and manuring the land and perhaps taking one or two preliminary crops from it before the prospective tenant moved in. An early instance was the reclamation of 5,000 acres of such land around Collon, Co. Louth, by the local landlord John Leslie Foster, who converted it into eighty-acre farms with fields of ten acres each and in the process laid out 70,000 perches of new fence. The Collon project was enthusiastically welcomed by Arthur Young – for all his vigilance and optimism it was almost the only totally new farmscape in his book – and he himself took part in a similar campaign on the Galtee Mountains of Tipperary.[75] Another advocate of the ten-acre field was Bernard Scalé on the Devonshire estate: although it never materialised, his plan has the further interest of coming from a professional surveyor.[76] In fact, to judge from the ratio of 'evolved' to 'planned' landscapes on Ireland's former bogs and mountains, this method of reclamation was less important in practice than in theory.

A special case of rural landscape making was the division of commons, at first by private or local arrangement, later by act of Parliament. The former method had a long history, an early example being John Young's survey of the commons at Naas in 1679–81.[77] Parliamentary enclosure was a familiar process in eighteenth-century Westminster. Its importation to Ireland foreshadowed the coming political union, and after two parishes had been dealt with individually (Dromiskin, Co. Louth, in 1800 and Garristown, Co. Dublin, in 1803) a general Irish Enclosure Act was debated by the United Kingdom Parliament.[78] The general legislation was a failure,[79] but the trickle of parochial acts went on for several decades, mainly affecting certain areas of common land that had survived in the English Pale (Fig. 7). Each act nominated commissioners who were free to appoint any surveyor with no personal interest in the commons, though (as often with official map-making in the nineteenth century) they were also empowered to use any existing survey that they believed to be accurate and authentic. The surveyor's duty was to map the surface features at an appropriate scale or scales, and then to divide the common

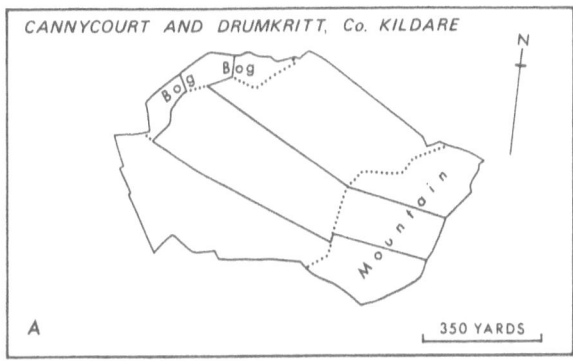
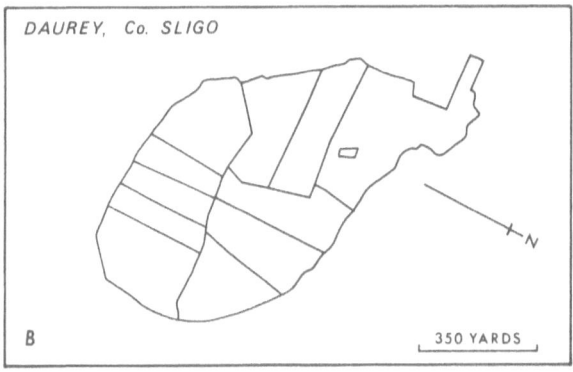
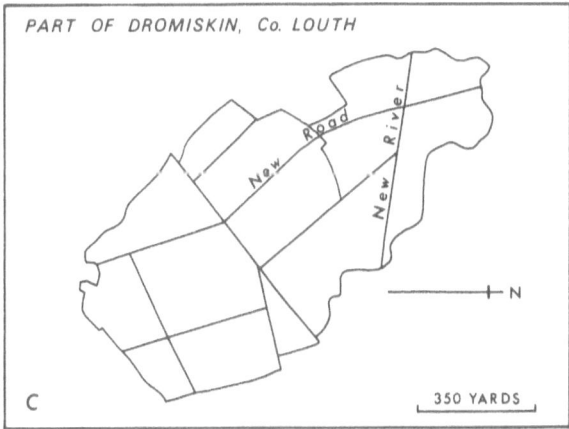

Figure 6. Farm boundaries laid out by surveyors.
A. Co. Kildare, 1703. Source: NLI, 16.H.14(8).
B. Co. Sligo, c. 1800. Source: NLI, 21.F.2.
C. Co. Louth, c. 1800. Source: NLI, MS 9041.

into lots so that each party who had an interest in it could be given land in corresponding proportion, a deduction being made to cover legal expenses and the cost of the survey. Lots to be offered for sale would be shown on a map exhibited at the Exchange coffee house in Dublin.[80] Though simple enough in theory, enclosure did not always go according to plan. At Ballymore Eustace, the official surveyors were driven off with threats of murder and the local people divided the common among themselves, presumably with the help of a somewhat apprehensive country surveyor. In this case, according to the commissioners, it would have taken a force of fifty soldiers to enforce the act.[81]

The surveyor's most dramatic achievement was replacing old farm boundaries by new ones in land already under cultivation, a process often combined with the 'dividing' considered in an earlier chapter although logically distinct from it. An elementary case was the 'balance' survey, in which a crooked boundary was straightened by a 'give-and-take' line with equal amounts of land exchanged between neighbouring proprietors. This kind of bargain was recognised by the Irish Parliament in 1721;[82] it could thenceforth be imposed by any improver upon a recalcitrant neighbour provided that the resulting change of ownership did not affect more than two plantation acres in every hundred perches of fence.[83]

As landlords came to assume a more direct responsibility for undertenants' farms, so the task of setting out equivalent areas became more complex. After the Napoleonic wars, in particular, disapproval of the middleman, an attitude which for many years had produced few results apart from a feeling of self-satisfaction among non-middlemen, at last began to achieve some practical consequences. Absentee tenants were disliked as a drain on income especially obnoxious in a period of agricultural depression; and condemned in an increasingly high-minded age for the crippling rents they extracted from the undertenant without having done anything to earn them. Their original function, to save the landlord administrative trouble, was becoming less useful as estate management grew more professional. Eliminating the middleman confronted the landlord with aspects of rural Ireland that may not have been shown on his maps and rentals, and especially with the effects of recent population growth. Townlands that had been let as single farms around 1780 were suddenly found to be teeming with subtenants in a state of quarrelsome poverty and squalor. For when life was short and families large, the effects of partible inheritance among small farmers could be spectacular. If unplanned and unsupervised it could quickly

Figure 7. Parliamentary enclosure, 1800–29. Sources: *Statutes at Large, Ireland; United Kingdom Statutes, Local and Personal.* An act for the enclosure of Castleisland, Co. Kerry, was passed in 1824. The act for Callan also included the parishes of Coolagh and Knocktopher.

bring chaos to the layout of farms and fields. In particular, it could reduce the rundale system to a shambles.[84]

The term 'rundale' is used in Arthur Young's *Tour* to denote the intermixture of different farmers' plots in a single arable field. The word was by no means universally familiar – it meant nothing to one intelligent farmer in Co. Louth as late as 1845[85] – but country people everywhere in Ireland knew the phenomenon to which it was applied. What rundale seemed most to express was a desire for equality, each farmer being required to share the various soil types in his townland: this at least was the motive imputed by Sir Henry Piers in the amusing account of Westmeath agriculture that he wrote in 1682.[86] But subdivision could increase the degree of intermixture beyond all reason when every separate plot was split into two or more pieces at each change of tenure. It could also cause rundale to appear from nowhere, belying the theory that it is necessarily a practice of great antiquity. Another local report from 1845 was that 'there is no rundale except a man has two or three sons, and lets them have some of the land'.[87]

The normal unit of rundale settlement was the 'village'. Modern Irish scholarship has been reluctant to apply this term, because although the houses of rundale farmers stood close together in groups of half a dozen or so, perhaps many more, the clusters were too poor to support the triad of church, inn and blacksmith's shop which geographers educated outside Ireland associate with traditional village life. Nor were the houses of the cluster necessarily aligned along definite streets: more often the grouping was formless and irregular. For these reasons a quasi-technical term – 'clachan' – has been generally adopted for a rundale village. What the clachan-dwellers did with their land is more easily discovered in modern academic literature than in any authentic historical source. The usual version is that adjoining the houses, gardens and farmyards, often on the downhill side of them, lay an arable field, fertilised every year and so kept always in cultivation, normally for oats. Within this single spread of tillage the land of any one farmer might be divided into ten or more separate plots, perhaps no larger than a rood in size, more or less rectangular in shape but not so long or sinuous as the plough strips of medieval villages in England and the English Pale. Instead of stockproof barriers, the plots of different farmers were divided by a low grass balk or a line of stones. In winter, after harvest, all the farmers' cattle would be allowed to graze freely on the weeds and stubble of the open field. In summer they fed on the common rough pasture to which most clachans had access in their immediate neighbourhood.[88]

Whatever may have happened in earlier epochs, around 1800 most rundale farmers were the under-tenants of middlemen on large and neglected estates with absentee landlords. The result was that rundale survived mainly in Ireland's less accessible and less productive rural backwaters. It was especially common among the peninsulas and islands of north and west Donegal, west Mayo and Galway, west Kerry and west Cork. There were also many clachans on the lowlands of Connaught. East of the Shannon the clusters were fewer and smaller and the farmland less open and intermixed, though typical rundale features reappeared in certain small peninsulas and upland glens, even within a few miles of Dublin. Extensive bog-free lowlands were largely without rundale.

The rundale system was condemned by almost every author who wrote about it, mainly because it caused disputes among farmers and impeded the amelioration of agriculture (it was a great hindrance to wheat growing) and the reclamation of hill pastures. As contemporaries remarked, it bore some resemblance to the open-field system of the English midlands, and its extinction was the nearest thing in Irish agrarian history to an 'enclosure movement' in the English sense. One difference however is that despite all the attentions of modern geographers nobody claims to have unearthed a pre-Famine Irish equivalent for the kind of English village plan in which each individual selion and furlong is identified, measured, named and ascribed to its owner or tenant. Most of the rundale maps published in twentieth-century academic books and articles are drawn from the comparatively recent records of the Congested Districts Board, the Land Commission or the Valuation Office, or from recent field research by university lecturers – and have thus been financed directly or indirectly by the taxpayer.[89] When two contemporary writers wished to illustrate the niceties of rundale they had to invent their own (very unconvincing) example.[90] Even the well-known map supplied by John Pitt Kennedy to the Devon Commission of 1845 was drawn for demonstration purposes rather than as part of normal estate management.[91] The fact is that since rundale usually developed without the approval of estate managers, and in a sense beyond their reach, it cannot be expected to come under the notice of the estate surveyor, and where the farmers themselves saw its disadvantages and decided to eliminate them the resulting documents (if any) can hardly be expected to survive. At this level one can only be grateful for the stray reference, like the passage in Tighe's *Statistical Survey* of Kilkenny which describes how common rundale farmers were beginning to partition their holdings into halves and quarters.[92] Presumably the process referred to was a dissolution of small partnerships rather than an increase in fragmentation. Whatever it was, Tighe reports that country surveyors got a profitable living from it.

Where rundale was abolished by landlords there can be little doubt about the usual course of events. The whole system yielded at a stroke to something completely new, the only obstacle to change being such resistance as might be put up by the farmers themselves. Given that many landlords were anxious for reform and braced for local opposition, and given that their efforts date mainly from a period when records of various kinds are comparatively well preserved, it may seem strange that maps of the rundale system on the verge of extinction are so hard to find.[93] Perhaps they always have been. One expert said in 1883 that nobody could deal with rundale without the aid of maps,[94] but experts are not necessarily right: people have always been better at doing without maps than later and more enlightened generations would have thought possible. In Scotland, where estate maps have been collected and catalogued with enviable diligence, there is a corresponding shortage of detailed maps that show the equivalent custom known as runrig.[95] Of course if rundale holdings were about to be swept away there was no point in wasting paper on their baffling complexity, especially when the cost of plotting and drawing them was so large compared with ordinary farms. Instead the surveyor could make and map his changes in a single operation.[96] Where the parcels were rectangular all that need be done was measure the length and breadth of each plot, assign it an acreable value, and then combine the results to get the extent of each farmer's new holding. If the tenants already agreed about each other's existing farm-sizes the old pattern might perhaps be ignored altogether.

Somehow, at any rate, the work was done, and the reports of government committees and commissions include a number of first-hand references to its progress by reforming landlords. An early mention is by J. L. Foster in 1825, describing land held from Trinity College.[97] A later but more vividly documented case is that of Philip Reade of Woodpark, Co. Galway.

> Are there many farms held in joint tenancy, or in common, near you?
> Very extensively.
> What is the effect of that system?
> Most injurious to the peace of the country, its improvement, and, I may add, to its morality.

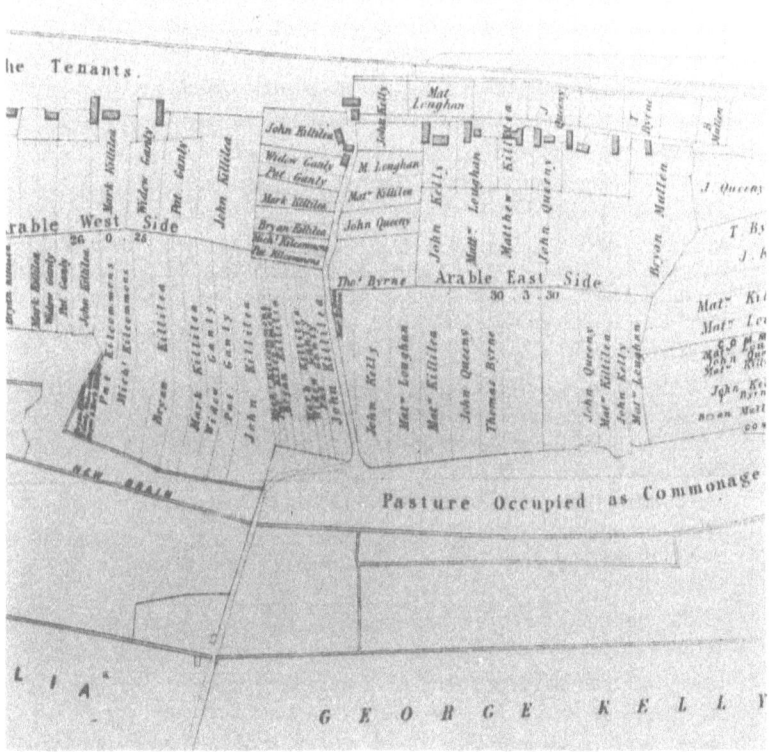

Plate 17. Lands at Boughill, Co. Galway, surveyed by Charles P. Brassington, 1850 (see chapter 7, note 89). Scale of original 20 statute perches to one inch. Maps of intermixed holdings are uncommon at this period. Boughill was a rare example of small farmers holding directly from the Crown at the time of the Famine and consequently becoming the subject of an official investigation.

> Can you suggest any remedy for such a system, further than the improved condition of the peasantry?
>
> I cured it myself. I got the whole of my estate, three years and a half ago, in joint tenancy, and I separated every holding. First, I induced every tenant on 3,000 acres to give me up possession; and I then went with a surveyor, a very clever man, certainly, and marked out every farm separately.
>
> Did that give rise to dissatisfaction among the tenantry?
>
> In the first instance, every man said he got the worst allotment, because his neighbour got some of his improvements; but within a month they were satisfied ... As an example, on one townland of 227 Irish acres, there were sixteen families who held their farms each of them in seventeen different places ... Now, each of those men got the same quantity of land, but together, and certainly to their general satisfaction.
>
> Is the system of joint tenancy disappearing every day?
>
> It has been very much lessened, except upon some very great estates.
>
> Did you make any roads through the property when you subdivided it?
>
> Yes ...
>
> Were you obliged to remove many of the houses ...?
>
> I avoided that as much as possible; but I had to remove a considerable number ...
>
> At present, does every man's house stand upon his own ground?
>
> I think so.[98]

With a clever surveyor to help him Reade could afford to be a little vague.

Another witness from the same period said that the first thing he did with a townland ripe for improvement was to throw it into squares. As a shape for either farm or field a square needed no justification, but in practice squaring seems to have been less common than striping. The stripe had the straight sides characteristic of the modern land improver (thus distinguishing itself from the curved strips attributable to a medieval ploughman) but its form was narrowly rectangular, sometimes grotesquely so. One dedicated striper admitted: 'I was blamed ... for making them so long and narrow, and they certainly appear ridiculous upon the map.' This was on an estate where the houses were allegedly built endways to fit onto their farms and where a man could avoid trespassing on his neighbour's land by jumping over it.[99] But the professional surveyor who laid out these farms had known what he was doing. Stripes were

Figure 8. Consolidation of rundale holdings in Rathlackan townland on the Palmer estate, Co. Mayo, 1918. Sources: NLI, 16.I.3(21, 22): E. E. Evans, *Irish Folk Ways* (London, 1957), pp 24–5.

meant to satisfy the aspirations of the former rundale tenants by allowing them to share all the various qualities of land, an object best attained by running the farm at right angles to the contours and soil boundaries and at the same time equalising access to rivers, sea coasts, main roads and the edges of pasturable bog or mountain. The stronger the commitment to egalitarianism, and the smaller the farms, the narrower would be the new holdings. Almost everywhere in Ireland physical geography provided some kind of linear pattern to justify the new arrangement, though fashion may also have made stripes popular for their own sake regardless of practical necessity.

Striping and squaring were the most important forces that sustained and sometimes even increased the demand for surveying expertise in early nineteenth-century Ireland. Both processes continued up to and after the making of the first Ordnance Survey maps: indeed their prevalence was one of the main reasons for publishing a second edition of these maps. It was the land surveyor's last major contribution to the rural landscape (Fig. 8). The contrary modern process of amalgamating depopulated stripes can be achieved without his help.

Notes

1. *Dublin Journal*, 30 June 1759, 17 Jan. and 7 Nov. 1761, 19 Nov. 1765, 30 Mar. 1784, 7 Nov. 1795; *Leinster Journal*, 10 July 1779; *Dublin Evening Post*, 4 Dec. 1784, 3 Jan. 1786, 10 Nov. and 15 Dec. 1787.

2. *Appellants' Case. House of Lords. From the Exchequer in Ireland. Between Richard Vicars, Esquire & Owen Grace, Esquire, Appellants and Timothy Colclough, Lawrence Adams, and William Lyster, Esquire (Executors of Thady Carroll, Deceased), Respondents* ([Dublin], 1779), p. 9.

3. *Freeman's Journal*, 2 Aug. 1768 (Royal Exchange, Dublin); *Dublin Journal*, 30 July 1772 (Blue Coat Hospital, Dublin); *Saunders's News-letter*, 28 May 1785 (new gaol, Dublin).

4. Annotated index to six-inch Ordnance Survey map of Co. Antrim, 1833, reproduced in C. E. B. Brett, *Historical Buildings, Groups of Buildings, Areas of Architectural Importance in the Glens of Antrim* [Belfast, 1971], p. 6.

5. *Cal. S. P. Ire.*, 1625–32, pp 301, 515–16, 529, 541.

6. Loeber, *Architects*, pp 48–51.

7. E. Malins and the Knight of Glin, *Lost Demesnes: Irish Landscape Gardening, 1660–1845* (London, 1976), pp 22–3. Another geometrical

design, from *c.* 1740–50, is illustrated in Knight of Glin and John Cornforth, 'Kilruddery, Co. Wicklow, Ireland', *Country Life*, 162 (1977), p. 80. For later maps of this kind, see Horner, *Bull. Ir. Georgian Soc.*, 18 (1975), Figs. 11, 12.

8. Reproduced in W. Fitzgerald, 'Carton', *Jour. Kildare Arch. Soc.*, 4 (1903–05), p. 12; discussed in A. A. Horner, 'Some Examples of the Representation of Height Data on Irish Maps before 1750, Including an Early Use of the Spot-Height Method', *Ir. Geogr.*, 7 (1974), pp 72–8.
9. Examples are Robert Moody (*Richard Reilly's Irish News-letter*, 29 Nov. 1740); George Dean (Malins and Glin, *Lost Demesnes*, p. 24 (1746)); Thomas Keightley (*Dublin Journal*, 14 Mar. 1752). Anonymous gardeners advertised in *Dublin Journal*, 30 Nov. 1776; *Volunteer Evening Post*, 31 July 1784; *Dublin Evening Post*, 3 Feb. 1787, 29 June 1793; *Northern Star*, 17 Nov. 1794.
10. Falkiner, *Irish History and Topography*, p. 68 (quoting Austin Cooper's diary, Nov. 1782); *Dublin Evening Post*, 6 Jan. 1781.
11. *Dublin Journal*, 31 Aug. 1765.
12. Private suits of Ireland, S.P. 63/22/62.
13. S.P. 63/84/29. Malby's plan is M.P.F. 95.
14. The Derry map is reproduced in [T.F.] Colby, *Ordnance Survey of the County of Londonderry*, 1 (Dublin, 1837), opposite p. 98. For the realistic portrayal of an intended town see Christopher Jefford's plan of Bandon, Co. Cork, in 1613 (TCD, MS 1209(39)).
15. Thomas Raven, 24 June 1621, in D. A.Chart (ed.), *Londonderry and the London Companies* (Belfast, 1928), p. 51.
16. *Cal. Anc. Rec. Dub.*, 4, p. 456.
17. Reproduced by R. Loeber, 'Irish Country Houses and Castles of the Late Caroline Period: an Unremembered Past Recaptured', *Bull. Ir. Georgian Soc.*, 16 (1973), plate 7.
18. E. R. R. Green, 'A Catalogue of the Estate Maps, etc., in the Downshire Office, Hillsborough, Co. Down', *Ulster Jour. Arch.*, 12 (1949), pp 1–25. These maps are now in PRONI.
19. *Maps and Plans. c.1580–c.1830, Co. Tyrone (How to Use the Record Office*, No. 16, PRONI, Belfast, n.d), p. 12.
20. *Dublin Journal*, 21 Apr. 1759. A map of Ballymote was mentioned in a contemporary lease (RD, 199/105/131704) but does not appear to survive.
21. Pembroke Estate Office, Dublin: Fitzwilliam estate, rent rolls and accounts, 31 Oct., 5 Nov. 1751; 3 July 1763; 'A Plan of Merrion Square with the Intended New Streets', 1764.
22. *Dublin Evening Post*, 25 Aug. 1791. Neville had also made a survey of Monaghan and its surroundings (A. P. W. Malcomson, ' The Earl of Clermont: a Forgotten Co. Monaghan Magnate of the Late Eighteenth Century', *Clogher Record*, 8 (1973), pp 25–6, 63).
23. *Cal. Anc. Rec. Dub.*, 5, p. 42 (1674); 8, pp 286, 350 (1738–9); 9, p. 357 (1750); 12, pp 156, 224 (1771–2); 13, p. 132 (1780), p. 377 (1784).

24. E. McParland, 'The Wide Streets Commissioners: their Importance for Dublin Architecture in the Late 18th-early 19th Century', *Bull. Ir. Georgian Soc.*, 15 (1972), pp 1–32.
25. This application of Rocque's map occurs in a report of 1773 quoted by J. T. Gilbert, *A History of the City of Dublin*, 2 (Dublin, 1859), p. 142.
26. Lord Carhampton, quoted in *Leinster Journal*, 22 Sep. 1798.
27. Report of Colonel Burton Conyngham's speech in the Irish House of Commons, *Volunteer Evening Post*, 12 May 1785.
28. E. MacDowel Cosgrave, 'On Two Maps, Dated 1751 and 1753, of the Essex Bridge District, Dublin', *Jour. R. Soc. Ant. Ire.*, 6th ser., 8 (1918), pp 140–49. There are many references to Semple in contemporary newspapers, one of them a complaint that his plan erred by three feet in the width of the complainant's house (*Dublin Journal*, 18 Nov. 1755). See also M. Craig, *Dublin, 1660–1860* (London, 1952), pp 139–40, 170.
29. Public Record Office of Northern Ireland, *Sources for Local History*, p. 60 (1968). For Priestley see M. Craig, *The Architecture of Ireland from the Earliest Times to 1880* (London, 1982), p. 209.
30. *Cal. Anc. Rec. Dub.*, 12, p. 425.
31. *Volunteer Evening Post*, 12 May 1785.
32. PRONI, T.2862/9, pp 130–33 (Midleton, 1799), pp 219–21 (Cove, 1801).
33. For Booth see J. S. Curl, *Moneymore and Draperstown: the Architecture and Planning of the Estates of the Drapers' Company in Ulster* (Belfast, 1979). Plans by Tite occur in *Report of a Visit to the Estate of the Honourable the Irish Society, in Londonderry and Coleraine* (London, 1834), appendices 4, 5; and *Report of the Deputation Appointed by the Honourable the Irish Society to Visit the City of London's Plantation in Ireland, in the Year 1838* (London, 1838), p. 46.
34. J. C. Curwen, *Observations on the State of Ireland*, 1 (London, 1818), p. 173. Curwen saw these plans in the possession of a local landowner and was impressed by their antiquity, doubting whether there were any earlier ones to be found at Newcastle in England.
35. 1 George II, c.13, sec. 3.
36. Road division by Mat. Meagher, Co. Kildare, 1779, NLI, 14.A.30. According to the author of *Some Considerations for the Promoting of Agriculture* (Dublin, 1723, p. 28), it was not unusual for Irish landlords to stop up public roads for the convenience of their estates. An example appears in William Wogan's atlas of the Clements estate, Co. Leitrim, in 1750 (NLI, 14. A. 16). Examples of designs for new roads occurring in private estate collections are those by Thomas Cuttle in Westmeath in 1752 (NLI, 21.F.80(38)) and by Owen Hall in Louth in 1839 (NLI, 21.F.154(7)). Some estate collections, like that of Lord Cloncurry (NLI, 21.F.50(31)), include maps of land taken for railways.
37. Road maps and road surveyors are frequently mentioned in the printed abstracts of grand jury presentments for Co. Westmeath, available in the Royal Irish Academy from 1804 to 1816.

38. J. H. Andrews, 'Road Planning in Ireland before the Railway Age', *Ir. Geogr.*, 5 (1964), pp 17–41; 'The Use of Half-Inch Ordnance Survey Maps in Irish Historical Geography, with Special Reference to Road Patterns', *Geogr. Viewpoint*, 5 (1976), pp 20–29.

39. When used for delimiting a permanent territorial boundary the mile might be accurately defined, as in James I's charter to Derry, which granted the city land to the extent of three miles in every direction from the 'old church walls', each mile containing 1,000 geometrical paces and each pace five feet (Colby, *Ordnance Survey of the County of Londonderry*, p. 121). Otherwise, travellers were expressing their awareness of the variability of the mile around the end of the seventeenth century. John Dunton in 1699 found in Co. Galway that the miles grew longer as the country grew worse, 'as if the badness of the commodity made the inhabitants there afford better measure' (quoted in E. MacLysaght, *Irish Life in the Seventeenth Century* (Cork, 1950), p. 326). Samuel Molyneux made the same point in 1709; he also noted a tendency for the mile to lengthen with increasing distance from Dublin (TCD, MS 884, p. 72). Lawyers were slower to take the point. Unspecified miles appeared in several early eighteenth-century statutes, e.g. 4 Anne, c. 6, sec. 2, 4 Anne, c. 9, sec. 2, 4 George I, c. 7, sec. 1. 'Mile or reputed mile' (6 Anne, c. 14, sec. 5) recognised the problem without doing much to solve it, and confusion must have been further confounded when the common Irish mile was defined in 1715 as twelve furlongs (2 George I, c. 12, sec. 5).

40. Hugh Boulter, *Letters to Several Ministers of State in England, and Some Others; Containing an Account of the Most Interesting Transactions which Passed in Ireland from 1724 to 1738*, 1 (Dublin, 1770), pp 169, 176, referring to a six-mile radius specified in a statute relating to parish churches and chapels of ease (6 George I, c. 13, sec. 3). Parliament inaugurated a new regime in 1727 (1 George II, c. 19) by in effect condemning its own use of the vague expression 'country mile' only twelve years earlier (2 George I, c. 14, sec. 12).

41. Gebbie, *Abercorn Letters*, p. 276 (1751); *Dublin Journal*, 12 May 1753, 31 July 1759.

42. Controversy on distances from Navan to Moynalty, Co. Meath, in relation to the Black Lion Inn, Carlanstown, involving the land surveyors Joseph O'Brien and Patrick Smith, *Dublin Chronicle*, 29 Mar., 2 Apr. 1791.

43. *Report from Select Committee on Turnpike Roads in Ireland*, q. 2401, H.C. 1831–2 (645), xvii.

44. 25 George II, c. 10, sec. 5.

45. 2 George I, c. 12. sec. 21.

46. Gabriel Stokes, *Observations on a Late Essay of Mr Richard Castle, Collected from Some Remarks Made in my Travels, on his Latest and Best Works of This Kind now Subsisting* (Dublin, 1735), p. 9. For Neville see Loeber, *Architects*, pp 79–80.

47. W. A. McCutcheon, *The Canals of the North of Ireland* (London, 1965); V. T. H. and D. R. Delany, *The Canals of the South of Ireland* (Newton Abbot, 1966).

48. Advertisement of Grand Canal Company, *Dublin Journal*, 18 Mar. 1773.
49. Advertisement of Fintan Doran of Cloyne, Co. Cork, *Cork Evening Post*, 4 Feb. 1782.
50. For Brownrigg see below, ch. 8. His survey of the Grand Canal from the city of Dublin to the River Barrow at Monasterevan (1787) is a manuscript book of maps in the possession of Coras Iompair Eireann at Pearse Station, Dublin. The same collection includes maps of the Royal Canal in 1819–20 by Joseph James Byrne.
51. *Dublin Evening Post*, 7 Nov. 1786 (Cuttle); *Commons Journals, Ireland*, 5, pp 370–72; 6, p. ccxxxiii; Delany and Delany, *Canals of the South of Ireland*, pp 32–3 (Williams). Williams's pretensions as an engineer were attacked by Peter Callan in *Universal Advertiser*, 21 Oct. 1758.
52. J. H. Andrews, 'Charles Vallancey and the Map of Ireland', *Geogr. Jour.*, 132 (1966), pp 48–61.
53. *Dublin Journal*, 22 Dec. 1772, 27 July 1773.
54. 45 George III, c. 43, secs. 2, 6.
55. *Sixth Report of Commissioners for Auditing Public Accounts in Ireland*, p. 201, H.C. 1818 (154), x. Taylor had been recommended for this appointment by J. L. Foster, the moving spirit behind much contemporary road legislation (PRONI, D.207/30/32). Some administrative details of the surveys appear in *Nineteenth Report of the Commissioners of Inquiry into the Collection and Management of the Revenue Arising in Ireland and Great Britain*, appendix 112, pp 532–6, H.C. 1829 (353), xii. Taylor's work on the military road is mentioned in W. Greig, *Strictures on Road Police, Containing Views of the Present Systems, by which Roads are Made and Repaired, Together with Sketches of its Progress in Great Britain, from the Earliest to the Present Time* (Dublin, 1818), p. 183.
56. H. Townshend, *A General and Statistical Survey of the County of Cork*, 2 (Cork, 1815), addenda, p. 69.
57. Irish road maps, NLI, 15.A.3–15.
58. 58 George III, c. 67, sec. 11 (1818).
59. *Newry Commercial Telegraph*, 5 Sep. 1828.
60. F. M. L. Thompson in Greig, *Gosford Estates*, pp 11–14; above, n. 55.
61. N. Gamble, 'The Dublin & Drogheda Rly', *Jour. Ir. Railway Rec. Soc.*, 11 (1974), p. 227. The surveyor was Joseph Byrne, presumably the Joseph James mentioned above in note 50. It was not long, however, before Byrne appeared as an 'engineer' (*Report ... [on] Dublin Improvement Bill and Dublin Consolidation, Improvements and Waterworks Bill*, H.C., 1847–8 (135–35.36), xxxi).
62. W. King, 'Of the Bogs and Loughs of Ireland', *Phil. Trans. R. Soc.*, 15 (1685), p. 960.
63. Correspondence on the draining of Annagh bog, Add. MS 46964A, f. 10; 46965, f. 32. For Perry see *Cal. Anc. Rec. Dub.*, 7, pp 176, 185,

328–39 and R. Loeber, 'Biographical Dictionary of Engineers in Ireland, 1600–1730', *Ir. Sword*, 13 (1977), pp 254–5.
64. Fitzwilliam estate correspondence, 14 Dec. 1748 to 14 Mar. 1749, NLI, mic. P.1020.
65. NLI, 21.F.171(2, 4).
66. A map of the early or middle eighteenth century, by Henry Weston, of lands 'annoyed by the River Brickey' in Co. Waterford, gives equal attention to parts of five different estates (NLI, 16.J.6(26)). Another communal venture was Samuel Bouie's map of the Boyne estuary in 1771, 'surveyed at the request of the proprietors' (BL, Egerton MS 1760).
67. *Reports of the Commissioners Appointed to Enquire into the Nature and Extent of the Several Bogs of Ireland, and the Practicability of Draining and Cultivating Them*, H.C. 1810 (365), x; 1810–11 (96), vi; 1813–14 (130, 131), vi.
68. Minutes of bogs commission, MS volume in the possession of Mr John Griffith, Shannon Grove, Pallaskenry, Co. Limerick.
69. H. F. Berry, *A History of the Royal Dublin Society* (London, 1915), especially ch. 4 and app 2. Early announcements relating to the Society's premiums are in *Dublin News-letter*, 24 Nov. 1741; *Pue's Occurrences*, 2 Mar. 1742; *Dublin Gazette*, 21 June 1743 (the last naming Lawrence Byrne and John Lane as surveyors of lands in Co. Kildare).
70. *Pue's Occurrences*, 4 Dec. 1742.
71. *Drogheda Journal*, 27 Aug. 1796, a report on the dismissal of the Linen Board's surveyor for taking exorbitant fees.
72. W. Blacker, *Prize Essay on the Management of Landed Property in Ireland* (Dublin, 1834), p. 17. The more common preference for straight edges appears in *Irish Farmers' Journal*, 5 Oct. 1822, and in W. R. Townsend, *Directions on Practical Agriculture, for the Working Farmers of Ireland* (Cork, 1837), p. 55.
73. For example the diagram given by John Hamilton in *Irish Agricultural Magazine* (Dublin, 1799), p. 24.
74. Tighe, *Kilkenny*, p. 428.
75. Young, *Tour*, 2, pp 95–100.
76. Bernard Scalé, Remarks and observations on the manor of Lismore in the county of Waterford, NLI, MS 6201, entry for Ounishade and Ballyrafter woods.
77. TCD, MS 2251, 21 Apr. 1679–30 Aug. 1681.
78. 43 George III, c. 29 (1803), local and personal. There are papers relating to the execution of this act in PROI, 2A.11.43.
79. *Cobbett's Parliamentary Debates*, 5, cols. 28–9 (20 May 1805).
80. *Saunders's News-letter*, 1 July, 14 Aug. 1819; 11 Apr. 1821; 4 July 1822. An example of a Parliamentary Enclosure map is John Brownrigg's survey of the commons of Dromiskin, Co. Louth, in 1816, NLI, MS 9041.

81. Correspondence on the survey of Ballymore Eustace commons, State Paper Office, Dublin, O.P. 574/507/7, 575/510/7, 7A.
82. 8 George I, c. 5, sec. 7.
83. An exchange involving two acres from each of two townlands in Co. Meath, and using a survey by Thomas Cuttle, is recorded in RD, 120/269/82567 (1745). A map made by Patrick Fogarty in 1826 for the purpose of straightening boundaries on the Trant estate in Tipperary is NLI, 21.F.24(25).
84. George Hill, *Facts from Gweedore* (London, 1845) is the most famous account of this subject and is reviewed in E. E. Evans, *The Personality of Ireland: Habitat, Heritage and History* (Cambridge, 1973), pp 85–105.
85. *Devon Report*, 1, p. 377 (Ardee, Co. Louth). The word 'rundales' had been used on the Abercorn estate in 1779 (D. McCourt, 'The Decline of Rundale, 1750–1850' in P. Roebuck (ed.), *Plantation to Partition: Essays in Ulster History in Honour of J. L. McCracken* (Belfast, 1981), p. 131). An earlier writer had described townlands where 'all plough and graze in common, making no ditches, or planting, but every man has his dale (as it is termed)' (*A Scheme Humbly Offer'd to the Consideration of Parliament, to Make the Inhabitants of that Kingdom a Happy and Flourishing People, without Interfering with Anything that Might Affect the People of England* (Dublin, 1751), p. 5).
86. Piers, *West-Meath*, pp 115–20.
87. *Devon Report*, 1, p. 816.
88. The classic paper is E. E. Evans, 'Some Survivals of the Irish Openfield System', *Geography*, 24 (1939), pp 24–36. Much subsequent literature is reviewed in D. McCourt, 'The Dynamic Quality of Irish Rural Settlement' in R. H. Buchanan, E. Jones and D. McCourt (eds.), *Man and His Habitat, Essays Presented to Emyr Estyn Evans* (London, 1971), pp 126–64, and in R. H. Buchanan, 'Field Systems of Ireland' in A. R. H. Baker and R. A. Butlin (eds.), *Studies of Field Systems in the British Isles* (Cambridge, 1973), pp 580–618.
89. Evans, *Geography*, 24 (1939), pp 31, 35; D. McCourt, 'Surviving Openfield in County Londonderry', *Ulster Folklife*, 4 (1958), p. 26; J. H. Johnson, 'Studies of Irish Rural Settlement', *Geogr. Rev.*, 48 (1958), p. 564; R. H. Buchanan, 'Common Fields and Enclosure: an Eighteenth-Century Example from Lecale, County Down', *Ulster Folklife*, 15/16 (1970), p. 105; R. Fox, *The Tory Islanders, a People of the Celtic Fringe* (Cambridge, 1978), maps 8, 19. All these maps belong to periods later than *c*. 1890. The earliest true rundale map noticed is a survey of Boughill, Co. Galway, in 1850 in *30th Report, Commissioners of Woods and Forests*, app 3 (B), H.C. 1852–3 (34), lv. See Plate 17.
90. Mr and Mrs S. C. Hall, *Ireland: Its Scenery, Character etc.*, 3 (London, 1843), p. 262, reproduced in R. D. Edwards and T. D. Williams (eds.), *The Great Famine, Studies in Irish History, 1845–52* (Dublin, 1956), p. 112.
91. *Devon Report*, 1, app 14, p. 59.
92. Tighe, *Kilkenny*, pp 419–20.

93. This judgement applies to rundale in the strict sense. In the case of ordinary farms with irregular boundaries, 'before and after' maps are not uncommon: an example is Thomas Jourdan's 'design of remodelling' farms in Co. Clare in 1884 (NLI, 21.F.150(17)).
94. *Third Report from the Select Committee of the House of Lords on Land Law (Ireland)*, q. 1108, app B, p. 197, H.C. 1883 (204), xiii.
95. I. H. Adams, 'Sources for Scottish Local History – 5. Estate Plans', *Local Historian*, 12 (1976), p. 26; and *The Mapping of a Scottish Estate* (Edinburgh, 1971), p. 2. See, however, the same author's 'The Land Surveyor and his Influence on the Scottish Rural Landscape', *Scot. Geogr. Mag.*, 84 (1968), p. 252.
96. *Report of the Deputation of the Court of Assistants of the Drapers' Company Appointed to Visit the Company's Irish Estates, in the Year 1873* (London, 1873), p. 7.
97. *Minutes of Evidence Taken before the Select Committee Appointed to Inquire into the Disturbances in Ireland*, p. 243, H.C. 1825 (20), vii.
98. *Devon Report*, 1, p. 327.
99. *Report from the Select Committee on Destitution (Gweedore and Cloughaneely)*, q. 6772, H.C. 1857–8 (412), xiii.

8
Surveyors in society

THE WORLD'S FIRST LAND MEASURER had no one to teach him his business, which makes the emergence of a surveying fraternity by spontaneous generation a hypothesis not to be ruled out in seventeenth-century Ireland or anywhere else. The alternative scenario (starting with a population that is assumed to be devoid of surveyors) is for an immigrant, or a returning emigrant, to introduce the craft from some foreign country in which it has already been developed. For those who look at Irish history through ethnic glasses, both kinds of innovator – endogenous and exogenous – may be further classified as either Gaelic, old English or new British. Later a surveyor in any of the six resultant categories may be supposed to have taught pupils of either his own or some other ethnic group. At this point the reader can be left to decide how many different 'breeds' of practitioner might exist after any given number of generations, and then to calculate how many possible combinations of types might occur among any given number of individuals. Hopelessly unrealistic though such an exercise may be, some theorising seems inevitable when throughout the formative period of the Irish surveying profession there is not a single surveyor whose place or mode of education is recorded in contemporary documents.

In this sea of uncertainty there float two rafts of somewhat insecure fact. One is a notable lack of Irishness at the beginnings. The great majority of seventeenth-century surveyors in Ireland have 'New English' names (which may be taken to include a small number of Huguenot names) and the proportion of such names increases as the record is followed backwards (Table 8). Secondly, there seems to be only one seventeenth-century reference to the deliberate importation of surveyors from England to Ireland and that is in the not very successful adventurers' survey done under the Commonwealth.[1] Furthermore hardly any of the earliest Irish surveyors are known to have practised in England at a previous stage of their careers, let alone to have achieved eminence there – not even those

TABLE 8
SURNAMES OF IRISH SURVEYORS

	Percentage of Sample		Size of Sample
	British	Irish	
1610–19	100	—	7
1620–29	100	—	3
1630–39	77	23	13
1640–49	71	29	7
1650–59	100	—	6
1660–69	69	31	13
1670–79	69	25	16
1680–89	78	17	23
1690–99	75	19	32
1700–09	67	33	55
1710–19	64	35	74
1720–29	59	38	108
1730–39	64	30	103
1740–49	64	31	135
1750–59	57	36	167
1760–69	59	37	186
1770–79	54	40	202
1780–89	51	44	215
1790–99	56	38	198
1800–09	53	41	202
1810–19	55	40	211
1820–29	54	39	250
1830–39	58	37	246
1840–49	61	34	198
1850–59	69	23	141

Only the makers of private farm and estate surveys are included. Names of uncertain origin are omitted.

who can be identified as immigrants like Jobson, Robins, Raven and Pynner.[2] A possible interpretation of these facts, if they really are facts, would postulate an English immigrant arriving newly-trained or half-trained (and perhaps driven by the languishing demand for his abilities at home) or simply predisposed towards surveying by some kind of 'mechanical' education. Once in Ireland he is recruited by the state to help execute a plantation scheme; or by one or more private landowners, perhaps as a part-time surveyor who may become a full-timer with increasing experience and success. One place where this sequence of events can be easily pictured in the early Stuart period is on the Earl of Cork's estate: here quite large numbers of men are described as joining forces to measure land – or sometimes as refusing an invitation to participate in such activities – in what looks like an amateur fashion, but certain names are found to recur, at first mere measurers such as Baldwin Carpenter, and later producers of finished maps like Augustine Atkins.[3]

A much larger number of surveyors must surely have been attracted to Ireland by the great land boom that began in the 1650s, some of them no doubt remaining in touch with their home country, like the 'geometrician' who was reported to cross the sea often on estate business in 1654.[4] Whatever education the newcomers brought with them, in this difficult and hectic period the problems to be faced in Ireland were so unusual that an immigrant surveyor's professional habits were more likely to be influenced by the environment he moved into than by the one he left behind. In the eighteenth century the mists grow thinner, without ever actually clearing. Surveyors now began to compose advertisements (Plate 18), to write books, and in one case even to keep a diary.[5] Of the books, Peter Callan's *Dissertation on the Practice of Land-Surveying in Ireland* (1750) is the most informative and the most readable, though not many modern social scientists would approve his classification of his colleagues as complete surveyors, grand surveyors, bungling surveyors, compulsatory surveyors, foppish surveyors, and pretenders.

What these sources suggest most forcibly is that few Irish surveyors were self-taught. Josias Bateman of Tallow may have been an exception, and so perhaps was Christopher Colles of Kilkenny, who 'made the mathematics his particular study' and later (immune from inherited professional insularity, it might be argued) became almost unique among native eighteenth-century Irish surveyors in winning cartographic fame outside his own country.[6] Other independent commentators claimed that surveying could be learned very quickly – Petty thought that a month's study ought to be long enough[7] – but, once they had finished learning, the surveyors themselves were not inclined to endorse this view. They were more likely to accept William Bald's nineteenth-century estimate of three to four years.[8] Callan wrote waspishly about fops who had learned their surveying out of an old book, and his own book certainly did nothing to help the armchair aspirant: like most Irish surveying authors he devoted nearly all his space to new or controversial topics, assuming his readers to have already acquired the rudiments through some other channel. In fact, far from attracting recruits, Callan claimed to have driven out of

P. BERNARD SCALLE

TAKES this Method of acquainting the Nobility and Gentry, That he surveys Counties, Cities, Gentlemen's Estates, &c. topographically, after the Manner of Mr. John Rocque his Brother-in-law, by whom he was instructed. He gives an accurate Drawing of his Survey, on which is laid down the just Bends of the Roads, Rivers, Brooks, Hedges, Banks, &c. &c. As also the true Bounds and Quality of each Field. He assures those Gentlemen that shall please to honour him with their Commands, That he will take a particular Care to acquit himself to their Satisfaction, and his own Credit.
☞ Plans and Maps copied, enlarged or reduced, and Plans for Leases, carefully drawn. Gentlemen shall be waited on by directing for him to Mr. Sleater, Bookseller, on Cork-hill; or at Miss Lyons, Milliner, in Skinner-row.

TO THE PUBLIC,

RICHARD BARRY of Killeagh, Dancing-master, having lately surveyed a lot of meadowing, at Ballylyng, for Mr. Molton, containing 1A. 3R. 9P. I returned it to Dr. Fitzgerald, 1A. 3R. 18P. This great genius, instead of acknowledging his error, lost no time in furnishing the public with a series of falsities, and invincible ignorance, pregnant with malice, calculated it to prejudice my character, and to support a false survey in direct opposition to truth and science. I employed Mr. Doran of Cloyne, a young man of a fair character, and of unquestionable abilities in the line of his profession, and he returned it 1A. 3R. 21P. I will hold Barry or any of his friends a wager of twenty guineas, that his survey is false, at least by the difference of his and my return, as above specified, but if he refuses closing the bett I now propose, shall pity him for his ignorance, despise him for his malice, and think him unworthy my notice.

Ballyprunna, May 3, 1784
(:) WILLIAM HIGGINS

Plate 18. The main purposes of newspaper advertising by eighteenth-century Irish surveyors were to attract custom (above, *Sleater's Public Gazetteer*, 23 Sep. 1758) and to repel competition (below, *Hibernian Chronicle*, 3 May 1784).

the profession, presumably by sheer force of invective, a number of men who he thought had no business to be there.

Of course an Irish surveyor could still read an English textbook, as Callan himself acknowledged by citing some half a dozen.[9] Joshua Wight had his own copy of Love's *Geodaesia* in the field with him in 1753, and by that time he could have found a home-produced substitute in Robert Gibson's *Treatise of Practical Surveying*, the one Irish book that expounded the whole subject in an orderly and systematic fashion. Although it took Gibson twelve years to build up a viable list of subscribers his book went through many editions and finally achieved an international reputation. But it did not kill the prejudice against the self-taught. Any surveyor who 'sprang up like a mushroom', with nothing known of his education or early experience, was greatly suspect, even if (perhaps especially if) he happened to be a schoolmaster. Thus Lawrence Nowlan of Carlow was ridiculed for having served his time as a worsted spinner, and for not 'coming at a smattering notion of figures' until he was twenty years of age, his mis-spent youth in no way counter-balanced by a certificate of proficiency from the Surveyor-General's office.[10]

The position of the eighteenth-century immigrant is not so clear. On the whole the foreign professional or craftsman, and the Englishman or Scotsman in particular, had a good name among Irish employers, as can be seen from the eagerness shown by many gardeners, architects and engineers to emphasise their cross-channel antecedents. But surveying was a less difficult and therefore less exotic skill, its practitioners being more akin to ordinary workmen, as Petty had implied; and by the late eighteenth century Ireland was regarded as a country to which no workman ever migrated.[11] Inevitably there were a number of oddities. Monsieur de Sceleback came to Cork as a surveyor expecting a welcome in what he described as a 'land of hospitality' but nothing more was ever heard of him.[12] Other exceptions can be accounted for by special circumstances. One new arrival, J. Hoctor (1773), turned out to be an Irishman with some English experience;[13] another in the same year, Robert Lewis, was a Dubliner returning after a spell as a schoolmaster in London.[14] A genuine Englishman, Robert Sharland (1809), was not only a land surveyor but also an architect, engineer and valuer of timber. Sharland's versatility was typical of a new immigrant generation, many of them qualified as agriculturalists and valuators but appearing too late to exert much influence on ordinary systems of Irish land surveying, which by this time were deeply entrenched.[15]

In the eighteenth century it was probably more usual for English or Scottish surveyors to arrive not for permanent residence but for some specific task, such as to map the Irish estate of a proprietor who held land on both sides of the water. Such transients could come and go without leaving any trace other than their maps. James Paine was well known in England but totally unheard of in Ireland apart from one small atlas,[16] and the recorded Irish activities of the eminent Scotsman Peter May did not extend beyond a single property.[17] Once Irishmen were firmly in control of their own surveying tradition, the best chance for a visitor to make his mark was in some remote corner of the country where a demand for surveyors had arisen without yet being satisfied. Such apparently was the course of events on Lord Donegall's Inishowen estate in the 1760s. There was no doubt about the provenance of his surveyors: as one journalist put it (with characteristic Irish superiority towards the non-aristocrat), they were 'boors brought from England'.[18] This rustic expression does not quite fit James Crow of Northumberland Street, London, whose maps of the Donegall properties are dated 1769–70.[19] Appropriately enough, Crow's first Irish appearance had been on the London Companies' properties in Co. Londonderry, and it was in the city of Londonderry that his visit proved most influential. His local pupil David McCool remained in business there for many years, and if McCool's apprentices, Robert and David Nolan, are taken into account the Crow influence was effective for nearly a century.[20]

The rarity of Crow's achievement gives added lustre to that of John Rocque as conqueror of the Irish surveying community in its own metropolis. One of the few typically Irish features of Rocque's career was the part played by family ties in transmitting professional knowledge, the only one of his pupils to reach the first rank being his brother-in-law Bernard Scalé.[21] In England the importance of such connections is said to date from the eighteenth century.[22] But in 1640 the son of the Earl of Cork's surveyor, Augustine Atkins, was sufficiently well established for his charges to become a subject of complaint.[23] In Cromwellian times, too, there are a few family names, such as Hunter, which occur among Irish surveyors with more than their expected frequency. A century later the relationships are better documented. By this time consecutive generations are occasionally found practising independently of each other, but the usual pattern was for son to follow father, first as pupil, then as partner and finally as successor, inheriting home, maps, instruments and goodwill – though not necessarily talent: the psychologist's principle of regression explains why few dynasties of surveyors sustained a really powerful position for more than two generations. It was in the middle ranks of the profession that family teams predominated. Sometimes the exact relationship is spelt out in the contemporary record, as when William and Conyngham McCrea worked under the inspection of their father Samuel.[24] More often the unimaginative baptismal habits of the eighteenth century have left a surveyor's identity perilously dependent on the actuarial preconceptions of the historian. Can George Hillas in 1755 be the same person as George Hillas in 1813?[25] How many Thomas Cuttles were making surveys between 1722 and 1772?[26] But the proven recurrence of an unusual surname – Sloane, Purfield, Neville, Roe, Hood – tells at least part of the genealogical story, and in any large sample of Irish land surveyors a substantial percentage will show some sign of being related by kinship to some other member of the sample. It is also safe to say that none of the sample will be a woman.

Even when professionally-associated land surveyors bore different names, the evidence is seldom sufficient to prove that they were not related by marriage. Lawrence Nowlan (already mentioned) and John Humphrey, for example, who formed a partnership in Carlow in 1769, may have been either uncle and nephew or brothers-in-law.[27] As it turns out such cases are rare. In a sample of 82 advertisements between 1760 and 1800, only three had been inserted by pairs of surveyors with different surnames. (The occurrence of two or more names on the same map throws little or no light on this question, for reasons explained in previous chapters.) The usual way of finding recruits outside the family was by apprenticeship. Not that advertising for apprentices was very common among surveyors: in the sample just cited it appears only five times. But the rather demanding tone assumed by some employers – 'none need apply but a lad of taste, ability, and good connections, who has been suitably educated'[28] – suggests that no shortage of applicants was considered likely. Even a certified surveyor might hope to benefit from a spell with an acknowledged master like John Brownrigg,[29] and younger apprentices were ready enough to pay for their training, though not all of them stayed to finish the statutory seven years.

Another way of becoming a surveyor was to go to school. In Cromwell's time it was the imminence of the plantation surveys that had seemed to justify the appointment of a mathematical professor at Trinity College.[30] But although at this period there was a serious lack of arithmetic teaching elsewhere in Ireland, the subject later began to move down the educational scale. An early example was the school conducted on Wood Quay, Dublin, in 1694 by Andrew Cumpsty (a recent immigrant who later worked on the Trustees' Survey) and his partner John McComb, which covered surveying and the use of instruments and a variety of other subjects.[31] Throughout the eighteenth century and into the nineteenth surveying continued to be taught by pedagogues, not in classical academies but in the numerous writing and mathematical schools that flourished in Dublin and other towns (not least in seaports where intending navigators could receive instruction) and even in country villages.[32] It was a rural polymath who boasted that

> I can teach mensuration and the elements of geometry,
> Dialling, navigation, and likewise trigonometry:
> My daily occupation is surveying and astronomy;
> Those branches I perform with the easiest economy.[33]

In a typical eighteenth-century mathematical school the curriculum would include accounts, arithmetic, astronomy, book-keeping, dialling, English, gauging, geography, geometry, navigation, surveying, trigonometry and writing. Thomas Holland of Cork also offered 'the use of maps, with their application to history'.[34] The unexpected emphasis often placed on writing deserves a comment as it probably explains the long-lived but otherwise pointless (and aesthetically dubious) habit among late eighteenth-century surveyors of including as many different scripts as possible on the same map. By the 1790s some schools had begun to prepare their pupils for a more exciting life with courses on fortification and gunnery, though it was a Londoner and not an Irishman who had anticipated this trend with lessons in 'the throwing of bombs'.[35]

To judge from Callan's book there was a prejudice among practising surveyors against what he called town schoolboys and petty teachers of the mathematics. But Callan was by temperament prejudiced against everyone. Other surveyors were willing enough to advertise their educational attainments. Such were Samuel Byron and James Williamson, both products of the Dublin Society's drawing school which, although mainly associated with the fine arts, also offered geographical, nautical, mechanical, commercial and military studies.[36] Williamson was equally proud of the classes which he later conducted himself; so, among other surveyor-teachers, were Robert Gibson[37] and Robert Lewis.[38] In the sample of advertisements quoted above, nearly a quarter of the surveyors claimed to be teachers. Similarly men who spent most of their lives as teachers found it worthwhile to be seen keeping their hand in, even if (like R. Montague of Belfast) the only time they had for surveying was on Saturday afternoons.[39] Whether or not the schoolmaster in Goldsmith's *Deserted Village* was meant to be an Irishman, he certainly typified the Irish teaching profession in his ability to 'measure lands'.[40] The same combination of talents was as common in the nineteenth century as it was in Goldsmith's day.[41]

No doubt mathematical schools produced as many failures and drop-outs as any other kind of school.[42] But one testimony to the effectiveness of such an education was the ease with which surveying capacity came to straddle Ireland's hereditary ethnic and religious boundaries. For Petty, or at any rate for his critics, to be a surveyor was to be a Protestant: his plan for staffing the Down Survey with non-surveyors was unpopular in some quarters because it opened the way to employing Catholics, an argument that would have cut no ice if Catholicism had been prevalent among the trained practitioners who were the alternative source of personnel.[43] The small proportion of native Irish names among recorded mid-seventeenth-century surveyors is thus probably a fair reflection of the facts. Perhaps it was an awareness of this imbalance that prompted James II's Parliament to encourage the teaching of mathematics and navigation.[44] Although this legislation proved ineffective, at least surveying was never one of the professions banned to Catholics, and its history shows no positive evidence of the discrimination often encountered by stewards, gardeners and other full-time estate employees.

By the early eighteenth century Josias Bateman could complain about 'surveyors of the natives' being hired by unscrupulous agents to the detriment of an estate in Co. Waterford.[45] So now the native practitioner was a recognised phenomenon. Meanwhile educational reformers began to favour surveying as a suitable subject (more suitable than the classics, anyway) for pupils of inferior social status.[46] Some of the reformers may never have met a landlord who believed in keeping farm-sizes hidden from the lower orders; others, after about 1800, may have noticed that acreage disputes were becoming less common and secrecy less desirable. One commentator of the new century found a more even balance between Catholics and Protestants at schools which taught mathematics and surveying;[47] another, more explicit, attributed the high standard of arithmetic and geometry in 'common Catholic schools' to the practical application of these subjects in the measuring of land.[48] In fact heresy and popery were almost the only disqualifications that Irish surveyors did not make a habit of publicly holding against each other.[49] The best evidence on the subject is the steady increase throughout the eighteenth century in the number of reputable map-makers with 'native' names, though perhaps never to quite the same ratio as among Irishmen in general. When the official census took up the story in 1861, 74 per cent of Ireland's land surveyors were Roman Catholics as compared with 78 per cent of the population at large.[50] Here was a tribute to the success of the Catholic schools over many generations, though the highest levels of the profession were to all appearances more solidly Protestant, throughout the nineteenth century, than these figures would suggest. It must also be admitted (turning to another favourite Irish cultural indicator) that there appear to be no Gaelic-language estate maps. If any such were known, cartographic history might have assumed a different significance in modern Ireland.

The geography of land surveying is an even more difficult subject than its cultural affiliations (Figs. 9–15). The largest numbers of surveyors might reasonably be sought in areas of intensive New English settlement, for it was in just such an environment that modern systems of agriculture and land tenure would create the strongest demand for land measuring as well as eliciting the largest supply of measurers. This hypothesis can be rather too easily proved, for it is precisely the same areas that provide most of the available evidence for seventeenth-century economic and technological activity of any kind. There are also biases in Irish historical research, most of which, in this as in some other fields, has been done in Dublin by students unversed in the Irish language. The only region immune from a Dublin bias is Ulster, where the collecting and calendaring of local records has been done more vigorously than anywhere else in Ireland and where at most periods the density of recorded surveyors' names is correspondingly high. The comparative shortage of Ulster names from the seventeenth and early eighteenth centuries is therefore particularly remarkable, and may reflect the low state of professional surveying in those parts of Scotland and northern England from which the Ulster planters were mainly recruited. However it was caused, the shortage had not yet been made good in 1721, when Colonel Richard Molesworth contemplated going to Ireland, not to the Dublin region but to 'some remote parts in the north', where he proposed to employ his time in practical and speculative geometry, surveying, levelling and map-making, presumably because there were more opportunities than in the midlands or south.[51] This was the first time in the history of land surveying that the north of Ireland revealed itself as a distinct cultural region.

But it was not long before a good network of surveyors had covered most parts of the country, north and south. Even Callan admitted by implication that it was only in abnormally out-of-the-way places that a pretender could hope to impose on ignorant farmers with a promise of saving them rent by reducing the size of their farms. By 1758, in a remote area like the Neale in Co. Mayo, where the pace of life is traditionally slow, surveyors could be produced at three days' notice to measure the 65-mile distance to Athlone by road.[52] The identity of these Mayomen is unknown, but in general the occurrence of well-established local surnames among the surveying community makes clear that skills were being spread as much by acculturation as by migration. There were Austens, Barrys and Sullivans surveying in Cork, Sloanes in east Ulster, Lynes and Stacks in Kerry, Hillases in Sligo, Laffans in Tipperary. Yet none of them can be shown to have formed a regional school in a stylistic sense, which suggests that the dispersal of plantation surveys and plantation surveyors must have imposed a measure of homogeneity throughout the country. No doubt the same could be said of the surveyors appointed by the Surveyor-General and the recipients of his certificate. Although the latter came mainly from Leinster and east Munster, the examination is also known to have been taken by men from the counties of Galway, Roscommon, Cavan and Down (Fig. 10). An additional cause of uniformity was the employment of the same surveyor on all the outliers of a far-flung property, or conversely of several independent parties on a tract too large for any one of them to tackle alone. Yet another relevant practice was for each new surveyor of an estate to study, and perhaps to gain possession of, the maps drawn by his predecessors on the same land: the only surveyor's map archive to be preserved in Ireland (that of John Longfield and his associates, mainly from the early nineteenth century (Fig. 11)) includes a body of work by cartographers unconnected with the firm, some of it nearly a hundred years old. One earlier surveyor, Josias Bateman, had actually visited friends of his employer with the object of learning something from their map collections.[53]

Whether by precept or example, then, the art of surveying surmounted both cultural and regional barriers with remarkably little difficulty. Its progress was due not only to the skill of Ireland's educationists and the comparative simplicity of their task, but also to the small capital requirements of the surveying industry. An eighteenth-century chain could be had for seven shillings, an azimuthal instrument of some kind for less than five pounds, a copy of Gibson's *Treatise* for 6s.[54] A surveying business

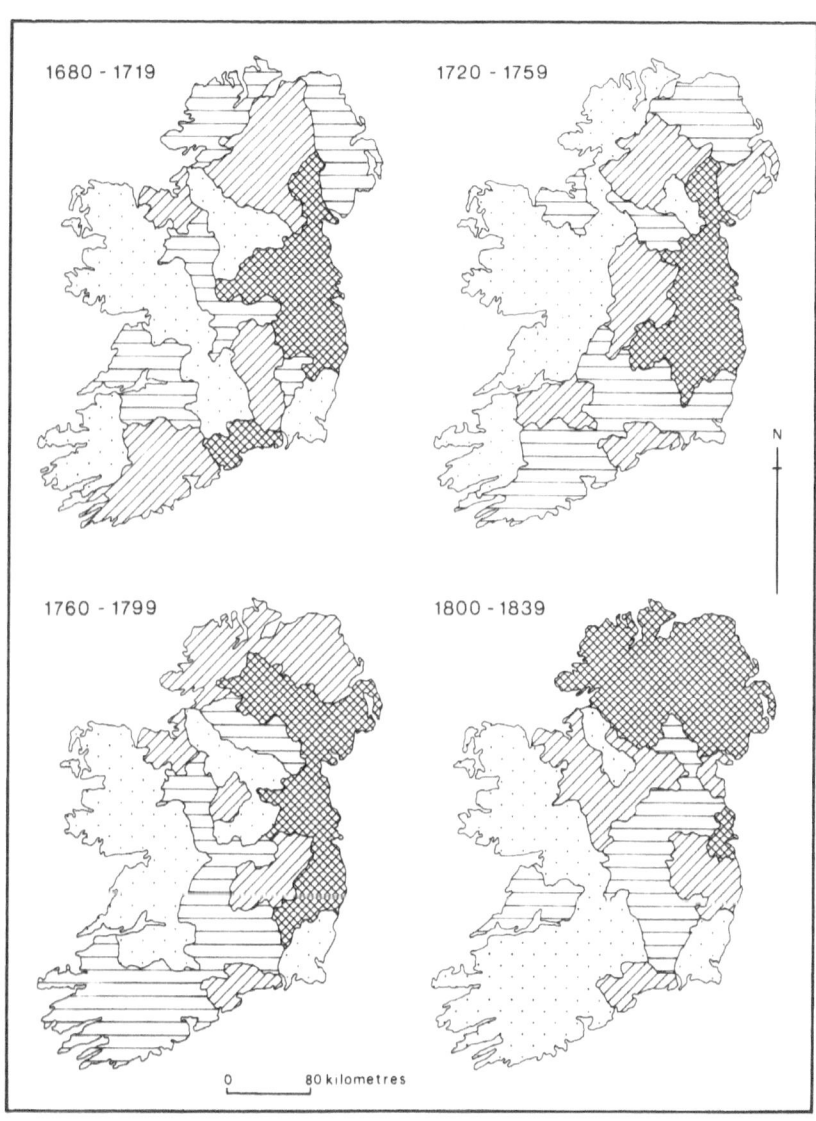

Figure 9. Geographical distribution of surveying activity, 1680–1839. Shading indicates the number of surveyors per 1,000 acres (excluding areas of uncultivated land as recorded in the 1841 census), with counties ranked in four groups of eight counties each and the regions of highest density shown by the darkest shading. Only surveyors known to have worked in private practice are included.

could also be conducted by a single man, hiring unskilled labourers to hold the chain or act as mark-men at daily rates that varied from 8d a day in Petty's time to 1s. 1d in the 1820s.[55] Admittedly the one-man firm was at a disadvantage in times of sickness, holidays or abnormally heavy work-load, and surveyors would often apologise for delays and absences through the medium of the press. And although sub-contracting was by no means unknown, it did little to solve this last problem in a business where so much depended on personal reputation. On the other hand both discipline and organisation would have been at risk if too many surveyors were combined under one head. In measuring land as in cultivating it, and for the same reason, the optimum size of firm is small. Later the optimum showed signs of increasing, but until the late eighteenth century the ideal was probably a master with one or two apprentices or a father with one or two sons. Thus William Steile of Kilkenny found a place for his sons William and Richard, but not for his third son Blennerhassett.[56] John Rocque's team of five or six assistants was a rule-proving exception, geared to general map production rather than just land surveying, and in any case it disintegrated into smaller units soon after Rocque's departure.

The growth of large firms was inhibited by geographical constraints on the amount of work that could be organised from a single base. Employers were sometimes advised to avoid recruiting from their own neighbourhood in the interests of impartiality,[57] but since travel and subsistence costs were usually passed on to the customer as separate items in an itinerant surveyor's account they provided an easily identifiable reason for disregarding this advice. How far it was worth bringing a surveyor in purely monetary terms depended on the size of his assignment: the greater the fee, the further he would willingly travel to collect it, especially if a few small surveys could be fitted in en route.[58] What makes the 'sphere of influence' a difficult concept is the unmanageable variety of the fees: at one extreme, several hundred pounds for a 50,000 acre estate mapped as a unit; at the other, sixpence for surveying a single field.[59] At first sight the intervening continuum might seem to defy analysis. But a surveyor who could be trusted with anything could probably be trusted with a townland of two hundred acres, and it is somewhere above the townland, nearer to the size of the complete estate, that a threshold might be expected to interpose itself between different professional categories.

In a survey of two hundred acres the surveyor's travel time would form a considerable addition. Callan suggested that he should charge for it at a rate of twopence per mile. Given a surveying charge of twopence per acre

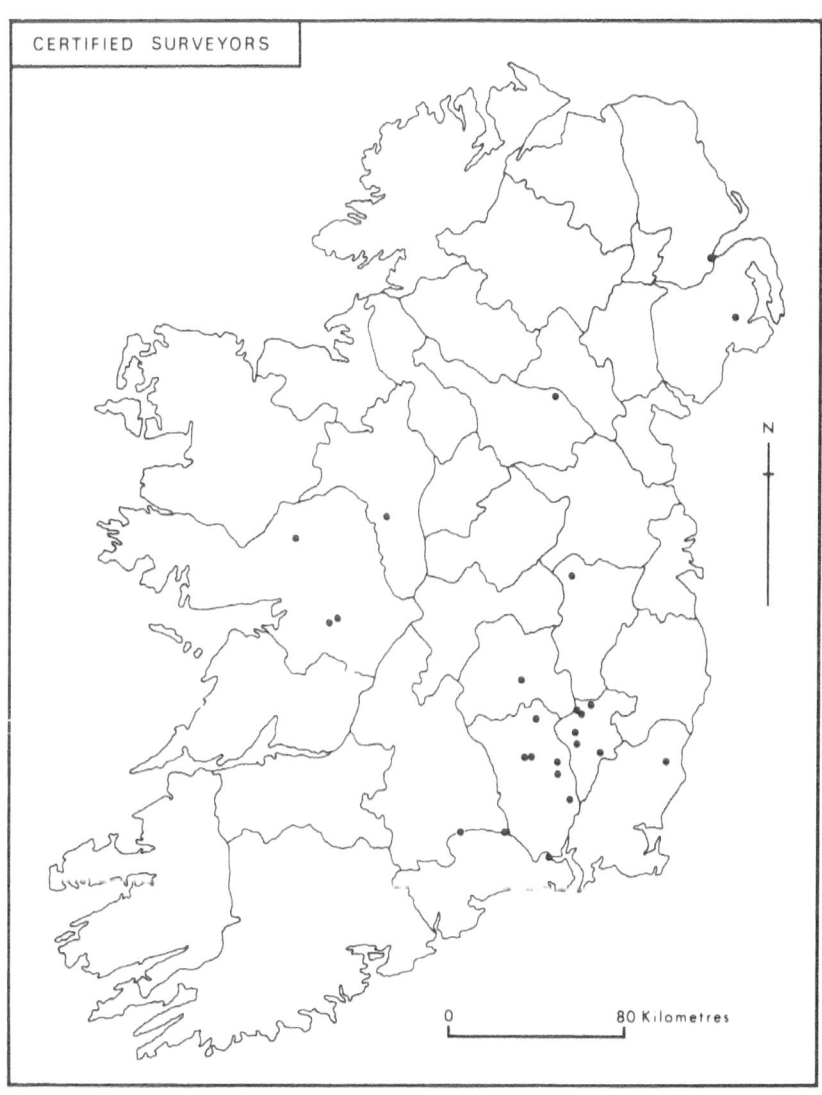

Figure 10. Certified surveyors,1750–1810. Most of the references come from the *Leinster Journal*, which was published at Kilkenny in the area of greatest apparent concentration; but since the newspapers of Dublin, Cork, Belfast and Londonderry have been sampled to the same extent, and since all these papers included numerous surveyors' advertisements not mentioning certificates, the distribution can probably be accepted as genuine.

a journey of ten miles and back would add ten per cent – a fair maximum allowance for contingencies – to the total cost. An overnight stay might seem in itself to make this cost prohibitive, but many surveyors were probably accommodated free of charge in local farmhouses. The problem is to translate such reasoning into practical terms. There is no denying that by the early eighteenth century a large part of the profession was made up of regional or 'country' surveyors. Thus in Table 9 the practitioners who appear more than once in the same county are at least fourteen times as numerous as chance coincidence would dictate. The table also enumerates surveyors recorded in two counties, and these counties adjoin each other five times more often than if they were chosen at random. Such figures may be better than nothing as a measure of geographical concentration, but most surveyors' *oeuvres* are too imperfectly recorded to be worth mapping as distribution patterns. Even a healthy-looking scatter of sites may be vitiated by the influence of one or two estates (Fig. 12). Among possible substitutes, the addresses at which a surveyor could be contacted might give an over-optimistic impression of his territorial range (Fig. 13); so might his claim to have surveyed such and such major estates, or to be recommended by the gentlemen of this or that county (Fig. 14). The most that can be said at present is that some spheres of influence were no larger than the hinterland of a regional capital or a market town

TABLE 9

TERRITORIAL RANGE OF EIGHTEENTH-CENTURY SURVEYORS

Single-unit hinterlands	Hinterlands of more than one unit	Number of counties in largest unit
101	23	1
99	13	2
25	6	3
5	4	4
2	1	5 or more

The tendency for surveyors to work in compact territories is roughly measured by the ratio of single-unit hinterlands to multiple-unit hinterlands. A single unit is defined as either one county yielding more than one independent reference to the same surveyor, or a group of adjacent counties each yielding one or more such references. Units counted in the centre column include counties with only one reference.

The table omits all surveyors recorded only once, and metropolitan influence is excluded by ignoring all surveyors known to have practised in Co. Dublin.

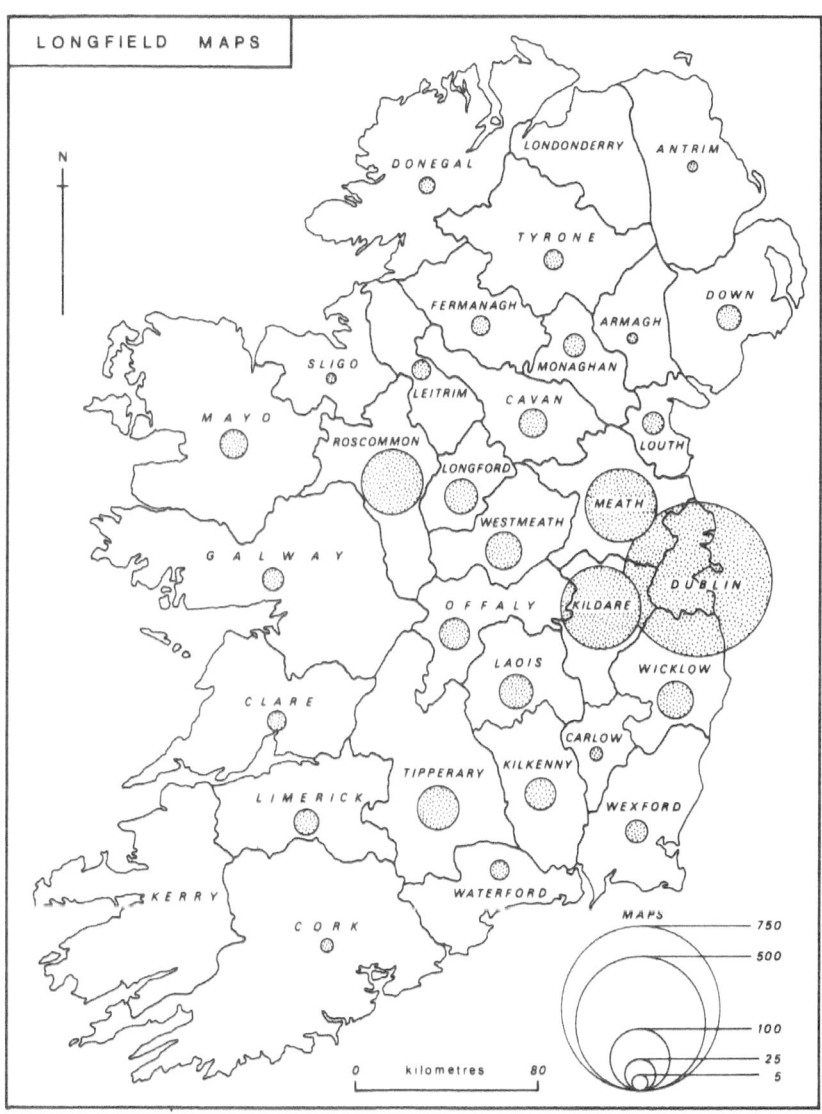

Figure 11. Maps preserved by John and William Longfield, mainly c. 1810 to c. 1840, but including many earlier maps by John Brownrigg and some by other eighteenth-century surveyors. For source see National Library of Ireland, *Report of the Council of Trustees for 1908–1909*, p. 15.

– perhaps a town as small as Dingle which stood perched with its resident practitioner not far from the tip of a narrow peninsula.[60]

Hinterlands as small as this were unlikely to provide enough work for firms with several partners or employees; they might not even provide enough for one man. The last statement cannot be amplified without some highly arbitrary provisoes. But those who enjoy such calculations may note the opinion of William Bald that one surveyor could tackle from 50 to 150 acres in a day depending on the character of the terrain,[61] a high estimate by cross-channel standards but one that may reflect the comparatively small amount of topographical information that the Irish surveyor was expected to put on his maps. In converting a daily output of approximately one hundred acres into its annual equivalent, account must be taken of bad weather and bad ground conditions (which at one period prevented Joshua Wight from working more than six months out of fifteen)[62] as well as of office duties. Allowing every other weekday for field work would give an annual total of about 15,000 acres, yielding a gross mid-eighteenth-century income of about £125 per year. To judge from his diary, Wight was exceptionally industrious and enviably active in both body and mind; for a closer approximation to the average, further allowances should be made for illness and holidays and for the kind of 'frictional' unemployment that must have been inevitable when work was divided in such small units. All in all it was reasonable for David McCool to have been pleased with a total output exceeding 70,000 acres in the period 1766–72,[63] and for his fellow-northerner Joseph Boyd to have felt the same about achieving comparable quantitative standards a decade later with more than 10,000 acres in a single season;[64] neither of them would have risked putting off potential customers by making claims that were improbably or discreditably large. If farms needed surveying once every twenty-one years (a common term for a lease), then someone like Boyd would have a territory of around 210,000 acres, or say 240,000 acres (with a radius of about eleven miles) to take account of land that was uncultivated and therefore let 'in bulk'.

Since most Irish properties fell far below this limit, the preceding paragraph at least explains why it was rare for a pre-nineteenth-century surveyor to be attached to one particular estate as a regular employee. This is another difficult field of investigation. Before 1700 there is no problem because the only two proven exceptions are obviously special cases.[65] The scene of Thomas Raven's six years' service with the city of London in the 1610s was clearly more like a plantation than an estate.

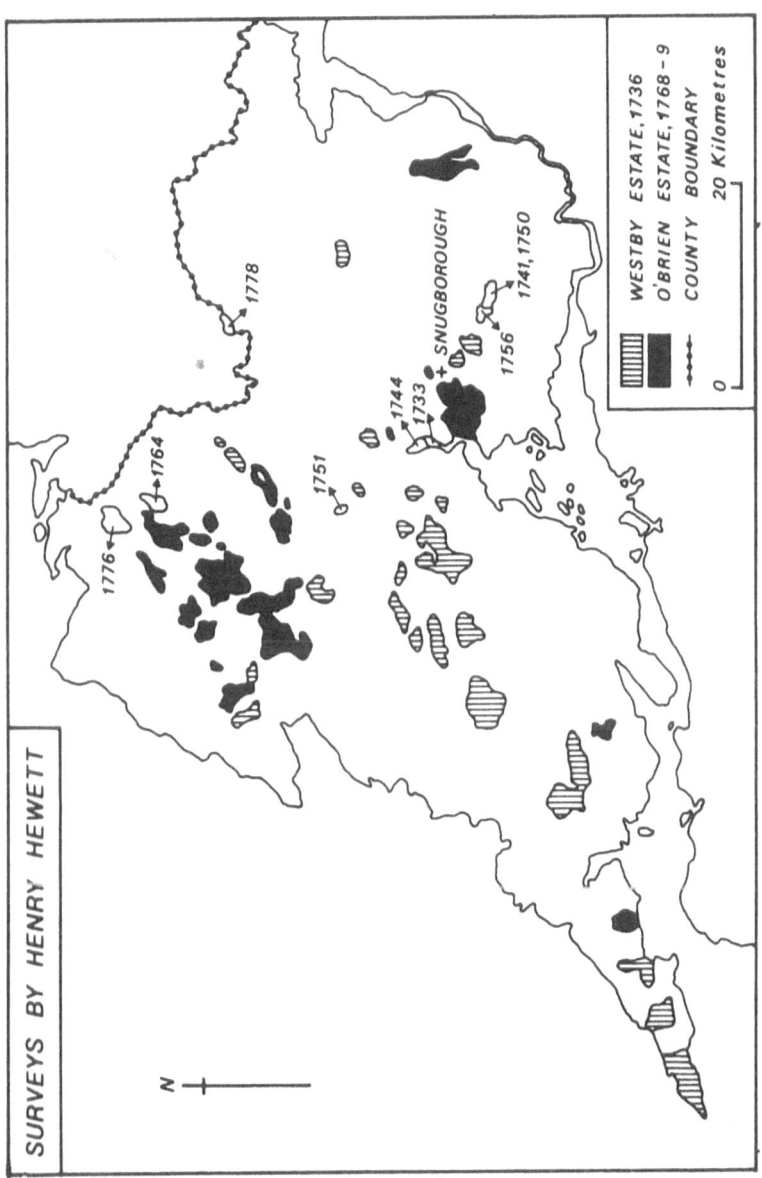

Figure 12. Recorded surveys by Henry Hewett of Snugborough, Co. Clare.

And the reason why Dublin needed its own City Surveyor (first appointed in 1679) was the unusual complexity of the municipal holdings, both in a purely geometrical sense and in the amount of quasi-engineering and quasi-architectural work involved. In the eighteenth century such overlapping of occupations made it difficult to classify the employees on rural estates, where surveying was often combined with managerial duties of various kinds. The salaried surveyor on the Fitzwilliam property in Co. Wicklow may have been justified by the abnormally large area of demesne woodland;[66] on the Abercorn estate it was the turf bogs that had need of salaried supervision;[67] at Lismore the same person was employed as surveyor and under-agent.[68] Another problem is to distinguish part-time from fulltime activity. The first Dublin City Surveyor, John Greene, absented himself so often on his own affairs that there was talk of having to find him a deputy.[69] A surveyor on salary was probably expected to do a moderate amount of private work on the side. In any case, without positive evidence of salary payments 'my surveyor' may mean no more than comparable modern middle-class expressions like 'my doctor' and 'my bank manager'. Perhaps the most revealing evidence on the subject of permanent surveyors is the number of very large and rich estates – Kildare, Abercorn, Devonshire and others – that were mapped in the later eighteenth century by men who are known to have been freelances.

Another possibility requiring comment (to return to the concept of the hinterland and its implications) is that the number of independent surveyors in Ireland may have been uneconomically large. If the foregoing calculations can be relied upon, about seventy surveyors would have been theoretically sufficient to keep the country going. The actual number was certainly greater. In 1750 Callan put it at a hundred, and those were only 'practical' surveyors and not the fops and pretenders whom he accused of wandering about the country in swarms. Eighteenth-century occupational censuses are rare in both time and space; since they are also likely to be incomplete, the three land surveyors recorded at Carrick-on-Suir in 1788 are more significant than the nil return received from Armagh in 1770.[70] The first such census of a whole barony was for Rathvilly, Co. Carlow, in 1825.[71] It enumerated six surveyors, a share of the baronial population that would imply an all-Ireland total in the same year of 2,350. This extrapolation has the possible disadvantage of treating urban and rural areas alike,[72] but as it happens the number of land surveyors given in the national census for 1841 is remarkably similar at 2,230. The problem here is that the 1841 figure included a number of

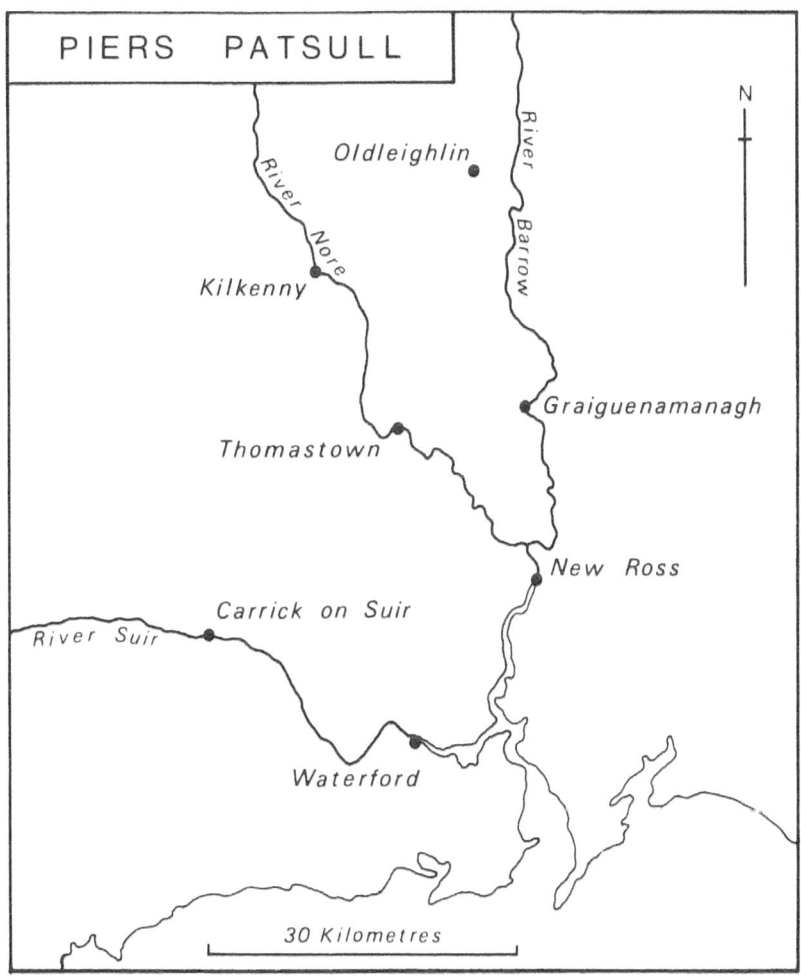

Figure 13. Business addresses of Piers Patsull. Source: *Dublin Journal*, 16 Aug. 1760. Patsull lived at Graiguenamanagh. The other places were advertised as 'the most convenient towns for his employers to direct to him'.

Ordnance Survey personnel for whom no proper allowance can be made owing to uncertainty about how the various ancillary duties of the Survey were classified for census purposes.[73] The number of office workers to be deducted could be as many as 500. But at least we have an uncontaminated total of more than 1,400 private surveyors for those counties in which the Ordnance Survey is known to have been unrepresented either indoors or outdoors at the time of the census. Assuming once more a constant ratio of surveyors to total population, the 1841 census can be projected backwards to give a total of about 500 in the middle of the eighteenth century. Of course this fails to reckon with whatever increase in per capita surveying activity accompanied the age of improvement, but even if such allowance were possible the mid-eighteenth-century total would surely be larger than seventy.

An alternative approach is to list all the individual surveyors' names and dates discovered by historical research and so to estimate the number at work in any one year. Two assumptions are necessary. One is the length of an average surveyor's career, which for the sake of argument has been put at thirty years. The other is the proportion of known to unknown surveyors: since in any new cache of names it is common to find that about half have not been previously encountered, the number of names on record should probably be doubled to give a realistic estimate. The result is a mid-eighteenth-century total of about 530. If the same method is pursued within a regional framework, by mapping surveyors' residences (Fig. 15), it yields the same general conclusion, namely that there were more surveyors in Ireland than a time-and-motion expert would have been happy with. The most obvious explanation for the surplus is that not many surveyors were kept constantly at work. It has been suggested for instance that the paucity of extant maps by certain practitioners – often only one map, sometimes none – shows that they cannot have drawn many maps in the first place. This argument might seem to overestimate the enthusiasm of later generations for preserving and recording Ireland's cartographic heritage and it must be admitted that a surveyor could be 'very eminent' (like Jeremiah Molony in 1791)[74] or at least able to earn a 'decent livelihood' (like William Higgins in 1784)[75] without managing to find a place in any modern map catalogue; which in turn suggests a positively gluttonous appetite for working overtime among those cartographers, such as the Frizell family, whose maps turn up in almost every large collection.

A more satisfying possibility is to look for the surveyor's other occupations. As already mentioned, many estate workers laid claim to

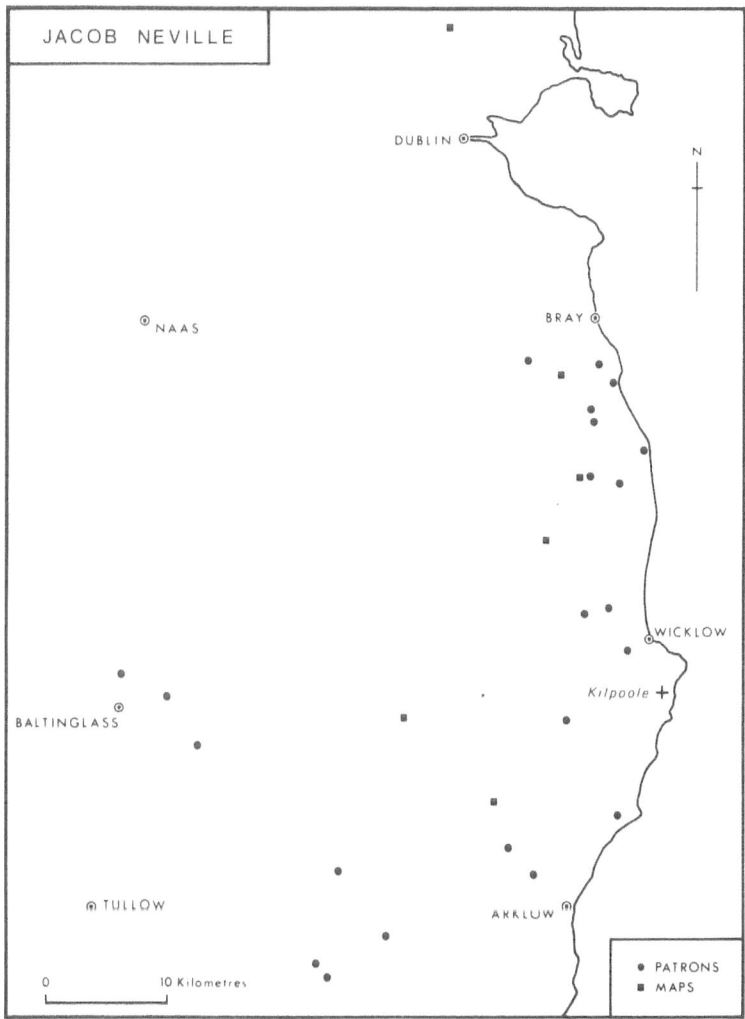

Figure 14. Patrons and maps of Jacob Neville. Symbols show the known addresses of those recommending Neville, just before his move to Dublin from Kilpoole, Co. Wicklow, for having 'given us general satisfaction in surveying our lands' and for having published a map of Co. Wicklow. In announcing his move Neville promised to make surveys in any part of Ireland; hitherto his only recorded surveys had been in Cos. Wicklow and Dublin, with a few in Cos. Armagh and Tyrone. Source: *Dublin Journal*, 9 Apr. 1773.

measuring ability, and Callan's attack on what he called compulsory surveyors ('agents, gardeners, menial servants, common bailiffs, fosterers, followers, and tenants, sons to landlords') implies that a good deal of mapping was done by men with other and unrelated calls upon their time. Then there was a range of occupations having one or more technical links with land measurement: engineers, architects, 'measurers' (of timber or building work), teachers, artists, instrument-makers. On the other hand Irish surveyors seem to have avoided the kind of offbeat second career (brickmaker, musician, plumber, sickle-smith etc.) that diversifies the muster-roll of their opposite numbers in England. In Co. Cork for a surveyor to have been a dancing master was an invitation to ridicule,[76] his mockers presumably forgetting that the great English cartographer, John Ogilby, had once gained a livelihood by this means. Such narrow-mindedness reflects the simpler occupational structure in Ireland and especially the dominance of farming in the countryside and shop-keeping in the towns. It seems significant that the earliest surviving letter from an Irish surveyor to a private client should make an excellent start with survey stations and map scales and then quickly deteriorate into a long-winded farmer's grumble about the price of corn.[77] If a surveyor's agricultural background is not betrayed in documents (as the tenant named in a lease or rental, or perhaps in the reference column of one of his own estate maps)[78] then it can often be deduced from his address, for many surveyors preferred to live at some distance from the amenities of town or village. Apart from the general Irish desire to hold land, farming suited the surveyor by not being itself a necessarily arduous or time-consuming occupation; and surveying suited the farmer because a surprisingly large amount of it was done in the winter months (Table 10). At the same time residence on a family farm would allow the aging surveyor to make his exit gradually and gracefully; we can hope that this is what happened to John Patsull of Graiguenamanagh, whose professional reputation was still in a healthy state when he died at the age of eighty-five.[79]

In estimating manpower requirements there is one more complication to be remembered. It was assumed on a previous page that each farm would be surveyed once at each letting; in reality, as has already been shown, many farms were separately measured by landlord and tenant, and then perhaps a third time if the first two surveys disagreed (Appendix B). A single piece of work might be checked and rechecked by its author, as when Mr Sanderson of Drogheda strove to meet academic standards of accuracy by three successive surveys of a farm belonging to Trinity

SURVEYORS IN SOCIETY 245

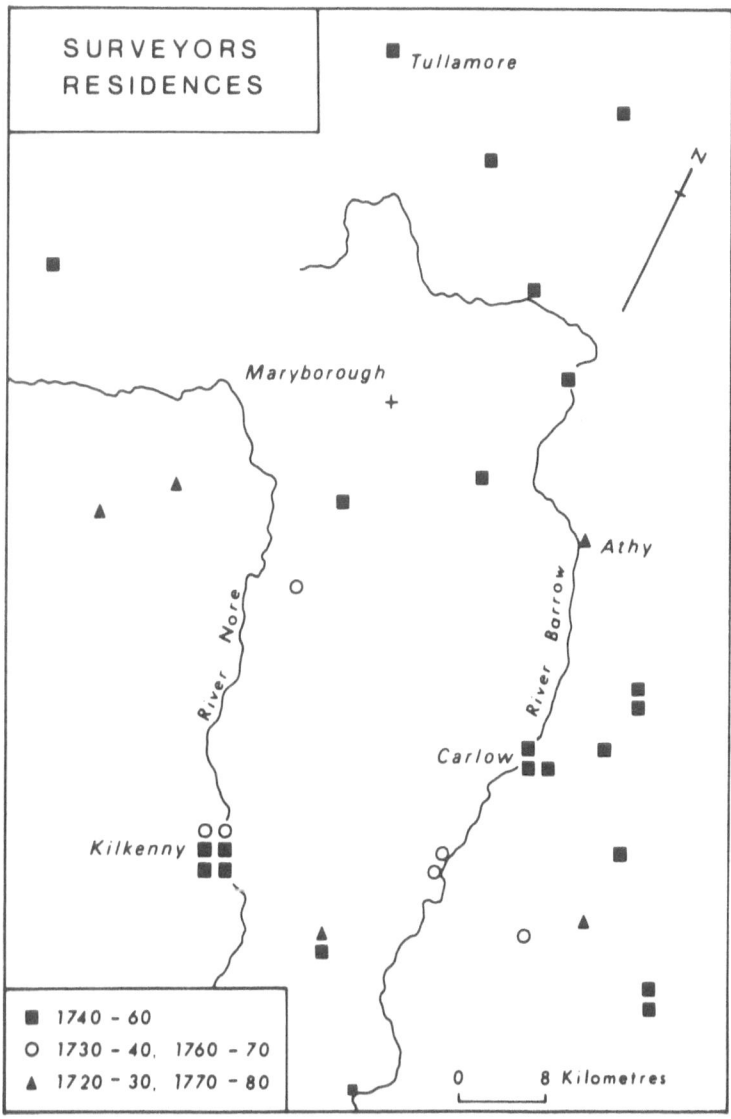

Figure 15. Surveyors' residences in the middle Nore and Barrow Valleys, 1720–80. The map does not take account of surveyors whose surviving output makes it likely that they lived somewhere in this district but whose precise addresses are not recorded. On the assumptions stated in the text, the number of surveyors probably resident here in 1750 was fifty, with a mean hinterland of about 30,000 statute acres.

College.[80] On another property in 1756–7 six independent surveyors were concerned in measuring a farm of less than a hundred acres, with two more mathematicians to calculate the acreage from the field notes.[81] (It sometimes seems as if the popular Irish technique of calculation from field notes was expressly designed to increase the number of disputes both near and far in which a single practitioner could participate.) It was thus common for surveyors to speak of 'defending' or 'making good' their surveys or of 'defeating' their opponents. At times their craft began to look like a spectator sport, with the two surveyors, the two employers, the mearsmen and a straggle of witnesses all perambulating the same boundary at the same time.

'Sport' is used here in its late twentieth-century sense: unlike lawyers, well known for fraternising after a clash in court, rival surveyors remained fiercely competitive and fanatically jealous of their reputations.[82] It was all in the day's work to be taunted with the offer of a bet, or threatened with an old law against 'deceitful pretenders to crafty sciences', or at any rate 'posted and gazetted'.[83] Unskilful or erroneous were then the mildest of the epithets that an Irish surveyor might expect to read about himself. Over areal differences of five per cent or less (Appendix B) he could be branded by his professional brethren as backbiting, base, blockheaded, bungling, calumnious, cobbling, crackbrained, crazy-headed, evasive, false, foolish, gasconading, groping, ignorant, impertinent, lying, malicious, notorious, obstinate, officious, pompous, purblind, scandalous, scurrilous, silly, sinister, sophistical, splenetic, spurious, stupid, unjust, vain, villainous, wanton, and worthless. (The victim would be surprised to find his lifetime appearing in a modern historical geography book as part of the 'silent century'.) These controversialists wrote more than enough to produce a book of their own (Appendix C) – a somewhat repetitive work it would be, for despite the size of their vocabulary the subject of their quarrels was always the same. It was one more battlefront in the war of landlord versus tenant, higher or lower rents, more or fewer acres. Yet surveyors could sometimes be found still locked in combat long after their employers had come to an agreement.[84] Their posture revealed a state of professional overpopulation that the availability of other livelihoods had done little to cure.

Despite the attractions of an evenly-matched contest, the horizontal cleavages between superior and inferior surveyors are of more serious interest than the vertical lines within a single peer-group. From the cartographic standpoint the most important 'class' distinction is between those who concentrated mainly on farm surveys and those who also surveyed entire estates. An estate surveyor could be brought from further afield; in fact for a job that might last a year or more he would be happy to travel from Dublin to any part of Ireland. And Dublin was clearly a good base from which to specialise in mapping estates, not only for access to clients and rumours of clients, but also for ease of purchasing and repairing instruments and other materials.[85] Among country surveyors drawn to Dublin in the eighteenth century were Archibald Stewart from Antrim or thereabouts,[86] Richard Frizell from Wexford,[87] Jacob Neville from Wicklow[88] and Joseph Ravell from Drogheda.[89] But like so many differences among surveyors the dichotomy of big city and small town was also a matter of degree. A practitioner of high repute might thrive in a provincial town (in that case our theory would require him to spend less time on estate surveys than the Dubliner, and more on farm surveys), and it was an independent current of migration that brought Samuel Andrews[90] and James Healy[91] to Cork, which, unlike for example Waterford, had its own instrument-makers.[92] Subsequently, as might be expected, Belfast became an equally powerful magnet, attracting among others James Williamson and John McArthur.[93] Ireland's estate-farm dichotomy thus recalls the distinction observed by another map historian between the town-dwelling surveyors of eighteenth-century France and their less proficient country cousins.[94]

The surveyor of whole estates needed a reputation for accuracy and impartiality. He would hope to hold himself above what Scalé described as an altercation in a newspaper, or at least to conduct such an altercation with his own touch of urbanity, as Scalé on the whole succeeded in doing.[95] The estate surveyor was also capable of waiting for his fee. In short, he was a person of more than usual substance, for in land surveying, as in all kinds of cartography, the status of the map-maker varies with the size of the area being mapped. Another factor of importance was a gift for neat and stylish draughtsmanship, especially after the aesthetic revolution set off by Rocque, though well before Rocque's time it was possible for reputations to be damaged by untidiness. 'I have no opinion of this Bourke', wrote Sir John Perceval (never one to mince matters), 'whose pitiful draft shows him to be a mean person in his profession'.[96] The remedy was a division of labour either between firms or within firms. Thomas Moland's maps of the Courtenay estate were said (perhaps mistakenly) to have been fair-drawn in England,[97] but later in the century the specialist draughtsman could be found nearer home. A well-known Irish artist like Gabriel Beranger might

TABLE 10

SEASONAL DISTRIBUTION OF SURVEYING

January	6.5%	July	9.7%
February	6.9	August	7.9
March	10.6	September	8.8
April	9.7	October	8.9
May	9.1	November	7.5
June	10.0	December	4.4

Percentages adjusted to allow for different lengths of month and calculated from a sample of 1,009 maps of various dates from 1633 to 1884.

copy maps as a side-line;[98] so did some school masters who were too busy in the daytime to undertake surveying,[99] and also of course a number of surveyors who happened to be more adept than their colleagues. Michael Kenny underlined the element of metropolitan sophistication in this activity by offering to draw maps for 'country' surveyors;[100] but it was in Belfast that James Williamson found himself so pressed by his fellows to 'ornament and finish' their maps that he had to refuse any further orders, and it was in Belfast, too, that a local land surveyor made the drawings for a world atlas being prepared for publication in 1828.[101]

While 'drawing' could include the initial plotting of a surveyor's fieldwork, it was sometimes subdivided into outlining and writing. Both possibilities are illustrated in the following advertisement:

> Maps and penmanship. Mr James Wheeler, long in the practice of surveying in Great Britain and Ireland, respectfully informs the nobility, gentry, and land-surveyors, that after school hours he devotes his time in delineating and embellishing maps of estate[s,] farms, etc. from the field notes or copies, old maps accurately done according to the present taste; and being assisted by that celebrated penman, Mr Darby, gentlemen may be assured, that nothing shall be wanting to render it the most useful and convenient institution of the kind offered to the public. Mr Darby is determined not to change his situation in future; informs gentlemen of the law and College, that he teaches the court, chancery, mixed and running secretary hands, German text, etc. etc. and on reasonable terms.[102]

With work thus divided, the most successful surveyor was the one who could commission the best artists. To be even more successful he had to bring the artists under his own roof. When an anonymous but apparently flourishing surveyor announced a vacancy for a clerk in 1773 it was made clear that neat drawing would count as a qualification;[103] and Thomas Sherrard evidently had draughtsmanship in mind when he advertised for two assistants simultaneously, one as an apprentice surveyor and the other to work in the office.[104] Sherrard's expansive gesture might have looked like an attempt to bring back the spacious days of Rocque. In fact he was giving a foretaste of the next century, for it was now that the size of the more successful land surveying practices began to increase. Occasionally the new trend was well publicised, as in the trinities of Sherrard, Brassington and Greene, and Brownrigg, Longfield and Murray. Sometimes the employees remained anonymous, and the only hint of expansion was the appearance of a branch office, as when James Vaughan practised in both Dublin and Athboy, and William Armstrong in both Dublin and Armagh. Some of the evidence is even vaguer, like the words 'and Co.' after a cartographer's name.[105]

But while a trend towards larger firms seems credible enough, in general the nineteenth century is a more difficult period to study than the eighteenth. For one thing, public controversy among surveyors appears to have declined. The drop in temperature was partly a matter of fashion in the media, not least among newspaper editors; but there were also a number of more substantial changes. The most noticeable was a rise in the surveyor's fees (Appendix E). If all prices were rising equally, the real cost of surveying would remain the same, but a 'perceived' rise may have been sufficient to curb the waste of labour indulged in by earlier generations and so to eliminate some of the ferocious – but often historically informative – wrangling to which disputed and duplicated surveys so often gave rise.

The most influential concomitant of the Irish price revolution, however, was an acceleration in the decline of the middleman. When landlords tried to administer their estates directly they soon became dependent on salaried professional assistance. The Devon report of 1845 includes references to Lord Hertford's 'own surveyor', to the surveyor 'belonging to' the Portglenone estate, to the surveyor 'attached to' Lord O'Neill's estate, and to the surveyor paid 'by the year' for regulating Lord Clanricarde's estate.[106] The ambiguity of such descriptions has already been noted, but in one case, at least, a genuine full-time staff-member can be identified beyond all doubt. This was Thomas Murray, apprentice and subsequently partner to John Brownrigg, who served the Marquess of Downshire as salaried surveyor from 1809 to 1850. His pay was £300, later rising to £350, and his duties included the revision of earlier surveys to correct inaccuracies or to take account of reclamation, the drawing and custody of maps, the making of valuations for new tenancies, the laying out of new farms and the subdivision of old ones, the construction of roads, and the planting of trees. It all kept him busy enough to need the assistance of his brother Henry at a salary of £150.[107]

Thomas Murray's work schedule highlights another feature of closer landlord control, and that was the increasing use of independent valuation – as opposed to competitive proposals – as a means of fixing rents. Of course in the late Middle Ages to survey and to value were almost synonymous, but by the eighteenth century the relations between the two ideas had grown more complicated. When land needed valuing at this period, it was often done by a professional surveyor – Moland, Neville, the Frizells, Scalé and Sherrard were all favourite choices – but equally often by the owner or his agent, or by a superior tenant farmer. The new tendency in the nineteenth century was for valuing to be regarded as a separate skill, not teachable through textbooks, but in which a man could nevertheless be apprenticed and instructed. A similar development was observable in England, and the fixing of more Irish rents by valuation brought an influx of 'quality men' westwards across the channel.[108] Other valuers – or valuators as they were now generally called – appeared in Dublin and in various parts of Ulster.[109] The valuator was not necessarily enough of a surveyor to make his own base maps: an Englishman who valued the Locke estate in Kerry in 1823 admitted without embarrassment that his maps had been made by somebody else.[110] On the other hand, the land surveyor was not necessarily qualified for both mysteries: 'surveyors we find are not so much accustomed to value', reported an assistant Poor Law commissioner in 1844, 'as some other men; they are more surveyors than valuers'.[111]

For those surveyors who could manage it there was much to be gained from combining the two jobs; especially as the valuator could take a separate fee (in the 1820s it was usually $2^{1}/2$ percent of his valuation)[112] for work which added very little to the time spent covering the same ground as a surveyor. With luck he might clear as much as five pounds a day for valuing on top of his acreable surveyor's charge. Of course money generally goes to money, but there was also a more specific reason for a valuator's clients to be attracted by a degree of affluence and status (as opposed to tangible merit) that would not be thought necessary in a surveyor pure and simple: status promised immunity from corruption, and corruption was much harder to test objectively with pounds, shillings and pence than with acres, roods and perches. For this reason it was the large firm of 'gentlemen' surveyors, as typified by Sherrard, Brassington and Greene, that had most to gain from the new importance attached to valuation.

Engineer was another title favoured by 'land surveyors, or as they call themselves, "civil engineers and land valuators"', to quote an impartial observer who seemed less happy about throwing these words around.[113] As his comment suggests, the relationships of valuing and engineering to ordinary land surveying were in some respects alike. There was also a difference. Few surveyors would positively refuse to be called engineers; but when the letters 'C.E.' appear on an estate map (a common occurrence from the 1830s onwards) the name in front of them is seldom as familiar to the map historian as those of the best-known valuators of the same period. The 'C.E.' might be a common surveyor aiming above his station – there was nothing except conscience, or fear of ridicule, to prevent the initials being flaunted by anyone who took a fancy to them[114] – or he might be a real engineer filling a blank space in his engagement book; in neither case could he claim a central position on the cartographic stage. It was a vocational split that had been widening for more than half a century. In Gabriel Stokes's time a surveyor could still win respect as an engineer while retaining eminence within his own profession, but from about 1770 the two occupations began to draw apart. The transitional figure here was Scalé's pupil John Brownrigg. He has already found a place in this study as a land surveyor closely concerned with canals. His own self-assessment made him 'the father of all the engineers in Ireland',[115] though he did little engineering apart from canal work and even in this restricted sphere he has failed to win a very good opinion from the most recent historian of the subject.[116] The truth is that in Brownrigg's lifetime engineering was moving rapidly ahead of land surveying in technical complexity, in educational standards, and in the cost and precision of the apparatus required; also in prestige and profitability. Any genuine engineer could measure an estate if he turned his hand to it; but given the talent and training for both activities he would naturally prefer the one that could pay up to ten guineas per day instead of only one or two guineas.[117]

The gap might seem to have been bridged by the 'topographical engineers' (as Alexander Nimmo called them) who surveyed the bogs of Ireland between 1809 and 1813. Such men, and in particular Nimmo himself, along with Richard Griffith, William Bald and William Edgeworth, could present themselves as all-round engineers who had developed a special interest in trigonometrical surveying – they might have added the expression geodetic surveying if it had been in common use. Nimmo was quick to distinguish his own role from that of the land surveyor, a difference perhaps signalled by allowing his employees to sign their own estate maps.[118] Among his generation there were some topographical engineers, notably William Edgeworth, whom it is almost impossible to visualise in an agrarian setting: when one's ambition is to measure a degree of latitude, triangulating a farm is not a very attractive substitute. Edgeworth was an extreme case, being rebuked by a famous English engineer for his lack of practicality.[119] Most of his Irish confreres were prepared to relieve the common land surveyor of some of his heaviest burdens, as has already been seen in the case of road planning.

This last subject throws light on the whole issue of professional demarcation. When it was proposed in the 1810s to create a new official class of county road supervisors, the ordinary land surveyor found himself frozen out and the plan was deemed to have broken down for lack of suitable applicants.[120] When it was successfully revived in 1833, a reputation in land surveying pure and simple made no better impression than before: the appointments were based on competitive examination, said to be the first use of this method in any branch of the public service either British or Irish.[121] Although the new post was officially described as that of 'county surveyor', the second of these words soon came to be regarded as a misnomer (and an offensive one at that),[122] and most of the county surveyors revealed their own opinion of themselves by joining the new Institution of Civil Engineers of Ireland, a body that no mere land surveyor seems ever to have aspired to.[123]

It was among the junior engineers that the overlap of functions lasted longest. Despite the sharp distinction he drew between the two activities, Nimmo saw an engineering apprenticeship as a good background for a land surveyor,[124] and some young men, even those with university training,[125] were less reluctant than their elders to undertake routine surveys when building a career. A famous case is the railway promoter William Dargan, the only Irish surveyor (if he can qualify as such) to have a statue erected in his honour.[126] A better if less well known example is Nimmo's pupil William Johnston, who offered 'surveying, laying out roads, bridges and engineering generally' in the same advertisement as 'estates etc. surveyed, maps and plans drawn, improvements designed, estimated for, and executed; also maps copied, and reduced for attaching to leases etc.'[127]

Perhaps the only clear conclusion to emerge from the preceding pages is that there was no such person as the typical surveyor. For the same reason the middle eighteenth century, on which much of this chapter has focused, can in no sense be regarded as representative of any other period. The surveyor's place in society varied from one individual to another and also from one era to another. Petty had his own reasons for emphasising that up to his time surveyors had been 'commonly persons of gentle and liberal education, and their practice esteemed a mystery and intricate matter, far exceeding the most part of mechanical trades'.[128] But in spite of Petty's deflationary tactics gentility was still far from dead at the end of the eighteenth century. One thinks of William Beauford, best known as an antiquarian researcher, and nearer the centre of things, the former Wexford surveyor Richard Frizell, who by 1791 had graduated into a 'facetious and hospitable gentleman' with a fine library.[129] In the next decade surveying could still be considered a possible career for the son of an Irish clergyman.[130]

By that time, however, the word 'surveyor' was coming down in the world (like the word 'clerk' and, later, 'secretary') – not by a wholesale displacement from one class to another, but by being diffused through successive bands of society's stratigraphical column, with a thick deposit of 'common surveyors' overlain by a thinner caprock of 'gentlemen surveyors'. As Nimmo pointed out, common surveyor was a very wide expression.[131] It might suggest a parity with teachers, agents and gentlemen's servants – groups bracketed with surveyors as the kind of pedestrian frequenting the roads of western Ireland, important enough to travel on business but still too humble to have his own horse or carriage.[132] It could also embrace the unfortunate Daniel Moore, a surveyor described in 1775 as needing to be given a pair of trousers before he was ready to appear in court.[133] Surveyors and their families could move up and down this long social ladder with surprisingly little trouble. In Co. Limerick one of their sons was accorded a status so mean that a baronet's upper servants drew the line at dining with him, but that did not prevent his triumphant reappearance a few years later displaying the 'dress and appellation of a gentleman'.[134]

After this, many modern historians will be curious about the Irish land surveyor's record of service in the class war. When Callan complained of favouritism towards either landlords or tenants, he did not say outright that the same surveyors always served the same social class, though this may have been what he meant: in general the most talented members of the profession could be expected to hook the richest clients, with gentlemen measuring for gentlemen (and Protestants for Protestants), and inferiors for inferiors. Lord Abercorn's agent illustrated this kind of doublethink when he first named the only three local surveyors who were available for service with the Earl and then mentioned a fourth, anonymous, 'country surveyor' who had been working for some of the tenants on the same estate.[135] In similar vein, a witness before the Devon commission spoke contemptuously of surveyors whom no landlord or agent would employ – and who therefore must have been hired solely by farmers or cottagers.[136] Even so, the lack of tenant farmers' records (not to mention surveyors' records) makes this a risky generalisation. What does seem clear is that the surveyor's ability to serve both sides gave him a position of neutralism that was all too rare in rural Ireland. The threatening, attacking and murdering of map-makers are all commonplaces of Irish history; but the surveyor could not be branded as an oppressor by definition – unlike the bailiff, the agent, the tithe-proctor, the driver and for that matter the landlord. The variability of his income, status and political leanings placed him closer to the teacher than to anyone else: that was another occupation with a wide socio-economic span, from the schoolmaster-labourer on record in 1835 (interestingly enough he also measured land)[137] all the way up to the university professor of mathematics. When subversive literature was alleged to be flooding the country in the 1820s the two classes of agitator who took the blame were rural schoolmasters and 'low surveyors'.[138] On the borderline between high and low stood the Wexford surveyor Valentine Gill, who made himself famous by changing sides halfway through the rebellion of 1798.[139]

Political unreliability was not the only failing among surveyors. A more common complaint was drunkenness, though there is no suggestion that they out-drank anyone else in Ireland, and the map historian, if obliged to dwell on human frailty, will find something more appropriate in the troubles of Lord Abercorn's employee Henry Hood, attributed not to alcohol but to 'abstemious living'.[140] Hood's private life was unusual in the attention it attracted. Other surveyors maintained a barrier of discretion and self-effacement that posterity has so far been unable to break down. Despite their many hours spent in farmhouse or tavern waiting for the rain to stop, they nearly always managed to escape the notice of agricultural and social commentators like Arthur Young. Surveyors also held aloof from brawls and scandals outside their own profession, and even the most successful of them were seldom in the public eye. Few put their names on subscription lists, or petitioned Parliament, or took their neighbours to court, or got on to official boards and commissions, or employed fashionable architects, or sat for their portraits, or had poems written about them.[141] Though often charged by their colleagues with producing works of fiction, they made hardly any impact on imaginative art and very little on literature. Surveyors' virtues were every bit as humdrum as their vices. Punctuality, patience, common sense, reliability and accuracy are not always seen as distinctively Irish qualities, even among friends of Ireland; nor are the map-maker's keen visual sense and his economical use of words. But they were common enough to fill a book.

Notes

1. Larcom, *Down Survey*, p. 256.
2. See the appropriate entries in Eden, *Dictionary of Surveyors*. The absence of earlier British entries is especially remarkable in the case of Raven, who by his own reckoning would have had time for plenty of experience before he came to Ireland: he was 'upwards of sixty' in Jan. 1635 (Harleian MS 4297, f. 168; R Gillespie, 'Thomas Raven and the Mapping of the Claneboy Estates', *Bangor Hist. Soc. Jour.*, 1 (1981), pp 7–9).
3. Grosart, *Lismore Papers*, 1st ser., 2, pp 79, 139–40 (Baldwin Carpenter, 1622-3). A map of one of Boyle's townlands in Co. Cork, made by Augustine Atkins, is mentioned in a list of leases in NLI, MS 6179.
4. Jephson, *Anglo-Irish Miscellany*, p. 51 (8 Nov. 1654).
5. For a representative sample of advertisements see Lockhart, *Ir. Geogr.*, 11 (1978),pp 102–09. The diary is that of Joshua Wight: entries relating to his professional life range from Apr. 1752 to Aug. 1755, with a long essay on surveying technicalities under 25 Sep. 1752. There is an unpublished biographical study of Wight by Mary Pike in the Friends' Historical Library, Dublin. Two of his Co. Cork estate maps, one of 1712 and one of 1723, are in NLI, 21.F.73(5, 44), neither of them particularly interesting.
6. *Dublin Journal*, 22 May 1762. Colles appears in the *Dictionary of American Biography*, and there is a biographical introduction in W. W. Ristow's edition of his *A Survey of the Roads of the United States of America, 1789* (Cambridge, Mass., 1961); see also Ristow's 'Eliza Colles, America's First Female Map Engraver', *Map Collector*, 10 (1980), pp 14–17. The family is noticed in R. Colles, *In Castle and Courthouse, Being Reminiscences of Thirty Years in Ireland* (London, n.d). Many other eighteenth-century American surveyors were of Irish origin but apart from Colles the only one recorded as practising in Ireland was the little-known James Trimble (Hughes, *Surveyors and Statesmen*, p. 180).

7. Larcom, *Down Survey*, p. 2.
8. *Report on Survey and Valuation*, 1824, p. 73.
9. The books that Callan mentioned (citing only the author's name) were Aaron Rathborne's *The Surveyor* (1616); either William Leybourn's *Pantometria* (1650) or his *The Compleat Surveyor* (1653); Vincent Wing's *The Geodaetes Practicus* (1664); John Love's *Geodaesia* (1688); Samuel Wyld's *The Practical Surveyor* (1725); and Henry Wilson's *Geodaesia Catenea* (1732).
10. Replies to Laurence Doyle, of Ballon, Co. Carlow, a 'schoolmaster and a pretended surveyor', by Laurence Nowlan of Fennaugh, Co. Carlow, and by William Thornton of Burton Hall, Co. Carlow, *Leinster Journal*, 9 Jan., 20 Feb. 1771; Doyle's rejoinder, 9 Feb. 1771. For more about Nowlan, or another of the same name, see R. J. McHugh (ed.) *Carlow in '98, the Autobiography of William Farrell of Carlow* (Dublin, 1949), p. 162.
11. Young, *Tour*, 2, pp 196–7.
12. *Hibernian Chronicle*, 2 July 1781.
13. *Leinster Journal*, 15 Sep. 1773.
14. *Dublin Journal*, 22 June 1773.
15. *Belfast News Letter*, 19 Dec. 1809; E. R. R. Green and E. M. Jope, 'Patron and Architect: an Example of Relations in the Late 18th Century', *Ulster Jour. Arch.*, 24–5 (1961–2), pp 150–51. The immigration of Scottish surveyors to nineteenth-century Ulster remains a subject for future research. For an example see Lockhart, *Ir. Geogr.*, 11 (1978), pp 103, 107.
16. Royal Institution of Chartered Surveyors, *Five Centuries of Maps and Map-Making* (London, 1953), p. 63 (estate of John Bourke of Palmerstown, Co. Dublin, 1734). See also Sotheby & Co., *Catalogue of the Celebrated Collection, the Property of C. E. Kenney, Esq.* (London, 18 Oct. 1965), p. 39.
17. *Maps and Surveys, c.1600–c.1830, Co. Armagh (How to Use the Record Office*, No. 12, PRONI, Belfast, n.d), p. 21. An example of the opposite process was the mapping of Lord Abercorn's land near Edinburgh by the Lifford surveyor Samuel McCrea in 1764 (PRONI, T.2541/IA1/6c/15).
18. *Ennis Chronicle*, 11 June 1789.
19. James Crow and Thomas Marsh, maps of the Ironmongers' Company's Lizard estate, 1765, Guildhall Library, MS 17297/1. Crow's maps of the Donegall estate in Cos. Antrim and Donegal are in PRONI, D.835/1 .
20. *London-derry Journal*, 29 Dec. 1772, 15 Aug. 1815. Another of McCool's pupils was William McIntire (*London-derry Journal*, 28 May 1773).
21. *Sleater's Public Gazetteer*, 23 Sep. 1758.
22. Thompson, *Chartered Surveyors*, p. 21.
23. John Walley to the Earl of Cork, 30 May 1640, Chatsworth House, Lismore MS 2/20, a reference kindly supplied by Mr Michael McCarthy Morrogh.

24. Survey of Lord Erne's estate, 1768–9, PRONI, D. 1939/2/14. Samuel McCrea's commendation of his sons to the Earl of Abercorn is in PRONI, T.2541/IA1/8/174 (1 Dec. 1769).
25. Robert Gibson, *Course in Experimental Philosophy* (Dublin, 1755), list of subscribers; NLI, 16.1.3(19).
26. Map by Thomas Cuttle, 1722, Doneraile House, Co. Cork; *Dublin Journal*, 8 Sep. 1772.
27. *Leinster Journal*, 16 Sep. 1769.
28. Advertisement by Thomas Sherrard, *Saunders's News-letter*, 12 Dec. 1791.
29. *Leinster Journal*, 23 June 1787.
30. Barnard, *Jour. R. Soc. Ant. Ire.*, 102 (1972), p. 130.
31. E. Evans, *Historical and Bibliographical Account of Almanacks, Directories etc. etc. Published in Ireland from the Sixteenth Century* (Dublin, 1897), pp 36–42.
32. The history of educational advertising in Ireland runs parallel with that of land surveying as exhibited in the newspapers cited in the present work.
33. Quoted in P. Kennedy, *Evenings in the Duffrey* (Dublin, 1869), p. 104. Though evidently of nineteenth-century origin, the poem cannot be given a precise date.
34. Nothing else is known of this pioneer of historical geography except that he soon afterwards married 'a most amiable young lady, with a pleasing fortune' (*Hibernian Chronicle*, 30 May, 25 Nov. 1782). Another link between surveying and liberal studies was the advertisement for a teacher of English, writing and drawing at a 'classical institution' in the country, a post said to be suitable for a 'young man who had received the requisite education for a surveyor' (*The Patriot*, 4 Jan. 1820).
35. William Alingham's advertisement of 1706, quoted by E. G. R. Taylor, *The Mathematical Practitioners of Tudor and Stuart England* (Cambridge, 1954), p. 289.
36. *Dublin Journal*, 1 July 1783. Apart from Byron, Williamson, and Thomas Sherrard (all discussed in chapter 9), the only well-known surveyor named in the school's records was John Travers (*Proc. Dub. Soc.*, 1–2 (1764), p. 42).
37. *Public Gazetteer*, 17 Apr. 1759; see also below, ch. 9.
38. *Dublin Journal*, 24 Dec. 1754.
39. *Northern Star*, 30 Jan., 19 June 1794, 1 Feb. 1796.
40. Oliver Goldsmith, *The Deserted Village, a Poem* (London, 1770), p. 12. The location of Goldsmith's village is discussed by M. Beresford in M. Beresford and J. G. Hurst (eds.), *Deserted Medieval Villages: Studies* (London, 1971), pp 53–6. He thinks it was in England
41. Ireland's national school teachers were described in an undated memorandum of the 1840s as 'generally able to survey land' (PRONI, Benn papers, D.3113/6/21). Later, Matthew Kiernan of Co. Kildare

told the land court that as a schoolmaster, chain surveying was 'part of his business' (*Leinster Leader*, 21 June 1884).

42. One graduate of the Templemoyle Agricultural School in Derry who failed to give satisfaction as a surveyor appears in the *Devon Report*, 3, p. 195.

43. Larcom, *Down Survey*, pp 20–21.

44. An act for the advance and improvement of trade, and for encouragement and increase of shipping and navigation, reprinted in T. Davis, *The Patriot Parliament of 1689* (ed. C. G. Duffy, London, 1893), p. 61.

45. Bateman, *Just and True Relation*, p. 10.

46. For an early expression of this view, in relation to the 'poor youth' of Dublin, and for other details of elementary mathematical education in seventeenth-century Ireland see K. T. Hoppen, *The Common Scientist in the Seventeenth Century: a Study of the Dublin Philosophical Society, 1683–1708* (London, 1970), p. 17. Would-be surveyors are specifically catered for in many later schemes for practical as opposed to classical education, for example in *Some Thoughts on the General Improvement of Ireland, with a Scheme of a Society for Carrying on all Improvements* (Dublin, 1758), p. 8; in J. Giffard, *Mr Orde's Plan of an Improved System of Education in Ireland; Submitted to the House of Commons* (Dublin, 1787), p. 47; in R. L. Edgeworth's report on charter schools in *Reports ... from the Commissioners of the Board of Education in Ireland*, app 10, p. 110, H.C. 1809 (142), vii; and in *Report from the Select Committee on Foundation Schools and Education in Ireland*, p. 37, H.C. 1837–8 (701), vii.

47. *Fourteenth Report of the Commissioners of the Board of Education in Ireland*, app 3, p. 343 (letter from J. L. Foster, 22 Apr. 1811), H.C. 1812–13 (21), vi.

48. J. E. Bicheno, *Ireland and its Economy* (London, 1830), p. 285.

49. Among several thousand Irish surveyors known to the author, only one is expressly described in a contemporary source as either a Catholic or a Protestant. He was Martin Gerraughty (*Devon Report*, 2, app B, p. 40). Protestant surveyors sometimes seem to identify themselves by applying such words as 'popish' or 'Romish' to Catholic chapels or by discriminatory comments on the skill and diligence of the Catholic farmers in their survey area. But surnames (and to some degree Christian names) are probably the best guide – good enough to show that none of the surveyors discussed below in chapter 9 is likely to have been a Catholic.

50. Table of occupations by religious professions, *The Census of Ireland for the Year 1861*, part iv, ii, p. 715, H.C. 1863 [3204–III], lx. The apparent growth in the proportion of non-Irish names in the nineteenth century (Table 8) may be due partly to the increased amount of surveying done by Ulstermen and partly to the influence of large surveying, valuing and engineering firms whose subordinate members are unnamed in maps and directories.

51. Hist. MSS Com., *Various Collections*, 8, p. 324.

52. *Dublin Journal*, 12 Aug. 1758.
53. Bateman, *True and Just Relation*, p. 4.
54. Even a flourishing surveyor like Henry Hood might own no more than a single 'instrument' (Matthew Hood, 14 June 1801, PRONI, T.2541/IA3/2/38). The price of a chain in 1790 is given in P. Power, 'A Carrickman's Diary 1789–1809', *Jour. Waterford Arch. Soc.*, 15 (1912), pp 34–5.
55. Larcom, *Down Survey*, p. 35; NAI, 2B.44.61 (surveyors' bills, 1820–29).
56. Steile's sons were named as the three lives in a lease of land let to the surveyor (using his own survey) in 1759 (RD, 200/568/134352). After their father's death Richard and William announced themselves as 'professors of the same employment' (*Dublin Journal*, 8 Jan. 1760).
57. *Address to the Noblemen of Ireland*, p. 62.
58. An example was Jonathan Barker's offer to survey lands on his way from Dublin to Cork and Waterford (*Universal Advertiser*, 16 July 1754).
59. John Bannan's bills for surveying, Rolleston estate, 1810–17, NLI, MS 13794(6).
60. The Dingle surveyor Maurice Fitzgerald appears in 1779 in NLI, 21 F.24(2).
61. *Report on Survey and Valuation*, 1824, p. 59.
62. Wight's diary, 25 Sep. 1752.
63. *London-derry Journal*, 29 Dec. 1772.
64. *Belfast News-letter*, 4 Apr. 1783.
65. A deed of 1640 mentions the Earl of Ormond's surveyor but it is not clear that this was a salaried appointment (NLI, D.4207).
66. P. Lennon, *Eighteenth Century Landscape Change from Estate Records: Coolattin Estate, Shillelagh, County Wicklow*, B.A. dissertation, Department of Geography, TCD, 1979, ch. 4.
67. Gebbie, *Abercorn Letters*, p. 321 (1775).
68. This was a Welshman, Thomas Lowe, appointed in 1793 (*Rept. on Fisheries (Ireland)*, 1849, q. 5314).
69. *Cal. Anc. Rec. Dub.*, 6, p. 196 (1698).
70. R. ffolliott, 'Provincial Town Life in Munster', *Irish Ancestor*, 5 (1973), p. 35; M. Glancy, 'The Influence of the Plantation on the City of Armagh', *Seanchas Ardmhacha*, 1 (1955), pp 146–57.
71. *Return ... to an Order of the Honourable House of Commons, Dated 25 February 1825, for an Account, Containing the Names and Numbers of the Several Baronies ... of Ireland*, H.C. 1825 (214), xxii.
72. The number of surveyors in many of Ireland's early nineteenth-century towns appears to have been comparatively small, to judge from contemporary directories and from the occupational lists of freemen and voters in *Reports from the Select Committee on Fictitious Votes, Ireland*, H.C. 1837 (308, 480), xi (appendices).

73. County occupation tables, *Report of the Commissioners Appointed to Take the Census of Ireland for the Year 1841*, H.C. 1843 [504], xxiv. Land surveyors were distinguished from both civil engineers and measurers.
74. Obituary, *Dublin Chronicle*, 4 June 1791.
75. *Hibernian Chronicle*, 17 May 1784.
76. Richard Barry of Killeagh, Co. Cork, *Hibernian Chronicle*, 3 May 1784.
77. Thomas Kelly, 15 Nov. 1640, Add. MS 46924, f. 135. Loeber (*Architects*, p. 66) suggests that Kelly may have been an architect rather than a farmer.
78. Charles and Richard Frizell are perhaps the best examples of the autometric surveyor, notably at Askemore and Askebeg, Co. Wexford, where in 1768 they praised the improvements which they themselves had made as tenants (Kavanagh estate maps, NLI, mic. P.4645).
79. *Freeman's Journal*, 9 Feb. 1773.
80. TCD, MUN/P/28/108, n.d. (late seventeenth century). Later, Thomas Magnier was said to have made three surveys of Knockbrack, Co. Cork (*Cork Evening Post*, 15 Jan. 1784).
81. *Dublin Journal*, 14 Dec. 1756, 8, 22 Feb. 1757. The surveyors were Darby Dunne, Maurice Downer, Edward Kensals, James Keenan, John Jordan and John Travers; the mathematicians were Robert and George Gibson. Another case, near Carlow, involving four surveys and four additional calculations from field notes, all said to have been done 'lately', was reported in *Leinster Journal*, 31 Jan. 1798.
82. An illustration of this touchiness occurred in Carlow in 1753 following a trial at the assizes. The case involved the superimposition of the Down Survey on a modern survey and the acreages at issue were: in the Down Survey only, 1 acre; in the modern survey only, 6 acres; common to both surveys, 153 acres. One witness (the surveyor Daniel Byrne) was so afraid of mockery that he put an advertisement in the *Dublin Journal* (29 Sep. 1753) answering what seem to have been malicious accusations that he did not know the difference between 1 acre and 154 acres.
83. Joshua Wight's diary, 25 Sep. 1752. For the threat of prosecution under 33 Henry VIII, c. 15, see below, appendix C.
84. The controversy between John Mooney and Dennis Kinsella was not ended by the tenant's protestations that he had accepted his landlord's survey (*Pue's Occurrences*, 14 June 1757).
85. T. H. Mason, 'Dublin Opticians and Instrument Makers', *Dub. Hist. Rec.*, 6 (1944), pp 133–49. All the practitioners mentioned by Mason under dates earlier than 1796 are known to have made surveying instruments. He does not mention Alies and Bates (1773), Edward Spicer (died *c.* 1776), John Lort (Spicer's successor), Alexander Fitton (1784), P. Baron (1794) or Richard Spear (1794–1834).
86. Stewart's address is given as Mary Street, Dublin, in *Dublin Journal*, 19 Dec. 1747, but a large proportion of his earlier maps were of estates in Cos. Antrim and Londonderry.

87. Frizell's successive residences are recorded in the *Dublin Journal*: Mountfin near Enniscorthy, Co. Wexford (15 Aug. 1758), Askemore near Gorey in the same county (7 Mar. 1761), and Rathfarnham, Co. Dublin (14 Jan. 1777). In Wexford Richard partnered his brother Charles; at Rathfarnham he was agent to the Earl of Ely, a connection perhaps arising from his employment in 1771 to map the Earl's estates in the Frizells' home county (NLI, MS 4153).
88. *Hibernian Journal*, 9 Apr. 1773.
89. *Dublin Journal*, 8 Feb. 1755.
90. In the *Cork Evening-Post* for 5 June 1760 Andrews and his partner John Powell offered to survey estates while finishing a chart of Cork Harbour. Andrews advertised the chart in the same paper on 29 Sep. 1768 but so far as is known it was not published until 1792. In the meantime he made various surveys in and around Cork city (R. Caulfield (ed.), *The Council Book of the Corporation of the City of Cork* (Guildford, 1876), pp 822–3, 1010, 1055).
91. *Cork Evening-Post*, 15 Apr. 1784.
92. Cork instrument-makers included the immigrant craftsman Elias Voster, Daniel Voster, Nathaniel Sweeney and Edward Sweeney (*Cork Evening Post*, 16 June 1760, 6 Oct. 1763). For the lack of instruments at Waterford see S. S. de Val, 'Some Eighteenth-Century Petitions', *The Past* (Wexford), 9 (1972), p. 10. Paper seems to have been readily available in provincial towns, though vellum was sometimes scarce. Colouring materials, according to Gibson, were to be had in 'many druggists' shops' – sufficiently accessible for him not to include a discussion of them in his book (*Practical Surveying*, p. 319).
93. *Belfast News-letter*, 31 Oct. 1837, quoted by Lockhart, *Ir. Geogr.*, 11 (1978), p. 106.
94. R. Desreumaux, 'De l'Utilité des Arpenteurs du XVIIIe Siècle' in F. Barbier (ed.), *La Carte Manuscrite et Imprimée du XVIe au XIXe Siècle* (Munich, New York, London and Paris, 1983), p. 102.
95. Dispute between Scalé and Matthew Tannam over lands in Co. Kildare, *Dublin Journal*, 1 Sep., 1, 3 Dec. 1772.
96. 22 Mar. 1739, Add MS 46990, f. 36.
97. Joshua Wight's diary, 25 Sep. 1752.
98. *Volunteer Evening Post*, 27 Nov. 1783. As happened among map engravers, some draughtsmen confined themselves to marginal decoration. T. Godfrey signed a title-piece on a map of 1785 by Isaac Ringwood (NAI, M.3022), and Sisson Darling appears in the same capacity on maps by Thomas Sherrard (lands of the Archbishop of Armagh, Marley, Co. Louth, 1788, NLI, MS 2772; College lands in Co. Wicklow, 1786, TCD, MUN/ME/7). Darling also provided the cartouche for John Brownrigg's printed map of the Grand Canal (1788), which made it appropriate that he should later become one of the canal company's collectors.
99. An example was Thomas Ford of Dublin (*Dublin Spectator*, 14 Nov. 1768).

100. *Dublin Journal*, 26 Dec. 1771. The relationship was echoed when 'a land surveyor, living in the country' advertised for a person capable of drawing and colouring maps (*Morning Register*, 28 Oct. 1830).
101. The drawings done by Robert Pattison of Belfast for the 'atlas adapted to modern geography' by James Thompson were acknowledged both in Thompson's advertisements (*Newry Commercial Telegraph*, 5 Feb. 1828) and in the book itself (J. Anderson, *Catalogue of Early Belfast Printed Books, 1694 to 1830*, supplement to the third edition (Belfast, 1894), p. 15).
102. *Saunders's News-letter*, 12 June 1797.
103. *Dublin Journal*, 22 Apr. 1773.
104. *Saunders's News-letter*, 12 Dec. 1791.
105. *Dublin Evening Post*, 17 Jan. 1824 (Vaughan); *Devon Report*, 3, p. 854 (Armstrong). 'Mr Brownrigg's partners' are mentioned in connection with a canal survey in Co. Kilkenny in 1801 (*Leinster Journal*, 31 Jan.). G. Montgomery and son, at Lifford, wrote in 1815 of employing 'their usual number' of assistants, described as 'expert young men' (*L:Derry Journal*, 15 Aug.).
106. *Devon Report*, 1, pp 475, 550, 557, 562; 2, p. 554.
107. Maguire, *Downshire Estates*, pp 156, 178–80, 188, 255; *Devon Report*, 3, pp 671–3 (Murray's evidence).
108. For this term see Thompson, *Chartered Surveyors*, pp 36–7.
109. *Devon Report*, passim: most witnesses were asked who, if anyone, valued the land in their district. For the special importance of valuation in parts of Ulster, see Richard Griffith's evidence in *Report from the Select Committee on Townland Valuation of Ireland*, q. 26, H.C. 1844 (513), vii, and in *Report from the Select Committee on General Valuation, etc. (Ireland)*, qq. 1335, 1578–80, H.C. 1868–9 (362), ix.
110. *Report on Survey and Valuation*, 1824, p. 117. Professional surveyors were seldom employed to value Church land, according to the *Report ... on the Revenues and Condition of the Established Church (Ireland)*, app, p. 64, H.C. 1867–8 [4082-I], xxiv.
111. *Report on Townland Valuation*, 1844, q. 1403. For the emergence of valuing as a distinct profession see also *The Landlord and Tenant Question in Ireland Argued, in a Dialogue between Tom and Dick* (Dublin, 1853), p. 38.
112. John Longfield's account with the Bishop of Limerick, 1825, NLI, MS 860; Sherrard, Brassington and Gale, printed circular, c. 1830, in NAI, 2B.44.61, which also includes a report of 1824 by John Brownrigg, the government's examiner of surveys of Crown lands, accepting the rate of $2^{1}/2$ per cent as normal.
113. *Devon Report*, 3, p. 328.
114. An early Irish use of the initials 'C.E.' is in the maps by Richard Lovell Edgeworth and Alexander Nimmo engraved in 1811–13 for the bogs commission.

115. Brownrigg to Lord Downshire, 1 Sep. 1827, PRONI, D.671/ C. 141/44, quoted by J. F. Fulton, *The Roads of County Down, 1600–1900*, Ph.D. thesis, Queen's University, Belfast, 1972, p. 349. One of Brownrigg's advertisements, for an apprentice, was headed 'Land surveying and levelling' (*Dublin Journal*, 1 Jan. 1801).
116. Heard, *Public Works in Ireland*, p. 199.
117. This estimate of an 'eminent' engineer's earning capacity comes in a letter to the Marquess of Downshire of 2 Mar. 1836 (W. A. Maguire (ed.), *Letters of a Great Irish Landlord, a Selection from the Estate Correspondence of the Third Marquess of Downshire, 1809–45* (PRONI, Belfast, 1974), p. 177).
118. *Report on Survey and Valuation*, 1824, p. 77. Maps by John Hill of the Cavan estate of Sir Robert Hodson (1828) described themselves as made under Nimmo's direction (George Mealy & Sons, *Catalogue* (Castlecomer, 14 Oct. 1982), no. 205).
119. Edgeworth's desire to measure a degree of latitude for his 'fame and amusement' is mentioned in his diary under 4, 21 Aug., 6 Sep., 27 [Oct.] 1821. He was criticised by Thomas Telford on 19 Oct. 1822 (NLI, MS 14124).
120. *Parliamentary Debates* (Hansard), 37 (1818), col. 111. This was in spite of the 'considerable school of civil engineering' said to be growing up in Ireland as a result of the bogs surveys and other public works (*Report from the Select Committee on Grand Jury Presentments, Ireland*, p. 20, H.C. 1826–7 (555), iii).
121. A. M. Carr-Saunders and P. A. Wilson, *The Professions* (Oxford, 1933), p. 313.
122. *Dublin Evening Mail*, 25 Jan. 1860. This and other press cuttings on the same subject are in NLI, Larcom papers, MS 7747.
123. Institution of Civil Engineers of Ireland, printed list of members and associates, 1849. The county surveyors are listed by name in *Report of the Commissioners Appointed to Revise the Several Laws under or by Virtue of Which Moneys are Now Raised by Grand Jury Presentment in Ireland*, app B, pp 10–19, H.C. 1842 [386], xxiv.
124. *Report on Survey and Valuation*, 1824, p. 75.
125. Advertisement by J. King, 'having just finished his education in the University of Glasgow', *L:Derry Journal*, 23 May 1820.
126. K. A. Murray, 'William Dargan', *Jour. Ir. Railway Rec. Soc.*, 8 (1950), p. 94.
127. *Morning Register*, 14 Mar. 1832. One of Nimmo's own subordinates, James Clarke, advertised himself as a land surveyor in the *Roscommon and Leitrim Gazette* for 6 Sep. 1823. Another example was Patrick Leahy of Thurles who took pride in having been mentioned by the bogs commissioners(*3rd Report*, p. 162) as an assistant to their engineer Thomas Townsend (*Clonmel Advertiser*, 17 Oct. 1818).
128. Larcom, *Down Survey*, p. xiv.
129. C. T. Bowden, *A Tour through Ireland* (Dublin, 1791), p. 67. See also below, ch. 9.

130. A. Friendly, *Beaufort of the Admiralty: the Life of Sir Francis Beaufort, 1774–1857* (London, 1977), p. 112.
131. *Report on Survey and Valuation*, 1824, p. 82.
132. J. B. Trotter, *Walks through Ireland, in the Years 1812, 1814 and 1817* (London, 1819), p. 532.
133. *House of Lords. Charles Ward Esquire – Appellant. Robert Hartpole Esq – Respondent. The Appellant's Case* ([Dublin], 1775), p. 9.
134. Diary of Sir Vere Hunt, 7 May 1813, NLI, mic. P.5527.
135. PRONI, T.2541/IA1/4/7 (27 Feb. 1756) and IA1/6B/50 (18 Sep. 1761).
136. *Devon Report*, 2, p. 363 (Joseph Sandford, Co. Roscommon). For an earlier comment on the proclivity of the lower class to hire impostors rather than 'real practitioners', see *Cork Evening Post*, 20 June 1785.
137. *First Report on the Condition of the Poorer Classes*, app A, p. 570 (Michael Shanley, Co. Longford), H.C. 1835 (369), xxxii.
138. *Minutes of Evidence Taken Before the Select Committee on Disturbances*, 1825, p. 65.
139. W. H. Grattan Flood, *History of Enniscorthy* (Enniscorthy, 1898), pp 130–31.
140. Gebbie, *Abercorn Letters*, p. 202 (1798). Hood was also said to spend too much time studying. His diffident personality had been remarked upon by Lord Abercorn's agent in 1784 (PRONI, T.2541/IA1/14/34, 38).
141. James Delany, a surveyor of Melitia, near Clonegal, Co. Carlow, had a 'charade' (rhyming riddle) addressed to him in Grant's *Almanack for 1822* (Dublin, p. 35), but it is not worth quoting.

9
Heads of their profession?

IN ONE SENSE THERE WAS NO PROFESSION for any Irish surveyor to be head of, and that is the sense in which professional status depends on membership of some officially recognised society or institution.[1] Such rigorous conformism should perhaps be rejected as an Englishman's criterion of acceptability, not necessarily exportable to lands of milder social climate. It would still have appealed to Ireland's most articulate surveyor, Peter Callan. In 1753 he was deploring the absence among his countrymen of 'judges, ... magistrates, or incorporated society, who legally assume to themselves the power of administering justice in matters of surveying' (Appendix C). His own remedy was that every surveyor should join a professional body administered by an Inspector-General (who would be chosen by the Dublin Society) with the assistance of four examiners, the whole system to be financed by subscriptions from the surveyors themselves. At the annual meetings of this corporation each surveyor would be required to show his instruments and likewise the whole of his previous year's work, which would then be scrutinised in the presence of the Dublin Society and the full assembly of his colleagues. After the pros and cons of each candidate had been solemnly put on record an official list of surveyors would be published by the Inspector-General. Presumably Callan's own output was expected to pass muster, though (as with most surveyors who took pleasure in polemical writing) his maps had little to offer by way of technical interest or aesthetic merit.[2] In any case his advice was probably intended more to irritate than to enlighten or convert;[3] and its results, if any, did not go beyond the doubtfully effective system of certificates operated by the Surveyor-General in the second half of the eighteenth century. Otherwise Irish surveyors showed no particular zest for professional unity, not even when the government finally gave them common cause by mobilising a rival power in the shape of the British Ordnance Survey; and except for passing judgement on inventions the Dublin Society took surprisingly little interest in their work.

Yet to withhold 'professional' status from these rugged individualists would be to ignore two centuries of linguistic usage among both clients and practitioners. And the differences of rank within the profession were no less real for not being formally defined. Some surveyors earned more than others; were more fully employed and more widely travelled; were more respected by their colleagues and better known to the general public; were more often consulted by persons in authority. Any reader of the signatures on Irish estate and farm maps will sooner or later draw his own line between major and minor figures, and the various 'top twenties' arrived at in this way would unquestionably show a large area of overlap. The following pages are not intended to preempt this kind of judgement. For one thing they deliberately exclude a number of influential personalities who have already been noticed elsewhere. They also seek to avoid repetition by placing at least as much emphasis on individuality as on typicality. And finally they offer a general comment, if only implicitly and in passing, on the technical problems of Irish 'cartobiography'. Despite its ill-repute among the pundits, the biographical approach will probably continue to influence a good deal of what is written about Irish maps, and for the newcomer to historical research there are worse ways of getting started: in the biography of land surveyors he may be encouraged by the modesty of the standard that needs to be surpassed.

Thomas Moland is the first Irishman known to have been considered a more capable surveyor than any of his compatriots. He won this accolade in 1724 from Sir John Perceval (not a man from whom praise came easily)[4] and it marked a new way of looking at surveyors as a structured community. In other respects, one must admit, there was nothing very new about Moland's career, which closely parallels that of the early seventeenth-century cartographer Thomas Raven. He resembles all previous Irish surveyors in the mystery that surrounds his early life. A Joseph Moland appears a few years before Thomas, but he is more likely to be brother than father, since he ranked below Thomas among the employees of the Williamite trustees; for both Molands fit the seventeenth-century stereotype in being products of the plantation surveys. Having been sworn by the trustees in July 1700, Thomas was among the first surveyors of the establishment to be appointed a 'protractor', in September of that year, with an annual salary of one hundred pounds. Eventually the survey was employing five such officers under its chief protractor, John Greene.[5] Apart from Greene (who was also unusual in arriving with well-documented pre-plantation credentials, as Dublin City Surveyor),

Moland was the only protractor to remain conspicuously active after 1703, and his former rank may have given him an advantage over those junior members of the trustees' team – not protractors but simply 'surveyors' – who entered independent practice at the same time.

Almost immediately after completing his official duties Moland secured a major private assignment on the Perceval lands in Co. Cork.[6] His maps cover only part of the property, the rest being surveyed at the same time by one Nugent (perhaps Oliver Nugent, recorded on some other estates), but there seems to have been no formal partnership between the two men, and Perceval always refers to them separately. Nugent, like several other surveyors, inspired conflicting emotions in his plain-speaking employer. On one occasion he was 'very knowing in his art'; on another, 'I did not look upon Mr Newgent or his assistant to be the best of their profession'. The assistant in question was evidently a third party, for the same letter looks forward to employing Moland again, and when doubts were cast on any of his surveys Perceval generally sought some other cause than inefficiency on the part of the surveyor; such causes are seldom hard to find, but genuine or not they showed how much a man like Moland could depend on his reputation once he had earned it.

The Perceval survey is said to have cost more (presumably not much more) than eighty pounds. Whether this estimate referred to Moland's part, or Nugent's, or both, it was soon to be left behind. The next few years saw Moland mapping for Sir William Courtenay, for the Earl of Thomond, and for the governors of the Erasmus Smith schools, a progress that took him into seven counties and three provinces.[7] The Courtenay maps hold the distinction of having been put to the test by a later surveyor, Joshua Wight. They stood up well, with many townlands, by Wight's account, showing an agreement that was 'near rational'.[8] The Thomond maps included the towns of Carlow and Skerries and carried a fee of £376. 15s. To judge from its effect in diversifying his subsequent career, this may have been the biggest survey that Moland ever made, but in later life he undertook at least two more major commissions, for the Earl of Malton in Co. Wicklow and for the Earl of Mountrath in the midlands.[9] In Wicklow Moland paid more attention to houses and fences than in his earlier maps. Given a longer career he might even have developed into a 'topographer'.

He certainly owned himself susceptible to the 'elegance and beauty' that came with planting and improving, though where improvement had not yet begun he kept his psychological distance from the local population, very much in the manner of an immigrant – which may of course have been what he was. Of Bealaghbehy on the Courtenay estate he wrote:

> the dwellers on the mountains are all Irish natives, and live wretchedly; this farm has a multitude of these cottages, and the inhabitants get good oats and potatoes out of these lands, without thought of any further improvement of which these mountains are more capable than any mountain lands in Ireland that I have yet seen.

As already suggested, the survey of entire estates in widely separate parts of the country is probably the best single criterion for distinguishing the superior from the inferior grades of land surveyor. It does not imply however that a surveyor like Moland would take no part in measuring ordinary farms. In 1706 he made maps of St Sepulchre's in Dublin that brought him no more than £2. 10s;[10] and surveys by 'Mr Moland' are cited in several deeds that relate to single townlands and are unlikely to have come from atlases of whole estates.[11] Nor did he decline the secondary role of copying other men's surveys, as appears from a case of 1714 recorded among the maps of Christ Church cathedral. Admittedly the Mr Moland of these years may sometimes be Joseph and not Thomas. As City Surveyor Joseph is known to have lived and worked in Dublin,[12] but then so probably did Thomas at this period. It was from Dublin that Perceval hoped to bring him in 1713 to measure several townlands whose areas were still uncertain or in dispute,[13] though in fact Thomas never appeared and the task fell to a local surveyor: presumably there was not enough of it to merit a trip from Dublin to Co. Cork.

Like many surveyors, in maturity Moland transferred some of his energies from measurement to management. Already in 1707–08 he was collecting rents for Lady Henrietta Bindon in Queen's Co. and Carlow and advising her on the prospects of a local linen industry.[14] About 1710 he became steward and receiver of rents on the Earl of Thomond's lands in the same two counties, and in the following year he was chosen as a person of integrity and ability to serve as clerk with a commission at work on the Thomond estates in Clare.[15] His duties as steward must have involved residing for considerable periods in or near Carlow, where he had a house and other property.[16] Although he was still drawing maps in the 1730s,[17] these more sedentary pursuits probably provided the bulk of his income in later life, and perhaps laid the foundations of the substantial estate enjoyed by another Thomas Moland forty years later.[18] Moland the cartographer died in 1737 and was remembered by his professional successors as 'an eminent hand'.[19]

Although his career was shorter than many, Moland is a notable case of a surveyor attaining a national reputation purely as a surveyor. He published nothing – though he was doubtless the author of the engraved index to the Perceval estates – and his only known link with the mechanical side of the surveyor's profession is the sum of 12s. 6d he earned for cleaning and mending surveyors' instruments for the Archbishop of Dublin.[20] There was almost no originality in his maps and not much in the remarks he wrote to accompany them. The effect he sought was that of a smartened-up Down or Trustees' Survey map, and much of his decoration was printed from anonymous copper plates – of which he must take the credit of being an early user. The most obvious merit of his maps is the fineness of their drawing and writing. In other words Moland succeeded by being good at his job.

Gabriel Stokes's maps look very much like Moland's, but he managed to become considerably better known, ranking today as one of the most fully documented of all eighteenth-century Irish surveyors, for what that is worth, thanks partly to the influence of his more famous descendants in stimulating genealogical research.[21] Among the fruits of that research are Stokes's parentage and date of birth (1682), both rare prizes in Irish cartobiography. Disappointingly, he was the son of a tailor, but after attending the King's Hospital School in Dublin he took up an apprenticeship in 1696 with Joseph Moland, then employed in the same school as steward and teacher of navigation.[22] Although old enough to have served on the Trustees' Survey, Stokes has not yet been found anywhere in its records. In fact he had reached his thirties and attained a solid position in life before he became an active map-maker.

He was married in 1711, and after another ten years, for 'skill in his profession', received a grant of arms with a surveyor's forestaff as his crest. The profession referred to was that of mathematical instrument-maker, which is the only description he gave of himself when witnessing a deed as late as 1720.[23] His wife, Elizabeth King, is thought to have belonged to another family of mid-eighteenth-century instrument-makers, but the germ seems likely to have passed from Stokes to his in-laws rather than the other way round. He was good enough to be chosen by the fellows of Trinity College to repair their quadrant, telescope, and other instruments, and to rectify their globes, on more than one occasion between 1715 and 1724.[24] He also published a pamphlet on hydrostatics,[25] and an essay on

The Description and Uses of the Universal Ring Dial (1731), by means of which (uncharacteristically for a Dublin shopkeeper), he hoped to avoid lengthy explanations of his product to those who came to buy it. His shop was still open more than twenty years later, at the 'Sign of the Dial' in Essex Street, when Stokes advertised an instrument of his own devising known as a pantometron, similar to a theodolite only more portable.[26]

Like many later surveyors Stokes could also claim the status of engineer. One of his books was *A Scheme for Effectually Supplying Every Part of the City of Dublin with Water* (1735), another offered a commentary on a rival scheme put forward by the architect Richard Castle. By this time he had lengthened his title to 'mathematical instrument maker and surveyor of lands'. His first choice of designation reflects the rapid growth of Irish land surveying in the years following the Williamite victory and the resultant need for an accessible supply of instruments. His second choice suggests that the growth in question may have been bewilderingly fast and that some landowners were looking behind the scenes for a map-maker of more than average authority. Exactly when Stokes took the cartographic plunge is impossible to say. His first signed map dates from 1716,[27] and the time of his greatest activity lasted from the middle 'twenties to the middle 'thirties. Most of his maps are of lands near Dublin, and he was perhaps more closely associated with the city than any previous private surveyor, as he hinted in 1737 with a complacently metropolitan reference to the cheapness of surveyors in Co. Cork. On his own ground he was happy with quite small commissions, like the plot in Francis Street which he surveyed for Trinity College at a charge of 11s. 6d. For longer assignments he was willing to go further: as far as Tipperary and Kerry in 1733 for surveys of College land costing £77. 15s.[28]

In combining the manufacture of instruments with their use Stokes was not alone. A contemporary Dubliner who did the same was Thomas Cave;[29] and both men produced equally versatile apprentices: Stokes's was Thomas Reading and Cave's was Jonathan Barker.[30] More unusual at this period was the interest shown by Stokes in geographical matters. He made an original survey of Dublin Bay and Harbour in 1726,[31] though none, strangely enough, of the city itself: the measurements of pipes in his scheme for supplying it with water came from the map published by Charles Brooking in 1728.[32] Nor was there any wider outlet for the map of Ireland which he made for the use of the Post Office at some time before 1755;[33] but which was lost before anyone had time to say whether it incorporated the latitudes and longitudes for Irish cities given in his book on the ring dial. He finally got into the catalogues, however, with his map of Co. Dublin published in 1750.

Cartographic originality was at a low ebb in Stokes's Ireland. His map of Co. Dublin treated its subject almost as if it was at the disposal of would-be leaseholders, the county boundary being given all the complexity of a farm survey traversed from one ditch-corner to the next while roads and other interior detail were sketchy to a fault. (Despite the author's reputation as a man of science the latitudes and longitudes are also very poor.) If Stokes's topographical survey looked rather like his estate maps, his estate maps looked much like any one else's, causing him to have been more than once held responsible for the work of other surveyors.[34] Outside their engraved cartouches – themselves a step towards impersonality – his maps are plainly and carefully drawn and written, though he lacked Moland's talents as a miniaturist.

It was with his tenure of the Deputy Surveyor-Generalship of Ireland from 1748 to 1752 that Stokes belatedly achieved public recognition. Now an old man, he nevertheless brought off a major administrative innovation, the certificate of competence awarded to private surveyors. If, as seems likely, Stokes himself set the examination by which the certificates were won, he may be said to have wielded more power than any previous surveyor of his century. He was soon to pass on the torch, however, though remaining alive until 1768.

Robert Gibson went one better than Stokes by publishing the first comprehensive surveying text book ever to appear in Ireland. Almost everything else about him is obscure, and one can only guess at his possible kinship with the Trustees' surveyor, John Gibson, who had made fleeting appearances as a private land surveyor and teacher of mathematics in the 1700s.[35] Robert's career began a generation later: he surveyed a Kilkenny farm in 1738 and soon afterwards was taking the first subscriptions for his *Treatise of Practical Surveying*, published in 1752.[36] Perhaps it was the appearance of Callan's very different book that prompted Gibson finally to put out his own. Both men in their different ways felt uneasy about current professional standards. Like most other surveyors Gibson used the firm as a medium of education – instructing among other apprentices his own nephew Robert Lewis[37] – but he probably won more prestige through the mathematical school he kept for both boarders and day-pupils in Anglesea Street, Dublin, through his book on experimental philosophy,[38] and through the public lectures he delivered on physical geography together with the use of globes and maps.[39] He died in December 1760.[40] It was a career that underlined the ineffectiveness of university mathematics, not to mention university geography. But the only map associated with Gibson that might be held to count as geographical was a chart of Dublin Bay and Harbour by his son George ('surveyor and hydrographer') for which both father and son failed to win support from the Dublin Society in 1756. Published nine months later, this little-known survey was more than usually rich in scientific data, including tidal phenomena and magnetic variation. In launching it George did not trade on his father's reputation except to commend the chart as 'this undertaking of a native, who is the son of a citizen'. Did this distinction between native and citizen imply that Robert Gibson had been born outside Ireland? The main thrust of the words quoted was against a rival cartographer who fell into neither category, namely John Rocque.[41] It was another case of Rocque coming off best: his map of the bay and harbour was still in print and under revision nine years after Gibson's plate had gone for scrap.[42]

The *Treatise of Practical Surveying* had more success – indeed it turned out to be one of the most popular introductions to surveying ever published both in Ireland and elsewhere (Appendix D). Perhaps its greatest triumph came in 1824 when the Ordnance Survey's Irish headquarters told one of its officers to study a rule in Gibson's book – an ironic tribute considering the Survey's low opinion of its non-military professional brethren in Ireland.[43] The *Treatise* is not only comprehensive, its tone is reasonable and temperate, with none of the attacks on colleagues and competitors that other Irish writers found so hard to resist. The exposition was also suitably idealistic, in the manner of textbooks, making no allowance for the kind of error inevitable in real life. It was this that led Callan to accuse Gibson of neglecting the 'mysteries of practice'. The charge was unjustified. Gibson's cartographic output never rivalled Stokes's, but examples of his work are by no means uncommon, mainly of lands within easy reach of Dublin.[44] His successor William Gibson, probably a nephew, offered in 1761 to exhibit copies of all the surveys done by Robert, doubtless as specimens of the style in which William, as a fellow land surveyor, was proposing to continue.[45] As would be expected from the advice given in the *Treatise*, the style in question was serenely conservative. Gibson's only break with the past was the emphasis he put on terrestrial magnetism, a topic now being forced by natural circumstances on the attention of every conscientious map-maker as the variation of the needle at Dublin widened to twenty degrees. The frequency with which magnetic north appears under its own name on later Irish estate maps may be at least partly attributable to Gibson's authority.

This authority won official acknowledgement in 1752 when the Surveyor-General, praising Gibson's skill, appointed him to examine a candidate for a certificate of the type introduced two years earlier by Stokes.[46] He had already been chosen by his peers as one of two eminent surveyors (the other was Jonathan Barker) who could be trusted to calculate the field notes of colleagues in dispute,[47] as well as being invited by one landlord forty miles from Dublin to add a fourth independent verdict to three conflicting local surveys.[48] Throughout the 'fifties Gibson continued to monitor the work of other surveyors, both officially and unofficially, his judgements sometimes being published by contestants in triumphant rebuttal of the opposition.[49] It was a status shared with few of his rivals (apart from Barker the one who came nearest to it was the Dublin City Surveyor) and which did not long survive him, for it soon became customary for certificates to be signed by the Deputy Surveyor-General himself, bringing the role of the private practitioner as *de facto* 'inspector general' to a disappointingly early end.[50] Perhaps there was some spirit working among Irish surveyors against the idea of an impartial assessor who might actually settle the disputes that they enjoyed so much. As a tail-piece to the Gibson story a reference should be made to the later but comparable figure of Thomas Harding, a member of the new Royal Irish Academy, an author of various books and articles, and an enthusiast for the remapping of Ireland on truly scientific foundations, as well as a maker of ordinary estate surveys when he had the time.[51] The point is that for all his knowledge and experience Harding never seems to have wished, or been asked, to set up as arbiter in the style of Stokes and Gibson. Perhaps by the 1790s Ireland had enough practising surveyors of good repute.

Samuel Byron represents what was left of public surveying in the Harding era, being one of a long line of able practitioners employed by the city of Dublin from the 1670s onwards.[52] Among the more distinguished of his predecessors were John Greene, subsequently chief protractor of the Trustees' Survey; Roger Kendrick, verger of St Patrick's Cathedral and author of an unpublished map of Dublin; and Thomas Matthews, sometime seller of magnets whom at least one successful private surveyor was glad to acknowledge as master.[53] In an age of low opinions their prestige stood high: that was demonstrated in 1758 (Appendix C) when an unusually disputatious map-maker in Co. Cavan agreed to submit his field notes to the Dublin City Surveyor for adjudication instead of to the Surveyor-General.

Matthews's successor was a Dublin man. Byron had no family connections with surveying, and it was probably his draughtsmanship that won him his post with the city in 1781, his land surveys having been good enough to go on public display at the Dublin Society's drawing school in 1779.[54] In the following year some of his pictures were exhibited by the Society of Artists in Dublin, though it was for skill in his main profession, apparently, that he gained the freedom of the city's ancient guild of cutlers, painter-stainers and stationers, an honour not known to have been shared by any other surveyor.[55] Increasing prosperity followed these tokens of recognition, as also did Byron's marriage in 1787 and his move from Eustace Street to the more fashionable quarter of St Stephen's Green.[56] It was an appropriate step. Some of his work was flagrantly derivative – his imitations of Scalé could have fooled Scalé[57] – but the Green had already brought out the best in him. According to a news item of 1783:

> The survey of Stephen's Green, which was presented by Mr Byron to the Lord Mayor ... is the most singular as well as beautiful production of the kind that can be imagined. Surveys and plans give in general little more than sites, boundaries, and contents; while this artist has extended his art infinitely beyond the mere rule and compass. In the above view mathematical accuracy, it seems, is not only critically preserved, but by a pencil unknown before in this line, we are delighted with an actual portrait of the celebrated square, in its most beautiful dress.[58]

Although no such plan is known to survive, the meaning of this passage is clear from Byron's plan of Trinity College, an isometric treatment which shows the roofs and elevations of the buildings as well as their locations in an interesting revival of a seventeenth-century cartographic mode.[59] The same feeling for the third dimension is likely to have been evident in his design for the gardens in Merrion Square, adopted with pleasure by the square's inhabitants in 1788.[60] Altogether it is odd that a more famous contemporary artist, James Malton, should have proposed the appointment of a 'city delineator' as a distinct office from that of City Surveyor, for Byron was living proof that the two faculties could be combined in one person.[61]

Nothing in the Trinity College vein is known to have been printed in Byron's lifetime, but unusually among City Surveyors he did achieve publication in the field of orthodox cartography with two small plans of Dublin for Wilson's annual directory, one appearing from 1783 to 1788 and the other from 1789 to 1792, and with a plan of Kilkenny dated 1786.[62] No doubt these borrowed much from the plans published by Rocque a generation earlier. In the case of Kilkenny the element of plagiarism is unmistakable: like other mid-eighteenth-century holders of his office Byron seldom strayed far from headquarters, the surveys he did in his own right being mainly confined to the counties of Dublin, Kildare and Queen's Co. Many of his rural plans, in any case, were drawn for a metropolitan clientele. In 1794, for example, he mapped the land belonging to Christ Church cathedral at Kilcullen, Co. Kildare, a good choice for a historically-conscious Dublin City Surveyor, including as it did the semi-legendary capital of the ancient kings of Leinster on Knockaulin Hill. Not that Byron knew about the kings, though he did describe the hill top as an 'ancient carne [cairn] or place of public worship'.[63]

One biographical problem common to several surveyors is how much of Ireland's present-day capital city can be attributed to any one man. Eighteenth-century newspapers give the impression that Byron's term as City Surveyor coincided with the proudest period in the development of the Dublin street pattern. Fittingly for an age that frowned on individualism, most of this activity was anonymous; yet someone must have fixed the direction and width of each new street. Buckingham Street can perhaps be credited to Byron: in a rare piece of 'personalised' reporting he is found connecting the North Strand with Summerhill by two lines of stakes a generous eighty feet apart.[64] Unlike so many Dublin streets, this one has kept its obtrusively English and aristocratic name: nobody seems to have thought of rechristening it Byron Street.

In 1795 Byron died in office.[65] There is said to have been some eager competition for his job, though the man who got it, David Worthington, was not particularly distinguished. Next came Arthur Richards (or Richard) Neville, who had already built up a large surveying and valuing business which he managed to combine with his official duties. Neville was the last tenant of his office to make any important contribution to cartography: once Dublin had its own large-scale Ordnance map the City Surveyor underwent a metamorphosis into City Engineer – without the appointment leaving the Neville family, as things turned out.[66]

Thomas Sherrard was appreciably older than Byron – his enrolment in the Dublin Society's drawing school had taken place some six years earlier[67] – but the firm that he established in the 1770s was to last until the end of the nineteenth century. He belonged to the third generation of the 'French school' that took its name from Rocque and Scalé; but although these founding fathers had transformed the Irish estate map they seem never to have felt themselves completely Irish: both sought their final retirement not in the villa-belt of Co. Dublin (or in France) but in England, and without leaving any successors of their own name. Scalé could claim to be more of an Irishman than Rocque, not only by virtue of staying longer but by recruiting his assistants in Dublin. Twice in two years he advertised for apprentices.[68] Presumably Sherrard was one of the respondents, and his future partner, John Brownrigg, another, but not long afterwards, in March 1773, the twenty-three-year-old Thomas made a brave attempt to strike out on his own:[69]

> Lands surveyed. By Thomas Sherrard, in the most accurate and careful manner, in the various methods, which give such entire satisfaction, practised by Mr Scalé, to whom he served his apprenticeship, and during which time had constant practice on the estates of several of the nobility and gentry of this kingdom; which enables him now, being perfectly versed in the business, to offer himself to their favour and protection; and hopes from his probity, care, and attention, to the justice of his returns, neatness and precision in his maps (exhibiting at one view the quantity, quality, state, and improvement of each farm) which, he presumes, will be found equal to any practitioner's, and his moderate charges, to merit the encouragement and countenance of those who shall please to honour him with their commands. Traces made from the Down or other surveys; farms divided; old maps copied, enlarged or reduced, and transferred into books, in the neatest manner, for perpetuation.

This catalogue of fine promises carried the address of William Sherrard, who was probably the surveyor's father, but a few months later Thomas married a lady from Drogheda and may be presumed to have set up house for himself.[70] It was not long, however, before Scalé, his business rapidly increasing, took both his former apprentices into partnership.[71] Given Scalé's reputation, this was not necessarily a retrograde step for Sherrard and Brownrigg. The trio, unique in eighteenth-century Ireland among surveyors not ostensibly related by blood or marriage, produced a number of complete estate surveys before Sherrard and Brownrigg left to establish a separate firm of their own in 1777.

It was an interesting juncture in Irish map history. Scalé like Rocque saw himself as a cartographic general practitioner, with a published output ranging from plans of individual buildings to maps of the whole country. The only hint that Sherrard and Brownrigg might do the same was when they appeared briefly in 1777 as retail tradesmen, advertising a map of Ticonderoga in North America.[72] Otherwise, although their careers lasted longer than Scalé's, their own publications were few. But they both kept up the tradition of surveying whole estates in a 'topographical' style, well exemplified at this early stage by their joint survey of a demesne near Oldcastle, Co. Meath.[73]

In spite of sharing a house the partners do not appear to have formed a permanent friendship.[74] By 1780 Sherrard was again in business for himself, the main difference from seven years earlier being the emphasis he now placed on agency and valuation work.[75] What remained the same was the belief in publicity inherited from his former chief. Almost any of life's experiences could form the basis for a Sherrard advertisement or news item: in February 1782, his change of address from Abbey Street to Capel Street, a time for reminding the public of the advertiser's 'accuracy, taste, and punctuality'; in the following November an admission of failure under the last of these heads, fulsomely turned to advantage by seeking further opportunities to serve those patrons who had called during the surveyor's absence; in 1784, a request for an apprentice to help solve this inevitable problem of a one-man business. Nothing is known of the apprentice, if there was one: it would have been a promising start for any surveyor. Employees were not in evidence when any one wishing to deal with Sherrard in the month of August 1785 was invited to contact him in Galway. Even the loss of a map to a pickpocket was worth reporting: a Sherrard map deserved its reward. There were others to give the bandwagon a push. When Nicholas Walsh of Waterford launched his new treatise on surveying in 1787 he thought it worthwhile to advertise Sherrard's approbation; and when Miss Maria Sherrard married the secretary of the Irish Linen Board in 1796 her father made sure that the newspapers took note. There was no escaping Sherrard.[76]

The most interesting of these public appearances was Sherrard's quest for a new assistant in 1791,[77] for it came at a critical time in his long and fruitful secondary career with the Dublin wide streets commission. He had first come to the commission's notice as one of its jobbing land surveyors in the late 1770s and then gradually made himself indispensable – drawing new maps, adding new detail to old maps, taking levels, laying out streets and dividing them into plots, preparing elevations and architectural drawings, and eventually managing to find time for a large amount of purely administrative work. After receiving a number of generous *ex gratia* payments on top of his surveying fees, he was given the salaried post of clerk to the commission in 1789.[78] Further research might prove Sherrard to be responsible for the courses of the present-day streets around Dublin's O'Connell Bridge. His main cartographic achievement as the commission's surveyor and clerk was a map of the whole city and its environs at the huge scale of eighty feet to an inch. Produced between 1791 and 1797 and mounted on six rollers, it was surely the largest of Dublin's pre-Ordnance Survey maps – and at £1,200 the most expensive. Despite pressure from its admirers the map never appeared in print, but as late as 1891 it was said to be carefully looked after: not carefully enough, to judge from more recent inquiries (Plate 19).[79]

All this left little time for rural interests, and it was here that the balance was redressed by Sherrard's associate, Richard Brassington. In later life Brassington was to manage a large farm of his own not far from Dublin, and to give sound advice to a parliamentary committee on agriculture.[80] After completing his apprenticeship in the 1790s he remained with Sherrard on a contract basis and at the dawn of the new century the two men became partners, moving at the same time to a more distinguished suburban address in Blessington Street.[81] In advertising the move Sherrard put his usual emphasis on the utility of surveying to the improver, but on this occasion he also announced that in response to many applications his office was now open for the receipt of rents and for the sale and letting of houses and estates. Cartographically his resources were soon being stretched to the limit, literally so in the sense that they ranged within two years from Dunbrody in Co. Wexford to the Inishowen peninsula in Co. Donegal, a leap unlikely to have been achieved by any earlier Irish surveyor.[82] With Sherrard now well into middle age, another accession of manpower was the only way forward. Clarges Greene appears as one of the firm's assistants in 1805 on a parliamentary enclosure map (at present in private hands) of the parish of Portrane, Co. Dublin. Between *c.* 1810 and *c.* 1829 he was a full partner, though for the latter part of this period he led a double life, running his own independent business from a house in Dominick Street. On Greene's departure, the firm was rechristened Sherrard, Brassington and Gale; in 1832 it became Brassington and Gale. (Nothing is known about Gale except that his first name seems to have been Samuel.) Even then the founder did not lose his gift for being noticed: he now gave his address as Coolock Lodge near Dublin and in

HEADS OF THEIR PROFESSION? 279

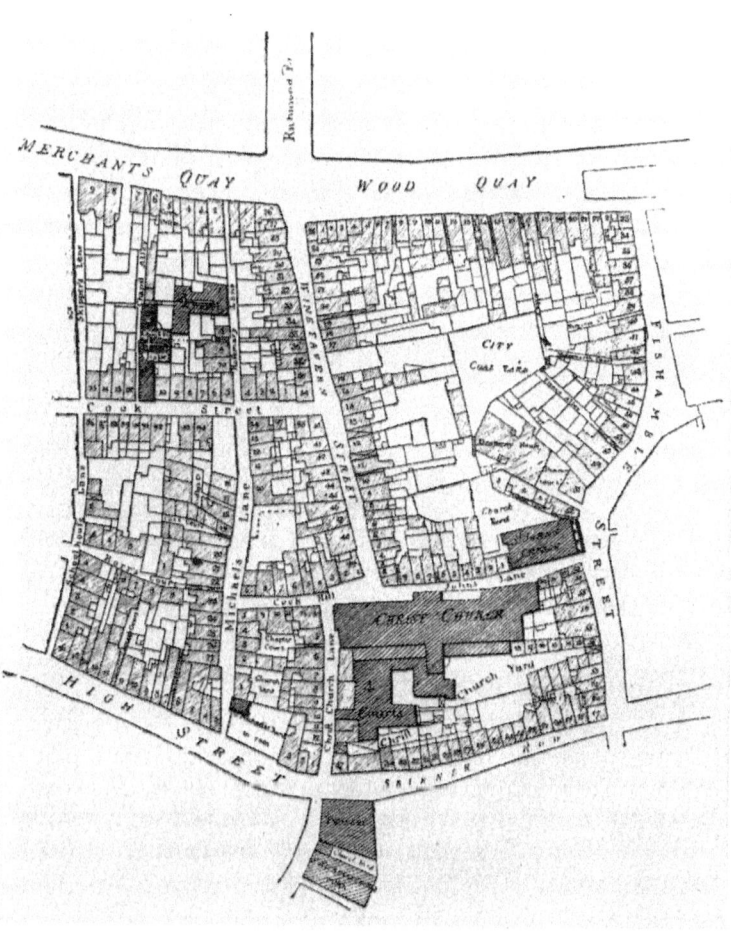

Plate 19. From Thomas Sherrard's plan of Dublin, 1791 (see chapter 9, note 79). Scale of original 80 feet to one inch. Sherrard showed more detail than John Rocque's *Exact survey* of Dublin (1756), but his map was never published and cannot now be traced: this is a late nineteenth-century extract.

1837 he appeared – fittingly but posthumously – as a subscriber to Samuel Lewis's topographical dictionary of Ireland.

His firm's status had long been measured by its fees. Already in 1792 Sherrard could ask a shilling per acre for survey, map and valuation,[83] and by the 1820s his rate for government work was two guineas per day instead of the one guinea which his ex-partner Brownrigg, now safe in retirement, told the authorities was the ancient and moderate rate (Appendix E). Another mark of vigour was the firm's ability to defend the borders of its hinterland. In 1836 Brassington could still speak of visiting every part of Ireland at regular intervals,[84] and his statement is borne out by the many surviving mid-nineteenth-century maps and atlases that carry his and his partners' names – not excluding maps of northern properties, despite the rise of several independent Ulster valuators at this period.

At least one modern secondary road in the Dublin region (L25A, east of Kilcullen) can apparently be credited to Sherrard,[85] but not much of his work could be described as engineering, even in the topographical sense. He and Brassington offered their services to the bogs commission, but withdrew when the commission refused to negotiate with partnerships as distinct from individuals.[86] (Perhaps this incident was a sign that surveying partnerships were still not very common.) Nor did Sherrard develop any serious interest in publishing. Nothing came of his offer to supply a grand jury map of Co. Dublin, though it preceded the influx of clever young trigonometrical surveyors who later won a near-monopoly of such work;[87] and his proposal for mapping Co. Carlow came so late that it was overtaken by the advent of the Ordnance Survey.[88] He never troubled to put his map of Dublin into publishable form. When his name did appear in print, on maps of Glasnevin and of Phoenix Park, it was at the instigation of other promoters.[89] Sherrard was thus content for his firm to stand as Ireland's leading land surveyors and valuators. As such its prosperity (like its founder's private fortune)[90] owed much to an expert knowledge of property management; and not a little, up to the middle nineteenth century anyway, to its draughtsmen's command of a lively style of cartography derived from Rocque.

James Williamson was the first Ulsterman, perhaps the first Irishman anywhere outside Dublin, to match the most eminent of his metropolitan rivals in historical interest if not quite in cartographic merit. The middle-rank surveyor, of sound reputation but limited territorial scope, had emerged in other parts of Ireland soon after 1700. Before long surveyors in several northern counties were winning their fair share of

HEADS OF THEIR PROFESSION? 281

Plate 20. Title page by James Williamson, 1784 (NLI, 14.A.24). A display of writing as well as drawing skills. In addition to Williamson's own maps this volume includes copies of surveys done in 1720 by Alexander Stewart.

success at this level, some of them as far west as the Foyle valley. By the early nineteenth century, however, a headquarters east of the Bann and preferably in Belfast had become increasingly attractive for any Ulster surveyor anxious to keep a full range of professional contacts in repair. From a historian this judgement may look like hindsight, but Williamson for one would probably have agreed with it. Like Sherrard he was quick to develop a feeling of self-importance, and a long series of newspaper advertisements left little of his career in the dark as it progressed from Armagh to Ballymena and from Ballymena to Belfast.[91]

Conceivably Williamson was related to the Armagh carpenter Matthew Williamson,[92] but his first appearance is as a fifteen-year old entrant to the Dublin Society's school of figure drawing in 1771.[93] The school left a strong impression and Williamson must be one of the earliest Irish surveyors to claim the quality of picturesqueness for his maps, though in general they show less aesthetic flair than the best productions of contemporary Dublin. In the 1790s it was still his intention to spend half his time as an art teacher, with a sideline in selling 'designs done in hair, either for bracelets, lockets, or mourning rings'. As a cartographer he welcomed the artistic challenge of demesnes and whole estates, and was often called upon by clumsier draughtsmen to copy and improve their maps, reserving the unusually explicit signature, 'Surveyed and drawn by James Williamson', to show where the responsibility was wholly his (Plate 20).[94]

The earliest surviving example of Williamson's work, a map of urban property in Armagh, dates from 1781, and in a later reminiscence it was at about this time that he placed the start of his surveying career. But even the most accomplished artist is unlikely to have remained at drawing school for a whole decade. Like Shakespeare, Williamson has some 'lost years' to account for. The strongest probability is that he spent them apprenticed to a local surveyor. Did he suppress these homely origins (a source of pride in the advertisements of many young entrants to his profession) with a view to sketching in some more cosmopolitan background? A broader hint to this effect was his offer in 1784 to colour maps on 'the most approved London method'. And it was plainly no mere country boy who some seven years later carried his first publishable manuscript to the workshop of Samuel Neele – the best map-engraver in London, as Williamson told readers of the *Belfast News-letter*. Another bid for superiority from the same period was his acquisition of a George Adams theodolite.

Of course there is no eighteenth-century Irish surveyor for whom the hypothesis of an early visit to London can be positively disproved, but for the immediate source of Williamson's cartographic style it is unnecessary to look outside his home district. Among the trademarks he shared with the Co. Armagh surveyor Robert Livingston were rococo cartouches of generally symmetrical lay-out, a range of tasteful lettering styles of which the roman and gothic were especially effective, a backward-reading scale bar, a compass star ornamented in the manner of a contemporary circumferentor, and wide decorative borders with unfashionably stylised patterns in grey watercolour. All these elements had appeared in Livingston's maps while Williamson was still a child.[95] Afterwards the younger man kept abreast of the times with hachured relief, naturalistic title-pieces (including some fine mountain scenery at Ben Bulben) and what he called 'the form of rigs in each field', all features of which not much can be said genetically except that they owed little to any Dublin exemplar.

Livingston was content to be associated with a single town. Williamson had larger ambitions. He began in Abbey Street, Armagh, seeking employment in the same and neighbouring counties, but after a spell in *c*. 1788–90 near Ballymena, Co. Antrim, he settled in Belfast, where he eventually built himself a large house as well as maintaining a retreat at Lilliput on the Carrickfergus road.[96] Williamson had thus placed himself in the two most privileged categories known to modern historians of his craft – gentleman surveyor and town-dwelling surveyor. In 1805 he was appointed (whether by the municipal authorities or the Marquess of Donegall is not clear) as surveyor 'for the purpose of laying out the new streets, intended improvements etc.', changes now proceeding so fast that his own new town plan never managed to catch up with them and consequently never got published.[97] Outside Belfast he was ready to make maps of anywhere in Ulster and in 1821 looked forward to widening his range still further as a surveyor of the Crown lands now up for sale in various parts of Ireland.[98] But at sixty-five it was time for Williamson to slow down and although he lived until 1832[99] no maps of his have been recorded from these final years. Of his surviving output the most remote from home were the maps of the Ben Bulben district near Sligo surveyed in 1813–14.[100]

Williamson's generation was the last that could prosper as land surveyors without apparently taking much interest in either engineering or valuing. (He had hoped to be succeeded by his son, but there is little sign that he ever was.)[101] For cartographers of this disposition the most congenial path to advancement was bigger and better maps. His own first step beyond the ordinary estate survey was to help prepare a little-known map of Lough Neagh in 1785,[102] but it was probably his plan of Belfast in 1792, the most ambitious yet published, that did most to impress the grand jurymen of the adjacent counties. In 1796 he was chosen to revise a map of Co. Antrim first published fourteen years earlier.[103] Revision in this instance took the form of new detail added, not quite harmoniously, to the original plates, so it was understandable that Williamson should also seek the satisfaction of mapping a whole county by himself. In 1803 he was given this task by the grand jury of Co. Down, with results which appeared to general acclaim in 1810.[104]

In Down Williamson showed the Ulsterman's respect for an emergent regional personality by his careful presentation of both Presbyterian meeting houses and linen manufacturers' bleach greens (also of a road named after King William III) and by preferring genuine local views as marginal decoration to the kind of imaginary or unrecognisable landscape favoured by many earlier cartographers. His chief weakness was that, apart from punctiliously recording the magnetic variation in Down and on most of his other maps, he made little attempt at mathematical refinement. It would have been too much to expect a triangulation diagram on an Irish county map of 1810, even from a surveyor with an Adams theodolite; but there was no excuse for meridians that diverged northwards instead of converging. For all its charm, and its considerable value as a topographic record, the map of Down marked the end of an era. So did its author.

William Bald was one of the half-dozen ablest, most hard working and most creative map-makers ever to practise in Ireland.[105] A separate chapter would be needed to summarise his many cartographic enterprises, a whole book to appraise his contribution as a civil engineer. Here it will be enough to provide a context for one sentence abstracted from the great mass of his writings and speeches, namely the unequivocal but tantalising announcement that by 1824 he had surveyed a 'vast deal' of property in Mayo, Sligo, Galway, Roscommon, Queen's Co. and King's Co.[106] His maps showed nine kinds of land, they generally distinguished fields, there was a lively demand for them, and that is all there is to say about Bald as an Irish estate surveyor. That not one of these surveys can now be produced makes a mortifying comment on a whole nation's map historiography. Bald's native country is more fortunate, with several excellent specimens of his work in Argyll and the Hebrides from the period 1805–07.[107] These and other of his early surveys, amounting to some 300,000 acres, were later incorporated into Aaron Arrowsmith's map of Scotland.

By the time Bald got to Mayo in 1809 he could be described by his old employer as a 'very big man'.[108] Coming from the famous Scottish cartographer John Ainslie, this was no ordinary tribute to a twenty-year-old, even allowing for a dash of irony. Bald had been well prepared for professional success on Ireland's Atlantic fringe. The Argyll maps, in addition to sensitive grey-wash slope shading, depict a complex mesh of townships (comparable to Irish townlands) with settlement as clusters of red block-plan symbols and arable land as simulated cultivation ridges, all at a scale of 1:8,444.

Like his fellow-Scotsman Alexander Taylor, Bald shifted his cartographic focus when he came to Ireland. His first commitment was a grand jury map of Co. Mayo, a task for which he had been proposed to the local member of Parliament by the officers of the British Ordnance Survey.[109] This appointment did not deter him from applying for a post under the bogs commission, apparently with the idea of working for each employer in alternate months.[110] In practice the arrangement turned out well, the two enterprises being combined in a trigonometrical survey of a sophistication hitherto unknown either in the boglands of Mayo or anywhere else in Ireland. A number of Irish county maps will be noticed in a later chapter. Bald's was in a class by itself. It was plotted on the exceptionally large scale of five inches to an Irish mile (1 : 16,128); its base measurement and triangulation were impeccably accurate and scientific; its careful hill shading was underpinned by barometric spot-heights, by levelled sections, and in a few areas by separate relief models. In spite of showing innumerable farm houses and a multitude of bogs it had little affinity with the typical Irish estate map.[111] In the 1820s Bald's masterpiece was engraved with appropriate skill and artistry in Paris, on a smaller scale than the original but still very slowly and at great expense. The field work had been completed in 1816, and by that time and for several years afterwards Bald was a familiar presence in the Mayo town of Castlebar, admired by many for his public spirit,[112] mistrusted by others for taking vast sums of money (estimated in 1830 at £6,372) from the pockets of the county's cess-payers.[113] The anti-Bald party was also moved by ethnic or territorial considerations of a kind not unfamiliar in Ireland's cartographic history. One writer combined several individuals, and several kinds of slur, in an attack on

> surly Taylor, the paver, slim Nimmo, the scurvy, or sly little Billy the Bald, knights of the chain and compass, or mere land surveyors, transported or imported here from Scotland.[114]

It is easy to guess which of these descriptions would have most annoyed the 'topographical engineers'. Meanwhile Bald's income was being drawn from both national and local government service on a number of Mayo roads and bridges, and popular or not he would almost certainly have been given charge of all of them if the current scheme for appointing county surveyors had been proceeded with. It was either in this Castlebar period, or during the main Mayo survey, that he found time for his elusive Irish property surveys, perhaps delegating some of them to his assistant Patrick Knight.[115] Meanwhile his own ambition had been set on more distant goals, for besides planning two more county maps (of Down and Clare) he now saw visions of a general triangulation of Ireland and of a huge chart depicting the western British Isles at a scale of one inch to one mile.[116] He may also have planned his own geological map of Ireland, to judge from his harsh criticism of the one produced by Richard Griffith.[117]

Clearly Bald's professional life was lived, in reality as well as fantasy, at a level beyond the reach of any eighteenth-century Irish surveyor. But when the Ordnance Survey came to Ireland all his cartographic dreams dissolved and he was soon giving his whole attention to roads (notably his famous Antrim coast road), bridges, canals, harbours and finally railways. The turning point in his career can be found in a select committee report of 1824 which gave approval to a widespread public demand for a national survey and valuation of Ireland. Bald was a principal witness. His evidence took in the whole of Irish cartography ancient and modern, and included many detailed suggestions for the management of the new survey. But perhaps the most memorable feature of his contribution is not so much what he said as the fact that he was present at all, especially when one notices who was absent. The main purpose of the proposed official survey was to find the boundaries and acreages of all the townlands in Ireland and to map the surface features that affected their economic value. To that extent it could be seen as a national estate survey, and Bald for one expected the results to look like his own estate maps. But the resemblance would be only superficial. If the select committee had its way, estate surveying would now be merged with small-scale cartography, even with world cartography. It was not a new alliance: a similar relationship had been adumbrated centuries earlier by Francis Jobson, whose panoramic vision of Irish mapmaking Bald and his contemporaries were about to restore after a long period of more partial views. But history had put Jobson's progression into reverse. Thanks to trigonometry and all that it implied, this time the national framework would come first, the land surveyor's local detail second; and it was the engineers' knowledge of the greater survey that qualified them to pass judgement on the lesser. Meanwhile, no evidence was heard in 1824 from any of the leading Irish land surveyors whose area of competence the government had now decided to invade. Bald and his like had become the heads of someone else's profession.

Notes

1. Carr-Saunders and Wilson, *Professions*, p. 298; but see also G. Millerson, *The Qualifying Associations, a Study in Professionalization* (London, 1964), p. 9.
2. There are examples of Callan's work in NLI, 16.M.2(8, 16).
3. A modern writer describes Callan's book as 'whimsical' but admits that the whimsicality was unintended (J. W. Foster, 'The Topographical Tradition in Anglo-Irish Poetry', *Irish University Review*, 4 (1974), p. 175).
4. 22 July 1724, Add. MS 46975, f. 72.
5. Moland was appointed a surveyor on 12 July 1700 and a protractor (at a salary of £100 sterling per year) on 28 Sep. (Annesley MS, NLI, mic. P.259).
6. 'A Book of Maps of the Estate of Sir John Perceval ... Together with Observations and Notes of what Improvements are on the Same this Present Year', Add. MS 47043. Some of the maps are undated, others carry the date 1702.
7. Courtenay estate maps, 1709, NLI, 16.F.2. The Thomond survey (for which see Ainsworth, *Inchiquin Manuscripts*, p. 638) is in Petworth papers, 6500. Part of it is discussed in A. A. Horner, 'Two Eighteenth Century Maps of Carlow Town', *Proc. R. Ir. Acad.*, 78C (1978), pp 115–26. The Erasmus Smith maps are at the High School, Rathgar, Dublin.
8. Joshua Wight's diary, 25 Sep. 1752.
9. Malton maps, 1728, NLI, 21.F.162 (photocopy), with book of reference, NLI, MS 4944; Mountrath maps, 1730, TCD, Armytage deposit.
10. Archbishop William King's accounts, TCD, MS 751(2).
11. *House of Lords. Appeal from the Court of Exchequer in Ireland. Charles Vipont Charles, Esq; – Appellant. The Right Hon. Hercules Langford Rowley, Esq; – Respondent. The Respondent's Case* ([Dublin], 1774), p. 3; RD, 118/225/80564 (Co. Meath, 1745).
12. *Cal. Anc. Rec. Dub.*, 6, pp 349–50, 378–9, 403–04. In 1710 Joseph's address was given as the city of Dublin (RD, 3/266/910). He surveyed

the harbour by chain and instrument in 1706–08 and was one of the lessees of the reclaimed area of the North Strand mapped for the corporation in 1717, but by January of the following year he was dead (*Cal. Anc. Rec. Dub.*, 7, p. 54).

13. 14 Aug. 1713, with agent's reply, 27 Aug. 1713, Add. MS 46965, ff. 171,179.
14. Rent roll of the lordship and manor of Carlow, 1705–08, NLI, MS 3071.
15. Ainsworth, *Inchiquin Manuscripts*, pp 109, 557. [House of Lords], *Henry Earl of Thomond, Appellant. James Hamilton, & al. Respondents. The Respondent James Hamilton's Case* ([Dublin], 1733), p. 3.
16. Horner, *Proc. R. Ir. Acad.*, 78C (1978), p. 116.
17. Map of lands in Grangegorman parish, Dublin, 22 Apr. 1734, NAI, TAB 9/43.
18. *Dublin Journal*, 24 July 1773.
19. A. Vicars, *Index to the Prerogative Wills of Ireland, 1536–1810* (Dublin, 1897), p. 329. Wight's diary, 25 Sep. 1752.
20. Archbishop King's accounts, 20 Aug. 1709, TCD, MS 751(2).
21. Mason, *Dub. Hist. Rec.*, 6 (1944), pp 138–9.
22. L. Whiteside, *A History of the King's Hospital* (Dublin, 1975), p. 16.
23. RD, 27/7/14899.
24. TCD, MUN/P/4/20, 23, 28.
25. *The Mathematical Cabinet of the Hydrostatical Ballance, Unlock'd: or, an Easy Key to all its Uses.* This essay has its own title page, but is paginated as part of Stokes's pamphlet, *A Scheme for Effectually Supplying Every Part of the City of Dublin with Pipe-Water* (Dublin, 1735).
26. Gibson, *Practical Surveying*, p. 160. A later calculating device with a similar name appears to have had no connection with Stokes's instrument (*Description of the Panmetron, or Universal Measure; Approved of by the Royal Dublin Society. Invented by James Jordan, of Downpatrick* (Dublin, 1823)).
27. Map of land near St Patrick Street, Dublin, St Patrick's Cathedral map collection, 17.
28. TCD, MUN/P/23/1440, MUN/P/4/37.
29. For Cave see *Dublin Journal*, 23 May, 10 June 1749. He and Stokes had been joint authors of a plan of Chichester House, Dublin, drawn in 1734 and reproduced in Haliday, *Scandinavian Kingdom of Dublin*, p. 239.
30. For Barker see *Dublin Journal*, 23 May 1749, *Universal Advertiser*, 16 July 1754; also the claim of a specialist instrument-maker, William King, that Cave had instructed no pupils apart from himself (*Pue's Occurrences*, 29 Sep. 1759). For Reading's relationship to Stokes see Gibson, *Practical Surveying* (3rd ed., [Dublin], 1768), p. 160 (not in earlier editions).

31. Add. MS 35391; *Cal. Anc. Rec. Dub.*, 7, p. 327; *Representation for the Improvement of Dublin Harbour, Submitted by the Directors General of Inland Navigation* (Dublin, 1805), p. 5.
32. *A Scheme for ... Pipe-Water*, pp 4, 21.
33. *Dublin Journal*, 7 Jan. 1755.
34. The Trinity College estate maps of 1715 are attributed to Stokes in a note forming part of the College archives (MUN/ME/16/41) and in Aalen and Hunter, *Hermathena*, 98 (1964), p. 91. But Stokes stated (MUN/ME/16/4) that the townland of Kilcoolytoghy had been returned as 40a. 1r. by Mr [John] Greene, compared with his own value of 39a. 1r. 10p., and it is the first of these figures that appears in the 1715 volume for Kerry. The Trinity muniments show that Greene was paid various sums in 1716–24 for surveying the College lands (TCD, MUN/P/4/21–8), but there were no such payments to Stokes at this early period.
35. John Gibson was sworn as a Trustees' surveyor on 12 July 1700 (Annesley MS, NLI, mic. P.259). His mathematical school is mentioned in *Dublin Intelligence*, 17 July 1708, and his map of lands in St Michael's parish, Dublin, is reproduced in *Irish Builder*, 33 (1891), p. 111. He calculated the road distances given in *Watson's Almanack* for 1736.
36. TCD, Barker Ponsonby MSS, map 1a. Callan, *Dissertation*, p. 22. There may be some link between Callan's remark and the unsupported publication-date of 1739 sometimes given for the *Treatise* (below, Appendix D).
37. *Dublin Journal*, 22 June 1773.
38. *A Course in Experimental Philosophy; Being an Introduction to the True Philosophy of Sr. Isaac Newton* (Dublin, 1738). A book with a similar title was published in Dublin by Gibson in 1755, with a subscription list that included twenty mathematicians and thirteen land surveyors. Gibson's teaching activities are mentioned in *Watson's Almanack* for 1743 (end-paper). For his school in Anglesea Street see *Dublin Journal*, 16 Sep. 1755.
39. *Public Gazetteer*, 10 Apr. 1759.
40. *Dublin Gazette*, 30 Dec. 1760.
41. *Dublin Journal*, 21 Mar. 1752, 2 Nov. 1754, 21 Sep. 1756; Dublin Society, MS minutes, 15 Jan.–12 Feb. 1756. George's marriage was reported in *Dublin Journal*, 17 Sep. 1754.
42. *Dublin Journal*, 10 Nov. 1764. Bernard Scalé's new edition of Rocque's map of the bay and harbour appeared in 1773.
43. OSO, letter registers (out-letters), 78 (1 May 1825). The continued popularity of the *Treatise*, 'particularly among the humbler class of surveyors', is confirmed in the preface to Patrick O'Shaughnessy's *Practical Surveying* (Limerick, 1843). For the many American editions of Gibson's book see L. C. Karpinski, *Bibliography of Mathematical Works Printed in America Through 1850* (Ann Arbor, 1940), pp 82–5, which describes it as an 'English' textbook.

44. For example his map of Mundown, Co. Dublin, 1749 (with printed cartouche), NLI, MS 11937.
45. *Dublin Journal*, 20 Jan. 1761.
46. *Dublin Journal*, 25 July 1752, 26 Aug. 1760.
47. *Dublin Journal*, 12 Dec. 1749.
48. Comparison of Gibson's survey with those of Joseph Coates, George Hibbard, and Matthew Slater, *c.* 1747, Fitzwilliam estate papers, NLI, mic. P.201.
49. Examples are in *Dublin Journal*, 14 Dec. 1756 (Downer vs Dunne); *Pue's Occurrences*, 16 Apr. 1757 (Mooney vs Kinsella); *Dublin Journal*, 15 Aug. 1758 (Frizells vs Connor).
50. *Dublin Journal*, 19, 23 Mar. 1765; *Leinster Journal*, 7 Mar. 1767.
51. Dials by Thomas Harding were advertised in *Hoey's Dublin Mercury*, 5 July, 30 Aug. 1766. Harding's new surveying and/or plotting instrument is mentioned in *Freeman's Journal*, 3 Apr. 1770, and in the 1780s and 1790s he was writing a book on surveying, compiling an almanac, experimenting with balloons, preparing a perpetual calendar, and practising as a writing master (*Hibernian Chronicle*, 8 Jan. 1784; *Hibernian Journal*, 2 Feb. 1785; *Dublin Evening Post*, 3 Feb. 1785; *Dublin Chronicle*, 28 Sep. 1790, 26 July, 9 Aug. 1791; RD, 491/190/317636 (1795)). His plan for a new trigonometrical survey is mentioned in the Council minutes of the Royal Irish Academy for 1792 (1, pp 250, 252). Harding estate maps of 1795 are in NLI, 21.F.108 (following p. 33), and he later took part in making a map of the Goldmines River in Co. Wicklow (O.P.517/106/29). See also Bowden, *Tour*, pp 58–9, and below, ch. 10. Perhaps there was more than one Harding.
52. M. Clark, *The Book of Maps of the Dublin City Surveyors, 1695–1827, an Annotated List* (Dublin, 1983), *passim*.
53. Advertisement by Isaac Ringwood, *Leinster Journal*, 8 Sep. 1784. Matthews served from 1764 to 1782. He began the map-books of the city estate (see above, ch. 6) and also made a survey of the city limits mentioned in 23 & 24 George III, c.17, sec. 4 (1773). His advertisement for magnets ('very proper to be in the possession of navigators, land surveyors, goldsmiths, jewellers, as also those afflicted with the gout, rheumatism, etc.') is in *Public Gazetteer*, 25 Sep. 1764.
54. *Proc. Dub. Soc.*, 15 (1779), p. 132; 17 (1781), p. 126; *Dublin Journal*, 7 Mar. 1780.
55. Gilbert, *History of Dublin*, 3, p. 369; *Dublin Journal*, 18 Oct. 1780; 'An Alphabetical List of the Freemen of the City of Dublin, 1774–1824', *Irish Ancestor*, 15 (1983).
56. *Dublin Chronicle*, 2 Oct. 1787. In 1791 Byron also owned a house in Great Britain Street, Dublin (RD, 513/451/338528).
57. Map of 1781 added to Scalé's atlas of John Hely Hutchinson's estate, Knocklofty, Co. Tipperary, 1771, NLI, MS 2735; Parnell estate maps, 1789, NLI, 21.F.18.
58. *Dublin Journal*, 21 Aug. 1783.

59. E. McParland, 'Trinity College', *Country Life*, 159 (1976), pp 1167, 1168, 1244.
60. *Dublin Chronicle*, 7 Oct. 1788.
61. James Malton, *A Picturesque and Descriptive View of the City of Dublin Described in a Series of the Most Interesting Scenes Taken in the Year 1791* (Dublin, 1799), p. ii.
62. Edward Ledwich, 'The History and Antiquities of Irishtown and Kilkenny', in C. Vallancey (ed.), *Collectanea de Rebus Hibernicis*, 9 (Dublin, 1781), frontispiece.
63. NLI, MS 2790(35), a copy by John Longfield. Other examples of Byron's work outside Dublin are in MSS 2735, 2789, 16.H.14(18) and 21.F.18.
64. *Dublin Chronicle*, 2 Aug. 1788.
65. *Dublin Evening Post*, 8 Sep. 1795.
66. Arthur Richards Neville became City Surveyor on Worthington's death in 1801 (*Cal. Anc. Rec. Dub.*, 15, p. 216). His tenure of the office is recorded in the directories until 1828, when he was followed by Arthur Neville, who in 1857 was followed by Parke Neville after sharing the post with him for a few years. In 1857 Parke was described as 'city engineer and local surveyor'. All three Nevilles conducted their private business from the same premises in York Street; presumably they were father, son and grandson.
67. Sherrard enrolled in the school of figure drawing on 27 Feb. 1766 and in the school of ornament drawing on 17 Mar. 1768; Byron in the school of figure drawing on 2 Apr. 1772 (*Proc. Dub. Soc.*, 1–2, p. 288; 4, p. 109; 8, p. 17).
68. *Freeman's Journal*, 13 Jan. 1770, 12 Sep. 1771. For the various Sherrard partnerships see the directory evidence cited in Andrews, *Ir. Geogr.*, 5 (1967), p. 287.
69. *Hibernian Journal*, 24 Mar. 1773. Thomas was in his 87th year when he died on 11 Mar. 1837 (*Dublin Evening Mail*, 13 Mar. 1837).
70. *Public Gazetteer*, 12 June 1773.
71. *Freeman's Journal*, 19 Mar. 1774; *Dublin Journal*, 1 Oct. 1774.
72. *Hibernian Journal*, 17 Sep. 1777.
73. J. Hanly, 'Oldcastle & Loughcrew 1778', *Riocht na Midhe*, 3 (1965), pp 249–52 (with reproductions).
74. Brownrigg's report on fees charged by Sherrard, Brassington and Greene, 1 July 1824, NAI, 2B.44.61.
75. *Dublin Journal*, 29 Feb. 1780.
76. *Dublin Journal*, 9 Feb., 12 Nov. 1782, 28 Feb. 1784; *Dublin Evening Post*, 30 July 1785, 27 Dec. 1796; *Saunders's News-letter*, 20 Nov. 1799.
77. *Saunders's Newsletter*, 12 Dec. 1791.
78. Wide streets commission minutes, City Hall, Dublin, volumes 4–8, *passim*, and especially 8, p. 245 (13 Mar. 1789).

79. Wide streets commission minutes, 10, p. 161(1791); 12, p. 210 (1794); 13, p. 36 (1795); 'Viator', *Letters to the Right Honourable Robert Peel ... Relating to the Improvement of 'the District of the Metropolis' and Principally the Earl of Meath's Liberties; By Making Therein Wide and Convenient Streets* (Dublin, 1816), p. 7. There is an extract from the map in *Irish Builder*, 33 (1891), p. 165. It was presumably a smaller version of this map that Sherrard made for the Irish government in 1801 (O.P. 521/142/4). His manuscript style at the 80-foot scale is seen in the plan of Athlone he drew in 1784 for an atlas of the Earl of Ranelagh's estate (Representative Church Body Library, Dublin, MS 151).
80. *Third Report from the Select Committee Appointed to Inquire into the State of Agriculture*, qq. 14589–14786, H.C. 1836 (465), viii.
81. *Saunders's News-letter*, 17 June 1800.
82. Chichester estate maps, NLI, 21.F.20 (Dunbrody, 1803), 21.F.19 (Inishowen, 1805).
83. Account for surveying College land in Co. Down, 1792, TCD, MUN/ P/4/69(20).
84. *Third Report on State of Agriculture*, 1836, qq. 14671–3.
85. NLI, 16.M.8(1–3).
86. Bogs commission minutes, 17 Oct. 1809. Nevertheless the signature 'Sherrard, Brassington and Greene' appeared on the map illustrating a report from Richard Brassington published by the commission.
87. H. Dutton, *Observations on Mr Archer's Statistical Survey of the County of Dublin* (Dublin, 1802), pp 166–7.
88. *Report on Survey and Valuation*, 1824, p. 186.
89. *Survey of His Majesty's Park the Phoenix, Dublin* (1773), revised by Sherrard, Brassington and Greene in 1811. A survey of the park was credited to Scalé in *Commons Journals, Ireland*, 8, p. cxxx, and in *Public Gazetteer*, 1 May 1773, when it was said to have been presented to the King. See also *Twelfth Report of Commissioners of Inquiry into Fees, Gratuities, Perquisites and Emoluments in Public Offices in Ireland*, p. 191, H.C. 1812(33), v. Sherrard's *A Survey of the Botanic Garden at Glassnevin* was engraved by John Taylor in 1800. His *A Survey of Part of the City of Dublin Shewing Several Improvements Intended by the Commissioners of Wide Streets* appeared in *Extracts from the Minutes of the Commissioners Appointed by Act of Parliament, for Making Wide and Convenient Ways, Streets, and Passages, in the City of Dublin* (Dublin, 1802).
90. Examples of Sherrard's dealings in property are in RD, 555/236/371172 (1803) and 769/97/521432 (1821). It was his activity as a speculator, apparently, rather than as a surveyor, that caused Dublin's Sherrard Street to be named after him.
91. Lockhart (*Ir. Geogr.*, 11(1978), pp 104–07) lists thirteen of Williamson's advertisements in the *Belfast News-letter* and prints three of them in full. Others appeared on 25 Oct. 1791, 9 Apr. 1805, 21 Apr. 1809 and 10 Apr. 1810. Except where otherwise stated the following account is

based on this material. News items in the same paper record the death of Williamson's mother in Armagh (13 June 1784), the death of his wife (22 May 1795) and his remarriage (17 July 1797).
92. Glancy, *Seanchas Ardmhacha*, 1 (1955), p. 150. A Quaker surveyor named William Williamson had practised in Co. Armagh in 1685 (William Molyneux, notes on the Castle Dillon estate, Southampton city archives, NLI, mic. P.1586).
93. *Proc. Dub. Soc.*, 7 (1 Aug. 1771), p. 211.
94. A number of Williamson's maps are listed in the booklets on maps of Antrim, Armagh, Belfast and Down in the *How to Use the Record Office* series.
95. Robert Livingston, map of Maghery, Co. Armagh, 1768, PRONI, D.291/2. Williamson's favourite border motif, a simulated moulding with beads arranged in groups of three, appears in a Livingston map of 1782 (NLI, 15.B4(1)).
96. Lease of land in Frederick Street, Belfast, 1805, PRONI, D.509/1572. Other Williamson property transactions are recorded in RD, 600/216/409105, 653/235/453202, 632/265/433069, 816/102/549638 and 814/367/548702.
97. G. Benn, *A History of the Town of Belfast from 1799 till 1810*, 2 (London, 1880), p. 68. No post-1792 plan by Williamson is listed in L. M. Ewart, 'Belfast Maps, a Record of Plans of the Town Chronologically Arranged ...', *Ulster Jour. Arch.*, 2nd ser., 1(1895), pp 99–105.
98. Application for employment, 20 June 1821, NAI, 2B.44.61.
99. Williamson's death at the age of seventy-six is recorded in the Shankill parish registers (PRONI, T.679/242, p. 17) and in the *Guardian and Constitutional Advocate*, 25 May 1832.
100. Palmerston estate maps, NLI, 16.F.17.
101. A civil engineer named Alexander Williamson appears in Martin's *Belfast Directory* for 1839, but he is not known to have produced any maps.
102. PRONI, D.604. The cartographer whom Williamson assisted on this map is unidentified. What was presumably a published version of it was advertised in *Dublin Evening Post*, 7 Apr. 1787. Maps based on the same source were the one in C. Coote, *Statistical Survey of the County of Armagh* (Dublin, 1804), pp 96–7, and William Allen's 'reduced' map of the lough dedicated to Lord O'Neill (undated, but later than 1800).
103. *Northern Star*, 5 Aug. 1796. James Lendrick is not otherwise known as a cartographer. His map of Antrim carries the date of its completion (1780) as well as the publication date of 1782.
104. Payments to Williamson for this survey between 1803 and 1806, totalling £600, are recorded in PRONI, C. & P. DOWN 4/2/5. This and the PRONI references cited in notes 96 and 99 above were kindly supplied by Dr Brian Trainor. According to *Report on Survey and Valuation*, 1824, p. 195, the cost of the map was £1,100. In 1984 it was reprinted by the Linen Hall Library, Belfast.

105. M. C. Storrie, 'William Bald, F.R.S.E., *c.* 1789–1857; Surveyor, Cartographer and Civil Engineer', *Trans. Inst. Br. Geogr.*, 47(1969), pp 205–31.
106. *Report on Survey and Valuation*, 1824, p. 57.
107. M. C. Storrie, 'The Man who Built the Antrim Coast Road', *Geogr. Mag.*, 43 (1971), p. 249.
108. Storrie, *Trans. Inst. Br. Geogr.*, 47 (1969), p. 207.
109. Bald to Lord Annesley, 16 Jan. 1819, PRONI, D.671/C/12/211.
110. Bogs commission minutes, 22 May 1810.
111. William Bald, 'An Account of the Survey and Map of the County of Mayo', *Proc. R. Ir. Acad.*, 1 (1836–40), pp 245–7.
112. Trotter, *Walks through Ireland*, pp 524–5, on his meeting with Bald at Castlebar in 1817.
113. *Telegraph or Connaught Ranger*, 6, 27 Oct. 1830.
114. *A Letter to the Nobility, Gentry, and Landholders, of the County of Mayo, on the Waste or Misapplication of the County Cess, or Acre Money* ([Castlebar?], 1822), p. 27. The sobriquet 'paver' for Alexander Taylor was a reference to his position as chief commissioner of the Dublin paving board.
115. Trotter, *Walks through Ireland*, p. 525; P. Knight, *Erris in the 'Irish Highlands'* (Dublin, 1836), p. 3.
116. Bald to Lord Annesley, 16 Jan. 1819, PRONI, D.671/C/12/211.
117. *The Times* (London), 23 and 30 August 1838. Bald's comment was anonymous but Griffith had no difficulty in recognising its author.

10
Tricks of the trade

'MR WISEACRE THE SURVEYOR, with his circumferentor and chain' was a sight familiar to every Irishman not only in the 1780s, when this half-friendly phrase appeared in print,[1] but for many decades before and after. The same two devices, and no others, had been specified in a seventeenth-century document as 'the names of such instruments as are used in surveying land';[2] and it was in an ostensibly more enlightened age that an Irish surveyor took both of them to England for a spell of work on the railways.[3]

Some uncertainty attends the circumferentor, but the chain is one of the few surveying appliances that seems to present no serious historical problem. In Ireland it was first mentioned at the time of the Wexford plantation survey of 1617 (Jobson and his generation had called their measuring standards ' lines', not necessarily implying that they were without links)[4] and from Petty's time onwards there is no decade without abundant proof of its use. Two minor points remain for exploration. The first is a matter of metrology. The standard yards made by the Dublin City Surveyor in 1720[5] were evidently meant to be identical with their British counterparts, but three different combinations of yards – the 'plantation', statute and Cunningham perches – appear to have co-existed in post-medieval Ireland. Chains in multiples of the seven-yard perch were doubtless being used, and probably manufactured, in many parts of Ireland at the time of the plantation surveys, though even in the eighteenth century some surveyors were working with chains imported from England and converting the results arithmetically into Irish measure.[6] Otherwise the only important distinction was between two-pole (50-link) and four-pole (100-link) chains, for nobody seems to have liked John Hood's suggestion, put forward in 1777, that one-hundredth of an Irish mile would provide a convenient alternative length.[7] Two-pole chains are on record at the time of both the Down and Trustees' Surveys, and there is ample evidence of their popularity (including many of the

TABLE 11

TRAVERSE SURVEYS: CHAINS AND CHAINING

Date	Number of lines in survey	Length of chain	Mean length of line in 4-pole chains	Source
SURVEYS				
1654–9	[20 stations per mile]	...	2.11	Hull (ed), _Economic Writings_, 2, pp 614–15
1711	81	2-pole	3.42	NAI, IA.37.13
Early 18th century	70	4-pole	3.83	" "
" "	163	2-pole	4.62	NLI, 14.A.30
" "	182	" "	5.21	NLI, MS 8030 (l)
" "	388	" "	12.18	NLI, MS 13739
1770	13	" "	8.66	NLI, MS 2793
TEXTBOOKS				
1654	15	4-pole	18.32	Osborne, _Exact Way_, pp 2, 5
1724	15	" "	2.52	Burgh, _Method_, p. 17
1763	13	" "	14.61	Gibson, _Practical Surveying_, p. 235
1764	7	2-pole	18.65	Noble, _Geodaesia_, p. 40
1768	19	4-pole	8.17	Hood, _Tables_, p. 19
1843	9	" "	19.67	O'Shaughessy, _Practical Surveying_, p. 41

The use of a 2-pole chain is assumed when all fractions of a chain are less than 50 links. All distances are assumed to be in Irish plantation measure. The figures quoted by Noble purport to be those of an actual survey; in the other textbooks the figures are probably invented.

entries in Table 11) until some way into the nineteenth century. The reason for preferring them, as Benjamin Noble pointed out, was that four Irish perches, amounting to 28 yards, made a somewhat 'unhandy' length compared with the traditional English 22 yards.[8] In towns, where the perch was a less appropriate unit, some surveyors favoured a chain of exactly forty feet.[9]

According to Robert Gibson, bad chaining was the most common source of error among surveyors.[10] One wonders how much of the error sprang from the practice of hiring local labourers to help with this task. Joshua Wight told how in one especially important survey he gave his men 'a special charge to carry the chain, as I taught them always to cut the pole before them and to beware of the least mistake or slip of the chain'.[11] By 'cutting the pole' he meant ensuring that the chain was laid out in a straight line from one station to the next. This was an obligation that the surveyor himself could sometimes enforce from a distance while he took the bearing of the same line, but it still left plenty of scope for the chain-men to go wrong in other ways. They might fail to identify sticks put in the ground at the end of each chain-length; metal 'arrows' were used for this purpose in Wight's time instead of sticks, though his own preference was for fourteen-inch rods with iron points, painted like barbers' poles to be easily visible. Another danger was to miscount the rods or arrows and so commit an error of a whole chain – a notoriously easy mistake, as Noble pointed out. What Wight called slips must have been gaps or overlaps between successive measured lengths. He might also have warned against holding the chain too tightly or too loosely.

Other weaknesses could be blamed on the manufacturer. Wight suffered much from chains that broke, sometimes two or three times a day, and from the difficulty of getting them repaired in country districts. He was accordingly proud of his 'excellent plantation chain, made by the ingenious Daniel Voster of [Cork]; the wire was well tempered and strong and the rings true, and so well turned that it never broke with me all the while nor seldom a chink [?] in the chain, nor never opened but once in one of the rings'. The usual criticism of a chain was that it either exceeded or fell short of the standard measure, perhaps through accidental stretching or bending of the links, perhaps by the deliberate choice of its owner. Peter Callan and Richard Frizell were two mid-eighteenth-century surveyors who blamed erroneously long chains for the kind of undermeasure that was now seen to be characteristic of their predecessors.[12] (Their explanation ignored one striking feature of this general propensity to understatement, illustrated for the Down Survey in Table 12, namely that large areas were often less affected by it than small areas.)

Once such irregularities had been detected a suitable allowance could be made for them: a map by John Bell of Cavan reports how he had altered the number of acres as a result of the chain being two inches too short.[13] Whether a chain should intentionally be made too long to allow for sag was a more difficult problem. Bell's note may have been obliquely referring to this issue, and also to his habitual critic Callan, who had advocated a built-in excess of two inches instead of the four to eight inches allegedly common in the past. Callan's view was unusual, even among his contemporaries. Noble for instance considered that the chain-lengths in a surveyor's field book were more likely to be excessive than deficient (presumably through misalignment or insufficient tension or both), an unwarrantable assumption if the chain had been deliberately lengthened to compensate for this tendency.[14]

Another question that long remained open, in this case until the nineteenth century, was whether to measure horizontally or along the slope of the ground. Callan distinguished natural surfaces, artificial surfaces (perhaps meaning the surfaces of roads and buildings) and horizontal surfaces; he even seems to have distinguished horizontal distances at sea level from those at higher altitudes. He castigated colleagues who took the chain along the slope with the argument that plant-stems and walls stand vertically and water lies horizontally, and that it is plants, buildings and water, rather than space in the abstract, that ought to give the land its value. Needless to say, an appeal to money as the ultimate criterion was typical of Callan and his colleagues: allowing an average difference of three per cent between surface and horizontal area, he calculated that the amount of rent at stake on this decision in Ireland came to something like £168,000 in a year. That his was the usual Irish attitude to slopes seemed evident when the Dublin Society made no award for a new way of surveying uneven ground: one of its reasons was that 'the method used by surveyors in surveying hills by raising up the chain is much more easy and ascertains very well the horizontal level'.[15] Later the existence of a contrary practice was attested by the Ordnance Survey's disclosure that when its own acreages were compared with those in 'old deeds etc.' any considerable inclination of the ground would be taken into account.[16]

Despite Gibson's anxieties, chaining was generally considered to be capable of high precision. Noble claimed that a distance of ten chains was measurable to within half a link of the truth. A maximum error of half

TABLE 12

EXAMPLES OF DOWN SURVEY ERRORS

Number of denominations in sample	Area of denomination in statute acres	Mean percentage error
15	0–99	–18.79
20	100–199	–13.25
21	200–299	–11.76
8	300–399	–7.59
9	400–499	–9.30
9	500–599	–13.86
3	600–699	–6.95
8	700–799	–8.39
1	800–899	–6.31
3	900–999	–5.85
6	+1,000	–1.15

a link was also quoted by Callan, without saying whether or not such a maximum might be expected to vary with the total distance measured; even in a single two-pole chain-length it would not amount to more than one per cent. Callan was an opponent of unrealistic minuteness among textbook writers; even so, link-splitting in surveys on any normal scale would have struck some of his predecessors as over-meticulous. The half-link does appear in surveyors' field notes of the early and middle eighteenth century, it is true. But in a surprisingly large number of entries there are no links at all.[17] This state of affairs is explicable in two ways. Either the surveyor was content to see his distances booked to the nearest chain, or else his stations really were separated by an exact number of chain lengths. The first suggestion, apart from being no more than a guess, implies a sadly unambitious approach to map accuracy – even if distances were being rounded down as a deliberate counter to loss of tension or bad alignment.[18] (Though over-compensatory rounding down might help to explain why early acreage figures are more often too small than too large.) The second has some contemporary support: at least two eighteenth-century writers advised the Irish surveyor to simplify his arithmetic by keeping measured main-line distances to an exact multiple of two perches, instead of bringing his stations as near as possible to some relevant landscape feature in the manner of a modern chain survey.[19] Whatever its other merits, this advice did nothing to ease the process of offset measurement discussed below.

Despite the imperfections attending its manufacture and use, there is no sign that the chain was ever seriously challenged by alternative methods of linear measurement. The wheel or odometer formed the subject of a characteristically original paper by Richard Lovell Edgeworth,[20] but in surveying no less than in other subjects the research paper is often a poor guide to what happens in real life. Boundary traversing gave little scope for the wheel and even on good road surfaces it did not entirely displace the chain.[21] Still stronger reservations apply to tacheometry, repeatedly advocated as a bold innovation throughout the modern history of surveying. No doubt this was the principle behind Joseph Ravell's machine of 1754 for measuring distance from a single station: like many such inventions it was never heard of again, in spite of winning a thirty-guinea reward from the Dublin Society.[22]

Mr Wiseacre's other instrument, the circumferentor, seems to have made its Irish literary debut in Petty's history of the Down Survey.[23] If other and more timid writers avoided the word, it was less through unfamiliarity with what it denoted than in deference to the difficulty of spelling it, as illustrated by the eighteenth-century forms 'circumvalenter'[24] and 'sircomfrontor'.[25] The usual term for a surveying device other than a chain, in Francis Jobson's day and later, was simply 'instrument', though this word is by no means orthographically foolproof either and it must sometimes have been chosen out of respect for the reader's ignorance, a state of mind that the expert is always happy to tolerate among the employing classes. In this case the ignorance has also afflicted some modern historians, so it may be advisable to provide a definition of a circumferentor, not necessarily valid outside Ireland, as an instrument for measuring compass bearings. Petty makes the magnetic connection implicit by his frequent references to the needle.[26] With Molyneux it becomes explicit – 'magnetic instruments (such as the circumferentor …)'[27] – and the same is true of various later authorities, including practical surveyors from Joshua Wight to William Bald.[28] The only other clue to the form and function of the Irish circumferentor is Callan's remark that its line of sight could not deviate from the horizontal by more than a few degrees. While there is no case for imposing this criterion of horizontality on modern usage, Callan's statement will serve for a much longer period than his own, the observation of vertical angles with a circumferentor being considered a novelty as late as 1809.[29] Our initial definition may thus be extended to give a magnetic compass swinging horizontally in a circular box, mounted either on a single rod or on a tripod, with a pair

TRICKS OF THE TRADE 301

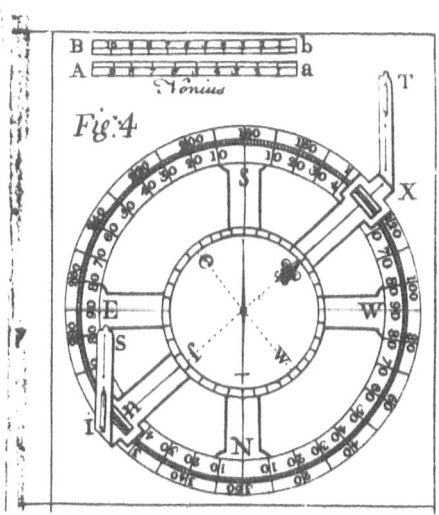

Plate 21. Two ways of depicting the Irish surveyor's 'instrument', the first unfortunately more common than the second. (a) above: a circumferentor, from an engraved compartment in a manuscript farm map by Dennis Carty, 1728 (Cork Archives Institute, U.137, Box 30). (b) below: 'a theodolite as it is now made', from Benjamin Noble's *Geodaesia Hibernica*, 1768, p. 30 and Fig. 4.

of open sights that were fixed to the box and consequently rotated with it, leaving the difference between needle and line of sight to be read in degrees and parts of a degree.

For Irish azimuthal instruments pre-dating the Down Survey almost the only explicit evidence is Petty's comment that land in Ireland had 'hitherto' been admeasured by the circumferentor. In this as in other respects, then, Petty himself was no pioneer. But it is not until later that information about Irish angle-measurement begins slowly to accumulate. Some of it is indirect, such as the fact that the Down Survey prompted the manufacture of circumferentors in Ireland and the presumption that a number of usable instruments must have been left behind by Petty's surveyors.[30] The only recorded specimens with seventeenth-century Irish associations are two instruments of unknown provenance, one at the Ashmolean Museum in Oxford and the other at Maynooth College.[31] However, pictures of surveyors at work start to become more common at about the same time (Plate 21). A circumferentor appears in the margin of Petty's small-scale map of Ireland, and another in a manuscript map of $c.$ 1700 attributable to Sir William Robinson.[32] Others, more to the point, are pictured in a number of eighteenth-century farm or estate maps, often in company with a surveyor's chain,[33] as well as in the newspaper advertisements of the Dublin instrument-maker William King.[34] Less predictably, what look like circumferentors were sometimes carved on surveyors' tombstones.[35]

Another premise for deductions about the circumferentor is the typical Irish surveyor's field book, in which a single measurement in degrees refers to a single line without mention of any second limb for the angle in question, apparently because this second line is assumed to lie in the direction of magnetic north. Some historians have also tried to determine a cartographer's choice of instrument from the north-points given on his maps. Although most Irish farm and estate surveyors showed north without any qualification, the kind of meridian that they had in mind can usually be established by comparison with an Ordnance Survey map of the same area. In a large sample of pre-Ordnance Survey maps, including work by most of the surveyors named in this book, compass north appears much more often than true north (Table 13). The increase in maps showing true north after about 1770 was too slight to invalidate James Weale's claim for the prevalence of the magnetic meridian more than half a century later.[36] Such evidence is by no means immune to scepticism. It is true that the line-plot of a compass survey must necessarily

TABLE 13
NORTH POINTS IN A SAMPLE OF FARM AND ESTATE MAPS

	Number of Maps	
Date	Magnetic north	True north
1690–1739	33	3
1740–1769	29	1
1770–1799	29	1
1800–1829	29	9

include a number of parallels that give the direction of the needle (and not the geographical pole), but the mere occurrence of a magnetic meridian on the final map is not enough to prove that more than a single bearing was observed with a magnetic instrument. Contrariwise, taking a circumferentor sight on the sun's noonday shadow could add what one cartographer called a 'solar' meridian to a compass survey without the aid of more sophisticated apparatus.[37]

A final point to note is the keen if intermittent interest shown in magnetic variation as a subject for scientific inquiry by Irish philomaths. Petty dropped them a hint by recommending a comparison of the true and magnetic meridians:[38] the fact that his own maps made no mention of this difference cannot be held against him, for in mid-seventeenth-century Ireland the two kinds of north happened to be nearly coincident. In the 1690s, when the variation stood at about seven degrees west, terrestrial magnetism received more formal attention from William Molyneux, as also did the cognate problem of superimposing surveys done at different dates.[39] After this, silence fell until the middle of the eighteenth century, a hiatus first made a subject of historical comment by Thomas Harding, who expressed some self-righteous surprise at the absence of magnetic data from the maps of his predecessors, including those drawn by the official Dublin City Surveyors in the early post-Molyneux decades.[40] Whatever its cause this neglect is hardly relevant to the present purpose. It is not before Harding's time but later, when more accurate instruments were being recommended and manufactured, that corroborative evidence for the use of the circumferentor is most necessary.

The first Irish estate maps to carry a statement of the variation appear to date from the 1740s, by which time the compass in Dublin was pointing about eighteen degrees west of north.[41] Shortly afterwards the subject began to be ventilated in print, first by Robert Gibson[42] and then by Benjamin Noble,[43] and thenceforth it was not unusual for both norths to appear on the same map. Although Harding's researches on geomagnetism were done with an eye to pure science (the Royal Irish Academy eventually published some of them) he also stressed their practical value to the land surveyor, and silenced a critic, who had questioned the utility of such work, with a confident appeal to expert opinion.[44] As a theoretician Harding was living through a difficult time. No sooner had he worked out a definitive law of westward movement (by twelve minutes and twenty seconds per year) than the compass began to defy all known precedents by veering in the opposite direction. Harding first noticed a lessening of the westerly variation in 1793–4. His new findings were made known with commendable speed,[45] but they seem to have left the ordinary Irish land surveyor unmoved. What did most to modernise professional orientations was the exclusive use of non-magnetic north on the widely-copied Ordnance Survey maps of the 1830s and after.

All this time the circumferentor was flourishing in the face of well-articulated criticism – from men of science as early as the 1700s,[46] and by the middle of the century from many practising surveyors.[47] Its main handicap, the danger of magnetic interference, had been known for many years: in discussing the provision of armed guards for the Down Survey, Petty had feared that their weapons would attract the surveyors' compass needles.[48] Permanent local anomalies were equally familiar to Petty's generation. Island Magee in Co. Antrim was one notorious example, explained first by magical powers at work in the peninsula and later by hypothetical iron ore deposits.[49] More geomagnetic traps lay in wait near Slane, Co. Meath; and Wight knew many in other parts of the country that involved deviations of two degrees, especially among the mountains.[50] Callan, mercenary as ever, thought that surveyors should be paid extra for working in areas subject to local attraction. Then there was the problem of diurnal variation.[51] Mindful of such hazards, eighteenth-century observers seldom booked their angles to less than half or a quarter of a degree, and instrument-makers were generally content with this modest level of precision on their compass dials. Reading the circumferentor to one minute, with the aid of a vernier scale, could still be treated as unusual in the early nineteenth century.

Outside Ireland, some eighteenth-century writers relegated the circumferentor to wastes and commons – 'much used in America, and in some other foreign countries for surveying woods and forests', ran one rather condescending comment in 1773.[52] The colonial image was partly a recognition of the instrument's labour-saving properties. Its portability was one of these. Another was that angles could be fixed with only one landmark instead of two (the magnetic pole took the place of a second landmark), a feature which also proved particularly useful in wooded country where long-range visibility was poor. Seen in this light the early adoption of the compass in England's Irish colony was natural enough; but as population grew larger and farms smaller its continued dominance presents a historical problem. Even contemporaries found the compass-surveyor's addiction hard to explain, and many of them wrote emphatically in praise of other instruments such as the theodolite and the semi-circle.

Most modern writers would probably define a theodolite as an azimuthal instrument in which the line of sight can rotate both horizontally and vertically, and which while often incorporating a compass is customarily used for finding the angle between two rays without reference to magnetic north. For several well-known eighteenth-century Irish surveyors, however, the essence of the theodolite was the rotation of sights on a flat circle, its superior efficiency being due partly to an index that was steadier than a compass needle and partly to the finer subdivision made possible by a longer circumference (Plate 21).[53] On such a circle the bearing of one sight-line from another could be found independently of the compass. In fact an arc of only 180 degrees is sufficient to determine any angle or its complement, and the advantages of a semi-circular instrument were urged in more than one contemporary textbook. How many readers took this advice is impossible to say. One observer mapped a farm in Co. Kilkenny with a semicircle in 1702, but since he was a sailor as well as a surveyor his choice of instruments may have been unusual;[54] and half a century later Joshua Wight thought it worthwhile to mention, as something not to be taken for granted, his own habit of annexing a semi-circle to the circumferentor when geomagnetic conditions were particularly bad.[55]

When the theodolite proper made its appearance in Ireland remains uncertain. Perhaps it was with Richard Castle in c. 1730; his combined surveying and levelling instrument was said to be the first of its kind.[56] The Armagh surveyor Robert Livingston was using a 'new improved theodolite' in 1759,[57] and the earliest pictorial clue comes from the same decade in the modern-style theodolites drawn by Rocque as marginal decorations, though even these are difficult to interpret: in one of the Rocque estate maps a later hand has pencilled in a pair of tall open sights as if to convert the theodolite into a circumferentor, without making clear whether it was the cartographer or the graffiti-artist who stood revealed in this cryptic gesture as behind the times.[58] The episode signals the danger of bias in early evidence on surveying techniques, which often consists of praise, usually self-praise, for somewhat vaguely-characterised inventions and improvements. What the Irish historian needs is Irish names, dates and places for each stage in the progress celebrated in so many standard histories of technology – telescopic sights, stadial wires, engine-divided circles and the rest. What he gets from the year 1811 is:

> A statistical survey of Lucan, by Major Sandys, with a correct map, on which is marked the produce of every acre, half acre, rood and perch in the town and vicinity, with the size, number of apartments and accommodation of every whiskey house, from accurate drawings and actual measurements, made by the assistance of observations had at every hour ... by the aid of different glasses; of the most approved diameters.[59]

Even as parody this is almost too specific to be convincing. Few non-satirical writers did more than define the standard of accuracy currently attainable, and the only instrumental improvements that they itemised – the nonius and the vernier – were in fact of considerable antiquity. Thus Noble told how the nonius made 'modern' instruments readable to a tenth of a degree. In 1786 another theodolite-user took the trouble to advertise a limit of five minutes (not much of an advance),[60] but only a year later James Irwin mentioned a new theodolite that could reduce this to one minute, unfortunately not saying what else was new about it.[61] However, one's overall impression is that, accurate or otherwise, the theodolite was rather slow to assert its supremacy. If William Bald is to be taken literally, no Connaught surveyors had yet adopted it when he first came to Mayo in 1809.[62] And in Limerick, thirty-four years later, Patrick O'Shaughnessy had to tell his readers where they could find a picture of the instrument. (For circumferentors he offered no such advice: they were already 'in the hands of every surveyor'.)[63]

The last azimuthal instrument to be noticed is the plane table, in which the angle was not read as a number on a scale but drawn in the field with sight-rule and pencil as a pair of intersecting rays. Though common in seventeenth- and eighteenth-century England, the plane table was ignored by most Irish authors,[64] and its two appearances in Irish maps and atlases are unacknowledged borrowings from non-Irish textbooks – the picture in Thomas Raven's Essex estate survey of 1635 from Aaron Rathborne,[65] and the one on a map of 1700 by Owen Swan from William Leybourn.⁶⁶ Of course no method of plotting maps in the field can be said to have the Irish climate on its side. A more revealing criticism would be that a plane-table determination of acreage, once complete, cannot be checked without being entirely done again. In Ireland, where so many surveys were disputed, it was an advantage for field and office work to be independently verifiable: hence the emphasis placed on field notes in almost every Irish survey that became a subject of disagreement.

The normal method of using the circumferentor may have seemed sufficiently obvious from its Latin name; at any rate few Irish writers took the trouble to describe it, and this reticence is even more characteristic of the earliest experts, like Henry Osborne (1654) and Thomas Burgh (1724), than of their more internationally-minded successors who were aware of other possibilities – a further sign of how much the Irish land surveyor owed to a single tradition. The first comprehensive statement is Benjamin Noble's: 'in taking a survey, the land is always surrounded with stations'.⁶⁷ This idea of the survey as built on a single polygon, called by Noble 'the body of the land', finds expression in many Irish farm maps of eighteenth-century and earlier date, in which the outer boundary is carefully and prominently drawn with the interior left almost empty. The same impression is given by surviving field notes, of which the earliest are some seventy pages preserved for the Thomond estates, apparently from the 1630s and belonging to the surveys of William Sapperton, Henry Ellsworth or Simon Garstin.⁶⁸ Each page shows two columns of figures arranged in pairs, some of them headed respectively 'degrees' and 'lengths'. Occasionally there are also references to landmarks, such as 'the gate' or 'the garden corner', placed in a third column opposite a pair of numbers. The entries are grouped in sets beginning with a denomination-name and not infrequently ending with a phrase of the form: 'here closes the map of Donsallagh'. On some pages the surveyor has drawn a rectangle to show the measured length and breadth of a small enclosure, but the main surveys are booked entirely without sketches or diagrams. It is impossible to resist the conclusion that each pair of numbers represents the length and bearing of one side of the survey polygon.

In 1654 Henry Osborne printed an extract from a specimen field book in exactly the form just described, and interpreted it in exactly the same way.⁶⁹ Later Irish field notes follow a similar pattern, at least until the middle of the eighteenth century: a column for distances, a column for angles, and one or more columns for remarks (Plate 22). Further corroboration comes from those maps – admittedly not very plentiful – on which the cartographer has identified his survey stations by numbering them or by joining them with straight 'construction' lines distinct from the boundaries on the ground. Such stations almost always 'surround' the land in the manner prescribed by Noble.[70] Finally, and not to forget the layman, there is the casual statement thrown out by one landowner that surveyors always kept the land on their right.[71] It appears then that the boundary traverse, as practised in the plantation surveys, was also customary among private surveyors at least as early as the 1630s.

On the other hand the private sector can do little more than the plantation surveys to show just how the traverse worked. There are two problems, in particular, on which both literature and documents have disappointingly little to say. The first is the elimination of what Petty called the perclose.[72] In traversing all the way round a farm or townland the surveyor's initial station is necessarily recorded twice, once as the beginning of his first line and again as the end of his last line. When all the lines and angles have been plotted these two points should of course be found to coincide on paper as they do in nature. A gap between them is evidently due to one or more errors in surveying or plotting or both and if it is wide enough the survey must be done again. But a small misclosure can hardly justify the cost of re-surveying, for without perfect instruments and perfect observers the second attempt will produce another error of comparable magnitude though probably in a different direction. No surveyor is so fanatically honest as to leave his closing error on the finished map. Instead he gets rid of it by distributing the appropriate distances around the polygon, changing the position of each angle by successively larger amounts from start to finish until no gap remains.

The dearth of simple and unequivocal descriptions of this procedure is not to be wondered at, for surveyors probably felt that to advertise it would be to shake the public's faith in their skill. Even when they set out their field work in a map-margin or on a reference-page the closing error had always been disposed of in advance. But if they wanted to argue about the merits of each other's work they still had to agree among themselves about the limits of the permissible. Here as usual Callan gave the game away by openly challenging the ivory-tower assumption that misclosures could be completely avoided. But having said that it was 'morally impossible to handle a chain, and field instruments, over the bounds of a large parcel of irregular lands, without differing the least fraction of a link, or degree', he concluded rather feebly that 'all experienced practitioners' allow 'small

Distances.	Angles.	South.	North.	East.	West.	X		Z	
14	:70	73 :00 S W	4	29					14 :05
20	:40	75 :30 S W	5	10		14 :06	4	:29	33 :85
10	:50	87 :00 S W	0	55		19 :79	9	:39	44 :34
9	:70	73 :30 S W	2	76		10 :49	9	:94	53 :64
29	:00	75 :30 S W	7	25		9 :30	12	:70	81 :75
7	:40	74 :30 S W	1	98		28 :11	19	:95	88 :87
10	:60	South.	10	60		7 :12	21	:93	88 .87
14	:60	28 :30 S W	12	84		00 00	32	:53	95 :84
33	:95	82 :00 N E			4 :74	33 :61	6 97	45 :37	62 :23
25	:00	72 :00 N E			7 :74	25 :75		40 :63	38 :48
21	:40	78 :30 N E			4 :28	20 :97		32 :89	17 :51
21	:00	65 :30 N E			8 :71	19 :11		28 :61	1 :60
:0	:00	4 :30 N W			19 90	1 60		19 :90	00 :00
238. 25			45. 37	45. 37	97. 44	97 :44	X		Z

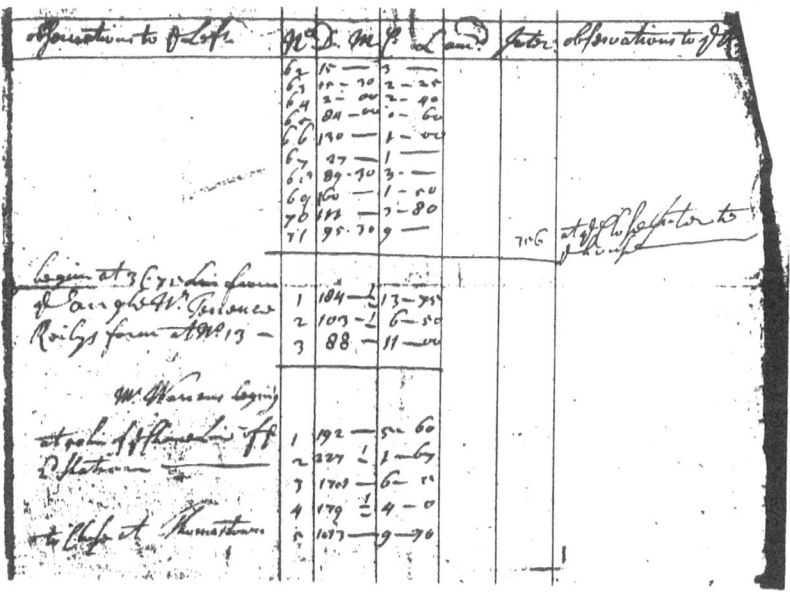

Plate 22. Irish surveyors' field notes. (a) above: from Henry Osborne's *Exact Way*, 1654 (see Plate 23). Distances are in chains and links, bearings in degrees and minutes. Latitudes and departures appear in columns 3–6. (b) below: anonymous survey of Kilmore, Co. Kildare, early eighteenth century (NAI, IA.37.13). D signifies degrees, M minutes, C chains, L links, 'Inter' intersections. The blank column headed 'am'd' (amended) was evidently intended for corrections.

fractions ... provided it does not amount to large fractions'.[73] Here, one would have thought, was a fruitful source of disagreement when the field notes of a controverted survey came under critical examination. Perhaps the derogatory epithet 'cobbling' implied a tendency to carry the process of adjustment too far. But how far was too far? Only two authors answered this question, neither of them quite unambiguously.[74] Both were willing to accept an error of about seven links, with no suggestion as to how the significance of any such absolute magnitude might depend on the extent of the survey area. The precise effect of a seven-link 'perclose' is hard to specify. Suppose, however, for the sake of simplicity, that the whole of this error can be attributed to the last line of the polygon, and that the line in question is ten chains long. The polygon must then be corrected by an addition or subtraction of something like 0.035 acres, surely an inconsiderable quantity, even among Irishmen, in a townland of average size. But the seven links come from the textbooks: what happened in real life is another matter.

The other problem with the traverse, and indeed with most kinds of survey, was to choose the right distance between successive stations. Once again Noble was ready with an aphoristic comment, but he was as vague on the subject of actual lengths as Callan had been about closing errors: 'the fewer stations you make ... the less labour you have, the less chance you have of making mistakes, either in the field-work or the chamber-work; so that I would recommend it to you, to make your stations as long as you possibly can, without having your off-sets or in-sets too large'.[75] In a traverse survey offsets and insets are the short, perpendicular measurements taken respectively outwards or inwards from known points on the main polygonal lines to fix the positions of places on the territorial boundary so that the boundary can be completed by joining up the ends of the offsets and insets. Of course Noble was self-evidently right to suggest that the lengths of these perpendiculars would vary inversely with the number of sides in the polygon. He was also right in implying that, other things being equal, a single long line is easier to measure accurately than a series of short ones. Yet he put less emphasis than a later surveyor would have done on the danger of long offsets, which in the early years of the Irish Ordnance Survey, for instance, was one of the commonest subjects for technical discussion,[76] and which in English surveying literature had been broached as early as 1725.[77] What brought offsets under suspicion was firstly that the perpendicular angles between the side lines and the main lines were customarily laid off by eye (though in theory they could have been done with a theodolite, a circumferentor, a surveyor's cross or an optical square), so that the longer the offset the greater the probable misplacement of the feature with which it connects; and secondly that each offset was left so to speak hanging in mid-air, without forming part of any polygon that could be made to check itself.

All of which makes it strange that the subject had not been raised by Gibson, Callan, Petty or Osborne. But there is worse to come. Offsets are by no means uncommon in the field work of the 1760s and 1770s,[78] and there is an earlier incidental reference to them in Joshua Wight's diary (for 16 April 1752), when in traversing round a particularly irregular boundary he complained that the main lines were 'nothing but like small offsets'. Here then was one surveyor of the pre-Noble period who knew an offset when he saw it, but some of the earlier evidence is less reassuring. The Thomond field books of the 1630s contain scarcely a single figure that can be interpreted as an offset measurement. It seems most unlikely that these would have been kept as a separate record: no surveyor wants to fumble with two field books at the same time, especially when he has plenty of room for secondary measurements in the remarks column of his first book. In any case, speculations about missing field documents can do little to explain the many farm and estate maps that show straight lines joining point to point along a boundary in just the kind of unconvincingly simple shape that would come from plotting the Thomond field books as they stand. It is possible that some of the angles in these polygons are the terminals of offset measurements taken from main lines that do not appear on the map, but apart from being unsupported by any surviving field books this supposition would deprive the offsets of their principal role, which is to provide realistic boundaries: the reader would still be looking for offsets from the offsets. On the other hand to tread or set forth a boundary with the chain is a seventeenth-century phrase which seems to envisage the surveyor as keeping so close to a ditch or stream that no offsets were necessary,[79] and some townland boundaries did indeed run straight enough for the chain literally to be laid along them or very close to them. 'Direct', i.e. straight, lines occur in many non-cartographic boundary descriptions, and in certain bogs and mountains they can still be seen on the ground. But this argument is hardly applicable to the unnatural-looking zig-zags by which river meanders are shown on many an early estate map.

One last possibility remains to be disposed of. If the chief purpose of a map was to find the number of acres in a given denomination (as seems more often than not to have been the case) then offsets could theoretically be avoided by making the measured polygon cut the boundary in a series of give-and-take lines: while the polygon would comprise fewer lines than the denomination its area would be the same. But apart from the difficulty of setting out such an equivalent polygon on the ground, to chain it would entail an intolerable crossing of banks, ditches and rivers as the line repeatedly moved in and out of the survey area.[80] Such crossings are sometimes preferable to the further multiplication of stations, but on the whole it is easier to run a main line on one side of the boundary or the other. And the average surveyor would rather take offsets (in Noble's terminology) than insets, partly to reduce the total distance measured and partly to facilitate the mapping of houses and other objects within the denomination under survey. If surveyors had been in the habit of taking insets from a circumscribing polygon they would not have complained as often as they did about being unable to measure a farm whose tenant had denied them admittance. This argument can be tested on the small number of maps which happen to show the principal survey lines as well as the townland boundaries or which happen to be accompanied by their field work. In one group of surveys by John Travers, for example, there were 257 offsets and only 58 insets.[81]

Finally, a point of more evident socio-economic importance: if surveyors were sometimes tempted to economise on offset measurements by cutting off the corners of a townland, their acreage values would necessarily fall short of the truth, which of course is what did very often happen in seventeenth-century Ireland. There are two reasons for not drawing the obvious conclusion, however. First, it is difficult to imagine a surveyor habitually shortening his boundaries without interested witnesses becoming aware of the fact. Next, the 'cut-offs' can hardly have been large enough to explain the worst differences between contemporary and modern area values. This too is a difficult subject to quantify, for the size of the omitted area would depend on the distance between traverse stations and on the character of the boundary being measured. Some information on distances is presented in Table 11. It suggests that calculations based on Petty's figure of twenty stations per mile will not be unfair to his fellow surveyors. In the matter of boundaries some kind of average between simple and complex cases can be struck by postulating a townland of circular outline. Another source of variation is the size of the parcel under survey: the larger the area, the smaller are its aggregated offset spaces as a proportion of the whole. But in all except the smallest townlands the loss would be comparatively insignificant: about one per cent in 100 Irish acres, on the above-mentioned assumptions, and about 0.25 per cent in 450 acres – a less important influence on levels of error, it would seem, than the alleged use of excessively long chains at the same period; and conceivably less important than the chain surveyor's omission of odd links.

Offsets to boundaries were not the only way in which a traverse survey could be extended outwards or inwards from its skeleton. Another possibility was to measure lines into or across the body of the land. The most probable reason for taking such measurements was to incorporate additional detail – like the centrally-placed lake which a surveyor of 1778 was accused of failing to deduct from his acreage, possibly because he had walked round the townland boundary without seeing it.[82] The Thomond field books include a number of bearings enclosed in circles (to distinguish them from those of the main traverse) and accompanied by such notes as 'parting the mountains … and the arable' or 'the intersecting line parting the bog from the highland'. (To treat soil and land-use boundaries as single bearings was another way of disregarding the subtleties of the offset.) The second reason for such measurements was as a check on the main traverse. Some check lines appear on the maps themselves;[83] others figure in contemporary disputes. Thus in one controverted survey, done by John Mooney of Geashill and Dennis Kinsella in 1757, the landlord checked Kinsella's map, which was threatening to cost him the rent of nine acres, by getting 'skilful people to measure several diagonal or cross lines from the extreme points of the land from their own marked stations, and I do hereby certify to the public that no one line agrees with Kinsella's map'. In one such diagonal the difference complained of was seven perches, which assuming a scale of forty perches to the inch would imply an error on the paper of 0.175 inches.[84]

Supplementary lines in a traverse survey were measured in two ways, as John Bell made clear in 1739 when asked to interpret another surveyor's map. The large 'pops' (dots or circles) signified the mearing of the property, he said, and had been fixed by the chain; the small pops had been either chained or intersected.[85] Intersections, formed by bearings taken from two or more known points without the aid of linear measurement, had been envisaged by Petty as part of the Down Survey. The alternative was either to chain a straight line all the way across the body of the land, as in the Mooney-Kinsella case; or else to take the bearings and distances of new traverse lines, perhaps singly as a kind of non-perpendicular offset, perhaps as a succession of legs which might or might not connect at both ends with the rest of the work. Given enough lines of this kind, a farm or townland survey could be converted into a survey of fields, houses and roads with no change of principle. An example was the survey of Upper and Lower Ahowle and part of Ballycullen in Co. Wicklow made by Edward Johnson in 1827. Besides the usual landscape features Johnson showed a number of circled points and broken lines which it seems safe to identify with the positions occupied respectively by the instrument and the chain.[86] The lands form a block of about thirty farms surveyed by a mesh of traverse lines. All the lines include at least two legs, so that there are no triangles; but every line is connected with two other lines. The same method could be used for networks of urban streets as well as for fences and farm boundaries. Apart from the extra time needed to measure the interior lines, the main burden on the surveyor was to design his field book not just as a continuous succession of tabulated numbers but as a mixture of tables and line diagrams, perhaps with the columns of numbers themselves arranged to form a diagram. This may have been the 'topographical' manner of taking field notes mentioned by Thomas Power in 1767.[87] Before the arrival of the Ordnance Survey such notes are rare in Ireland: the best example seems to be the book kept by William Hampton in a topographical survey of Co. Roscommon in 1813.[88]

Increasing the density of lines in a traverse survey was a natural evolutionary trend, in the face of which no completely new system stood any real chance of success. (One such system, advocated by a Dublin mathematical teacher, was to treat every station as the apex of its own triangle, with all the triangles springing from a single line laid out on one side of the survey area.[89] There is no evidence that any practising Irish surveyor adopted this rather cumbersome procedure.) It was also a trend which could eventually produce a difference of kind rather than degree; that would happen when there was no quadrilateral in the network without its measured diagonal. The resulting triangular mesh is stronger than any simple traverse in the sense of being more easily checked, and it provides an opportunity for further development in one of two possible ways, either by increasing the proportion of measured angles to measured lines or by doing the exact opposite. One variation described by Irwin was to measure a complete round of angles with a corresponding set of radiating distances, all taken from a single point in the middle of the survey area.[90] Harding brought the idea a stage further with his unpublished account of a simple triangulation (using the word in its modern sense) in which it was only the angles that had to be measured, together with one line, the 'base line', which served to give the map its scale.[91] It was not unknown for a base line to be shown on the finished plan;[92] but most surveyors erased all traces of their line-plot, thus making it hard to judge how often triangulation was applied in practice.

At the other extreme stood the chain survey (again anticipating modern terminology) in which only the sides were measured except for the one angle necessary to give the map a north-point. One Irish surveyor apologised for returning a mere sketch with the excuse that having left his instrument at home he was forced to depend on the chain,[93] apparently unaware that the solution to his problem lay in the teachings of Robert Gibson and James Morphett on how to make a survey without measuring angles.[94] Such ignorance must have been fairly widespread, for when John and Thomas Prynallt of Belfast undertook in 1827 to do their surveying 'by the chain only' they urged this seemingly unfamiliar practice on their readers as 'the approved English system'.[95] One reason for the prevalence of chain surveying in England was the survival there of large and finely divided open fields which offered no obstacle to the laying out of complex patterns of linear measurement. In most of early nineteenth-century Ireland the enclosures were small and the fences hard to negotiate. However, conservatism was too strong for many Irish surveyors to go very far towards minimising the use of the chain, and from the 1820s the method of strict chain survey was successfully applied to almost the whole country, fences or no fences, by the field staff of the Ordnance Survey department.

Until that time some kind of traverse survey continued to hold sway in Ireland, which meant that the simplest method of plotting an Irish survey was with scale and protractor. If the result produced a serious misclosure, successive replottings would confirm that the error lay with the surveyor and not the draughtsman. At the same time there were some sources of inaccuracy, such as a badly divided scale, that would not necessarily reveal themselves in the line-plot. Thomas Kelly's errors in 1638 on the Perceval lands in Co. Cork were not made known until the tenants cast doubt upon his survey, and then he blamed his 'base instruments ... and false scale'.[96] Among Kelly's successors on the same estate the diagnosis was more explicit. Mr Slattery's scale came from the best instrument-maker in London; Mr Smith (whose acreage for the same farm was four per cent greater) had made his own scale, on which as he later admitted 'the diagonal line was by a small matter too far distant from the other lines'.

Having been once caught out Smith tried hard to save his reputation by a show of zeal: he ordered three new scales from Dublin and rejected all of them as not good enough.[97]

It must have been experiences like Smith's that led Irish surveyors to try calculating the area of a polygon without the aid of either scale or protractor. The orthodox procedure for many years had been first to plot the measurements, then to convert the resulting outline into a mosaic of regular figures whose areas could each be calculated from some simple formula, and finally to add these figures together. A common way of doing this was by what Petty called a 'laborious prostapheresis' of triangles,[98] such as can be seen drawn on the Inchiquin plantation map of 1589[99] and on a number of early seventeenth-century plots.[100] Eventually John Mooney devised a machine for converting irregular figures into triangles,[101] but by that time Petty's alternative method of squares had proved its adequacy in numerous private farm surveys as well as in the Trustees' Survey of 1700–03.[102] Callan's suggestion for printing standard gridded paper as a government service to surveyors fell predictably flat, but private enterprise had no trouble in making up for the deficiency.[103] He also mentioned some less commonplace techniques of area measurement: one method, subsequently made familiar by the Ordnance Survey, involved dividing the outline into parallel strips, each with a give-and-take line at both ends; another was to cut out the map and weigh it.[104] All of which makes it remarkable, though in view of what has already been said hardly surprising, that Callan had nothing to say about the measurement of offset spaces. It was left to Noble to state the simple rule that the areas between successive offsets could each be treated as a trapezium.[105]

The search for non-graphic methods of area calculation goes back to the traverse tables produced by the English surveyor Richard Norwood in 1637.[106] Norwood got rid of the protractor by converting the position of each traverse point from a distance and bearing into a pair of rectangular co-ordinates known as northings and eastings or latitudes and departures; to find the cordinate values the distance between stations was multiplied by either the sine or cosine of the bearing. Apart from making the survey easier to plot accurately, the co-ordinates provided a simple way of checking the field work, for in a properly closed traverse the sums of both northings and eastings should be zero. The great appeal of Norwood's book for Irishmen, however, was his hint that coordinates could be used to calculate the area of a closed traverse 'very exquisitely'. The mathematics of this operation are simple enough, requiring only a knowledge of sines

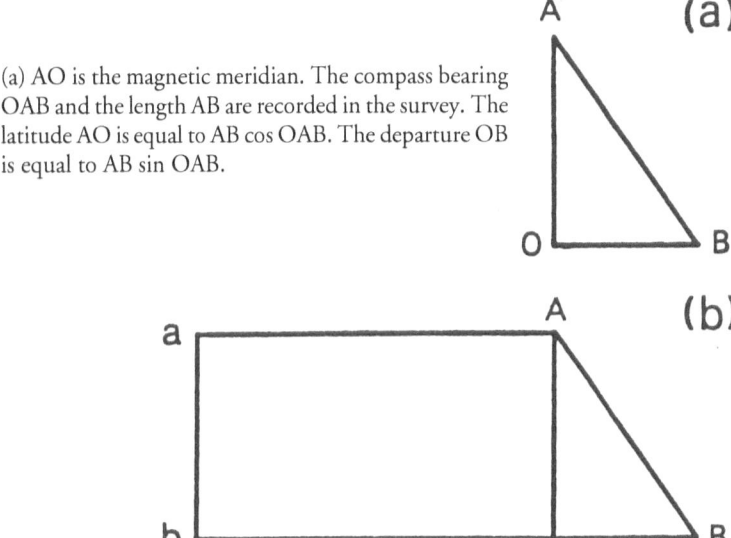

(a) AO is the magnetic meridian. The compass bearing OAB and the length AB are recorded in the survey. The latitude AO is equal to AB cos OAB. The departure OB is equal to AB sin OAB.

(b) Aa is a perpendicular to the meridian, of arbitrary length, known as the meridional distance. The area of the trapezium aABb is that of the rectangle AOba (AO x Ob) plus that of the triangle OAB (AO x OB/2). In traverse terminology this is the product of (i) the latitude and (ii) the sum of the meridional distance and half the departure.

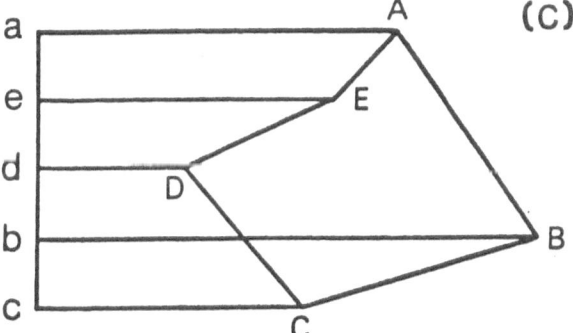

(c) ABCDE is the complete traverse. Each of its limbs defines the non-rectangular side of a trapezium whose area can be calculated from its latitude and from the meridional distance together with the accumulated departures of itself and the preceding limbs. The 'south areas' are ABba and BCcb. The 'north areas' are CDdc, DEed, and EAae. The sum of the north areas subtracted from the sum of the south areas gives the area of ABCDE.

Figure 16. Calculation of area by latitude and departure

and cosines and of how to find the area of a trapezium (Fig. 16); the real problem was to choose a method of tabulation that kept the arithmetic as quick and straightforward as possible. The pioneer of polygonometry (as a nineteenth-century writer christened it) was Henry Osborne, who wrote in 1654 with an eye to the coming Down Survey (Plate 23). But Osborne's tables are not known to have been used in the Survey and they were certainly never mentioned by its director, unless it was by implication in Petty's forecast that future Irish surveyors would benefit from some old geometrical theorems, together with a new property of a circle demonstrated by Dr R. Wood. Trigonometrical functions might just be described as properties of a circle, but it seems hazardous to interpret 'Dr R Wood' as a misreading of 'Norwood', especially as there was a real Dr Robert Wood at Oxford.[107]

At all events it was an Irish architect and engineer, Thomas Burgh, who finally took the credit (plus a generous official reward) for the method of latitude and departure after devoting a book to it in 1724.[108] Not all his countrymen were willing to give him the last word: between 1762 and 1791 there were four more books exclusively concerned with the same topic, and in advertisements for several other surveyors' manuals it was singled out as a major selling point (Appendix D). Some of these books seem never to have found a publisher, but those that did were not just left on the shelf, five errors in Benjamin Noble's tables of 1767 being publicly pounced upon by his local competitor, Kyran Fitzpatrick.[109] Noble and his fellow polygonometrists were mainly concerned with matters of detail. In the first place, the older tables of latitude and departure could be elaborated by incorporating smaller subdivisions of chains and degrees. Then the calculations using the tables could be both simplified and diversified, in the latter case apparently with the object of treating the area of an uncorrected traverse as the mean of several different results. Alternatively, advice could be given on deducing the most erroneous lines and bearings from the pattern of misclosures, and for distributing the corrections in the most appropriate way. Later experts were inclined to treat these discussions as unimportant,[110] and it would certainly be difficult to gauge their effect in improving standards of accuracy, or to estimate how many surveyors adopted the system of latitudes and departures in any form. On the one hand, from the very year after the appearance of Burgh's book a map declares itself to be based on 'Mr Burgh's new method'.[111] Yet forty years later another writer was regretting that the 'more than ordinary exact and much approved of method in calculation' had made so little headway.[112]

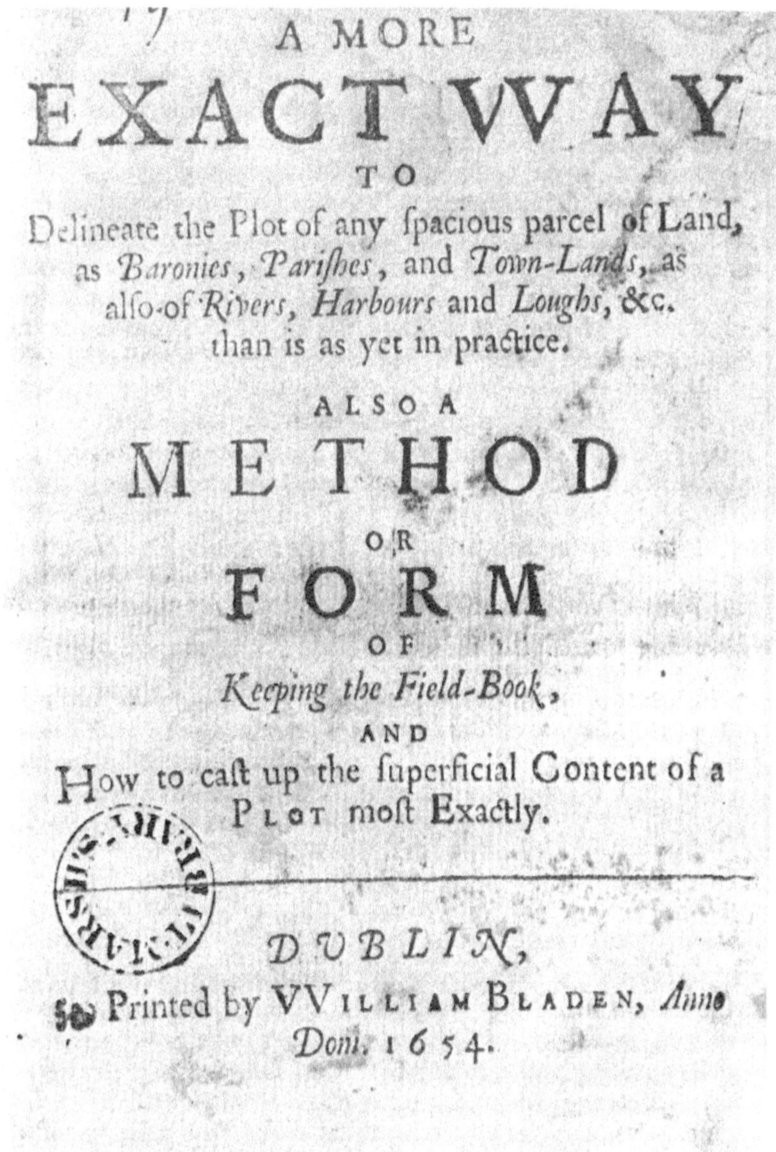

A MORE EXACT WAY

TO

Delineate the Plot of any spacious parcel of Land, as *Baronies*, *Parishes*, and *Town-Lands*, as also of *Rivers*, *Harbours* and *Loughs*, &c. than is as yet in practice.

ALSO A

METHOD

OR

FORM

OF

Keeping the Field-Book,

AND

How to cast up the superficial Content of a PLOT most Exactly.

DUBLIN,

Printed by WILLIAM BLADEN, *Anno* Dom. 1654.

Plate 23. The first book on land surveying known to have been published in Ireland, unnoticed by other textbook-writers and by most modern historians (but see Hoppen, *Common Scientist*, p. 13).

The tables also had their critics. Joshua Wight took an unshakable stand in favour of graphic admeasurement, even after being told he was a dunce by a rival who had obtained larger acreages than Wight's by applying the method of latitude and departure. Wight did not do himself justice on this occasion. His argument was that Burgh took no account of the slope of the land; but the same is true of ordinary protraction when the chain has been held horizontally, and if Wight had been chaining along the slope his areas should have been larger than his opponent's and not smaller. Perhaps he meant that to map the land at a scale of one to one (which is what Burgh's method amounted to, as Noble saw) entails introducing differences between surface area and horizontal area which at smaller scales would disappear. That seems an arguable point – the same point made by an English military surveyor, Sir James Carmichael Smyth, in his criticism of the acreages shown on the earliest Ordnance Survey maps.[113] But to plead the merits of approximation in Ireland would have been acting out of national character. It was the exactitude of the tables that made them attractive to Wight's countrymen.[114]

Not that the mathematicians' triumph can ever have been quite complete. If all Irish traverse surveys had been calculated non-graphically, someone would surely have said as much in the 1820s when the methods of the Ordnance Survey came under review, and when the Survey's distrust of 'computation from paper' was seen in many quarters as provokingly eccentric. Among private surveyors the new (and apparently less argumentative) century began by giving an impression of peaceful co-existence, with one method being used to check the other in the spirit of Callan's dictum that calculation should be demonstrated by protraction, and protraction proved by calculation. It is also possible that graphic methods were now being facilitated by the use of larger sheets of paper, and therefore of larger-scale plots, as well as by better plotting instruments.

The apparent decline of professional bellicosity among Irish surveyors has been mentioned in a previous chapter. How far was it genuine? Much of their wrangling had been conducted in the newspapers and (as we have seen) its disappearance after about 1800 was mainly a matter of editorial policy. Textbooks are less vulnerable to fashion, however, and here the decline in output is plain to see in any major library catalogue or bibliography. It was also noticeable at the time: when a visitor to Dublin asked about books on surveying in 1825, the best the bookshop could offer him was a 'survey' of the Christian religion.[115] Finally there

TABLE 14

ACREAGE ERRORS IN A SAMPLE OF ESTATE MAPS

	Size of sample	Percentage of sample with excesses of			
		0–0.5%	0.5–1%	1–1.5%	>1.5%
1. T. Moland, 1709	27	7.4	—	3.7	3.7
2. J. Greene, 1715	11	—	9.1	—	18.2
3. J. Rocque, 1756–8	28	7.1	7.1	—	3.6
4. M. Kenny, 1773	15	6.7	—	6.7	—
5. R Frizell, 1774–5	15	6.7	—	6.7	13.3
6. T. Sherrard, 1787–8	16	18.7	18.7	—	—
7. J. Healy, 1812	14	—	—	—	—
8. J. Williamson, 1813–14	21	9.5	9.5	4.8	—
9. J. J. Byrne, 1819	12	8.3	—	—	—

	Percentage of sample with deficiencies of						
	0–0.5%	0.5–1%	1–1.5%	1.5–2%	2–2.5%	2.5–3%	>3%
1. Moland	3.7	11.1	3.7	—	14.8	14.8	37.0
2. Greene	—	—	9.1	9.1	—	9.1	45.5
3. Rocque	17.9	10.7	14.3	3.6	14.3	3.6	17.9
4. Kenny	—	13.3	13.3	46.7	13.3	—	—
5. Frizell	20.0	20.0	6.7	6.7	6.7	13.3	—
6. Sherrard	25.0	18.7	—	18.7	—	—	—
7. Healy	21.4	28.6	28.6	14.3	7.1	—	—
8. Williamson	9.5	9.5	14.3	33.3	9.5	—	—
9. Byrne	25.0	25.0	41.7	—	—	—	—

Each surveyor is represented by one or more estate atlases. Error is defined as percentage difference above or below the acreage recorded on the first edition of the six-inch Ordnance Survey maps (1833–46). Townlands whose boundaries were changed before the making of the Ordnance maps have been excluded on the basis of visual comparison. To allow for changes not detectable by this method, the most erroneous twenty-five per cent in the resulting selection of each surveyor's maps have also been excluded from the sample.

SOURCES: (1) NLI, 16.F.2; (2) TCD, MUN/ME/1/2; (3) NLI, mic. P.4032; (4) NLI, MS 3101; (5) TCD, MUN/ME/4; (6) NLI, 21.F.105; (7) NLI, 21.F.139; (8) NLI, 16.F.17; (9) NLI, 14.A.21.

is the evidence of nineteenth-century government inquiries relating to agriculture and landed property. The Devon report of 1845, in particular, was a huge compendium of every Irish rural grievance, real or fictitious. Surveyors did not escape its attention altogether. Doubts were cast on their incorruptibility, and on their skill in valuing farms and houses.

But not a word was said against their effectiveness as measurers and map-makers, either by their fellow surveyors or by the various other witnesses who were in a position to judge their performance. The same is true of contemporary inquiries into the relation between land area and tax assessment: the surveyor's ability to give an accurate account of the contents of a farm or townland was everywhere taken for granted. But for the impact of the Ordnance Survey the profession might almost have been described, by early Victorian observers with short memories, as happy in its lack of history.

In the longer term, a possible interpretation of what was written and left unwritten is that the later eighteenth century had been a period of rapid improvement, faster than anything since Elizabethan times and perhaps not subsequently equalled until the coming of the Ordnance Survey. Apart from a general tightening up of standards due to professional rivalry and buoyant land values, several lines of progress were observable in the two or three decades that followed the year 1760: advances in instrumental design; a more educated interest in the behaviour of the compass; increased precision in the booking of angles and distances; a new approach in measuring and calculating offsets; better mathematical tables, used with more discrimination. In the end, of course, both the surveyor and his method must be judged by their results (Table 14). Comparison of contemporary and 'correct' (i.e. Ordnance Survey) acreages would be rejected by modern theorists as too lenient a test, allowing opposite positional errors to cancel each other out. To the vast majority of Irishmen, however, it was on this comparison and very little else that any Irish map would stand or fall. Making it is a task which unfortunately becomes more difficult as history unfolds, for the surveyors of the eighteenth and nineteenth centuries may have been better at taking measurements than the modern non-surveyor who aspires to test their accuracy. Then there is the need for strict comparability of areas mentioned in an earlier chapter – a nightmare for the historical researcher but a loophole for any surveyor who chooses to answer a charge of error by insisting that he had been shown the wrong bounds. For the statistician this difficulty may well be insuperable. For the non-statistician the only solution is simply to ignore all differences above some arbitrary threshold on the argument (logically circular, but still acceptable to common sense) that no professional surveyor could be bad enough to deserve the blame for them. Both parties can agree that it was by no means uncommon for pre-Ordnance Survey maps of Irish farms and townlands to come within 0.5 per cent of the Ordnance Survey values.

Better figures than those of Table 14 have been recorded from seventeenth-century England.[116] But the post-seventeenth-century histories of the two kingdoms were not the same: while English farms were being enlarged, the trend across the channel was for smaller units and keener competition. As the slices cut from Ireland's agrarian cake grew thinner, so more eyes were beadily fixed on every movement of the surveyor's knife. Hence the verdict, in 1824, that 'in measuring small farms and fields, the Irish surveyors seem the most [*recte*, more] rigorously accurate, owing, perhaps, to the greater value attached to land in Ireland, and to the constant rivalship which exists there amongst surveyors'.[117] Until more research has been done in both countries, this judgement may be allowed to stand.

Notes

1. *Strictures on a Pamphlet Signed Theophilus*, p. 15.
2. Undated sheet in a bundle of late seventeenth-century documents, Lane papers, NLI, MS 8646(1).
3. 'Fingal', 'Some Passages from the Life of an Architect', *Irish Builder*, 24 (1882), p. 129.
4. The 'wyer line' described by Cyprian Lucar in 1590 could be folded into sections (A. W. Richeson, *English Land Measuring to 1800: Instruments and Practices* (Cambridge, Mass., 1966), p. 80).
5. The City Surveyor from 1718 to 1735 was James Ramsay, a pupil of Joseph Moland (*Cal. Anc. Rec. Dub.*, 7, pp 54, 121; 8, p. 188).
6. Noble, *Geodaesia*, p. 25.
7. *Proc. Dub. Soc.*, 13 (1777), p. 95. Hood's chain was 22.4 yards long. He recommended it especially for surveying roads and counties.
8. Osborne, *Exact Way*, pp 6–7; Gibson, *Practical Surveying*, pp 129, 135; Noble, *Geodaesia*, p. 25; Irwin, *Treatise*, p. 128. *Report on Survey and Valuation*, 1824, p. 84 (Patrick Kelly). Surveyors announcing their use of the two-pole chain range from Pat Bath in 1722 (Co. Meath, NLI, 21.F.144(1)) to Samuel Byron in 1791 (Co. Dublin, NLI, MS 2789(17)).
9. A 40-foot chain is recorded in notes of 1763–4 associated with no. 563 of the wide streets commission maps, formerly in NAI, now in Dublin City Hall. This document was not available in 1984.

10. Gibson, *Practical Surveying*, p. 131.
11. Joshua Wight's diary, 25 Sep. 1752.
12. Callan, *Dissertation*, p. 24; Frizell, Report on Courelicky and Cappagh. A controversy involving an excessively long chain was reported in *Dublin Journal*, 16 Dec. 1749, 6 Jan. 1750.
13. Map of lands in Co. Meath, 1741, NLI, 21.F.31(18). See also below, Appendix C.
14. Noble, *Geodaesia*, p. 85; Callan, *Dissertation*, pp 8–9.
15. Dublin Society, MS minutes, 28 Apr. 1743; Gibson, *Practical Surveying*, p. 132; Noble, *Geodaesia*, pp 45–7.
16. 13 Feb. 1864, OSO, file 3010. In the reference to a map of 1795 by Pat Ware (NLI, 14.A.30) one parcel is described as 'an inclined surface', but without saying whether Ware had returned the sloping or the horizontal area. This is a reference of some rarity: in general Irish surveyors seem to have been much less preoccupied with horizontality than their English counterparts.
17. In one set of early eighteenth-century field notes (NLI, MS 13739), fractions of a chain are specified in only 27 out of 390 recorded distances.
18. Reckoning lengths in whole chains was common in eighteenth-century Virginia (Hughes, *Surveyors and Statesmen*, pp 47, 118).
19. *An Essay on the Origin and Use of Tables of Latitude and Departure* (Dublin, 1770), p. 9; John Hood, *Tables of Difference of Latitude and Departure for Navigators, Land Surveyors etc.* (Dublin, 1772), p. 7.
20. R. L. Edgeworth, *Memoirs*, 1, pp 175–6. Edgeworth's instrument was tested in *c.* 1768; about twenty years later the credit for its invention was being claimed by someone else. There is no evidence as to how it differed from the kind of wheel mentioned in Gibson, *Practical Surveying*, pp 134–5, and in earlier writings.
21. An act of 1785 concerning post roads (23 & 24 George III, c. 17, sec. 9) refers to the measurement of roads 'by the wheel, or otherwise'. Another writer of the same period appears to have regarded the use of 'wheelbarrow perambulators' as a generally accepted method (*Belfast Mercury*, 17 Dec. 1784).
22. Dublin Society, MS minutes, 19 Dec. 1754; *Dublin Journal*, 12 Oct. 1754. Another instrument which failed to emerge from obscurity was one that measured an unknown distance by comparing it with a known base as described with approval by W. McMenamy of the Marine School, Dublin (PRONI, D.562/8930C). The same is true of the method by which Charles Dunroche was reported in 1791 to survey land without using any instruments (Bowden, *Tour*, p. 110).
23. Larcom, *Down Survey*, p. 53.
24. 'Stage-Irish' account of a new relief model of the Killarney district, *Hibernian Chronicle*, 8 May 1786.
25. Advertisement by John Alment, *Hoey's Dublin Mercury*, 28 Mar. 1767.
26. Larcom, *Down Survey*, pp xiv, 17, 45, 53.

27. Molyneux, *Phil. Trans. R. Soc.*, 19 (1697), p. 625.
28. Joshua Wight's diary, 25 Sep. 1752; *Report on Survey and Valuation*, 1824, pp 58, 66.
29. Richard Freeman, 'On the Improvement of the Circumferentor', *Trans. Dub. Soc.*, 6 (1810), pp 47–68; Callan, *Dissertation*, p. 32.
30. Petty, *Political Anatomy*, p. 113. Petty wrote of instruments being pawned by his surveyors and stolen by tories (Larcom, *Down Survey*, pp 122, 125).
31. St Patrick's College, Maynooth, Museum, *Third Tostal Display Souvenir Catalogue* (1955), no. 801. McLaughlin, *Irish Ecclesiastical Record*, 73 (1950), p. 133. For another example in Ireland, not necessarily of Irish manufacture, see Mason, *Dub. Hist. Rec.*, 6 (1944), p. 134.
32. NLI, MS 1437, reproduced in Andrews, *Irish Maps*, 8.
33. Surveyors depicting both observers and instruments include Dominick Donnelly (1703: Dublin, St Patrick's Cathedral maps, 5 and 7); Dennis Carty (1728: Cork Archives Institute, U.137/Box 30); James Graham (1729: NAI, M.1175); James Costello (1753: NLI, 21.F.44(77); 1768: Longfield, *Bull. Ir. Georgian Soc.*, 20 (1977), p. 66 – two almost identical pairs of pictures); John Moloney (1801: NLI, 15.B.14(17a), reproduced in National Library of Ireland, *Ireland from Maps*, p. 10). Instruments without surveyors appear in maps by Robert Thompson (1718: PRONI, D.3053/2/3), Thomas Matthews (1773: NLI, 16.G.16(38)), and John Roe (1806: Lt. Col. Manners Fitzsimons, Glencullen, Co. Dublin).
34. *Pue's Occurrences*, 29 Sep. 1759.
35. Andrews, *Irish Maps*, 10.
36. Weale, in NLI, MS 864, p. 31.
37. Laurence Magennis, maps of properties in Co Dublin, 1786 and 1804, NLI, 21.F.146(4, 8).
38. Marquess of Lansdowne, *Petty Papers*, 1, p. 83.
39. Molyneux, *Phil. Trans. R. Soc.*, 19 (1697), pp 625–31. The same subject was discussed by Irwin, *Treatise*, p. 122.
40. T. Harding, 'Observations on the Variations of the Needle', *Trans. R. Ir. Acad.*, 3 (1791), pp 107–18. One surveyor, John Heylin, reported finding the variation shown on a map of 1724 (*Freeman's Journal*, 13 Oct. 1787).
41. The first such map seen by Harding was one of Roger Kendrick's dated 1745, but a variation of $16^{1/2}$ degrees had been noted in 1740 on Robert Gibson's map of Borreen, Co. Kildare (NLI, 21.F.34(22)).
42. Gibson, *Practical Surveying*, pp 299–301.
43. Noble, *Geodaesia*, pp vi–viii.
44. *Dublin Journal*, 3 Oct. 1786; *Dublin Evening Post*, 30 May 1786, 25 Oct. 1787. Harding's controversy with his pseudonymous opponent 'Magneticus in Angulo' was in *Hibernian Journal*, 29 May, 26 June, 30 Aug., 4, 8, 13 Sep. 1786. It was ended by a rather sharp 'correspondence closed' note from the editor. Harding was also attacked in the *Freeman's*

Journal by a critic signing himself 'Linen Draper' (1, 11, 22 Sep., 11, 16 Oct. 1787). He was accused among other things of ignoring diurnal changes in variation, and of not proving that the longer-term changes occurred at a uniform speed. He persevered, however, both in the newspapers (e.g. *Dublin Chronicle*, 28 Sep. 1790) and in his paper to the Royal Irish Academy (see above, n.40). In 1816 Harding's work was cited in the margin of an estate map by John Longfield (NLI, 21.F.47(7)).

45. T. Harding, 'On the Variation of the Needle', *Anthologia Hibernica*, 3 (1794), p. 292. Harding's estimate for the variation in Nov. 1800 is quoted by Matthew Handcock in BL, Maps C. 24.d.10. The subject is also treated in G. V. Sampson's *Statistical Survey of the County of Londonderry* (Dublin, 1802), app , pp 1–2. Sampson cited observations by the Derry surveyors Colhoun and McCart, the latter apparently a misprint for McCool. Another Ulster reference to the variation is *Northern Star*, 1 Oct. 1795.

46. William King, 'Some Thoughts of a New Way of Making a Map of Ireland', quoted in J.H. Andrews, 'Science and Cartography in the Ireland of William and Samuel Molyneux', *Proc. R. Ir. Acad.*, 80C (1980), p. 250.

47. Callan, *Dissertation*, pp 27, 32; Noble, *Geodaesia*, p. 33.

48. Larcom, *Down Survey*, p. 45.

49. Richard Dobbs, Description of Co. Antrim, in G. Hill, *An Historical Account of the Macdonnells of Antrim* (Belfast, 1873), p. 379.

50. Callan, *Dissertation*, p. 27; Wight's diary, 25 Sep. 1752; Irwin, *Treatise*, pp 118–19. John Piers, a surveyor known to have worked in Co. Cavan (NLI, 21.F.8(1)), wrote an essay on the treatment of local attraction which seems to have remained unpublished (*Proc. Dub. Soc.*, 10 (1773–4), pp 310, 361–2).

51. Hood, *Tables*, pp 5–6; Freeman, *Trans. Dub. Soc.*, 6 (1810), p. 6.

52. J. Waddington, *A Description of Instruments Used by Surveyors* (London, 1773), p. 5; George Adams, *Geometrical and Graphical Essays* (2nd ed., London, 1797), p. 216. See also Hughes, *Surveyors and Statesmen*, p. 31.

53. Thomas Burgh, *A Method to Determine the Areas of Right-Lined Figures Universally. Very Useful for Ascertaining the Contents of Any Survey* (Dublin, 1724), p. 13; Callan, *Dissertation*, pp 27, 32; Noble, *Geodaesia*, pp 30–3; Gibson, *Practical Surveying*, p. 155. Other references are less explicit, like John Bell's mention of his twelve-inch theodolite in 1752 (*Dublin Journal*, 7 Oct.).

54. NLI, 16.H.33(6).

55. Joshua Wight's diary, 25 Sep. 1752.

56. Richard Castle, Essay on artificial navigation, c. 1730, NLI, MS 2737. Samuel Molyneux's theodolites did not count, not being used for professional purposes (*A Catalogue of the Library of the Honble Samuel Molyneux deceas'd* ([London, 1730]), pp 56, 61.

57. *Belfast News-letter*, 9 Nov. 1759. Since this advertisement also dealt with the regulation of running water it seems likely that Livingston's instrument could measure vertical angles.
58. Reproduced in A. Horner, 'Cartouches and Vignettes on the Kildare Estate Maps of John Rocque', *Bull. Ir. Georgian Soc.*, 14 (1971), pp 66–7.
59. *The Irish Magazine, and Monthly Asylum of Neglected Biography*, January 1811, p. 2.
60. Advertisement by Thomas Power, *Cork Evening Post*, 13 Apr. 1786. In the following year Nicholas Walsh was claiming an accuracy of three minutes for a semi-circle with a vernier (below, Appendix D).
61. Irwin, *Treatise*, p. 136.
62. *Report on Survey and Valuation*, 1824, p. 58.
63. O'Shaughnessy, *Practical Surveying*, pp 30, 55.
64. Gibson (*Practical Surveying*, pp 162–5) is an exception.
65. Reproduced in Andrews, *Irish Maps*, 9; Aaron Rathborne, *The Surveyor in Foure Bookes* (London, 1616).
66. Map of part of Clonmaning, Co. Wicklow, Truell papers, NLI, mic. P. 1560; William Leybourn, *The Compleat Surveyor* (London, 1674).
67. Noble, *Geodaesia*, p. 11.
68. Petworth papers, C.27.D. These field books are not included in the microfilm of Irish material at Petworth supplied to the National Library of Ireland.
69. Osborne, *Exact Way*, pp 2, 5.
70. Stations are numbered in the map of 1768 reproduced in Longfield, *Bull. Ir. Georgian Soc.*, 20 (1977), pp 59, 62–3. For a Down Survey example, see above, ch. 3, n. 64.
71. James Franck Rolleston, 17 June 1784, NLI, MS 13797; confirmed by Burgh, *Method*, p. 13; Gibson, *Practical Surveying*, pp 172, 269; Noble, *Geodaesia*, p. 107; Irwin, *Treatise*, p. 116; O'Shaughnessy, *Practical Surveying*, p. 33. John Travers described his field notes as following the sun (NLI, MS 2793).
72. Larcom, *Down Survey*, p. 49. Later authors used the word 'perclose' as synonymous with 'closure' and without any implication of an error. For an example see below, Appendix C.
73. Callan, *Dissertation*, p. 28.
74. Trotter, *Gibson's Treatise*, p. 127; O'Shaughnessy, *Practical Surveying*, p. 40.
75. Noble, *Geodaesia*, p. 47.
76. Andrews, *Paper Landscape*, pp 58–9, 74, 81.
77. Samuel Wyld, *The Practical Surveyor, or the Art of Land-Measuring, Made Easy* (London, 1725), p. 84.
78. Irwin (*Treatise*, p. 116) recommended the booking of offsets in a single column with plus and minus signs to distinguish left-hand and right-hand measurements. Hood preferred separate offset and inset columns,

one on either side of the main or 'visual' line (*Tables*, p. 19) and this layout had already appeared in 1763–4 (Wide streets commission maps, see note 9 above) and in John Travers's Mountrath estate maps of 1770 (NLI, MS 2793).

79. For example a landowner of 1633 wrote of ditching and quicksetting a boundary that the surveyors had set forth with the chain (Harleian MS 4297, f. 132).
80. As it happens, exactly this situation is shown on a map of Newbay, Co. Kilkenny, in 1697 (NLI, 21.F.157(3)), in which the straight lines of the survey make fourteen crossings of a meandering river at the rate of about one crossing per chain-length.
81. NLI, MS 2793. Besides his eight sets of field notes in this volume, two of Travers's maps show the main lines of the survey. In one map the inside and outside lines are about evenly balanced, in the other almost every line is inside the townland.
82. Crawford, *Ulster Land Agent*, p. 21. The excuse for omitting the lake (regarded by the agent on the Annesley estate as an improbable error) was that the work was done 'late in the evening by the surveyor who was in a hurry'.
83. Diagonal measurements are shown in William Bassnett's map of Curragh, Co. Tipperary, in 1725 (NLI, 21.F.113(21)).
84. *Pue's Occurrences*, 2 Apr. 1757. The farm under survey by Mooney and Kinsella contained about 175 acres.
85. Notes on cases in the court of Exchequer, Ireland, May 1739, Add. MS 19858, f. 64; Hood, *Tables*, p. 19.
86. In private possession, made available by Dr Anngret Simms of University College, Dublin. For another example see NLI, 21.F.38 (12).
87. *Cork Evening Post*, 26 Oct. 1767.
88. NLI, MS 3242. The book includes what appears to be a survey of private property at Cappagh, beginning on 25 Aug. 1813, done as an interlude in Hampton's work on the county map.
89. McMenamy, *Trans. Dub. Soc.*, 1 (1800), pp 3–10.
90. Irwin, *Treatise*, p. 140
91. T. Harding, 'Survey of the Botany Gardens belonging to the College done Mar. 1796', PRONI, D.562/8924G.
92. For example, *Plan of the Town of Magherafelt Situate on the Estate Belonging to the Worshipful Company of Salters, Londonderry*, Waterlow & Sons, London, 1837.
93. PRONI, T.2541/IA2/1/36 (1775).
94. Gibson, *Practical Surveying*, pp 141–7; Morphett in *Belfast News-letter*, 13 Mar. 1760 ('surveying by the chain, whereby that instrument is made to answer (in all capacities) the use of the theodolite'). See below, Appendix D. A diagram of 1769 by George Miller of lands in Co. Cork seems to be the record of a chain triangulation (NLI, 21.F.73(54)).
95. *Belfast News-letter*, 11 Sep. 1827.

96. Kelly to Sir Philip Perceval, 15 Nov. 1640, Add. MS 46924, f. 135.
97. Add. MS 46972, ff. 48, 75, 78, 81, 87 (Apr. to Aug. 1721).
98. Larcom, *Down Survey*, p. xvi.
99. Dartmouth maps, 38.
100. There are examples in the Petworth papers, C.27.D., and in M.P.F. 268.
101. Dublin Society, MS minutes, Jan.–Feb. 1742; *Pue's Occurrences*, 6 Feb. 1742; Berry, *History of Royal Dublin Society*, p. 59. Robert Lewis later invented an instrument for finding areas without protraction or the use of tables (*Dublin Journal*, 22 June 1773).
102. Squares as well as triangles appear (once each) in the Burdett estate maps of 1674–82 (NLI, MS 2727). John Bell used a square grid in 1741 (NLI, 21.F.31(18)). Numerical annotations on several maps of various dates show that parts of a square were usually reckoned in hundredths.
103. 'Chequered paper', as sold by the Dublin instrument-makers Edward Spicer and James Lynch, was advertised in John Hood's *Tables* and in *Hibernian Journal*, 3 Apr. 1772.
104. Callan, *Dissertation*, p. 11. The method of weighing is explained in 'A mechanical problem for finding the areas of mapps usefull for surveyors of lands' (n.d., eighteenth century?), PRONI, D.562/8924A.
105. Noble, *Geodaesia*, pp 107–08.
106. Richard Norwood, *The Sea-Man's Practice, Contayning a Fundamentall Problem in Navigation, Experimentally Verified* (London, 1637), pp 31–8.
107. Petty, *Political Anatomy*, p. 113; Larcom, *Down Survey*, p. 323; Goblet, *Transformation*, 1, p. 263. For Wood, see Taylor, *Practitioners of Tudor and Stuart England*, p. 226.
108. *Commons Journals*, Ireland, 3, i, pp 322, 327, 333; Burgh, *Method*. Gibson (*Practical Surveying*, preface) paid tribute to Burgh without mentioning Osborne. For more on Burgh, see Loeber, *Architects*, pp 31–9.
109. Noble's only reply was to continue advertising the *Geodaesia* (*Leinster Journal*, 29 Sep. 1773, 18 Dec. 1773 to 25 Jan. 1775).
110. McMenamy (*Trans. Dub. Soc.*, 1 (1800), p. 3) considered that 'no material improvement' in methods of area calculation had taken place since the 1720s.
111. Tim Bridge, map of Castle Otway, Co. Tipperary, June 1725, NLI, 21.F.129(4). In 1746 D. M. Sullivan thought it worthwhile to point out that the content shown in his map of lands in Co. Tipperary was found 'independent of scale and compass' (NLI, 21.F.113(25)), and in 1773 a Co. Clare estate map was said to be 'laid [down] by a scale of 40 but the area found by numerical calculation' (NLI, 21.F.160(19)).
112. Advertisement by William Jordan of Downpatrick, *Belfast News-letter*, 5 Oct. 1764. Ignorance of trigonometrical calculation was an issue in the Bell-Callan controversy of the 1750s (below, Appendix C).
113. Sir James Carmichael Smyth's report on the Ordnance Survey of Ireland, 1828, PRO, W.O. 44/519.

114. Outside Ireland, the calculation of area from latitudes and departures seems to have been especially common in colonial North America, where it was known as the Pennsylvania method (J. B. Love, *The colonial surveyor in Pennsylvania*, Ph.D. thesis, University of Pennsylvania (1970), p. 253).
115. Diary of Lt. Col. C. W. Pasley, 9 July 1825, Add. MS 41984.
116. W. Ravenhill, 'The Mapping of Great Haseley and Latchford', *Cart. Jour.*, 10 (1973), p. 111.
117. *Report on Survey and Valuation*, 1824, p. 85 (Patrick Kelly). One by-product of the Irish interest in area determination was James Whitelaw's 'Essay on the Best Method of Ascertaining the Areas of Countries of Considerable Extent' (*Trans. R. Ir. Acad.*, 6 (1795), pp 65–76), an interesting contribution to a subject which most eighteenth-century geographers had ignored.

11
Breaking into print

THERE HAVE BEEN THOUSANDS of competent Irish surveyors, but most of Ireland's published cartography has been the work of foreigners. The best way of resolving this paradox is to classify each map in terms of its probable sales. For most of an ordinary surveyor's output, the clientele comprised not more than two customers, landlord and tenant: although estate and farm maps must often have been shown to visitors, there was generally no prospect of publishing them except perhaps as 'case studies' in textbooks on surveying or agriculture (Plate 24).[1] At the other end of the market stood the small-scale atlas map, the marine chart and, in wartime, the news-map. It would have seemed reasonable for a great metropolis like Dublin to nurture at least one or two publishers of map-types as popular as these, and some of their raw material for maps of Ireland could be expected to come from Ireland's own surveyors. Any additional costs due to publishing in a small and peripheral country should have been balanced by easier access to local information and by closer contact with the Irish purchasers who would form a large proportion of the market for a map of their own country. The only manifest weakness in this argument is that Irish operating costs were not in fact particularly high: on the contrary, Dublin was a relatively favourable site for map production, to judge from the cartographic careers of George Grierson and several of his relations. Though mainly letterpress printers (they held the office of king's printer in Ireland) this family began publishing maps as a sideline in about 1730 – just how actively became clear some thirty years later when buyers were invited for the plates of 250 Grierson maps covering 'all the empires and kingdoms, states, nations and principalities in the world'.

As cartographic subject-matter his homeland held little interest for Grierson, the few maps he made of it being all imitations of originals imported from elsewhere.[2] The fact is that the Irish cartographic market was too weak to influence the location of the map-making industry even for maps of Ireland itself, partly because of its small population and poor living standards, and also (some map-makers might have claimed in moments of exasperation) because Irishmen were not very interested in geography. This unpromising picture was relieved by the facility with which foreign publishers were able to obtain all the information about Ireland that they needed. Although the channels through which it reached them are seldom precisely known, communication must have been eased by the political links between Ireland and Britain and by the absence of a language barrier. Much material destined for publication came ultimately from a source that might have been expected to remain inaccessible to foreigners, namely the military engineer. His contribution included not only siege and battle maps, and plans of fortified towns, but also regional surveys of considerable extent. The history of this traffic went back to Robert Lythe and Francis Jobson, both of whom were sources, probably at several removes, for Speed's well-known series on the four provinces and through Speed for the majority of early and middle seventeenth-century maps of Ireland.[3] In the 1770s and after there was a revival of regional mapping by military surveyors and notably by Charles Vallancey, whose results reached the public through the printed maps of Ireland by Alexander Taylor and Aaron Arrowsmith.[4]

The long interval between these two spells of war preparation was commanded by the uniquely versatile figure of William Petty. The plantation surveys, while resembling early estate maps in form and content, had between them covered a large enough area to influence the shape of Ireland as a whole. It was Petty's achievement (perhaps inspired by his predecessors in the Strafford Survey)[5] to effect this modification in the county and provincial maps which he published in London under the title *Hiberniae Delineatio* in 1685.[6] The *Delineatio* gave a basis for innumerable later maps of Ireland down to the time of the Ordnance Survey. Many of them professed to go beyond Petty – sometimes mentioning recent estate surveys as among their sources[7] – but most of their innovations were roads, barracks and other sharply localised features that could easily be interpolated into small-scale adaptations of his work without the need for further admeasurement.

Between the estate map and the national map lay an area of cartography that included Ireland's dioceses, counties, towns, rivers, canals and tourist resorts. For such sub-national maps Irishmen could be presumed to comprise a larger share of the world market than for ordinary atlases, but there were still one or two awkward questions to answer before this apparently comforting fact could be turned to advantage. Would a

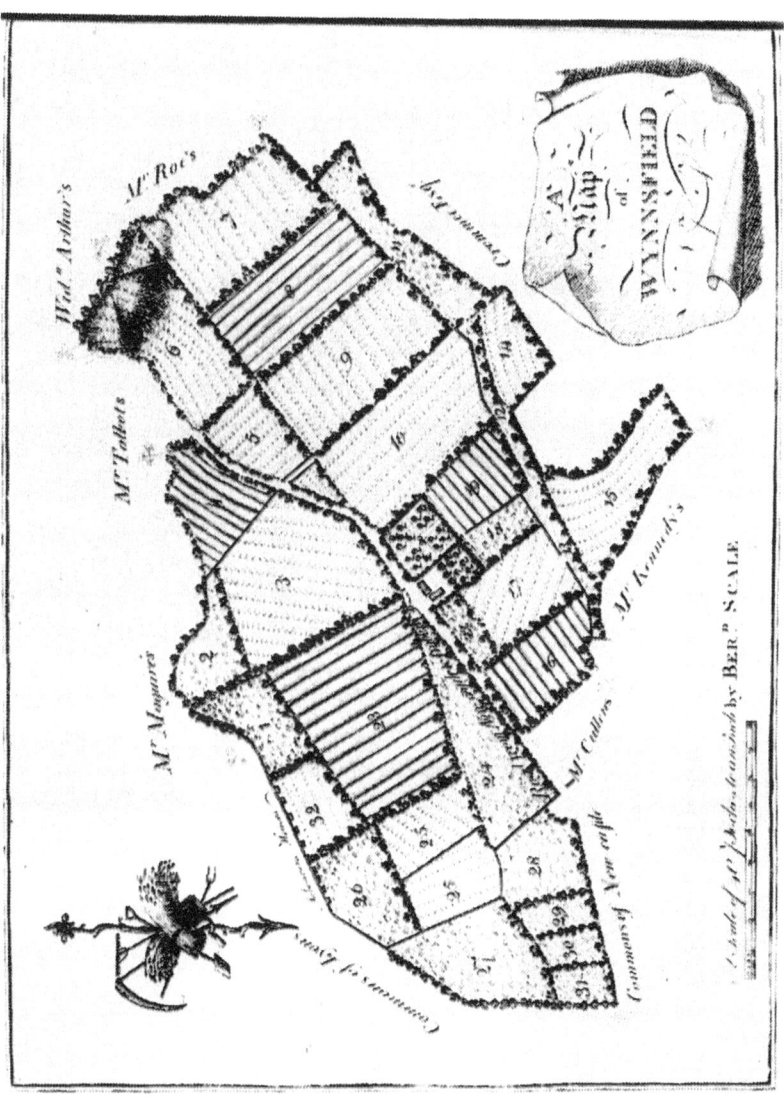

Plate 24. Wynnsfield otherwise Loughlinstown, Co. Kildare, by Bernard Scalé, 1772 (see chapter 11, note 1). Scale of original 40 perches to one inch. The area represented was a model farm managed by John Wynn Baker, 'experimenter in agriculture', on behalf of the Dublin Society. The engraver, identified only as Butler (perhaps Peter Butler of Cork) has captured much of the letter and spirit of Scalé's manuscript estate maps.

regional map sell enough copies to pay its way? And who would make such a map – especially if it could not be put together from maps already extant? Here at least the land surveyor might be expected to play a part, but there were two other Irish contenders for authorship in this sphere, the amateur scientist and the professional engineer or architect. Each of these three classes reached its cartographic zenith at a different period but they all remained more or less active throughout the era of regional-map publication, and the role of the land surveyor cannot be properly defined without devoting some attention to his rivals.

The cartographic amateur emerged in the seventeenth century and continued to flourish until the nineteenth. He had knowledge and talent; also enough money to support himself while working on his maps, though not necessarily enough to hire additional labour or to pay for printing and publication. His deficiencies were in business ability and managerial skill, and sometimes in capacity for sustained effort. If Petty had been given to historical formulations, he might have seen himself as the first Irish cartographer to merit the status of scientist (or natural philosopher, as he would have put it), though at this high level his maps were not of outstanding importance and more than one scientific thinker in the Dublin of the 1680s saw how they might be improved or superseded. Their main weakness was the absence of a proper control survey and the consequent omission of latitude and longitude. Although there were some ambitious and enlightened schemes for remedying these defects, in the end it was Petty's instinct that showed the best blend of science and practicality. Even an accurate survey of a single town could prove maddeningly difficult for a mere man of science to organise without government support, as William Molyneux found when he tried to act as impresario for a large map of Dublin which seems never to have been drawn, let alone published. His failure was one of many, both in its lack of results and in the semi-anonymity and subordinate position of the surveyor ('one Farel') who took the measurements.[8]

The cartographic disappointments of the Restoration era were especially acute where the input of scholarship and philosophy might have seemed likely to reach a maximum, which was among the ecclesiastics. As early as the 1660s the Irish Parliament had been struck by the geographical absurdity of expecting parishioners to worship on small and perhaps uninhabited islands,[9] and the Bishop of Kilmore had begun to use map evidence in considering the best locations for new churches.[10] Cloyne, Tuam and Armagh all have diocesan maps from this period,[11] and a map of Elphin was mentioned in 1703.[12] There is no sign that any new field work went into these compilations: part of the Armagh map declares itself to be based on the Down Survey, and the Cloyne outline plainly owes much to the same source, its only visible claim to superiority being an episcopal preference for latinised place-names. The seventeenth-century diocesan style still held its popularity more than a hundred years later, even among professional surveyors like Walter Laffan of Co. Tipperary:[13] in essence it recalled the skeletalism of the ordinary estate index, with parishes taking the place of farms. Daniel Beaufort's map of the diocese of Meath was unusual in its emphasis on topography; it was also the only pre-Ordnance Survey specimen of the genre to be published in its own time.[14]

Meanwhile, among the laity, the scientific spirit had remained dormant until the foundation of the Dublin Physico-Historical Society in 1744.[15] By now there was increasing dissatisfaction with Petty's maps (mainly on the ground of their factual obsolescence), but the aspirations of the new society were more modest than those of the Molyneux period. Its county descriptions were to be illustrated by maps, but the maps did not have to meet the time-limit of four to five years that the society thought reasonable for the authors of purely literary material. The physico-historians soon came to accept that 'this poor country is not yet ripe for so weighty and extensive an attempt' as a new series of county admeasurements.[16] Instead their spokesman hoped that correspondents would submit corrections to existing maps, or better still follow the example of certain gentlemen in Antrim and Down who, while stopping short of a complete survey, had at least caused the roads of their respective counties to be measured with the chain.

By this time gentlemen and professionals had come together. In Co. Down the chaining of the roads had probably been done by the local land surveyor Oliver Sloane, whose neat but open-textured manuscript map of the county bearing the date 1739 survives in the Linen Hall Library, Belfast. Networks of road traverses are hardly models of scientific rectitude, but even when the Physico-Historical Society was able to employ its own assistants they chose to start with Sloane's outline, supplemented by several existing canal and coast surveys and revised by three surveyors 'each in the parts where they were most conversant'.[17] Despite the flaws inherent in such eclecticism, it would be hard to deny that the result (issued as an illustration to Walter Harris's *Antient and Present State of the County of Down* in 1744) was the best Irish county map of its time

– not that this was saying much, of course. The first separate sheet map of the same progressive county was published in 1755 with no surveyor's name. Its reputed author was a Dr Kennedy, of whom little is known apart from his being an 'ingenious gentleman'.[18] A doctor was no doubt more of a man of science than any land surveyor, but all Kennedy did, it seems, was put together surveys of different estates supplied to him by the proprietors, and in this task (admittedly more difficult than it sounds) he may have been helped by a local surveyor, John McClatchey, whose special relationship with the map was exhibited in his advertisements offering to frame and glaze it.

The Physico-Historical Society also sponsored maps of the counties of Waterford, Cork and Kerry, and of the towns of Waterford, Cork and Tralee, all by Charles Smith and all published as book illustrations.[19] Smith was another doctor (of medicine) who appears to have practised as an apothecary; but he claimed to have made his own triangulations and then to have filled them in with new road surveys augmented by recent hydrographic charts. While the results were indisputably original, their coverage of basic geographical features was sketchy, their scale unsatisfactorily small, and their presentation rough and old-fashioned. By now the society had been forced to admit that its cartographic ambitions could go no further than roads, towns, villages and gentlemen's seats; and in Tyrone and Fermanagh, the next counties on its agenda, the maps made little progress.[20] But at least Smith had done more than the Reverend Richard Barton, who set himself the strictly limited objective of a single line (the coast of Lough Neagh) and then failed to achieve even that.[21] Another fruitless co-operative venture was Charles Vallancey's Society of Antiquaries. Although Vallancey himself was a better cartographer than antiquarian, the only map eventuating from this little-known enterprise was the one in his own edition of Henry Piers's essay on Westmeath, and most of that had been copied from Petty's atlas.[22]

Even the best of Ireland's amateur map-makers – Daniel Augustus Beaufort and George Vaughan Sampson – had considerable difficulty with their field work and in their relations with the surveying community. Beaufort found employment for several minor practitioners when preparing his general map of Ireland and his diocesan map of Meath. One of them, named Heavy or Heavey, was given some kind of base-line to measure, but Beaufort seems quickly to have raised his control network above the common land surveyor's ken by deciding to use astronomical data instead.[23] He did pay some very small sums to other surveyors (their names were Connel, Killaly and Hood, the last two well-known in other contexts),[24] but his maps were basically compilations, however careful and scholarly. Sampson's subject was the county of Londonderry. Although unable to find a surveyor to work on the map accompanying his *Statistical Survey* of the county, published in 1802,[25] he did get some professional help for his excellent grand jury map of eleven years later. Unusually in such circumstances, he also acknowledged the help, albeit in the obscurity of a dead language.[26] But no ordinary surveyor can have contributed much to the remarkable store of geological information that Sampson had the precocity to put on his map; and only an amateur would have dared to reckon his longitudes from the meridian of a provincial city, even one as proudly named as Londonderry.

Sampson's Londonderry was the first Irish county map to be made by a gentleman-cartographer since the time of Dr Kennedy: the efforts of this leisured community had clearly left plenty of scope for the professionals. In fact the estate surveyor's incursion into commercial cartography dates mainly from the 1720s and reached its maximum strength at the period of his greatest impact on such non-cartographic media as newspapers and books. He seldom took the initiative, however, preferring to meet a demand which came chiefly from the county and municipal authorities. The lack of documentary evidence for the working of eighteenth-century Irish local government would surprise and dismay the majority of non-Irish historians, but it takes no great depth of scholarship to appreciate the cartographic implications of paving, cleaning, lighting, policing and water supply in the towns and of the many new roads and bridges now appearing in the countryside. As might be expected it was the towns that took the lead. Subscriptions were being collected for a new map of Dublin as early as 1703,[27] but no such map is known to have been made until an example had been set in 1726 by John Carty's plan of Cork.[28] Carty is one of the earliest provincial surveyors whose manuscript work survives in any quantity, and some of the faults of the Cork map can safely be attributed to its engraver. Two years later, Charles Brooking's plan of Dublin was on sale – more attractively presented, more successfully publicised, but not, apparently, the work of a professional land surveyor.[29] Other published town plans are shown in Figure 17.

Among the counties the first to get a land surveyor into print was, predictably, Dublin. Here Archbishop King had sponsored a map by Gabriel Stokes and given fifty guineas towards its cost.[30] The Physico-Historical Society adopted Stokes's survey and sought to raise another thirty guineas in voluntary subscriptions. The map was finished by 1747 – after many years of near-completion – and published in 1750.[31] Outside Dublin an early example of local enterprise came in 1749 from John Noble of Carlow and James Keenan of Castledermot. Their proposals for a map of Kildare, though perhaps drawing some inspiration from reports of work by Stokes and others, envisaged a mainly topographical treatment with no particular emphasis on roads or other individual thematic elements.[32] In Meath the impetus came a month later from the grand jury, but the objectives were equally wide-ranging and the competition was open to any surveyor offering security for his performance and willing to write down his proposals. The Meath map was to include 'all roads public and private, the divisions of each barony, the exact chart of the sea coast, with the soundings on the same, boroughs, market towns, parish churches, gentlemen's seats etc. etc.'[33]

Next, perhaps encouraged by the publication of Noble and Keenan's map in 1752, the new wave spread south-westwards into Queen's Co., Tipperary and King's Co., its cartographic essence somewhat diluted by a growing preoccupation with routine grand jury business. In Queen's Co., in May 1753, proposals were requested for 'an actual survey of said county, with an exact description of all roads therein'.[34] In Tipperary, a few days later, the invitation was for 'surveying and making proper and correct maps of the high roads of said county, with necessary observations concerning the convenience of materials for repairing the same' – the last phrase an interesting reference to geological possibilities which in this case seem to have come to nothing.[35] Nor is there any satisfactory record of John Mooney's map of King's Co. apart from the fact that he made it.[36] Mooney, like Noble and Keenan, was a local man; but both Meath and Queen's Co. were surveyed from a headquarters in Co. Down,[37] an early hint of the kind of specialisation that was to characterise much county map-making later in the century (Plate 25).

The same issue of locals versus strangers was raised to an international plane by the arrival of John Rocque in 1754. By this time Brooking's map of Dublin had outlived its usefulness. Brooking had shown parishes, but the parish soon proved an unsuitable unit for the organisation of street-cleaning and in 1749 the City Surveyor, Roger Kendrick, was asked to re-divide the built-up area into nine districts. When set up in the Tholsel office the new district maps presumably showed a considerable improvement on Brooking, of whom the City Surveyor held a not very high opinion; they probably came from a prototype of the city map at twenty Irish perches

Plate 25. From *Map of the Queen's County* by Oliver Sloane of Hillsborough. Scale of original one inch to one Irish mile. The map carries no date, but is usually assigned to 1763. The substance of the map is typical of this period (except for the early occurrence of a steam-engine), but the use of profile symbols for hills and houses was already becoming obsolete.

to the inch (1:5,040) which Kendrick was proposing to publish in the summer of 1754 and which he hoped to follow by another map, on a smaller scale, extending three or four miles into the adjacent countryside. Rocque came just in time to forestall this project with a city plan of his own at double Kendrick's scale. Kendrick was not without supporters. A patriotic newspaper pointedly remarked that he had better qualifications to survey the city 'than any other person could possibly have'. More surprisingly, there were even some Dublin surveyors who volunteered to help him beat Rocque into print. Kendrick rejected their offers, choosing to stand on his own knowledge and reputation, on his decision to publish at an even larger scale than originally intended, and on the thoroughly authentic Irishness of his engraver, his paper and himself.[38]

Notwithstanding these advantages, Kendrick's map of Dublin was never heard of again. Rocque won the metropolitan battle and went on to publish not only five separate maps of the city and its surroundings but also maps of several other Irish towns together with the counties of Dublin and Armagh.[39] Apart from the quantity and quality of his output he was the first man in Ireland to have successfully and lastingly joined the two occupations of surveyor and publisher, and to have shown complete cartographic facility on almost every scale. In print as in manuscript Rocque's great contribution was his attachment to planiformity, profile symbols being eliminated from his maps except for certain minor conventional signs (Plate 26). Many of the attractions familiar from his coloured estate maps could be carried onto the copper plate, and where planiform engraving conventions already existed he was often able to improve on them, for instance in his use of stipple for large building blocks instead of the harsh diagonal ruling favoured by Brooking's engravers. The worst feature of his county maps was that the surveying was not quite as exact as the scale required, a fault which culminated in the fictitious fields and hedges of his rural landscape. As might be expected from a surveyor employing a number of assistants, the standard of his maps was uneven. His Armagh was criticised by Beaufort,[40] and had presumably come under attack from within the county before the grand jury decided to replace it in the 1770s;[41] his Co. Dublin was good enough to survive unchallenged for over sixty years; his town plans were excellent.

Cartographically Rocque's career was a triumph. His stature as a businessman is more questionable: he left Ireland rather suddenly in 1760 without finishing his four-sheet map of the country round Cork and Kinsale, and died two years later in not very affluent circumstances. This

BREAKING INTO PRINT 341

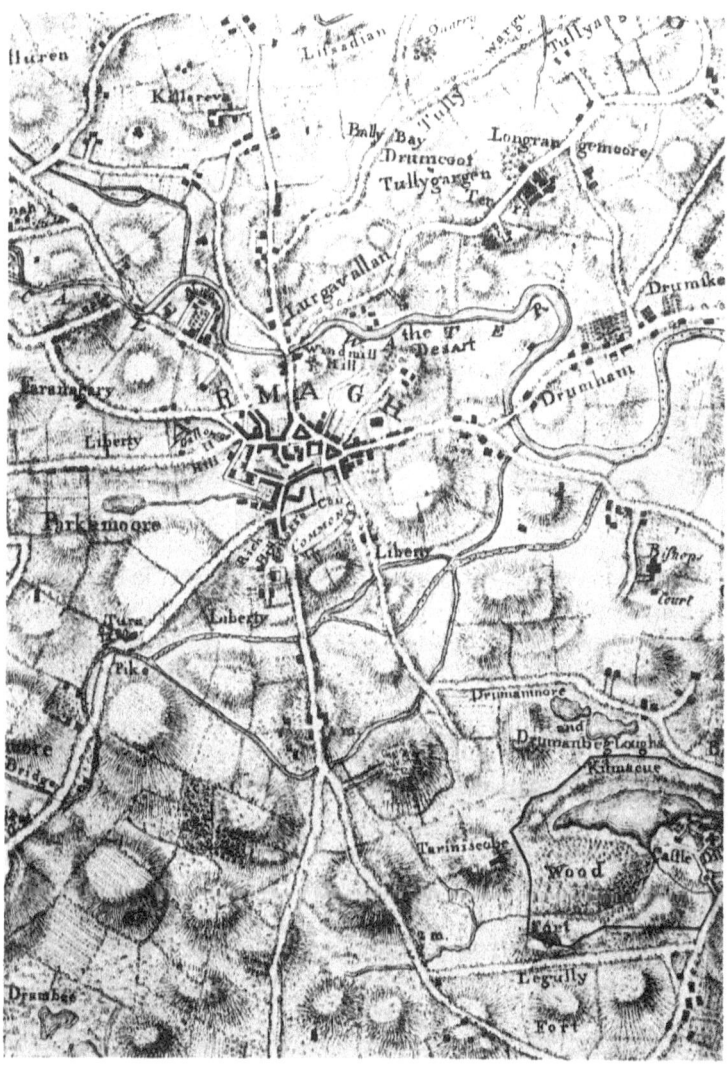

Plate 26. From John Rocque's *A Topographical Map of the County of Armagh*, 1760. Scale of original two inches to one Irish mile. The topographical style as adapted to county cartography. The field boundaries are shown diagrammatically without regard to individual fences, as can be seen by comparison with the large-scale plans of Armagh and Newry printed as insets to this map.

did not deter his pupils from trying to mix a similar blend of cartographic functions. Bernard Scalé in 1758 was already undertaking maps of counties, cities and gentlemen's estates;[42] Samuel Andrews, John Powell and Matthew Wren were even bolder, offering kingdoms and provinces as well as counties and cities.[43] Of the four only Scalé had much luck, notably with revised versions of some of Rocque's town plans, an original map of Waterford and a chart of the coast from Balbriggan to Arklow.[44] Like Rocque he was willing to sponsor other men's work, as in his chart of Wexford harbour and town, based on a survey by Joseph Allen.[45] But it was a smaller output than Rocque's (Scalé's production of manuscript estate plans was larger) and much of it depended on London publishers. Nor, despite the advertisement noticed above, did Scalé produce a single original county map – perhaps an acknowledgement that Rocque's activities in rural Ireland had been financially disappointing. The best that the younger man could do for the counties was his tiny *Hibernian Atlas* of 1776. Scalé put the best possible face on this diminutive publication by pointing out how few of his Irish competitors were qualified to equal it and by claiming to have drawn on his own experience in every part of the kingdom. As might be forecast from the elegance of his other maps, the atlas was beautifully designed and engraved (by the London firm of Ellis and Palmer), which no doubt helps to explain how it weathered a good deal of hostile criticism to reach a fourth edition.[46]

Despite the extent of his own estate surveys (not in fact a very useful source of information at the small scale of the *Hibernian Atlas*) Scalé disposed of little original data from the counties. Only three of them are known to have made any cartographic progress since Rocque's departure, none with spectacular results. Jacob Neville's map of Co. Wicklow looked pleasant enough in the Rocque manner; its engraver, George Byrne of Dublin, had previously worked for Rocque and knew how to imitate the kind of field and hedge that had embellished the master's maps of Dublin and Armagh. But Neville had much to contend with. Appointed in 1754 by the Wicklow grand jury, he found it hard to raise the necessary subscription of £180 (presumably equivalent to 360 copies) and by 1757 he was almost ready to give up. In the end the subscribers had to wait until 1760. Neville, a land surveyor from Kilpoole near Wicklow town, had evidently been promised a lump sum as well as an interest in the sale of the map; three months after publication he was telling the press that his bill remained unpaid.[47] All the same Wicklow was more fortunate than Kilkenny. There, conceivably under the influence of Rocque's survey of

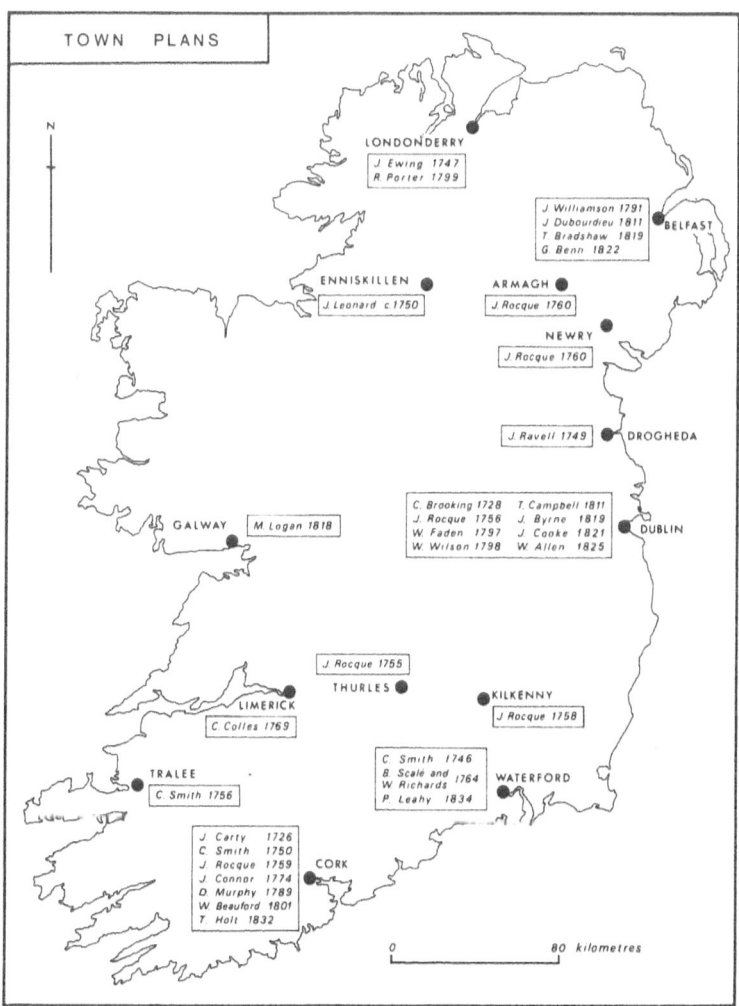

Figure 17. Printed town plans, 1700–1840. Revised editions and small-scale reductions are omitted. The lists for Dublin and Belfast are selective.

the city in 1758, a county survey was planned by a local surveyor, William Steile, who died in 1760 and whose successors, John Wright and William Steile Jnr., proved unable to complete the map – perhaps unable to begin it, for they wanted three hundred subscriptions at a guinea each before starting work.[48]

The last county project of the sixties was another slow starter, a map of Co. Louth which had been under consideration for at least four years before the grand jury decided to go ahead in 1763.[49] Instead of a local surveyor (one of the Bells would have been an obvious candidate) the jury chose Rocque's former assistant Matthew Wren, who now lived in Dublin and could claim no special connection with Louth apart from having recently drawn a plan of Newry just across the county border.[50] Whatever else he had been doing since last heard of in 1760–61, Wren continued to profit from his reputation as a Rocque alumnus. His publisher for Louth was another member of the old firm, Andrew Dury, and the map appeared under Rocque's name in several contemporary catalogues.[51] It was also engraved in the Rocque style though without the diagrammatic fields and hedges. None of these associations could save Wren's survey from being less than accurate, or from the odium of being replaced after only twelve years. Wren returned to England,[52] and with him went the Rocque school's habit of making, engraving and publishing county surveys as a single operation.

Since the days of the Physico-Historical Society, county maps had been either announced, drawn or actually published for a block of eleven prosperous counties in the hinterland of Dublin, and all the cartographers known to have been concerned in them were professional land surveyors, with the single exception of Dr Kennedy. The appointment of two mapmakers with somewhat different backgrounds to resurvey the county of Louth in 1777 inaugurates a new period in Irish topographical mapping. Even in the 'fifties the local surveyor could not rely on being honoured in his own country. Twenty years later, at a time of rising cartographic aspirations, his weaknesses were becoming more evident. He still had one advantage, it is true, and that was an intimate knowledge of his home ground. Some of the knowledge was in his own head, some in the drafts and copies of local estate maps which he prudently kept for future reference as duplicates of those delivered to his clientele. Not all of it was usable, however, at county scales which were almost always less than a quarter that of the normal estate map. Even the most basic feature of an estate survey – the owner's name – was for some reason less popular with Irish than with English county map-makers; and it was only in Londonderry that anyone adopted George Semple's suggestion for showing estate boundaries on a grand jury map as well as or instead of administrative divisions.[53]

What might have seemed more relevant was the insider's knowledge of 'geographical values'. Many of Ireland's most significant landmark-types – fair greens, ancient forts, holy wells, ruined churches and so on – show surprisingly little variation from one county to another, but there was surely some room for the genius loci in even the least pretentious of home-produced county maps. One such opportunity appears in the map of Co. Wexford produced by the Enniscorthy surveyor Valentine Gill: 'Strongbows camp', ' Earl of Essex camp', ' Lieut Buckley killed', ' Colonel Walpole killed' – a stranger might have felt it tactless to dwell on old (and not-so-old) scenes of violence with quite the same gusto. And who but a local cartographer could have thought of mapping 'Ten in a hundred' or 'McNab's tree' or 'Pierce's leap 14 yards'? A resident observer was also better able to choose appropriate subjects for the kind of marginal view that helped enlarge the market for many eighteenth-century maps. Finally, he was more likely to discover the most acceptable forms of local placenames. The metropolitan surveyor's routine precaution of circulating names in advance among the inhabitants was by no means fool-proof in Ireland, at least according to the author who complained of 'want of correction by the gentlemen of the county, few of whom but would rather laugh at than set one right'.[54]

Against these assets must be set the local land surveyor's narrowness of intellectual vision. Insensitive to the scholarly and scientific demands of the wider map-buying public, he proffered little geological or archaeological or even hydrographical information beyond the call of duty, and seldom supported his map with any kind of explanatory memoir above the standard of a copywriter's blurb. Even Rocque's publicity for his theodolite and chain[55] (a modest enough revelation beside the flow of cartographic confidences that was to characterise the nineteenth century) raised hardly an echo among his Irish contemporaries or their immediate successors. In the whole century before 1800 the only technical reference to county maps came from a surveyor who had never made one, Benjamin Noble. Writing in 1768, too late to have much excuse for his ignorance, Noble saw the county survey as no more than a series of traverses, uncontrolled by any trigonometrical skeleton. To a largely conventional account of estate surveying he added:

After this, or a similar manner, an actual survey of a county or province may be made; taking your stations along the different roads; and the various objects as castles, churches, or country seats, may be taken in, as you chain along, by taking the bearing of each object at two different places on the chaining.[56]

If this was how the typical Irish county map-maker worked, and it probably was, then he did well to keep quiet about it. But no amount of reticence could prevent his superiors in the engineering profession from dismissing the ordinary land surveyor as fit for a townland or perhaps a parish and unfit for anything larger.

Some of the local surveyor's handicaps were more social and psychological than technical. To cover a county quickly and efficiently was best done by teamwork, as John Noble and James Keenan had recognised by forming a temporary partnership for this purpose. But most eighteenth-century surveying firms were one- or two-man affairs, their members too under-capitalised to hire extra staff and temperamentally too self-sufficient to co-operate on equal terms. In any case, as a lifelong inhabitant of his town or county the indigenous surveyor was under no strong pressure to get it finished. His subject-matter lay waiting: why should the map not wait as well, left on the Irishman's 'long finger' until some new road or canal was ready for inclusion? From a business point of view, simply to have been chosen as county cartographer might be enough to establish one's reputation with the landowners who commanded the most inviting channels of future employment; and with maps, as with some other kinds of publication, to travel hopefully might sometimes be more beneficial than arriving. Finally, no country surveyor could be expected to double as engraver or printseller, and few can have had much familiarity with the processes and personnel involved in reaching a mass market. A number of useful maps were consequently doomed to languish in manuscript, and those that did achieve publication were often marred by inefficient editing or by rough and unsympathetic engraving.

Such afflictions could easily outweigh the joys of authorship. In any case most land surveyors would have found something flighty and vainglorious about the desire to see one's name at the top of a printed map. As an earlier chapter has shown, there was little desire for public acclaim even among those who had the best chance of winning it – the Gibsons, Barkers, Frizells, Sherrards, Hardings and their ilk, to say nothing of Joshua Wight, who grumbled that nobody had made a good plan of his own city without ever attempting to fill the gap himself.[57] On the contrary, it was apathy among the fashionable surveyors that helped to give the eccentrically-ambitious local practitioner his chance.

This, however, is where the 1770s marked a new departure. The contexts of the change were both legal and administrative. Grand juries had been involved in county mapping from the start; but now their cartographic role was to be recognised by Parliament. In 1774 the counties were empowered to spend up to £100 on getting themselves surveyed.[58] In 1778 this almost derisory sum was increased to £100 per 100,000 acres,[59] and in 1796 the £100 became £300 with an additional ten pounds each for separate barony maps. The 1796 act also allowed a sum of £20 per 50,000 acres for revising the grand jury maps on a fifteen-year cycle.[60] The result was that an Irish county map now stood a better chance of being published at a profit: in 1797 the making of such maps could even be described with no hint of sarcasm as a gateway to fame and fortune.[61] Certain land surveyors accordingly sought to overcome their lack of relevant experience by specialising in county surveys, choosing counties that were close together so as not to lose the benefit of their local knowledge. At the same time grand juries began to take more interest in applicants who were not primarily estate surveyors and whose talents seemed commensurate with larger territories and longer distances.

The land surveyors who did most county mapping under the new dispensation were the McCreas of Lifford in Co. Donegal. The family's interest in this neglected branch of Irish cartography dated from as early as 1751, when Samuel McCrea undertook a map of Co. Tyrone. Conceivably this venture had some connection with the Physico-Historical Society; but like so many projects of its period it hung fire – eight years later the author was still being urged to make a start[62] – and appears to have made little progress until taken up by Samuel's sons William and Conyngham in 1773. Their proposed scale of 100 perches to an inch (1:25,200 or 1:19,800) was unusual for a county map-maker; but then the McCreas at this stage of their careers were still essentially estate surveyors. Their manuscript maps were ornately decorative in a style that owed nothing to the French school,[63] a degree of independence that they emphasised by surveying the adjacent county of Armagh less than twenty years after it had been mapped by Rocque. However, it was not their estate work but the specimens they could offer of parts of Tyrone that won them their commission in Armagh,[64] followed soon afterwards by a similar appointment on the other side of their home town, from the grand jury of Co. Donegal.[65] All three counties may be assumed to have

TABLE 15
IRISH COUNTY MAPS

Author	County	Date	Scale	Triangulation	Graticule	Projection	Hills	Building Symbols	Settlement
Land Surveyors									
O. Sloane	Down	1739	0	0	0	0	0	0	0
G. Stokes	Dublin	1750	0	0	1	0	0	0	0
J. Noble & J. Keenan	Kildare	1752	0	0	0	0	0	0	0
J. Rocque	Dublin	1760	1	0	0	0	1	1	1
J. Rocque	Armagh	1760	1	0	0	0	1	1	1
J. Neville	Wicklow	1760	0	0	1	0	1	0	0
O. Sloane	Queen's	[?1763]	0	0	0	0	0	0	0
M. Wren	Louth	1766	1	0	0	0	1	1	0
J. Lendrick	Antrim	1782	0	0	0	0	1	0	0
P. & R. Butler	Carlow	1789	1	0	0	0	1	0	0
W. McCrea	Monaghan	1793	0	0	0	0	1	0	0
A. Neville	Wicklow	1798	0	0	1	0	1	0	0
W. McCrea	Donegal	1801	0	0	0	0	1	1	0
D. Cahill	Queen's	1805	1	0	0	0	1	0	0
J. Williamson	Down	1810	0	0	1	?	1	1	0
V. Gill	Wexford	1811	0	0	1	1	1	0	0
N. Bath	Cork	1811	0	0	0	0	1	1	1
W. McCrea & G. Knox	Tyrone	1815	0	0	1	1	1	1	0
Engineers & Others									
Dr Kennedy	Down	1755	0	0	1	0	0	0	0
G. Taylor & A. Skinner	Louth	1777	1	0	1	1	1	1	1
A. Taylor	Kildare	1783	1	0	1	1	1	1	1
H. Pelham	Clare	1787	0	0	0	0	1	0	0
W. Larkin	Westmeath	1808	1	0	1	0	1	1	1
G. Sampson	Londonderry	1814	1	0	1	0	1	1	1
W. Edgeworth	Longford	1814	1	1	1	1	1	1	1
W. Larkin	Meath	1817	1	0	1	1	1	1	1
W. Larkin	Waterford	1818	1	0	1	1	1	1	1
W. Larkin	Galway	1819	1	0	1	1	1	1	1
W. Larkin	Leitrim	1819	1	0	1	0	1	1	1
W. Larkin	Sligo	1819	1	0	1	0	1	1	1
W. Duncan	Dublin	1821	1	1	1	1	1	1	1
R. Griffith & W. Edgeworth	Roscommon	1825	0	1	1	1	1	1	1
W. Bald	Mayo	1830	1	1	1	1	1	1	1

Maps on scales smaller than 1:100,000 are omitted. Points are scored for scales larger than 1:50,000, for triangulation diagrams, for marginal latitude and longitude divisions, for non-rectangular projections, for the representation of hills by hachures, for the representation of buildings by planiform symbols, and for the inclusion of cabins as well as larger buildings. Dates refer to the publication of the map and not to the making of the survey.

---

taken advantage of the new legislation on grand jury maps, but the sums allowed by the 1774 act were not enough to finance the kind of four-sheet engraving that the McCreas had rightly chosen as a suitable medium; nor were the subscriptions contributed by the local gentry, despite their admiration for the maps.[66]

Nevertheless the McCrea in residence had not given up hope of publication when Daniel Beaufort came to Lifford on cartographic business of his own in 1787. His host's initial reaction was to promise Beaufort transcripts of Armagh, Tyrone and Donegal, together with 'remarks upon the other counties in Ulster', but when the visitor returned in the following year and began to make copies for use in a forthcoming map of his own, McCrea's welcome lost some of its cordiality: 'McCrea comes in and waxing hot made me a very long speech upon the great injury he was now likely to suffer'. He calmed down, however, when shown the small scale of Beaufort's map of Ireland, and ended by renewing his assistance, to be paid in the fullness of time by a gift of original latitude and longitude values, by a letter recommending him for the forthcoming survey of Co. Monaghan, and by a printed encomium on his 'great skill and accuracy'.[67] McCrea duly mapped Monaghan in 1790–3, completed the survey of Donegal (where in 1793 he was paid a hundred pounds for finishing the barony maps and inserting new roads),[68] and finally moved on to Londonderry, where he was financed by a succession of hundred-pound payments at the county assizes from 1792 to 1799. The resulting map was soon to be made redundant by Sampson's aforementioned survey of 1813. Nevertheless McCrea's Londonderry added its influence to the evolutionary stream: Sampson valued it enough to borrow it from the grand jury, and the jury valued it enough to be still pressing for its return in 1824.[69] In Donegal, Tyrone and Monaghan the McCrea achievement was more fully acknowledged: in the end these counties were all published, the first two with additions by another Lifford land surveyor, George Knox.[70] Recognition of the McCreas did not however extend to their pupil Gabriel Montgomery, who delayed his map of Fermanagh while awaiting the completion of canals and post roads. He waited too long: the map never appeared.[71]

In south-west Ireland, another sphere of influence comparatively remote from Dublin, the McCreas' opposite number was Neville Bath, a land surveyor who lived in or near Cork city and who also had connections with north Kerry;[72] First heard of in the 1770s near Listowel, he was master of a neat cartographic style which drew much from metropolitan models and which no doubt helped him to secure more than ten years of grand jury work in the counties and cities of Cork and Limerick (in 1787–9), in Co. Tipperary (1795–7) and in Co. Kilkenny (in progress, 1799). Financially these operations were profitable enough: the £1500 each paid for Co. Cork and Tipperary represented a better-than-average income for a country estate surveyor at the same period. Outside the grand jury room Bath was less fortunate. In 1796 he proposed to publish the city of Cork, the liberties of the city, the county of Cork and the individual baronies of the county, at scales ranging from two inches to the mile (1:40,320) up to twenty perches to the inch (1:5,040), the whole amounting to twenty-three maps, and undertook to start engraving as soon as a hundred sets were subscribed for. In the event only the county map was published and this not until fifteen years later with a scale half that originally planned. Bath finished by trying to extend his sphere of influence into Roscommon – apparently without success, for the only known post-plantation survey of this county is the one made in 1813 by Richard Griffith and William Edgeworth. Despite his setbacks it had been an impressive career.

The closest parallel to Bath and the McCreas was James Williamson, whose work on Antrim and Down has been discussed in a previous chapter. Although these three firms supplied a total of thirteen grand juries they were not the only Irish exponents of the county map between the years 1780 and 1815. There were also several practitioners of more strictly local allegiance, as shown in Table 15, who continued the 'one-off' tradition of the 'fifties and 'sixties. Prolific or otherwise, the nineteenth-century land surveyor inherited many of the limitations of his predecessors. He (or his publisher) was readier to commit himself to latitudes and longitudes, but not to a triangulation diagram or other trigonometrical data; and by the standards of the 1800s his map could look suspiciously rough, giving little impression of land cover, oversimplifying relief, and omitting most of the smaller settlements. And his popularity never lasted very long. To the next generation, Valentine Gill's Wexford seemed very

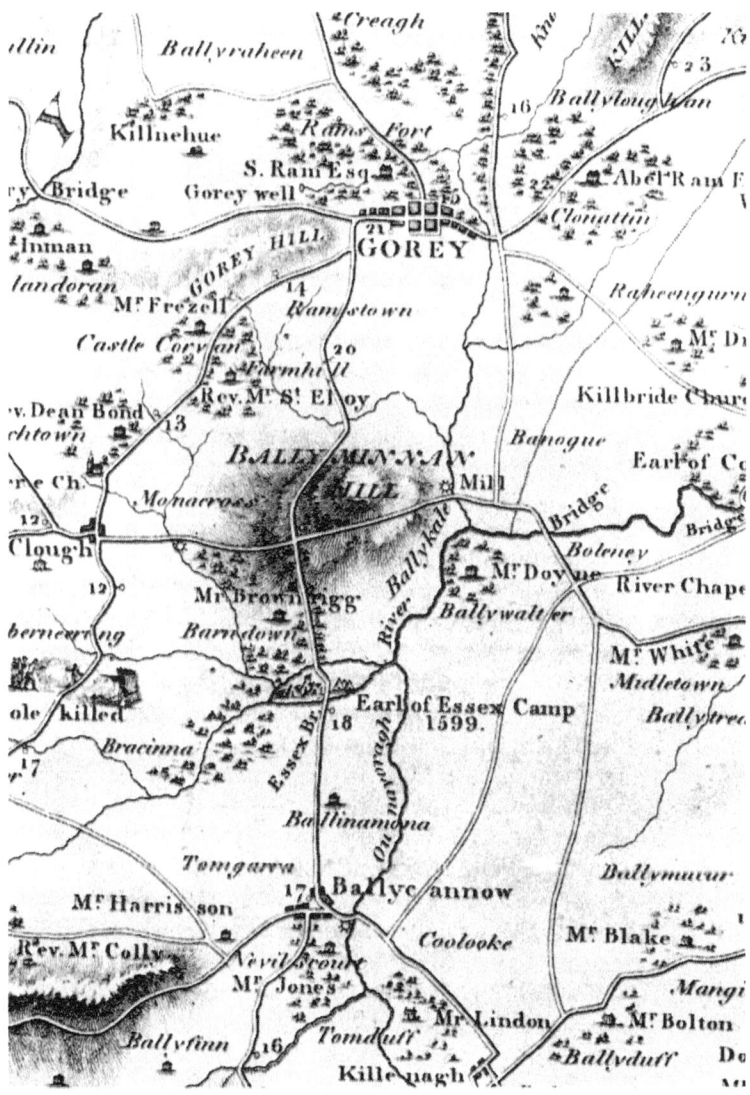

Plate 27. From *A New Map of the County of Wexford* by Valentine Gill of Enniscorthy, 1811. Scale of original one inch to one statute mile. One of the last Irish county surveys to be completed by a local practitioner (at the relatively modest cost of £400), Gill's map is unusual in its choice of historical information and in its emphasis on the names of resident gentry. His minor roads obviously make no claim to planimetric accuracy.

incorrect; Daniel Cahill's Queen's Co. an original survey but an indifferent one; the McCreas' Tyrone a compilation of old surveys; Williamson's Down imperfect in its representation of 'ground' (i.e. relief); and Bath's Tipperary so inaccurate that it was never referred to.[73]

Gill, publishing in 1811, was the last local practitioner to get a county map finished (Plate 27). From now on the country surveyor's ambitions, being for the most part without practical effect, can no longer be expected to leave much trace for posterity apart from the occasional newspaper advertisement[74] or accident of diary-keeping. An example of the latter occurred in 1813 when two local surveyors were applying to make a new survey of Co. Tipperary and when one of them, Pat Leahy, was noted as steady and meritorious by Sir Vere Hunt, who happened to be visiting Clonmel for the assizes.[75] The outcome of this encounter remains unknown (Sir Vere was so impressed by his next engagement, a visit to the female ward of the Clonmel house of industry, that he forgot all about surveying), but it was now becoming difficult for men like Leahy to be given charge of a whole county by any grand jury that claimed to be abreast of the times. The most likely reason for this further change of outlook was the influence of certain government cartographic projects that were reaching their culmination around 1815. Henceforth county maps were to be made by nationally-known engineers, town maps by engineers or architects. As always, different periods overlap, and only by means of a forty-year flashback can the first signs of the new movement be picked up. It was in 1774 that Joseph Connor's map of Cork city, though seemingly the work of a land surveyor, came bearing the approval of local architects.[76] Nine years later another Cork surveyor (Patrick Aher) and an architect were planning a joint map of their home town, and it was the architect Daniel Murphy who brought a similar plan to execution in 1789.[77] In Dublin, often behind Cork in cartographic progress, the first documented architect's map is that of J. Cooke in 1821,[78] though Dublin cartographers of the period from 1790 onwards were so often anonymous that the comparison is not wholly fair.

In the engineering profession it was the military branch that first assumed a definite cartographic identity as commanders began to ask for topographical maps as well as town and fort plans. It is tempting to include the Anglo-American Henry Pelham in this class, his famous plan of Boston, Massachusetts, being so obviously a soldier's map in style and subject.[79] But Pelham was too versatile to be pinned down. He was enough of a scientist to plan a series of astronomical observations at Loop Head, Co. Clare, including the transit of Mercury as a means of longitude determination, in 1786;[80] enough of a scientist, perhaps, to anticipate the Ordnance Survey of Ireland in refusing to publish a less-than-perfect graticule; and also enough of an artist to take a boat trip up the Shannon later in the same year for the purpose of painting the scenery and antiquities.[81] Soon afterwards he was appointed agent to the Earl of Shelburne in Kerry. There he seems to have left the estate surveying to others,[82] but his map of Clare appeared in 1787 and his map of Kerry was ready for the engraver when Pelham was drowned in Bantry Bay nineteen years later.[83]

With William Byers and Alexander Taylor the military associations are more explicit.[84] Byers served as an assistant to Charles Vallancey on the military survey of Ireland; his grand jury map of Co. Down was never finished, but enough of it survives to show a close resemblance to Vallancey's style.[85] Taylor began in Scotland as an estate surveyor[86] before coming to work on the Irish road surveys that were published by his brother George, with Andrew Skinner, in 1778.[87] The same team also made a map of Co. Louth, engraved like the road book by Garnett Terry of London, which may be regarded as Ireland's first modern county map. Alexander's subsequent career had two strands. In 1781 he joined the army as a lieutenant in the 81st Regiment of Foot, later finding a more congenial habitat in the Corps of Engineers. In this capacity he deputised in Vallancey's military survey for much of the 'eighties and 'nineties. At the same time, though less happily, Taylor was trying to specialise in county cartography. In 1783 his map of Kildare maintained the standards set in Louth a few years earlier, and in Longford he collaborated with the versatile amateur Richard Lovell Edgeworth in laying the trigonometrical foundations for another first-class county survey.[88] The Longford operation was absorbed anonymously into William Edgeworth's grand jury map of 1814, and Taylor's plans for other counties are known only in the form of preliminary advertisements.[89] From 1800 onwards he contented himself with the road surveys described in an earlier chapter.

Taylor himself never quite blended into his Irish environment; to some he was still a 'thorough Caledonian' even after half a century.[90] But he and his brother, along with their one-time partner Andrew Skinner, were given credit for training an Irish school of road surveyors to use the theodolite instead of the circumferentor.[91] No doubt the pupils in turn begot their own professional progeny, but neither of these later generations can be identified with any confidence. Taylor's best-known subordinate in the

Post Office surveys of *c*. 1805, William Larkin, was categorically accused of preferring the circumferentor, but Larkin's output was so large as to leave room for a variety of methods and a variety of critical opinions. In King's Co., at least, his skeleton map for the bog commissioners could be described as 'trigonometrical'.[92] Elsewhere he worked by joining up his Post Office strip maps, and in this way, on his own initiative and with his own subordinates, he was able to assume in the second decade of the new century the role of universal county map-maker that Taylor seems to have been coveting twenty years earlier. Altogether Larkin surveyed nearly a dozen counties, six of which were engraved with consummate professionalism by Samuel Neele of London (at a slightly larger scale than they were worth) and published with a promptitude that would have made any earlier Irish surveyor envious. In other respects, too, Larkin aimed to impress: his readers in the maritime counties of Waterford and Galway, perhaps more cosmopolitan than the rest, were treated to a scale of myriometres, chiliometres, hecatometres and decametres. His popularity with the grand juries may illustrate the descent of scientific ideas about road making, and road mapping, from central to local government level, but among surveyors he was at best a transitional figure. Even if he kept the compass for by-roads and traversed the main roads with a theodolite, his maps were still not trigonometrically quite respectable, and despite their clarity and large scale they failed to satisfy the experts.[93] (Their neglect by modern landscape historians is less defensible.) The same was true of Edward Carte's less well known proposal, in Co. Limerick, for a new kind of county or barony survey that would show the relation of roads to townlands.[94]

The makers of military maps and post-road surveys provoke a question that has already been asked of the topographical engineers: were they also 'land surveyors'? The answer is, only just. They certainly made a few estate maps – Byers in Co. Down,[95] Taylor in Kildare and Cork,[96] Larkin in Leitrim[97] – but their closest affinities were with the world of William Bald, Richard Griffith, William Edgeworth and William Duncan, and this is a world that deserves its own book. The four last-named individuals produced a total of only four county maps, but to the ordinary land surveyor they presented a challenge as unbeatable as that of the Ordnance Survey a few years later. His easiest response was to work for one of the new supermen (as William Hampton worked for William Edgeworth),[98] relying on later historians to rescue this modest role from obscurity. Another loophole was the kind of survey in which scientific exactitude was not yet considered necessary. Such surveys might include the revision of an existing map, as Arthur Richards Neville revised Jacob Neville's map of Wicklow[99] and as the map of Dublin city was kept constantly up-to-date for use in guidebooks and directories. There was also still room for original work, especially in areas small enough to be surveyed by elementary methods and interesting enough to command a market – watering places, sites of antiquities or natural curiosities, beauty spots, military training grounds, sporting venues and places of pilgrimage. Such surveys are not very numerous and not very good. Gabriel Montgomery's map of Lough Erne is perhaps the most elaborate, Henry Walker's map of the Curragh race course the most enjoyable.[100]

With these lesser maps the problem of attribution is made more difficult by the emergence (or re-emergence) of the desk-bound cartographic entrepreneur. Surveyors like Rocque had sold their own maps, either single-handed or with the assistance of one or more booksellers whose contribution might sometimes merit a note of acknowledgement in very small print. By the 1770s the independent publisher was taking a larger share of the credit, and even the most genuine of originals might find his identity suppressed, like the creator of the crowd-pulling relief model of Killarney exhibited round the country in the following decade.[101] Generally speaking, as Irish maps grew smaller so their publishers' names grew more obtrusive. Some of the firms in question had interests among various other graphic arts, like the Dublin establishment of William Allen founded in 1779.[102] Others belonged more to the world of books. But when composing credits both groups were inclined to give publicity to a map-engraver – perhaps because they themselves had more contact with him – rather than to those responsible for the field work. Among the large output of early nineteenth-century maps of Dublin city, for example, it is hard to find even one that features the name of a land surveyor.[103] Why the men who printed and sold Irish maps were now becoming better known than those who did the actual cartography is a problem for another occasion. However unhelpful to modern scholarship, the change must be accepted as historically appropriate: the land surveyor's anonymity matched his declining status, a decline that would eventually extend from the print-shop to the estate office and the farm.

Notes

1. Engraved map of Wynnsfield, Co. Kildare, by Bernard Scalé, in John Wynn Baker, *Experiments in Agriculture, Made under the Direction of the ... Dublin Society in the Year 1771* (Dublin, 1772). The only Irish properties whose estate maps can be said to have been published in any quantity are those of the London Companies. Here the status of landlord was divided among a large enough number of individual company-members to justify the printing of maps, and much other information, of a kind that would normally have remained in manuscript. Apart from town plans (for which see above, ch. 7, n. 33; ch. 10, n. 92), the published Londoners' maps include full-size townland maps (e.g. *Report to the Court of Assistants of the Drapers' Company, upon the Meath Estate* ... (London, 1868)) and reduced townland maps with appropriate indexes (e.g. *Rental of the Manor of Sal, in the County of Londonderry, for the Year 1845, Printed for the Use of the Members of the Salters' Company* (London, 1846); *Report of the Deputation Who, in Pursuance of a Resolution of the Court of Assistants of the Skinners' Company ... visited the Manor of Pellipar in the County of Londonderry* (London, 1853); *Report of the Deputation Appointed by the Court of the Worshipful Company of Skinners, to View the Manor of Pellipar, in the County of Derry* (London, 1874). The 1853 Skinners' report includes a topographical location map at 1:253,344 and their 1874 report a small-scale regional map (*c.* 1:515,000) showing proposed railways in the north of Ireland.
2. Examples of Grierson's advertisements are in *Dublin Journal*, 4 Dec. 1744; *Dublin Courant*, 18 Jan. 1746; *Watson's Almanack*, 1746. His publications included new editions of Henry Pratt's and Herman Moll's maps of Ireland and of Petty's *Hiberniae Delineatio*. Grierson died in 1753 and his map plates were put on sale twelve years later (*Dublin Journal*, 29 Dec. 1759, 19 Nov. 1765).
3. For Lythe see Andrews, *Imago Mundi*, 19 (1965), pp 22–31; for Jobson, S. Ó Ceallaigh, *Gleanings from Ulster History* (Cork, 1951), pp 50–51 .
4. Andrews, *Geogr. Jour.*, 132 (1966), p. 58.
5. TCD, MS 1209(69). See above, ch. 3, n. 36.
6. Reprinted, with introduction by J. H. Andrews (Shannon, 1969).
7. See the advertisements for Philip Lea and Herman Moll's map of 1690 and for Robert Morden's map of 1691 in S. Tyacke, *London Map-Sellers, 1660–1720* (Tring, 1978), pp 47, 49.
8. Andrews, *Proc. R. Ir. Acad.*, 80C (1980), p. 239.
9. 14 & 15 Charles II, c. 10, sec. 1.
10. Correspondence of Bishop of Kilmore and Provost of Trinity College, 1662, TCD, MUN/P/24/144. There is a rough map of the diocese of Kilmore in Bodleian, Rawlinson MS B.487, f . 75 (noted in McNeill, *Analecta Hibernica*, 1 (1930), p. 143).
11. The Cloyne map is reproduced in T. G. H. Green, *Index to the Marriage Licence Bonds of the Diocese of Cloyne* (Cork, 1899–1900). There is a facsimile of a map of the diocese of Tuam, at two miles to an inch, with an accompanying letter from the Deputy Diocesan Registrar of 15

Jan. 1935 in NAI, T.2639. The letter describes the map as dating from the time of Archbishop Samuel Pullen (1660–67) and as having cost £150. The diocese of Armagh is represented in two maps of 1662 at the Diocesan Registry (D.104/22/4/1, 2), one of which is stated to be based on the Down Survey.

12. Bishop King, 16 Jan. 1703, TCD, MS 1489(2). Bishop of Elphin's maps of 1740 and 1817 are quoted as authorities in the Ordnance Survey's field name book for the parish of Aughrim, Co. Roscommon (townlands of Rockville and Coolnahinch), but these may have been local estate maps.

13. Skeleton map of Cashel diocese, 1782, scale about two Irish miles to one inch, Hampshire County Record Office, Winchester, Normanton papers, 21.M.57, 245.

14. Editions of 1797 and 1816 are recorded in E. M. Rodger, *The Large Scale County Maps of the British Isles, 1596–1850* (2nd ed., Oxford, 1972), pp 43–4. A manuscript diocesan map of Ardagh (Representative Church Body Library, Dublin, D5, n.d., watermarked 1796) appears to be based on Beaufort's ecclesiastical map of Ireland

15. G. L. Herries Davies, 'The Making of Irish Geography, IV: the Physico-Historical Society of Ireland, 1744–1752', *Ir. Geogr.*, 12 (1979), pp 92–8.

16. *A Topographical and Chorographical Survey of the County of Down* (Dublin, 1740), preface. This passage is absent from the complete version of the *Survey* published in 1744.

17. [W. Harris and C. Smith], *The Antient and Present State of the County of Down* (Dublin, 1744), pp ix, xi.

18. J. Dubourdieu, *Statistical Survey of the County of Down* (Dublin, 1802), p. 254. Dubourdieu seems to be the earliest authority for Dr Kennedy's authorship of this map.

19. *The Antient and Present State of the County and City of Waterford* (Dublin, 1746); *The Antient and Present State of the County and City of Cork* (Dublin, 1750); *The Antient and Present State of the County of Kerry* (Dublin, 1756).

20. Dublin Physico-Historical Society's questionnaire, *Dublin Journal*, 28 Oct. 1746. Almost the only evidence relating to maps of Tyrone and Fermanagh at this time is that the Bishop of Clogher offered to pay ten guineas each towards the cost of them.

21. Richard Barton, *Lectures in Natural Philosophy, Designed, to be a Foundation, for Reasoning Pertinently, Upon the Petrifactions, Gems, Crystals, and Sanative Quality of Lough Neagh in Ireland* (Dublin, 1751), p. 91.

22. Vallancey, *Collectanea*, I. Vallancey gives no account of how his map of Westmeath was compiled.

23. Diary of Daniel Beaufort, 1 Sep. 1787, TCD, MS 4026, f. 6. A surveyor named G. Heavy appears in *County Westmeath, a Schedule of Presentments Applied for at Spring Assizes* (1816), p. 10.

24. Beaufort account books, NAI, 1A.37.96, pp 7, 62.

25. Sampson, *Londonderry*, p. vii.
26. 'J. OKane Delin^t adjuvante concilio et opera auctoris'. O'Kane is not mentioned in Sampson's *A Memoir Explanatory of the Chart and Survey of the County of London-derry* (London, 1814).
27. C. T. Keatinge, 'The Guild of Cutlers, Painter-Stainers and Stationers, Better Known as the Guild of St Luke the Evangelist, Dublin', *Jour. R. Soc. Ant. Ire.*, 5th ser., 10 (1900), p. 142.
28. E. Carberry, 'The Development of Cork City (as Shown by the Maps of the City, Prior to the Ordnance Survey Map of 1841–42)', *Jour. Cork Hist. & Arch. Soc.*, 48 (1943), p. 73.
29. J. H. Andrews, '"Mean Pyratical Practices": the Case of Charles Brooking', *Bull. Ir. Georgian Soc.*, 23 (1980), pp 33–43.
30. *Dublin Journal*, 12 June 1744, 28 Oct. 1746.
31. Minutes of Dublin Physico-Historical Society, 6 Jan. 1746 *et seq.*, Royal Irish Academy, MS 24.E.28; *Dublin Journal*, 16 Jan. 1748; *Watson's Almanack*, 1748, p. 69; 1750, p. 70; 1751, p. 67.
32. J. H. Andrews, 'Proposals for Eighteenth-Century Maps of County Kildare', *Jour. Kildare Arch. Soc.*, 16 (1979–80), pp 89–90.
33. *Dublin Journal*, 12 Sep. 1749.
34. *Dublin Journal*, 29 May 1753.
35. *Dublin Journal*, 5 June 1753.
36. The 'enlargement of a trace taken from Mooney's map of the King's County' in PRONI, D.671/M6/12, is too sketchy to give an impression of the original.
37. Queen's Co. was surveyed by Oliver Sloane of Hillsborough. The Meath map, never published and now not to be found, was attributed to John Sloane in Robert Thompson, *Statistical Survey of the County of Meath* (Dublin, 1802), p. 2.
38. *Dublin Courant*, 15, 26 Aug., 2 Sep. 1749; *Dublin Journal*, 31 Aug., 14 Sep., 2 Nov. 1754.
39. Andrews, *Ir. Geogr.*, 5 (1967), p. 279.
40. Beaufort, *Memoir*, p. vii.
41. Coote, *Armagh*, p. 284. It was the Rocque survey, however, and not its replacement that provided the basis for Coote's own small map of the county.
42. *Public Gazetteer*, 23 Sep. 1758.
43. *Dublin Journal*, 12 Jan. 1760.
44. Andrews, *Ir. Geogr.*, 5 (1967), p. 284.
45. 'Done from an actual survey' by Allen, engraved by J. Mackoun, and published by Scalé and his partner William Richards, 1764.
46. The atlas was advertised in *Hibernian Journal*, 2 Jan. 1775, and published in 1776. Scalé's errors were innumerable, Richard Gough was told by J. C. Walker on 30 Oct. 1787 (Nichols, *Literary History*, 7, pp 701–2); but they were still uncorrected in the editions of 1788 and

1798. A. Bonar Law (*Three Hundred Years of Irish Printed Maps* (Belfast, 1972), p. 29) mentions an edition of 1824.
47. *Dublin Journal*, 14 Sep. 1754, 26 Apr. 1759, 17 Nov. 1759, 9 Dec. 1760, 14 Mar. 1761.
48. *Dublin Journal*, 18 Oct. 1760.
49. Subscription list, 1 Aug. 1759, NLI, MS 10350; surveyor's appointment, *Dublin Journal*, 16 Aug. 1763.
50. PRONI, T.618/327.
51. Wren's Louth is included among lists of Rocque's maps in *A Catalogue of the Genuine and Valuable Collection of Copper Plates of the Ingenious Mr. John Rocque* (n.p., 1771); in *Hibernian Journal*, 4 Mar. 1774 (an advertisement for Rocque's Irish maps as revised by Scalé); and in Robert Sayer and John Bennett's printed catalogue of 1775.
52. For Wren's English maps see R. V. Tooley, *Tooley's Dictionary of Mapmakers* (New York and Amsterdam, 1979), p. 674.
53. George Semple, *Hibernia's Free Trade* (Dublin, 1780), pp 162–3, 186. For Sampson's mapping of the London Companies' proportions see Moody, *Londonderry Plantation*, pp 453–5.
54. Hely Dutton, *Statistical Survey of the County of Clare* (Dublin, 1808), pp 353–5.
55. Proposals for map of harbours of Cork and Kinsale, *Dublin Journal*, 12 Feb. 1760.
56. Noble, *Geodaesia*, pp 50–51.
57. Wight's diary, undated description of Cork city.
58. 13 & 14 George III, c. 32, sec. 22.
59. 17 & 18 George III, c. 22, sec. 10.
60. 36 George III, c. 55, secs. 29–32.
61. Thomas Lane, 1 Oct. 1797, on William Byers's lack of progress in mapping Co. Down, PRONI, D.607/E/319.
62. PRONI, C. & P. TYR 6/1; Gebbie, *Abercorn Letters*, pp 109,113.
63. William and Conyngham McCrea, maps of the Forbes estate, Co. Tyrone, 1777, PRONI, T.1132/1 (photocopies).
64. William and Conyngham McCrea to Earl of Abercorn, 10 Jan. 1777, PRONI, T.2541/IA1/12; Coote, *Armagh*, pp 284–5. Later Sir Charles Coote made an arrangement with the grand jury of Co. Armagh to publish this map. The scheme broke down, but not for reasons that brought any discredit to the McCreas (*The Newry Magazine*, 1 (1815), p. 152).
65. *Freeman's Journal*, 21 Dec. 1776; the original notice was dated 29 Aug.. The Donegal map was nearly finished by the time of the summer assizes of 1785 (PRONI, T.2541/IA1/15/27). The determination of parish boundaries for what was presumably this map, in 1783, is mentioned in some anonymous notes on Co. Donegal placenames dating from 1836 (NAI, Valuation Office letter books, 2A.26.71).

66. The financial history of the maps from 1773 to 1785 is documented in letters from various local correspondents to the Earl of Abercorn (PRONI, T.2541/IA1: 10/108, 112; 11/26A; 15/27). For the Tyrone map see also John McEvoy, *Statistical Survey of the County of Tyrone* (Dublin, 1802), p. 126.

67. TCD, MS 4028, ff. 12,18 (8, 13 Nov. 1787), MS 4029, ff. 18–21 (11–14 July 1788); Beaufort, *Memoir*, p. viii. Presumably the McCrea mentioned by Beaufort was William, who seems to have been the elder of the two brothers, but the later history of the family is obscure. The William McCrea who had died a few years earlier(*Volunteer Evening Post*, 12 Feb. 1784) may have been Samuel's brother, who in 1775 was said also to survey 'a little' (PRONI, T.2541/IA2/39). No Christian name was recorded for the 'Mr McCrea, a land surveyor, and an old man', who kept the school at Lifford, in 1812 (*Twelfth Report of Commissioners of Education*, p. 8, H.C. 1812 (218), v).

68. R. MacDaid, Typescript copy of grand jury presentments, Co. Donegal, 1793–8, p. 25, NLI, Ir. 94113.d.2. For the Monaghan survey see Malcomson, *Clogher Record*, 8 (1973), p. 63.

69. PRONI, County warrant books, Derr. 8/1 (1792–9); Grand jury to Revd G. V. Sampson, 20 Aug. 1824, Derr. 10/1.

70. Rodger, *Large Scale County Maps*, pp 41–4.

71. G. Montgomery, 20 Feb. 1813, PRONI, D.725/1.

72. J. H. Andrews, 'A Cork Cartographer's Advertising Campaign', *Jour. Cork Hist. & Arch. Soc.*, 84 (1979), pp 112–18.

73. For the sources of these verdicts see J. H. Andrews, 'Ireland in Maps: a Bibliographical Postscript', *Ir. Geogr.*, 4 (1962), p. 243, n. 59.

74. Nicholas Sinnott advertised a county map (otherwise unknown) of Waterford in *Waterford Mirror*, 7 Nov. 1804.

75. Hunt's diary, 7 Aug. 1813, NLI, mic. P.5527. Hunt spelt the name 'Lahy'. Proposals for a county map of Tipperary were subsequently invited (*Clonmel Advertiser*, 23 Apr. 1814), but no map later than Neville Bath's was mentioned in the grand jury's return to the select committee on the survey and valuation of Ireland in 1824. However, Patrick Leahy's map of the Killenaule coal district, 1824, mentions his survey of the barony of Slieveardagh made for the grand jury (NLI, 16.I. 17(1)).

76. *Hibernian Journal*, 1 July 1774. O'Connor's sponsors included Lorenzo Nixon, Christopher Myers and John Morrisson.

77. *Hibernian Chronicle*, 27 Aug. 1781; *Cork Evening Post*, 20 Apr. 1789.

78. *Saunders's News-letter*, 2 Feb. 1821.

79. British Library, *The American War of Independence, 1775–83* (London, 1975), p. 63.

80. *Hibernian Chronicle*, 6 Apr. 1786.

81. *Leinster Journal*, 27 Sep. 1786. See also R. M. Elmes, *Catalogue of Irish Topographical Prints and Original Drawings* (Dublin, 1975), p. 227.

82. In 1790 Pelham was instructed to employ one John Doud as a surveyor (Marquess of Lansdowne, *Glanerought*, p. 81). He did

however produce a map of Bearhaven in 1804 (Scottish Record Office, Edinburgh, RHP/3194).
83. Proposals for Pelham's map of Kerry, *Cork Advertiser*, 18 Aug. 1801. The map was not published but is said to have been the source for William Larkin's county map (also unpublished) of 1814. Neither of these surveyors seems likely to have been responsible for the anonymous pre-Ordnance Survey townland map of Kerry that survives in the National Library of Ireland (16.H.7). A number of references to Pelham are assembled in M. G. Moyles and P. de Brun, 'Charles O'Brien's Agricultural Survey of Kerry, 1800', *Jour. Kerry Arch. & Hist. Soc.*, 1 (1968), pp 73–100. His death 'last week' is reported in *Cork Mercantile Chronicle*, 1 Oct. 1806.
84. Andrews, *Geogr. Jour.*, 132 (1966), pp 53, 60.
85. 'Part of Mr Byers's county survey …', n.d., PRONI, D.671/M7/5A. Byers was paid a total of £150 in 1788–9 for a map that never materialised; in 1798 the grand jury was demanding its money back (PRONI, D.607/F/143).
86. I. H. Adams, 'George Taylor, a Surveyor o' Pairts', *Imago Mundi*, 27 (1975), pp 55–6.
87. J. H. Andrews, *Alexander Taylor and his Map of County Kildare* (Royal Irish Academy, Dublin, 1983).
88. Beaufort, *Memoir*, p. ix. Edgeworth's application for Taylor to be given leave to finish the map of Longford, O.P. 517/106/27. There are photocopies of Taylor's work on the map in NLI, 16.H.28.
89. *Belfast News-letter*, 27 May 1785 (Down); *Dublin Evening Post*, 23 Apr. 1793 (Co. Dublin).
90. *Robin's London and Dublin Magazine*, Mar. 1827, p. 229.
91. *Report on Survey and Valuation*, 1824, p. 77 (Alexander Nimmo).
92. Bogs commission minutes, 21 Sep. 1809.
93. *Report on Survey and Valuation*, 1824, pp 33 (J. L Foster), 64 (William Bald); H. Dutton, *A Statistical and Agricultural Survey of the County of Galway* (Dublin, 1824), p. 509. Apart from the maps mentioned in the reports on the bogs, and on survey and valuation, there are maps of Louth, Meath and Monaghan by Larkin at Headfort House, Kells, Co. Meath. His published maps of Galway and Meath were not very favourably noticed in Add. MS 40612. Much of his work must have been done by assistants. One of these, Mr Clarke, appears in Sir Vere Hunt's diary for 3 Sep. 1813 (NLI, mic. P.5527). He may have been the James Clarke who worked as a road surveyor for Alexander Nimmo and who later settled at Carrick-on-Shannon (*Roscommon and Leitrim Gazette*, 6 Sep. 1823).
94. Carte's proposals of 1 Jan. 1814, with related correspondence, NLI, MS 7825. *A Survey of the Publick Roads in the Barony of Upper Connelloe, County of Limerick, Divided by Parishes and Townlands. Projected and Arranged by Edward Carte, Esq., of Newcastle, in Said County, in the Year 1813* (Limerick, 1814). The folding map in T. Rice, *An Inquiry into the Effects of the Irish Grand Jury Laws* (London, 1815), may be based on

Carte's survey, which is unenthusiastically noticed in Jeffries Kingsley, *Standard County Book* (Dublin, 1838), p. 40.
95. Green, *Ulster Jour. Arch.*, 12 (1949), pp 14, 18–20.
96. NLI, Ainsworth reports, 15, p. 2955 (no. 435, Aylmer papers); *New Cork Evening Post*, 28 Jan. 1796. Taylor's map of Tully, Co. Kildare, is reproduced in NLI, mic. P.7086.
97. NLI, 16.F.11.
98. NLI, MS 3242. Griffith said that he had employed 'country surveyors' in all his surveys (*Report on Survey and Valuation*, 1824, pp 43–4).
99. James [*sic*] Neville's map was said in *Report on Survey and Valuation*, 1824, p. 374, to have been improved by Richard Neville in 1789 – but this was evidently a printer's transposition, for the publisher was collecting subscriptions in 1795 and the map does not seem to have been published until three years later (*Dublin Evening Post*, 13 June 1795, 31 Mar. 1798).
100. *Map of the Curragh of Kildare Shewing the Race Courses, Gentlemen's Seats etc. Accurately Described*, surveyed by Henery Walker, engraved by Kersting, in two sheets, 1807. The plates of this map (with patterns for printed linen engraved on the back) are in the Ordnance Survey Office, Dublin, where they are noticed in File 22970 (14 Dec. 1932). See also A. K. Longfield (Mrs Leask), 'Old Patterns for Irish Printed Linen', *Jour. Kildare Arch. Soc.*, 15 (1975–6), p. 494.
101. The model showed forty square miles of country on a platform measuring eight feet by five feet. Admission cost one shilling (*Hibernian Chronicle*, 27 Apr. 1786; *Cork Evening Post*, 21 Aug. 1786; *Dublin Evening Post*, 16 June 1787). All we know about the author is that he was 'a little outlandish ingenious fellow' (*Hibernian Chronicle*, 8 May 1786).
102. Allen's map and print business in Dame Street also dealt in 'masks, fancy dress, bows, quivers etc. for the masquerade' (*Dublin Journal*, 6 July 1780). A few years later Allen decided to retire (*Dublin Evening Post*, 6 July 1784) but changed his mind quickly enough and thoroughly enough for his firm to maintain an unbroken existence for another sixty years or so. It published a number of grand jury maps as well as Allen's own map of Dublin.
103. An example is Joseph James Byrne's 'Modern Plan of the Metropolis of Ireland' (1819). A new set of parish maps of Dublin was advertised in *Dublin Evening Post*, 18 Mar. 1828, by Lewis Hilton, surveyor and engineer, but they seem never to have been published. Hilton's prospects of success were poor, to judge from his very bad record in the government's Boundary Survey (Richard Griffith, 24 Oct. 1827 *et seq.*, NAI, 2A.26.67). An example of an important map that was not credited to any surveyor was William Faden's *A Plan of the City of Dublin Surveyed for the use of the Divisional Justices* (London, 1797). It seems likely that this was based on surveys by John Brownrigg, whose manuscript maps of three of the Justices' divisions are in NLI, 21.F.90.

12
Taxes and tithes

THE IRISH COUNTY CESS WAS A TAX levied on the owners or occupiers of land and used to pay for courts, gaols, the salaries of county officials, and the upkeep of roads and bridges. Its origins are unknown, but it is undoubtedly older than the practice of mapping or measuring land for public purposes. Even in the nineteenth century, when the cess was still being collected, no one seemed ready to venture much information about its history or about the principles on which the burden was shared. That became clear when Parliament tried to discover those principles, first in 1822 and later in 1824.[1] Not more than two counties were altogether unresponsive, but the facts supplied by the others proved disconcertingly meagre. Of the three – Armagh, Dublin and Limerick – that had based their scale of liability on recent information, only Armagh was in possession of an accurate survey.[2] Other counties had lists of numerical acreages without being able to say where they came from: they were for parts of Kildare and Longford, and for Meath, Kilkenny, Leitrim, Louth, Queen's Co. and Westmeath. In another seven counties or part-counties the cess was calculated on unknown principles or levied from ancient units of uncertain magnitude. These were Cavan (carvaghs), Fermanagh (tates), part of Longford (cartrons), Kerry, Cork and Waterford (all ploughlands), and Donegal (unspecified).

Then there were counties whose representatives simply consulted a book or key of uncertain inspiration and dubious provenance. In most cases the document in question was described as old or ancient or immemorial or of unknown date, Londonderry coming nearest to historical precision with the theory of a link between its cess and the seventeenth-century plantation.[3] Finally, some statements actually contained the word 'survey'. In the inquiries of the 1820s, the only counties that mentioned the Down Survey by name were Down, King's Co. and Tipperary, though Westmeath may be added on the basis of other evidence and in 1808 it was said of Ireland in general that 'in many instances' the apportionment of the cess depended on Petty's maps.[4] Monaghan cited a survey of William III's time, perhaps a copy of some earlier original. The Wicklow surveys were 'very old', but nobody said how old. Of all the assessments, the earliest that can be identified was the Strafford Survey, still doing duty in Clare, Galway and Mayo – and probably also in Sligo and Roscommon, where there is evidence of its use in the eighteenth century.[5]

None of this gave a very firm foundation for a tax which by the 1820s was raising about £750,000 per year.[6] Everyone knew that Irish local taxation had got seriously out of line with the realities of acreage and productivity. Not only had surveying methods improved, but cultivation had been greatly extended, leaving huge tracts of inhabited country untaxed and others wrongly taxed. In Waterford for example there was one ploughland of 180 acres and another of 8,000 acres paying the same amount.[7] A county short of revenue had the same motive for surveying its townlands as a landlord short of rent had for surveying his farms, and the same hope that the profits arising from such a survey would be proportional to the lapse of time that had preceded it.

Similar irregularities beset the administration of another time-honoured impost that was meant to be based on agricultural productivity. Tithes, which had originally amounted to one-tenth of the produce of each parish, were as old as the parochial system itself.[8] In Ireland they aroused much dissatisfaction, partly because so few Irishmen adhered to the established church and also because of irregularities in the way they were collected. Whatever may have been justified in the past, by the eighteenth century there was little to be said for the current practice of exempting pasture from tithe, or for the unpredictability of certain other exemptions, with potatoes for instance being tithable in some districts but not in others. As a further anomaly, in some parishes payment was in kind and in others by a fixed sum, while elsewhere the crops were subject to a process of annual valuation which might require a more or less accurate reckoning of the area under tillage. As one writer pointed out, it would hardly become a minister of the gospel to go about his parish carrying a chain;[9] instead the crops were valued by an official called the tithe proctor. Because of the unpopularity of tithes the position of proctor often went to a person 'of a very inferior situation, and not of the best character'.[10] No doubt some surveyors could be thus described but the proctor was seldom a professional measurer, and his survey probably consisted of walking over the land to look at the crops or at most of pacing the length and breadth of the fields.[11]

Such were the circumstances, civil and ecclesiastical, that led eventually to a complete admeasurement of Ireland by the officers of the Ordnance Survey. Before that, the land surveyor's relationship with taxing and tithing may be divided into four periods, or rather four overlapping sequences of events and non-events. The first, in the later seventeenth century, included some remarkably thoroughgoing attempts to solve the whole problem. The Commonwealth government, geographically radical in so many ways, made a gesture towards discovering the acreage and corn output that was tithable in each parish,[12] but the main preoccupation of the 1650s was with the counties. In July 1657 commissioners for the assessment of Co. Antrim decided to obtain estimates and surveys from each barony. In the following year steps were taken instead to measure the same baronies afresh and it was not long before bets were being laid on the relative sizes of two of them.[13] This was evidently a distinct operation from the Down Survey, most of which had been completed for Co. Antrim two or three years earlier. (Perhaps Richard Dobbs's reference, in 1683, to a Major Carrol Bolton who had measured Island Magee was occasioned by this later survey.)[14] There is no record of the interiors of the Antrim baronies being mapped by the commissioners, but it is perhaps significant that in the south of the county Petty's printed maps of 1685 show more detail than any of his own manuscript barony and parish maps.

Though not part of the Down Survey, this Antrim admeasurement may have been done at least in part by surveyors who had previously worked for Petty. Further south a similar inference is supported by a book of Co. Dublin maps bearing the date 1658 and the signatures of the two former Down Surveyors, Thomas Taylor and Edward Lucas. The maps profess to have been 'performed in pursuance of a contract made with the honourable commissioners for the assessment of the said county'. They are drawn at scales of eighty or sixty perches to the inch in typical Down Survey style, but show much that the original surveyors had omitted, notably the names, outlines and areas of a number of unforfeited townlands.[15] Elsewhere the evidence is sparser. From Queen's Co. comes a printed map of the barony of Upper Ossory described as 'a particular survey of all the lands, forfeited and unforfeited Protestant lands, church and glebe lands, school house lands etc'. It carries the name of R. Bolton as well as those of five members of Petty's original staff.[16] Its eighteenth-century editor considered this to have been one of the maps given to debenture-holders at the time of the Down Survey, but the inclusion of Protestant lands suggests that further work had been done on it later. There is also a manuscript map of the barony of Scarawalsh in Co. Wexford which includes Protestant townlands not mentioned in Petty's parish maps, along with acreage figures that differ from those of the Civil Survey.[17]

The purpose of these various maps and assessments is a problem for future research (perhaps it was the maintenance of the army under a government order of 1654), but they cannot have given adequate coverage of the whole country, for in 1665 Parliament still considered Petty's maps and descriptions to be incomplete.[18] By this time Petty himself was otherwise engaged, and evidence of further progress at either national or local level is disappointingly sparse. Some of it comes from Westmeath, where Protestant lands absent from the Down Survey were said to have been 'discovered' in 1675 and where other tracts got into the county book after being newly surveyed by 'Major Garstin' (perhaps the Simon Garstin of the Down Survey or a relation), possibly in the first instance for private estate purposes.[19]

Another interesting case was that of Cork. Here the question of county cartography was raised in a letter of 1670 from John Kealy, evidently a surveyor, to Philip Ford. Kealy's immediate subject was two townlands which had been left unsurveyed – in the Down Survey, he meant – as reputedly Protestant. He added that he had these areas on a barony map, but could not bring them to the scale of the 'great map' without committing an error. He also mentioned a 'book survey' of the Protestant interest in Cork which he and Mr Taylor (this must be Thomas Taylor) had made up in 1659, and asked to be sent a trace from this book. Since Kealy was in Dublin and Ford in Cork, the book would seem to have been in the possession of the county authorities. Once he got the trace, Kealy concluded, 'your maps will be as perfect as your heart can wish'.[20] Here, unmistakably, is an attempt at a complete county map, possibly the source of the barony map mentioned by Sir Richard Cox in 1687[21] and of the copies that Sir John Perceval was seeking in 1712.[22] At the time of Perceval's inquiry the originals were in Bandon, and one of them had 'every gentleman's names to the several denominations that were then given out to them'. All of which suggests an amended Down Survey rather than the kind of small-scale topographical county map that became familiar after the middle of the eighteenth century. Perceval left no such map among his papers, though he did own a book listing the acreages of all the denominations in the county.[23] The Taylor 'book survey', or a copy of it, was acquired by an early eighteenth-century bishop of Cork.[24] The main point of the story is that a hundred years later Cork was assessed at a fixed value per ploughland, its representatives denying that there had ever been such a thing as a county book.[25] Whoever made off with the county's last copies of these records went somewhat further than was requisite to show how Cromwellian *dirigisme* had dissolved into a much longer second period of inaction and timidity.

The new eighteenth-century mood had already received statutory expression. Earlier Irish legislation on the subject of road maintenance had appeared to lay special emphasis on the ploughland as a territorial unit,[26] and after eighty years or so the law was proving difficult to impose on counties where the ploughland was unheard of. The remedy, according to Queen Anne's Parliament, was for counties with ploughlands to translate them into acres, and for other grand juries to do the same with whatever corresponded to a ploughland under their jurisdiction.[27] The phrasing of the new act, with its rather casual reference to 'what number of acres ... shall be taken for, and construed to consist of, and be, a ploughland', seems to make this a quite arbitrary equation, analogous to those that had proved so troublesome in the plantations of a hundred years earlier, and there is little sign that any county saw the act as an invitation to make a new survey. Public attitudes to the resulting lull were mixed. One writer on agriculture took it for granted that the high constables' barony books would show the exact number of acres in every denomination.[28] In other quarters these local records inspired a certain amount of mistrust. It was not that the old surveys were themselves inaccurate or out of date, but rather that Justices of the Peace had deliberately understated the number of acres in many denominations and then covered their tracks by amalgamating more than one denomination under a single name, thus reducing the burden of tax on those proprietors whom they wished to favour. This at least was the opinion of the well-known antiquarian Edward Ledwich.[29] Mayo was one county whose officials were suspected of tampering with the county book.[30]

Confronted with this kind of fiscal gerrymandering (real or imaginary) in the counties, several writers recommended a return to whatever statistics might be obtainable from some more central repository. A local historian in Co. Tipperary, quoting the county books as for the moment the most accessible source, hoped later to correct his barony acreages from data in the Surveyor-General's office.[31] More noteworthy was a proposal addressed to the grand jury of Galway in 1786. Its author welcomed the prospect of a new county map for road planning purposes as contemplated by Parliament twelve years earlier. He also deplored the burden of the cess and what he thought to be the consequent danger of Ireland's acquiring too many roads. The overcharge was due, he contended, to the subdividing of townlands since the compilation of the county books, so that a sum meant for a whole townland was now being levied several times from different proprietors.[32] It was the exact opposite of Ledwich's argument, but each criticism may have been true of its own area. The Galway writer's quixotic remedy for out-of-dateness was to disinter the Strafford Survey, whose acreage figures he would have been happy to see printed in the margin of a 1780s county map. Such palpable antiquarianism was not unusual. The Kennedy map of Co. Down published in 1755 undertook to show the 'original' denominations but not the ones into which so many of them had since been subdivided. Rocque in Armagh and Wren in Louth were other county cartographers who went back to Petty for some of their territorial boundaries.

The next attempt by Parliament to probe the roots of Ireland's administrative geography was not very vigorous either. An act of 1809, regretting that some counties had no county book at all, or none that gave the contents of the denominations, empowered the grand juries of such counties to produce a 'table' of names and areas to fill the gap.[33] Since the results had to be compact enough to fit onto a church door it seems unlikely that 'table' was still carrying its old sense of map. And at this point it must be emphasised (what should be fairly clear already) that the 'grand jury' maps discussed in the previous chapter were not meant to give the areas of anything smaller than a parish, the money allowed by Parliament for such maps amounting to only an insignificant fraction, per unit area, of the average land surveyor's charge for measuring a townland. Not even the most careful contemporary methods could reach that far down the territorial hierarchy on a map of only one or two inches to the mile. To measure a barony or parish at such a scale was perhaps rather more reasonable, and some perfectionists objected when the acreages of these divisions were omitted from their county map.[34] But grand juries did not necessarily take advantage of such figures even when they already had them. In Mayo William Bald's barony areas varied from twice to eleven times those of the county books, yet nothing was done to eliminate the differences.[35]

Meanwhile church had been no more active than state in applying cartography to its financial problems. Ireland's nearest approach to an ecclesiastical Petty was William King, who circularised his archdiocese requesting names and acreages for the townlands in each parish.[36] He is unlikely to have supposed that many of his respondents would pay a surveyor to tell them the answer. It is true that in due time Ireland produced a large number of parish maps: in one period of fifteen months the Ordnance Survey's boundary department inspected ninety-eight of them.[37] But far from serving as a source of acreages, such maps seem generally to have treated townlands in the same way that parishes were treated on the more modest kinds of diocesan map.[38] The only accurate cartographic surveys that an incumbent could be expected to have in his possession were maps of the Church's own property. From the seventeenth century these were made in the manner and by the methods of ordinary estate cartography – sometimes involving clergymen in the kind of unseemly territorial dispute familiar among their parishioners.[39] The most common ecclesiastical survey was the glebe terrier, done to show the bishop on his visitation, in which one or more small maps accompanied a description of the church and its appointments with a note on the rector's sources of income.[40] In some dioceses glebe maps were carefully preserved[41] but few glebes were larger than a normal-sized townland and some were only drops in the parochial ocean; where a terrier gave the area of the entire parish it is probably safe to assume that this had been copied from the county books. The latter at any rate were the source from which parish acreages had to be obtained when the Board of First Fruits made new rules for the building of churches in 1759.[42]

Terriers and glebe maps did nothing to solve the problem of tithes, and until the nineteenth century neither did any other kind of map. But it was tithes that inaugurated a third and more eventful (though still not very constructive) period in the history of Irish official cadastralism, a period in which public and private surveys were linked in a new mesh of shifting and uneasy relationships. The trouble started with the tithe controversy of the 1780s. One point emerging from the polemics of that decade is that tithe owners seem to have disclaimed any legal right to survey land of which they were neither the tenant nor the proprietor in fee; or rather they hesitated to exercise this right for fear of arousing hostility. Yet many of the opposing party – in this pre-revolutionary period more concerned with equalising the charge than with abolishing it – were anxious to see the process of valuing for tithes improved. There were the inevitable appeals to the Down Survey and the county books, but the agitators known as 'Rightboys' who challenged the tithe system in Co. Cork insisted in their manifesto that the incumbent should employ two honest sworn appraisers, 'and if one of the two be not a surveyor, it may be lawful for the people to exclaim against the valuation', a consummation no doubt meant to be less anti-climactic than it sounded.[43] In the end the only practical outcome, for surveyors, of this early attack on tithes was an act of Parliament which in 1793 gave a seven-year exemption from tithe on all land reclaimed from the waste.[44] With typical Irish bipartisanship the applicant for such exemption had to produce a survey verified by the oaths of two surveyors, one nominated by the proprietor or occupier of the reclaimed land and the other by the incumbent of the parish.

These troubles of the 'eighties and 'nineties revealed a wide spread of opinion on official large-scale cartography. A few commentators, like Henry Grattan in 1788, favoured some kind of general government survey.[45] For others, such an expensive luxury had been rendered unnecessary by private estate maps already in existence.[46] Forty years later the issue was rejoined, more intensely and more conclusively. The tithe composition act of 1823 allowed the tithe payers and the tithe owner in any parish each to nominate a commissioner, these two officers then fixing a sum for the entire parish and a proportion of that sum for each contributor.[47] The amounts might be determined either by simple agreement, or from an average of earlier payments, or by a calculation based on recent corn prices. The act empowered commissioners to make their own admeasurement if they thought fit, or else – in what had now become a common formula – to use any existing plan, survey, estimate or valuation of whose authenticity and accuracy they were satisfied. A hundred years earlier, the Surveyor-General might have been directed to choose the necessary surveyors. Now no instructions were given – not even for the assessment of authenticity and accuracy in earlier surveys. It was quite unlike the procedure adopted for the English tithe maps less than two decades later,[48] but by this time the prospect of a new all-purpose official survey may have inhibited Parliament from discussing Ireland's cadastral problems in any detail.

The immediate sequel to the act of 1823 was described by George Lidwill[49] in the following year:

> The Down Survey is capriciously defective; but every landlord, and most of the tenants in each parish, have correct surveys of their respective properties; and, some might be inclined to leave the [tithe] commissioners to the Down Survey, when that would give an advantage in the applotment, if he could get no other but that; but when the commissioner has the power, at an expense to the parish, to cause a new

survey, the landlords will, to save expense, give the maps and surveys; which will, to an acre, tell the exact number the parish contains.

'County book' figures of Down Survey origin do sometimes appear in the tithe applotments,[50] though in most parishes they were evidently rejected as inaccurate; they would certainly have kept the average tithe-payer's liability well below its rightful figure. But even without the Down Survey, composition was expected to favour the parishioner, and by 1830 more than half the country's parishes had compounded.[51]

An early instance of Lidwill's speculations being translated into reality came from the parish of Ballinahagliss, Co. Mayo, in February 1824. After a warning that a new survey might be imminent, proprietors were at once reminded that the use of existing information would 'of course' save the expense of an *ad hoc* admeasurement.[52] To judge from the meagre published data, such reminders often proved effective in discouraging extravagant outlay on surveyors. David Aher, valuing for tithes in Co. Kilkenny, found some farmers unwilling to produce their maps, but when he sent men to measure the small holdings (the implication being perhaps that it was only the small farms that would not already have private maps) the other occupiers changed their minds. Another commissioner used not maps, but tenants' leases and receipts, to establish the acreage and rent of each farm. A third simply asked both owner and tenant to state the quantity of their lands; only if the answers were contradictory did he have a surveyor 'run the chain round the land, without making a minute survey of each person's holding'.[53] Such methods were unlikely to produce much creditable cartography, even from a professional surveyor. Nicholas Sinnot was employed by a tithe commissioner to measure part of a parish in Co. Kilkenny with a chain, but the only map he agreed to hand in was 'a sketch'. The sketch was allegedly never produced. In the rest of the parish it may never have been promised: there, all Sinnot did was assist in the calculation of areas – without the chain, as our informant makes a point of remarking.[54]

In theory this fragmentary evidence could be checked against the tithe applotment books themselves, many of which are preserved in the Public Record Offices of Ireland and Northern Ireland. Unfortunately the only person known to have gone through more than a small proportion of them and given some account of his findings is the man later appointed as the government's chief valuator, Richard Griffith. In his opinion, out of 1,539 parishes compounded only 498 had been accurately valued, while in 1,468 parishes there were only 384 valuations for which he was able to find any use in his own work.[55] His report at least proves, if proof be needed, that the tithe valuations had not been made on uniform principles, and that for general public purposes it would still be necessary to conduct the kind of centrally-directed survey that Griffith himself had now been commissioned to carry out. Otherwise his remarks are not very helpful. A bad valuation does not imply a bad survey, badness being in any case an elusive concept where a valuator's talents are in question.

Nor did Griffith distinguish the relative merits of the existing surveys and those that had been specially made for tithe purposes, and indeed the form of the documents would have made this difficult and perhaps impossible. To begin with an apparently attractive line of inference, nothing can be deduced from the identities of the commissioners. Even when they were known land surveyors (which was not often, though both Robert Nolan and Richard Brassington served as commissioners on occasion)[56] it does not follow that the applotment required them to practise their craft. The books also say little of methods and sources, let alone of their indebtedness to particular surveys by particular individuals. One exception occurred at Lismore, Co. Waterford, where the commissioners said that a general survey would have cost double the statutory maximum expense allowed for the applotment.[57] Another exception was at Ballyshannon and Kilrush, Co. Kildare, which unlike Lismore did acquire a complete set of farm maps, though since the surveyor was one of the local churchwardens his charges may have been unusually low.[58] In general, most commissioners appear to have taken a course that happens to be documented at Tumna in Co. Roscommon. Here it was only a few farms that were explicitly said to have been surveyed afresh, either because they had been recently reclaimed from the waste (too recently to appear in the landlord's private surveys) or else because of exceptional unresponsiveness among the locals – as on the farm that was 'surveyed in consequence of Mr Corr the agent not giving the map of the Coothall property after sending a special messenger for it to Frenchpark, a distance of 25 miles'.[59]

For most parishes the only evidence of method comes from the acreages and values that the applotters entered in their book. The great disappointment here is the maps that accompany a proportion of the applotments. Some are glebe terriers, some are general location diagrams, some are old estate maps that seem to have found their way into the tithe books almost by accident. But by far the largest category are what might be called 'certificate maps'. Under a statute of 1832 (which among other things had the effect of making tithe composition obligatory for the first time) certain kinds of landholder could qualify for a reduction in liability by means of a formal undertaking to pay the composition for a specified portion of a parish. Such persons would then receive a certificate to that effect from the incumbent, together with what the act called a 'map or terre chart or ground plan' of the lands in question.[60] The purpose of these maps, which in practice were probably supplied by the tithe payer, was to show the location of the lands and not their quality or quantity. In one sense they are far from uninformative, for they make it painfully clear that whatever may be said about other departments of estate cartography, there was no Irish tradition of the separate boundary map. Even ignoring anomalous maps that were copied from originals made for some different purpose, the certificate maps show an extraordinary range of variation. A few are full of detail, correctly scaled and oriented, and drawn with care and artistry by professional surveyors.[61] Others are mere outlines showing only the names of bordering denominations.[62] Some cartographers, still within the letter of the law, unblushingly reduced the shape of their parish to four straight lines;[63] this was playing safe with a vengeance, though even with a simple rectangle it is possible for east and west to be shown the wrong way round (Plate 28).

What all the certificate maps fail to throw light on is how the composition was actually applotted. But it is clear from the tabulated figures that there was support among the commissioners for both the systems of land assessment favoured by contemporary Irish farm and estate surveyors. One was to return an acreage and value for each kind of land use or land capacity – arable, pasture, mountain and so on. The other did the same for grades of land labelled simply first-class, second-class, and in at least one remarkable case all the way down to an eighteenth class. In both kinds of classification the tithe applotters' farm acreages look remarkably precise, specific numbers of roods and perches being appended in the style of a true land survey.

Tithes were not the last official valuation problem which private surveyors could be expected to help solve. When grand juries started awakening to their responsibilities in this field the experience of the tithe composition was closely paralleled. A former Cork county treasurer, boldly stating the area of Ireland's largest county to the nearest perch in 1830, appears to have derived his information not from any comprehensive survey, but from 'the kind of knowledge which is very general in Ireland, the actual territorial extent of every man's tenure'.[64] He did not say what

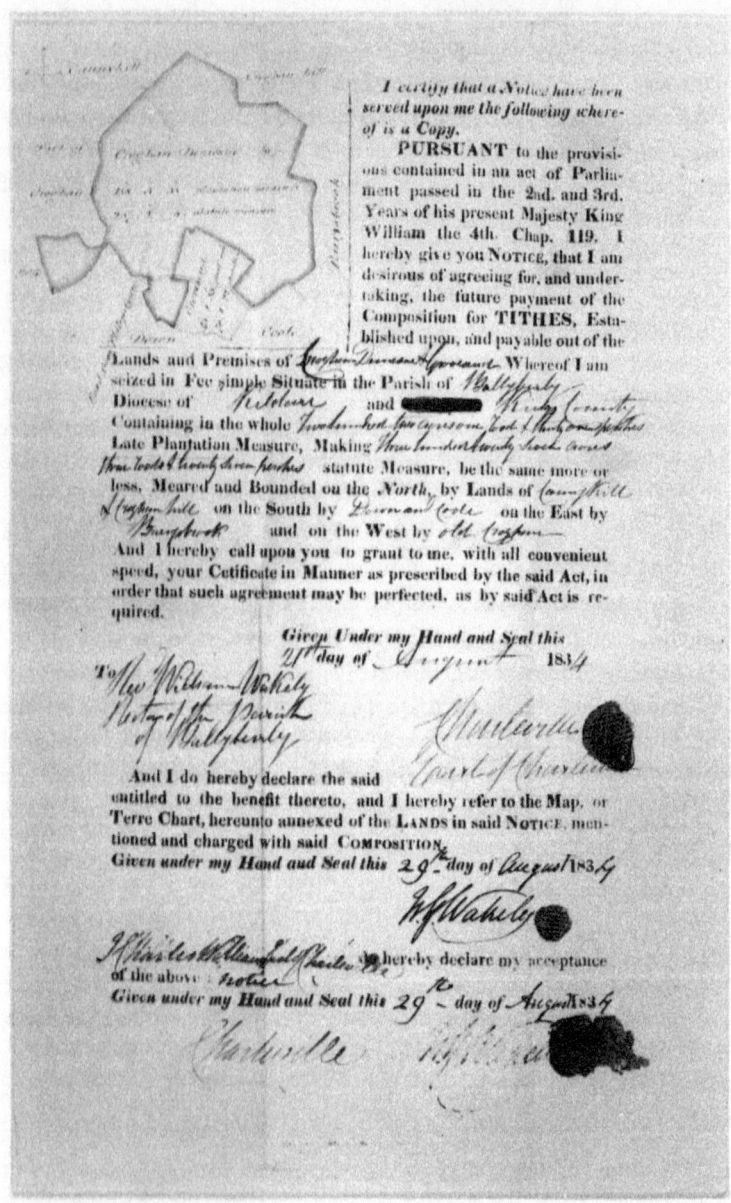

Plate 28. Manuscript map of part of Ballyburly parish, Co. Offaly, 1834 (NAI, TAB 15/6), on a printed tithe certificate signed by the rector and the landowner. Scale of original about 3½ inches to one statute mile.

had been done about the mountains, where much land was still measured by its stockraising capacity and not by acres, let alone perches. At this point it must be remembered that the official survey conducted by the Board of Ordnance (of which more later) had started at the other end of the country and that its initial progress was disappointingly slow. The Ordnance Survey had still not reached Waterford when that county was made the subject of its own special valuation in 1837, another venture in which the calculation of acreages from local sources was not felt to present an insurmountable problem.[65] A number of other counties were still without an Ordnance map when the poor relief act was passed in 1838. This laid a new charge on the land, for which each holding had to be separately valued. The act authorised every Board of Poor Law Guardians to make a valuation of its allotted territory or 'union'.[66] The guardians were not positively forbidden to make their own surveys, but in a useful summary of the current state of Irish cartography the government made it clear that so costly an expedient was unlikely to be needed:

> Wherever the Ordnance Survey is not completed, it is probable that from one or other of the following sources the means of estimating the quantities of land may be derived: 1st, the maps, by which leases are frequently accompanied; 2nd, other private surveys and maps; 3rd, the valuations made under the several acts relating to tithes. And should all these fail, recourse may be had to the local knowledge of parties, or to the evidence which common reputation frequently supplies, of the quantity of land in any given enclosure or farm.[67]

Of course, acreages and valuations which passed muster in pre-Ordnance Survey times were not necessarily good in an objective sense. Even so, the experience of the 1830s and 1840s shows how much had been done by private Irish surveyors, unsupervised and unco-ordinated, since the days of the Down Survey. What they had effected was nothing less than a quiet revolution in the Irishman's knowledge of his country. Yet the revolution was far from complete. Many bogs and mountains remained unaccounted for, not all the lowlands had been covered in full and equal detail, and much of the information collected was still hidden from the public at large. In any case the idea of a strictly uniform survey of Ireland, familiarised so long ago among indoor map-enthusiasts by Petty and others, had not been totally buried by this vast accumulation of data. Sooner or later such an enterprise would have to be taken seriously enough for the details of its procedure and organisation to be discussed in depth, thus initiating a fourth phase in the development of a national cartographic policy. This last period, in which the prospect of some great public gesture was generally taken for granted, may be said to begin in 1815 with a classic report from the select committee on grand jury presentments and to culminate nine years later with an even more memorable inquiry on the forthcoming survey and valuation of Ireland.[68] But even now the break with the past was not quite final. There was still a lingering belief among both experts and laymen that earlier maps might somehow be spliced into a new all-Ireland survey. And no one envisaged such a survey as doing all that was to be done by the men of the Ordnance when it came to the point.

At first the discussion of these matters was less important than the problem of who should do the discussing. As the debate developed three parties became distinguishable. In one corner stood a small but influential group of politicians and administrators, some with first-hand experience of employing land surveyors and of studying large-scale maps in a private capacity on their own Irish estates. None of them would claim any great depth of cartographic knowledge, but all seem to have felt the attraction of a fully scientific map, and it was their respect for scientific integrity that gave prominence to a second, more exotic, group comprising the military officers and other senior staff of the British Ordnance Survey department. In this concentration of talent there was inevitably little knowledge of Irish land tenure or Irish public finance; few Ordnance Survey officers knew much about Ireland at all. But they could colourably claim an almost total monopoly, among witnesses accessible to the United Kingdom government, of expertise in military mapping and in the higher reaches of trigonometrical surveying and geodesy. Both parties, political and military, agreed that any new survey of Ireland, whatever its detailed character, should attain the high mathematical standards that had been governing the Ordnance Survey's work in Britain since its foundation in the 1790s.

Between the Irish laymen and the British experts stood the topographical engineers who had been working so tirelessly on Ireland's bogs, roads and harbours. They knew the Irish landscape and the problems of mapping it. It is true that they lacked the highest scientific qualifications, and that in the absence of a professional institute or society they had no means of speaking with one voice. But it would have been foolish to disregard their advice, and nobody did. It was different with the Irish land surveyors proper. Their advice was ignored by everybody. The only one of their number to address the committee of 1824 was Patrick Kelly, a person otherwise almost unknown to map history who happened to be a doctor of laws and may have been chosen as spokesman on that account. The rest of the profession was limited to a shadowy offstage existence in the generally disapproving or condescending observations of its betters. This was undeniably a snub, and the Irish surveying community never got over it.

Not that the surveyors would have disagreed with the government's other sources of cartographic wisdom. They may have felt that the scale of 1:10,080 suggested by Richard Griffith was too small for a national survey, preferring William Edgeworth's recommendation for 1:5,280 or 1:6,720 (depending on whether Edgeworth's miles were English or Irish) or even Bald's advocacy of 1:3,024. Any of these scales would have been sufficient for denomination-boundaries, roads, buildings and the essentials of land quality. Support could also have been mustered among land surveyors for the various classification systems put forward at this time, most of them combining use (e.g. woods), capacity (e.g. arable), value (e.g. good, ordinary) and character (e.g. boggy, mountainous). It was all firmly in the tradition of Irish estate surveying – though not of the French school, for the depiction of field boundaries still seemed undesirable to many map-users, including the select committee of 1824 itself.

The main subject of debate was not the end-product of the survey but its organisation, the problem being to decide at which level of the Irish territorial hierarchy executive control should be concentrated or divided. In this respect what interests the map historian most is the actual unit of mapping, in other words the largest parcel of land that was to appear on one sheet or as a block of filled-up rectangles capable of being assembled into a mosaic. Some witnesses favoured the parish, others the barony. The idea of the multi-sheet county map (which is what the Ordnance Survey ultimately supplied) does not seem to have arisen at this early stage, though neighbouring parishes or baronies could be regarded as marriageable and one writer suggested erecting inscribed stones along the parish boundaries to ensure a network of common points.[69] For contemporary cartographers the relevant question was how many baronies would come under one surveyor's authority, which depended in turn on whether his employer was a county or the state. In Ireland neither of these bodies was ready with its own surveying agency. The counties could claim more experience of employing surveyors (notably for the grand jury maps) but they could not always claim more success. To put the verdict at its kindest, they had failed to create a uniform standard in either style, content or merit; and although Ireland's best topographical engineers were generally thought capable of remedying these defects, there were not enough of them for every county to be employing one at the same time.

At the national level there were two possibilities. On the one hand a committee of Irish engineers could have agreed on a general specification and then divided the country among themselves into a manageable number of districts, which is how the bogs survey of 1810–13 had been organised to most people's satisfaction. Although it would have been generally acceptable in Ireland, this course had been eliminated in advance by calling in the Ordnance Survey. The officers of the Royal Engineers had little enthusiasm for devolutionary principles; they distrusted any kind of surveying except their own. But like their civilian colleagues they were not numerous enough to survey the whole of Ireland in the time required by the government. The solution, most observers thought, was some kind of partnership in which the Ordnance would be the dominant member, supplying not only the trigonometrical and other scientific foundations for the new map of Ireland but also the rules and discipline under which its boundaries and topography would be filled in. No one expected the silent majority of Ireland's common surveyors or even its gentlemen surveyors to have much influence on the final specification. Even without their conspicuous absence from nineteenth-century committee rooms, there were many earlier precedents for passing them over when senior staff were under recruitment for major cartographic programmes. But however discriminatingly chosen, and however closely supervised, a number of ordinary land surveyors would surely be given at least a subordinate role. That was what every Irish commentator would have wrongly predicted, even after the Ordnance had been placed in charge of the new survey in June 1824. However, the immediate effect of this last decision was to bring all arguments and predictions to an end. The Ordnance Survey was to incur much criticism in Ireland for proceeding too slowly and too expensively; but only a few Irishmen complained in public about the way it chose its personnel, and fewer still had any complaints about the content or format of the resulting maps.

All this demonstrates the massive and indeed intimidating prestige enjoyed in the early 1820s by the Ordnance Survey in general and in particular by the Duke of Wellington, who happened to be the government minister in charge of it. What sort of maps the Irish authorities would have got if the Survey had stayed in Britain may be an inadmissably hypothetical question. Yet the answer seems fairly clear: they would have been maps like William Armstrong's. This gifted but little-known surveyor deserves more than a passing mention. Beginning soon after the new century, his career showed that it was not just the bogs and Post Office surveyors who could claim the highest places in Irish cartography. By 1821, with offices in both Armagh and Dublin, and with assistants good enough to work without supervision, he was advertising a full span of services, among them valuation and the quasi-legal task of 'examining the original titles from the ancient records'.[70] He surveyed roads as well as estates and his close attention to slopes recalls the best work of the military engineers and their civilian disciples. He too described himself as an engineer, and there is something reminiscent of mechanical drawing in the strongly shaded capital letters by which he simulated three-dimensional artifacts cut out of metal or cast in relief. Doubtfully attractive in itself, this stylistic detail helps to indicate the breadth of Armstrong's cartographic synthesis.[71]

With such a background Armstrong was equipped to tackle the most widely-evaded task in the whole of post-medieval cartography, that of integrating the regional map with the estate map – or, in practical Irish terms, of making a map that could be used by both cess-applotters and road planners. It was a challenge that carries the mind back through several centuries of map history. Jobson, Raven and the authors of a host of estate indexes had sought the same object by a marked reduction of scale and an equally ruthless simplification or omission of detail. Petty had solved the problem, or rather sidestepped it, by means of a cartographic hierarchy in which the defects of each scale could be remedied at one of the other scales. But Petty had inherited a tradition of degrading the estate map into a network of frontiers, the equivalent of a political map. Rocque, a century later, had done exactly the opposite: his county maps were meant to look like a mosaic of farm surveys, but commercial pressures forced him into smaller scales and quicker methods than his topographical sense required, and the resulting element of deception in his work was easily detectable. No one would have tried to use Rocque's map of Co. Armagh for purposes of local valuation, and the same could in all probability be said of the McCreas' lost successor to it, for after Rocque the landscape of the individual townland was largely ignored by county cartographers, and the few townland boundaries shown on their maps were frankly diagrammatic.[72] Even William Bald's magnificent and expensive map of Mayo was useless for the valuation of townlands, as his local critics kept pointing out.[73]

Armstrong brooked no compromise. In scale, style and substance the map he embarked upon in 1818 for the grand jury of Co. Armagh was exactly like the maps he made for individual landlords: its only 'regional' feature was the amount of space it covered. Of course it is never desirable (though very common) to praise a large-scale map without first applying some test of planimetric accuracy, but there is nothing ridiculous about comparing Armstrong's map with the earliest six-inch sheets of the Irish Ordnance Survey (Plate 29). Such a comparison must be carefully structured, however, and the familiar six-inch engravings must be left out of it. The Survey's original intention had been to furnish the government's valuators with a series of manuscript six-inch plans, to be followed some time later by a one-inch military and topographical map of Ireland. As a way of unifying different cartographic conceptions, this was just as evasive as Petty's, especially as different parishes were to be drawn on different sheets. By contrast each of Armstrong's maps covered a whole barony, and his scale (forty statute perches to an inch or 1:7,920) was considerably larger than six inches. Like the Ordnance Survey he shows a full range of territorial divisions with an acreage figure written across each townland. He omits field boundaries – but then so do the earliest Ordnance maps. The two surveys are likewise on a par in their treatment of roads, houses, rivers, bogs, marshes and woods; almost on a par, too, in displaying their mathematical framework, for Armstrong included a number of base lines and a selection of rays drawn from trigonometrical stations. He also scores with the kind of capricious extra detail attractive to all but the most puritanical of map-readers, such as the holy well that was frequented on the first three Sundays of May and August. Some of this information would have been eschewed on principle by the Ordnance Survey (the names of local residents for example), but its officers would have been jealous of Armstrong's subtle and delicate hill shading, particularly as they had decided after some heart-searching to omit relief from the earliest versions of their own six-inch plans.

Like several of his fellow land surveyors Armstrong offered his services to the Ordnance Survey soon after its arrival, not realising that their pay for civilians would be four shillings a day[74] instead of the two guineas that he could earn for personal attendance on private clients. The Survey chiefs for their part had nothing to offer Armstrong, but they did need his maps as evidence for the townland boundaries of Co. Armagh, and took it amiss when he insisted on keeping them in his own possession. (He even refused to allow the maps in the grand jury room except

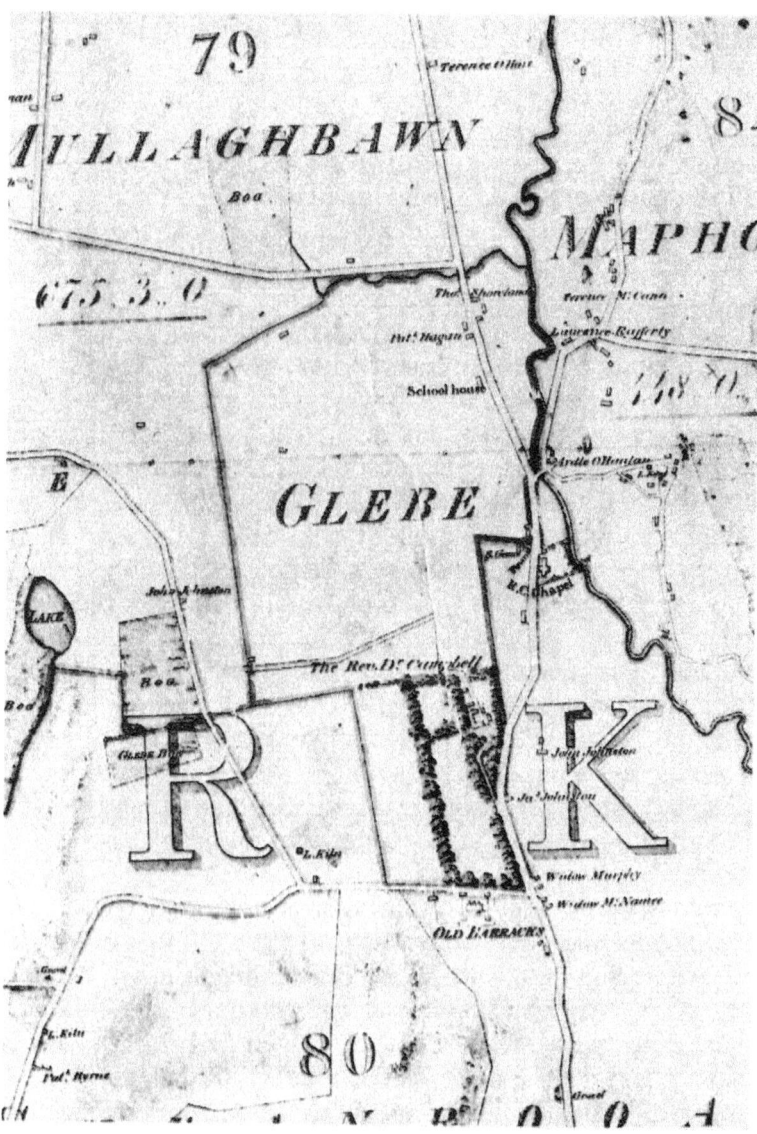

Plate 29. Part of the parish of Forkill, from William Armstrong's manuscript map of the barony of Orior, Co. Armagh, 1827 (see chapter 12, note 75). The two-digit numbers refer to a separate list of townlands, printed for certain other baronies of Armagh in *Report on Survey and Valuation*, 1824, pp 166–80. Other numbers give townland areas in statute acres, roods and perches.

during the assizes, which may help to explain why they are not now in the county offices, and why indeed only one of the baronies appears to survive.)[75] There followed an unfortunate misunderstanding about the Survey's right of access to Armstrong's work, with the author allegedly trying to exact payment for showing it and the Ordnance officers poised to retaliate by postponing their own survey of Armagh as a 'mark of discredit'.[76] It was a dramatisation in brief of the conflict between old and new cartographies, but Armagh got its Ordnance map in the end and so did every other Irish county. No other county got a privately-made map like Armstrong's. He had solved Ireland's cartographic problem, but he had solved it too late.

Notes

1. *Reports from the Select Committee on Grand Jury Presentments*, Ireland, H.C. 1822 (353, 413, 451), vii. *Report on Survey and Valuation*, 1824.
2. One 'county of a city' should be included in this reckoning. Under local acts of Parliament (53 George III, c. 111; 55 George III, c. 82) two surveyors were hired to survey the liberties of Cork city in *c.* 1813 (*Southern Reporter*, 11 July 1815; W. Parker, *Observations on the Intended Amendment of the Irish Grand Jury Laws ... to which is Added, a Plan for the General Survey and Valuation of Ireland, and for the Commutation of Tithes* (Cork, 1816), p. vi).
3. *Report on Townland Valuation*, 1844, q. 457 (Sir R. A. Ferguson).
4. *Cork Mercantile Chronicle*, 1 Jan. 1808.
5. Charles O'Hara, A survey of the economic development of Co. Sligo in the eighteenth century, transcripts in PRONI, T.2812/19/1, and TCD, MS 7685. Transcript of Roscommon county book, 1721, NLI, MS 3119.
6. *Report on Survey and Valuation*, 1824, p. 3.
7. *Report on Survey and Valuation*, 1824, p. 350.
8. G. O'Brien, *The Economic History of Ireland from the Union to the Famine* (London, 1921), pp 494–502.
9. *A Letter from an Irish Dignitary to an English Clergyman, on the Subject of Tithes in Ireland* (Dublin, 1822), pp 32–3.
10. *First Report from the Select Committee on Tithes in Ireland*, qq. 136–42, H.C. 1831–2 (177), xxi.
11. *A Defence of the Protestant Clergy in the South of Ireland in Answer to the Charges against them, Contained in the Rt Hon. Henry Grattan's Speeches Relating to Tithes* (Dublin, 1788), p. 20; *Freeman's Journal*, 21 Feb. 1788.

12. Dunlop, *Commonwealth*, 2, p. 661 (1657).
13. *Cal. S.P. Ire.*, 1647–60, pp 641, 660–1, 665, 684.
14. Hill, *Macdonnells*, p. 379.
15. 'A Booke of the Survey of the County of Dublin …' by Thomas Taylor and Edward Lucas, 25 May 1658, in the possession of the Earl of Iveagh. A book with a similar date and title in NAI (M.2475) includes acreage figures but no maps.
16. Edward Ledwich, *A Statistical Account of the Parish of Aghaboe, in the Queen's County, Ireland* (Dublin, 1796), pp 9, 16–17.
17. Map of barony of Scarawalsh, Co. Wexford, 1657, NAI, Clayton MS, 27 (1A.41.40), reproduced in A. P. Smyth, *Celtic Leinster* (Dublin, 1982), Plate B.
18. 'Commonwealth State Accounts, Ireland, 1650–1656', *Analecta Hibernica*, 15 (1944), pp 742–5. 17 & 18 Charles II, c. 2, sec. 100.
19. Copy of Westmeath Down Survey, with additions, NLI, MS 2296.
20. John Kealy to Philip Ford, 5 Aug. 1670, *Cal. S.P. Ire.*, l669–70, p. 209. For the background to this letter see I. Grubb (ed.), *My Irish Journal, 1669–70, by William Penn* (London, 1952), p. 80. The lands in question were part of Penn's estate.
21. 10 Jan. 1687, R. Day, *Jour. Cork Hist. & Arch. Soc.*, 2nd ser., 8 (1902), p. 67.
22. George Crofts to Perceval, 8 Apr. 1712, Add. MS 46964B, f. 185.
23. 'Survey of the Co. Cork', Add. MS 47048.
24. W. M. Brady, *Clerical and Parochial Records of Cork, Cloyne, and Ross*, 1 (Dublin, 1863), pp lviii–lix.
25. Report by Robert de la Cour on procuring materials for a county book, 1825, in *Papers Relating to the Valuation of Cork County*, p. 4, H.C. 1825 (87), xxii.
26. 11 James I, c. 7, sec. 6.
27. 9 Anne, c. 9, sec. 1.
28. *A Dissertation on the Inlargement of Tillage, the Erecting of Public Granaries, and the Regulating, Employing, and Supporting the Poor in this Kingdom* (Dublin, 1741), p. 39.
29. Ledwich, *Aghaboe*, pp 20–21.
30. *Telegraph or Connaught Ranger*, 5 May 1830.
31. Royal Irish Academy, MS 24.G.9, p. 278.
32. *Dublin Evening Post*, 6 July 1786.
33. 49 George III, c. 84, sec. 23.
34. R. L. Edgeworth, 1 Jan. 1814, NLI, MS 7825, p. 51.
35. *Telegraph or Connaught Ranger*, 30 June 1830.
36. *Questions, to which each Incumbent is Desir'd to Give an Answer, in Order to the Making of a Terrier, According to the Forty Fourth Canon of the Church of Ireland, and in Order to the Understanding the True State of the Province of Dublin* (Dublin, 1709). Thomas Moland may have

been involved in these inquiries. In an undated letter addressed to 'Mr Moland', the naturalist Samuel Molyneux referred to 'the employment you have under My Lord Primate' and requested a list of the parishes or baronies in each diocese of Ireland (TCD, MS 888/1, f. 8).

37. *Second Report from the Select Committee on the Public Income and Expenditure of the United Kingdom*, app 23, p. 351, H.C. 1828 (420), v.
38. Parish maps occur in ecclesiastical collections (see for example J. Dean, *Catalogue of Manuscripts in the Public Library of Armagh* (Dundalk, 1928), pp 11 (Clones) and 17 (Inish McSaint)), in estate collections (e.g. Ardstraw by William McCrea and Clonfeakle by John Hill in the 'Glebes' volume of the TCD muniments), and among the tithe applotment books, e.g. Calary (TAB 32/23) and Delgany and Kilmacanogue (TAB 32/11). A number of such maps were published in Mason's *Parochial Survey*. Later, plans of new parishes were required to be lodged in the council office in Dublin Castle (*Established Church Rept*, 1867, app , p. 96).
39. *Leinster Journal*, 28 Mar., 22 Apr. 1778.
40. In 1764 a terrier was defined as a kind of map, and said to be 'always admitted as evidence in law, to prove the boundaries of the glebe', in *Debates Relative to the Affairs of Ireland*, 2 (London, 1766), pp 647–8. Examples are TAB 17/95 (Dromin, Co. Limerick, 1787), and TAB 17/77 (Kilkeedy, Co. Limerick, 1755).
41. Returns of maps from nine dioceses appear in Irish Record Commission, *2nd Rept*, supplement (1812), p. 354. See also *Twenty-first Report of the Commissioners ... [on] ... Courts in Ireland*, pp 71, 120, 142, H.C. 1831 (146), x. In the early 1820s the Archbishop of Dublin ordered a survey of all the glebes in his diocese (Charles Lindsay, 12 May 1830, NLI, MS 859), but it is not known whether the results were collected in any central repository.
42. *Dublin Journal*, 6 Mar. 1759.
43. Copy of Rightboys' manifesto, *Hibernian Journal*, 10 July 1786.
44. 33 George III, c. 25, secs. 3 & 4.
45. *A Full Report on the Speech of the Right Hon. Henry Grattan in the House of Commons, on Thursday, the 14th of February, 1788, in the Debate on Tithes* (Dublin, 1788), p. 6. Report on Grattan's speech of 8 May 1789, *Parliamentary Register*, 9 (Dublin, 1790), p. 450.
46. *Defence of the Protestant Clergy*, p. 57.
47. 4 George IV, c. 99, secs. 21 & 22.
48. R. J. P. Kain, 'R. K. Dawson's Proposal in 1836 for a Cadastral Survey of England and Wales', *Cart. Jour.*, 12 (1975), pp 81–8.
49. *Dublin Evening Post*, 13 Jan. 1824.
50. The acreage column for Creeve parish, Co. Roscommon, is headed 'as per county survey' (TAB 25/13).
51. R. C. Simington, 'The Tithe Composition Applotment Books', *Analecta Hibernica*, 10 (1941), pp 295–8.

52. *Ballina Impartial, or Tyrawly Advertiser*, 16 Feb. 1824.
53. *First Report on Tithes*, 1831–2, qq. 1471, 2117; *Second Report from the Committee of the House of Lords, Appointed to Inquire into the Collection of and Payment of Tithes in Ireland*, pp 46–7, H. C. 1831–2 (663), xxii.
54. Tithe commissioner's certificate [1833], parish of Kilcoane, Co. Kilkenny, NLI, mic. P.7116.
55. *First Report on Tithes*, 1831–2, qq. 2896–7, 2941–7. The only published review of any large number of tithe books by a modern scholar appears to be J. H. Johnson's survey of Co. Londonderry ('The Irish Tithe Composition Books as a Geographical Source', *Ir. Geogr.*, 3 (1958), pp 254–62).
56. Nolan: Raymonterdoney, Co. Donegal, 1836 (TAB 7/9); Brassington: Dunany, Co. Louth, 1833 (TAB 20/43). Nolan did make some tithe surveys: in Sep. 1830 he offered them to the Ordnance Survey (OSO, letter register 8838).
57. TAB 29/14.
58. TAB 13/91, a large vestry book containing maps interspersed with other parochial records. The surveyor was Edward Conlan; there is another large book of his maps in TAB 13/64 (Ballysax parish, Co. Kildare).
59. TAB 25/5.
60. 2 & 3 William IV, c. 119, sec. 22. An interesting letter on the working of this act is printed in Maguire, *Letters of a Great Irish Landlord*, pp 94–6.
61. Examples are maps by David Vaughan of Kilbegnet, Co. Galway (TAB 11/20), Clarges Greene of Drimseragh, Co. Mayo (TAB 21/62), and J. D. Hall of Ardcarne, Co. Roscommon (TAB 25/4).
62. For example Mostrim, Co. Longford (TAB 19/10) and Kilaspick, Co. Sligo (TAB 26/6).
63. For example Rathdrum (TAB 32/26) and Rathnew (TAB 32/31), both Co. Wicklow.
64. *First Report ... on the State of the Poor in Ireland*, q. 2586, H.C. 1830 (589), vii. This information was collected by an arrangement in which surveys were to be made only where a 'satisfactory estimate' of acreage was not available (*Papers Relating to the Valuation of Cork County*, 1825, p. 7).
65. *Report on Townland Valuation*, 1844, qq. 527–30 (Sir Richard Keane).
66. 1 & 2 Victoria, c. 56, sec. 66.
67. *Copies of all Instructions Issued by the Poor Law Commissioners to the Valuators in Ireland ...* (25 Mar. 1839), p. 5, H.C. 1841 (353), xxi. A circular of 8 May 1839 printed in the same source (p. 8) admitted that a survey would have to be made if the occupier did not consent to an estimate.
68. *Report from the Select Committee Appointed to Examine ... the Grand Jury Presentments of Ireland*, H.C. 1814–15 (283), vi. *Report on Survey and*

Valuation, 1824. Similar ideas had already been suggested by private authors, for instance in *State of Ireland Considered with an Enquiry into the History and Operation of Tithe*, pp 71–87.

69. Parker, *Observations*, p. 98.
70. NAI, 2B.44.61 (31 Mar. 1821). Armstrong's pupils included Thomas Noble of Armagh (*Belfast Newsletter*, 30 Apr. 1822) and Philip Clare of Camden Street, Dublin (*Dublin Evening Post*, 24 July 1824).
71. Part of one of Armstrong's estate maps is reproduced in W. R. Hutchinson, *Tyrone Precinct: a History of the Plantation Settlement of Dungannon and Mountjoy to Modern Times* (Belfast, 1951), frontispiece.
72. Townland boundaries are shown on the McCreas' map of Co. Monaghan and in an extract from David Aher's map of Co. Kilkenny printed in Mason, *Statistical Account*, 3 (1819), pp 582–3.
73. *Telegraph or Connaught Ranger*, 30 June, 27 Oct. 1830. Bald's proposals for a map of Co. Down were criticised on the same grounds (PRONI, D.671/C/12/212).
74. Advertisement of vacancies in the Ordnance Survey, *Dublin Evening Post*, 25 Nov. 1826.
75. Armstrong had surveyed four of the eight baronies of Co. Armagh by 1822 (*Report on Survey and Valuation*, 1824, pp 165–80). His survey is described as complete in 'The memorial of William Armstrong', 8 Jan. 1830, in NAI, 2B.44.4 (bundle labelled 'Brassington & Gale's a/cs'). The only section of it at present available is the barony of Orier, dated 1827, in PRONI, D.916.
76. Foreman of Co. Armagh grand jury to Under-secretary of Ireland, 17 Apr. 1827; Superintendent of Ordnance Survey, Dublin, to same, 8 May 1827: NAI, Chief Secretary's office, registered papers, 1827, nos. 560, 932.

13
Mapping without surveyors

TODAY MAPS ARE BEING MADE AND USED for almost every purpose known to the seventeenth and eighteenth centuries (and for many purposes then unknown) but the independent professional land surveyor has been lost to view. While the map-makers employed by the government can clearly take much of the credit or discredit for his submergence, the precise character and timing of their impact have yet to be established in detail. The Ordnance Survey's own departmental history is easily summarised.[1] Its headquarters staff arrived at Phoenix Park, Dublin, in the autumn of 1824, and by 1846 its field parties, working from north to south, had mapped the whole of Ireland on a scale of six inches to one statute mile. The making of their maps was preceded by an official delimitation of every townland in the country and followed by an official valuation of the land and buildings within each of these divisions as the basis for a revised county cess. Although the bounding and valuing were done by a separate department they are often attributed to the Ordnance Survey – an error which in the present context it would be pedantic to insist on correcting.

All of which is straightforward enough. The difficulty may be illustrated by comments from two contemporary surveyors: one, an Ordnance Survey officer's claim in 1838 that his department's maps were providing more work for independent Irish surveyors than they had ever had before;[2] the other, sixteen years later, a lament by one of the surveyors concerned to the effect that his occupation was now 'nearly a nominal one'.[3] To harmonise these judgements is a task unlikely to arouse much sense of urgency among map scholars of the present generation. The Ordnance map still gives most local historians all the cartographic data for its period that they seem conscious of needing; only with increasing specialisation will the relationships between different kinds of nineteenth-century cartography become an object of serious inquiry. Meanwhile it seems safe to suggest that the 1830s brought a new division between public and private in Irish map-making, and that subsequent decades have seen a gradual encroachment of the public sector on the private.

To all appearances the Ordnance Survey incurred only one debt to the past and that was in using earlier maps to help identify the territorial boundaries on which its own best efforts were now to be spent. (The debt was unacknowledged except in the brief remarks written by Ordnance Survey personnel on certain estate maps that were subsequently restored to their private owners.)[4] Any further use of earlier maps would have been considered gravely reprehensible, for although the Survey's developing notions of cadastral accuracy may have been influenced in a general way by Irish attitudes, its procedures in field and office were quite unlike anything described in earlier chapters of this book. At Phoenix Park the compass needle was banned almost from the start and traverses were kept to a minimum.[5] Instead each boundary was fixed by short offsets from the sides of interconnecting chain triangles, the largest of which could be checked against the trigonometrical distances of a meticulously accurate national control survey.

Not only the old practices but the old practitioners were studiously ignored. As in Petty's survey, the cost of the new admeasurement was kept down by a strict division of functions within a pool of largely non-professional manpower, much of it filled from outside Ireland by members of the Corps of Royal Engineers and the Royal Corps of Sappers and Miners. To begin with, Irishmen were employed mainly as labourers, though it was expected to find places for some of them in due course as civilian draughtsmen and engravers. As a check on accuracy, field work and plotting were to be held separate: 'I have never plotted a line in my life', one member of a Survey field party was later to write in indignant self-defence.[6] Both the defence and the indignation would have bewildered an ordinary land surveyor, and it is in acknowledgement of this feeling that the new enterprise might be called cartography without cartographers, even surveying without surveyors. When the Ordnance began to augment its military staff with an intake of Irish 'civil assistants' one enthusiastic young man enrolled as a means of qualifying as a land surveyor, only to complain later that it was like trying to learn boat-racing in a man-of-war.[7] The same paradox was given more uncompromising expression by a famous German cartographic scholar who visited Phoenix Park in 1844:

> I was forcibly struck by the great inferiority, in point of intelligence and education, of the persons engaged in the execution of this great work. In similar undertakings in Germany, as, for example on the great

map of Saxony, which has for a long time been in progress at Dresden, all those employed are taken from the educated classes. Here, on the contrary, all the inferior artists are merely common workmen, who probably understand nothing more than that particular part of the work on which they are actually employed.[8]

These comments did not apply to the Survey's boundary and valuation departments, which could boast several names familiar from earlier estate maps and road surveys (including Robert Warwick, Henry Buck and John Hampton)[9] and which were later to be headed by a former apprentice of Sherrard, Brassington and Gale.[10] And even on the Survey proper a mettlesome recruit could achieve a measure of versatility by moving from one sub-department to another; he might eventually enter private practice on the strength of such experience, though graduates from Phoenix Park were never numerous enough to stage a take-over of the whole profession or to form a recognisable school within it. There was no mass exodus from the Ordnance Survey when its six-inch coverage of Ireland was complete: most of the staff were put to work preparing similar maps of northern England.

Indirectly, however, the Ordnance Survey had a far-reaching influence on other Irish map-makers. In the typical estate office this effect must have been in many ways unexpected. After all, the government's operations had been designed for a mixture of fiscal, military and scientific purposes without much thought for the private needs of landlord or tenant; yet the end-product was found to look more like an estate survey than anything else. It showed the boundary, name and acreage of every townland, together with roads, buildings and the edge of cultivation or improvement. Interior fences were excluded after some argument (recalling the distinction between 'in farms' and 'in fields' observed in private practice) but within a few years, and with less argument, they were beginning to find their way on to the maps until in the midlands and south of Ireland the Survey's record of field patterns was virtually complete.

Apart from their topographic content the main advantage of the six-inch Ordnance maps for estate use lay in combining extremely accurate planimetric information with an extremely low price. The accuracy was taken for granted almost from the beginning, but for any reader who has purchased an Ordnance Survey map in the late twentieth century the price is worth dwelling on. In 1833 a full-size six-inch sheet could be bought for five shillings, or about 0.004d per statute acre, which was several hundred times cheaper than a map of similar standard supplied by a contemporary private surveyor. Equally strange from a modern standpoint is the effectiveness of the Survey's publicity in the 1830s and early 1840s. Thanks to the enthusiasm of the booksellers Hodges and Smith, its official Dublin agents, sales were reasonably gratifying and many proprietors are known to have bought the sheets that included their estates.

Yet for all its popularity the six-inch map had certain limitations as an aid to landlords and their agents. Its most unusual feature was the division of each county into rectangular blocks. Every map-user knows that however small the area of his interest it never seems to fall within one sheet of a multi-sheet lay-out. Farms thus divided were an obvious nuisance; conversely, instead of its margin being free for non-cartographic information the normal Ordnance sheet was filled to the brim with land belonging to other proprietors. It was a difference full of historical portent, eliminating the various badges of identity (owner's name and rank, disposition of his farms etc.) that normally accompanied the estate map, and reducing the whole landscape to a condition of nameless uniformity in which every occupier stood equal in the eyes of the cartographer, the cartographer's employer and mankind as a whole. More important in a practical sense, the new map failed to tell the whole agrarian story. Part of the trouble was simple obsolescence, the fate of all maps. It is true that the Ordnance Survey department remained in being after 1846 and that its earliest maps were coming under revision even before the last of the counties made its initial appearance in print; but the revision went more slowly than the original survey (less than five counties per decade instead of about twenty-five), too slowly to match the rapid landscape changes of the great famine and its sequel. The Ordnance map of 1850 was already showing too many houses and too few public works, as well as misrepresenting streams that had been straightened and farms that had been squared or striped.

Even on its first publication the new survey had fallen short of earlier estate maps by omitting tenurial boundaries and acreages. (The farm boundaries on the maps in the government's Valuation Office existed only in manuscript.)[11] Of course this reticence was wholly deliberate, and the Survey took some satisfaction in reminding litigious correspondents of its strict proprietorial neutrality. Lawyers put the same point in a less flattering form: for them, if for nobody else, the Ordnance Survey was inferior to the Down Survey.[12] Another source of weakness was the Survey's unfashionably austere approach to agrarian typology. Its draughtsmen distinguished bog, mountain and marsh, but made no attempt to separate tillage from grassland, let alone to divide these categories into different grades. Eventually, it is true, the Valuation Office made a monetary assessment of each farm on the basis of its soil, local climate, fertiliser supply, and other intrinsic and extrinsic characteristics, but little of this information ever reached the maps.[13] Finally there was the much discussed question of scale. Six inches to the mile came close to the ratio of 1:10,080 adopted in the Down Survey and in many early landlords' maps, but by the nineteenth century this scale was generally considered inadequate for ordinary estate use. Opinions differed as to just how small an acreage could be satisfactorily measured on a six-inch map, but whatever the limit a good many farms could be expected to fall below it, and even on large farms there might not be room for tenants' names, field acreages, proposed new roads or buildings, and the various other details which landowners were in the habit of inserting on their maps.

For several reasons, then, the Ordnance Survey could not be welcomed without reservation as a complete and ready-made printed estate map, whatever its value to landlords as an index and a topographical portrait. But did it need the supplement of an entirely separate estate survey in traditional Irish style? This was a question that each private land surveyor and his clients had to answer in their own way. To an ultra-conscientious estate manager the Ordnance map might appear as a spur to independent surveying rather than as a substitute for it. Faced with a difference between the government's new survey and his own old ones, he would order a third admeasurement (in the manner of his eighteenth-century forebears) to find out who was right. That was the reaction of the Drapers' Company in Co. Londonderry, for example.[14] For an ultra-conscientious surveyor the third map might involve doing everything that the Ordnance officers had done from the mathematical roots upwards. This was Robert Manning's course of action on the Marquess of Downshire's property in 1848: gaining access to the unpublished field books and calculations at Phoenix Park, he then faced the duty or pleasure of drawing the Survey's attention to one of its errors, 42 links in a distance of 18,082 links. Not many employers would have relished subsidising such virtuosity, especially if the resulting maps were to resemble Manning's in being priced at several hundred pounds.[15]

At the other extreme a landlord might just buy a set of six-inch maps for his county, stamp his name on the cover next to the Ordnance Survey coat of arms, and colour in his own property on the appropriate pages.[16] Or the various townlands comprising an estate could be cut out of the six-inch map and pasted on blank leaves to produce an atlas of conventional pre-Ordnance Survey form, with farm boundaries and the names of adjoining townlands added in manuscript.[17] Between the extremes, an atlas could be made by tracing each denomination from the Ordnance map and enlarging it, thus allowing farm or field areas to be measured on a less restricted and more convenient scale. In Ordnance Survey circles this kind of graphic enlargement was regarded as a 'bad trick',[18] though the authorities did nothing to stop it. For the customer it had the disadvantage of producing acreages that were less accurate than they looked, at a price that sometimes included non-existent field work as well as genuine draughtsmanship. Nevertheless there was a vigorous trade in derivative estate maps, some of it emanating from Hodges and Smith, some from the many firms of lithographic printers and law stationers that flourished around the mid-century in both Dublin and the major provincial towns. The scale of the enlargements varied, the most common being twenty statute perches to an inch (1: 3,960). Charges would also vary, from fourpence an acre down to a penny.[19]

An estate map's dependence on the Ordnance Survey was sometimes left for its reader to see for himself, as when a cartographer of 1850 recorded without acknowledgement not only the depth of a lake but also the exact date on which the lake had been plumbed (by the Survey, needless to say) some twelve years earlier.[20] For draughtsmen of contentious temper the best way of disclaiming plagiarism was to take the offensive: a not uncommon ploy was to mention some supposed error on the Ordnance map – the misspelling of a name, perhaps, or a difference in acreage so tiny that no third survey was likely to eliminate it.[21] Other private cartographers, probably a majority, preferred to assert some kinship with their government colleagues, like the Dublin firm which boasted of a staff that understood the Ordnance Survey's methods.[22] Meanwhile some draughtsmen were trying to disguise their debt to the Survey with a display of Victorian ornamental script or similar marginal irrelevancies; others, more brazen, made no attempt at concealment. The most obvious resemblances between the new official and the new unofficial maps were of a purely negative character, like the omission of shading for relief and for the most widespread kinds of rural land use. Less conspicuous but more revealing was the private draughtsman's habit of imitating the minor symbols of the six-inch map, for instance those for forges and lime-kilns, and of copying its spot heights and trigonometrical stations. Another kind of Ordnance Survey influence was seen when estate maps were printed instead of being drawn by hand:[23] by the 1850s the same person might advertise himself not just as engineer, surveyor and valuator, but also as lithographic printer.[24] It was printing that inspired the only mid-nineteenth-century cartographic innovation among Irish estate surveyors that had no apparent connection with the Ordnance map, namely the dotting of farm boundaries as a substitute for the traditional hand-coloured boundary tint.

Between total independence and slavish copying lay a domain (so far unexplored by historians) whose complexities were suggested as follows in 1844:

> The nobility and gentry are respectfully informed that Messrs Heffernan and Co. supply surveys of estates, enlarged and calculated from the Ordnance plans, at fifty per cent under the ordinary charge. The Ordnance Survey, (which is on a very diminutive scale) not being a field or a farm, but a townland survey, has supplied nothing available for the purposes of the proprietor, but Messrs H. & Co., supplying all deficiencies by actual measurement on the ground, and transferring these to an enlargement of the Ordnance maps, will furnish plans so enlarged, and so completed, which, in point of execution, will be found very superior, and in point of accuracy, strictly correct.[25]

Apart from farm boundaries and up-dated Ordnance Survey detail, the deficiencies supplied by practitioners of the Heffernan type were few. Some surveyors and valuators made an effort to find useful information beyond the reach of the official map, an extreme case being the several hundred profile drawings of houses and cabins presented to the Earl of Carysfort in 1877.[26] But the only new subject to engross much attention was geology, and that was not for very long.

Searching for useful minerals had been a common eighteenth-century preoccupation: this was now combined with a new interest in soil types as well as with purely scientific motives. Thus in 1853 a Dublin valuator of much experience began to offer surveys and opinions on 'agricultural and mineral capabilities', a service which he and his partner took the trouble to announce in the *Mining Gazette*.[27] This enterprise had to be abandoned for personal reasons, but another 'pretender to geology' won a measure of professional fame: he was Dr John Irwine Whitty, whose 'general engineering, geological and valuation office' in Henrietta Street, Dublin (with a branch in Trafalgar Square, London), was said by his detractors to be advertised with all the pertinacity of a pill-manufacturer.[28]

Whitty did manage to produce a number of geological estate maps.[29] He was not the first Irish surveyor to be mocked for his originality, but in one sense the mockers were right, for there was little staying power in the cause that the doctor had so busily espoused. Landowners' aspirations on the subject of rocks and soils began to weaken as Ireland's post-Famine agriculture lapsed towards undifferentiated pastoralism, and in any case the government had struck a near-fatal blow at the private geologist by starting an authoritative geological survey of its own. Independent late nineteenth-century valuators usually followed the example of the official tenement valuation by attaching a single sum of money to each field or other enclosure with no attempt at scientific commentary or exegesis.[30]

In the long run, the tasks that blended best with land surveying were the same as they had always been, namely valuation, agency, engineering and architecture. Like their predecessors, the practitioners of the 1850s mixed these activities in varying proportions and with varying degrees of success. As the experience of James Lynam made clear, it remained possible in this decade to lay the foundations of a long career. Lynam spent a year looking for work after leaving the government's valuation department in 1851 and was still 'awfully poor' seven years later, but eventually progressed to the highly responsible post of drainage engineer on the Rivers Shannon, Suck and Erne as well as farming 160 acres of land on his own account.[31] Others began with even less experience, like the youthful partnership of Fleming and Locke founded in 1854; within a year they had extended their hinterland to the south-west corner of Co. Cork and were soon afterwards banking a profit of one hundred pounds, presumably in excess of whatever they had been paying themselves by way of salary.[32] Meanwhile the old firm of Brassington and Gale remained as prominent as ever, and so did Clarges Greene, Joseph James Byrne, William Armstrong and others – some of them being consulted by the government of the 1850s on the right scales for future Ordnance Survey maps.[33]

Outside Dublin a large estate could still find a niche for the salaried practitioner, especially if he was also a builder or an engineer. The Lansdowne property in Kerry had its own surveyor as late as *c.* 1870, though admittedly not for very long.[34] At the other end of the country Lord Leitrim paid a pound a week to an ex-Ordnance Survey sergeant for thirteen years, and that was in a district which the Survey had already mapped twice over.[35] The Duke of Abercorn was another northern proprietor who spent large sums on Ordnance maps without giving up his own 'exceedingly intelligent surveyor and valuator'.[36] In the salaried sector, as well as among the fee-earners, there was room for a mixture of public and private.

Finally, a reservoir of freelance surveying knowledge was still available in rural Ireland, ranging from country schoolmasters to well-qualified practitioners working out of large provincial towns. Attached to the latter group was an anonymous assistant of the Londonderry surveyor Robert Nolan, whose work diary survives for part of the 1850s.[37] For a daily income of between three and six shillings, this man measured individual fields and gardens as well as complete farms; he drew plans and elevations of houses and measured painting work; he surveyed roads, took sections, laid out mearings, mapped tree plantations, cast up valuations, enlarged old maps or mounted them on canvas, and generally found plenty to do except when making himself scarce to avoid a *sub poena* in an awkward court case. Twenty-five years later another such record, from Co. Tipperary, makes very similar reading. Here too the surveyor's assignments were small, 101 of them being recorded in the space of twenty-two months. The largest was evidently for building and not surveying; the next largest was worth £19 and the great majority of the others brought only £5 or less apiece.[38]

In some surveys the prior existence of an Ordnance map probably had little effect on the amount of skill required. Given that the ground had to be gone over anyway for the recording of new detail it must often have been more convenient to survey a whole farm or townland afresh than to map it by combining one's measurements with somebody else's. And even for the apparently simple task of running new lines across the Ordnance map the surveyor had to be properly qualified, as he could be quick to tell a government committee if given the chance.[39] One young surveyor in 1882 was happy to put 'striking out lines' at the top of his list of skills. (The other skills were levelling, chaining, using the theodolite, and laying down and colouring maps.)[40] Another witness to the abilities involved in this kind of operation was the poet Percy French:

> He finds out the holding and what it contains,
> Then maps out his system in furlongs and chains
> And points out positions for 'minors' and 'mains' –
> Such wisdom has William, Inspector of Drains.[41]

In both Dublin and the country, then, the impression from early and middle Victorian Ireland is of a *modus vivendi* between the independent land surveyor and the state. On closer inspection the Ordnance Survey is found to have been gradually enlarging its influence. From the 1830s its officers grew steadily in self-confidence (not that they had ever been short of this commodity) and also in public esteem. It is unnecessary to range over their whole output, much of which lay outside the purview of the land surveyor in the ordinary sense of the term: the only maps of the post-1844 period which matter in the present context are those on scales of more than six inches to a mile.

The Survey's five-foot (1:1,056) plan of Dublin city appeared in 1840–48 and in the course of the next decade the authorities began to issue similar or larger plans of other Irish towns – of every town that might have had any chance of attracting a private publisher. The Ordnance town plans shared some of the disadvantages of the revised six-inch maps, notably their slow rate of publication and the awkwardness of their sheet lines, as well as a size that most non-specialists found excessive. To that extent they left a gap for private enterprise to fill, especially in Dublin, Cork and Belfast, but the relationship between official and private town plans is far from clear. Matters began badly when Hodges and Smith were found to be selling a government street-map of Dublin which had been supplied to a small number of public bodies for purely internal use. For some reason the Survey worked itself into a state of corporate rage over this harmless act of piracy: the resources of textual criticism were mobilised to identify the culprit and Hodges and Smith only just escaped being punished with the loss of their right to sell the Survey's other maps. Later a more indulgent view prevailed. Guy's plan of Cork (1852) was received at Phoenix Park with no more comment than that it had been made by a number of civil engineers. And at Belfast in 1864 the Survey appeared coolly indifferent to a challenge from the local bookseller Marcus Ward. The department had intended to sell a small index sheet (to the new five-foot Ordnance plan of Belfast) as a separate publication, but this proposal lost most of its credibility when Ward dismissed it as 'the small government map' in an advertisement for a superior new city map of his own.[42] Ward's and other private town plans owed a lot to the Ordnance Survey, however much they might obscure their debt by simplifying topographical detail or by adding marginal views and other salesmanlike embellishments.

The truth is that the Survey had now made such a far-reaching commitment to estate cartography that it could afford to forget about private town plans. The period of this coup was the early 1860s; its scene was the Irish Landed Estates Court, previously known as the Incumbered Estates Court and subsequently rechristened the Land Judges' Court. Of course there was nothing new about Irish courts of law directing the sale of landed property. It was the upsurge of sales following the famine that led to the creation of a court solely intended for this purpose in 1848. The Land Judges quickly saw the necessity for maps of the properties being conveyed, and agreed to allow a maximum of threepence per acre as payment for the necessary surveys as well as the cost of lithographing the results in editions of two or three hundred copies.[43] At this point Hodges and Smith antagonised a number of Dublin's principal surveyors by urging the court to take advantage of the Ordnance Survey maps.[44] In fact, as recent estate experience had been showing, the standard Ordnance scale was often too small for the court's purposes and the judges expressed a preference for sixteen inches to the statute mile (1:3,960).[45]

Whatever the scale – and in the event it varied from one purchase to another – the Incumbered Estates Court maps were mainly copies or enlargements of the Ordnance Survey, indeed there was reputedly a greater demand for Ordnance maps in the street where the sales took place than anywhere else in Ireland.[46] And it was in the court that the issues raised by the enlarging process were brought into the open and finally resolved. As one surveyor put it, expressing professional prejudices as well as professional knowledge:

> When the Incumbered Estates Court required maps of the holdings for sale to a scale of 20 perches to an inch, a new trade sprung [sic] up, and the Survey maps were copied and enlarged to two and two-thirds the original scale, and foisted on the public by attorneys' clerks and others as correct maps of the estates. Smart scriveners and draughtsmen made money by this process, till at last the heads of the Survey office saw a way of getting the grist to their own mill, and set to work to supply by zincography the maps for any future sales.[47]

In 1859 the Ordnance Survey was authorised to supply the judges with their maps.[48] It avoided the perils of graphic enlargement by calculating parcel areas on large-scale replots from its own six-inch field books, similar replots being used as a basis for updating the original six-inch detail in the field. The results were less accurate than if the scale had been chosen before taking the measurements, but the whole arrangement found favour with all parties (except private surveyors) as long as the court remained in being. Throughout the later nineteenth century the making of these maps was a major preoccupation of the Survey authorities, and by the 1880s they were said to have covered one-seventh of Ireland.[49]

Even the operations of the Landed Estates Court were overshadowed by the massive late nineteenth-century land reforms in which Irish tenant farming finally gave way to owner occupation. These reforms destroyed the great estate. Apart from the plantations (of which they might be seen as a reversal) they constitute the most important event in the history of Irish land surveying. They began in the 1870s, and the head of the Ordnance Survey in Ireland was quick to grasp their cartographic implications. His verdict: 'each tenement will have to be mapped as if it were a distinct property'. He also foresaw some of the difficulties likely to arise in the field: 'there are plenty of places where no fences appear on the ground ..., and the whole district is nevertheless cut up into narrow strips of holdings with undefined boundaries'.[50] One object of the coming revolution was to consolidate the strips and mark the boundaries with fences.

It was not until the next decade, however, that estates began to break up fast enough to affect the structure of Irish surveying. The body then charged with financing and organising the various tenant purchase schemes was the Irish Land Commission, established in 1881. Like the Incumbered Estates Court, the commission soon felt the need for maps and was soon finding it hard to obtain them. In several country districts it was impossible to get farms privately surveyed at less than exorbitant rates,[51] and where it did prove possible the resulting maps often failed to meet their recipients' expectations.[52] Once more the government cartographers came to the rescue. But history did not quite repeat itself. A critical difference between the 'eighties and the 'fifties was that the Ordnance Survey had now made considerable progress in publishing cultivated areas at the huge scale of 1:2,500. Most of these areas were in England but in Ireland the new scale had been adopted for Co. Dublin in the 1860s, apparently at the request of the Valuation Office, and had also played a part in the making of many Landed Estates Court maps. To facilitate the management of very small farms, and especially those held in rundale, the Treasury agreed in 1887 to map the whole of Ireland's cultivated area at 1:2,500, to publish the results in the form already adopted for England and at the same time to reduce them to a new and more expeditious revised six-inch map. In the 1890s the Land Commission decided to use the 1:2,500 where the six-inch was too small[53] and by 1914 the new survey had been completed for the whole country.

For lands left unsold or sold outside official channels the effect of Ireland's cartographic revolution was to pose once more the old question of protecting titles in some kind of official registry that would preserve a record of all the relevant documents. According to Robert Torrens, a leading authority on such matters, the Ordnance Survey had made Ireland the aptest of all countries for reform in this complex field.[54] But as it turned out the Irish programme of registration did little to improve matters. Maps were given passing recognition when Parliament reorganised the Registry of Deeds in 1832,[55] and eighteen years later the Ordnance Survey was brought into the legislative limelight by an amending act on the registration of lands. The statute of 1850 was chiefly notable for its acceptance of cartographic possibilities, including not just the Ordnance map as such but also 'copies or reprints ... with any additions to or variations in the matters marked on the said maps ... and ... maps on any enlarged scale or scales',[56] a display of subtlety which all went to waste when the Treasury neglected to put the new law into force.[57] The next act for the registration of Irish land titles, in 1891, was not much more adventurous, despite the imminence of the new 1:2,500 survey:

> Registered land shall be described by the names of the denominations on the Ordnance maps in which the lands are included, or by reference to such maps, in such manner as the registering authority thinks best calculated to secure accuracy, but, except as provided by this act, the description of the land in the register or on such maps shall not be conclusive as to the boundaries or extent of the land.[58]

What this clause amounted to, in modern international terminology, was that in Ireland as in England Parliament had chosen 'general' (i.e. generalised or not fully determinate) property boundaries instead of the 'guaranteed' boundary as advocated by Torrens.[59] Again, no authoritative reasons were given for the choice. It might have been defended as preserving the Ordnance Survey's now-traditional impartiality on property questions and as protecting it from conflict with such cartographically inaccurate but legally potent sources as the Down Survey. History apart, the 'general' boundary could be approved as a realistic assessment of the Ordnance Survey itself, for the 1:2,500 maps, like the six-inch, were bound to leave some planimetric questions unanswered. Since the Ordnance map had deliberately omitted property boundaries an independent cartographic operation would be needed to insert them. The most awkward omissions of this kind were the balks and mearing stones of the rundale system, but the same problem would also affect features already printed on the map, for the Survey had always shown fences by invisible lines along the middle, ignoring the true width of the barrier and leaving others to determine the precise course of a boundary that was legally defined in words, for instance as following the edge of a ditch or the face of a bank.[60]

Finding the 'thread' of a property boundary was not the only problem for users of the 1:2,500 map. Slowly though the Irish landscape was changing in the early years of the twentieth century, the need for ordinary topographical map-revision could not be underestimated indefinitely. In fact the country was about to acquire its first modern suburban housing estates, a change unluckily coincident with the serious decline in Ordnance Survey output which began with the first world war and which was then prolonged by the change from United Kingdom to Free State. Both changes meant that the building and registration of new houses and new garden fences would usually necessitate a separate act of admeasurement to put these objects on the map.

There were evidently several parallels between the aftermaths of the first six-inch maps and the first 1:2,500 maps. How did the two periods compare in respect of map accuracy? Resurveying the country at four times the original Ordnance Survey scale might seem to have disposed of such questions once and for all. The planimetric standards of the Ordnance map did undoubtedly improve between the middle nineteenth century and the early twentieth. But so, it might be urged did the standards of the map-using public in an age of agricultural, industrial and residential development. And just as the competition for space is capable of being intensified without limit, so the kind of error that causes inconvenience can grow indefinitely smaller. The nightmarish prospect of corrections chasing errors without ever catching them is perhaps a trifle unrealistic. In practice the Survey admits the possibility of a root mean square error of up to two metres on its 1:2,500 maps;[61] not very much, perhaps, but there are those who consider it excessive. In that sense the similarity between the enlargements of *c.* 1850 and the resurvey of *c.* 1900 is still perceptible, however faintly: both left the more exacting map-user with a latent source of dissatisfaction.

Meanwhile for the private land surveyor history was again declining to repeat itself. In the 1850s he had suffered, fought back, and scored a few points. The framework of his profession had been left intact. Fifty years later the position was different. Now, according to the government's Commissioner of Valuation, the Irish branch of the Surveyors' Institute consisted altogether of land agents, and in or out of the Institute Ireland had so few surveyors that he was unable to maintain his staff without seeking recruits from England and Scotland.[62] This was perhaps a rather pessimistic view. Various public and semi-public departments were still employing non-Ordnance surveyors, and continued to do so even after all the 1:2,500 maps had become available; outside the public service altogether, land surveying facilities remained on offer from civil engineers as well as from estate agents. Until they too pass into history, the performance of these later generations will be hard to measure. But one thing is clear: none of them is now at work on the kind of monumental estate atlas – so conspicuous in its consumption of cartographic resources – that once marked the summit of the land surveyor's skill. The great landlords who commissioned those atlases have gone; so, in consequence, have the 'gentlemen surveyors' who created them. And it was the gentleman surveyor, had he survived, who might eventually have laid the basis for a modern professional organisation and who might in due course have been succeeded by the graduate surveyor.

As it is, although surveys are still being made in Ireland by numerous 'technicians' of different kinds, no attempt to give the subject a third-level educational status has been very successful.[63] Other countries have done better in this respect, and Irish map-makers were unusual in being squeezed from both sides of the supply-demand relationship, their old clientele no longer wanting what they had to offer and their new rival being in any case better able to supply it. In a long enough view, this change may doubtless be accepted with equanimity. Fields and house-plots were being measured before the land surveyor was heard of, and will continue to be measured after most people have forgotten his existence. Historians should not be too quick to forget him, however, for in some respects he suits the anti-romanticism of their own profession in the late twentieth century. Once Irish history books celebrated the ideals of brotherhood and self-sacrifice, but today it seems easier to recall how obsessively the soil that nourished bygone patriots was being divided and packaged, priced and labelled. The man who most embodied this obsession may seem an unsympathetic figure. Among lovers of cartography he needs no defence.

Notes

1. Andrews, *Paper Landscape*.
2. T. A. Larcom, memorandum on proposed Ordnance Survey memoirs, NLI, MS 7553.
3. J. Henderson (land surveyor, Dungiven, Co. Londonderry), 29 Sep. 1854, OSO, file 1369.
4. The circular sent to landowners by the Survey's boundary department included a request for maps (copy in NAI, M.3533). The head of the same department described estate maps as 'essential to the accuracy as well as rapidity of our progress' (*Second Report on Public Income and Expenditure*, 1828, pp 349, 351).
5. Andrews, *Paper Landscape*, pp 55, 58–9, 74.
6. From a Survey employee's answer to a charge of faulty work, OSO, file 11378 (1907).
7. 'Fingal', *Irish Builder*, 24 (1882), p. 101.
8. J. G. Kohl, *Travels in Ireland*, (London, 1844), p. 289.
9. The employees of the boundary department in 1825–8 are listed by name in *Second Report on Public Income and Expenditure*, 1828, pp 351–8. Among those recorded, previously or later, as independent land surveyors were Peter Blake, William Clutterbuck, Charles Cooper, John Gaynor, Dennis O'Connor and William Stokes. For Hampton and Buck see A. C. Mulvany (ed.), *Letters from Thomas J. Mulvany R.H.A. to his Eldest Son William T. Mulvany Esqre Royal Commissioner of Public Works Ireland from 1825–1845* (Dusseldorf, 1907), pp 30–31, 42–7.
10. *Report on General Valuation*, 1869, q. 96. The officer in question, John Ball Greene, may have been related to the Greene who had partnered Sherrard and Brassington earlier in the century.
11. Andrews, *History in the Ordnance Map*, pp 56–7. What seems to be an unusual case of a Valuation Office map in private possession is the five-foot plan of Kildare town in *c*. 1850 among the Duke of Leinster's records now held by Messrs Huggard & Brennan, solicitors, Wexford. The six-inch Valuation Office farm maps were printed in a very small edition in the 1870s: few people seem to have known of their existence, though in fact they constitute Ireland's closest approach, at any period, to the concept of a national estate survey. An earlier collection, now seemingly lost, that merited the same description was the set of six-inch maps annotated under the orders of Captain T. A. Larcom as an aid to the delimitation of poor law unions (Andrews, *Paper Landscape*, p. 140).
12. R. G. N. Combe, *Hunt's Law of Boundaries, Walls and Fences* (London, 1912), p. 242. In 1863 the Lord Chief Baron denounced 'the extravagance of the proposition, that what was done in the making of the Ordnance Survey had or can ever have the least effect on title' (Tisdall vs Parnell, *Irish Common Law Reports*, 14 (1864), p. 28).
13. 'Outline of the system according to which the general valuation of Ireland ... is carried into effect', *Devon Report*, 1, app 1, pp 1–4.

14. *Reports to the Court of Assistants of the Drapers' Company, upon the Estate of the Company, in the County of Londonderry, in Ireland, in the Years 1853, 1856, 1862, 1865, and 1867* (London, 1868), p. 71.
15. R. Manning, 'A Method of Correcting Errors in the Observation of the Angles of Plane Triangles, and of Calculating the Linear and Surface Dimensions of a Trigonometrical Survey', *Min. Proc. Inst. Civ. Eng.*, 73 (1882–3), pp 290, 308. Manning's personal account book for the period covered by the Downshire survey is in the possession of Professor J. C. Dooge of Dublin.
16. Nicholas Westby, maps of Co. Clare, NLI, 21.F.85.
17. Hodges and Smith, maps of the Earl of Clonmell's estate, 1854, NLI MS 4754. Maps of John G. Adair's estate, 1865, NLI, 16.M.20.
18. Colonel T. F. Colby, 18 May 1844, NLI, MS 7569.
19. *Reports of Drapers' Company* (1868), p. 71; *Report to Drapers' Company upon the Meath Estate*, pp 12–13.
20. Hodges and Smith, printed map of Kylemore estate, Co. Galway, 1850.
21. Hodges and Smith, printed maps of Tinny Park and Ballyhorsey, Co. Wicklow, 1850, and of John P. Dell's estate, Co. Limerick, 1850.
22. O'Neill and Duggan, *A Mining Map of Ireland* (Dublin, n.d., probably 1853).
23. Examples are the six-inch non-Ordnance Survey maps used by Lord Carberry for what seem to have been purely internal estate purposes. Two 'editions' of these are represented in NLI, 16.H.19.
24. Advertisement of J. McArthur, *Irish Economist*, 24 Dec. 1855.
25. *Evening Packet*, 5 Mar. 1844.
26. Valuation and illustration of the town of Arklow the property of the Earl of Carysfort by J. Townsend Trench, Kenmare, 1877, original in the museum of Arklow Vocational School, photostat in NLI, MS 2703.
27. Diary of John Locke, 20 Aug. 1853, NLI, MS 3728.
28. J. B. Greene, 11 Apr. 1857, OSO, file 1952. Some of Whitty's maps carried the impressive inscription: 'By John Irwine Whitty LL.D. C.E. Valuator and Agriculturalist ... Lithographed at the General Engineering Geological Survey and Valuation Office and Printing and Lithographing Establishment 1 & 16 Henrietta St, Dublin. Director – John Irwine Whitty LL.D. C.E.' Whitty's trade card is among the topographical prints in NLI, 549TA.
29. J. I. Whitty, Report on the coal district of the northern part of the county of Dublin, read at a general meeting of the Geological Society of Dublin, held March 8 1854; also 'Geological Map of Bear Island, Rosmacowen and Ballhusky, Part of the Estates of the Earl of Bantry', 1853.
30. 'Aleph', *The Irish Agriculturalist's Guide to the Principles of Land Valuation* (Dublin, 1871). Geological influence is evident in the remarks on soils attached to several estate maps of the middle and late nineteenth century, for instance those of 1865 by James Julian in the library of

University College, Cork, and an undated anonymous map (watermark 1854) of Brownstown, Co. Kildare, in NLI, MS 8796(3).
31. Transcript of Lynam family diary, in the possession of Mr J. P. O'F. Lynam, Dublin.
32. John Locke's diary, 18 Dec. 1854, 12–17 Mar., 18–23 June, 22 Dec. 1855, 25 Jan. 1856.
33. *Correspondence Respecting the Scale for the Ordnance Survey, and upon Contouring and Hill Delineation*, p. 61 (Maurice Collis, Dublin), p. 332 (James Deering, Midleton, Co. Cork), H.C. 1854 [1831], xli.
34. Reports, accounts and rentals from Lord Lansdowne's estate, NLI, mic. P.1020.
35. OSO, files 3332 (1867), 4230 (1880).
36. PRONI, D.623/327 (Dec. 1835); R. Donnell, *Chapters on the Leaseholders' Claim to Tenant Right and Other Tenant Right Questions with Land Act Reports* (Dublin, 1873), p. 85.
37. PRONI, D.1197.
38. NAI, TIPP 12/1.
39. *Report of the Commissioners Appointed to Consider the Subject of the Registration of Title with Reference to the Sale and Transfer of Land*, p. 407 (C. P. Brassington), H.C. 1857 [2215], xxi.
40. John Boyle, 24 May 1882, OSO, file 4400.
41. Percy French, *Prose, Poems and Parodies, Edited by his Sister Mrs De Burgh Daly* (London, 1929), p. 59. French too had been an inspector of drains.
42. OSO, files 566 (1849), 868 (1852), 2300 (1860–64).
43. *Report of the Progress of the Ordnance Survey and Topographical Depot, to the 31st December 1858*, p. 10, H.C. 1859 [2482], viii; *Report from the Select Committee on the Cadastral Survey*, q. 296 (Mountifort Longfield), H.C. 1861 (475), xiv.
44. Letter signed by William Longfield, Neville & Son, Joseph James Byrne, Clarges Greene & Son, and James Brassington, 11 Apr. 1850, OSO, file 644.
45. R. C. MacNevin, *The Practice of the Incumbered Estates Court in Ireland* (Dublin, 1854), p. 115.
46. J. I. Whitty, 24 May 1858, OSO, file 1952.
47. 'Fingal', *Irish Builder*, 24 (1882), p. 101.
48. OSO, file 2777 (1862).
49. *Report of the Progress of the Ordnance Survey, to the 31st December 1889*, p. 14, H.C. 1890 [C-5959], lviii.
50. Major B. A. Wilkinson, 17 Nov. 1870, 22 June 1871, OSO, file 3576.
51. Proposal by Thomas Adair for making enlargements of six-inch Ordnance Survey maps to be used in the land courts, 3 Jan. 1882, OSO, file 4357.

52. K. Buckley, 'The Records of the Irish Land Commission as a Source of Historical Evidence', *Ir. Hist. St.*, 8 (1952), p. 31. Another ominous feature of the 1880s was the lack of interest in surveying shown in the *Second Report of the Royal Commissioners on Technical Education, vol. iv: Evidence, etc. Relating to Ireland*, H.C. 1884 [C-3981.-III], xxxi.
53. R. R. Cherry, *The Irish Land Law and Land Purchase Acts 1860 to 1901* (3rd ed., Dublin, 1903), p. 822.
54. *Report from the Select Committee on Land Titles and Transfer*, q. 3131, H.C. 1878 (291), xv. Torrens's essay, *Transfer of Land by 'Registration of Title' as now in Operation in Australia under the 'Torrens System'*, had been published in Dublin in 1863. He was himself an Irishman and a graduate of Trinity College, Dublin.
55. 2 & 3 William IV, c. 87, sec. 29.
56. 13 & 14 Victoria, c. 72, sec. 1.
57. E. Graves Mayne, *An Inquiry into the Foreign Systems of Registering Dealings with Land by Means of Maps and Indexes* (Social Inquiry Society of Ireland, Report no. 4), p. 5; [G. A.] Leach, *Suggestions for Improving the Mode of Registering Deeds in Ireland* (Dublin, 1861), p. 16; [R.] Donnell, 'Report on the Best Means of Facilitating Land Transfer, by Means of Local Registry', *Jour. Stat. & Soc. Inq. Soc. Ire.*, 6 (1874), p. 295.
58. 54 & 55 Victoria, c. 66, secs. 55, 56.
59. S. R. Simpson, *Land Law and Registration* (Cambridge, 1976), ch. 8.
60. N. J. Synnott, 'The Proposed Re-valuation of Land in Ireland', *Jour. Stat. & Soc. Inq. Soc. Ire.*, 12 (1910), p. 350.
61. 'Mapping and the Role of the Ordnance Survey', *Estates Gazette* (Dublin), Jan.–Feb. 1979, p. 14.
62. *Report from the Select Committee on Irish Valuation Acts*, qq. 1050–51, 1075, H.C. 1902 (370), vi.
63. M. J. Long, *Mapping for the Management of National Resources in the Irish Republic*, M.Sc. thesis, TCD (1980); A. L. Allan, *The Education and Practice of the Surveyor in the Private Sector within the European Economic Community*, University College, London (1980); R. C. Cox and J. A. Dixon, 'The Development of Land Survey Education in Ireland', *Survey Ireland*, 1 (1983), pp 21–7.

Appendix A

A surveyor's advice to farmers

(NLI, MS 3876, ff. 61–7. Spelling and punctuation modernised.)

Husbandry in epitome or a method of farming recommended by which in seven years, a farmer on coarse land worth between five and ten shillings per acre, may make it worth twenty shillings per acre and be fully paid his expense with interest. Recommended to the perusal of Theobald Wolfe Esquire for the improvement of his estate. By Charles Frizell a County of Wexford farmer 1760.

Of Soils

These I shall reduce under three heads, that is a loam, a clay and a light turf soil.

A loam is a loose dry soil intermixed with sandy particles and if the soil is deep is capable of the highest improvement, but if thin, the under strata is generally so loose and porous that manure without great care runs through it. This soil is easily known at first view, by its mossy coat, furze and poor weak grass.

A clay entirely differs from the former by its stiffness, occasioned by the under strata being a binding clay or inclinable to a marl which holds the water that weeps over it, and perhaps this is occasioned for want of skill to cut off the head springs, which occasions a poor sour forked rushy grass with a brown mossy coat and very bad pasture.

The light turf soil differs from the two former, its parts are too fine and weak for want of the two former soils being intermixed with it.

That each of these different soils might be made useful to each other, the following method is recommended.

First that a compost of the loam and clay ground be drawn together and laid layer over layer about a foot to each layer and to every 20 load of each sort, a barrel of rock lime to be spread between. These layers to be continued to be raised to any discretionary height and after three months lying to be turned over and mixed with spade and shovel about two load to the square perch will be a choice manure for the turf soil.

Second, draw the turf soil, old ditches or any other kind of light soil and mix a barrel of rock lime to every 40 loads between layer and layer, let it lie about the same time of the former and turn it. The same quantity of this as of the former is a very good manure for the clay or stiff ground.

Third, draw off the clay or stiff ground like the former, mix a barrel of rock lime to every 15 load between layer and layer, let it lie as the former and turn it and allow three load to the perch square, which will be the highest manure for the loam.

Now to prepare each of these manures in the cheapest manner, lay a good row of lime round the headlands of the fields and spread it. Plough this in very deep and continue often to turn it with the plough and have this ready for the above use, remembering always to use it as before recommended and where the two soils are required to be mixed draw one to the other and mix them with the plough as before recommended.

To manage a farm of about 350 acres which may serve as a specimen for a greater or lesser quantity.

Suppose such a farm has been held by sundry tenants and their under tenants who have sowed their crops after them according to the custom of the country, and that such farm comes into the ensuing farmer's hands at Lady Day or May, so that he has the most of the ensuing year to regulate his future plan.

That he might not be quite idle, though it is not the right season, let at least ten or twelve acres of the oldest coarse ground be ploughed up in sets about 12 feet wide as soon as possible. About the beginning of June plough it back again which will lay the grass and rubbish side uppermost, then cross plough it very short and harrow it as well as possible and burn beat all the small clods and rubbish. Spread the ashes as hot as possible with about 40 corn barrels of rock lime to the acre, plough it very light, harrow it down and then sow about two pound of red turnip seed to the acre any time about Old St Peter's-tide. If you have a one horse roller run it over the whole to prevent the fly, and as soon as the turnips are each in their four leaves give them the first hoeing which is called chopping. By the time the field is thus served by two or three good hands, the first part of the field will be ready for the second hoeing at which time thin them to about a foot at least from each other. These will come to such a size that each acre will fatten about 25 sheep from December to the latter end of March by drawing off morning and evening to the adjoining meadow or pasture where there ought to be a cock of hay made for them with a centre post for fear of bad weather. Folding and eating them on the land would be of more benefit to the improvement of the field was there folds to change them every two or three days. As fast as the turnips are carried off, the ground ought to be ploughed, which when all is done, then harrowed down and sowed with flat barley, about a barrel and a bushel of seed to the acre. This ground thus managed will produce about 20 barrels of barley to the acre increase and may be sowed the ensuing year or laid down this with four barrels of hay seed to the acre and half a stone of white or red clover in like manner to the acre. Note to roll the land after sowing the grass seeds when the corn is about two inches high, which serves for a moulding to the plant. Be sure the land for turnips for the next year be ploughed some time in autumn and then managed as before directed. If at any time you plough up the weak turfy soil, the compost before recommended is best and after the crop of turnips are ate off, lay it out on the first crop of barley with grass seeds as before on account of the weakness of the soil.

As soon as the turnip field is completed as above, provide all the manures against autumn and lay it on the leys you design to plough up. That is lime on the loam, the light compost on the clay or stiff ground and the mixed on the turf soil, plough up these as soon as you can and let them lie in the ridge until the beginning of June and manage the remainder as you are directed for the turnip crop, only not harrowing down the last ploughing of the part designed for wheat until a short time before sowing the seed, three bushels of which will be sufficient to the acre.

An oat crop is best after wheat and a barley crop to sow the grass seeds on.

The number of acres that a farmer ought to break up every year on a farm of these dimensions should be at least 40 acres and every year after the third year, lay down 40 acres so that there will be 80 acres always in tillage.

To make this the least expensive there ought to be ten cotters with three acres of land for gardens to each and about 30 acres more set apart for their common grazing. Each of these would be worth in poor land about £4 per annum. Besides the cotters there ought to be ten good low squat horses of about five pound value each, ten wheeled cars with tumbrel boxes to be emptied by a tail board under the back or hind part of the car. These car tumbrels will draw the corn, furze, etc. as well as collect the manure.

Likewise, tackling for two ploughs of four horses each and three different ploughs for each set, that is the breaking up plough, the back stirring plough and the seed plough.

With these cotters and materials I begin as follows in the beginning of November after the former tenants' crops are taken away. I would plough up all their old stubbles and gardens and let them lie to mellow until February at which time to harrow them down and then sow the whole with grey peas under the plough allowing sufficient seed of about a barrel and a bushel to the acre. When these are in full bloom or blossom in July to plough them entirely in, and have a bat man to keep them well under the plough, let the land lie so until the ensuing spring, harrow the ground down and lay it down with a spring crop of barley or oats and harrowing it as level as possible and sowing 4 barrels of grass seeds and seven pound of white or red clover to the acre.

Though this management does not strengthen the ground like the other manures, yet it will bring immediate meadowing and sweet pasture and prepare it to be manured when the rest of the farm is completed.

Note this is the proper method for harassed worn out ground because manure is entirely lost on it until it comes to heart to bear it.

When only three crops are taken off the land allowing the manures before recommended, they will be very good in their kinds, from which and the great quantity of stock the manured ground will feed and the profit of fattening sheep with turnips will abundantly recompense the industrious farmer.

These working horses should never be kept in a regular stable but have a house built convenient to their work and pasture open at both ends with a wall in the middle against which a rack and manger on each side. When the horses are cleaned after work leave them a sufficiency to eat as long as they please to stay at it, and then go to their pasture and return at pleasure. Don't forget their morning's feed and by this method they will be hardy and never get cold or surfeits and will work perpetually, never be out of order and hold above seven years, the time prescribed for the first improvement of the farm.

Of Dung

As dung is of the most general use to the farmer, it's a pity that what is called dung is not of the tenth part of the value it might be brought to, nor half the quantity collected that with good management might be.

To have it in its full perfection sink a foundation like a cellar about four or five feet deep, about 100 feet long (or larger according to your fancy) and 20 feet wide, let a roof on knees or feet be put on this and thatched, the sides wattled close with furze or brush wood and a passage for a tumbrel left open at each end with a wattled gate for the same. Into this draw all the dung, straw litter, weeds, ashes, parings of the yards and garden walk, sweepings, clay and every other thing that can be collected and throw all together now and then a load of dry lime spread over it, and be sure that all waters, suds, wash and all others of the kind be thrown into it. Let it be so situated that any sudden shower shall convey the fat water of the yards etc. into it by paved channels from each and a way to turn off great rains when too much falls. This will ferment altogether and one load taken out in its full strength is better than ten. A small quantity of it will go a great way for your kitchen garden, potatoes, weak meadows, poor weeping ground etc. Cleanse it every spring and begin anew.

Note this dung on poor worn out stubbles will produce a good crop of turnips and is the best manure for clay or stiff ground.

It is to be supposed in a few years that there will be a sufficiency of sheep walk on the farm at least so much as will rear the sheep designed for turnips, and as it will require a shepherd or man to attend them who most of his time is idle, to prevent which and to make the most profit of the shepherd and the sheep, let a hovel on knees or feet be raised proportionable to the flock, when they lie down in the evening. This may be covered with furze or any other thing that will keep off the rain, the sides to be wattled with furze or any kind of brush wood and the passage into it stopped at night with a gate, the sheep to be drove in at night fall during the dry months of summer and let out early in the morning. The shepherd then with his wheel barrow, spade and shovel, to cover the whole floor with dry earth brought from some old ditch or bank adjoining or some angle of the field and this renewed every day and the sheep at night will raise the floor to a great height of good mould well manured with their dung and urine. This ought to be laid out for manure on some meadow or barren ground before winter comes on and the next year the hovel to be removed to some other place for the benefit of the mould as aforesaid. By this method a good deal of ground might be manured yearly, the shepherd well employed and no way hurtful to the sheep because they always lie still at night, and this also prevents the rot in them.

Appendix B
Surveyors in dispute, 1743–1798

The use of published advertisements, or (more rarely) news items, as a medium for conducting professional disputes among Irish surveyors appears to have begun in the 1740s, to have remained popular for about four decades, and then to have declined, virtually disappearing by the early nineteenth century. Pamphlets or broadsheets were also printed for the same purpose, but none of these is known to survive. Apart from being unusually long and complex the example printed in Appendix C is typical of the genre in both tone and content. Other controversies of the same kind are listed below. Where possible, the difference at issue is reckoned as a percentage of the smaller of the two rival acreages.

Surveyors	Locality	Difference between disputed acreages	Source
Anon, John Bell of Carrickmacross, Co. Monaghan	—	—	*Dublin Journal*, 17 March 1743
William Thornton, John Noble	Capanaboe, Queen's Co.	1.91%	*Dublin Journal*, 16 December 1749, 6, 16 January 1750
Arthur Lilly, William Mitchell, John Naghten	Crievemully, Co. Roscommon	3.14%	*Dublin Journal*, 1 October 1751
Peter Callan, John Bell	Gravelstown and Carnalstown, Co. Meath	2.72%	See below, Appendix C
Darby Dunne, Maurice Downer	Queen's Co.	1.34%	*Dublin Journal*, 4, 14 December 1756, 8, 22 February 1757
Dennis Kinsella, John Mooney	Clubbin, King's Co.	5.37%	*Pue's Occurrences*, 26 March, 2, 16 April, 14 June 1757
Charles and Richard Frizell, Andrew Connor	Co. Wexford	11.57%	*Dublin Journal*, 15 August 1758
Peter Callan, Thomas Williams	Navan, Co. Meath	—	*Universal Advertiser*, 21 October 1758
Dennis Kinsella, John Mooney	Corrmore, King's Co.	5.88%	*Dublin Journal*, 18 November 1760, 9 March 1762

Surveyors	Locality	Difference between disputed acreages	Source
John Brenn of Clonmel, Thomas Thornton	—	8.33%	*Leinster Journal*, 1 July 1767
William Thornton, Thomas Brown	Low Grange, Co. Kilkenny	1.82%	*Leinster Journal*, 20 July 1768
Lawrence Doyle, Lawrence Nowlan	Ballon, Co. Carlow	0.62%	*Leinster Journal*, 22 December 1770, 9 January, 9, 20 February 1771
John McGennis, Bernard Scalé	Robertstown, near Navan, Co. Meath	*c.* 1.00%	*Freeman's Journal*, 25 June 1771
Mathias Tannam, Bernard Scalé	Cloncurry, Co. Kildare Raheendough, Co. Meath	4.47% 3.05% 3.76%	*Dublin Journal*, 1 September, 1, 3 December 1772
Peter Mulvihill, Thomas Cuttle	Newpark, Co. Longford	—	*Dublin Journal*, 8 September, 28 November 1772
Kyran Fitzpatrick, Maurice Downer	Donaghmore, Queen's Co.	4.00%	*Leinster Journal*, 28 March, 22 April 1778
John Daly, Thomas Magnier	Castle Kivan, Co. Cork	0.04%	*Cork Evening Post*, 15, 19 January, 15 April 1784
William Higgins, Richard Barry	Ballylyng. Co. Cork	3.11%	*Hibernian Chronicle*, 3, 10, 17 May 1784
John Sullivan, Michael Farrell, John Dowly	Kilgobin, Co. Cork	17.65%	*Cork Evening Post*, 20 June 1785
Cor. Callaghan, Robert Croake	Scaragh, Co. Cork	8.62%	*New Cork Evening Post*, 24 May 1792
Thomas Berne, Mr Waddein, Ben Butler, Mr Conroy	Old Derig, Queen's Co.	—	*Leinster Journal*, 22 January 1798

Appendix C
Peter Callan versus John Bell, 1753–60

Universal Advertiser, 1 December 1753
Whereas the general regularity of the affairs of landlords and tenants in this kingdom, chiefly depends on the skill, diligence and integrity of surveyors of land; since there are no judges, no magistrates, or incorporated society, who legally assume to themselves the power of administering justice in matters of surveying: But every man, who is pleased to undertake the occupation of land-surveying, (without any regular qualification) is at free liberty to impose on the public in the most important affairs, without any regular means of redress, but the liberty of the press; to expose to public view, the unaccountable proceedings of such surveyors as obstinately persist in known errors, to the general prejudice of landlords and tenants; for which reason, the three following instances are here exhibited against Mr John Bell of Cootehill in the county of Cavan, who by insinuating address, and want of opposition, has acquired the reputation of a good surveyor, in the most parts of Ulster and Leinster these thirty years past. One instance of which happened in the part of the lands of Horistown, in the parish of Rathkenny, barony of Slane, and county of Meath, held by Andrew Fitzpatrick and partners; which had been formerly surveyed by Mr Peter Callan of Drogheda, (author of the dissertation on the practice of land-surveying) after which it had been surveyed by the said John Bell, who returned it several acres less, for which the said tenants stopped payment these seven years past. Another instance happened in the part of the lands of Gravelstown, in the parish of Kilbeg, barony of Kells, and county of Meath, held by Bryan McConnell, which land had been formerly surveyed by Mr Garret Hogan, and several other surveyors, who all agreed in their surveys of the same, till six years ago it was surveyed by the said John Bell, who returned it several acres less, for which the said tenant stopped payment these sixteen years past; and the said land had been surveyed since by the said Peter Callan and others, who all agree with the said Garret Hogan's return. An other instance happened in the part of the lands of Carnalstown, in the parish of Drumcondra, barony of Slane, and county of Meath, held by George Elliot; which land had been formerly surveyed by the said John Bell, and since by the

said Peter Callan, who returned it several acres less, for which an under tenant stopped payment these ten years past. Concerning all, and every one of the above-mentioned instances, the said John Bell hath been often served with proper notices, to come and meet the said Peter Callan and others, on the said several lands, in order to make proper vindications in favour of his said surveys, or submissive apologies for errors committed; to which the said John Bell obstinately refuses complying, and still encourages the said parties to insist on his said surveys. By means of which refractoriness, the said tenants unavoidably involve themselves into debt and law-suits, out of which it is probable they shall never be able to extricate themselves, without the utter ruin of themselves and families, which shall be attended with considerable loss and trouble to their landlords, if not speedily prevented by bringing the said John Bell to compliance. To accomplish which, and deter others from the like practices, this notice is given to the said John Bell, and all others whom it may concern, that I will proceed against him the said John Bell, pursuant to the sta[tute] of the 33d year of K. Hen. the 8th, 1st sess., 15th chap[ter] against deceitful pretenders to crafty sciences, if he the said John Bell does not come to proper compliance before the 20th day of January next. Dated November 30th 1753. Peter Callan.

Universal Advertiser, 15 December 1753

Whereas one Peter Callan, of Drogheda, who takes upon him to survey land, did publish in the *Universal Advertiser,* the first of this instant, that John Bell, of Cootehill, in the county of Cavan, land surveyor, surveyed the lands of Horistown, part of the lands of Gravelstown, and part of the lands of Carnalstown, all in the county of Meath. And that likewise, the said Peter Callan, and others, surveyed said lands, and differed in their surveys, from said Bell's surveys; and said, that Bell refused to meet said Callan, to adjust the said surveys. Now this is to give notice, to the said Peter Callan, and all others, that I the said John Bell, will at the proper request, of those gentlemen that employed me, to take those surveys, fix a proper time, and give a month's notice before, of the day that I will meet said Peter Callan, on said lands, to defend and make good my surveys against him: And will before any two honest skilful surveyors, make it appear, that Callan is considerably mistaken in each survey. Dated at Cootehill, the 4th of December 1753. John Bell.

Universal Advertiser, 1 January 1754
I, John Bell, of Cootehill, in the county of Cavan land surveyor, do hereby give notice to Peter Callan of Drogheda, who takes upon him to survey lands, to meet me on Monday the 4th day of March next, on the lands of Gravelstown, in the parish of Kilbeg, barony of Kells, and county of Meath, held by Bryan McConnell. Also, to meet me upon Friday the 8th day of March next, on the lands of Horistown, in the parish of Rathkenny, barony of Slane, and county of Meath, held by Andrew Fitzpatrick and partners. Also, to meet me upon Tuesday, the 12th day of March next, on the lands of Carnalstown, in the parish of Drumcondra, barony of Slane and county of Meath, held by George Elliot, these being all the lands mentioned in said Callan's malicious and false advertisement, against me the said Bell. These meetings I appoint in order that we may survey all those lands over again, fairly and honestly; so that justice may be done between landlords and tenants, to prevent them from having any law-suits or disputes; where I will make it appear before any two skilful honest surveyors, that said Callan is considerably mistaken in his surveys of those lands. Dated at Cootehill, the 22nd day of December, 1753. John Bell.

Universal Advertiser, 24 October 1758
Whereas the legislature having not as yet provided or enacted particular laws to establish a regulation or uniformity in the practice of land-surveying, or to punish impostors therein; and for want of recent precedents, Justices of the Peace, and other proper magistrates, are timorous in punishing such impostors, by virtue of the general act of the 23rd of Henry VIII, by which means many of the most abandoned wretches arrogate to themselves the said occupation, to the great prejudice of the nation, without any immediate remedy for the sufferer, but publicly to expose the offender: Therefore the following instances are exhibited against Mr John Bell, of Cootehill, in the county of Cavan, and Mr John Bell, of Walterstown, in the county of Louth, by whose means my affairs have been kept in one continual chain of trouble and confusion, these 11 years past, concerning the lands of Gravelstown, in the parish of Kilbeg, barony of Kells, and county of Meath, held by Bryan Connell; which land had been formerly surveyed by Mr Garret Hogan, and several other eminent surveyors, at different times, and employed by different men, and every one of the said surveyors returned it 136 acres, or upwards, and the rents were settled and paid accordingly: Till the year 1747, the ten-

ant employed the said John Bell, of Cootehill, to survey said lands, who returned it 132a. 1r. and 24p. The said tenant afterwards employed said John Bell, of Walterstown, who returned it 133a. 2r. 30p., upon which I employed Mr Peter Callan, author of the dissertation on the practice of land-surveying, who returned it 136 acres; after which several notices had been given to said Bell to meet said Callan on said land, to which he absolutely refused complying, till the said Callan was obliged to expose him for that, and several other articles, in the *Universal Advertiser*, the 1st, &c. of December, 1753; upon which both the said Bells, accompanied by several other surveyors, met said Callan on said land, in March, 1754, and, after attempting several evasive tricks, (which the said Callan immediately detected) they unanimously agreed on a correct set of field-notes. The degrees of every angle being taken with two different instruments, and the length of lines taken with a chain of 42 feet and 2 inches (being the established two-pole practical chain, plantation measure) both the said Bells then absconded, and never since appeared, either to me or to said Callan; but sent a map, containing 134a. 2r. 20p. alleging it to be the contents of the said field-notes; which notes had been calculated by several other surveyors, who all agree that they contain 136a. and the said Bells have been often served with proper notices, to come and meet on that occasion, to which they still refuse complying: Therefore it is humbly submitted to the consideration of the public, whether it appears that the said Bells are guilty of premeditated partiality, or intolerable defect in capacity? and whether a man guilty of either, is fit to undertake business of such important consequence as the surveying of land? This public notice is given to the said Bells, that if they do not make a public defence, or a submissive apology, to undeceive the public, and pay all the expense that was occasioned by this dispute, that I will proceed against them according to the said general act. Dated October the 23rd, 1758. Bartholomew O'Brien.

Universal Advertiser, 7 November 1758
Mr Bartholomew O'Brien, of the lands of Gravelstown, in the parish of Kilbeg, barony of Kells, and county of Meath, I do hereby let you know, and give you notice, that you had no occasion to publish, in the *Universal Advertiser*, so malicious and false an advertisement, against me and my nephew, John Bell, of Walterstown, in the county of Louth, concerning the survey of your lands of Gravelstown, held by Bryan Connell; for that I and my nephew always were, and now are, ready to appear on said lands,

to defend our survey, according to the field-notes and chain-work, taken by us, and your surveyor, Peter Callan, in March, 1754, which field-notes were cast up by two eminent practical surveyors, and a mathematician, who all agreed the contents to be 134a. 2r. 20p. the map of which was sent to you, which, I find, you are not willing to abide by; Therefore let the same exact field-notes be sent to be cast up by the Surveyor-General, or by the City Surveyor of Dublin, which, I think, will determine that affair; or let any other two skilful, honest surveyors, meet on the land, and cast up the said notes, and chain the land over again, if they please, and determine the contents of that survey. This is what my nephew and I were, and is always, satisfied to agree to. Dated at Cootehill, October 28, 1758. John Bell.

Universal Advertiser, 21 November 1758
To the public, concerning Mr John Bell of Cootehill, and Mr John Bell of Walterstown.

Formerly, gentlemen had no certainty in matters of surveying, but implicit dependence on the reports of such men as were pleased to style themselves surveyors of land; but now, (by means of the dissertation on the practice of land-surveying lately published) every gentleman can vindicate his own cause, in the most obscure punctilios that can possibly occur in the practice of surveying: Therefore, as the said Bells have not published a clear answer to my advertisement against them in the *Universal Advertiser* the 24th, &c. of October last; but the 31st, &c. of said month, had published in the said paper some lines, (very much resembling the evasive juggle formerly used by pretended surveyors) wherein they declare in general terms, that my said advertisement is malicious and false, without attempting to contradict any of the many irregularities that are there exhibited against them; for which reason I am obliged (in vindication of my character and property) to require of them to publish a full and clear answer to each and every one of the following questions, without evasion or equivocation; by which the impartial reader may soon judge, whether the said Bells have been judicious, honest men, in their occupation, or fraudulent impostors.

1. By what motive was the said John Bell of Cootehill induced to return a false survey of the lands of Gravelstown, in the year 1747, after surveying it with the greatest caution and deliberation, knowing he was to be opposed by several eminent surveyors? 2. By what motive was the said John Bell of Walterstown induced to return another false survey of

the said lands, in the year 1750, being under the same circumstances? 3. By what motive was the said John Bell of Cootehill induced to refuse answering any of the several notices with which he hath been served, to come and meet Mr Callan on said lands, till Mr Callan was obliged to have him exposed in the *Universal Advertiser*, the 1st of November, &c. 1753? 4. By what motive were the said Bells induced to have their chain 42 feet and 4 inches, when they met Mr Callan on said lands, in March, 1754? 5. By what authority did the said Bells then cut 2 inches off their said chain, and no more? 6. By what motive had it been contrived to have the hand-loops of the said Bells' chain afterwards stretched forth, so as to have increased its length above 2 inches, which Mr Callan detected and confuted on the first line of the said survey, who then obliged them to lay it by, and abide by his own chain, handled by himself, under the inspection of the said Bells, and all the spectators? 7. By what motive were the said Bells induced to refuse depositing a fair copy of the field notes (then taken and unanimously agreed on) in proper hands, for an unalterable memorial? 8. By what motive were the said Bells then induced to abscond, and never since met either me or Mr Callan, in order to calculate the contents of the said field-notes notwithstanding the many notices with which they were served, on that occasion? 9. By what motive was the said John Bell of Walterstown induced (in March 1754) to carry away from the said tenant a map of said lands, for which the said tenant had formerly paid him a guinea; the said map was signed by one of their eminent practical surveyors? 10. By what motive were the said Bells then induced to apply to two eminent practical surveyors, and a mathematician, in order to help them to find the true contents of the said field-notes, when in reality, any schoolboy who understands plain trigonometry, can (in the most accurate and invariable manner) calculate the contents of good field-notes, to the hundred thousandth part of a perch, which appears by the sixth general rule of the above dissertation? 11. By what motive were the said Bells induced to refuse having the said field-notes calculated by the said sixth general rule? 12. By what motive can we be induced to believe, that an accurate, invariable calculation, conformable to a mathematical demonstration, should not be the only uncontrollable determination of the contents of field-notes? 13. By what motive should we be induced to believe, that it is not now the indispensable duty of the said two eminent practical surveyors and mathematician, to produce such a calculation of the said field notes, in a fair, methodical order? 14. By what motive can we be induced to believe, that there is a

Surveyor-General, and a City-Surveyor of Dublin, lawfully empowered to determine the contents of field-notes? And if there be such superior officers, how can we know who they are, and by what law are they so established? 15. By what authority can the said Bells refuse paying all the expense that was occasioned by this dispute?

This public notice is given to the said Bells, that if they refuse or neglect answering the foregoing 15 questions, as aforesaid, that I will proceed against them as the law directs. Dated November the 19th, 1758. Bartholomew O'Brien.

Universal Advertiser, 19 December 1758
Mr Bartholomew O'Brien, of the lands of Gravelstown, in the parish of Kilbeg, barony of Kells, and county of Meath, in answer to all your trumpery of rhapsody and sophistical questions, maliciously published against me and my nephew in the *Universal Advertiser*, to injure our characters, concerning the survey of your lands of Gravelstown, held by Bryan Connell, we give you this public and timely notice, that upon the 22nd of January next, at 12 o'clock, we will meet you upon the said lands; and there will defend our survey, according to the field notes and chainwork taken and agreed to by us, and your surveyor, Peter Callan, in March 1754; and we will make it appear, before any two skilful, honest surveyors, that the said Callan is mistaken in casting up the contents of said field-notes, for that the contents thereof will not amount to 136 acres, as you assert from said Callan's survey. Dated at Cootehill this 9th of Dec[ember] 1758. John Bell.

Universal Advertiser, 7 April 1759
To the public. Whereas, in October and November last, there were contrived, forged and published, two malicious, false and scandalous advertisements, in the *Universal Advertiser*, against Mr John Bell, of Cootehill, land-surveyor, and Mr John Bell, of Walterstown, concerning the surveying of the lands of Gravelstown, in the barony of Kells in the county of Meath, and one Mr Barth. O'Brien's name subscribed thereunto, as the publisher, who is a gentleman of good character. The printer being applied to, to know who gave it to him, declares himself, and proved by his man, that one Peter Callan, of Drogheda, who styles himself land-surveyor, delivered it, with Mr O'Brien's name subscribed thereunto, to the printer, and said Bells taking Mr O'Brien to account for publishing the same, Mr O'Brien declared, before gentlemen and others,

more than once, upon his honour and reputation, that he was not the publisher, nor gave any direction for publishing the same, and that he would horse-whip Callan for daring to make use of his name to so villainous a thing. And whereas the said Mr O'Brien, the 15th of March last, hath given under his hand, that he hath rebuked Callan for it properly, for presuming to make use of his name without his knowledge; the public may readily judge what kind of a person Callan is, and that he ought to be prosecuted and sued for defamation and damages. The said Cootehill Bell sets forth, as he hath surveyed many lands in his 43 years practice, and ended many disputes amongst land-surveyors and kept his reputation, and hath had the approbation of the best surveyors and mathematicians in the kingdom in his favour, and is ready, where any of his surveys are disputed, to appear on the lands, and defend and make his survey good, before any honest, skilful surveyor, whomsoever, that the public will not judge of him the worse for being scandaled, undeservedly, by any splenetic professor of surveying, who strives to injure said Bell's character. Dated at Cootehill, the 4th of April, 1759. John Bell.

Universal Advertiser, 19 May 1759
To the public, concerning Mr John Bell, of Cootehill, and Mr John Bell, of Walterstown.

In conformity to the general method of punishing impostors, in the practice of land-surveying, the said Bells had been exposed in the *Universal Advertiser* the 23rd, &c. of October, and the 19th, &c. of November last, for intolerable evasions and prevarications by them used in the survey of the lands of Gravelstown, in the barony of Kells, county of Meath, and as the kind of vindication by them published in the said paper the 28th, &c. of October, the 12th, &c. of December, and the 7th, &c. of April last, so nearly resembled the frantic expressions of miserable objects in Bedlam, I hitherto considered them as objects of compassion, rather than of further opposition. But now I am importuned by several of the nobility and principal gentry of this kingdom, to set forth this affair in the clearest light – knowing that great part of mankind have the misfortune of being infatuated by habitual prejudice, and abhor all reasonable inquiries after such truths as are beyond the limits of their prejudiced inclinations; it is now plain to all common readers, (except such as are so infatuated) how far the said Bells have transgressed, since it appears that they have no subterfuge but their atrocious, scurrilous invectives, against me, for not being properly authorised by Mr O'Brien to publish the said two advertisements in his name. Therefore I humbly submit it to the consideration of the public, whether that should mitigate the enormity of the said Bells' proceedings in the said survey, more than if the said advertisement had been published in any other name, since there is nothing therein set forth against the said Bells but undeniable facts by them committed; and as Mr O'Brien, in the presence of several gentlemen, has made a verbal promise, (often repeated these twelve months past) to pay me the sum of nine pounds, sterling, on condition that I should use the most effectual means of obliging the said Bells to comply to an impartial decision of the said dispute, in which nothing but exposing them would prevail; therefore it was impossible for me to have executed my orders by any other scheme but the method I have used; which I was obliged to use before with the said John Bell of Cootehill, (in the *Universal Advertiser*, the 1st, &c. of November, 1753) concerning the said land of Gravelstown; and the part of the lands of Horistown in the parish of Rathkenny, county of Meath, held by Mr Fitzpatrick, &c. and one of the principal gentlemen of the county of Cavan was likewise obliged to expose the said John Bell of Walterstown, in the *Dublin Journal*, about 15 years ago; by which it appears, that the said Bells have often deserved to be used in this manner. And it seems, now, that it is a happiness of some importance to me, the said Bells cannot charge me with any deficiency in capacity, diligence or integrity, in anything relative to my occupation; and since they have not, as yet, attempted to account for any part of the enormity laid to their charge on this occasion, I require of them now to publish a proper answer to each and every one of the fifteen questions (relative to their conduct in this dispute) which were published in the *Universal Advertiser* the 19th, &c. of November last; which questions, if properly solved by the said Bells, would fully clear up the point. Now, the said John Bell of Walterstown declares, that he ought to be exempted, as he has taken away his map of the said land, and refunded the money he received for it: But let it be observed, that he ought, in like manner, to have taken up all the maps he ever returned, and refund all the money he received for them, if he cannot vindicate the truth of any of his surveys, when brought to a proper test. As it is the predominant opinion of the generality of our civil magistrates, that the statute does not sufficiently authorise them to inflict personal punishments on impostors in surveying land, nothing can prove more effectual on that occasion, than pecuniary punishment; therefore I propose the following scheme to the said Bells, to which, if they refuse to comply, it may be easily judged what confidence the public can have, in the truth, of any part of their 43 years practice, &c. I will deposit 35 guineas in the hands of a gentleman, on the said lands of Gravelstown, at 8 o'clock in the morning, the 5th day of June next, which sum is to be divided into seven different bets, viz. 1st, I will lay five guineas that the said land contains more than 132a 1r. 24p. which is the return made by the said John Bell of Cootehill in the year 1747. Secondly, five guineas that the said land contains more than 133a. 2r. 30p. being the return made by the said John Bell of Walterstown in the year 1750. Thirdly, five guineas that the said land contains more than 134a. 2r. 20p. being the joint return made by both the said Bells in March 1754. Fourthly, five guineas that the said land contains 136a. which is the only return made by me. Fifthly, five guineas that the said land of Horistown contains more than 70a. which is the return made by the said John Bell of Cootehill in the year 1752. Sixthly, five guineas that the said land contains more than 71a. 1r. being the joint return made by both the said Bells in March 1754; And seventhly, five guineas that the said land contains 72a. 1r. which is the only return made by me; and, in order to avoid the imputation of inaccuracies in instruments, or errors in tables, as the said land is clear and level, let it all be reduced into right-angled triangles, and the base and perpendicular of each triangle exactly chained, and multiplied one by the other, throughout the whole polygon; all which being added together, the half thereof shall be the exact content of the said land; (Euclid 41.1) all which to be impartially performed in the presence of two gentlemen of considerable property in the country, who shall be men of learning, and experience in the art of surveying, and men that neither of them ever signed any false map of the said lands; and if either of us be condemned in each and every one of the foregoing seven articles, the party so concerned may be rationally allowed to be altogether unworthy of the privilege of living any longer in any part of His Majesty's dominions in Europe: Therefore, let proper bonds be reciprocally executed between us the said day, on the said land, obliging the party who shall be so condemned, to pay unto the other party, the sum of one hundred pounds sterling, provided the person or persons so condemned, can be found in any part of the said dominions, any time ever after the said first day of August; by which means the imposture will be fairly ascertained, and the impostor deservedly punished: Now I desire that the said Bells may (without evasion or equivocation) publish either their acceptance of these proposals, or their objections against them. Dated, May the 7th, 1759. Peter Callan.

Universal Advertiser, 22 May 1759
Mr Peter Callan of Drogheda, that surveys land, in answer to your magnanimous advertisements published in October and November last, against me and my nephew John Bell, to injure us, I published another on the 9th of December last, that we should all meet on the lands of Gravelstown the 22nd of January following, to settle that survey. You did not come there to meet me, nor any from you. I and my nephew, with two surveyors, stayed that day, on those lands waiting for you, from ten in the morning, till about four in the afternoon, to show you your mistake in casting up the contents of that land by the field notes taken by us together, when Mr O' Brien showed us the mearings, for those field notes will not per close the map by protraction, but stands wide of it; neither will they answer the easting and westing by trigonometrical calculation; so that upon this hypothesis, no exact survey can be ascertained, until the error in taking those notes be rectified in the field, which you hindered that day to be done, by not coming there to meet me. And as you did not come to meet me that day, to have the field notes set right, and the survey truly calculated, I will not give myself the trouble to meet you on Gravelstown the 5th day of June next; and as for your sophistical questions, scheme, bets and bonds, I reject them all, as not worth my notice, or any such like chimerical bravadoes, as the field work will not per close; for that I am better employed, than to enter into any disputes, or cavillings with you, about any of your surveys; and, for the future; I will not mind, nor answer, nor take notice, of anything you write or say, if it be not actionable. Dated at Cootehill, the 19th of May, 1759. John Bell.

Dublin Journal, 23 June 1759
Whereas the dispute concerning the survey of the lands of Gravelstown in the Barony of Kells, County of Meath, occasioned constant confusion and expensive law suits these 12 years past, between Mr Bartholomew O'Brien the landlord and Bryan Connell the tenant, which proved the utter ruin of the said tenant; the source of which appears now to have been a perfect juggle executed by John Bell of Cootehill, and John Bell of Walterstown, by the assistance of two eminent practical surveyors, and a mathematician, who joined the said Bells in signing several false maps of the said lands, etc., the falsity of all which maps is publicly acknowledged by the said Bell in the *Universal Advertiser* the 22nd &c. of May last, where the said Bells accuse me of negligence in not meeting them on the said lands the 22 of January last, in order to help them to

correct their errors in the said survey; after they had been served with timely notice that great part of the mears of said land had been then inaccessible by inundation, therefore, the 12th of March following was then unanimously appointed for our meeting on the said land; and they did not meet me that day, nor any time since; therefore I was obliged to publish a scheme (in the *Universal Advertiser* the 15th of last May) to oblige them either to submit or traverse, in a proper decisive manner, upon which they submitted as aforesaid; therefore Mr O'Brien desires me to serve said Connell with proper notice, that he will oblige him to pay for 136 acres (which is the contents of my map of the said land) if the said Connell will not employ some skilful surveyor or surveyors, who will fairly prove a deficiency in the said land before the 26th day of July next; and proper means shall be then used to oblige the said Bells to pay for all the damages that has hitherto been occasioned by this dispute – N. B. There never was any difference concerning the mears or bounds of the said land; and as the said Bells declaring that they will not attempt to survey any more land, is not sufficient satisfaction to the public for not having this dispute fully discussed I will pay a guinea unto any surveyor who will demonstrate (in my presence, any time before the said 26th of July) that the said land does not contain 136 acres, plantation measure. 14 June 1759. Peter Callan.

Dublin Journal, 21 July 1759
Peter Callan of Drogheda, who styles yourself land surveyor, notwithstanding all your false and malicious advertisements, and mighty bravadoes, published from time to time to injure my character, I give you this public notice, that, upon the 27th of August next, at eleven o'clock, I will meet you on the lands of Gravelstown, to defend my survey against all splenetic pretenders to surveying whomsoever, and will make it appear, upon a fair survey (if Mr O'Brien gives leave to survey that land) that Bryan Connell's part does not contain 136 acres, as you have asserted. Dated at Cootehill July 17, 1759. John Bell.

Dublin Cazette, 20 October 1759
Whereas the 27th of August, being appointed in the *Dublin Journal* of the 20th of July last, by John Bell, of Cootehill, for meeting me on the lands of Gravelstown, in order to have the long continued dispute concerning the survey of the said land, properly adjusted; and accordingly I have been met there that day by the said John Bell of Cootehill; John Bell of

Walterstown, and James Bell of Carrickmacross, attended by a teacher of mathematics, and several other gentlemen, &c. where it did not appear that either of the said Bells understood the method of investigating the contents of surveys by trigonometrical calculation; therefore they were obliged to beg leave to declare themselves off, and employ the said teacher to accompany me in settling the said dispute; that being granted, they then begged leave to have it postponed, for fifteen days, alleging, that the said teacher could no sooner be properly prepared, which was likewise granted; and accordingly the said teacher attended by three of his pupils, met me on the said land, the tenth of September last, where he would not be content with any method of measuring our chains without level boards! Therefore we were obliged to go two miles off the said land to adjust the length of our chains, and when that was effectually done, the said teacher declared that he could not attend the said survey till some other time; upon which he absconded without appointing any other time of meeting on that occasion; and he still refuses to appoint a day for that purpose: Therefore this notice is given to all whom it may concern, that the twelfth day of November next, at nine o'clock in the morning, I will have on the said lands several gentlemen of learning and experience in the art of surveying, who will survey the said land in the most public manner; the curious are requested to attend. To avoid the imputation of litigiousness, and convince the public, that I would take no advantage of the frailty, or inability of my fellow creatures, I hereby offer unto the said Bells the arbitration of two judicious, impartial gentlemen concerning all, and everything that ever happened between us in this dispute. Dated October 18, 1759. Peter Callan.

Dublin Gazette, 30 October 1759
Peter Callan who takes upon you, to survey land, and publish a Dissertation on the practice of surveying, I give you this public notice, that upon the 12th of November next, at 11 o'clock, I will meet you once more, on the lands of Gravelstown, (as you desire) and will defend and make good my survey against you, by calculation trigonometrically, arithmetically, and mechanically; and will likewise stand by my survey against any reputed crack brained, crazy-headed, lying splenetic pretender to surveying whomsoever. Dated at Cootehill, the 23rd of October 1759. John Bell.

Dublin Gazette, 19 August 1760

Whereas the man who (these 50 years past) has influenced the public to believe that he could (by conjuration) concert schemes for the discovery of stolen goods, &c. and that he was an infallible practitioner of surveying land &c. if such a man should be publicly detected, as John Bell of Cootehill, and John Bell of Walterstown, are now, concerning the dispute in the survey of the lands of Gravelstown, etc. it would be easy to calculate the efficacy of the honour and honesty of any man, who would afterwards employ or recommend such a man, in, or to, any job surveying land, or any other employment of public utility, where skill and integrity are absolutely necessary; notwithstanding the great influence of the opulent man who was employed, by the said Bells to solicit Mr O'Brien's interest (contrary to all humane principles) for them against his own surveyor. Mr O'Brien still positively declares, that he is ready to depose upon oath, (if required) the truth of every fact exhibited against them, (on this occasion) in the two advertisements in the *Universal Advertiser* of October and November 1758. I presume it is needless to expatiate on the enormity of the said Bell's behaviour in this dispute, since they have (by their advertisements) conveyed unto the public the most clear ideas of their own characters, etc. But it is necessary to observe, that the said John Bell of Walterstown is the principal [?] importuned others to sign two different false maps of the said lands and refused to appear the 12th of November last, according to appointment; when the said John Bell of Cootehill is concerned in no more than one of the said false combinations, and appeared on the said lands the said 12th of November, where he declared that the inclemency of the weather rendered it impracticable for such an old man as him to examine the said survey at that time; and that he would attend it any time after the middle of April following; and was ready to expend £400 on the said dispute, before he would acknowledge any more of his errors in the said survey; but could not, ever since, be persuaded to come to settle that affair.

 Therefore this notice is given to all whom it may concern, that the 27th of this instant August, at nine o'clock in the morning, I will have on the said lands, two gentlemen of learning and experience in the art of surveying, who will (upon oath) survey the said land in the most accurate manner, and give the clearest satisfaction to all curious spectators: This farther notice is likewise given to the two eminent practical surveyors, and mathematician who formerly joined the said Bells in signing two different false maps of the said lands, that if they do not appear the said day, on the said land, and publicly clear themselves of the imputation of forgery, that they shall be prosecuted as the law directs. Dated August the 18th, 1760. Peter Callan.

And lest Mr Bell should be tempted to apply his said four hundred pounds to bribes, I earnestly recommend him to lay out that sum in bets, viz £30 in each of 7 bets, and £190 in the main, as prescribed in my advertisement in the *Universal Advertiser* of May, 1759.

Dublin Gazette, 13 September 1760
Whereas the 27th of August last, being the day I have appointed in the *Dublin Gazette* of the 19th of said month, for the decision of the dispute which was most obstinately continued in the lands of Gravelstown these 13 years past, by Messrs John Bell, of Cootehill, and John Bell, of Walterstown: Accordingly I have been met there by the said John Bell, of Cootehill, attended by a teacher of mathematics, and a great number of surveyors and other gentlemen of curiosity; where Messrs Robert Berrell, and John O' Brien, had been unanimously appointed operators, at the said survey, which they have executed under the inspection and to the entire satisfaction of the whole assembly; by which it appears that the said land contains 136a. 2r. plantation measure, which is exactly equal to the return made of the said land in the year 1731, by Mr Garret Hogan and others; by which the impartial reader can easily judge how far the said Bells have transgressed, having in their first survey insisted on 132a. 1r. 24p. in their second survey 133a. 2r. 30p. in their third survey 134a. 2r. 20p. and now are obliged to acknowledge that the said land had been truly surveyed before them; but the said John Bell, of Walterstown, did not appear on the said dispute since his inability had been detected and set forth in the *Dublin Gazette* of the 20th of October last, for which discovery (if he resents it) I am ready with the utmost pleasure to give him any reasonable satisfaction, as I have given to the said John Bell, of Cootehill, in the presence of the said assembly, by offering to recant and insert in the public papers at my own expense, every allegation that he could prove false or ill-grounded against him in any of my advertisements on this occasion these seven years past; upon which it appeared that he could not point out so much as a single syllable either false or ill-grounded in the said advertisements. Dated September 12, 1760. Peter Callan.

Dublin Gazette, 20 September 1760

To the public. John Bell, of Cootehill, accompanied by three mathematicians whose names are hereunto subscribed, did upon the 27th of last month, on the disputed lands of Gravelstown, meet Peter Callan, with his two surveyors, which two surveyors, with their own instrument and a chain three inches too short, did survey and took field notes round the said lands; upon which, Peter Callan, in his advertisement of the 12th inst, says that the content is 136a 2r. which I do insist upon and deny that it is the true content nor exact survey of that land, for that those field notes and survey will neither calculate mathematically nor perclose a map by protraction mechanically. These three mathematicians having examined the field notes, finds that there is an error of 36 links in the easting and westing, and another error of nine links in the northing and southing, and in the protracting, the degree leads not within eight degrees of the point, and the chain line above 25 links to one side, which they will stand by before the best trigonometrical calculators in the kingdom, so no survey can be made by these field notes; so Peter Callan, you may go to the field and correct your errors, and learn (if you can) to publish truth, and find me out a remedy for an enthusiastic crazy soul. September 15 1760. John Bell, James Corran, William Corran, Michael McKinlie.

Dublin Gazette, 27 September 1760

Whereas we cannot expect propriety nor connection in the advertisements of a man who is inflicted with a compound of mental disorders, as Mr John Bell of Cootehill in his advertisement in the *Dublin Gazette* of the 20th instant, publicly declares himself to be; for whom I cannot think of a better remedy than the use of St Patrick's Hospital but if his said declaration appears to be calculated with a view of getting himself exempted from being obliged to pay the damages that was occasioned by his refractoriness in the dispute of the survey of the lands of Gravelstown, better lawyers shall be employed to determine it; as the said dispute is now determined according to law; by two gentlemen of considerable properties in that country, who are men of learning, profound mathematicians, and thorough experienced practitioners in the art of surveying; unanimously chosen by both parties, and upon oath as to their care and integrity; but if any of Mr Bell's friends will choose to carry this affair to a higher pitch, I am still ready to lay out (in bets on that occasion) any sum not exceeding four hundred pounds, as prescribed in my advertisement in the *Universal Advertiser* of May 1759. Given under my hand, September the 26th, 1760. Peter Callan.

Appendix D
Books on land surveying
published or advertised in Ireland

1654 Henry Osborne. *A more exact way to delineate the plot of any spacious parcel of land, as baronies, parishes, and townlands, as also of rivers, harbours and loughs, etc., than is yet in practice. Also a method or form of keeping the field book and how to cast up the superficial content of a plot most exactly* (Dublin: William Bladen). British Library; Marsh's Library, Dublin.

1724 Thomas Burgh. *A method to determine the areas of right-lined figures universally. Very useful for ascertaining the contents of any survey* (Dublin). British Library; Trinity College, Dublin.

1750 Peter Callan. *A dissertation on the practice of land-surveying in Ireland* (Drogheda). Stated in the 1758 edition (see below) to have been published in 1750. No copies known. Advertised *Dublin Journal*, 9 Mar. 1751.

1752 Robert Gibson. *A treatise of practical surveying* (Dublin). No copies known. Advertised *Dublin Journal*, 9 May 1752. In Richeson, *English Land Measuring*, p. 154, this work is said to have been first published in 1739.

1752 Jacob Neville. 'Proposals for printing by subscription, A treatise of practical surveying, shewing everything that is useful in that art; particularly, seven various methods of calculation to determine the content of ground; one of which, with tables of difference of latitude and departure, proceeding gradually from 1 to 100 chain, calculated for every degree in the quadrant, (including quarter, half, and 3 quarters of each degree) never yet published. Note, these tables is so fitted to the foregoing methods, that one (by them) may determine the content of any field notes with great ease & exactness, in quarter the time now spent by surveyors, etc. also to measure the several works of building and with dialling. By Mr Neville, Professor of Mathematics. N.B. The book will contain about 300 pages octavo, price six British shillings bound' (*Dublin Journal*, 28 Mar. 1752). No copies known. In a later advertisement

(*Dublin Journal*, 9 May 1752) the book was said to contain eight methods of calculation, of which two had never previously been published.

1754 Jacob Neville. 'In the press, and speedily will be published by subscription, Mr Neville's Treatise of surveying, shewing everything useful in that art, particularly, eight entire new, and much more concise methods of calculation (to determine the contents of surveys from the field notes) than any heretofore made public; with two other geometrical methods, and a new table of difference of latitude and departure, proceeding gradually from 1 link to 100 chains, fitted for said methods of calculation to every degree, quarter and third of a degree in the quadrant, which will render practical surveying much more expeditious, easy and certain than it is at present. Said table shews the base and perpendicular lines of any hill, which is exceedingly useful in surveys, &c. The book will contain 340 pages, large octavo. Price to subscribers six British shillings, (and seven to others). Half to be paid at subscribing (*Dublin Journal*, 7 Sep. 1754). No copies known.

1758 Peter Callan. *A dissertation on the practice of land surveying in Ireland, and an essay towards a general regulation therein in two parts by Peter Callan, student & practitioner in the art of surveying* (Drogheda). National Library of Ireland. Advertised as lately published and sold by Peter Lord of Cook Street, Dublin, at one British shilling, *Dublin Gazette*, 20 Oct. 1759.

1760 James Morphett. '... The said James Morphett has now ready for the press (and will be published as soon as a sufficient number of subscribers is found) A compleat practical system of surveying. In this system, besides what is shewn in other authors, is added – First, a method to find the east or west points from the field notes, very useful for protracting. – Secondly, to determine the angles of the field from the bearings taken by the quartered compass, or circumferentor. – Thirdly, to find the area of all right-lined figures by a new method of calculation, without the help of map, instrument, or table, having only the field notes as commonly taken. – Fourthly, surveying by the chain, whereby that instrument is made to answer (in all capacities), the use of the theodolite, semicircle, or plain table; wherein it is proved, that the degrees of angles may be, and with less trouble, taken as well with the chain as with any instrument whatever. – Fifthly, an infallible method to find out from the field-notes any one error committed in taking them, the station wherein it was committed, and how to rectify it. – Sixthly, a demonstration that there never was a true method given of dividing of land and an infallible method given how to perform the same. To these are added several other useful things; all which the curious are welcome to see at the author's house aforesaid. The whole illustrated with copper plates and useful tables. Price to subscribers 5s 5d. one half to be paid at subscribing, and the remainder at delivery of the book …' (*Belfast News-letter*, 13 Mar. 1760). No copies known.

1762 Jacob Neville. 'Neville's new tables, of ninety pages in very large octavo, for determining the areas of surveys from field notes, arithmetically, in sixteen different methods; also six geometrical ones; (being in all thirteen methods more, and more concise than ever were published by any person that has wrote on the science) and a table of ten pages for changing several measures; and everything else useful in the practice of that art. Price six British shillings; half to be paid at subscribing, and the remainder on the delivery of the book, which will contain upwards of 320 pages' (*Dublin Journal*, 2 Mar. 1762). No copies known.

1763 Robert Gibson. *A treatise of practical surveying; which is demonstrated from its first principles. Wherein every thing that is useful and curious in that art is fully considered and explained. Particularly four new and very concise methods to determine the areas of right-lined figures arithmetically, or by calculation, as well as the geometrical ones heretofore treated of; with two other new geometrical methods much more accurate and ready than any of the former, never before made public. Also the method of tracing defaced boundaries from the Down (or any other) Survey. Very useful to persons who have any property in land, to lawyers in controverted surveys, and to practical surveyors. The whole illustrated with copper-plates. The second edition* (Dublin: William Ross). National Library of Ireland.

1767 Thomas Power. 'Proposals for printing by subscription; The universal land-surveyor: containing, the elements of the art clearly demonstrated, with their application to the practical and useful part of it. Also, the topographical manner of taking field notes, never before published, by which the survey of harbours, fortifications, cities, manors, counties or kingdoms, may be taken, with as little trouble as that of a few fields.

To which is added, a new, extensive and correct set of tables, of latitude and departure, by which gentlemen of landed interests as well as surveyors, may (with very little trouble) prove the truth or falsity of any survey, from the field notes, and thereby prevent many expenses, attendant on the disagreement of surveyors.

By these tables also, any survey may be cast up, (without the assistance of mathematical instruments) in much less time, and with greater facility, than can be performed by any other method hitherto published.

The whole illustrated with copper-plates ... This work ... will make about seventeen sheets in quarto ...' [Price to subscribers, 5s 5d], (*Cork Evening Post*, 15 Oct. 1767). No copies known.

1768 Robert Gibson. *A treatise of practical surveying. The third edition* (Dublin: Laurence Flin and Robert Fitzsimons). British Library.

1768 Benjamin Noble. *Geodaesia Hibernica: or an essay on practical surveying. Which contains the following useful improvements. I. Protraction without parallels, &c. II. A description of a new instrument, by which any gentleman, tho' unskilled in surveying, may measure a map, or part of a map, almost in one view. III. Different methods for correcting surveys, and fitting them for calculation. IV. A new method and plan of calculation, proposed to practitioners, to give in return with their surveys. V. A new set of tables, in which may be found, by inspection only, the difference of latitude, and departure, for a station of any length and bearing that may happen in practice* (Dublin: Alex McCulloh). National Library of Ireland. Advertised *Dublin Journal*, 19 Apr. 1768; *Leinster Journal*, 16 July 1768, 31 Aug. 1773, 25 Jan. 1775.

1768 William Hawney. The complete measurer; or, the whole art of measuring. In two parts. 8th edition. To which is added, an appendix, 1, of gauging; 2, of land measuring (Cork: the Company of Booksellers). No copies known (E. R. McC. Dix, *List of Books, Pamphlets, Journals, etc., Printed in Cork in the 17th and 18th Centuries* (Cork, 1904), part 3, p.4).

1770 *An essay on the origin and use of tables of latitude and departure; particularly, as they are suited to the purposes of land surveying* (Dublin: James Porter). Library of Congress. Advertised *Waterford Chronicle*, 1 Jan. 1771.

Internal evidence suggests that the author was not the Robertson whose *Traverse tables* (see below) the *Essay* accompanied, but an

Irish mathematician whose interest in land surveying was more theoretical than professional.

1770 [Abraham?] Robertson. *Robertson's traverse tables; or, tables of difference of latitude and departure: constructed to every quarter of a degree of the quadrant, and continued from one to the distance of one hundred miles or chains. Originally applied to plane sailing; but now more particularly suited to the purposes of land surveying* (Dublin: James Porter). Library of Congress (bound with the previous item). Taylor (*Practitioners of Hanoverian England*, p.295) attributes this work to John Robertson, whom she describes as a land surveyor of Dublin; the Library of Congress prefers the English mathematician Abraham Robertson (1751–1826).

1772 John Hood. *Tables of difference of latitude and departure for navigators, land surveyors, &c. With their application to plane trigonometry, and their use in plotting and calculating surveys, which perfects the house-work of that art. To which is prefixed, an account of the diurnal variation of the magnetic needle, the error thence arising and its correction; the use of a new surveying instrument, &c. Being great improvements of the field-work. The whole almost entirely new. Compiled at the instance of a committee of the Dublin Society* (Dublin: William Sleater, for the author). British Library.

1772 A. Burns. *Geodaesia improved; or, a new and correct method of surveying* (Belfast: John Hoey and James Magee). No copies known. J. Anderson, *Catalogue of Early Belfast Printed Books 1694 to 1830* (Belfast, 1902), p.10. *Derry Journal*, 29 Oct. 1773.

1783 Garret Heagerty. 'Immediately ready for the press, and to be published, by Mr Garret Heagerty, land-surveyor and architect, as soon as there are a sufficient number of subscribers, A new and curious method of surveying inventively and mathematically demonstrated, and adapted to a simple and portable instrument of his own invention.

Notwithstanding that the branch has been treated of by some good authors, yet, the compiler of this treatise, flatters himself, that his method of ascertaining the areas of ground, although perfectly different from theirs, will be allowed to be less subject to error, more expeditious, and as mathematically true; as the accuracy of any survey taken by this method, can be proved in a few minutes on the spot, by the pen alone, without the help of tables, or any kind of instruments, to an incontrovertible certainty: To which is added, some curious improvements, which he has gained by an [?] state of practice and study, together with the method he used in calculating surveys, with tables of the difference of latitude and departure, for any station that may happen in land surveying by inspection only' (*Cork Evening Post*, 24 July 1783). No copies known.

1784 Thomas Harding. 'Speedily will be finished. The practical land surveyor's best companion, being a treatise on the construction of tables of latitude and departure, and their application to all the methods of calculation hitherto published, with a comparative view of Bourgh's [*sic*], Gibson's and Noble's methods, and the addition of two new concise ones, never before printed, by T. Harding, Meath-street, mathematician. To which is subjoined a description of his improved octant, an instrument designed to supersede the use of these tables in surveying and navigation. The price, stitched in blue paper, will be 2s 2d. neatly bound and lettered 2s 8^{1}/2d' (*Dublin Journal*, 31 Aug. 1784). No copies known.

1786 Thomas Power. 'Proposals for printing by subscription, The universal land surveyor, containing the elements of the art, with their application to the practical parts of it. The topographical manner of taking field notes and drawing maps. New and correct tables of difference of latitude and departure for any stationary distance and bearing to every five minutes of the quadrant by inspection only: a degree of accuracy not hitherto attempted by any writer on the subject. The instrument at present used by surveyors is the circumferentor, by which they can take angles (only by guessing) to every fifteen minutes of the quadrant: it is well known that a small error in an angle, may make a very considerable error in the calculation of a survey in proportion to the length of the station; moreover the circumferentor is subject to many other inaccuracies, as the attraction of iron mines, the agitation of the magnetical needle by every puff of wind: it is often prevented from playing freely by the moisture of the atmosphere, above all the centre pin in which the needle vibrates, is so liable to accidents, as to render it often totally useless, etc. all which call loudly for a reformation in the surveying instrument and calculation.

By the above new tables the surveyor will now be enabled to use the theodolite which gives the angles of the boundaries with certainty to every five minutes of the quadrant, an instrument which cannot be affected by any of those accidents attendant on the circumferentor, also by the above tables and theodolite the surveyor can (in the most expeditious manner) prove his field work both as to angles and chain lines.

This useful art being thus fixed on accurate and just principles, must equally succeed in the hands of every judicious practitioner. The work to be illustrated with handsome engravings by Thomas Power, master of the Academy of Arts and Sciences, Cork ... Subscribers to pay three crowns, viz. half a guinea at subscribing, and four shillings and ten pence halfp. on delivery of the book' (*Cork Evening Post*, 13 Apr. 1786). No copies known.

1786 Anthony Divir. 'A new book. And ready for the press, The mariner and land-surveyor's companion: showing the figure and use of three mathematical instruments, never before published; to which is added, an accurate abridgement of the tables of latitude and departure, adapted to the whole half and quarter degrees of the quartered compass; and to any stationary distance in leagues, chains, miles, &c. by which the northing, southing, easting, and westing of any field work may be obtained; consequently, a close before the surveyor leaves the field without any delay. The first of these instruments is a bassimeter, by which the basis or content of any hill or mountain may be ascertained, by inspection only, to the nicest accuracy. The second in order is a naval quadrant, by which, the meridian altitude of the sun and latitude of the place may be discovered without the least trouble to the skilful observer, independent of the horizon. Thirdly an universal level, by which, the depth of earth to be dug away in any ground designed for a canal or aquaduct may be ascertained in feet, inches, &c. before the ground is broke up. With an appendix to the foregoing inventions, taken from other authors, being tables of the sun's declination, and how to find the variation of the compass, &c. carefully compiled. Subscription five shillings and five pence. One half paid in hand, the other half on delivery of the book: and if no book, the money will be returned. Subscribers' names, titles, and places of residence, shall be carefully prefixed to this book. The above instruments and abridgements were invented, exemplified, and demonstrated by Anthony Divir, land-surveyor, nigh Donegal' (*Strabane Journal*, 28 Aug. 1786). No copies known.

1787 James Irwin. *A treatise on gunnery, in theory and practice ... to which is subjoined an appendix containing some useful remarks, &c.*

on surveying (Limerick: A. Watson & Co.). Royal Irish Academy. City Library, Limerick.

Irwin also published his method of calculating areas, in a letter to *Anthologia Hibernica*, 4 (1794), pp 133–6.

1787 Nicholas Walsh. 'Under the patronage of the Rt Hon. and Hon. the Dublin Society, and by the approbation of the Rev. Henry Usher ... and Mr Sherrard, an eminent land surveyor, will be published by subscription, A treatise on surveying, by Nicholas Walsh, of the city of Waterford, mathematician; which contains a short logarithmic method of calculating the area of any estate or farm, independent of magnetism, from the field angles and stationary distances only, without the least assistance from trigonometry: the field angles to be taken to the twentieth part of a degree with accuracy and expedition, by a plain semicircle and vernier, improved by him for that purpose; by which the errors resulting from the daily librations of the needle may be avoided. It contains a very short method of dividing land; Mr Burgh's and Mr Gibson's methods of magnetic calculations; short, accurate methods of finding the distance of any inaccessible object; the horizontal bases of hills; elegant new methods of computation, by a sliding vernier and computing circle, invented by him, etc. – Proposals at large may be had from all the booksellers of the kingdom, and subscriptions received by them; by the author, in Waterford; and Byrne, bookseller, in Dublin ...' (*Dublin Evening Post*, 14 Apr. 1787). Also advertised *Cork Evening Post*, 12 July 1787, price 8s $^{1}/_{2}$d bound, 5s 5d to be paid on subscribing. No copies known.

1787 Thomas Power. 'Now ready for the press, and will be published as soon as two hundred have subscribed, The universal land surveyor. The author of this work, having by very laborious calculations, constructed a set of tables of difference of latitude and departure to every five minutes of the quadrant, and thereby (with a complete theoretical and practical system) hath brought the art of land-surveying to a degree of perfection not hitherto attempted, most humbly solicits the patronage of the nobility and gentlemen of landed interest of this kingdom, whose properties are so intimately connected with the accuracy of this business.

It is humbly conceived the encouragement due to such performance, should be a national concern. Subscriptions are taken by the author, Thomas Power, master of the Academy of Arts and

Sciences, Academy Street, the printers hereof, and all the stationers and booksellers, Cork' (*Cork Evening Post*, 23 Apr. 1787). No copies known.

1787 Thomas Harding. Pamphlet on the variation of the compass. Mentioned in *Freeman's Journal*, 11 Oct. 1787. No copies known.

1790 Robert Gibson. *A treatise of practical surveying*. Fourth edition (Dublin: Richard Cross). Franklin Institute, Philadelphia.

1791 Thomas Harding. 'This day is published (price 4s 10^{1}/2d) at Sleater's, Dame-street, Tables of latitude and departure, with an essay on their origin and use; particularly as they are suited to the purposes of land surveying: – also, an appendix, containing an illustration of all the methods of calculation hitherto practised, and a specimen of eight new methods, never before published. By Thomas Harding. Designed to rescue calculation from the intricacy and obscurity in which it was too long involved; an impartial examination of the notes and remarks on the various methods hitherto published, will shew how far the author's endeavours have been successful. The practical surveyor, who would wish to be decided by arithmetical calculation, which cannot err, will find this small volume his best companion, and his employers must, of course, experience it their best friend' (*Dublin Chronicle*, 26 July 1791). No copies known. Harding later found an outlet for his 'An Elucidation of Eight Universal Methods for Determining the Areas of Right Lined Figures' in *Anthologia Hibernica*, 2 (1793), pp 212–16, 292–6, 372–6, 446–8, with a postscript in 3 (1794), pp 53–6.

1795 Robert Gibson. *A treatise of practical surveying*. Fifth edition (Dublin: P. Wogan). Catholic University of America, Washington D.C.; University of Michigan, Ann Arbor.

1802 Robert Gibson. *A treatise of practical surveying*. Sixth edition (Dublin: P. Wogan). University of Pennsylvania, Philadelphia.

1810 Robert Gibson. *A treatise on practical surveying*. Sixth edition, improved (Dublin: P. Wogan). New York State Library, Albany; University of Alabama.

1839 Marcus Trotter. *Gibson's treatise on land surveying developing the most approved methods of surveying, viz. by the circumferentor, theodolite and chain; also trigonometrical surveying* ... (Dublin: John Cumming, 1839). British Library; National Library of Ireland; Trinity College, Dublin.

1843 Patrick O'Shaughnessy. *Practical surveying. By the circumferentor, theodolite, and chain, demonstrated from its first principles. Wherein everything that is useful and curious in that art is fully demonstrated and explained, with many methods of calculation never before made public. Also, trigonometrical surveying, with different methods on levelling, together with its computation. Also, tables of natural sines* (Limerick: O'Brien, printer, 108 George Street). City Library, Limerick.

1847 Patrick O'Shaughnessy. 'A second edition of his own Treatise on surveying and engineering'. 5 shillings. Advertised *Limerick Reporter*, 2 Feb. 1847. No copies known.

Appendix E
The cost of surveying

'The business of surveying depends so much on circumstances and the nature of the ground', wrote William Armstrong in 1821, 'that it is extremely difficult to fix a price for business in general' (NAI, 2B.44.61). If that was a surveyor's view, then the mere historian must be wary of committing himself to anything as simplistic as a graph or table. His first problem is that surveyors' charges are recorded in two forms, as fees for specific assignments and as rates per unit of work. Among the latter, charges per acre relate more closely to the management of a farm or estate, while daily rates throw a more direct light on the economics of the surveying profession. Acreable rates are also recorded much more often, and have the advantage of being open to augmentation by modern research, for when the surveyor's total fee is known we often also know the number of acres in his survey.

However, all measures of cost are subject to one or more kinds of uncertainty. Not many sums of money are specified as Irish or sterling (Irish currency was worth less, though by varying amounts), and Irish, statute and Cunningham acres are frequently left undifferentiated; one can only assume that Irish measure was usually intended for both land and money. Other difficulties were caused by what Armstrong called the nature of the ground. Unit cost could be expected to vary inversely with area, especially since in a traverse survey the labour of measuring a perimeter is proportional to the square root of the acreage enclosed. In principle this kind of scale economy can be quantified by comparing the fees charged for maps of different sizes; in practice scale is hard to separate from other influences, such as slope, vegetation-cover, hydrology and (more important, as will be seen) the number of internal divisions. Finally, there is the definition of the work itself. Did a surveyor's fee include his travelling expenses, and the payments he made to mearsmen and chain-bearers, as well as his own professional services? And did the latter consist simply of measuring, or did they include the drawing and mounting of maps, the laying out of new farms, and the valuation of land and buildings? It is a rare bill or advertisement that answers all these questions. And the answers when we do have them are often too complex to be easily related to those given by other surveyors. So on the whole it seems safest to present the available data with a minimum of editorial interference.

The earliest recorded acreable charge appears to be the 1d per acre 'admeasurement money' adopted for the Longford plantation (Hickson, *Ireland in the Seventeenth Century*, 2, p.294). Later figures are somewhat higher. The fee that Thomas Raven proposed in 1634 for a government surveyor was 1.6d; and although Benjamin Worsley offered to make the Cromwellian plantation surveys for 0.54d, Petty regarded his own charge of 1.44d as more realistic (Larcom, *Down Survey*, pp 6, 9).

For private surveying Petty thought 10s a day a 'competent allowance' (Larcom, *Down Survey*, p. xiii). From the 1690s Josias Bateman was charging 1d per acre (probably statute) for rough plans in west Waterford, with another 1d per acre for fair plans (*Just and True Relation*, p. 16). On the Perceval estate in north Co. Cork the usual charge in the period 1701–53 was 2d per Irish acre for a townland, 1^1/2d for a larger area, and 3d for anything unusually complicated (Add. MSS 46964A–47003). Similar figures are found elsewhere, for instance 1d in Co. Cavan in 1726–8 (*Analecta Hibernica*, 20 (1958), p.173), 2d in Cork-Waterford (probably statute acres) in 1729 (PRONI, D.2707/A1/1/15B), 1^1/2d on the Kearney estate in Co. Cork in 1740–41 (NLI, mic. P.5306), 2d in Co. Wexford in 1745 (A. K. Longfield (ed.), *The Shapland Carew Papers* (Dublin, 1946), p.82), about 2.4d sterling in Co. Fermanagh in 1742 (NLI, 16.H.1(6)), and 2d in Co. Louth in the 1750s (PRONI, D.562/634–5).

Occasionally a surveyor's charges were questioned. Bateman's demands in Waterford were considered excessive (NLI, MS 7197(2)). Samuel McCrea told Lord Abercorn's agent that he normally got 12d per acre (this included dividing as well as surveying), which was elevenpence more than his employer regarded as fair. The agent was being more realistic: eventually the gap between them reduced itself to 1d versus 1^1/2d (PRONI, T.2541/IA1/3/17, 40: Apr. and Oct. 1754).

Most of the rates quoted above were broadly consistent with the general recommendations (the first of their kind) issued by Peter Callan in 1750. He suggested 2d per acre for a parcel of more than 100 acres in a single enclosure, 2^1/2d for 50–100 acres, 3d for less than 50 acres, and 4d for meadows, stubbles and land to be laid out in 'even acres'. In his second edition, dated 1758, Callan admitted that some readers had found these rates too low. Here was an early hint that surveying costs might now be responding to the increase in farm prices that had begun around 1750 (R. D. Crotty, *Irish Agricultural Production: its Volume and Structure*

(Cork, 1966), pp 282–4). Another such indication came with the first rate recorded by the French school, the 4d per English acre (about 6½d per Irish acre) asked by Samuel Andrews and John Powell in 1760 (*Cork Evening-Post*, 24 July), though this included drawing as well as surveying. Consistently with this trend, Piers Patsull in 1770 wanted 12d sterling per acre for surveying and mapping lots of 1–20 acres in Co. Kilkenny, 6d for 20–100 acres, and 4d for more than 100 acres (*Leinster Journal*, 28 Mar. 1770). At about the same time, James Miller of Thurles in the next county was making do with 3d per acre for farms and 2d for estates (*Leinster Journal*, 20 June 1770). To judge from the following figures the average probably lay somewhere in between.

	Date	Surveyor	Location	Acreable charge	Remarks
1.	1763	Robert Livingston	Armagh	3d	113 statute acres
2.	1771, 1773	John Barker	Belfast	4d	Including maps and valuation
3.	1772	David McCool	Londonderry	3d	Including maps
4.	1773	Charles Frizell, Jnr	Co. Westmeath	3d	606 acres 'very troublesome'
5.	1776	—	Co. Down	6–8d	Sterling
6.	1778	Sherrard & Brownrigg	Co. Meath	3d	Tenanted land, in farms
	"	" "	"	6½d	Demesne, in fields
7.	1779	—	Co. Galway	13d	
8.	1781	—	Co. Down	4d	Including maps
9.	1790	A.R. Neville	Co. Carlow	6d	Surveying only: map cost *c*. 2d per acre more
10.	1790	John Evans	Co. Galway	2.44d	223 acres
11.	1793	James Kean	Co. Clare	5.15d	12½ acres
12.	1795	John Leonard	Co. Galway	5.39d	152 acres
13.	1795	Michael McGawley	Co. Meath	3.59d	54 acres
14.	1796	—	—	12d	Maximum fee paid by Linen Board

SOURCES: (I) PRONI, D.959/M/50; (2) PRONI, D.572/2/52; *Belfast News-Letter*, 10 Aug. 1773; (3) *L:Derry Journal*, 29 Dec. 1772; (4) NAI, M.4726; (5) & (8) Crawford, *Ulster Land Agent*, pp 12, 33–4; (6) NLI, MS 1399; (7) NLI, MS 4920; (9) Monahan, *Carloviana*, I (1954), p.18; (10) & (12) NAI, M. 3588; (11) NLI, 21.F.160 (7); (13) NLI, 21.F.97(8); (14) *Drogheda Journal*, 27 Aug. 1796.

A new century does sometimes happen to mark a genuine historical divide, at least in the opinion of the Co. Kilkenny surveyor Patrick Mackey. In 1801 he urged his patrons to 'forget the old prices which only answered the last century' (*Leinster Journal*, 31 January), adding by way of explanation:

> Our daily subsistence is risen to thrice,
> Our instruments, and our apparel likewise;
> To be plain, for the future a shilling per acre,
> At the least should be paid to each lawful surveyor.

The next batch of figures suggests that Mackey was right about the direction of the change, wrong about its magnitude.

1.	1803	David McCool	Londonderry	8d	Including maps
2.	1804	Edward Reilly	—	5d	For dividing bogs and laying out potato grounds
3.	1808	David McCool	Londonderry	10d	Including maps
4.	1816	John Hill	—	4d	
5.	1818	Patrick Leahy	Thurles	10d	For townlands in ordinary sized farms

SOURCES: (1) & (3) *Derry Journal*, 11 Oct. 1803, 16 Feb. 1808; (2) NLI, 21.F.8 (23); (4) *Irish Farmers Journal*, 31 Aug. 1816; (5) *Clonmel Advertiser*, 17 Oct. 1818.

The 1820s yield a number of bills from firms employed in the survey of Crown lands, among them Sherrard, Brassington and Greene (the leading Dublin surveyors and valuators of the time), Joseph James Byrne (his career not yet far advanced) and William Armstrong (NAI, 2 B.44.6 1). Their prices may have been slightly inflated by the fact that the government was paying, but the comments of an official referee, John Brownrigg, are available as an antidote. For mountains and bogs the usual charge was now 6d (Brownrigg considered $4^{1}/2$d enough) and for ordinary farmland

12d or 13d. Brownrigg pronounced this last figure 'the highest ever charged', but he still thought it not unreasonable, in 1823, for a survey of individual fields; where the smallest divisions were farms of more than 30 acres he wanted it reduced to 9d. These figures were not far from William Bald's quotations of the following year (*Report on Survey and Valuation*, 1824, p.59), which were $9^{1}/_{2}$d for 'the most minute survey' in enclosed districts and 6d for 'other tracts with few divisions'.

All these figures reflected the rise in prices and rents precipitated by the Napoleonic wars, as Brownrigg recognised. His recommended figure of $1^{1}/_{2}$ guineas per day marks a significant contrast with those of Petty and also with his own recollections, as recorded on 1 July 1824:

> Some of the surveyors employed by the commission of Crown lands charge one guinea per day and are satisfied, and Messrs Sherrard and Brassington charge two, even for Sundays I imagine! If work coming from under their hands, was twice as well done as other people's, there would be no difficulty in the decision, but I have no idea this is the case! When Mr Sherrard and I lived together we were contented with one guinea per day clear of expenses! It must be admitted that a guinea forty years ago, and a guinea now, are different things. As lands rose in price, money sunk [*sic*] in value, however it is supposed, money and land are coming back towards their former standard, but not yet arrived at it.

The clearest evidence for a restoration of earlier standards comes from an advertisement issued by Sherrard's firm in 1827 reducing their fee of 12d per Irish acre to 6d per statute acre (9.7d per Irish acre). Three years later they changed their minds and started charging 4d per statute acre for mountains and large divisions, 6d for farms, and 9d for fields. The last value was equivalent to 14.6d per Irish acre, higher than any rate yet noted, though in 1837 an Ulster surveyor, John McCormick, was claiming to have charged 16d per Irish acre for the past twenty years (PRONI, D.1660/19). In reality, the general level of post-1820s charges seems to have been considerably lower.

1. *c.*1823	John Longfield	Co. Dublin	9.86d	609 acres, including map
2. 1823	Edward Conlan	Co. Kildare	3d	
3. 1832	—	Co. Cavan	10d	1,072 acres
4. 1833	George Sloan & Charles McQuaid	Co. Cavan	8d	866 acres
5. 1834	Pat McLoughlin	Co. Roscommon	6.89d	10 acres
6. 1835	Alexander Richmond	Co. Armagh	6d	Per English acre
7. 1835	David McArthur	Co. Armagh	6d	
8. 1836–40	George Sloan	Co. Cavan	6d	229 acres

SOURCES: (1) *First Report on Tithes*, q. 2130; (2) TAB 13/91; (3), (4) & (8) NAI, M.6178 (14, 27, 42); (5) NLI, 21.F.125(10); (6) & (7) PRONI, D. 1606/5/1.

The figures from the 1830s relate to particular transactions. The next general rate, in some ways the most general of all, was fixed in 1850 by the Incumbered Estates Court (MacNevin, *Incumbered Estates Court*, p.115). This was a mere 3d per statute acre, and clearly represented a tacit admission that henceforth a significant part of the land surveyor's work could be done by enlarging the Ordnance Survey maps of 1833–46.

Index of Personal Names

Personal names standing alone are those of Irish land surveyors.
Other personal names are distinguished by rank title or description.
References with 'n.' mean note no. (singular) and 'nn.' referes to notes nos (plural).
The indexes have been revised, rearranged and expanded,
especially for the second edition, by Dr Brian Lambkin.

Abercorn, Earls and Dukes of (*see also* Abercorn estate in Index of Place Names), 143 n.107, 147, 150, 192, 254, 256 n.17, 257 n.24, 264 n.140, 359 n.64, 360 n. 66, 394, 440
Adair, Thomas, 404 n.51
Adams, George, instrument-maker, 282, 284, 326 n. 52
Aher, David, 185 n.100, 371, 386 n.72
Aher, Patrick, 168, 352
Ahern, Denis, 107 n.80
Ainslie, John, Scottish cartographer, 285
Alen, John, Archbishop, 3–4, 8
Alen, John, constable of Maynooth, 19
Alen, Thomas, constable of Maynooth, 19
Alford, Lancelot, Surveyor-General, 29, 41
Alies, instrument-maker, 260 n. 85
Allen, Joseph, 342
Allen, William, map publisher, 293 n. 102, 343, 355, 358 n.45, 362 n.102
Alment, John, instrument-maker, 324 n.25
Andrews, Samuel, 161, 247, 342, 441
Antrim, Earl of, 148
Armagh, Archbishop of, 74 n, 3, 261 n. 98
Antrim, Marquess of, 181 n.46
Armstrong, William, 249, 379–82, 394, 439, 442
Arrowsmith, Aaron, map publisher, 284, 332
Arundel, Earl of, 112
Asser, James, 167
Atkins, Augustine, 224, 227, 255 n.3
Austen family, 232

Balfour, Blayney Towneley, landowner, 143 n.109
Bald, William, 102 n. 13, 224, 251, map-maker, 284, 293 n.105, 294 n.111, 368, 379
  opinions, 238, 300, 306, 443

Bannan, John, 141 n.87, 259 n.59
Barker, John, 140 n.72, 185 n.102, 187
Barker, Jonathan, 168, 185 n.102, 191, 259 n.58, 270, 273, 288 n.30, 346, 441
Baron, P., instrument-maker, 260
Barry family, 232
Barry, Richard, 260 n.76, 412
Basire, James, engraver, 201
Bassnett, William, 328 n.83
Bateman, Josias, 180 n.26, 181 n.45, 182 n. 58, 224, 230, 232, 258 n.45, 259 n.53, 440
Bates,—, instrument-maker, 260 n.85
Bath, Neville, 348, 350, 352, 360 n.75
Bath, Pat, 323 n.8
Baylie, Charles, 198
Beauford, William, 153, 183 n.70, 253, 343
Beaufort, Daniel Augustus, scholar and cartographer, 108 n.100, 335–6, 340, 349, 357–8 nn.14, 23, 24, 40, 360–61 nn.67, 88
Bell, James, of Carrickmacross, 425
Bell, John, of Cootehill, 298, 313, 326 n.53, 329 n.102, 411, 416–29
Bell, John, of Walterstown, 419–29
Bells (of Cootehill and Walterstown), 344, 416–27
Benn, G., author, 342
Bennett, John, map publisher, 359
Beranger, Gabriel artist, 247
Berne, Thomas, 412
Berrell Robert, 427
Billingsley, Henry, planter, 43
Bindon, Lady Henrietta, 268
Blake, Peter, 168, 402 n.9
Bodley, Sir Josias, 55–8, 60, 75 n.26, 82
Bolton, Carrol 365
Bolton, R, 365
Booth, W. J., architect, 193
Bouie, Samuel, 219 n.66

Bourke,—, 247
Boyd, Joseph, 238
Boyle, James, 184 n.93
Boyle, John, 404 n.40
Bradshaw, T., 343
Brassington and Gale, 168, 278, 397
Brassington, Charles.P., 211, 404 n.39
Brassington, James, 404 n.44
Brassington, Richard, 167, 202, 280, 292 n.86, 372, 385 n.56
Brien, John, 182 n.58
Brenn, John, 412
Bridge, Tim, 329 n.111
Brooking, Charles, 270, 337–8, 340, 358 n.29
Brown, Thomas, 412
Browne, John, 45
Browne, Valentine, planter, 29, 46 nn.6, 11, 48 nn.41, 52, 50 n.78
Brownrigg, Longfield and Murray, 181
Brownrigg, John, 101, 167, 228, 251
    canal surveys, 196, 264
    maps, 141, 219, n.80, 237, 261 n.90, 279, 362 n.103
    opinions on other surveyors, 130, 262 n.112, 276, 280, 442–3
    partners and employees, 184, 249, 262 n.105, 263 n.115, 278
Brudenell William, 69
Buck, Henry, 389, 402 n.9
Burgate, Thomas, 95
Burgh, Thomas, architect and engineer 307, 318, 326 n.53. 429, 436
Burghley, Baron, 28, 29, 34, 42, 45, 52
Burns, A., author, 433
Butler, Ben, 416
Butler, P., 348
Butler, Peter, engraver, 333
Butler, R, 348
Byers, William, 353, 354
Byrne, Daniel 260 n.82
Byrne, George, engraver, 342
Byrne, Joseph James, 199, 218 nn.50, 61, 221, 321, 345, 362 n.103, 394, 404 n.44, 442
Byrne, Lawrence, 219 n.69
Byron, Samuel, 127, 229, 273–5, 323 n.8

Cahill Daniel, 348, 350
Callaghan, Cor[nelius[, 412

Callan, Peter,
    book by, 96, 224, 226, 271, 429–30
    opinions, 96, 131, 218 n.51, 224, 229, 240, 244, 253, 265, 272, 413–28
    on surveyors' charges, 232, 234, 304
    on surveying techniques, 118, 130, 297–300, 308, 310–11, 316, 320, 411
Campbell T., 343
Carden family, 140
Carker [Carter?],—, 59
Carpenter, Baldwin, 224
Carroll, Barnaby, landowner, 188
Castlecomer, Earl of, 263 n.118
Carte, Edward, author, 354
Carter, Abraham, 101 n.6, 127
Carty, Dennis, 182, 301, 325 n.33
Carty, John, 182, 337, 343
Clonmell Earl of, 108 n.106, 403 n.17
Carysfort, Earl of, 393
Castle, Richard, architect, 189, 270, 305
Cave, Thomas, 127,168, 270
Cecil Sir Robert, 44
Chichester, Earl of, 149
Chichester, Lord Stanley Spencer, 169
Clare, Philip, 386 n.70
Clarke, James, 263 n.127, 361 n.93
Clutterbuck, William, 402 n.9
Coates, Joseph, 29 n.48
Cockayne, Thomas, 115
Colhoun, —, 326
Colles, Christopher, 224, 343
Collis, Maurice, 404
Coner, Charles 93, *see also* Connor
Conlan, Edward, 385, 444
Connel, —, 336
Connor, Andrew, 415
Connor, Charles, 93–4
Connor, Edward, 168
Connor, Joseph, 343, 352
Conroy, —, 412
Conway, Viscount, 189
Cooke, J., 343, 352
Cooley, John (17th century), 154
Cooley, John (18th century), 197
Cooper, Charles, 402 n.9
Corran, James, 428
Corran, William, 428
Cork, Earl of, 114,140, 145, 148, 224
Cosby, Pole, landowner, 148
Costello, James, 325 n.33

Cotton, Sir Robert, antiquary, 57
Courtenay, John, 69
Cowell, —, 130
Cowley, Walter, Surveyor-General, 19
Cox, Sir Richard, 148,150,161, 366
Croake, Robert, 412
Crow, James, 172, 227
Cuff, Sir Hugh, planter, 42
Cumpsty, Andrew, 229
Cunningham, Lieutenant General Robert, 192
Cuttle, Thomas, 195,197, 219, 220 n.83, 228, 412

Daly, John, 412
Danby, Thomas, 49
Darby, —, penman, 248
Dargan, William, 252
Darling, Sisson, artist, 261 n.98
Dean, George, gardener, 215 n.9
Deering, James, 404 n.33
Delany, James, 264
Delany, Mary, and landscape gardening, 189
De Renzi, Matthew, planter, 75 n.24
Desmond, Earl of, 28
Devonshire, Duke of, 128,140 n.80, 184 n.90, 204, 240
Divir, Anthony, 435
Dobbs, Richard, author, 326 n.49, 365
Dodson, William, architect, 189
Donegall, Earls and Marquesses of, 227, 283
Donnell, James, 190
Donnelly, Dominick, 325 n.33
Donovan, John, 106 n.64
Doran, Fintan, 218 n.49
Doran, — (of Cloyne), 225
Doud, John, 360 n.82
Dowly, John, 412
Downer, Maurice, 140 n.80, 260, 411, 412
Downshire, Marquess of, 148, 249
Doyle, Lawrence, 256, 412
Dublin, Archbishop of, 156, 269, *see also* Alen, John
Dubourdieu, J., author, 343, 357 n. 18
Duff, Peter, 101 n.6
Duncan, William, 348, 354
Dunne, Darby, 260 n.81, 411
Dunroche, Charles, 324 n.22

Dunton, John, author, 178 n.6, 217
Dury, Andrew, engraver, 344

Edgeworth, Maria, on estate maps, 180 n.35, 181 n.49
Edgeworth, Richard Lovell, engineer, 262, 300, 353
Edgeworth, William, 252, 348, 350, 353, 354, 357
Egmont, 76 n. 38, 136 n.15, *see also* Perceval
Ellis, —, engraver, 342
Ely, Earl of, 261
Ellsworth, Henry, 307
Erne, Lord, 257 n.24
Essex, Earl of, 43, 81,149, 306
Evans, Eyre, landowner, 1, 12, 13, 24 n.29
Evans, John, 441
Ewing, J., 343
Eyre, John, author, 76 n.28

Faden, William, map publisher, 343, 362 n.103
Falkland, Viscount, 52
Farel, —, 334
Farrand, William, 67
Farrell, Michael, 256 n.10, 412
Fingall, Countess of, 107 n.83
Fitton, Alexander, instrument-maker, 260 n.85
Fitzgerald, Maurice, 259 n.60
Fitzpatrick, Kyran, 318, 412
Flanagan, Owen, 107
Fleming, —, 394
Fogarty, Patrick, 137 n.31, 220 n.83
Ford, Philip, on map of Co. Cork, 366
Ford, Thomas, 261 n.99
Foster, John Leslie, politician, 204, 210, 218 n.55, 258 n.47, 361 n.93
French, Percy, poet, 395
Frizell family, 146, 202–03, 242, 250, 290 n.49, 324 n.12, 346
Frizell, Charles, 179 n.11, 182 n.57, 260 n.78, 261 n.87, 406, 415, 441
Frizell Richard, 90, 168, 179 n.11, 182 n.57, 185 nn.104 106, 247, 253, 260 n.78, 261 n.87, 297, 321, 411

Gale, Samuel, 278
Garstin, Simon, 81, 307, 366
Gaynor, John, 402 n.9

Gee, Henry, 59, 60, 96
Gerraughty, Martin, 258 n.49
Gibson, George, 98, 260 n.81, 272
Gibson, John, 271
Gibson, Robert, 261 n.92, 296, 297, 298, 346
   advice to surveyors, 93, 152, 160
   book by, 90, 91, 226, 232, 271-3, 303, 311, 315, 429, 431, 432, 434, 436, 437
   examiner of surveys, 98, 273;
   maps, 328;
   school, 229, 272
Gibson William, 272
Gilbert, Dr William, mathematician, 55–6, 59, 63
Gill, Valentine, 181 n.46, 254, 345, 348, 350, 351-2
Goblet, Y.M., map historian, 71
Godfrey, T., artist, 261 n.98
Goggins, James, 136
Goldsmith, Oliver, Deserted Village, 230
Graham, James, 325
Grattan, Henry, on tithes, 370
Greene, Clarges, 278, 282, 385 n.61, 394, 404
Greene, John, 94, 147, 240, 266, 273, 289 n.34, 321
Greene, John Ball, Commissioner of Valuation, 402 n.10
Greig, William, 172, 199
Grierson, George, map publisher, 331
Griffith, Richard, 202, 251, 286, 350, 354, 357, 371, 377
Guy, —, printer and publisher, 396
Gwinn, John, 75

Hall J.D., 385 n.61
Hall, Owen, 216 n.36
Hampton, John, 389
Hampton, William, 314, 354
Handcock, Matthew, Deputy Surveyor General, 86, 98, 102 nn.14,17

Harding, Thomas, 273, 303, 306, 314, 346, 434, 437
Hardinge, Henry, archivist, 100
Hardinge, W.H., archivist, 41, 86, 96, 99, 100
Hariot, Thomas, mathematician, 47 n.33
Harris, Walter, antiquary, 335
Hatton, Sir Christopher, landowner, 32
Hawney, William, 432
Heagerty, Garret, 433
Healy, James, 247, 321
Healy, Matthew, 109 n.110
Heavey or Heavy, —, 336
Heffernan, Messrs, 393
Henderson, J., 402 n.3
Hertford, Earl of, 173,174, 249
Hewett, Henry, 239
Heylin, John, 325
Hibbard, George, 290 n.48
Higgins, William, 242, 4162
Hill, John, 185 n.110, 263, 384, 442
Hillas family, 232
Hillas, George, 228
Hilton, Lewis, 365
Hoctor, J., 226
Hodges and Smith, booksellers, 390, 392, 396, 397
Hodson, Sir Robert, Cavan estate of, 263
Hogan, Garret, 97, 101 n.6, 107 n.83, 181 n.44, 413, 415, 427
Holland, Thomas, teacher, 229
Holt, T., 343
Honig, —, paper maker, 166
Hood family, 180 n.108, 228, 336
Hood, Henry, 141 n.85, 170, 171, 183 n.81, 254, 259 n.54, 264 n.140
Hood, John, 141 n.83, 170, 185 n.108, 295, 433
Hood, Matthew, 259 n.54
Humphrey [Humfrey], John, 107 n.89, 228
Humphreys, John, 69, 81,101 n.5
Hunt, Sir Vere, landowner, 131, 352
Hunter family, 227
Hunter, Thomas, 81
Hunter, William, 81, 93, 101 n.5, 106 n.74

INDEX OF PERSONAL NAMES   449

Irwin, James, 137 n.30, 142 n.96, 306, 314, 435
Ivory, Thomas, architect 193

Jackson, John, 117 n.89
Jackson, Philip, 183 n.75
Jenison, Thomas, and Munster plantation, 29
Jephson, Denham, landowner, 129
Jobson, Francis, 32, 33, 35–6, 40, 46, 56, 58, 81, 332
    maps and surveys, 39-44, 75 n. 24, 379
    cartographic merits, 45, 286
    methods of surveying, 34, 45, 295, 300
    opinions, 40, 41
    origins and background 32, 223
    17th-century references, 57–8
Jobson, Sir Francis, 32
Jocelyn, Viscount, estate of, 140 n.80
Johnson, Edward, 314
Johnson, Revd John, mathematician, 59, 63
Johnston, William, 252
Jordan, James, 288 n.26
Jordan, John, 260
Jordan, William, 180 n.38, 329
Jourdan, Thomas, 221 n.93
Julian, James, 403 n.30

Kavanah, Thomas, 98
Kealy, John, 366
Kean, James, 441
Keane, Sir Richard, 385 n.65
Keating, Geoffrey, historian, 15
Keenan, James, 260 n.81, 338, 346, 348
Keightley, Thomas, gardener, 215 n.9
Kelly, Patrick, 323 n.8, 329 n.96, 330 n.117, 376
Kelly, Thomas, 59, 260, 315
Kendrick, Roger, 137 n.36, 139 n.55, 141 n.81, 182 n.57, 273, 325 n.41, 338, 340
Kenmare, Viscount, 148, 150
Kennedy, Dr, and map of Co. Down, 336, 337, 344, 348, 357 n.18, 368
Kennedy, John Pitt, civil servant, 209
Kennedy, Robert, 74 n.6
Kenny, Michael, 169,181 n.52, 248, 321
Kensals, Edward, 260 n.81

Kerry, Earl of, 102 n.22, 148,161,179 n.12
Kildare, Earl of, 49,158, 159, 161,165,167
Kiernan, Matthew, 257
Killaly, John, 336
King, Elizabeth, wife of Gabriel Stokes, 269
King, William, Archbishop, 199, 287 n.10, 288 n.20, 337, 368
King, William, instrument-maker, 288 n.30, 302, 328 n.46
Kinsella, Dennis, 260, 313, 328 n.84, 411
Kinsella, Maurice, 107
Knox, George, 105 n.56, 348, 349
Knox, T., 182 n.63
Kohl, J.G., map historian, 388, 402

Laffan family, 232
Laffan, Walter, 335
Lane, John, 219 n.69
Lanigan, Joseph, 108 n.107
Lansdowne, Marquess of, 63, 74 n.4, 77 n.5, 78 n.67, 79 n.82
Larcom, Captain T.A., 402
Larkin, William, 197, 199, 348, 353–4, 361 nn.83, 93
Lawson, John, 32, 34, 43
Leahy, Patrick, 263 n.127, 343, 352, 360 n.75, 442
Leake, Sir John, landowner, 114
Ledwich, Edward, antiquary, 291 n.62, 367–8
Leinster, Duke of, 140 n.73
Leitrim, Earl of (Lord), 394
Lendrick, T., 293 n.103, 348
Leonard, John, 343, 441
Lewis, Robert, 96, 181 n.52, 226, 229, 271 329 n.101
Lewis, Samuel, topographer 280
Leybourn, William, author, 256 n.9, 307, 327 n.66
Lidwill, George, author, 370
Lilly, Arthur, 411
Livingston, Robert, 181 n.52, 283, 293 n.95, 305, 327 n.57, 441
Locke, John, valuator, 394
Logan, M., 343
Longfield, John, 121, 127, 141 n.84, 167, 202, 232, 237, 249, 262 n.112, 291 n.63, 326 n.44, 444
Longfield, William, 237, 404 n.44

Lort, John, instrument-maker, 260
Love, John, author, 226, 256 n.9
Lowe, Thomas, 259 n.68
Lucas, Edward, 365
Lynam, James, 394
Lynch, James, instrument-maker, 329 n.103
Lyne family, 232
Lythe, Robert, 28, 46 n.2, 332, 356 n.3

McArthur, David, 444
McArthur, John, 178, 247, 403
McCarthy, Daniel, 124–5, 156, 158–9
McClatchey, James, 181 n.52
McClatchey, John, 336
McComb, John, 229
McCool, David, 172, 180 n.35, 200, 227, 238, 256 n.20, 326 n.45, 441, 442
McCormick, John, 443
McCrea family, 347, 349, 350, 354, 379, 386 n.72
McCrea, Conyngham, 228, 349, 359 n. 63-4
McCrea, Samuel, 230, 257 n.24, 347, 440
McCrea, William, 228, 348, 349, 359 nn.63–64, 360 n.67, 384 n.38
McGawley, Michael, 441
McGennis, John, 412
McGillycuddy of the Reeks, 93
McIntire, William, 256
McKinlie, Michael, 428
McLoughlin, Pat, 108 n.107, 444
McMenamy, William, author, 143 n.144, 324 n.22, 328 n.89, 329 n.110
McQuaid, Charles, 175, 186, 444
McQuaid, Patrick, 175, 186
Mackey, Patrick, 442
Madden, Dr Samuel, improver, 203
Magennis, Lawrence, 325 n.37
Magnier, Thomas, 260 n.80, 412
Maguire, James, 183 n.74
Malby, Sir Nicholas, at Roscommon, 190
Malton, Earl of, 27 n.62, 267
Malton, James, artist, 274, 287 n.9, 291 n.61
Manning, Richard, 185 n.106
Manning, Robert, 391
Marsh, Thomas, 256 n.19
Massereene, Viscountess, 190
Matthews, Thomas, 182 n.57, 273–4, 290 n.53
May, Peter, 227
Meagher, Matthew, 216 n.36

Midleton, Earl of, 140 n.65, 158, 193
Midleton, Lady, 138 n.48
Miller, James, 108,143, 441
Mitchell, William, 411
Moland, Joseph, 266, 269, 323 n.5
Moland, Thomas, 27 n.62, 126,129, 155–7, 183 n.75, 202, 247, 250, 266–9, 271, 321, 383 n.36
Molesworth, Richard, cartographic ambitions, 231
Molesworth, William, Surveyor-General, 26 n.56, 86
Moloney, John, 325 n.33
Molony, Jeremiah, 242
Molyneux, Samuel, scientist, 217 n.39, 326 n.56, 384 n.36
Molyneux, William, scientist, 90, 300, 303 334–5
Montague, R, 230
Montgomery, Gabriel 262 n.105, 349, 355.
Montgomery, William, 141
Moody, Robert, gardener, 215 n.9
Mooney, John, 181,189, 260, 313, 316, 328 n.83, 338, 358 n.36, 411
Moore, Daniel, 109 n.109, 253
Moore, Garret, estate of, 181 n.51
Moore, John, 180 n.34
Moran, Nicholas, 138 n.44
Moris, —, 75
Morphett, James, 132, 317, 432
Morrin, James, 130
Mountrath, Earl of, 267
Mulvihill, Peter, 412
Murphy, Daniel, 343, 352
Murray, Henry, 250
Murray, Thomas, 249, 250

Naghten, John, 411
Neele, Samuel, engraver, 282, 354
Neville family, 228, 275, 408
Neville, Arthur, 293
Neville, Arthur Richards, 108 n.106, 185 n.97, 192, 250, 275, 291 n.66. 348, 354, 362 n.99, 441
Neville, Francis, 196
Neville, Jacob, 168, 243, 247, 342, 348, 354, 429, 430, 431
Neville, Parke, engineer, 291 n.66
Newcomen, Robert, 62, 81, 101, 115, 136 n.16, 191

INDEX OF PERSONAL NAMES 451

Niblock, James, 186
Niblock, John, 186
Nimmo, Alexander, 251–3, 262 n.114, 263 nn.118, 127, 285, 361 nn.91, 93
Noble, Benjamin, 23 n.2, 169, 185 n.98, 297, 301, 304, 306–08, 310–12, 316, 318, 320, 329 n.109, 345, 432, 434
Noble, John, 96, 338, 346, 348, 411
Noble, Thomas, 386 n.70
Nolan, David, 227
Nolan, Robert, 227, 372, 385 n.56, 395
Norden, John, English cartographer, 162
Norwood, Richard, English surveyor, 316
Nowlan, Lawrence, 226, 228, 256 n.10, 412
Nugent, [Oliver?], 267

O'Brien, Bartholomew, 416, 419–26
O'Brien, Charles, 361 n.83
O'Brien, Daniel, 67, 86
O'Brien family, 61, 102 n.16
O'Brien, John, 107, 182 n.58, 427
O'Brien, Joseph, 217 n.42
O'Connor family, 3
O'Connor, Dennis, 402 n.9
O'Connor [Connor], Joseph, 352, 360 n.76
O'Dempsy family, 3
O'Donovan, John, Irish scholar, 104 n.41
O'Driscoll, Timothy, 107 n.80
Ogilby, John, English cartographer, 244
O'Melaghlin family, 51
Omer, Thomas, canal engineer, 197
O'Molloy family, 51
O'More family, 3
O'Neill, Hugh, horse and chaise hire service, 197
O'Neill, Viscount, 249, 293 n.102
Ormond, Countess, 77 n.43
Ormond, Earl of, 43, 49 n.59, 81,136 n.15, 259 n.65
Orrery, Earl of, 115,133
Osborne, Henry, 69, 78 n.62, 307, 309, 311, 318, 329 n.108, 421
O'Shaughnessy, Patrick, 289 n.43, 306, 438

Paine, James, 227
Palmer, —, engraver, 342

Parsons, William, Surveyor-General, 54–5, 74 nn.5, 8, 9, 12, 75 n.25, 82
Patsull, John, 244
Patsull, Piers or Peter, 241, 441
Pattison, Robert, 172, 262 n.101
Pattison, Thomas, 172, 173,186 n.111
Payton, Christopher, and Munster plantation, 29
Pelham, Henry, 348, 352–3, 360 n.82, 361 n.81
Perceval, Sir John, later Earl of Egmont, landowner, 81, 114, 115, 118, 126, 132, 140 n.66, 142 n. 103, 144–8, 148, 155–6, 181 n.42, 200, 247, 266–8, 366
Perceval, Sir Philip, 101 n.2,136 n.15, 143 n.108, 329 n.96
Perry, John, engineer, 200
Petty, William, 52, 56, 59, 62–74, 148, 297, 311, 332, 368
    accuracy of surveys, 62, 71–2
    area calculation, 63–4, 68, 71–2, 86, 316
    as author, 62–3, 82, 84, 300, 334
    controversies, 62, 70–72, 93, 100
    earlier surveys, 62–3, 82, 302, 380
    finances, 62, 68, 70–71, 82, 84, 234, 388, 440, 443
    instruments, 65, 300, 302,
    land settlements, 83, 85–9, 91, 127–8
    maps, manuscript, 65, 82, 84, 89, 128, 144, 302, 335, 364, 366, 368, 379
    maps, printed, 85, 144, 332, 336, 365
    personnel, 68–70, 73, 81, 224, 226, 230, 253, 365, 388
    proposals for new maps, 54, 72, 161, 318, 375
    survey methods, 62, 64–6, 68, 72, 82, 88–91, 100, 120, 127, 152, 161, 295, 303, 308, 312–13, 316, 318, 334, 379–80
Pickles, Nathan, 77
Piers, Sir Henry, author, 24 n.24, 208, 336
Pine, Henry, planter, 50
Plunkett, Francis, 181 n.51
Porter, James, author, 432–3
Porter, Robert, 343
Powell, John, 161–2, 261 n.90, 342, 441
Power, Thomas, 314, 431, 434, 435
Pratt, Henry, 94, 161, 356 n.2

Priestley, Michael, architect, 192
Prynallt, John, 315
Prynallt, Thomas, 315
Purcell, James, 138 n.50, 203
Purfield family, 228
Pynner, Nicholas, 55, 59, 223

Raggett, Dr Patrick, 69
Raleigh, Sir Walter, and Munster plantation, 32, 36, 43, 45, 114, 140 n.80
Ramsay, James, 323 n.5
Rathborne, Aaron, author, 256 n.9, 306
Ravell, Joseph, 247, 300, 343
Raven, Thomas, 54, 58, 81, 223, 255 n.2, 266, 379
    maps and surveys, 58–9, 74 n.8, 75 n.24, 96, 101 n.2, 126, 139 n.60, 149, 154, 155, 306
    official surveyorship, 54–5, 140 n.74, 191, 202, 238, 440
Reade, Philip, landowner, 210, 212
Reading, Thomas, 127, 181 n.52, 270
Reeves, Messrs, solicitors, 86, 99
Reilly, Edward, 442
Richards, William, 343, 358
Richmond, Alexander, 172, 444
Ringwood, Isaac, 261, 290
Roberts, Edward, landowner, 149
Robertson, Abraham, 433
Robertson, John, author, 432
Robins, Arthur, 29, 30, 31, 36, 41, 42, 43–4, 49, 225
    maps and surveys, 32–4, 38–9, 42, 46 n.10, 47 n.20, 47 n.33, 48 n.37
Robinson, Sir William, and map of Ireland, 302
Rochfort family, 86
Rochfort, Robert, 26 n.56
Rocque, John, 119, 148, 159–60, 227, 249, 338, 340, 368, 379
    cartographic style, 160–68, 170–71, 247, 279–80, 305
    employees and pupils, 160, 234, 276, 344
    influence on successors, 160, 185 n.100, 275–6, 342, 345, 347, 358 n.41
    maps, 140 n.73, 164, 184 n.93, 191–2, 216 n.25, 272, 289 n.42, 321, 340, 341, 348, 355, 359
Roe family, 228
Roe, John, 183, 325 n.33
Rotherham, Sir Thomas, military engineer, 55

Sampson, Revd George Vaughan, 181 n.46, 326 n.45, 336–7, 348, 349, 359 n.53, 360 n.69
Sanderson, —, of Drogheda 244
Sapperton, William, 154, 307
Sayer, Robert, map publisher, 359 n.51
Scalé, Bernard, 128, 159, 227, 247, 250, 276, 342
    cartographic style, 160–69, 171–2, 184 nn.84, 90, 93, 219 n.76
    employees and pupils, 166, 196, 227, 251, 274, 276–7
    published maps, 136 n.12, 167, 179 n.15, 181 n.47, 289 n.42, 290 n.57, 342, 356 n.1, 359 n.51
    surveys, 128, 159, 162, 204, 292 n.89, 333, 342, 358 nn. 45, 46, 412
Sceleback, Monsieur de, 226
Semple, George, projector, 137 n.27, 192, 216 n.28, 345
Sharland, Robert, 226
Shelburne, Earl of, 102 n.22, 115, 353
Sheres, Sir Henry, and Trustees' Survey, 56, 72
Sherrard and Brassington, 169, 402 n.10, 443
Sherrard, Brassington and Gale, 179, 262 n.112, 278, 389
Sherrard, Brassington and Greene, 71, 138 n.49, 167, 172, 181 n.46, 186, 201, 249, 251, 278, 292 nn.86, 89, 442
Sherrard and Brownrigg, 276–7, 441
Sherrard, Maria, 277
Sherrard, Thomas, 167, 249, 257 n.36, 261, 275–84, 321, 346, 436, 443
Sherrard, William, 276
Shine, —, teacher, 184
Sinnot, Nicholas, 360 n.74, 371
Slater, Matthew, 290 n.48
Slattery, —, 315
Skinner, Andrew, road surveyor, 348, 353

Sloan, George, 444
Sloane family, 228, 232
Sloane, John, 358 n.37
Sloane, Oliver, 335, 339, 348, 358 n.37
Smith, Charles, natural historian, 336, 343
Smith, Erasmus, 267, 287 n.7
Smith, John, projector, 191

Smith, John, of Charleville, 130, 142 n.94, 155, 199, 315
Smith, Patrick, 217 n.42
Smith, Thomas, 199
Smyth, Sir James Carmichael, military engineer, 320
Southwell, Edward, landowner, 155
Southwell, Robert, landowner, 78 n.67, 144–5, 149
Spear, Richard, instrument-maker, 260
Speed, John, English cartographer, 332
Spicer, Edward, instrument-maker, 260 n.85, 339 n.103
Stack family, 232
Starrat, William, 118,125,170, 185 n.108, 202
Steile, Blennerhassett, son of William Steile, 236
Steile, Richard, 138, 236
Steile, William, the elder, 181, 234, 259 n.56, 344
Steile, William, the younger, 234, 344
Stephens, Lieutenant Henry Sykes, 183 n.70
Stewart, Alexander, 281
Stewart Archibald, 120, 138 n.51, 247, *see also* Stuart
Stokes, Gabriel, 91, 156, 271-3
    as Deputy Surveyor-General, 96–8, 274, 273
    as engineer, 251, 270
    maps, 117, 158, 269–72, 337, 338, 348
Stokes, William, 402 n.9
Stone, Richard, Surveyor-General, 61
Stuart or Stewart Archibald, 183
Stubs, —, 75 n.24
Sullivan family, 232
Sullivan, D.M., 329
Sullivan, John, 412
Swan, Owen, 307
Sweeney, Edward, instrument-maker, 261 n.92

Sweeney, Nathaniel, instrument-maker, 261 n.92
Swift, Jonathan, on utility of surveys, 145
Symner, Miles, mathematician, 63

Tagen, John, measurer, 12
Tannam, Mathias or Matthew, 261 n.95, 412
Tarrant, Colonel Charles, engineer, 193
Tasker, John, measurer, 12
Taylor, Major Alexander, 103 n.26, 197–8, 218 n.55, 285
    published maps, 202, 332, 353-4
    road surveys, 198, 294 n.114, 348, 361 n.88
Taylor, George, the elder, 348, 353
Taylor, George, the younger, 177
Taylor, John, 292 n.89
Taylor, Thomas, 77 n.58, 85, 102 n.15, 103 n.23, 149, 181 n.40, 362, 365–6, 383 n.15
Telford, Thomas, engineer, 263 n.119
Terry, Garnett, engraver, 353
Thomas, John, military cartographer, 45,
Thomond, Earl of, 81, 115, 154, 267–8, 288 n.15, 311, 313
Thompson, James, world atlas, 262
Thompson, Robert, 325 n.33, 358 n.37
Thornton, Thomas, 412
Thornton, William, 96, 256 n.10, 411–12
Tighe, William, author, 136 n.9, 209–10
Tite, William, architect, 193
Torrens, Robert, author, 399
Townsend, Thomas, engineer, 263
Townsend, W.R., author, 219 n.72
Travers, John, 168, 257 n.36, 260 n. 81, 312, 327 n.71, 328 n.78
Trench, J. Townsend, 403 n. 26
Trimble, James, 255
Trotter, Marcus, author, 327 n.74, 437
Trotter, J.B., author, 264 n.132, 294 nn.112, 115
Tyrone, Earl of, war with, 44, 51, 55

Ussher, James, correspondent of William Gilbert, 56

Vallancey, Charles, 85, 99, 103 nn.25–28, 197, 291 n.62, 332, 336, 353
Vaughan, David, 385 n.61
Vaughan, James, 249, 262 n.105
Voster, Daniel instrument-maker, 261 n.92, 297
Voster, Elias, instrument-maker, 261 n.92

Waddein, Thomas, 412
Walker, Henry, 167, 184 n.94, 355
Walker, J.C., 358 n.46
Wallop, Henry, Treasurer-at-War, 29
Walsh, Nicholas, 277, 327 n.60, 436
Ward, Marcus, publisher, 396
Ware, Sir James, Auditor-General, 25 n.42, 57, 75 n.23, 79 n.70
Ware, Pat, 324
Warwick, Robert, 389
Weldon, —,190
Wellington, Duke of, 378
Westby, Nicholas, landowner, 403
Weston, Henry, 219 n.66
Whatman, James, paper maker, 166
Wheeler, James, 248
White, John, of Virginia, 43
Whiteacre, *see* Whittaker
Whitelaw, James, historian and statistician, 330 n.117
Whittaker, Richard, 32, 34, 43
Whitty, John Irwine, 393
Wiggins, John, 179 n.21
Wight, Joshua, 91, 119, 138 n.45, 226, 267, 297, 300, 304–05, 320
  diary, 91, 138 n.42, 182 n.60, 238, 288 n.19, 311, 346
  quoted, 151, 255 n.5, 259 n.62, 260 n.83, 261 n.97, 287 n.8
Willes, Lord Chief Baron, 158–9, 167
Williams, Thomas, 197, 411
Williams, William, 182 n.61
Williamson, Alexander, engineer, 293 n.101
Williamson, James, 183 n.71, 185 n.110, 229, 247–8, 257 n.36, 280–84, 321, 348, 350
Williamson, Matthew, carpenter, 282
Williamson, William, 292 n.91
Wilson, Henry, author, 256 n.9
Wilson, John, 134
Wilson, William, publisher, 275[?], 343
Wing, Vincent, author, 256
Wiseman, Thomas, lawyer, 29–30
Wogan, William, 216
Wolfe, Theobald, landowner, 406
Wood, Dr Robert, mathematician, 318
Woodhouse, —, 75
Worsley, Benjamin, Surveyor-General, 56, 62–4, 69–70, 440
Worthington, —, lawyer, 5
Worthington, David Burleigh, 277
Wren, Matthew, 342, 344, 348, 368
Wright, John, 344
Wyld, Samuel author, 256

Young, Arthur, agriculturalist, 145, 154, 202–04, 205, 208, 254
Young, John, 81

Index of Place Names

Academy of Arts and Sciences, Cork, 435, 436
Adair estate, Ballymena, Co. Antrim, 139 n.60, 403 n.17
Ahowle, Lower and Upper, Co. Wicklow, 314
Allen, Lough, canal to, 197
America, surveying in, 32, 35, 47 n.30, 255 n.6, 289 n.43, 304, 330 n.114, 352
Annesley estate, Co. Down, 142 n.103
Antrim, County, 247, 286
   acre-units, 124
   grand jury maps of, 284, 348
   17th-century surveys in 86, 174, 365
   survey of, 335
   surveyors in, 173, 260 n.86
Ardcarne, Co. Roscommon, 385 n.385
Ardfert Commons, Co. Kerry, 141 n.91
Ardstraw, Co. Tyrone, 384 n.38
Argyll, 284
Arklow, Co. Wicklow, 25 n.44, 342, 403 n.26
Armagh, city, 293
   surveyors in, 240, 282
   Abbey Street, 283
Armagh, County maps of, 340, 341, 342, 348, 363, 368
   property in, 284, 379, 381
   roads, 199
   surveyors in, 146, 249, 283, 305, 444
Armagh, diocese, 334
Ashbourne, Co. Meath, 194
Ashmolean Museum, Oxford, 302
Ash Park Dublin, 141 n.84
Askebeg, Co. Wexford, 260 n.78
Askemore, Co. Wexford, 260 n.78, 261 n.87
Athboy, Co. Meath, 249
Athlone, Co. Westmeath, plan of, 292
Athy, Co. Kildare, 168
Aughrim, Co. Roscommon, 357 n.12

Balbriggan, Co. Dublin, 197, 342
Baldoyle, Co. Dublin, 12
Ballahanaskadan, Co. Limerick, 76, 107 n.90

Ballamore, see Ballymore Eustace
Ballhusky, Co. Cork, 403 n.29
Ballinahagliss, Co. Mayo, 371
Ballinasloe, Co. Galway, 168
Ballon, Co. Carlow, 256, 412
Ballybrittig, Co. Cork, 155
Ballyburly, Co. Offaly, 374
Ballycastle, Co. Antrim, 193
Ballycullen, Co. Wicklow, 314
Ballygrace, Co. Cork, 130,142 n.94
Ballyhorsey, Co. Wicklow, 403 n.21
Ballylyng, Co. Cork, 412
Ballymena, Co. Antrim, 139 n.60, 139 n.60, 282, 283
Ballymore Eustace, Co. Kildare [Ballamor], 3, 121, 138 n.53, 206, 220 n.81
Ballymote, Co. Sligo, 191
Ballynacragga, Co. Clare, 61
Ballyroan, Co. Leix, 98
Ballysax, Co. Kildare, 385 n.58
Ballyshannon, Co. Kildare, 372
Banagher, Co. Offaly, 75 n.24
Bandon, Co. Cork, 155,165, 215 n.14, 366
Banefune, Co. Cork, 120
Banemore (alias Rathanane), Co. Cork, 107 n.82
Bantry Bay, Co. Cork, 46 n.2, 353
Barbawn Bog, Co. Kildare, 143
Bath estate, Co. Monaghan, 179 n.15
Bealaghbehy, Co. Limerick, 268
Bearhaven, Co. Cork, 361 n.82
Belfast, 113, 235
   maps of, 284, 293 nn.94, 97, 343, 396
   surveyors in, 230, 247–8, 262 n.101, 282–3, 293 n.101, 315, 335, 343, 441
Ben Bulben, Co. Sligo, 283
Bestwood Park, Nottinghamshire, 66
Bibliotheque Royale, Paris, 85
Blake estate, Co. Mayo, 136 n.12
Blessington, Co. Wicklow, 191
Borreen, Co. Kildare, 325 n.41
Boston, Massachusetts, survey of, 352
Boughill, Co. Galway, 211
Boyne, River, 291 n.66

Brenanstown, Co. Dublin, 183 n.71
Brickey, River, Co. Waterford, 219 n.66
Brooke estate, Co. Fermanagh, 140 n.66
Brownstown, Co. Kildare, 404 n.30
Bunratty Park, Co. Clare, 154
Burlington estate, Co. Cork, 181 n.45
Burton Hall, Co. Carlow, 256 n.10

Caherbane, Co. Cork, 155
Calary, Co. Wicklow, 384
Callan, Co. Kilkenny, 25
Capanaboe, Co. Leix, 411
Cappagh, Co. Cork, 105 n.61, 324
Cappagh, Co. Roscommon, 328
Carlanstown, Co. Meath, 217
Carlow, County, 240, 268
  maps of, 46 n.2, 280
  surveyors in, 226, 228, 256, 338, 348, 412, 441
Carlow town, 104 n.38, 184 n.95, 260 nn.81–2, 267, 287 n.7, 288 n.14
Carnalstown, Co. Meath, 411, 413–15
Carndonagh, Co. Donegal, 171
Carrickfergus, Co. Antrim, 283
Carrickmacross, Co. Monaghan, 154, 411, 425
Carrick-on-Shannon, Co. Leitrim, 361 n.93
Carrick-on-Suir, Co. Tipperary, 240
Carrollstown, Co. Offaly, 188
Cloncurry, Co. Kildare, 412
Carton, Co. Kildare, 154,158,189–90
Castlebar, Co. Mayo, 285–6, 294 n.112
Castle-Craig, Co. Leitrim, 137 n.37
Castledermot, Co. Kildare, 338
Castle Dillon, Co. Armagh 293
Castle Kivan, Co Cork, 412
Castle Otway, Co. Tipperary, 329
Cavan, County, 5, 79 n.86, 125, 137 n.37, 138 n.49, 232, 363, 421, 440
  surveyors in, 175, 186 n.112, 263 n.118, 274, 298, 326 n.50, 413–15, 444
Celbridge, Co. Kildare, 137
Charleville, Co. Cork, 130,191
Clancarroll, Co. Monaghan, 49 n.59
Clandeboye, Lower and Upper, Co. Down, 55
Clare, County, 140 n.71, 189, 221 n.93, 268, 352

maps of, 83, 140 n.67, 286, 329 n.111, 353, 364, 403 n.16
plantation surveys of, 51, 61
surveyors in, 108 n.107, 239, 348, 441
Clements estate, Co. Leitrim, 216 n.36
Cloncurry estate, Co. Kildare, 216 n.36, 412
Clonegal Co. Carlow, 264
Clones, Co. Monaghan, 384 n.38
Clonmaning, Co. Wicklow, 327
Clonmel, Co. Tipperary, 352, 412
Clontarf, Co. Dublin, 186 n.113
Cloyne, Co. Cork, 218 n.49, 335, 356 n.11
  diocese, 334
Clubbin, Co. Offaly, 411
Cobh (Cove), Co Cork, 193
Coleraine, Co. Londonderry, 120,154
Collon, Co. Louth, 204
Connaught, 18, 51, 58, 60, 125, 209, 306
  maps of, 44, 45
  surveys, 52, 55, 59
Connello, Co. Limerick, 18
Cookstown, Co. Tyrone, 191
Coolnahinch, Co. Roscommon, 357 n.12
Coolock Lodge, Co. Dublin, 278
Cootehill, Co. Cavan, 413–28
Coothall, Co. Roscommon, 372
Cork city, 113, 333, 366, 396
  Academy of Arts and Sciences, 435, 436
  instrument makers, 247, 261 n.92, 297
  maps of, 336–7, 340, 352, 396
  surveyors in, 168, 226, 227, 229, 232, 235, 350, 352, 396
Cork, County, 122, 132, 369, 373
  land units, 6, 123, 125, 209, 268, 363
  maps of, 7, 30, 37, 43, 91, 336, 354
  plantations, 29–33
  surveying, 33, 34, 87, 366, 440
  surveyors in, 29, 118, 119, 124, 156, 244, 270, 297, 348, 394
Cork Harbour, 44, 91
Corraneary, Co. Cavan, 175
Corrmore, Co. Offaly, 411
Courelickey, Co. Cork, 105 n.61, 324 n.12
Courtenay estate, Co. Limerick, 157, 247, 267
Craigtown, Co. Leitrim, 137 n.37
Creeve, Co. Roscommon, 384

INDEX OF PLACE NAMES   457

Crievemully, Co. Roscommon, 411
Crumlin, Co. Dublin, 121
Curracanderry, Co. Cavan, 138
Curracombera, Co. Cavan, 138
Curragh, Co. Tipperary, 328 n.83
Curragh of Kildare (racecourse), 355

Dalkey, Co. Dublin, 121,138 n.53
Delgany, Co. Wicklow, 384 n.38
Delville, Co. Dublin, 189
Dingle, Co. Kerry, 238
Dodder [Dodir], River, Co. Dublin, 3
Domville estate, 185 n.103, 184 n.92
Donaghmore, Co. Leix, 412
Donegal County, 51, 82, 125, 185 n.108, 209, 347, 363
   maps of, 171, 256 n.19, 349
   surveys and sureyors in, 278, 348, 349
Donegal town, 435
Donsallagh, Co. Clare, 307
Down, County, 16, 232, 338, 363
   maps of, 284, 286, 335–6, 348, 350, 353, 368
   surveys 55,155, 354, 441
Downpatrick, Co. Down, 155, 180 n.38, 181 n.43, 329 n.112
Drimseragh, Co. Mayo, 385
Drogheda, 108 n.96, 135 n.4, 194, 199, 276
   maps of, 101 n.5, 115, 136 n.17, 184 n.92, 343
   surveyors in, 96, 108, 182 n.61, 244, 247, 413–19, 423–4
Dromin, Co. Limerick, 384
Dromiskin, Co. Louth, 204
Dromoland, Co. Clare, 189
Drumcondra, Co. Meath, 413, 415
Dublin Bay and Harbour, 6, 202, 270, 272, 287 n.12
Dublin city, 6, 14, 88, 127, 194, 199, 218 n.50, 231, 268, 280, 316, 334, 350, 387, 393
   book shops and print shops, 320, 355, 390
   corporation, 99, 113
   engravers, 151, 342
   environs of, 1, 44, 209, 272, 278, 280, 344
   instrument-makers, 302
   map collections, 82, 83, 86
   map production 282, 331, 352, 392,
   maps of, 271, 276, 278, 279, 280, 334, 337, 340, 343, 352, 355, 355, 396
   streets, 192, 275, 278
      Abbey Street, 277
      Anglesea Street, 271
      Aston's Quay, 113
      Botanic Garden, 292 n.89
      Buckingham Street, 275
      Camden Street, 386 n.70
      Capel Street, 277
      Chichester House, 288 n.29
      Christ Church Cathedral, 179 n.11, 268, 275
      Cook Street, 430
      Dame Street, 362 n.102, 437
      Dominick Street, 278
      Essex Street, 83, 270
      Fitzwilliam Street, 191
      Harcourt Street, 108
      Henrietta Street, 393, 403 n.28
      King's Hospital School, 269
      Meath Street, 434
      Merrion Square, 185 n.102, 191, 215 n.21, 274
      Moore Street, 192
      North Lots, 113
      North Strand, 275, 288 n.12
      O'Connell Bridge, 278
      Oxmantown Green, 114, 136 n.16, 191,193
      Parliament Street, 192
      Phoenix Park, 189, 190, 280, 387, 388–9, 391, 396
      Registry of Deeds, 99, 115, 140 n.68, 399
      Royal Exchange, 113, 214 n.3
      Royal Irish Academy, 101 n.2, 180 n.33, 216 n.37, 273, 290 n.51, 304, 326 n.44
      St Mary's Abbey, 12
      St Michael's Parish, 289
      St Patrick's Cathedral, 182 n.57, 273
      St Patrick's Hospital, 428
      St Patrick's Street, 288 n.27
      St Stephen's Green, 102 n.22, 136 n.16, 191, 274
      Sherrard Street, 292 n.90

Wood Quay, 229
York Street, 291 n.66
surveyors in, 94,161, 168, 172, 200, 226, 246, 250, 268, 269–70, 342, 366, 379, 393, 396
teachers in, 96, 229
Dublin, County, 15, 18, 276, 363;
maps of, 271, 280, 340, 342, 348, 398
surveys in, 117, 275, 365, 444
Dunany, Co. Louth, 385
Dunbrody, Co. Wexford, 169, 278
Duncannon fort, Co. Wexford, 44
Dunfanaghy Bay, Co. Donegal, 200
Dungarvan, Co. Waterford, 121, 165
Dungiven, Co. Londonderry, 402
Dunleer, Co. Louth, 107
Dunloe, Co. Kerry, 94
Dunmore, Co. Leix, 153,183 n.70

Elphin, diocese, 335
Ely O'Carroll, Co. Offaly, 51, 74 n.12, 75 n.25
English Pale, 25, 43, 110, 115, 120, 204, 208
Enniscorthy, Co. Wexford, 261, 345, 351
Enniskean, Co. Cork, 186 n.112
Enniskillen, Co. Fermanagh, 343
Erne, Lough, 45, 355
Erne, River, 394

Farney, Co. Monaghan, 49
Fermanagh, County, 5, 125, 363
maps of, 336, 349, 359 n.20
surveys in, 140 n. 66, 440
Fermoy, Co. Cork, 191
Fethard, Co. Tipperary, 121
Fingal Co. Dublin, 15,18
Fingall estate maps, 97
Finglas, Co. Dublin, 156
Fitzwilliam estate, Co. Wicklow, 200, 240
Fox's Country, Co. Offaly, 51
Foyle Valley, 282
France, 85, 247, 276
Frenchpark, Co. Roscommon, 372
Friars Wood, Co. Dublin, 3
Gale (parish), Co. Tipperary, 107 n.85
Galtee Mountains, 204
Galway, County, 7, 209–11, 217 n.39, 220 n.89, 232, 284, 354, 451

maps of, 59, 348, 361 n.93, 368
surveys, 210, 364, 441
Galway town, 277, 343
Garristown, Co. Dublin, 107 n.87, 204
Geashill, Co. Offaly, 313
Germany, official surveys, 388–9
Glasnevin, Co. Dublin, 280
Glenavy, Co. Antrim, 122
Goldmines River, 290
Gore estate, 137 n.26, 137 n.34, 179 n.17
Gorey, Co. Wexford, 261 n.87
Graiguenamanagh, Co. Kilkenny, 241, 244
Grand Canal, 197, 218 n.50, 261 n.98
Gravelstown, Co. Meath, 411, 413–28

Hamilton estate, Co. Down, 81,101 n.2, 139, 155
Haroldstown (parish), Co. Louth, 108 n.106
Hebrides, William Bald in, 284
Herbert estate, Co. Kerrry, 149
Hillsborough, Co. Down, 191, 339
Horistown, Co. Meath, 413, 414–15, 421–2
Howth, Hill of, 180 n.22
Hughes estate, Co. Wexford, 181 n.46
Hutchinson estate, Co. Tipperary, 136, 290 n.57

Ileagh, Co. Tipperary, 89
Inchiquin, Co. Cork, 36, 41, 47 n.33, 316
Inish McSaint, Cos Donegal/Fermanagh, 384 n.38
Inishowen, Co. Donegal 149, 227, 278
Ireland, general maps of, 162, 270, 276, 286, 302, 331, 332, 336, 349
Irishtown, Co. Westmeath, 139 n.59
Islandbridge, Co. Dublin, 184
Island Magee, Co. Antrim, 304, 365

Kanturk, Co. Cork, 155
Kearney estate, Co. Cork, 106 n.66, 440
Kells, Co. Meath, 85
Kenry, Co. Limerick, 48 n.53
Kerry, County, 29, 40, 70, 79 n.82, 115, 123, 125, 207, 209, 350, 353, 363
maps of, 179 n. 12, 336, 353, 361 n.83

surveys in, 93–4, 133, 141 n.91, 232, 250, 270, 394
Kilaspick, Co. Sligo, 385 n.62
Kilbarron, Co. Tipperary, 106 n.62
Kilbeg, Co. Meath, 141 n.86, 413, 415, 416, 419
Kilbegnet, Co. Galway, 385 n.61
Kilbrew, Co. Meath, 67
Kilcoane, Co. Kilkenny, 385
Kilcullen, Co. Kildare, 275, 280
Kildare, County, 16, 240, 261 n.95, 363
    maps of, 166–7, 202, 205, 338, 348, 353, 361 n.87
    surveys in, 148, 161, 201, 219 n.69, 275, 309, 354, 412, 444
Kildare, manor of, 161,163
Kildare town, 138 n.51, 402 n.11
Kilgobin, Co. Cork, 412
Kilkeady (Kilkeedy), Co. Limerick, 384 n.40
Kilkenny, County, 27 n.63, 123, 136 n.9, 363
    maps of, 77 n.43, 104, n.38, 138 n.50, 182 n.56, 328 n.80, 343, 350, 386 n.72
    surveys in, 141 n.86, 181 n.52, 203, 209, 262 n.105, 271, 305, 371, 412, 441, 442
Kilkenny town, 115, 224, 234, 235, 275, 342
Killarney, Co. Kerry, 148, 355
Killenaule, Co. Tipperary, 138 n.50, 360 n.75
Killivarig, Co. Cork, 155
Killyleagh, Co. Down, 154
Kilmacanogue, Co. Wicklow, 384 n.38
Kilmore, Co. Kildare, 309
Kilmore (Co, Waterford), 37
Kilmore, diocese, 334
Kilpoole, Co. Wicklow, 243, 342
Kilruddery, Co. Wicklow, 215 n.7
Kilrush Co. Clare, 193
Kilrush, Co. Kildare, 372
Kiltiernan, Co. Dublin, 24
Kilcoolytoghy, Co. Kerry, 289 n.34
King's County, see Offaly
Kinsale, Co. Cork, 49 n.58, 155, 340
Kinsale Harbour, 44, 359 n.55
Knockaulin Hill, Co. Kildare, 275
Knockbrack, Co. Cork, 260

Knocklofty, Co. Tipperary, 290 n.57
Knockmealdown Hills, 128
Knocknadozen Co. Wicklow, 140 n.72
Knocktemple, Co. Cork, 155
Kylemore, Co. Galway, 403

Lackendarragh, Co. Cork, 142
Lancashire, land measures in, 17
Lanesborough, Co. Longford, 191
Lansdowne estate (Kerry), 63, 102 n.22, 394, 404 n.34
Lansdowne (Somerset), 77 n.53
Leinster, 57, 60, 232, 275
Leinster, estate, 140 n.73
Leitrim, County, 18, 51, 55, 57, 75, 80 n.92, 104 n.38, 142 n.100
    map of, 348
    surveys in, 354
Leix, (Queen's) County, 52, 98, 268, 365
    maps of, 338, 339, 348, 350
    surveys in, 55, 275, 284, 338, 350
Leix, territory, 3, 11, 20, 21, 30
Levitstown, Co. Kildare, 140 n.73
Lifford, Co. Donegal, 256 n.17, 262 n.105, 347, 349
Lilliput, Belfast, 283
Limerick city, 306, 343, 350
Limerick, County, 16, 18, 29, 51, 253, 363
    maps of, 50, 104 n. 38, 157, 352
    surveys in, 57, 93, 95, 123, 131, 354
Limerick diocese, 262 n.112
Lisburn, Co. Antrim, 191
Lismore, Co. Waterford, 128, 165, 181 n.47, 219, 240, 372
Listowel, Co. Kerry, 148, 350
Lizard estate, Co. Londonderry, 181
Locke estate, Co. Kerry, 250
London, 113, 190
    city of, Irish estates, 81, 110, 238
    map production in, 31, 282, 332, 342, 354
    surveyors from, 172, 226, 227
Londonderry, city, 219, 235, 337
    maps of, 120,154,181 n.46, 349
    surveyors in, 174, 180 n.35, 200, 227, 395, 441, 442
Londonderry, County lands, 110, 146, 157, 182, 229, 263, 363, 391
    maps of, 183 n.75, 260 n.86, 337, 344, 348, 349

plantation, 51, 59, 366
surveyors in, 172
Longford, County, 94, 264 n.137, 363
  maps of, 104 n.38, 348, 353,
    361 n.88, 412
  plantation surveys, 51, 57, 58, 59, 82,
    440
Loop Head, Co. Clare, 352
Lough Lean (Logh Lean), 150
Loughlinstown, Co. Kildare, 333
Louth, County, 11, 106 n.68, 141 n.88,
  204, 208, 363, 415, 440
  maps of 108 n. 106, 205, 261 n.98,
    344, 348, 353, 359 n.51, 361 n.93,
    368
  surveys in, 107 n.86, 207, 216 n.36,
    219 n.80, 385 n.56
Low Grange, Co. Kilkenny, 412
Lucan, Co. Dublin, 306
Lynch Blosse estate, Co. Mayo, 137 n.33
Lyons, Co. Kildare, 183 n.69

McCoughlan's Country, King's Co.
  (Offaly), 51
Maganey, Co. Kildare, 140 n.73
Mallow, Co. Cork, 129
Marley, Co. Louth, 261 n.98
Maynooth, Co. Kildare, 19, 158,184 n.90,
  191
Maynooth College, 302, 324 n.31
Mayo, County, 209, 232, 284, 364, 367,
  370, 371
  maps of, 50 n.75, 59, 80 n.92,
    136 n.12, 137 n.33, 179 n.17, 285,
    348, 368, 379
  surveys in, 213, 285–6, 306
Mealiff (Mealiffe), Co. Tipperary, 105
Meath, County, 16, 217 n.42, 363
  maps of, 7, 338, 350, 358 n.37,
    361 n.93
  surveys in, 67, 97,177, 411–12, 413,
    414–23, 441
Meath, diocese, 336
Melitia, Co. Carlow, 264
Midleton, Co. Cork, 193, 404
Minchin estate maps, 106
Mitchelstown, Co. Cork, 191
Mogeley (Mogeely), Co. Cork 37, 43, 45,
  140 n.80
Molahiffe, Co. Kerry, 40

Monaghan, County, 5, 367
  maps of, 7, 43, 44, 179 n. 15, 348,
    349, 361 n.93, 386
  surveys in, 43, 49 n.62, 149,
    215 n.22, 360 n.68, 364, 411
Monaghan town, 192
Monasterevan, Co. Kildare, 201, 218 n.50
Mostrim, Co. Longford, 385 n.62
Mountfin, Co. Wexford, 261 n.87
Mountrath, Co. Leix, 108
Mountrath estate (Cos. Roscommon
  Leitrim, Westmeath), 183 n. 75,
  185 n.105, 287 n. 9, 328 n. 78
Moynalty, Co. Meath, 217 n.42
Mullingar, Co. Westmeath, 190
Mundown Co. Dublin, 289 n.44
Munster, 18, 60, 64, 110, 232
  plantation, 21, 28–44, 51, 55, 56, 57,
    58, 70, 122, 139 n.60
Muskerry, Co. Cork, 48 n.53

Naas, Co. Kildare, 204
National Maritime Museum, Greenwich,
  35
Navan, Co. Meath, 217 n.42, 411, 412
Neagh, Lough, 196, 284, 336, 357 n.21
Neale, the, Co. Mayo, 232
Newbay, Co. Kilkenny, 328
New Birmingham, Co. Tipperary, 142 n.92
Newcastle, Northumberland, mining maps
  at, 216 n.34
Newcastle, Co. Limerick, 361, n.94
Newcastle Lyons, Co. Dublin, 121,
  138 n.53
Newpark, Co. Longford, 412
Newry, Co. Down, 191, 196, 341, 343, 344
Newtown Forbes, Co. Longford, 191

O'Brien estate, Co. Clare, 61, 102 n.16
O'Byrne's Country, Co. Wicklow, 51
O'Dunne's Country, Co. Leix, 51
Offaly, (King's) County, 58, 363
  maps of, 104 n.38, 338, 354
  surveys in, 57, 58, 59, 75 n.24, 96,
    138 n.44, 142 n.105, 190, 287
Offaly, territory, 3, 11, 19, 20, 21, 30
Oldcastle, Co. Meath, 277
Old Derig, Co. Leix, 412
Omagh, Co. Tyrone, 154, 179 n.20

INDEX OF PLACE NAMES   461

O'Melaghlin's Country, Co. Westmeath, 51
O'Molloy's Country, Co. Offaly, 51
Orior, Co. Armagh, map of, 381
Ormond, territory (estate), 25, 114, 136 n.15
Ossory, Upper, Co. Leix, 365

Paris, 79 n.83, 84–5, 103 n.24, 285
Pellipar, manor of, Co. Londonderry, 183 n.75
Pembroke estate, Dublin, 24 n.19, 147,168, 179 n.9, 180 n.22, 185 n.102, 215 n.21
Perceval (Egmont) estate, Co. Cork, 81, 199, 440
   maps of, 132, 144–6, 181 nn.42, 49, 266–9, 287 n.6, 315, 366
   surveys in, 101 n.2, 114–15, 118, 126, 140 n.66, 142 n.103, 147–8, 155–6
Portarlington, Co. Leix, 191
Portglenone estate, Co. Antrim, 249
Portrane, Co. Dublin, 22 n.1, 278
Powerscourt, Co. Wicklow, 189
Public Record Office, Ireland, 25 n.38, 86
Public Record Office, London, 30
Public Record Office, Northern Ireland, 86, 138 n.51, 183 n.74, 216 n.29
Public Record Office, Scotland, 361, n.82

Queen's County, *see* Leix.

Raheendough, Co. Meath, 412
Rathanane [alias Banemore], Co. Cork, 107 n.82
Rathconnell, Co. Westmeath, 195
Rathcoole, Co. Dublin, 121
Rathcoursey, Co. Cork, 91, 183 n.77
Rathdrum, Co. Wicklow, 385
Rathfarnham, Co. Dublin, 261 n.87
Rathkenny, Co. Meath, 413, 415, 421
Rathlackan, Co. Mayo, 213
Rathmore, Co. Kildare, 121
Rathnew, Co. Wicklow, 385 n.63
Rathvilly, Co. Carlow, 240
Raymonterdoney, Co. Donegal, 385
Red Island, Co. Cork, 138

Registry of Deeds, Dublin, 99, 115, 140 n.68, 399
Robertstown, Co. Meath, 412
Rockville, Co. Roscommon, 357 n.12
Rolleston estate, 139,141 n.87, 142 n.105, 259 n.59
Roscommon, County, 9, 111, 382 n.5
   maps of, 102 n.16, 107 n.83, 348, 350, 385 n.61, 444
   surveys in, 168, 185 n.105, 232, 268 n.127, 264 n.136, 284, 314, 364, 372, 384 n.50, 411
Roscommon town, 14, 190
Rosmacowen, Co. Cork, 403
Royal Canal, 135 n.4
Royal Exchange, Dublin, 113, 214 n.3
Royal Irish Academy, Dublin, 101 n.2, 180 n.33, 216 n.37, 273, 290 n.51, 304, 326 n.44
Royal Society, London, 90

St Sepulchre's, manor of, Dublin, 268
Saxony, map of, 389
Scaragh, Co. Cork, 412
Scarawalsh, Co. Wexford, 366
Scarwilliam, Co. Limerick, 157
Scotland, 17, 144, 172, 210, 231, 284, 285, 353, 401
Shannon Grove, Pallaskenry, Co. Limerick, 219 n.68
Shannon, River, 59, 63, 110, 209, 353, 394
Sheephaven, Co. Donegal, 200
Shuldham estate, Co. Cork, 185 n.106
Skerries, Co. Dublin, 267
Slane, Co. Meath, 191, 304, 413, 415
Slewvarise (Tallow, Co. Waterford), 36
Slieveardagh, Co. Tipperary, 360 n.75
Sligo, County, 98, 151, 284, 364
   maps of, 80 n.92, 98, 104 n.42, 108, n.102, 151, 348
   surveys in, 137 nn.26, 34, 197, 205, 232, 382 n.5
Sligo town, 197, 283
Southwell estates, Cos Cork and Down, 144, 149
Strabane, Co. Tyrone, 125, 138 n.51, 170, 192
Suck, River, 394
Summerhill, Co. Dublin, 275
Swords, Co. Dublin, 121

Tallaght, Co. Dublin, 117
Tallow, Co. Waterford, 36, 37, 165, 224
Templemore, Co. Londonderry, 78 n.59
Templemoyle Agricultural School, Derry, 258 n.42
Termon McGrath [Termond Magragh], Co. Donegal, 182 n.63
Thames, River, 200
Thomastown, Co. Kilkenny, 156
Thomond estate, 182 n.66, 267, 268, 287 n.7, 307, 311, 313
Thomond's Park (Bunratty), 154
Thurles, Co. Tipperary, 263, 343, 441, 442
Ticonderoga, map of, 277
Tinny Park, Co. Wicklow, 403
Tipperary, County, 5, 11, 16, 51, 82, 204, 363, 367
   maps of, 49 n.59, 79 n.72, 104 n.38, 105 n. 56, 106 n.62, 123, 136, 137, n.31, 138 n.50, 143 n.117, 220 n.83, 290 n.57, 328 n.83, 329 n.111, 338, 352, 354, 355, 360 n.75
   surveys in, 43, 49, 76 n.40, 108, 121, 142 n.100, 203, 232, 270, 335, 350, 352, 395
Tooms, Co. Kerry, 94
Tralee, Co. Kerry, 48, 336, 343
Trant estate, Co. Tipperary, 137 n.31, 143 n.117, 220
Trinity College, 192, *see also* Dublin,
   accounts, 82
   as proprietor, 110, 148, 185 nn.104, 106, 210, 244, 270
   estate maps, 289 n.34
   fellows, 56, 228, 269, 356
   graduates, 405 n.54
   plan of, 274
Tuam, diocese, 334, 356 n.11
Tullow, Co. Waterford, 47
Tully, Co. Kildare, 362 n.96
Tyrone, County, 185
   maps of, 104 n.38, 215 n.19, 336, 347, 348, 349, 357 n.20, 359 n.63, 360 n.66
   surveys in, 243, 350

Ulster, 44, 61, 231
   Bodley's survey, 55, 56, 57, 58, 87
   estates in, 110, 174
   maps of, 44, 45, 49, 50 n.71, 172, 283, 349
   plantation of, 45, 51, 55, 56, 58, 60, 106 n.69, 122
   surveys in, 55, 58, 159, 176, 232, 250, 256 n.15, 262 n.109, 280, 326 n.45, 413, 443

Virginia, surveying in, 43, 47 n. 30, 324 n.18

Walterstown, Co. Louth, 415–27
Waterford city, 247, 261 n.92, 277, 436
   maps of, 336, 342, 345
Waterford, County, 29, 36, 122–3, 126, 219, 357 n.19, 363, 364, 372, 375
   maps of, 37, 47 n.33, 104 n.38, 165, 182 n.58, 184 n.90, 219 n.66, 336, 348, 354, 360 n.74
   surveys in, 24 n.33, 33, 230, 259 n.58, 440
Waterford Harbour, 44, 49 n.65
Westmeath, County, 24 n.24, 51, 57, 75 n.25, 106 n.77, 208, 336, 363
   maps of, 104 n.38, 139 n.59, 183 n.70, 338, 348, 383 n.19
   surveys in, 27, 57, 78 n.62, 134, 185 n.105, 195, 216 n.36, 357 n.23, 366, 441
Westport, Co. Mayo, 191
Wexford, County, 51, 104 n.37, 112, 406
   maps of, 104 n.38, 169, 181 n.46, 345, 348, 350, 351, 366
   plantation of, 55, 56, 75 n.19, 295
   surveyors in, 168, 202, 247, 253, 254, 260 n.78, 278, 411
   surveys of lands in, 56, 57, 58, 86, 114, 142 n.103, 280, 369, 440
Wexford town (and harbour), 342, 402 n.11
White Knight's Country, 43, 49 n.58
Wicklow, County, 16, 51, 76 n.31, 202
   estates in, 27 n.62, 140 n.72, 200, 215 n.7, 259 n.66, 385 n.63, 403 n.21
   maps of, 104 n.38, 245, 261 n.98, 290, 327 n.66, 346, 348, 355
   surveys and surveyors in, 55, 58, 59, 168, 240, 243, 247, 267, 314, 342, 364

Wicklow Mountains, 197
Wicklow town, 342
Woodland, Co. Meath, 97
Woodpark, Co. Galway, 210
Wynnsfield (alias Loughlinstown), Co. Kildare, 333

Yorkshire, West Riding, Irish perch in, 26 n.49
Youghal, Co. Cork, 36, 47 n.33, 165

Index of Subjects

Academies, *see also* Societies,
   Academy of Arts and Sciences, Cork, 435
   classical academies, 229
   Royal Irish Academy, 273, 304, 436
Access, (right of admittance), 131, 312, 382
Access, to
   common rough pasture, 208, 214
   clients, 247
   colouring materials, 261 n.92
   documentation, 132, 147, 367, 391
   earlier records, 77 n.54
   instruments, 270
   rivers, sea coasts, main roads, 214
   witnesses, 376
Accessibility, 209, 331–2, 424, 436
Accession (policies of libraries and archives), 178 n.2
Accuracy, 255, 389, *see also* Precision, Error,
   of advertising, 247, 277, 349, 393
   of measuring process, 15, 35, 44, 130, 274, 299, 388, 400
   checks on, 59, 130, 147, 177, 194, 244, 250, 306, 318, 322, 370, 388, 399, 433–6
Acre,
   aggregative, 10, 13, 21
   origin, 12, 13
   in placenames, 24 n.29
   size variations 14–16, 76 n.29, 123, 124
   use, 125–6, *see also* Plantation measure
Acreable penalties, 128
Acreable rents, 13, 125, 128
Acreages (and footages), 14, 30, 42, 72, 124–6, 411–12
   accuracy, 299, 307, 312–13, 391, 92
   county lists, 363, 366–7
   demesnes, 145, 154
   Down Survey, 71
   estimation of, 39, 89, 372, 375
   'fiscal', 12
   Gross Survey, 62
   in deeds and leases, 87, 115, 125, 126, 127, 130, 371
   in official surveys, 286, 363, 364, 389, 390
   in 16th- and 17th-century maps, 71, 72, 89, 93, 114, 366, 367, 369, 373, 375
   'laying off', 93
   non-arbitrary systems of, 14
   Ordnance Survey, 71, 298, 320, 322, 390, 392
   parish (townland and field), 368–9, 391
   statute-acreages, 14
   'surveyor's', 19
Acts, of,
   admeasurement, 400
   historical judgement, 1
   partition, 10
   perambulation, 8
   piracy, 396
   plagiarism, 64
   Surveyor-General, 100
Acts of Parliament, 84, 100, 128, 204
   Explanation (1665), 89
   General (23rd of Henry VIII), 415
   Grand Jury (1727, 1809), 193, 368
   Making Wide and Convenient Ways, Streets, and Passages, 292 n.89
   Post Roads, 324 n.21
   Satisfaction (Cromwellian), 21
   Settlement (1662, 1665), 88, 92, 95, 102 n.10, 108 n.102
   Tithes (1793, 1823), 370, 370
Adjustment, 95, 414, 424
   arbitrary, 37
   chains, 425
   irregular (fudging, coaxing, humouring; 'cobbling'), 91, 310
   orthogonal axes, 91
   percentages, 248
   rent, 39
   scale-ratio, 90
Adjudication, 135, 274, *see also* Boundary disputes
Admeasurement money, 57, 82, 440
Adventurers, 60, 62, 88, 92, *see also* Soldiers
   adventurers' survey, 70–71, 222
Advertisements in newspapers (mapping-related), 25 n.39, 120, *see also* Newspapers

INDEX OF SUBJECTS 465

acreages, 140 nn.66,73
books, 105 n.57
'compartments for surveyors', 151
educational, 257 nn.28,34
farms, 135
land sales, 105 n.45
maps, 112–13, 127, 277, 336, 342, 396
Peter Callan *versus* John Bell, 1753–60, 413–28
plot-numbers cited in leases, 120
property, 112
sales-particulars map, 112–13, 411
Advertisements of surveyors (in manuals), 318
Advertisements of surveyors (in newspapers), 25 n.39, 87, 106 n.64, 109 n.110, 235
acknowledgements, 262 n.101
anonymous, 190
answering malicious accusations, 260 n.82, 393, 411, 415–17, 419, 421, 423–4, 426–8
atlases, 358 n.46
books on surveying, 429–38
benefits to improvers, 278
business addresses, 241, 277
campaign, 360 n.72
charts, 261 n.90
competences, 188, 252, 263 n.127, 308, 393,
composing, 224
copying of old surveys, 127
educational attainments, 229, 263 n.125
fees, 443
homely origins, 282
instruments, 270, 290 n.51, 306, 327 n.57
instrument-makers, 302, 329 n.103
for apprentices, 228, 263 n.115, 276–7
for assistants, 249, 262 n.100
invitation to survey, 131, 142 n.100, 259 n.58
invitation to 'unite' surveys, 149
'lands traced from the Down Survey', 90
magnets, 290 n.53
map-framing and glazing, 336
maps, 248, 293 n.102, 342, 356, 359 n.51, 360 n.74, 116
marriage, 277

motifs in, 130
Ordnance Survey vacancies, 386 n.74
parish maps, 362 n.103
penmanship, 248
preliminary (survey plans), 353
purposes (attract custom), 225
representative samples, 255 n.5
sample of 82 (1760–1800), 228–9
series of, 282, 292 n.91, 352
span of services, 379
survey charges, 142 n.103
surveyors' manuals, 318
testimonials, 277
Advertising, 393
Aesthetic appeal (of maps), 150, 160, 164, 229, 247, 265, 282
Affinities, between
map makers and land surveyors, 354
map drawing and park design, 189
county and estate maps, 285
Agents, 187, 244, 253, *see also* Bailiffs, Land Agents, Stewards,
agents' offices, 113
estate agents, 401
landlord agents, 87, 116, 124, 147–8, 250, 254, 353, 372, 390, 440
official Dublin agents of booksellers Hodges and Smith, 390
under-agents, 240
unscrupulous agents, 230
Agrarian,
activities, 121
affairs, 4,
cake (slices from Ireland's), 323
historians, 17
history (story), 92, 209, 390
landscape terms, 24 n.23
practices, 4
profit, 164
settings, 252
societies (communities), 2, 11, 132
trends, 6
typology, 390
Agricultural,
background, 244
depression, 206
development (improvement, revolution), 89, 190, 202, 393, 400
implements, 160
socio-agricultural hierarchy, 31, 112, 170, 364

Agriculturalists, 20, 187, 202–03, 226, 254
Albums, 146, 152, 166, see also Atlases
Altars, 176, see also Chapels, Churches, Religion
Aliases, 120, see also Names
Alidade, 35
Altitude,
  emphasis on (and slope), 202, 298
  meridian (of sun), 435
Alumni, 344
Amalgamation, 10, 189, 214, 367, see also Dividing, Fragmentation, Partition
Amateur, see also Professional,
  interest, 98
  fashion, 223
  brilliant, 63
  cartographers, 334
  draughtsmen, 28
  enthusiastic, 192,
  fashion, 223
  gentlemen, 45
  interest, 98
  map-makers, 71, 334, 336
  scientists, 334
  surveyors, 133, 337
  versatile, 353
Amateurs,
  architects, scientists, engineers, 334
  draughtsmen, 28
  map-makers (cartographers), 71, 334, 336
  measurers, 224
  surveyors, 45, 63, 98, 133, 192, 337, 353
'Ancient' (not modern), 155
  cartography, 286
  documents (records), 363, 379
  guild, 274
  'Irish', 156, 158
  local family, 176
  maxim, 118
  monuments, 66, 275, 345
Antiquities
  rate, 280
  royal titles, 51, 275
  sources and influences, 54
  surveys (of record), 87, 90
  territorial units, 6, 12, 32, 363
  traditions, 11, 116
  universities, 100
  writers, 10
Animals, 10, 154, see also Cattle, Horses, Sheep
Angle measurement, 35, 57, 300–07, see also Bearings
Anglo-Normans, 4, 11, 14, 120
Anonymous, see also Naming,
  activities, 275
  advertising, 190, 215 n.9
  attendance, 33
  copper plates, 269
  documents, 79 n.71, 148, 294 n.117, 309, 352–3, 359 n.65, 361 n.83, 404 n.30
  employees (clerks) 19, 199, 395
  surveyors, 248, 254, 355
  namelessness, 196, 258 n.50, 336, 390
  semi-anonymity, 334
Antiquarianism, 368
Antiquaries (antiquarians), 85, 153, 253, 336, 367
Antiquities, 66, 353, 355, see also Ancient monuments, Castles,
  cairns, 275
  forts (Danish) or raths, 65, 116, 176, 202, 345
  giants' graves, 176,
  standing stones (Long Stone), 118
  town walls, 176
Apothecaries, 336
Appendages to leases (maps), 115, 139 n.55, 373
Applotment, 370–71, see also Composition, Tithes,
  tithe applotment books, 371, 373
Applotters, 370, 373
  cess-applotters, 379
Apportionment (cesss), 9, 56, 363
Apprentices, 184 n.94, 227, 234, 249, 270–71, 276–8, 282, 389
Apprenticeships, 228, 250, 252, 269, 278
Architectural,
  competition, 189
  drawings, 277
  quasi-architectural work, 240
Architects, 17, 187, 189, 193, 226, 244–5, 270, 318, 334, 352, 433
Architecture, 189, 191–3, 394
Area calculation, 316–322, see also Estimation of area
Areas of,
  cartography, 332

closed traverses, 316–8
competence, 287
concentration, 235
counties, 373
demesne woodland, 240
denominations, 299
estates, 436
interest, 185 n.108, 390
irregular figures (polygons), 41, 316, 430
farms, 11, 436,
fields, 203
overlap, 188
ploughlands, 39
reclamation, 288 n.12
surveys, 143 n.114
Arrows, in chain surveying, 297
Atlas 'factices', 146
Atlases (manuscript), 3, 124, 282, 283
contents, 146, 148, 156
format, 152, 162,169,170,180, 309, 394
functions, 149, 150, 161, 404, *see also* Map-Book
Atlases (printed), 71, 87, 146, 251, 333, 336, 344
Auditor-General's office, 80 n.93, 84
Avenues, 154–5, 188–9
Azimuth,
azimuthal instruments 232, 302, 305–06

Backs of houses (privy, dust-hole, dairy yard, cock pit, dog kennel), 176
Badges of identity, 390
Bailiffs, 18, 187, 254
common bailiffs, 244
Balance surveys, 206
Balks, 399, *see also* Mearing stones, low grass balks, 208
Balloons,
ascents, 176
experiments with, 290 n.51
Ballybetagh (knight's fee), 5, 8, 10
Ballyboe (land division), 8, 12, 13, 14
Bailiffs, 18, 187, 244, 254, *see also* Agents
Bank(s), 6, 65, 118, 162, 312, 400, *see also* Ditch(es),
use of 'old' banks, 410

Baptism,
'equivalent of baptism' ('laying on of the chain'), 56, *see also* Metaphor
'unimaginative baptismal habits of the eighteenth century', 228
Barren, *see also* Waste,
grounds, 36, 41, 410
lands, 36, 94
mountains, 21
Barony,
books, 367
boundaries 56
courts of survey, 21
maps, 28, 43, 57, 60, 71, 84–6, 144, 145, 149, 338, 347, 349–50, 365–6, 380–82
payment by, 69
statistics (census, population, acreages), 57, 240, 365, 367–8
surveys, 354, 365, 377
Baronies, 5, 59, 114–15, 413, 415–23, 429
Base, 42, 104 n.41, 203, 234, 247, 324 n.22, 422, 430, 436, *see also* Debasing,
base-skeleton of roads, 150
lines, 34–5, 198, 315, 380
maps, 167, 192, 202, 250
measurement, 285, 336
of the Nelson Pillar (Dublin), 200
Battles, *see also* Conflict, War,
battlefronts, 246
battle-maps, 332
battle-views, 50 n.76
Boyne, 51, 128
cartographic, 125, 199, 246, 340
Cath Mhuighe Leana or the Battle of Magh Leana, 23 n.9
landlord-tenant (cartographic) battle, 132, 246
Bays, 149, 272
unreclaimed, 200
Beacons, 152
Bearings, 8, 303, 309, *see also* Angle measurement and Compass,
compass, 35, 300, 305, 317
correcting, 318, 434
intersection of, 66, 313
laying down of (taking), 90, 297, 346, 430
mapping of, 120, 307
statement (recording) of, 116, 313, 316

Beautiful (production of maps, atlases),
    274, 342
Beauty, 196, 267, *see also* Elegance,
    scenic, 170,
    spots, 355
Beneficiaries, of
    surveys, 133,
    premiums, 203
Benefits, of
    apprenticeship, 228
    corrupt practice, 45
    county cartographers, 346
    folds (to the improvement of fields),
        408
    geometry and trigonometry, 318
    local knowledge, 347
    mailcoach road maps, 198
    quasi-academic labels, 100
    removing hovels (to other places), 410
    surveyors (daily allowance), 38
    surveys, 131
Bias (regional), 231
Bias, in
    early evidence on surveying techniques,
        306
    Irish historical research, 231, *see also*
        Historians
Bigotry, 176
Bleach greens, 152, 284
Blending, of, *see also* Overlapping,
    cartographic functions, 340–41
    economic promise with military and
        social motives, 154
    'foreigners' into Irish environment, 353
    science and practicality, 334
    valuation, agency, engineering and
        architecture with land surveying, 394
Blocks,
    block-headed, 246
    block plans, 171, 285, 377, 390
    block-plan symbols, 155, 285
    building, 192, 340
    wood, 182 n.57
Blocks, of
    connecting sheets, 179 n.9
    counties, 344
    farms, 314
    forfeited area, 60
    land, 110, 114
    rectangles, 377, 390

territory, 51, 344
townlands, 66
Book (in titles),
    *A Book of Maps of the Estate of Sir John
        Perceval*, 287 n.6
    *A Booke of the Survey of the County of
        Dublin*, 383 n.15
    Book(s) of the Corporation of Drogheda,
        101 n.5, 136 n.17
    Book(s) of the Mercers'Company,
        182 n.62
    *Council Book of the Corporation of the
        City of Cork*, 261 n.90
    Red Book of Ormond, 24 n.26
    Standard County Book, 362 n.94
    *The Book of Maps of the Dublin City
        Surveyors*, 290 n.52
    The Surveyor in Foure Bookes, 327 n.65
Book-illustrations, 336
Book-keeping, 229
Booking,
    angles, 304, 322
    distances, 299, 322
    offsets, 327 n.78
    without sketches or diagrams, 307
Books, 337
    world of, 355
Books (types) of, *see also* Atlases,
    Field-books, Manuscripts, Map-books,
    Registers, Textbooks,
    academic, 209
    account, 357 n.24, 403 n.15
    'barony books', 367
    'book survey', 366
    boundary remark-books, 8
    'county books', 9, 366–9, 371,
        382 n.5, 383 n.25
    'county warrant books', 360 n.69
    engagement, 251
    extracts (Down Survey), 96
    fair-books, 68
    guidebooks, 355
    letter-books, 74 n.8, 359 n.65
    map-booklets (PRONI), 293 n.94
    parcels (of land), 47 n.22
    reference, 63, 82, 287 n.9, 363
    road, 353
    survey and distribution, 22, 25 n.36,
        78 n.62, 92, 102 n.16, 106 n.67
    this (present) book (JHA), 2, 4, 22, 69

tithe applotment, 371–2, 384 n.38, 384 n.51, 385 n.55
travel, 178 n.6
vestry, 385 n.58
Booksellers, 107 n.95, 355, 390, 396, 432, 436–7
Bookshops, 320
Book subscribers, 236
Bog, 124, 152, 162, 168, 209, 313, 376, 380
    boglands, 285
    bog-maps, 143 n.32, 285, 354, 390
    bog-surveys, 200, 251, 378–9, 442
    bogside (as boundary), 65, 118
    deterioration into, 64
    non-rented, 128
    reclaimable, 6, 204
    spreads (tracts) of, 6, 116
Bogs, 65, 70, 198–9, *see also* Curraghs, Heaths, Marshes, Moors, Waste,
    dividing (partitioning) of, 72, 133, 442
    quantification (acreage, surveying) of, 13, 15, 40, 62, 72
Bogs (types of)
    'pasturable', 214
    'unprofitable', 6, 21–2, 40, 66, 79 n.77, 145, 170, 311, 375, 377
    turf bogs, 112, 133, 240
Bogs Commission, 200-02, 280, 285, 354
Bordering (denominations), 373
Borderlines,
    between people, 254
    on maps, 160, 174, 181 n.52
Borders, 150, *see also* Boundaries, Hinterlands,
    county, 344
    decorative, 283
    defence of, 280
Boroughs, 338
Boundary,
    bog, 118
    changes, 71–2, 89
    characters (types, names, colours), 312, 389, 393
    cutting ('give-and-take'), 206, 312
    crosses, 23 n.14, 116, 166
    denominations, 10, 72, 119, 166
    descriptions (verbal, written, non-cartographic), 3–4, 83, 121, 311
    disputes, 8, 89, 90–91, 94, 114
    information (collecting), 33, 116
    junctions, 61, 152, 168
    landmarks, 118, 120
    lines (extent of, course), 31, 95, 119, 206, 400
    maps, 373
    marks (linear, non-linear), 66, 116, 206
    perambulation, 246
    reconstruction, 118
    remark books and registers, 8
    stones, 118
    streams, 119
    tracing, 40, 57, 95, 118
    traverse, 35–6, 41, 57, 59, 300, 308, 311
Boundaries, 11, 13, 45, *see also* Landmarks, Traverse,
    'badly-fitting' (incompatible) sections of, 91, 93
    barony, 56
    common, 59, 68, 73
    county, 271
    defining (delimiting, fixing), 40, 116, 388, 399
    Down Survey, 89
    diagrammatic sketches of, 30, 116
    ditching and quicksetting of, 328 n.79
    establishing, 29, 115
    estate, 88
    farm, 119, 175
    geometrical, 32
    house-plot, 176
    leasehold, 116
    legal, 6
    maritime, 6
    medieval (modern), 15, 90
    nature (theoretical) of, 121
    outer, 36, 38, 307
    record of, 85, 90
    straight-line, 6, 206
    territorial, 15, 64, 66, 72, 83, 310
    townland, 66, 71, 97, 313
    treading (setting forth), 311
    visible (invisible), 6, 116, 118, 121–2
    well-known, 4
Boundary department (OS), 369, 389
Boundary Survey (Griffith), 362 n.103
Bounding, 8, 22, 32, 172, 387, *see also* Dividing, Naming, and Valuing
Bounds, 21–2, 38, 65, 121, 308, 424
    drafts for, 144
    'extreme' (outer), 36, 89, 124

known, 36, 96
of confiscated areas, 56
settling of, 95, 322
true, 23
Brickmakers, 244
Bridges, 152, 162, 187, 252, 286, 337
as landmarks, 137 n.30
upkeep of, 363
Broadsheets, 411, *see also* Pamphlets, Sheets
Building,
assignments, 395
banks, 6
block-plans, 171
careers, 252
churches, 369
covenants in leases about, 203
estates, 63
houses, 400
plans, 188, 190–91, 277
roads, 6, 198
symbols, 48–9
walls, 6
work, 11, 244, 429
Buildings,
character of buildings, 125, 155, 391
elevations of, 274
Irish, 17
'conducting', 190
on maps, 174, 298, 340, 377, 389
roofs of, 274
surveyors of, 17, 22, 191
types of, 164, 187
urban building-plots (blocks, lots), 124, 192–3
valuation of, 20, 387, 439
visualisation of, 188
Bulk rents, 127,128,134 , *see also* Renting
'Burgage acre', 15, 25 n.43
Burning, of, 407
faulty maps, 181 n.42
land, 128, 141 nn.86, 87, 130
By-
laws (on surveying), 115
products (of plantation, surveys), 48 n.53, 76 n.36, 113
roads, 354

Cabins, 112, 152, 155, 183 n.75, 349
Cadastral,
problems, 119, 370

sources, 44
specifications (accuracy), 65, 388
surveys (maps), 139 n.57, 161, 384 n.48, 404 n.43
Cadastralism, 369
Cadastre, 52
Cairns, 275
Calculating devices, 288 n.26, 428
Calculation, of, *see also* Estimation, Protraction, Reckoning,
areas, 14, 15, 31, 39, 41, 56, 59, 64, 68, 86, 116, 119, 273, 316, 330 n.114, 375, 391, 393, 397, 416, 418
areas (non-graphic methods), 316–18, 320, 371, 423, 425, 428–38
boundary lines, 31
cess, 363
input and output, 20, 82, 203
manpower resources, 4, 34, 222, 238, 240, 248
offsets, 322
rent, 298
road distances, 289 n.35
taxation, 4
tithes, 370
traverse stations, 312
'Callowe measure', 15
'Callows' (river meadows, from Ir. *caladh*), 170
Calm, 349, *see also* Conflict, Quiet, Rage
Canal,
developments (proposals), 196–7
engineers, 193, 202, 251, 286
levels, 197
maps, 322
new map feature, 135 n.4, 154, 346, 349
surveys, 197, 335, 435
Canals, 187, 200
Grand Canal, 196–7, 218 n.48, 261 n.98
'Carbre acre', 25
Careers, *see also* Professions,
ends, 71, 100, 350
parliamentary (of landlords), 146
second (secondary), 244, 253, 277
stages (parts), 81, 103 n.26, 222, 282, 347, 353
starts, 10, 130, 252, 271, 282, 394, 442
turning points, 286

Careers, of
    cartographers, 331, 340
    surveyors, 48 n.53, 56, 71, 172,
        184 n.86, 227, 242, 266–7, 269,
        272, 277, 282, 350, 379
Carriage, of
    bedding, 39
    corn, 194
    field provisions, 39
    furniture, 39
    tents, 39
    victuals, 39
Carriages (and horses), 253
'Carrows' (quarters), 10
'Casting', 59, 68, 73 *see also* Calculation
Cartography, 2, 45, 98, 179, *see also*
Historiography,
    and land tenure, 158
    aggressive and defensive, 148
    attraction of, 84
    'cartography without cartographers',
        388
    commercial, 337
    county, 353, 366
    contemporary state of, 42, 156, 166,
        174, 189, 192, 202, 275, 355, 371,
        379, 387
    ecclesiastical (church), 368
    elements (parts) of, 68
    estate, 149, 152, 369, 373, 396
    English, 66, 168
    governmental (official) and non-
        governmental, 84, 94, 96, 99, 370
    Irish, 22, 114, 125, 159, 190, 275,
        286, 331, 347, 375, 379
    lawyers' attitude to, 88, 115
    lovers of, 401
    plantation, 114
    road, 196
    sale and lease, 121
    'schools' of, 172
    styles of, , 280
    systems of , 167
    types (kinds) of, 247, 332, 341, 353
'Cartobiography', 266, 269
Cartouches, 151, 160, 161, 174, 182 n.57,
    261 n.98, 271, 283
'Cartrons' (quarters), 9,10, 11, 363, *see also*
    Carrows, Quarters
Carucates, 8, *see also* Sessiaghs, Ploughlands

Catholic, *see also* Protestant,
    'common Catholic schools', 230–31
    farmers, 258 n.49
    Irishmen (removing across Shannon),
        63
    landlords, 110
    pupils (learning mathematics and
        surveying), 230
    reservations (110)
    surveyors, 230–31, 258 n.49
Catholicism (prevalence of), 230
Catholics
    innocent (claims of), 88
    northern (remonstrances of), 74 n.10
'Carvaghs' (Cavan), 363
Castles, 10, 19, 21, 36, 39, 65, 86, 152,
    156, 160, 346
Catalogues,
    map cataloguing, 191, 210, 242, 271,
        320
    printed catalogues, 359 n.51, 344,
        359 n.51
Catalogues, of
    improvements, 64
    manuscripts, 384 n.38
    maps, 80 n.93, 180 n.30, 182 n.64,
        215 n.18, 359 n.51
    printed books, 262 n.101, 326 n.56,
        433
    private surveys, 43
    promises, 276
Cattle, 9, 71, 112, 119, 125, 208, *see also*
    Animals
Censuses, of
    baronies, 240
    farm and estate maps, 145
    nations (official), 231, 233, 240, 242
    occupations (18th century), 240,
        258 n.50, 260 n. 73
'Certificate maps', 372–4
Certificates, of
    acreage, 74 n.12, 75 n.25, 83
    proficiency (competence), 98–100,
        226, 228, 232, 235, 265, 273
Cess, *see also* County Cess, Tax,
    apportionment, 363
    burden, 367
    calculation, 363
    collection, 363
    theory of link with plantation, 363
Cess-applotters, 379

Cess-payers, 285
Chaining, 56–7, 68, 296, 298, 346, 395
   along slopes, 320
   bad, 297
   of roads, 335
   re-chaining, 90
   surveying by the chain only, 133, 315
Chainmen, 69, 95, 69, 95, 107 n.86, 114, 234, 297, 364, 415
Chains, 11, 14, 34, 232, 259 n.54, 285, 297–9, 302, 309–15, 320, 388, 416–19
   combined with circumferentor, 90, 91, 287 n.12, 295, 296, 300, 308, 318, 345–6
   in farm surveys, 122, 129, 130, 131, 133, 367, 371
   for plantation maps, 56, 57, 68, 72, 75 n.25, 311
   in road surveys, 299–300, 335, 348
Chapels, 176, *see also* Churches, Religion
   of ease, 194, 217 n.40
   'Popish' or 'Romish', 258 n.49
Charts and marine surveys, 261 n.90, 272, 286, 287 n.12, 331, 336, 338, 342, *see also* Terriers
'Cheshire acre', 17
Church,
   yards, 203
   doors, 368
   map symbols, 164, 176
   'old walls', 217 n.39, 345
   towers, 120
Church (Established), 4, 190, 194, 338, 364, 368
   Representative Church Body Library, 108 n.106, 292 n.79, 357 n.14
Churches, 10, 31, 36, 65, 90, 152, 162, 208, 346, *see also* Chapels, Religion, Dublin, 3, 179 n.11, 268, 383 n.36
   'new', 334, 369, 384 n.38
Church land, 62, 110, 262 n.110, 275, 365, 369, *see also* Crown land, Glebes
Churchwardens, 372, *see also* Vergers
Circles, 150, 174, 305, 313–14, *see also* Lines,
   computing, 436
   engine-divided, 306
   of officialdom, 55, 392
   properties of, 318
   red, 164
   semi-circles, 35, 305, 430, 436

Circumferentor, 283, 295, 300–07, 311, 353, 430, 434, 437–8, *see also* Instruments
City,
   archives, 115
   'big city, small town dichotomy', 247
   latitudes and longitudes of, 270
   properties (boundaries of), 114
City Engineer, 275
City Surveyors, 99, 146–7, 192, 240, 266, 268, 273–5, 295, 303, 338, 417, 419, *see also* Surveyors
Cities, 115
   maps of, 342, 350, 431, 338, 340, 342, 346, 350, 352, 355, 396
   provincial, 337
Civil concerns, 191, 365, *see also* Private
Civil Bill Court, 105 n.48, *see also* Courts
Civil engineers, 199, 201, 251–2, 260 n.73, 284, 378–9, 396, 401
Civil magistrates, 421
Civil Survey, 16, 25 n.46, 27 n.65, 60, 68, 366
Civil War (Irish), 86
Civilians, 380, 388
Civilization, 56, 75 n.24, 102 n.15
'Clachans' (rundale villages), 155, 208–09, *see also* Rundale, Scatters (scatterings)
'Clanwilliam acre', 16
Class, 174, 253
   class displacement, 253
   class war, 253–4
Classes,
   educated, 389
   employing, 300
   humblest (lowest), 11, 112
   landowning, 2, 110, 145
   middle-class, 240
Classes, of,
   county road supervisors, 252
   land surveyors, 188
   middlemen, 112
   tithe proctors, 133
Classifications, of,
   documents, 84
   employees on rural estates, 240
   ethnicity, 222
   land, 70, 72, 170, 373, 377
   land surveyors, 224, 246, 289 n.43
   maps, 28, 144, 159, 285, 331, 334, 352–3
   survey duties, 242

Cleaning, of, *see also* Lighting, Paving,
'dung cellars', 409–10
horses, 409
instruments, 269
records, 42
rivers, 199
streets, 337, 338
Cleavages (horizontal and vertical, between surveyors), 246
Clergymen,
careers of sons of Irish clergymen, 253
in territorial disputes, 369
Clerks, 253
anonymous, 19, 199
attorneys', 397
Surveyor General's, 19, 55
surveyors', 197, 268
Town clerk's office, 113
vacancies for, 249
Clerk of the Crown and Peace (county), 104 n.42
Clerk of Quit-Rents, 106 n.77
Clerk to Dublin Wide Streets Commission, 278
Climate, *see also* Weather,
Irish, 307
local, 391
social, 265
Clusters, 10, 31, 155, 209, 285, *see also* 'Clachans', Scatters (scatterings), Triads
Coaches, 198
mailcoach-roads, 119, 198, 199
Coasts, 214
changes in, 41, 176, 200
coast roads, 286
coastal (fishing) settlements, 112
coastlines as boundaries, 6, 119, 197
Coasts, of, *see also* Charts,
Donegal, 51
east Ireland, 115
Dublin and Wexford (Balbriggan to Arklow), 342
Lough Neagh, 336
surveys of, 65–6, 335, 338
Cocks,
cock pits, 176
hay cocks, 407
Collecting,
'admeasurement money' (fees), 82, 234
boundary information, 33
estate records, 113, 196, 231

figures (data), 14, 60, 375
manure, 408–09
maps, 42, 71, 75 n.24, 82–5, 87, 96, 99, 102 n.16, 103 n.24, 148, 210, 232, 242
rents, 93, 268
subscriptions, 337
taxes (revenue, cess, tithes), 9, 94, 363, 364
Colonial,
America, 35, 330 n.114
image, 304
Colonialism, 3, 122, 135
Colonists, 28, 32, 51, 120
Colonies, 31, 51, 75 n.24, 305
Colour, for
boundaries, 90, 116, 150, 152, 172
compass roses, 150–51
demesnes, 154
framing, 150, 174
land-use, 36, 124, 137 n.28, 162, 164, 174
Colouring (of maps), 160, 174, 340, *see also* Shading,
materials, 166, 261 n.92
'French style' of, 168
grey watercolour, 283
hand-colouring, 201, 262 n.100, 282, 391, 393, 395
superimposition in colour (Down Survey), 104 n.41
uncoloured, 83, 166, 172, 174
Colps (land measurement), 8
Commercial,
cartography, 337
dealers, 127
economy, 19
pressures, 379
studies, 229
Common lands, 1, 65, 160, 204, 252, 304
Commons (surveys), 162, 204, 304
Ardfert, 141 n.91
Ballymore Eustace, 220 n.81
division (survey) of, 204, 336
Dromiskin, 219 n.80
Naas, 204
Slewvarise, 36
Commonsense (judgement), 70
Companion,
map, 41
surveyor's book, 41 , 434–5, 437

Comparative surveys, 78 n.62, 90, 92, 290 n.48, 302, 352, 380, *see also* Surveys
Comparison, of
   admeasurement and valuation, 159
   ancient and modern, 41, 155, 209, 400
   areas (acreages), 13, 31, 71, 112, 298, 322
   boundaries, 59, 68, 341
   Catholics and Protestants, 231
   copies and originals, 85, 176
   executive organs, 54
   fees, 439
   lengths, 297
   map and ground, 113, 321
   rentals, 128
   roads, 198
   scarcity (rarity, shortage), 44, 124, 151, 231, 238, 259 n.72, 313, 350
   townships and townlands, 285
   true and magnetic meridians, 303
Comparisons, 187, 210, 238, 308
'Compartments' (engraved), 117, 151–2, 160, 301
Compass, 90, 274, 285, 305, 322, 354, 437, *see also* Circumferentor, Instruments,
   bearings, 35, 300, 317, 430, 435
   needles, 64, 300, 303–05, 388
   rods, 300
   roses (stars), 150, 182 n.57, 186 n.113, 283, 302, 304
   surveys, 302–03
   surveys without compass, 329 n.111
Complaints, 32, 49 n.60, 199
   Recusants', 26 n.60, 74 n.9
Complaints, about
   access (lack of), 312,
   checking (lack of), 345
   disregard of advice, 35
   drunkenness of surveyors, 254
   favouritism, 227, 230, 253, 378
   hazardous circumstances, 44
   inaccuracy of milestones, 194
   short measure, 40, 70, 136 n.16, 143 n.108, 216 n. 28
   skill (lack of), 28, 56, 311, 313, 388
Composition, *see also* Applotment, Tithes,
   applotment of, 373
   favouring the parishioner, 371
   obligatory (of tithes), 373
   of tithes, 373
   payment of (for portion of parish), 373

Tithe Composition Act (1823), 370
Tithe composition applotment books, 384 n.51, 385 n.55
Compositions,
   maps as, 172
Compromise, on
   survey extents, 147
   standards, 379, 388
Conacre, 119, 133
Concealments, 148, *see also* Encroachments,
   by false admeasurement, 92
   concealed lands, 54, 92, 94, 148
Conductors, of Down Survey, 68–9
Confiscation, 51, *see also* Redistribution, Restoration
   confiscated area, 30, 44, 56
   estates, 18, 29, 62
   kingdom, 81
   lands, 3, 19, 32, 58, 67, 88, 93, 94
Conflicting,
   emotions, 267
   surveys (cartographies), 128, 199, 273, 340, 382, 399
Conflicts, 118 *see also* Battles, Controversies, Disagreements, Rage, Troubles, Wars, and Calm, Quiet,
   altercations, 247
   arable *versus* pasture, 170
   combats, 246
   contests, 246, 273
   landlords *versus* tenants, 132, 246, 273, 247
   mapping of banks and ditches, 118
   rebellions, 20, 50 n.77, 114, 254
   writing on map contents of each farm or not, 125
Congested Districts Board, 209
Conspiracy, 85, 92, *see also* Secrecy
Contouring, 404 n.33, *see also* Hill delineation
Contours,
   contour-lines, 189–90
   profusion of contour-like 'natural' boundaries, 172
   running farms at right angles to the, 214
Controversial, *see also* Conflict,
   cases, 94–5
   sequences of events, 63
   topics, 224, 433
Controversialists, 246

Controversies (professional), 132, 194, 224, 249, 411
    controverted surveys, 310, 313, 431
    lands 'in controversy', 149
Controversies, about
    patents, 93
    tithes (1780s), 369
Copper mines, 178
Copper plates, 151, 269, 340, 431–2
Copies, 23 n.6, 67, 127, 75 n.22, 83 , 97, 232, 364, 366
    contemporary, 93
    fair, 418
    free, 113
    maps, 248
    personal, 226
    signed, 50 n.68
Copying, 42, 72, 83, 85, 127, 268, 282, 392 –3
Copyholders, 32
Copyists, 127, 188
Copywriters, 345
'Corcasses' (marshes, especially salt marshes along rivers Shannon and Fergus, from Ir. *corach*),70
Corn,
    barleycorn, 10
    carriage of, 194, 197
    corn barrels, 407
    output of, 71, 365
    price of, 244, 370
    seed corn, 8
Corn acre (con acre), 138 n. 43
Corners,
    ditch-corners, 271
    'garden corners', 307
    hedge-corners, 65
    townland corners, 312
Correspondence, of
    Downshire, 263 n.117
    Fitzwilliam, 142 n.106, 219
    Herbert, 138 n.46
    Bishop of Kilmore and Provost of Trinity College, 356 n.10
    Jonathan Swift, 178 n.6
    Perceval, 115
    Petty-Southwell, 78, 178 n.6
    Plantation commissioners, 47 n.24
    Quit-Rent Office, 103 n.30
    survey authorities, 52
    Vallancey, 103 n.26
Correspondence (in newspapers), 325, *see also* Newspapers
Correspondence, on
    boundary cases, 139 n.55
    copying of the Down Survey, 103 n.30
    draining of bogs, 218 n.63
    map surveys, 220 n.81, 361 n.94
    Ordnance Survey, 404 n.33
    Rathcoursey, Co. Cork
Correspondents, 29, 180 n.35, 194, 335, 360 n.66, 390
Costs, of, *see also* Charges, Fees, Prices, Salaries
    official surveys, 38–9, 45, 50 n.68, 58, 62, 439–40
    private surveys, 44, 133, 147, 236, 249, 280, 389–90, 392, 393, 439–44
Cotters, 408–09
County books, 9, 362 n.94, 367–9, 371, *see also* Books (types of)
County cess, 363, *see also* Cess, Tax,
    misapplication of, 294 n.114
    revised, 387
    waste of, 294 n.114
County maps,
    Elizabethan, 35, 44
    17th century, 71, 84, 85, 144, 366
    18th and 19th-century, 150, 196, 271, 284, 285, 286, 332, 335–6, 337–9, 340–42, 344–6, 348–54, 366, 368
County roads, 193, 252
County surveyor, offices of, 252, 263 n.123, 286
Court, *see also* Law, Legal,
    cases, 395
    challenges, 126, 255
    decisions (orders), 89, 95
    maps in court, 85, 397
    petitions, 96,
    seneschals of the, 19
    surveyors in, 95, 99, 135 n.7, 253
Court of (Named),
    Assistants of the Drapers' Company, 221 n.96
    Chancery, 96, 98–9
    Claims (Dublin), 5
    Incumbered Estates, 397–8
    Landed Estates (later Land Judges' Court) 135 n.7, 396–8
    Survey, 21
    The Exchequer, 19, 96, 98–9

476   PLANTATION ACRES: THE IRISH LAND SURVEYOR AND HIS MAPS

Courthouses, 190, 363
Courtroom,
   clashes, 246
   tricks, 100
Courts, *see also* Law, Legal,
   of law (Irish), 8, 88, 90, 94, 96, 126
   of survey, 18, 21–2
   manorial, 18
Cromwellian land settlement, 67, 70, 82, 89
   Act of Satisfaction, 21
   dirigisme, 367
   maps (lack of), 93, 114
Cromwellian surveys, 21, 60, 440, *see also*
   Down (Lansdowne) and Strafford surveys,
   care of, 56, 62
   data distribution, 114
   'divisional' lines, 129
   instructions, 22
   newspeak, 63
Crop,
   inspection, 364
   reaping, 407–09
   rotation, 202
   sowing, 204
   valuation, 364
Crops (barley, oats, turnips, wheat), 187, 203, 408, 410
Crosses,
   boundary, 23 n.14, 116, 117, 166
   Christian, 9, 155
   on maps, 61, 116, 152, 174
   surveyor's, 133, 311
Crown lands (estates), 4, 51, 62, 93, 100–01, 283, 442–3, *see also* Church lands
Cultivation, 6, 110, 125, 200, 206, 208, 234, 364, 389, 398, *see also* Uncultivated lands,
   potato ridges, 133
   ridges, 13, 162, 164, 172, 185 n.110, 285, 408
   spade ridges, 13
'Cunningham acre/perch' (measure), 17, 26 n.48, 122–4, 167, 295
'Currraghs' (bog, from Ir, *corach*), 170, 175, *see also* Bogs
Custodians (of maps, surveys), 113, 202
   contemporary (of successive Surveyors-General's maps), 96
   subsequent (of plantation maps), 86
Custodianship, 17, *see also* Overseeing, Supervision

Custody, of
   government surveys, 81
   maps, 41, 250
   plantation maps, 82
Cutlers, Painter-Stainers and Stationers, guild of, 274

Dairy yards, 176
Damming (of streams), 189
Danish forts, 176, *see also* Antiquities
Data,
   astronomical, 336
   cartographic, 387
   data-collection (accumulation), 60, 375
   data-presentation, 440
   height, 215 n.215
   magnetic, 303
   official, 72
   published, 371
   scientific, 272
   survey, 114, 367
   tenurial, 150
   topographical, 121, 166
   trigonometrical, 350
Datum, 91, 200
Day's ploughing, unit of measurement, 13, 25 n.36
Dead house, 178
Debasing (coinage), 170, *see also* Base
Decoration, 190
   caricatures, 151
   cartoons, 176
   circular bands of, 174
   decorative conventions, 86
   'decorative windows', 160
   marginal, 160, 261 n.98, 283–4, 305
   penumbra of decoration, 150
   styles, 127, 151, 160, 174, 347
   techniques, 269
   undecorated maps 150
   wall-decoration, 154
Demesnes, 145, 155, 161, 183 n.70, 189, 277, 282, 441
Demolition (of houses), 189
Destruction, escape from, 84, 159
Destruction, of
   evidence, 114
   government records, 83, 86
   great estates, 398

planner's work, 189
surplus material, 82
Deterioration, 128, 244, *see also* Improvement(s),
of maps, 86
of land into bog, 64
Devices (surveying), 40, 57, 295, 300, *see also* Instruments
calculating device, 288 n.26
clock-plan symbols, 155
compass star, 186
'concentric' waterlines, 155
engraver's cartouche, 151
for settling boundary disputes, 94
invention of, 126
Devon Commission and Report, 129, 141 n.86, 180 n.24, 209, 249, 254, 258 n.49, 321
Diagonal (cross) lines, 57, 164, 313–15, 328 n.83, 340
Diagrams, 30–32, 56–7, 146, 149, 162, 307
diagrammatic (field and townland) boundaries, 341, 344, 379
line, 314
location, 372
triangulation, 284, 328 n.94, 349, 350
Dictums, 81, 89, 320, *see also* Doctrines, Maxims,
'a grant by acres presupposeth a survey', 125
'custom is the best guide to the spelling of names', 119
'the apparent indestructibility of the townland unit', 159
'there are as many ways of mapping a property ... a country or continent', 144
'this is a world [of Bald, Griffith, Edgeworth, Duncan] that deserves its own book', 354
Differences, 65, 209, 390, *see also* Similarities, Indifference,
ethnic, 15
international, 17, 38
regional, 15, 174
terminological, 13
Differences, between, *see also* Conflicts,
landlords and tenants, 133
mapmakers, 62, 132, 190, 202, 247, 251–2, 277

Differences in,
boundaries, 89, 92
categories, 144
gradients, 197
maps, 57, 62, 83, 174
quality, 124, 154
quantity, 118, 124, 130, 156, 167, 194, 196, 246, 298, 312, 392, 411–12
rank, 266
technique, 20, 30, 70–71, 73, 302–3, 313–14, 320–22, 368, 391, 398, 433–6
Dioceses, 3, 368, 384 n.36
Diocesan maps, 332, 334, 335, 336, 356 nn.10, 11, 357 nn.12, 13, 369, 384 n.41
disjecta membra (road system), 121
Directories, 257 n.31, 258 n.50, 291 n.66, 355
annual, 275, 293 n.101
contemporary, 259 n.72
evidence of, 291 n.68
'general' (surveys), 148
Disagreement, about, *see also* Conflict, Controversy, and Agreement, Contract,
public and private surveys, 87, 116, 132, 142, 244
surveying fundamentals, 62, 96, 147, 307, 310, 377, 432
tithes, 95
Disputes, surveyors', 71, 225, 246–7, 273–4, 298, 308, 310, 313-14, 315, 320, 411–28
Distaste, 167, *see also* Taste
Districts,
coal, 360, 403 n.29
city, 216 n.28, 291 n.79, 338
congested, 209
country, 93, 125, 262 n.109, 297, 364, 378, 394, 398
county, 15, 122, 297, 202, 245, 283, 324 n.24
enclosed, 443
home, 283
town, 105 n.59, 148, 172
Ditches, 40, 65-6, 220 n.85, *see also* Banks, Hedges,
boundary, 400
dating, 176

measuring, 118–19, 138, n.43, 204, 271, 311–12, 328 n.79
'old' ditches, 407, 410
Diverging,
architectural and engineering professions, 193
meridians (on county maps), 286
provision for adventurers and soldiers, 60
Diverging, from
aboriginal standard (length), 17
mean (in size, wealth), 8
truth (Petty's area), 71
Diverse,
bogs (wastes), 48 n.44
measures (labour of), 74 n.12
Diversion (mapping demesnes), 183 n.70, see also Leisure
Diversity, of, see also Uniformity,
calculations, 318
careers (surveyors'), 244, 267
Diverting (streams), 189, see also Damming
Dividing, 3, 32, 45, 68, 72, 89, 106 n.69, 130, 133, 142 n.96 , see also Bounding, Partition,
bogs, 442
farms, 206
lands, 431, 436, 440
streets, 277
into strips, 316
townlands, 200, 368
unwanted roads, 193
Doctrines, see also Dictums, Maxims,
'cursed be he that removeth his neighbour's landmark', 121
'pegs are paramount to plans', 121
Dog kennels, 176
Dower, writs of, 94
Down Survey, 27 n.65, 52, 59, 67, 70. 144, see also Strafford Survey,
accuracy, 71–3, 79 n.86, 92–3, 100, 116, 164, 298–9, 302, 366, 370, 390, 391
content and style, 66, 78 n.58, 89, 116, 152, 161, 269, 365
copies and derivatives, 66, 82–7, 98, 100, 102 n.22, 106 n.68, 127, 149, 161, 181 n.49, 276, 335, 357 n.11
legal status, 88–96
name, 63, 72

personnel, 68–70, 79 n.74, 93–4, 230, 304, 365, 366
reconstruction, 90–93, 104 n.41, 118
surveying and cartographic techniques, 64, 78 n.62, 120, 295, 300, 313, 318, 375
uses, 365, 369, 371, 399
Drafts (preparatory, 'foul'), 77 n.47, 82, 84, 144, 247, 344
Drainage,
drainers, 187
engineers (inspectors), 394–5
land (bogs), 199, 200, 204, 218 n.63, 219 n.76
Drains (on income), 187, 200, 206
Drapers' Company, 146 , 216 n.33, 356 n.1, 391, 403 n.14
Draughtsmanship, 101, 247, 249, 274, 392, see also Drawing
Draughtsmen, see also Engravers, Scriveners,
amateur, 28
civilian (trained), 104 n.41, 388, 390
designers (planners, cartographers), 161, 191, 261 n.98, 280, 282
legal, 115
private (specialist), 151, 154, 156, 247, 315, 392, 397
topographical, 153, 166
Drawing, 30, 32, 188, 248, 262 n.100, 277, 281–2, 439, see also Painting,
hand, 151
instruments, 150
masters (teachers), 184 n.95, 257 n.34
mechanical drawing, 174, 379
offices, 168
plane table, 34
rooms, 167
schools (Dublin Society), 229, 274–5, 282, 441
Drawing of,
maps, 41, 128, 210, 248, 268, 434, 439
new towns, 190
pictures (views, prospects, on maps), 68, 116, 176, 182 n.53, 189, 250, 277
Drawings,
finished, 168
neat (fine, accurate) , 249, 269, 306
profile (of houses), 162, 393
sectional, 199
topographical, 161

Drawing, on (previous work, inspiration, attention, conclusions), 64, 66, 98, 161, 312, 338, 391, 407
Dust-hole, 176
Dutch,
  papermakers, 166
  trading vessels, 178
Dwelling houses, 10, 66, *see also* Houses,
  clachan-dwellers, 208
  'dwellers on the mountains', 268
  town-dwellers, 60, 247, 283

Ecclesiastical,
  circumstances, 365
  collections, 384 n.38
  'Pettys', 368
  map of Ireland, 357 n.14
  surveys (glebe terriers), 369
Ecclesiastics, 334, *see also* Clergy
Egestorff collection, of surveying instruments, 181
Elegant, 267, *see also* Beauty,
  maps, 150, 342
  portrayal, 182 n.57
  theorising (methods of computation), 32, 436
Employment, of (surveyors) 30, 232, 426, *see also* Unemployment,
  finding (seeking), 45, 188, 283, 336
  future, 346
  leaving, 70
  private, 44, 81
  professional, 193
Emptiness (blankness of maps), 124, 149, 151, 155–6, 164, 176, 307, 392
Enclosed,
  acreage, 439
  districts, 443
  gardens, 189
  parks, 155
  farms, 31
Enclosure,
  enclosing parcels of land, 91
  enclosure movement, 118, 206, 209
  Parliamentary (Irish Enclosure Act, maps), 204, 207, 278
Enclosures (small), 118–19, 151, 154–5, 307, 315, 375, 394, 440
Encroachments, 131, *see also* Concealments, covering up, 118

Irish acre on Cunningham acre, 124
public sector on private, 388
protection of outbounds from, 124, 148
unauthorised, 89
Engineering, 280, 283, *see also* Architecture, Surveying, Valuing,
  apprenticeships, 252
  General Engineering, Geological Survey and Valuation Office and Printing and Lithographing Establishment (Dublin), 403 n.28
  plans, 127
  profession, 174, 193, 200, 346, 352
  quasi-engineering, 240
  reasons, 119
Engineers,
  'architect-engineers', 318
  canal, 193, 202
  City, 275
  civil, 199, 201, 251–2, 284, 396, 401
  company, 196
  Corps of (Royal) Engineers (Sappers and Miners), 353, 378, 388
  engineer-surveyors, 137 n.27
  military, 55, 58, 81, 197, 332, 379
  proper (eminent), 28, 187, 192–3, 196, 199, 200, 226, 244, 251, 334, 348, 352, 379
  supremacy of, 199, 287
  'surveyor-engineers' (builders, valuators), 270, 362, 393–4, 438
  'topographical engineers', 251–2, 286, 354, 376, 378
Engines,
  engine-divided circles, 306
  engine-houses, 178
  steam-engines, 339
English, 29, *see also* Irish, Scottish, and Quarters,
  acre, 15–16, 122, 441, 444
  cartography, 39, 151, 244
  farms, 323
  language, 17, 162, 176, 229
  men, 17, 29, 60, 226
  mile, 18
  'New' English, 222, 231
  officials, 18, 34
  'Old' English, 43, 222
  'Pale', 25 n.42, 110, 115, 120, 204, 208
  perch, 31, 122, 297

plantations, 53, *see also* Scottish,
settlers (colonists), 3, 31, 32, 114, 223
soldiers, 28
statue measure, 57–8, 122
surveying practice, 29, 39, 122, 127, 135, 172, 227, 265, 315
tithe maps, 377
textbook, 18, 33, 132, 226, 310
village plan, 209
Engraving,
cartouches (compartments), 151, 174, 271, 301
counterfeit, 160
four-sheet, 349
index, 269
maps, 113, 149, 155, 262 n.114, 285, 342, 350, 356 n.1
ornament (leaf pattern), 150
planiform, 340
six-inch, 380
style, 344, 346, 353, 354
Engravers, 151, 182 n.58, 184 n.86, 201, 255 n.6, 261 n.98, 282, 292 n.89, 333, 337, 340, 342, 346, 353–55, 358 n.45, 362 n.100, 388, 435, *see also* Draughtsmen, Scriveners
Enlargement, of maps (traces), 276, 358 n.36, 393, 395, 397, 399, 400, 404 n.51
graphical, 177, 392, 397
Equal, *see also* Equality,
acrimony, 194
departures (mapping), 317
detail (simplification, omission), 375, 379
division (of survey costs), 131
enthusiasm, 190
familiarity (with local anomalies), 304
latitudes, 317
obscurity (of examination and certificate system; of enclosure; of parts of estates), 99, 118, 148
permanence (of landmarks), 90
price rises, 249
strangeness (effectiveness of publicity), 390
success (of survey), 435
terms (co-operation on), 346
validity (of primary and secondary maps), 84

value, 427
versatility (of apprentices), 270
Equalising (access to rivers, sea coasts, main roads, edges of pasturable bog or mountain, charges), 214, 369
Equality (other things being equal), 166, 310, *see also* Parity, Sharing,
desire for ('in the eyes of the cartographer'), 208, 390
of denominations (proportions, amounts of land), 8, 129, 206
of municipalities (in making and keeping resolutions), 115
quasi-equality, 8
unequal bargains, 83
unequalled improvements, 322, 342
Error, 70, 92, 272, *see also* Accuracy, Inaccuracy,
reasons for, 132, 143 n.108, 297, 299, 308, 310–15, 318
Errors by Ordnance Survey, 387, 391–2, 400, 403 n.15
Errors, in
estate maps, 97, 98, 121, 127, 149, 192, 250, 321–2, 413–28
plantation maps, 40–41, 71–3, 92, 105 n.49, 298, 297–9
published maps, 199, 358 n.46, 366
road surveys, 199
tracing Down Survey, 71, 91, 299
Estate maps, 28, 61, 68, 87, 98, 118, 127, 144–5, 148–52, 154–6, 158–62, 166–8, 174, 176, 191, 311, 331–2, 354, 372, 379, 388–90, 416–18, 421, 423–4, 428, 430, 432, *see also* Map categories (types),
coloured, 340
derivative estate maps, 392
errors in, 321
estate maps by civil engineers, 251–2
estate mapped as a unit, 234
Incumbered Estates Court maps, 397
multi-partite estate maps, 200, 227
'no Gaelic-language estate maps', 231
reference columns in, 244
signatures on, 266
statement of magnetic variation, 303
transformation of, 276
typical (normal), 271, 285–6, 344
very large and rich estates, 240
Estate papers, 82, 86, 113, *see also* Papers (collections of), State papers,

Fitzwilliam, 290 n.48
Gormanstown, 107 n.83
Estates, *see under* Mapping, Surveying
Estimation (of area), 1, 11, 13–15, 22, 36, 39, 40, 51, 56, 365, 370, 375
by sampling, 39
from local information, 30
mixing estimates and admeasurements, 60
viewing and estimating, 19, 21, 36, 39, 126
Estimation (of costs, resources, time), 198, 224, 238, 242, 244, 252, 267, 285, 318
'Eskers' (ridges of post-glacial gravel, from Ir. *eiscir*), 170
Ethnic,
differences (associations, boundaries, considerations), 15, 58, 230, 285
glasses (looking at Irish history through), 222
origin of surveyors, 222–3
Evaluation, 1, 8, 148, *see also* Valuation
Examination, of
premises (original titles), 28, 379
surveyors' work (critical, field notes), 65, 98–100, 310, 426, 428, 437
Examinations (competitive, setting of), 322, 252, 271, 273
Examiners (Down Survey, of Crown lands), 73, 85, 101, 262, 265
Exempting,
from liability, 421, 428
pasture from tithe, 364, 370
roads from rent, 119
Expert,
assistance, 55, 262 n.105
cartographers, 354, 376, 376
juries, 20
opinion, 304
Experts (professional), 31, 116, 210, 262 n.105, 300, 376, *see also* Laymen, British, 376
Experts, on
acres, roods, and perches, 12
arbitration, 199
fortification, 55, 119
landcape-planning, 202
military mapping, 376
rundale, 210
property management, 280

surveying, 99, 116, 133, 214, 318, 307, 354
time-and-motion, 242
waste land, 204
Explanation, Act of (1665), 88, 89, 95
Exports, 265, *see also* Importation
Eyeing,
'eye-marks', 6
'eye-catching', 150, 155, 159
judging 'by eye', 13, 34, 170, 197, 310

Factories, 193, *see also* Industries, Mines
Fair greens,
Fakes, 131, *see also* Forgery
False,
admeasurement
advertisements, 415–17, 419, 424, 427
combinations, 426
maps, 422–3, 426
scales, 315
starts, 30
surveyors, 246
surveys, 417
Family, 8, 140 n.80, *see also* Genealogy,
arms (distinctions), 77 n.53, 150
farms, 112, 244
history, 80 n.93, 150, 360 n.67, 404 n.30
family-imposed restraints, 110
junior members, 58
monuments, 78 n.67
resemblances, 202
papers, 86
residences (seats), 85, 176
Families, of
instrument-makers, 269
surveyors, 146, 202, 227–8, 242, 274–5, 331, 347
Famine, 112, 211, 390
pre-Famine Ireland, 123, 209
post-Famine agriculture, 394, 397
Farming societies, 203
Features (representations) on maps, 150, 152, 154, 160, 162, 164, 166, 181 n.52, 190, 390
appropriate, 121
basic (geographical), 336, 344, 355
common, 4, 40
control, 250
essential, 66

internal, 187
localised, 322
man-made, 153
marginal, 151, 166
memorable, 286
mentioned (in earlier records), 118
misplaced (effect of offsetting), 311
natural, 121, 160
new (landscape), 135 n.4, 193
ominous (lack of interest in surveying), 405 n.52
ordinary (geographical), 189
ornamental, 154
permanent, 167
persistent 6
physical, 172
'regional', 380
relevant (landscape), 299
revolutionary, 162
standard (normal, usual), 90, 133, 314
striking (propensity to understatement), 297
surface, 204, 286
typical (rundale, Irish), 209, 227, 283
topographical, 71
unusual (division of each county into rectangular blocks), 390
useful (magnetic pole as landmark), 305
worst (of county maps), 340
Fees, *see also* Costs,
as 'rates per unit of work', 439
annual average, 83, 291 n.74
'exorbitant', 219 n.71
for supplying map duplicates (traces), 83, 104 n.35, 439
measurement of status by, 280
rise in surveyor's, 249, 278
Surveyor General's, 102 n.12
'unmanageable variety of fees', 234
Fences,
damage to, 50 n.77
(included on maps), 45, 154, 164, 267, 314, 400
(omitted on maps), 36, 66, 172, 341, 389
repairing (improving), 118, 202–04, 398
suburban garden, 400
Fencing, 402 n.12, *see also* Pale, Paling
Fields
boundaries, 90

enclosures, 315
straight (lengths), 130, 206
Fertility,
fertile (land, source of ideas), 71, 128
fertiliser (spreading, supply), 202, 208, 391
infertile (land), 70
Field,
amalgamation, 189
boundaries, 162
names, 154
open-field agriculture, 25 n.37, 139 n.53
surveying 159, 401
systems, 220 n.89
Field-books, 8, 34, 19, 68, 78 n.62, 90, 92,122, 298, 302, 311, 327 n.68, 391, 397, 429
contemporary references to, 64, 84, 95, 273, 307, 314
surviving examples of, 307–09, 311, 312, 313
Field-notes, 55, 246, 248, 260 n.81, 273–4, 299, 307, 309–10, 313–14, 324 n.17, 327 n.71
sets of, 328 n.81, 416–19, 423, 428, 429–32
topographical manner of taking, 434
Field name-books, 357 n.12
First, *see also* Second, Third,
America's first female map engraver, 255 n. 6
Board of First Fruits, 369
world's first land measurer, 222
Fishing,
fishery, 10, 184 n.91, 259 n.68
fishing settlement, 112
Flooding, *see also* Rivers,
flood control, 200
mears inaccessible by inundation, 424
Folds (sheep), 407–08
Foreshadowing, of
coming political union (parliamentary enclosure), 204
modern vogue for hedge history, 176
partition into equal proportions, 129
Forests, 6, *see also* Trees,
Office of Woods and Forests, 86, 220 n.89
staff, 269
surveying, 304

INDEX OF SUBJECTS   483

Forgery, 419, 427 *see also* Fakes, False
Forges, 392
Forgetting, *see also* Remembering,
  by critics, 244
  details of policy, 42
  magnates, 215 n.22
  names, 120
  'old prices', 442
  proficiency certificates, 99
  surveying and surveyors, 352, 401
Forts, 65, 116, 176, 202, 345, *see also* Antiquities
Forty-shilling freeholders, *see* Freeholders
Fosterers, 244
Fragmentation, 10, 210, *see also* Amalgamation
Framing, 198
  map frames, 150, 152, 154, 336
  sampling frames, 39
Frameworks, 70, 89, 93, 160, 242, 286, 380, 400
Free,
  of charge (use of surveyor's office, map copy, accommodation), 98, 113, 236
  for non-cartographic information (map margins), 390
  from change (danger, undesirable associations, restraint), 4, 38, 58, 69, 110
Freedom from,
  bog (lowlands), 209
  ordinary surveyor's habitual secrecy, 64
  scrutiny, 73
Freedom, of
  artists, 160
  town/city, 192, 274
Freedom to,
  appoint surveyors, 204
  graze (cattle), 208
  publish, 64, 413
Freehold,
  interest, 129
  land, 36
Freeholders (forty-shilling), 30, 32, 129, 146–7
Freelance land surveyors (cartographers), 69, 81, 101, 240, 395
French,
  copyists, 103 n.26
  language, 17
  privateers, 84
  revolutionary calendar, 58
  school of surveyors, 167–70, 172, 276, 347, 377, 441
Friendships, *see also* Rivalry,
  'good friends to cartography', 98, 232, 255, 428, 437
  Petty and Taylor (Cox), 64, 77 n.58, 148
  Sherrard and Brownrigg, 277
Future, *see under* Time
Furze, 33, 406, 408–10

Gaelic, 222, *see also* Old English, New British (English), Scots,
  dictionary (1825), 24 n.28
  families (names), 110, 120
  Gaelic-language estate maps (none), 231
  Ireland, 4, 13, 17
  mensuration (early), 11
  renaissance (14th and 15th centuries), 4
Gallons (land measure), 8, *see also* Pottles
Gallows, 178, *see also* Murder, Punishment
Games, *see also* Leisure,
  rackets, 178
Garden,
  corners, 307
  design, 161, 189, 190, 274
  fences, 400
  plots, 25 n.43
  symbols, 164
  walks, 410
Gardeners, 190, 215 n.9, 226, 230, 244
Gardens,
  cherry, 154
  kitchen, 410
  of lowliest cottagers, 31, 112, 208, 408
  ornamental, 110
  potato-gardens, 133
  sparragrass, 154
  symmetrical, 189
  walled, 154
Gates, 307
  demesne (park), 112, 190
  gateway (to fame), 347
  passage, 410
  turnpike, 164
Gavelkind, 6
Genealogical, *see also* Family,
  'cartogenealogical' inference, 168, 172

continuity (between plantations), 58
research, 269
stories (of surveyors), 228
maps in 'genealogical histories',
    181 n.49
Genius loci, 345, *see also* Personality
Gentlemen surveyors, 251, 253–4, 283,
    335, 378, 401
Geodesy, 376
    geodetic surveying, 252, 432–3
Geographical
    distribution (diffusion, concentration),
        5, 110, 120, 233, 236
    divisions (administrative geography),
        144, 368
    'geographical values' (radical), 345, 365
    maps (advertisements), 35, 113, 145,
        149–50, 161, 189, 272, 336
    pole, 303
    realities (needs, aspirations,
        specifications, constraints, matters),
        39, 44, 60, 65, 234, 270
    use (purposes, absurdity), 71, 73, 334
Geographers,
    armchair, 196
    modern historical, 121, 160, 170, 187,
        208–09, 246, 330
Geography, 2, 17, 158, 161, 332
    of land surveying, 231, 233
    school subject, 229
    physical (human), 176, 193, 214,
        271–2
Geological,
    maps 286, 394
    societies, 403 n.29
Geology, 337–8, 345, 393, *see also* Stone,
    Rocks, Soils
Geometrical,
    boundaries, 32
    complexity (of municipal holdings),
        240
    measuring of land, 178 n.6
    position (eternal), 122
    road-making, 193
    theorems (methods), 318, 430–31
'Geometricians', 224
Geometry, 229–31, *see also* Trigonometry
Gerrymadering (fiscal), 367
Giants' graves, 176
Glebe, 90, *see also* Church,
    boundaries, 384 n.40

lands, 138 n.50, 365, 384 n.38
maps, 369
surveys, 384 n.41
terriers, 369, 372
Globes, 269, 271
Gneeves (land measure) 5, 10
Golden age, 129
Gradients, 199
    quantitative (gentler, less than 1 in 35),
        197
Grand juries, 187 , 193, 196, 199, 373,
        377, *see also* Jury, Maps,
    maps for, 187, 193, 196, 199, 280,
        284–5, 314, 337–8, 340, 342,
        344–5, 347, 349–50, 352–4,
        367–8, 377, 380
Grass, *see also* Meadows, Pasture, Tillage,
    deep (poor weak), 33, 406
    land (ploughing), 391, 407
    seeds, 408–09
    green, 170
    low grass balk, 208
    sparragrass, 154
Graticules, 150, 348, 353, *see also* Grids
Gravel,
    gravel-pits, 137 n.30
    gravelling, 204
    limestone-gravel, 128, 203
Grids,
    checkered (street), 190
    reference-grids, 150
    printed, 64, 72
    square-grids, 86, 329 n.102
    standard gridded paper proposal, 316
Grocers' Company, 179
Ground, 1
    back- (fore-, under-), 162, 167, 193
    back- (of surveyors), 19, 244, 252,
        282, 344, 379
    conacre-ground, 133
    covering-, 250, 298, 393, 395
    cutting lines in the, 13, 90, 93, 116,
        118–19, 297, 308, 312
    ground-plan, 4, 198, 373
    holes in the, 178
    home-ground, 103 n.24, 212, 270, 344
    representation of 'ground', 352
    roods (acres) of, 11, 133, 203, 429, 433
    types (nature) of, 168, 439
    variations on the, 31, 90

visible on the, 113, 121, 152, 162, 191, 311, 398
ground-work, 28–9, 435
Grounded,
  ill-, 427
  in popular consciousness, 32
Grounds, 65, 156, 335,
  bad (barren, burnt, uneven), 36, 41, 141 n.86, 238, 298
  geographical, 17
  good (fertile), 36, 199, 406–10
  potato-, 112, 442
  testing-, 99
  training-, 355
'Gross Survey', 60, 62, *see also* Surveys (Named)
Groves, 188, 219 n. 68
Guidance,
  custom as best guide to spelling of names, 119
  guidebooks, 355, 403 n.30
  maps as guides to comparisons, 59
  precedents as guides, 30
  research papers as poor guides to real life, 300
  surnames and Christian names as guides to religious affiliation, 258 n.49
  topographers as guides to land valuation, 170
  townlands as guides to location, 120
Guilds, 60, 274
Gunnery, 229
  connection with surveying, 137 n.30, 142 n.96, 435

Hachures, 162,166, 171–2, 283, 349, *see also* Shading and Colouring
Hamlets, 16, 31, 115, *see also* Villages, Precincts
Hands (court, chancery, mixed and running secretary, German text etc.), 248, *see also* Writing
Harbours, 10, 44, 60, 65, 91, 187, 200, 261 n.90, 270, 272, 286, 342, 376, 429, 431
Head,
  block-headed (crazy-headed), 246, 425
  come to a, 114
  danger of losing one's, 44

head of water (head springs), 199, 406
head landlords, 112, 187
headlands, 407
headquarters, 272, 275, 282, 338, 387
headway, 318
  over another man's, 158
  take into one's, 66,
  under one, 234
Headings (heads of instruction), 46 n.14, 187, 263 n.115, 277, 307, 309, 384, 397, 406
Heads of professions (organizations), 265, 287, 389, 398
Headfort map collection, 85, 87
Heaths, 33, 40, 65, 162, *see also* Bogs hedge, corners, 65
Hedge,
  history, 176
  hedge-rows, 203
  hedge symbols (diagrammatic), 342, 344
Hedges, 65, 118, 152, 162, *see also* Ditches, hedges (fictitious), 340
  quick-set, 118, 155
Hiberniae Delineatio, 71, 85, 103 n.30, 332, 356 n.2
Highways, 3, 65, 152, 198, *see also* Roads, Surveyors,
  cattle on, 119
  early eighteenth-century, 193
Hills, 3, 65, *see also* Relief ,
  delineation of, 404 n.33
  flanks of hills (downhill sides), 128, 208
  high hills ('notorious'), 66, 137 n.30
  hill pastures, 209
  hill tops, 202, 275
  lowering of hills, 198
  often disregarded (avoided), 193, 197
  parts of, 180 n.22
  representation of (shading, symbols, hachures), 197–8, 285, 339, 348–9, 380
  surveying of, 298, 430, 435–6
Hinterlands, 240, 245, *see also* Borders,
  defence of, 280
  Dublin, 344
  regional capital, 236
  small, 238
Hints, of, *see also* Subtleties,
  approximation, 14
  association, 270

disapproval, 82
expansion, 249
influence, 170
instructions, 59
methods, 35, 64, 66, 172, 277, 303, 316
origins, 282
primitivism, 174
specialisation, 338
Historians, 3, 71, 99, 120, 128, 176, 282, 401, 439
   agrarian, 17, 125
   architectural, 125
   demographic, 228
   economic (industrial), 20, 196
   landscape, 188, 354
   literary, 54
   local, 66, 221 n.95, 367, 387
   17th century, 15, 29, 63
   18th century (physico-historians), 335
   19th century, 64
   modern, 118, 164, 253, 283, 300, 319, 337
Historiography,
   of cartography, 82, 164, 284, 178 n.2, 247, 251, 254, 302, 306, 354, 377, 393
   of land surveying, 2, 4, 10, 15, 17, 52, 54, 69, 127
History, 8, 222, 322, 398, 399, 400
   autobiography, 62, 300
   biography, 71
   history books, 401
   periods of, 44, 51, 202, 204, 369
   place in, 33, 60–61, 115, 203, 254, 286, 401
   tide of, 6
History, of
   administration, 52, 387
   colonisation and settlement, 122
   hedges, 176
   land forfeitures, 72
   land surveying, 19, 126, 131, 231, 300, 322, 398
   maps (map-makers), 29, 30, 68, 71, 73, 87, 229, 231, 276, 285, 332, 377, 379
   medieval mensuration, 12
   religious discrimination, 230
   taxation (cess), 363
History (types of),
   agrarian (rural), 92, 189, 209
   archival, 81
   topographical, 6
Holometer, 34, *see also* Instruments
Holy wells, 176, 345, 380
Holy writ, 121
Hollow-ways, 137 n.30, 198
Home,
   county, 168, 261 n.87
   country, 224
   district, 283
   farm, 110, 145, 204
   government, 33
   ground, 103 n.24, 344
   land, 4, 331
   homeless, 158
   homely origins, 282
   home-made (produced), 133, 226, 345
   maps, 227
   towns, 347, 352
   permanent home, 86
Homes, 45, 85, 223, 247, 283, 315
Horse, *see also* Animals, Carriage,
   hire services, 197
   horsemeat, 38
   horse-rollers, 407
   horse-stealing, 190
   horse-whips, 420
   travel by, 253
Horses,
   low, squat, 408
   ploughs of four, 408
   working (cleaning of), 409
Hospitals, 178, 214 n.3, 269, 428
   fever ward (operating theatre, dead house, dissecting room), 178
House-,
   letting, 278
   mapping, 198, 267, 312, 390
   pictures, 150–51, 153, 160, 164, 170, 184 n.90, 189, 190, 393
   plots (urban), 72, 155, 176, 192, 401
   registration, 400
   surveys, 314, 380, 395
   symbols, 151, 172, 183 n.75, 339
   valuation, 321
Houses, 65, 95, 152, 162, 187, 189, *see also* Building,
   cabins, 183 n.75
   courthouses, 190
   'dead houses', 178

INDEX OF SUBJECTS   487

demolished, 189, 212
dwelling, 10, 22, 66, 112
engine-houses, 178
farmhouses, 31, 113, 125, 236, 254, 285
for horses, 409
hovels, 410
mansion (big), 110, 154, 156, 187, 283
meeting (Presbyterian), 284, *see also* Churches,
of industry, 352
poorhouses, 178
'remarkable', 137 n.30
rundale, 208, 212
school, 365
unfortified, 36
whiskey houses, 306
Huguenots, 222
Husbandry, 26 n.52, 406
Hydrographers, 272
Hydrographic,
charts, 336
information, 345
surveying, 23 n.2
Hydrology, 439, *see also* Drainage, Rivers
Hydrostatics, 269, 288 n.25
Hypotheses, about
activity of land surveyors, 33, 133, 188, 222, 231, 282
closed traverse, 36, 423
continuity in plantation surveys, 56
Cromwellian inspiration for attaching maps to leases, 114
lease as necessary condition of map, 145
mapping ('devolutionary hypothesis'), 145
Ordnance Surveys of Britain and Ireland, 378
undiscovered Atlantic islands (iron ore deposits), 51, 304

Image(s), 32, 132, 156, 304, *see also* Pictures, Signs, Symbols
Impartial,
adjudications, 135
assessors, 273
decisions, 421
examinations, 437
gentlemen, 425
observers, 251

performance, 422
readers, 417, 427
Impartiality, 234, 247, 399, *see also* Neutrality, Partiality
Impersonality, 271, *see also* Personality
Importation, of, *see also* Exports,
chains (from England to Wexford, Ireland), 57, 295
enclosure (from England to Ireland), 204
ideas (from other cartographic media), 166
maps, 331
surveyors (from England, Scotland), 43, 222, 285
words (from ancestral tongue, ie Irish), 170
Impostors, 264 n.136, 415, 417, 420–22
Imposts, 364, *see also* Taxes
Imprecision (typical), 197, *see also* Precision
Improvements, 210, 242, 267, 276, 322, *see also* Invention, Deterioration
'balance' survey of, 206, 212
catalogue of, 64, 202, 283, 406
conversion of non-rented bog or mountain, 128–9
maps of, 132, 154, 188, 212
rural (design of), 190–91, 252
Improvements, of
commission of perambulation, 94
land registration, 399
Petty's method, 72
technical (surveying), 130, 282, 305–06, 318, 334, 338, 340, 364, 369, 389, 400
Improving landowners, 145, 158, 159, 191, 278
Inaccurate,
'county book' figures, 371
maps, 91, 131, 139 n.56, 352
scale bars, 152
surveys, 367
Inaccuracies,
correction of, 250
of instruments, 422, 434
Inaccuracy, 40, *see also* Accuracy,
complaints of, 136 n.16
milestones, 194
planimetric, 121
sources of, 40, 131, 194, 121, 315, 351, 380, 399, 422, 434

Incorporated Society of Solicitors and Attorneys, 104 n.40
Incumbered Estates Court, 396–8, 404 n.45, 444, *see also* Courts, Law
Indexes, 20
    estate (small-scale) indexes, 146, 149–50, 154, 269, 335, 379, 391
    index maps, 149, 167, 396
    theodolite index, 305
    townland index maps, 7, 184
Indifference, 14, 115, *see also* Differences
Individual, 176, 253, 266, *see also* Typical,
    criticism, 130
    maps, 159
    notice (claim to), 52
    sites (identification, measurement of), 120, 172, 177, 209, 341, 395, 443
    titles (insertion of), 151
    treatment (of parishes), 204
Individualism, 275
Individuality (ignoring of), 379
Industrial,
    era (new), 174, 400
    historians (modern), 196
    maps, 193
Industries, *see also* Factories, Mines,
    ancient Irish, 156
    house of industry, 352
    linen, 112, 268
    local, 160
    surveying (map-making) industry, 2, 232, 238, 331
Inheritance, 89
    from earlier traditions (of surveying), 166, 224, 277, 350, 379
    from fathers, 99
    gavelkind system, 6
    of titles, 148
    partible, 206
Inheritors, 148, 227
Inns, 152, 208, *see also* Taverns,
    inn-keepers, 194
    inn-signs, 66
    local inns, 113
Inquisition (inquest), 4–5, 12, 20, 24 n.19, 95, *see also* Court of survey,
    inquisitorial structure, 22, 68
    Strafford inquisition (1630s), 60, 84
Inscribed stones (network proposal), 377
Insects, 176

Intellectual, 14, 161, *see also* Military,
    milieu, 55–6
    vision, 345
International, *see also* Local, Regional, National, Levels,
    plane, 338
    reputation, 226
    terminology, 399
Internationally-minded (successors), 307
Institution of Civil Engineers of Ireland, 252
'Instrument' (surveyors' term), 34–5, 52, 57, 59, 72, 90, 94, 133, 300–06, 314–15, 416, 422, 428, 430
Instrument making, 232, 244, 247, 269–70, 303–04, 315, 322
Instruments (surveying), 2, 34, 40, 45, 73, 116, 150–51, 197, 227, 229, 265, 295, 300, 305, 308, 320, 432–5, 442, *see also* Alidade, Chains, Circumferentor, Compass needle, Cross (surveyor's), Holometer, Lines, Odometer, Optical square, Pantometron, Plane table, Polimetrum, Protractor, Quadrant, Ring dial, Scale, Semi-circle, Theodelitus, Theodolite, Wheel
Integrate (regional and estate maps), 379, *see also* 'Unite'
Interpretations, 35–6, 73, 121, 164, 183 n.75, 189, 223, 318, 322
Interpretations, of
    deadlines, 31
    drawings of theodolites, 305
    field books, 307, 311
    form, 2, 12, 121
    length, 16, 57
    symbolism, 162, 313
Interpreters, 33
Intersections, 36, 65, 66, 192, 203, 309, 313, 345
Interviewing, 63, *see also* Viewing
Invention, of, *see also* Improvements,
    devices, 126
    examples of rundale, 209
    figures, 296
    fortifications, 44
    isopleth, 70
    new instruments, 73, 300
    new techniques, 306, 433
Inventions, 435,
    passing judgement on, 265

Inventors, 192, 288 n.26, 324 n.20, 329 n.101, 433, 435–6
Inventory (taking), 149
Irish language, 15, 17–18, 120, 170, 176, 231–2
Irish Manuscripts Commission, 87
'Irish measure', 16 , 58, 76 n.29, 88, 124, 295, 439, *see also* Plantation measure, Acre, Perch
Islands, 51, 65, 155, 209, 334, *see also* Peninsulas
Isometric treatment, 164, 274
Isopleth, 70
Issues, about
    competence of co-workers, 196, 329 n.112
    industrial maps, 193
    Irish estate cartographers, 159
    lengths of chains, 298
    locals versus strangers, 338
    method of boundary traverse, 59
    map enlargement process, 397
    planting of defensible civic communities, 154
    professional status (demarcation), 45, 232
    public versus private surveys, 370
Itinerant surveyors, 234, *see also* Migration

Jobs,
    combining two jobs, 250
    competition for jobs, 275
    good at job, 269
    job demarcation, 187
    job of Down Survey, 70
    jobbing land surveyors, 277, 426
    year-long jobs, 247
Judges, 265, 397, 413
Juggling, 417, 423, *see also* Forgery
Juries, 8, 20, 21–2., *see also* Grand juries, Inquisition
    findings, 25 n.39
    local, 14

Kilns, 137 n.30, 152, 164, 392
King's Inns, Society of, 104 n.37, 116, 137 n.27

Laity, 335, *see also* Laymen
Lakes, 14, 78 n.62, 119, 138 n.45, 152, 162, 181 n.40, 189, 218 n.62, 313, 328 n.82, 392, 429, *see also* Loughs
Lady Day, 407
Lament, 387
Land agents, 142 n.103, 180 n.34, 328 n.82, 400, 442, *see also* Agents
Land Commission, 107 n.82, 209, 398, 405 n.52
Landed Estates Court, 86, 136 n.7, 396, 398, *see also* Court (Named)
Landed Estates Record Offfice, 86
Land 'hunger' ('fever') 76 n.29, 178
Land Judges Court, 397
Landlord,
    'activity', 187
    agents, 254, 390, *see also* Land agent
    control, 250
    maps (surveys), 115, 124–5, 130–33, 145, 150, 154, 170, 188, 273, 313, 364, 372, 380, 391, 401
    parliamentary careers, 146
    tenant relations, 128–9, 131, 145, 147–8, 156, 166, 206, 244–6, 253, 331, 370–71, 389, 413–15, 423
Landlord's
    demesne, 32, 112
    estate, 112, 187, 249
    home-farm, 110
    rents (leases), 119, 125, 146, 203
    sons, 244
Landlords, 31, *see also* Proprietorship, Agents, Tenants,
    absentee, 209
    Anglo-Irish (Protestant Irish), 54, 110, 187
    Catholic landlords, 110
    improving (progressive, reforming), 159, 193, 204, 210, 230
Landmark(s), 8, 90, 116, 118, 120, 121, 193, 305
Land question, 1, 143 n.112
Land measurement methods, 34, 244
Land measures
    early Irish, 11
    eighteenth-century, 123
    problem of standard lengths, 57
    units, 15
Land measurers, 19, 199, 222, 244

Landscape, 13, 70, 90, 25, 156, 172, 376, 390
   landscape-approach (of historians), 170, 354, 390, 400
   features, 299, 314
   maps, 170, 173
   medieval, 120
   modern (contemporary), 97, 156
   rural, 187, 214
   subdivisions of, 159
Landscape-making (planning, modification), 187–8, 193–4, 202, 204, 284, 340
Landscapes,
   farmscapes, 121, 202
   fieldscapes, 130, 203–04
   lost, 189
   townland, 379
Land surveying, 1, see also Surveying,
   historiography of, 54
   occupational frontiers of, 43, 59
Land surveyors, 86, 119, see also Surveyors, Surveyors',
   advent of, 21, 33, 190, 401
   ancestors of, 8, 13
   average (ordinary, common, mere), 151, 202, 252, 268, 285, 304, 324 n.19, 336, 346, 368, 378, 388
   biographies (genealogies) of, 59 n.73, 228, 266, 272, 348, 360 n.67
   challenges (quarrels) of, 40, 194, 414–15
   decline of, 355, 376–7, 444
   definition (titles) of, 1–6, 18, 133, 168, 187–8, 190–91, 251, 262 n.100, 263 n.127, 289 n.38, 290 n.53, 334, 336, 354, 372, 424, 433
   difficulties of, 17
   eighteenth-century, 193, 240
   English, 127, 190, 226
   evidence of, 109 n.109, 286
   freelance, 69
   full-time (private, public, professional), 45, 56, 68, 100, 190, 193, 203, 240, 271, 337, 344, 376, 387, 391, 395, 400
   'golden age' of, 129
   Irish, 129
   leading, 126, 185 n.102, 268, 280, 286, 436
   livelihood (income), 32, 100, 342, 380
   mentality of, 31, 346, 396
   nineteenth-century, 355
   preoccupations of, 122, 286–7, 345, 401
   purpose (contribution) of, 44, 69, 187, 214, 248, 334, 337, 349–50, 352
   qualifications, 182 n.53, 250, 252, 388, 434, 436
   registered, 108 n.107
   relationship with taxing and tithing, 365
   religious affiliations of, 231
   specialisation of, 199–200, 251, 347
   school of, 159
   versatility of, 192, 196, 226
Land surveyor's companion, 431, 434–7
Lanes, 31, 155 see also Roads, Streets, Paths,
   back lanes, 176
Language,
   barriers, 332
   linguistic sense (usage), 12, 266
   in variety of placenames, 176
   original (of man), 12
Languages,
   dead (Latin), 12, 17, 307, 335, 337
   English, 15, 17
   Irish (Gaelic), 18, 120, 231
   'language of cartography' (originality in), 162, 168
Latitude, geographical, 252, 263 n.119, 270–71, 334, 349–50, 429–30, 432–7
Latitude and departure, 309, 316–18, 320, 330 n.114
Laughter, 70, 151, 345, see also Satire
Law (the), 88, 92, 95, 128, 197, 246, 367, 373, 399, 419, 427, see also Courts, Legal, Poor Law, Writs,
   by-laws, 115
   courts of, 8, 126, 397
   criminal, 110
   instrument of, 94
   law-abiding, 152
   law-suits, 414–15, 423
   law-tracts, 4
Law, of
   evidence, 88
   Irish property transactions, 99, 124, 194
   westward movement, 304
Lawyers, 1, 5, 84, 115, 120, 248, 428
   doctor of laws, 377

early Irish lawyers, 6
'lawful men', 8, 21, 370
'lawful surveyors', 442
law stationers, 392
non-lawyers, 121
Lawyers'
  conservatism, 126
  offices, 113, 166
  opinions, 139 n.55
  preference of words to maps, 89, 113, 116, 122, 127, 199, 390
  pronouncements, 88
  sense, 87
Laymen, 34, 308, 376, *see also* Experts, Laity, Irish (British experts), 372
Leasehold, 116, 145
Leaseholders, 133, 271
Leases, 112, 125, 129, 156, 371
  lease-maps, 99, 113–16, 121, 124, 127, 133, 149, 152, 158, 166, 187, 252, 375
  new, 131–2, 146–7
  of forfeited land, 94
  of twenty (twenty-one) years, 110, 128, 146, 158, 238
  plot-numbers, 120,
  pre-lease surveys, 137 n.26
  provisions (covenants) of, 23 n.17, 26 n. 61, 118, 131, 203, 244
  'staggering' of, 147
Legal, *see also* Law, Writs,
  authority (powers, rights), 188, 265, 369, 399, 413
  boundaries, 6, 200
  context, 347
  continuity, 89
  definition, 400
  documents, 5, 114
  draughtsmen, 115
  expenses, 206
  escape-clauses, 11
  evidence, 164
  fiction, 39
  inquiries, 30, 68
  opinions, 141 n.88
  proceedings, 107 n.87
  purposes, 166
  quasi-legal, 19, 188, 379
  reasons, 41
  status, 114
  validity, 85

Lettering, 150, 174, 283 *see also* Writing
Levelling, 231, 263 n.115, 395, 438
  instruments (level boards), 305
  for pavements (pipes, canals), 197
  sea level (Nelson Pillar datum), 200
  sections, 285
Levels, of, *see also* Local, Regional, National, International,
  accuracy, 130, 304, 313
  education, 33, 401
  fees, 443
  finance and decision-making, 187
  rent, 70
  taxation, 4
  urgency, 28
Levels, in
  public service (local government), 52, 354, 366
  surveying profession, 69, 128, 147–8, 161, 231, 282, 286, 334
  territorial hierarchies, 5, 135, 145, 209, 377–8
Light (see, shed, throw new), 35, 42, 114, 120, 162, 228, 252, 305, 373, 420, 439
  enlighten(ed), 116, 149, 210, 265, 295, 334
  delight(ed), 274
  highlight, 250, 399
Lighting, 337, *see also* Cleaning, Paving
Lime, 203, 408
  dry lime, 410
  lime kilns, 137 n.30, 164, 392
  limelight, 399
  lime-stone gravel, 128, 203
  rock lime, 406–07
Limner, 190
Linen Board, 203, 277
Lines, 130, 160, 164, 174, 194, 197, 308, 314–15, 395, 417, *see also* Circles,
  base, 380, 430
  boundary, 116, 119, 172, 190
  chain, 435
  check, 313
  coastlines, 6, 176
  'concentric' waterlines, 155
  contour, 190
  deadlines, 62
  diagonal (cross), 57, 313
  erroneous, 318
  give-and-take, 312
  imaginary (invisible), 172, 400

interior, 314
main lines, 310–11
measuring (laying down/out), 13, 34, 52, 73, 93, 295–6, 313, 416
new, 89, 95, 128, 196, 395
outlines, 2, 72, 129, 166, 365, 373
parallel, 186 n.113, 190
pencil, 45
Petty's, 90–91
polygonal, 310
protractors', 73
reprotracting, 68
rival, 118
scale-lines, 56
sheet-lines, 396
side, 310
straight, 107 n.83, 130, 133, 154, 193, 203, 308, 311, 373
supplementary, 313
survey, 312, 328 nn.80, 81
traverse, 66, 313, 314
vertical (perpendicular), 246, 430
Lines, of,
    levelling, 200, 202
    progress, 322
    stakes, 275
    wire, 36
Links,
    cartographic, 114, 158, 170, 174, 391
    chain , 295, 297, 298–9, 308–10, 313, 428
    cross-channel, 4, 31, 332
    cross-generation, 54, 295–6, 363
    occupational 244, 269, 369
Literature,
    academic (modern), 208
    dedicatory verses, 176
    English surveying, 310
    historical, 135 n.1
    Irish surveying, 190, 308
    openfield systems, 220 n.88
    'realm of', 150, 255
    subversive, 254
    topographical, 4
    wasteland reclamation, 204
Literary,
    debut (Irish), 300
    history, 358 n.358
    material, 335
    men, 178 n.6
    stylists, 63

Lithography, 103 n.30, 113, 174
    lithographic costs, 397
    lithographic printers, 392–3, 403 n.28
Livestock, 8, 178
Local, 144, 219, n.78, 366, *see also* Regional, National, International,
    acts of Parliament, 382 n.1
    agriculture, 40
    allegiances, 350
    anomalies, 304
    architects, 352
    arrangements, 204
    booksellers, 396
    cartographers, 79 n.73, 168, 345
    churches, 90,
    churchwardens, 372
    climate, 391
    communities, 125
    competitors, 318
    copper mines, 178
    correspondents, 360
    critics, 379
    detail (information, knowledge, sources), 30, 287, 331, 347, 375
    families, 172
    farm houses, 236
    farming societies, 203
    government, 87, 286, 337, 354, 405 n.57
    historians, 66, 221 n.95, 367, 387
    houses, 160
    industries (enterprises), 160, 268, 338
    inns, 113
    juries, 14
    labourers, 297
    landowners (landlords, gentry), 73, 82, 187, 204, 216 n.34, 349
    maps, 344, 357 n.12
    members of Parliament, 285
    opposition, 210
    placenames, 345
    pronunciation, 120
    records, 231, 367
    reports, 208
    residents, 113, 116, 149, 200, 206, 267, 338, 372, 380
    roads, 121, 150, 196
    scales, 5
    shortages, 114
    surnames, 232

surveyors, 60, 93–4, 128, 155, 172, 199, 227, 248, 254, 268, 273, 282, 335–6, 342, 344–6, 351–2
taxation (valuation), 9, 94, 102 n.15, 106 nn.77,79, 364, 379
town plans, 138 n.51
varieties (of land measurement), 124
views, 284
witnesses, 60, 95
Localities, 4, 17, 411–12
localised features, 332
London companies, 76 n.33, 146, 182 n.62, 193, 215 n.15, 227, 356, 359 n.53, 391
Longfield maps, 232, 237
Longitude, 270–71, 334, 337, 349–50, 352
Loops,
loopholes, 322, 354
hand-loops, 418
road loops, 197
Lost landscapes, 189, *see also* Landscapes
Lots, 92, *see also* Parcels,
division of common into, 206
mapping of, 441
new (for building), 192
North Lots (Dublin), 113
Loughs, 78 n.62, 152, 162, 181 n.40, 218 n.62, 293 n.102, 429, *see also* Lakes
Lowlands, 209, 375, *see also* Uplands

Magistrates, 265, 413, 415, 421
Mail, *see also* Post Office,
mail-coach roads (approval of), 119, 197, 199
mail-coach road maps, 198
Mainstream, of, *see also* Streams,
country's life, 188
Victorian large-scale cartography, 168
Magnetic,
calculations, 436
compass, 300
instruments, 300, 303
interference, 304–05
meridian, 302–3, 317
'magnetick-needle', 77 n.53, 105 n.49, 300, 433–4
north (pole), 153, 175, 273, 302, 305
variation, 90, 108 n.100, 272–3, 284, 303
'Magneticus in Angulo', 325 n.44
non-magnetic north, 304

Magnetism,
terrestrial (geo)magnetism, 272, 303, 304
towns as magnets, 247
Magnet sellers, 273, 290 n.53
Management,
art and design, 151
estate, 43, 110, 164, 206, 209, 391, 439
farm, 278, 333, 398, 407–09, 439
land (property), 18, 92, 133, 280
survey, 55, 95, 121, 199, 202, 234, 250, 254, 268–9, 283, 286, 378, 394
system, 62
Managers, 72, 73, 240
managerial load (duties, skills), 147, 240, 275, 334
Manifestoes, of
agricultural revolution, 202
'Rightboys', 369
Manorial,
courts, 18
maps (atlases), 48 n.44, 146, 163
surveys, 128
system, 146
villages, 31
Manors, 19, 21, 38, 95, 161, 431, *see also* Lordships
Manufacturers, of, 34
chains, 295, 297, 300
instruments, 270, 302–03
linen, 284
pills, 393
Manuring, *see also* Fertility,
preparation, 407
soils (loam, clay, turf), 406–10
with marl, lime, limestone, gravel, sand, 203–04
Manuscript,
additions on printed maps, 392
atlases, 144, 218 n.50
barony (parish) collections (maps), 71, 365–6, 374, 381
books, 44
cartography (Irish), 159
mapped townland surveys, 48 n.49, 77 n.44, 80 n.90
maps (advertisement, farm, estate), 113, 128, 151, 301–02, 333, 342, 347, 390
six-inch plans, 380

styles (neat, open-textured), 292 n.79, 335, 340
work, 337
Manuscripts, *see also* Scripts, Transcripts, Printing,
　'doomed to languish in manuscript', 346
　Irish Manuscripts Commission, 87
　publishable manuscripts, 282
Map,
　commentaries (remarks, notes), 170, 269, 298, 308, 335, 345, 349, 369, 388, 391
　copying, 248, 252, 276, 282
　conventions (symbols), 116, 119, 166, 172, 174, 178, 392
　drawing, 189, 248, 250, 268, 434, 439
　engraving, 282, 355
　enlarging (reducing), 98, 276, 395, 444
　fees, 83, 94, 147, 280
　history, 73, 276, 284, 377, 379
　ornaments, 68, 150, 160, 188, 248
　production, 234, 331
　reading, 42, 380
　scales, 41, 45, 59, 84, 122, 145, 151, 159, 161, 166–7, 204, 244, 315–16, 320, 342, 344, 349–50, 365, 377, 379, 394, 396, 399
　scripts, 229
　styles, 168
　testimony, 2
Map archives (collections), 232, 250
Map-books, 3, 63, 66, 84, 86, 89, 96, 99, 103 n.30, 141 n.81, 146–8, 150, 160, 179 n.17, 218 n.50, 281, 290 n.53, 365, 385 n.58, *see also* Atlases
Map catalogues (modern), 242
Map categories (by time),
　Elizabethan, 35–7, 40–45
　eighteenth-century, 345
　mid-nineteenth-century, 280
　Plantation, 41, 42, 52, 54, 56–7, 64, 66, 68–9, 72, 82–94, 114, 144, 152, 155, 316, 364
　post-Plantation maps, 99–101
　pre-Ordnance Survey, 302, 323, 332
　seventeenth-century maps, 332
Map categories (by type), 145, 188, 331, 378–9, 387
　advertisement map, 113–14, 127
　architects', 352

'anti-map', 125
barony, 43, 57, 84–6, 149, 347, 349, 365–6, 380–81
base, 167, 192, 202, 250
bog, 201
boundary, 373
canal, 261 n.98
city, 278, 280, 334, 338, 340, 350, 352, 355, 396
'certificate', 372–3
composite, 159
conveyance, 127
county, 44, 58–9, 84–5, 144, 150, 162, 166–7, 196, 271, 277, 284–6, 332, 335–55, 367–8, 377, 380
demesne, 154
'diagram', 150
diocesan, 334–6, 369
district, 338
'estate', *see under* Estate maps
'false', 417, 422–3, 426
farm maps, 117, 121, 131, 145–8, 159, 166, 266, 305, 307, 311, 331, 372, 395
finished, 224, 308
folding, 361 n. 94
'foreign', 277, 284–5, 389
'foul', 84, 150
general, 149
glebe, 369, 372
geological, 286, 394
government, 42, 55
grand jury, 280, 285, 337, 344, 347, 353, 368, 377, 380
harbour, 44, 272
improvement, 132, 154, 188
index, 149, 167
'in-fields', 164
industrial, 193
Ireland, 85, 88, 218 n.52, 270, 286, 302, 331, 337, 349, 378, 387
landscape, 170, 189–90
lake (lough) and river, 199–200, 284, 355
lease, 99, 113–16, 124, 133, 149, 152, 158, 187
location, 30
'manorial', 146
manuscript (hand-drawn), 48 n.49, 128, 151, 301–02, 333, 335, 346, 365–6, 374, 392

military, 1, 354, 376, 380
mining, 403 n.23
modern, 90
mountain tract, 100
news-maps (wartime), 331
national, 332
non-estate, 161
official, 66, 82, 84, 86, 156, 204, 392–3
Ordnance maps, 7, 135, 146, 153, 175, 177, 194, 214, 275, 302, 304, 316, 320–21, 375, 380, 382, 387–9, 391–401,
Parliamentary enclosure, 278
partition, 97
parish, 60, 67, 86, 365–6, 369, 371
picture-maps, 4, 144, 282, 302, 305–07
planners', 188, 277
printed, 174, 178 n.2, 261 n.98, 332, 346, 365, 392, 403 nn.20,21
private and public, 370–71, 375, 382, 388
political map, 150, 379
property, 4, 17, 22, 94, 115, 144, 227
provincial, 44, 56, 84, 172, 332
race course, 355
regional maps, 44, 145, 333–4, 379
'ridge', 172
road, 194, 198, 202
rundale, 209–12
sale-maps, 112–14, 206
scientific, 376
siege and battle maps, 332
signed, 188, 270, 273, 280, 282
site, 189
skeleton, 354
sketch-maps, 116, 121, 126, 371
soldier's, 352
specimen, 131
street, 396
strip (single-road), 139, 196, 354
sub-national, 332
'succession', 148
tenement, 154, 156, 159
terrier, 157, 369, 372–3
tithe, 370–71
topographical, 352, 366, 380, 400
town, 161, 164, 190–91, 267–8
townland, 48 n.49, 164, 395
'true' (correct), 43, 121, 306

unfinished, 150
unofficial, 392
unpublished, 273
urban property, 113
wall-maps, 144, 154
Mapping (map-making), 1–5, 8, 17, 20, 23 n.2, 28–9, 32, 42, 44, 52, 68, 161, 231, 331, 363
  accuracy, 299
  ad hoc, 114, 116, 244
  distribution patterns, 236, 242–3
  instructions, 120, 122, 238
  large-scale, 7, 41, 44, 72, 146, 155–6, 168, 275, 341, 370, 376, 380, 397
  local (placenames), 345
  lots, 441
  names (people, places, things), 228
  national, 30, 197
  originality in, 269
  panoramic vision of, 286
  'quality', 125
  regional, 332
  re-mapping, 88, 92, 94–5, 148, 232, 273, 277, 354, 367, 390, 394, 400
  road-mapping, 354
  time (future, present), 187
  tree plantations, 395
  'water lines', 118
  small-scale, 44, 48 n.53, 84, 189, 286, 302, 331
  specialist, 247
  splicing, 376
  straightforward map-making, 202
  survey lines, 311–13
  topographical, 344, 434
  transformation, 172
  ways of mapping (methods), 144, 318
Map-makers, 58–60, 65, 71, 95, 98, 145, 254–5, 332, 387, 400–01, *see also* Cartographers,
  Anglo-American, 352
  activity of, 269
  amateur, 336
  authoritative, 270
  anglicised, 120
  contemporary, 145
  corrupt, 322
  county, 346–7, 354
  creative, 284
  disputatious, 274
  effective, 322

English, 152, 344
female, 255 n.6
'French', 170, 347
late eighteenth-century, 159–61
'natives', 231
provincial, 94
status variation, 247
sources, 191
Map-users, 3, 12, 28, 42, 81, 84, 89, 113, 115–16, 127, 132, 148, 377, 390–91, 400
  architects, 352
  bishops, 334–5, 337
  collectors, 232
  commissioners of maps, 145, 192, 196, 201–02, 209, 371
  clienteles, 275, 331
  debenture-holders, 365
  estate managers, 391
  Grand juries, 347, 380
  Land Judges, 397–8
  landlords, 170, 206, 391
  lawyers, 166
  lecturers, 271
  map-buying (using) public, 345, 378, 400
  map-enthusiasts (indoor), 375
  map historians (students, scholars), 164, 176, 247, 251, 254, 266, 387
  map-sellers, 355
  Parliament, 368, 399
  proprietors, 188
  spies, burglars, pickpockets, 156, 277
  soldiers, 352
  sponsors, 336–7
  students, 229
  tenants, 166
  Treasury, 398
Marine charts, 331
Mariners, 435
Mariner's companion, 435
Maritime features, 6, 354, *see also* Seas,
  anchorage, 65
  bar, 65
  beds of seaweed, 119
  course of channels, 65
  harbour (haven), 10, 44, 60, 65, 187, 286, 376, 429, 431
  high water mark, 119
  sands, 65
  shelves, 65
  soundings, 65, 338
Markets,
  cartographic (map) market, 39, 331, 345, 355
  land market, 112
  market economy ('the market'), 10,
  market towns, 236, 338
  supply side of market, 167
  world (mass) market, 332, 346
Marks, 38, 65, 121, 127, 194, 196
  boundary marks, 66, 116
  'eye-marks', 6
  landmarks, 8, 90, 116, 118, 307
  mark-men, 34, 234
  trademarks, 168, 283
Marriageability (of maps), 377
Marshes, 198–9, 380, *see also* Bogs
Martlands (land measure), 8
Mathematical,
  frameworks, 380
  instrument makers, 270
  instruments, 197, 288 n.25, 432, 435
  limits (strict, accurate, refined, standards), 118, 274, 284, 320, 376, 433
  operations (calculations, demonstrations), 316, 418, 428, 433
  roots, 391
  scope, (Elizabethan, 19th-, 20th century), 41, 91, 289 n.43
  tables, 322
Mathematicians, 47 n.33, 56, 63, 91, 224, 246, 257 n.35, 260 n.81, 289 n.38, 417–18, 420, 423, 425, 428, 433, 434, 436
  mathematically-minded labourers (surveyors), 135
Mathematics,
  in schools (universities), 182 n.61, 229–30, 230, 258 n.46, 271–2, 289 n.35
  teachers (professors), 96, 228–9, 254, 271, 314, 425, 427, 429
Maxims, *see also* Dictums, Doctrines,
  'a large area should not fall out of lease at the same time', 147
  'greater or less' ('centuries old stipulation'), 126

INDEX OF SUBJECTS 497

'in England a bargain's a bargain', 132
'to him that hath shall be given', 118
May Day, 407
Meadows, 6, 13, 25 n.37, 65–6, 128,
    141 n.86, 152, 162, 407, 409–10, 440,
    see also Pasture, Tillage
Mearing (the line where 'the water would
    most naturally run'), 118, 120
    stones, 399
    symbols, 313
Mears (walls, ditches, banks, hedges, river,
    bogside, ridge, valley etc.), 38, 65, 127
    flooding of, 424
    of confiscated areas, 56
    settling (laying out) of, 95, 395
    'trodden with the chain', 57, 75 n.25
Mearsmen (mearers), 95, 116, 118, 127,
    137 n.34, 246, 423, 439
Measurement, *see under* Land measurement
Medical, *see also* Hospitals,
    doctors, 56, 240, 336,
    reports, 82
    treatment, 178
Medieval, 4, 12–13, 29, *see also* Post-
    medieval, Pre-medieval,
    acreage figures, 14
    boundaries, 3, 15
    colonialism, 3
    fortifications, 176
    Gaelic (English) families, 110
    Ireland (England), 4, 15, 17–18, 145,
        295
    landscape, 120
    m. sources, 4
    maps, 155
    mensuration, 12
    open-fields, 13
    ploughmen, 212
    property descriptions, 8
    time-traveller, 22
    townland, 15
    medieval-type strip fields, 121
    units
    villages, 208
Meeting houses (Presbyterian), 284
Memorials,
    of boundaries, 145, 418
    of tenants, 75 n.22, 79 n. 80,
        140 n.68, 141 n.82, 386 n. 75
Mentality, 31
Mercers' Company, 182 n.62

Merging (good and bad land), 70, 162
Meridians, 90, 160, 284, 302–03, 317, 337,
    435, *see also* North points
Merit, 268, 377, 402 n.11
    aesthetic (maps), 265
    arithmetical, 299
    artistic (estate atlases), 188
    cartographic, 280
    dualism of estate and farm, 144
    fineness of drawing and writing
        (maps), 269
    moderate charges (surveyor's), 276
    status of scientist, 334
    tangible (of suveryors), 259
Meritorious surveyors (booksellers), 352, 355
Merits,
    of approximation, 320
    relative (of surveys), 56, 308, 372
Messuages, 19, 21, 25 n. 43
Metaphors, *see also* Mosaic, Resemblances
Mimicry
    'advancing forces of the Ordnance
        Survey', 101
    'evolutionary stream', 349
    'rough was taken with smooth', 124
    'the laying-on of the chain was like a
        mystical rite', 56
    'the subterranean stream of cause and
        effect, 54
    'sea of uncertainty', 222
    'seeds of the surveying profession', 42
    'unwillingness to penetrate beneath the
        surface', 170
    'valuing farms, like marking
        examination papers', 159
Metes (and bounds), 11, 21–2, 96, 121,
    see also Boundaries
Methods (survey), 15, 30, 35
    choice, 45, 276, 354, 429–38
    laborious (Ordnance Survey), 120,
        320, 392
    new, 59, 364, 368, 372, 379
    old (time-tested, elementary), 62, 64,
        72–3, 200, 355, 369, 371
    'superficial', 35
Methods, of
    area calculation (graphic and
        non-graphic), 316, 320
    land measurement, 34, 75 n.25
    linear measurement, 300
    textual criticism, 127

Metres, 354, 400
Metric system, 354
Middlemen, 112, 133, 158, 159, 206, 209, 249
Migration, 232, *see also* Itinerant, Squatting,
    currents of, 247
    immigrants 17, 29, 38, 222, 223, 224, 226, 229, 256 n.15, 261, 268
    internal migration, 168
    migratory piece-working Irish harvesters, 135
    of archives, 96
    return, 222
Miles (length of), 194
Milestones, 164, 194
Military, *see also* Intellectual,
    cartographers, 45, 85
    engineers, 55, 58, 81, 197, 332, 352, 379
    maps, 1, 354, 376, 380
    milieu, 55, 56, 154, 229, 353, 376, 389
    non-military professional brethren, 272, 352, 388
    roads, 197
    science, 44
    sketches, 28, 170, 197
    surveyors, 320, 332
    surveys, 101 n.7, 170, 197, 353
    training grounds, 355
Mills, 10, 31, 137 n.30, 152, 166, 397
Mimicry, 168, *see also* Metaphors, Resemblances
Mines and minerals, 10, 22, 196, 393
    copper, 178
    iron, 434
    maps (plans) of, 193, 290 n.51
    sappers and miners, 388
Misrepresentations (of, streams), 390, *see also* Representations
Mistranscriptions (editorial), 15, *see also* Transcripts
Models, *see also* Re-modelling,
    legal, 95
    metropolitan, 350
    model farms, 333
    relief models, 285, 324 n.24, 355, 362 n.101
    Roman, 193
    scientific, 335

Modes, of
    control, 17
    draughtsmanship, 101
    verbal communication, 121
Modest
    aspirations, 335
    costs, 351
    decorations, 160
    inferences, 42
    revelations, 345
    roles, 354
    standards, 266, 304, 369
Modus vivendi, 395
Monasteries, dissolution of, 4
Mosaic, of
    farms (farm surveys), 159, 379
    regular features, 316, 377
Moors, 13, 168, 170, *see also* Bogs
Mounds, 203
    pagan burial, 6
Mountains 3, 6, 21–2, 65, 112, 128, 152, 162, 168
    access, 214
    classifying, 70, 170, 373, 377, 390-1
    improvement, 268
    geomagnetic deviation, 305
    measuring, 66, 204, 311, 313, 375, 435, 442–3
    scenery, 283
    terra incognita, 145, 375
    tracts, 100, 116, 125
Mourning rings, 282
Municipal,
    authorities, 283, 337
    holdings, 240
Municipalities, 110, 115
Murder, *see also* Gallows, Punishment,
    of map-makers, 254
    site of recent, 178
    threats of, 206
Musicians, 244
Mysteries, 266
    'surveying' and 'valuing' as mysteries, 20, 250, 253, 272
Mysterious,
    expression ('registered surveyor'), 99
    'plot', 43

INDEX OF SUBJECTS   499

Names, 4, 5, 21, 45
  aliases, 120
  authority for, 87, 117, 345
  authors', 69, 75 n. 24, 114, 151, 249,
    280, 344, 346
  Catholic, 258 n. 49
  'C.E' [Civil Engineer], 251, 254
  Christian, 360 n. 67
  common land, 65
  confusing, 60
  denomination, 307, 366–8, 373, 399
  family, 227
  familiar (famous, proud, well-known),
    202, 257 n.36, 337, 389
  field names, 129, 154, 357 n. 12
  first, 278
  Gaelic (native) derivation, 126,
    230–31
  good, 226
  hill and mountain, 66
  instrument, 295
  Irish, 306
  known, 45
  Latin (latinised), 307, 335
  Local place-names, 345, 359 n.65
  modern, 38
  named lives, 259 n. 56
  named territorial divisions, 9, 37
  'New English', 222
  nicknames, 203
  'non-Irish', 258 n. 50
  owners' (proprietors'), 66, 89, 111,
    116, 344, 352, 366, 390
  outlandish, 34
  placenames, 42, 71, 194
  publishers' (printers'), 355, 419–20
  recording, 30, 176, 222, 231
  relation between name and number, 10
  retained, 89
  same (namesakes), 33, 56, 58, 256 n.9
  similar, 288 n. 26
  single-denomination, 113
  street, 275
  surnames, 223, 228, 232, 276
  tenants' (local residents'), 198, 244,
    380, 391
  townland, 120, 365, 389, 392
  Ulster, 231
  uncertain (non-existent), 120, 189
Naming, 8, 22, see also Anonymity,
  ascribing names, 209
  assuming the name, 58
  bearing (carrying) the name, 24 n.29,
    365
  circulating names in advance, 245
  fields (parcels within fields), 5
  identified by name, 81
  given the name, 16
  listing names, 242, 254, 269 n. 71,
    263 n. 123, 302, 402 n.9, 428, 435
  making a name, 60
  mentioning by name, 33, 41, 196, 363
  nameability, 119
  named after, 72, 284, 292 n. 90
  pronunciation, 120
  script, 152
  taking name from, 276
  spelling (misspelling), 119, 360 n. 75,
    392
  stamping, 391
  using the name of another, 421
National 144, 366, see also Local, Regional,
  International, Levels,
  attitudes, 92
  bank, 99
  census, 240
  character, 320
  concerns, 436
  fame, 202, 352
  frameworks, 286
  government, 286
  mapping operations, 30, 71, 286, 332,
    376–8, 388, 402 n.11
  parliament, 88
  resources, 405 n.63
  reputation, 226, 269
  school teachers, 257
  sub-national maps, 332
Navigation, 229–30, 269, 329 n.106, 434,
  see also Rivers,
  inland navigations, 196, 288 n.31,
    326 n.56
  navigable rivers (waterways), 65, 196
  navigation boards, 187
  river navigations, 60, 200
Neutrality, see also Partiality,
  position of neutralism, 254
  strict proprietorial neutrality, 390
New British (English), 222, 231, see also Old
  English, Scots, Gaelic
News-map, 331, see also Maps

Newspapers, *see also* Advertisements,
    advertisements, 87
    announcements (of map
        consultations), 113
    evidence for eighteenth-century land
        measures, 123
    evidence for influence of eighteenth-
        century surveyors, 275, 337
    instrument-makers' advertisements,
        302, 326 n.44
    letters to, 96, 216 n.28, 247, 320
    obituaries, 185 n.102
    patriotic, 340
    properties for rent, sale, 149
    surveyors' advertisements, 90,
        108 n.96, 168, 225, 235, 257 n.32,
        277, 282, 352
    surveyors' testimonials, 98
Newspapers, Named (carrying map- and
    surveying-related advertisements),
    Ballina Impartial, or *Tyrawly Advertiser*,
        384 n.52
    Belfast Newsletter, 183 n.71
    Clonmel Advertiser, 263 n.127
    Cork Advertiser, 361 n.83
    Cork Evening Post, 327 n.60
    Dublin Courant, 366 n.2
    Dublin Evening Post, 293 n.102
    Dublin Gazette, 427
    Dublin Journal, 215 n.9
    Hibernian Journal, 329 n.103
    Hoey's Dublin Mercury, 290 n.51
    Kilkenny Moderator, 184 n.95
    Leinster Journal, 290 n.53
    Limerick Chronicle, 141 n.100
    Limerick Reporter, 438
    Morning Register, 142 n.103
    Newry Commercial Telegraph,
        262 n.101
    Northern Star, 215 n.9
    Roscommon and Leitrim Gazette,
        263 n.127
    Saunders's News-letter, 257 n.28
    Universal Advertiser, 141 n.88
    Volunteer Evening Post, 182 n.58
    Waterford Chronicle, 432
    Waterford Mirror, 360 n.74
    Watson's Almanack, 356 n.2
Newspaper editors, 249
Networks, of, 196
    ancient land divisions, 32
    common points, 377
    control, 336
    frontiers, 379
    road traverses, 335
    small territories, 4, 62
    straight lines, 130
    streams, 203
    surveyors, 232
    triangles, 35, 66
    townlands, 6–7
    urban streets, 314
No-man's land (ecological), 199, *see also*
    Overlapping
Nonius, 306, *see also* Instruments
North-points (indicators), 90, 151–2,
    160–61, 174, 302–3, 315, *see also*
    Compass
North Pole, 303, 305

Oblivion, *see also* Time (Past, Present,
    Future),
    consign to, 189
    rescue from, 203
Occupation, of
    land-surveying, 413, 415, 417, 421
    lands (from tenant to owner), 135, 398
Occupations, 190, 229, 240, *see also* Jobs,
    Overlaps,
    occupational censuses, 240
    occupational frontiers, 43
    occupational groups (categories, range,
        structure, specialised), 2, 187, 188,
        244, 244
    other (of surveyors), 242, 244, 251,
        254, 340, 387
Odometer, 300, *see also* Instruments
Offsets and insets, 299, 310–13, 316, 322,
    388, *see also* Measurement
Old English, 49 n.60, 222, *see also* New
    British, Gaelic
Old St Peter's-tide, 407
Omission, of
    areas, 312, 365, 368, 390
    boundary landmarks, 116, 118, 399
    detail, 379
    dwelling houses (small cabins), 66,
        155, 183 n.75, 350
    Elizabethan Munster surveys, 55
    field boundaries, 380
    lakes, 328 n.82

INDEX OF SUBJECTS   501

latitude and longitude, 334
odd links by chain surveyors, 313
pink or yellow tint on lease maps, 166, 390
provisoes, 127
quality and quantity, 125
roads from area calculation, 119
shading for relief, 380, 392
tenements, 167
Optics,
opticians and instrument makers, 260 n.85
optical squares, 311
Orchards, 10, 152, 155, 188
Ordnance Survey, 54, 388, 400
as standard of comparison, 54, 71, 101, 116, 125, 175, 199, 302, 322-3, 335, 353-4, 375-8, 380, 382, 387, 389-91, 395, 398-400
boundary records, 8, 116, 369
criticisms of, 320, 378, 390-93, 396-7, 399
history, 5, 9, 30, 172, 174, 194, 199, 265, 280, 286, 314, 322, 332, 378, 387
influence on private surveys, 389, 391-6, 399, 444
Landed Estates Court and, 136 n.7, 397-8
maps, 7, 85, 87, 128, 146, 153, 173, 175, 177, 214, 275, 278, 321, 375, 377, 390, 444
methods, 37, 120-21, 126, 128, 146, 168, 177, 179 n.9, 298, 304, 310, 315-16, 320, 388, 392, 398
staff, 96, 168, 174, 202, 242, 272, 285, 365, 375, 378, 380, 382, 387-90, 394, 401
uses of maps, 135, 136 n.7, 177, 389-91, 401
Ornamental Parks and Gardens, 110, 154, *see also* Parks
Ornaments (of maps) 68, 73, 86, 151, 174, 248, 283, 392
Overlapping, of, *see also* Blending, No-man's land,
certification and registration, 108 n.107
duties (functions), 95, 252
figures (major and minor), 266
maps (and building plans), 161, 189
measured lengths, 297

occupations (gardening and surveying), 190, 240
periods (sequences of events), 352, 365
territory, 64
Overseeing, 17, 193, *see also* Custodianship, Supervision
Oversimplifying (on maps), *see also* Simplifying and Diversifying,
landscape, 156
relief, 350

Pacing (fields), 133, 217 n.39, 364, *see also* 'Stepping out'
Painting, 68, *see also* Drawing,
painter-stainers (guild), 274
painting townlands (fourteen-inch rods, scenery, antiquities), 170, 297, 353, 395
Pale (English), 25 n.42, 43, 110, 115, 120, 204, 208
Pales (palings), 162
paling symbols, 154
Pamphlets, 108 n. 96, 143 n.113, 180, n.33, 323 n.1, 411, 432
on hydrostatics, 269, 288 n.25
on variation of the compass, 437
scandalous, 80 nn.91,94
Pantometron, 270, *see also* Instruments
Paper, 8, 184 n.93, 189, 308, 313, 320, 340,
availability, 261 n.92
blue, 434
'chequered', 329 n.103
end-papers, 289 n.38
gridded (standard), 316
pieces (scraps) of , 91, 113, 160
'paper of reference', 76 n.38
papermakers, 166
quality of, 114
reams of, 82
sheets of (unbroken), 166, 320
'strong' (royal), 114
waste, 210
Papers (collections of), *see also* Estate papers, Newspapers, Research papers, State papers,
Aylmer, 362 n.96
Benn, 257 n.41
Bowen, 142 n.103
Brown of Clonboy, 105 n.47

Caperccullen (Limerick), 101 n.3, 106 n.74
Cecil (Hatfield House), 49 nn.65,67
De la Cour, 383 n.25, 385 n.64
Domville, 184 n.93
Hartpole, 107 n.86
Lane, 323 n.2
Larcom, 263 n.122
Lismore, 26 n.60, 50 n.77, 103 n.23, 135 n.2, 136 n.14, 140 n.80, 178 n.5, 255 n.3
McGillycuddy, 106 n.71
Meath, 23 n.17, 107 n.89
Normanton, 357 n.13
Ordnance Survey, 78 n.59
Perceval, 366
Petty, 74 n.4, 325 n.38
Petworth, 101 n.2, 182 n.66, 287 n.7, 327 n.68, 329 n.100
Rolleston, 141 n.87
Sarsfield Vesey, 23.n.17
Shapland Carew, 440
Stephenson, 136 n.13
Truell, 327 n.66
Paradoxes (surveying and cartography), 161, 331, 389
Parchment (vellum), 8, 76 n.38, 114, 155, 166, 261, n.92
Parish,
    boundaries, 359 n.65
    churches, 194, 338
    commons, 204, 207
    field name books, 357 n.12
    incumbents, 370
    maps, 67, 86, 104 n.42, 108 n.106, 278, 365–6, 369, 374, 381
    memoirs, 78 n.59
    parishioners, 334, 369, 371–2
    registers, 293 n.99
    tithes, 364–5, 371
Parishes, 5–6, 21, 59, 114–15, 377, 429
    chapels of ease, 194
    mapping of, 60, 67, 95, 104 n.35, 335, 346, 372–3, 380, 413
    roads in, 195
    street-cleaning in, 338
    units of land reckoning in, 9, 368
Parity, 253, *see also* Equality
Parks, 67, 141 n.84, 145, 162, 210, 280, 372, 387–9, 403 n.20, 412, *see also* Gardens,

deer, 183 n.67
enclosed, 155
gentlemen's, 154
park-making (creation, design, laying out), 189–90
ornamental, 110
overlap (with demesnes), 189
park-designers, 161
park gates, 190
park surveys, 292 n.89
Parliamentary,
    bills, 76 n.29, 85
    careers, 146
    committees, 278
    debates, 219 n.79, 263 n.120
    elections, 129
    enclosures, 204, 207, 219 n.80, 278
    registers, 384 n.45
Partnerships (cartography and surveying),
    dissolution, 210, 238, 280, 353
    formation, 228, 276, 394
    informal (temporary), 267, 346
    local surveyors as partners of Ordnance Survey, 378
    seventeenth-century, 229
    eighteenth-century, 277–8
    nineteenth-century, 167, 185 n.110, 282, 393
    sons (friends) as (pupils), partners, (successors), 227, 249, 276
Patents, 39, 48 n.42, 93, 148
    letters patent, 36
Parcel (of land), 2, 14,
    area, 397
    acreage, 56, 122, 124
    rate per acre
    size, 20, 312
    treated as polygon, 35, 78 n.62
Parcelling, 144
Parcels, 42, *see also* Hamlets, Lots, Villages,
    books of, 47 n.22
    edges of, 122
    confiscated (but not granted), 94
    inclined (surface), 324 n.16
    large, 308, 377, 440
    naming of, 119, 120
    new, 89
    rectangular, 210
    resulting, 130
    small, 91, 120
    spacious, 78 n.62, 429

survey (resurvey) of, 92, 142 n.100,
 169, 312
threatened, 149
unnamed, 120
within fields, 5
Partiality (premeditated), 416, *see also*
 Impartiality, Neutrality,
 partial statements (views), 2, 286
 partial turning of the tables, 62
Partition, *see also* Amalgamation, Dividing,
 acts of, 10, 94
 cases of, 96
 maps of, 97
Partitions, of
 estates, 145
 farms, 187
 irregular outlines, 129
 properties (gavelkind), 6, 209
 uncultivated tracts (bogs), 112, 133
Past, *see under* Time
Paths, 152, 189, *see also* Lanes, Roads,
 Streets, Paving
Pastoralism, 394
Pasture, 13, 15, 36, 64–6, 152, 168, 407,
 see also Grass, Meadows, Tillage,
 common, 31, 112, 208
 conversion to, 128
 exemption from tithe, 364
 green, 170
 hill, 209
 low-lying, 61
 rough (bad), 208
 summer, 6
 sweet, 409
 versus arable, 170, 172, 373
Patterning,
 closely patterned maps, 156
 printed linen, 362 n.100
 repeated circles, pellets and spirals, 150
 rigidly patterned gardens, 189
 short pen or brush strokes, 124
 unfashionably stylised, 283
Patterns, *see also* Structures,
 common (similar), 52, 307
 farm, 210
 field, 121, 168, 389
 leaf, 150
 linear, 214, 315
 'pattern to make a town', 190, *see also*
  Grids
 road, 217 n.38

settlement, 168
street, 275
usual (son following father), 227
Patterns, of
 distribution, 236
 types of acre, 124
 English and Scottish influence, 122
 estates, 111
 misclosures, 318
 territorial variation, 15
Paving, 337, *see also* Cleaning, Lighting,
 paved channels, 410
 pavements, 192
 pavers, 285, 294 n.114
 Clerk for the Crown and Peace for the
  county, 104 n. 444
 Justices of the Peace, 203, 367, 415
Peaceful (co-existence), 320
Peacetime, 10, 55, 60, 73, 210, *see also*
 Wartime
Pedagogues, *see under* Schoolmasters
Peninsulas, 149, 209, 238, 278, 304, *see also*
 Islands
Penitential stations, 176
'Pennsylvania method', 330 n.114, *see also*
 Calculation
Perambulation, 6, 8, 11, 23 n.17,
 24 nn.18,20, 38, 56, 246, *see also* Riding,
 Walking,
 commission of, 94
 'wheelbarrow perambulators', 324 n.21
 writ of, 107 n.82
Perch (land measurement),
 'Cunningham' (Scotland), 17, 139, 295
 'English', 31
 'Lancashire', 17
 'Irish measure', 16, 57–8, 122, 295, 297
 'statute', 164, 211, 380, 392
 'woodland', 139 n.60
Perches, 11, 21–2 , 124, 251, 306, 375,
 418, *see also* Poles, Rods,
 'as both areal and linear measure',
  13–14, 130, 299, 381, 406–07
 'as map scale', 41, 43, 59, 61, 66–7,
  72, 85, 97, 117, 122, 134, 152–3,
  157, 163–9, 171, 173, 175, 195,
  198, 201–211, 333, 338, 347, 350,
  365, 380, 392, 397
 experts on, 12, 17
 origin as ploughman's goad (pole), 10,
  17

reckoning by, 203–04, 206
'squeezing out' of, 131, 194, 196, 313, 373
varieties of, 18, 33, 36, 57, 122
Perclose, 308, 428, *see also* Mapping, Surveying,
closure (misclosure), 308, 327 n.72
seven-link 'perclose', 310
Personality, *see also* Impersonality,
diffident, 264 n.140
national and regional, 220 n. 84, 284
Philologists, 12
Philomaths, 185 n.107, 303
Philosophers,
English, 127
natural, 64, 90, 334
Philosophy, 334, *see also* Scholarship,
experimental, 257 n.25, 271, 289 n.38
natural, 357 n.21
underlying, 162
verbalistic, 170
Pickpockets, 277
Pictures, 23 n.8, *see also* Images, Portraits, Signs, Symbols,
dismal, 127
maps compared to pictures of houses and portraits, 150
picture-maps, 4
exhibiting, 274
reassuring, 144
unpromising, 332
Picturing
cartographic inspiration, 145
sequences of events, 224
surveyors, 14, 54, 151, 302, 325 n.33
surveying instruments, 151, 306, 325 n.33
Picturesqueness (of maps), 282, 291 n.61
Pilgrimage (places of), 355
Placenames, 42
acceptable forms of local, 345
anonymous notes on, 359 n.65
consigned by planners to oblivion, 189
episcopal preference for latinised forms, 335
local pronunciation of, 120
on road maps, 194
reformed vocabulary of Irish placenames, 71
variety of otherwise unrecorded placenames, 176

Plagiarism, 64, 275, 392
surreptitious copyists, 127
Plane-tabling, 34, 307, 403 n.15, 433, *see also* Instruments,
plane table drawings, 34
plane tables, 34, 306
Plantation measure, 57–8, 296, 416, *see also* Irish measure, Acre, Perch
Plats, 54–5, *see also* Maps, Plots
Pleasure (and profit), 45, 148
in polemical writing, 265, 391, 427
special (aesthetic), 154, 164, 188, 274
Plots, 30, 45, 48 n.44, 49 n. 58, 56, 316
'draft', 84
'fair', 42–3
farmers', 208
garden, 25 n.43
labourers', 134
landowners', 166
line, 52, 302, 315
'original', 127
plot-numbers, 120
surveyors', 57
urban house-plots, 72, 124, 164, 176, 190, 270, 277, 401
Plotting, 34–8, 40, 59, 64, 69, 78 n.62, 172, 193, 210, 248, 285, 308, 311, 388, *see also* Surveying,
instruments, 290 n.51, 320
methods, 307, 315-16, 397, 429
Ploughing, 10, 13, 26 n. 36, 128, 138 n.43, 162, 164, 407–09
in common, 220 n.85
plough strips, 208
ploughteams, 8–9
unauthorised ploughing, 141 n.86
Ploughlands, 9, 42, 115, 125, 363, *see also* Acres, Perches,
average size, 39, 95, 114, 364
confiscated, 32
conversion to acres, 12, 29, 367
subdivisions of, 5, 11–12, 29, 37
Ploughmen, 152, 212
Plumbing,
plumbers, 244
plumbing (of lakes), 392
'Plus acres', 93, *see also* Acres
Poets, 56, 287 n.3, 395, *see also* Prose, poetic licence, 5
Pole star, 77 n.53, *see also* North Pole

INDEX OF SUBJECTS 505

Poles, 10, see also Perches, Rods, Surveying poles,
  origins of, 17, 26 n.49
  two-pole and four-pole chains, 295–6, 299, 323 n.8, 416
Policing, 337
Polimetrum, 34, see also Instruments
Polls (land measure), 5,10, 125 , see also Ploughlands, Tates, Quarters
Polygonometry (pioneers of), 318
Polygons, 35, 316, 422
  offsets and insets, 311–12
  survey polygons, 307, 310
Ponds, 162, see also Lakes/Loughs, fishponds, 152
Poor, 142 n. 103, 208 , 335, 394, see also Poverty,
  classes, 138 n.45
  farmers (tenants), 119, 133
  houses (Georgian), 178, 355
  living standards, 332
  'youth', 258 n.46
Poor Law (Poor Relief Act), 375
  Board of Guardians, 375
  Commissioners, 250, 385 n. 67
  Unions, 402 n. 11
'Pops', 119, 313, see also Mapping
Portable,
  instruments, 270, 305, 433
  volumes, 148
Portraits, of, see also Pictures,
  children, 150
  deer, 154
  self-, 3
  surveyors, 255
  topographical, 391
  town squares, 274
  wives, 150
Post-medieval,
  farmscapes, 121
  improving landowners, 145
  co-existence (of perches), 295
  cartography, 379
Post Office, see also Mail,
  mailcoach roads (laying out of), 197
  postal charges, 194
  road maps (maps of Ireland, strip maps), 202, 270, 353
  surveyors, 17, 199, 379
  surveys (c. 1805), 353

Potato, 268, 364
  gardens (patches), 112, 133, 410
  ridges, 133
Pottles (land measure), 8, see also Gallons
Poverty, 112, 204, 206, see also Poor
Precedents, 30, 107 n.84, 304, see also Unprecedented,
  early plantation schemes, 128
  one page per townland, 166
  passing over of common surveyors, 378
  regulation of land-surveying, 415
Precincts, 115, 386 n.71, see also Hamlets, Villages
Precise,
  chaining, 298
  comparison, 90, 231
  dating, 114, 257 n.33, 363
  definition of (perch acre, estate survey), 13, 73
  location (address), 134, 245, 400
  marking of townland divisions, 6
  recipes (spreading fertiliser, mixing seed), 202
Precision, 332, 387, see also Accuracy,
  degrees of, 2, 5, 251, 310
  numerical (acreage, angles, distances), 57, 125, 322, 373
  of compass dials, 304
  of maps, 276
Pre-medieval (sources), 4, see also Medieval
Premiums (for agricultural improvement), 128, 203
Prescribed,
  oaths (commissioners), 31
  proportions (land), 129
  stations (surveyors'), 308
  sums (money), 427–8
  times (for improvement), 409
Prescriptions
  Surveyor-General, 98
  Ordnance Survey), 202
Present, see under Time
Prevalence, of
  chain surveying in England, 315
  English acre in east Co. Cork and west Co. Wexford, 122
  magnetic meridian, 302
  processes of striping and squaring, 214
  Protestantism among trained practitioners, 230

Price,
  fixing, 439
  monopolies, 82
  pricing self out of market, 39
  revolutions, 249
  trends, 44, 83, 200, 249, 389, 442–3
Prices, of, *see also* Charges, Costs,
  books (surveying), 429–32, 434, 436–7
  chains, 259 n.54
  corn, 244, 370
  farms, 200, 440
  land (soil), 401, 443
  maps, 391–2
  surveying prices, 439
Printers, 419, 437–8
  king's, 331
  letterpress, 331
  lithographic, 392
Printing, 274–5, *see also* Publication,
  by subscription, 429, 431, 434
  from copper plates, 269
  getting cheaper, 167, 334
  getting into print, 150, 337, 340, 368
  'in print', 272, 278, 280, 295, 303, 340, 390, 434
  small print, 355
Printing, of,
  atlases, 144
  'compartments', 117
  county maps, 85, 150
  documents related to agrarian affairs, 4
  encomiums, 349
  estate maps, 391, 393
  extracts from specimen field books, 307
  impressions of surveyors' names, 151
  insets (town plans), 341
  maps, 128, 161, 174, 332, 346, 365, 399
  ornaments onto manuscript maps, 151
  property advertisements, 112
  squares (grids of), 64, 72, 316
  tithe certificates, 374
  townland lists, 381
  town plans, 343
Printsellers, 346, 355
  print-shops, 355
Private, 388, 395, *see also* Public,
  admeasurement, 174
  arrangement, 204
  assignment, 267
  atlas, 146

cartographers, 392
clients, 244, 380, 391
collections, 23 n. 17, 83, 216 n.36
draughtsmen, 392
disputes, 94
employment, 44–5, 81
enterprise, 100, 316, 396
estates, 4, 81, 366, 370–71
fortune, 280
geologist, 394
individuals (persons), 83, 87, 96, 145, 376
land transactions (dealings), 89, 125
landowners, 82, 223, 278, 388
life, 254
matter of concern, 191
office, 87
property, 55, 87
publisher, 396
roads, 198, 328
sector, 73, 308
surveyors, 58, 82, 94, 100–01, 116, 152, 233, 242, 270–71, 273, 308, 320, 373, 375, 389–91, 397, 400
surveys, 43–4, 62, 87, 132, 223, 316, 369, 372, 375, 382, 398, 440
town plans, 396
use, 86
work, 81, 240
Problems, 46, 91, 224, *see also* Solutions,
  cadastral, 370
  cartographic, 147, 376
  classificatory, 159, 331
  disagreement over tithes, 95
  disputes over boundaries, 115
  elimination of the perclose (misclosure), 308
  financial, 368
  integrating regional and estate maps, 379
  map deterioration, 86
  redundancy through boundary changes, 72
  terminological complexity, 6
  identification of boundary markers, 40
  statistical, 323
  taxing and tithing, 365, 369, 373
  technical, 266
  traverse offsets and insets, 310
  townland acreages (includes bog, wood, pasture with arable or not), 15

uprising, 28
under-measurement (over-granting), 40
Proctors, 143 n. 115
  tithe proctors, 133, 254, 364
Professional,
  admeasurement (mensuration) 10, 12
  allusions, 150
  ambitions (pretensions), 29, 68
  antecedents (descendants, successors, progeny), 33, 167, 269, 353
  brethren (fraternity, community), 246, 272, 377
  bodies (institutes, societies, framework, organisation), 265, 376, 400–01
  competition, 45
  contacts (range of), 282
  disagreements (controversies, bellicosity, disputes), 96, 132, 254, 320, 411
  fees (economics of profession), 199, 439
  help (expertise, knowledge. assistance), 2, 31, 133, 227, 249, 337, 397
  life, 286, *see also* Careers,
  mores (habits, insularity, unity, standards), 4, 224, 265, 271, 322
  overpopulation, 246
  prejudices, 397,
  reputation (eminence, talent, skill, success, fame), 244, 251, 254, 267, 269, 274, 285, 354, 393
  status, 46, 126, 174, 192, 228, 231, 234, 247, 252, 265, 265, 287, 335, 389
Professionalism, 172, 354, *see also* Amateurism,
  expulsion from professions, 226
  history of professions (lack of), 322, 376
  non-professional manpower, 388
Professionals, *see also* Land surveyors,
  foreign, 188, 193, 226, 334, 337
  full-timers and part-timers, 45, 223, 230, 249
Professions,
  architecture, 189
  engineering, 174, 193, 346, 352
  estate management, 206
  instrument-making, 269
  law, 30, 193
  surveying, 2, 28, 33, 42, 45, 59, 130, 140 n. 77, 222, 269, 282
  teaching, 230
Projectors (ignorant and incapable), 192
  of gardens, 190
Projections, 342, 348–9
Projects, 44, 51, 190–91, 193, 196, 204, 340, 344, 347, 352
Proprietors, 29, 70, 93, 110, 132, 146, 336, 371, 393
  agreements between, 118, 94, 118, 200
  as patrons, 164, 188, 390, 394
  institutional, 110
  interest in adjacent properties, 149, 206, 390
  keeping farms untenanted, 147
  names of, 89, 111
  'old', 24 n.18
  'papist', 67
  'philistine', 150
  'transnational', 227
Proprietorship, 1, 19, *see also* Tenure,
  property rights, 88, 187
  subordination to topography, 119
Proprietorial,
  affiliations, 6
  neutrality, 390
  significance, 89
  super-proprietorial authority, 200
  tax burden, 367, 368, 369, 370
  versus physical condition of land, 187
Prose (of lawyers and cartographers), 199, *see also* Poets
Prospects, *see also* Views, Vistas,
  fanciful, 44
  new, 370
  nightmarish, 400
  no, 70, 331
  not averse to, 85
  poor, 362 n.103
  prospective tenants, 204
  welcome, 367
Prospects, of
  houses, 151
  local linen industry, 268
  public gestures, 376
Prostapheresis (of triangles), 316
Protestant, *see also* Catholic,
  churches, 190
  clergy, 382 n.11, 384 n.46
  faith (members of), 194

'interest', 176, 366
'in religion', 110,
lands (forfeited and unforfeited), 365–6
landlords (typical), 110
surveyors (employment of), 230–31, 254, 258 n.49
townlands, 366
Protestants (in schools, learning mathematics, surveying), 230, 258 n.49
Protraction, 41, 43, 68, 320, 423, 428, 430, 432 *see also* Plotting, Surveying
Protractor (instrument), 315–16
Protractor (survey officer), 72–3, 101, 266–7, 273
Province maps, 10, 35, 50 n.71, 59, 84, 144, 149, 332, 342, 345
Public, 248, 387, 395, *see also* Private,
appearances, 277
attention (acclaim, eye, recognition, attitude), 190, 254, 271, 346, 367
bodies (departments), 114, 396, 401
buildings, 187
character, 94, 199, 230
collections, 99
confidence (faith, esteem), 98, 308, 313, 396
controversy, 249, 318, 378, 397, 415–31
demand, 286
display (hidden), 274, 375, 413
face, 190
general public, 82, 266
gesture, 375
image, 132
lectures, 271
life, 202
map-using public, 400
money, 101
places, 1, 113, 275
purposes, 363, 372
revenue (finance), 106 n.75, 376
road (highway), 198, 338
sale, 85, 345
sector, 101
service (servants), 52, 55, 252, 401
spirit, 285
surveys, 87, 273, 369
transport, 194
works, 17, 390

Publication, 63–4, 81, 248, 275, 277, 332, 334, 338, 342, 346, 349, *see also* Printing,
official, 100, 390
rate, 396
Publicity, 52, 66, 133, 168, 190, 192, 249, 355
campaigns, 161, 277, 337, 345, 390
Punishment, 178
escape from, 396
of imposters, 415, 420–22
pecuniary, 421
Purposes (mapping, surveying, valuing),
calculation of areas, 116, 286, 311
censuses, 242
delimitation of boundaries, 38, 95, 116, 120, 286, 297, 373
demonstration, 209
electoral, 146
fiscal, 389
legal, 166, 397
military, 389
present, 4, 20, 303
proprietorial, 393
public, 363, 372
road-planning, 367
scientific, 389
small-scale geographical, 73
tithe, 372
Purposes of,
identifying forfeited properties (mears and bounds), 30
land surveying (all-purpose), 29, 92, 370, 432–3, 437
laying out new streets, 283
local valuation, 379
map-making (quick, extensive), 68, 128, 172, 346, 366, 387
newspaper advertising, 225, 411
painting scenery an antiquities, 353
plane table, the, 34
stamp duty, 114
settling boundary disputes, 8

Quadrant, 269, 429–30, 433–6, *see also* Instruments
Qualitative,
distinction, 124
refinement, 170
spirit, 197
variation, 10

INDEX OF SUBJECTS   509

Qualities,
  best maps ever (arguably), 172
  boundary, 65
  dynamic (settlement), 220 n.88
  imaginary, 172
  land, 29, 60, 75 n.25, 122, 139 n.58,
     158, 172, 214, 377
  map, 28, 54, 114, 125, 282
  output, 340
  road-work, 199
  sharpness and neatness of detail, 172
Quality, 11, 20–21, 156, 159, 255, 276,
  see also Quantity,
  quasi-quality, 8
  'sanative quality', 357 n.21
'Quality men', 250
Quantitative,
  gradients, 197
  significance, 10, 310
  standards, 238
Quantities, of
  land, 11–12, 21, 40, 49 n. 49, 88, 122,
     158, 212, 371, 375, 407–10
  lead ore, 157
  maps, 8, 337
  output, 340, 356 n.1
  seed corn, 8
Quantity, 29, 95, 156, 276, 373, see also
  Estimation, Quality,
  true, 54
  subtraction, 48 n. 44, 125
Quarries and quarrymen, 10, 22, 137 n.30,
     152, 164, 194
Quarters (land measure), 9–10, 61, 115,
     125, 209, see also Cartrons, Carrows,
     Ploughlands,
  quarter-acres, 14
  quarters (in towns), 155, 274
Quiet, see also Calm, Conflict, Rage,
  country, 38
  keep, 346
  possession, 89
  quieten the sceptics, 199
  revolution, 375
  '... with the aid of a map to give rest
     and quiet to all the world', 127
Quit-Rent Office, 85, 87, 93–6, 104 n.41
  clerks, collectors, commissioners,
     106 nn.72, 77, 79
  correspondence, 103 n.30, 107 n.95
  letters, 106 n.72

Quit rents, 60, 70, 78 n.58, 79 n.78, 93–4,
     110
  arrears, 105 n.59

Rabbit warren, 10
Race,
  native race, 135
  of text-book writers, 57
Rage, see also Conflict, Calm, Quiet,
  corporate, 396,
  umbrage, 126
Railways, 113, 135 n.4, 141 n.85, 199,
     286, 295
  maps, 216 n.36, 356 n.1
  promoters, 252
Raths, 65, 116, 202, see also Antiquities
Reckoning, see also Calculation,
  increase in per capita surveying activity,
     242
  lengths, 324 n.18
  longitudes, 337
  parts of a square, 329 n.102
  rent, 135
  units of land (area), 9–10, 122, 135,
     203, 364, 411
Reclamation (drainage works), 131, 204
  taking account of, 250
Reclamation, of
  hill pasture, 209
  new land from the waste, 112, 128
  unprofitable land, 72
Recreation, see also Sport,
  leisured community, 337
  maypoles, 178
  rackets courts, 178
'Rectifier', 73,
Rectifying,
  globes, 269
  maps, 91
  notes ('in the field'), 423, 431
Redistribution, 1, 60, 79 n. 74, 88–9, see
  also Confiscation, Restoration
Regional, see also Local, National, Levels,
  Periods,
  capitals, 236
  barriers, 232
  early estate cartography, 114
  explanations, 15
  distributions, 122, 233
  features, 380

frameworks, 242
maps, 44, 145, 174, 332, 334, 356 n.1, 379
patterns of surveying activity, 235
personalities, 284
plantation schemes, 51, 114
scales, 5
schools, 232
significance, 5
standards, 17
surveyors and surveys, 236, 332
territorial hierarchies, 5
variations (land quality), 60
Regions, 114, 231, 280
'Registered surveyor', 99, 108 n.107, *see also* Surveyors
Registered,
land, 399
papers (Chief Secretary's office), 386 n.76
Registers, *see also* Newspapers,
annual, 102 n.20
Deeds, 405 n.57
General Register of Real Property, 140 n.78, 262 n.100, 263 n.127
Land, 399, 405 n.57
letter (out-letters), 289 n.43, 385 n.56
Morning Register, 142 n.103
Ordnance Survey, 8
parish, 293 n.99
Parliamentary Register, 384 n.45
see of Dublin, 3
Registrar (Deputy Diocesan), 356 n.11
Registration, of
lands (land titles), 309, 404 n.39, 405 nn.54,59
new houses, 400
surveyors, 107 n.107
Regression (psychologist's principle), 228
Relief, 66–7, *see also* Mapping, Poor relief act,
'ground', 352
hachures, 162, 171, 172, 283
irregularity of Ireland's, 203
models, 285, 324 n.24, 355
omitting, 380, 392
oversimplifying, 350
relief-conscious theory of road design, 197
symbols, 172
three-dimensional artefacts, 379

Religion, 176, *see also* Churches, Chapels, Catholic, Protestant,
Christian, 320
new (Protestant), 110
religious affiliations (of land surveyors), 232–3
Remapping, 273, *see also* Mapping
'Remarkable' boundary features, *see also* Boundaries,
barns, 137 n.30
beacons, 152
bleach greens, 152
bogs, 152
bridges, 137 n.30, 152
cabins, 152
castles, 152
churches, 152
gardens, 152
gravel-pits, 137 n.30
hedges, 152
hills, 137 n.30
hollow-ways, 137 n.30
houses, 137 n.30, 152
kilns, 137 n.30, 152
land-marks, 137 n.30
loughs, 152
meadow, 152
mills, 137 n.30, 152
old buildings, 137 n.30
old trees,
pasture, 152
paths, 152
quarries, 137 n.30, 152
rivers, 152
rivulets, 152
roads, 137 n.30, 152
tillage, 152
walls, 152
water-cuts, 137 n.30
woods, 152
'Remarkable',
entries in Dictionary of Surveyors, 255 n.2
maps, 149
synthesis, 167, *see also* Blending
shortage of Ulster names, 231
store of geological information, 337
surveying techniques, 316, 373
Remarks column, 156, 202, 219 n. 76, *see also* Maps

Remembering (not forgetting), 3, 6, 84, 308, 396, 409, *see also* Forgetting, Time (Past)
Remembering, by
    author (JHA), the, 78 n.64
    professional successors, 269
    reader, the, 34, 144, 156, 168, 176, 244, 375, 407
Re-modelling, of, *see also* Models,
    farms, 188, 221 n.93
    holdings, 204
    parks, 154
Rents, 124, 246
    collection of rents, 93, 268, 278
    Crown rents, 110
    high (crippling) rents, 138 n.43, 206, 443
    Irish rents (competitive bidding, fixing), 125, 159, 250, 415
    low rents, 20, 147
    'quit rents', 60, 94
    renting 'by the bulk' ('in the lump', 'in the gross', 'by the side'), 125, 132, 238
    rent rolls, 148, 215 n.21, 288 n.14
Repertoires (of mapmakers), 151, 168
Representing,
    lengths and bearings as numbers, 307
    'measurers' as scarce commodities, 43
Representation,
    absence of, 72, 164, 242, 253
    by surveyors in disputes, 92, 149
    in private collections, 83, 196
Representations, of, *see also* Misrepresentations,
    boundary junctions by crosses, 61, 116
    estate maps as single leaseholds, 145, 333
    income (surveyor's), 350, 444
    lands by 'denominations', 4
    landscape (sketchy, 'natural'), 70, 168, 172, 197–8, 349, 352
    local industries, 160
    north by fleur-de-lys, 150,
    provinces, 35
    roads by 'pops', 119
    sheets of OS map by numbered rectangles, 7
Representatives, of,
    counties, 363, 367
    public surveying, 273, 321

Research (original) papers, 300, 326 n.44
Resemblances, between, *see also* Metaphors, Similarities,
    Antrim maps and 'lost originals', 86
    Bogs commissioners maps and Post Office road maps, 202
    'current modes of draughtsmanship' and plantation surveys, 101
    Elizabethan Ireland and North America, 32
    estate maps and farm maps, 146
    landed property and sovereign state, 200
    midland and Ulster maps, 57
    plantation records and surveys, 36
    post-plantation adjustments and the plantations, 95
    rundale system and English midlands open-field system, 209
    surveyors in NE Ulster and Dublin, 172
    Thomas Raven and previous Irish surveyors, 266
    'topographical' artists and estate cartographers, 166
    'Trustees' Survey and Down Survey and estate maps, 72, 152
    William Bald's maps and Ordnance Survey maps, 286
Restoration, 51, 93, 118, 129
Resurveying, 62, 92, 127–30, 147, 344, 400, *see also* Surveying
Retrenchments, 88, 92–3, 106 n.69
Reviewing, *see also* Viewing,
    distinction between profitable and unprofitable land, 64
    evidence, 59
Reviewing, of
    duties, 95
    maps, 150
    methods, 320
    literature, 135 n.1, 220 nn.84,88, 385 n.55
    surveyor's influence, 187
Revision, 263 n. 123, 343, *see also* Remapping, Resurveying
Revision, of
    county cess, 387
    maps, 91, 128, 272, 284, 292 n.89 , 347, 354, 390, 396, 398, 400
    surveys, 147, 179 n.21, 249, 335, 354
    town plans, 342

Revolutionary,
  calendar (French), 58
  features (Roque style), 162
  period, 21
  pre-revolutionary period, 369
  single-road (strip) map, 196
  status (Petty), 68
  tasks, 26
  surveys, 52
Revolutions,
  aesthetic, 247
  agricultural, 202, 398
  cartographic, 399
  Irish price, 249
  quiet, ('Irishman's knowledge of his country'), 375
Ridges, 65, *see also* Cultivation, Potato, Spade, Valleys
Riding, 3, 126, *see also* Perambulation, Walking,
  triennial riding, 6, 23 n.16
Rightboys, 373
Ring dial, 272, 273
Ripeness,
  'this poor country is not yet ripe for ... new series of county admeasurements', 335
  'ripe for improvement' (townlands), 212
  gallon or pottle ('which could ripen a certain quantity of seed corn'), 8
Rival,
  cartographers, 272, 280, 401
  claims, 119
  landowners, 93
  lines, 118
  schemes, 196, 270
  surveyors, 93, 192, 202, 246, 265, 273, 320, 322–3, 334
Rivalry, 62, 69, *see also* Friendship
River,
  cleansing, 199
  courses, 200
  crossings, 312, 328 n.80
  lowering, 199
  maps, 199, 219 n.66, 290 n.51, 311, 332
  meanders, 311
  navigations, 60, 65, 200
  surveys, 72, 78 n.62, 152, 162, 168, 200, 218 n.50, 380
  widening, 199
Rivers, *see also* Canals, Lakes/Loughs, Streams, Flooding, Navigation, Water,
  access to, 214
  as boundaries, 6, 36, 65, 116
  breadth and depths, 65
  islands in, 65
  falls in, 65
  rivulets, 152
Roads, 1, 6, 283, 286, *see also* Lanes, Paths, Streets,
  areas of (inclusion and exclusion), 119, 135, 138 nn.43,45
  as boundaries, 40, 66, 116
  county, 193, 198, 252, 263 n.115, 335
  cross-sections of, 198
  dirt on, 119
  farm, 204
  laying-out of, 32, 193, 252
  legislation, 218 n.55, 324 n.21
  line of, 198
  local system of, 121, 150, 217 n.38, 367
  mail-coach, 119, 197–9
  main (high), 31, 36, 66, 199, 214, 338
  mapping of, 37, 137 n.30, 152, 162, 168, 170, 194, 198, 200, 271, 332, 338, 354, 376–7
  mileages, 194, 232, 289 n.35, 324 n.21, 335
  milestones, 194
  military, 197, 218 n.55
  minor (secondary), 36, 280, 351
  naming of, 284
  new, 119, 141 n.87, 196–8, 216 n.36, 337, 346, 349, 391
  old, 198
  on estate maps, 113, 119, 152, 193
  pedestrians, 253
  physical condition of, 187
  post (Post Office), 197, 202, 349, 354
  private, 198, 338
  public, 198, 216 n.326, 338, 361 n.94
  repairs (upkeep, maintenance), 218 n.55, 363, 367
  road books, 353
  roadmakers (designers, planners), 193, 196–9, 212, 216 n.36, 250, 252, 354, 367, 376, 379
  road surveyors, 216 n.36, 353, 361 n.93, 379, 395
  single-road (strip) maps, 196
  straightening of, 195

surfaces, 198, 298, 300
surveys of, 119, 195, 197, 255 n.6, 314, 323 n.7, 336, 345, 353–4, 380, 389
townland roads, 354, 389
traffic, 197
turnpike, 198, 217 n.43
Rocks, 8, 39, 65–6, 162, 164, 199, 394, 406–07, *see also* Soils, Stones
Rods, 10, *see also* Perches, Poles, Compass rods, Surveying poles,
half-perch and whole-perch rods, 17
laying down of, 13
Roods, 12, 124, 208, 251, 306, 381, *see also* Stangs,
four per acre, 13
'odd roods and perches', 14
of ground, 11
Rotation (crops, compass, theodolite), 202, 302, 305
'Rounding out' maps (eliminating bays, salients, enclaves, exclaves), 149
Royal Corps of Sappers and Miners, 388
Royal Engineers, 76 n.34, 378, 388
Ruination, of
churches, 345
tenants, 414, 423
Rundale, *see also* Runrig,
abolition, 210
consolidation (of holdings), 213
definition, 208, 220 n.85, 221 n. 93
development, 209
features, 209
farmers, 209
maps, 209–10, 220 n.89, 398
settlement (village – no church, inn, blacksmith's shop), 208
tenants, 213
system, 208, 210, 399
Runrig, 210
Rural, 240, *see also* Urban,
areas (landscapes, of Ireland, history of), 155, 156, 187, 189, 254, 340, 342, 395
backwaters, 209
consciousness, 12
estates, 240
grievances, 321
improvements, 170
interests, 278
landscape making, 204, 206, 214

land use, 392
life, 152
plans, 275
polymaths (schoolmasters), 229, 254
population, 112, 133
preoccupations, 190

Salaries, of
clerk to Dublin wide streets commission, 278
county officials, 363
prortractors, 287 n. 5
surveyors, 19, 26 n.53, 30–31, 68, 81, 240, 249, 250, 266, 394
Sales,
Crown land, 283
estate, 85, 95, 142 n.103, 397
map, 331, 337, 342, 390, 396–7
public, 85, 149, 278
sale-cartography, 121
sales-particulars map, 112–13, 206
Satire, *see also* Laughter,
non-satirical writers, 306
satirical comments, 192
Scale, 23 n. 2, 32, 45, 66, 122, 144, 244, 439, *see also* Map scales,
base line, 315
correctly scaled, 373, 394
county scales, 344
diminutive, 393
huge (exceptionally large), 278, 285, 398
large-scale, 7, 35, 76 n. 62, 285, 354, 357 n 14, 72, 155, 164, 166, 168, 275, 320, 370, 376, 380, 396
local and regional, 5
measuring, 10, 154, 167, 313, 318, 348, 354, 368
medium, 202
normal, 299
original, 397, 400
scale bars, 150, 160–61, 283
scale-choice, 45, 59, 149, 159, 200, 204, 285, 347, 365, 377, 387, 392, 398
scale-enlargement, 399
scale-index, 146
scale (instrument), 315–16
scale-lines, 56
scale-ratio, 36, 90, 152, 391

scale-reduction, 36, 78 n. 62, 343, 366, 379
scale-spectrum (pyramid), 44, 145, 350
small-scale, 35, 43, 342, 349, 73, 84–5, 113, 150, 161, 189, 196, 286, 302, 320, 331, 336, 340–41, 349, 366
standard, 397
unscaled maps, 4, 155
vernier scale, 304
Scatters (scatterings), of, *see also* Clusters, Clachans,
   dwelling houses, 10
   forfeited acres, 51
   open-field strips, 120
   sites, 236
   urban properties, 120
Scholars,
   map (contemporary, Restoration, Victorian), 41, 56–8, 81–2, 334, 337, 345, 388
   map (modern, recent), 13, 43, 71, 385 n.55, 387
Scholarship, *see also* Philosophy,
   present state of, 35, 176, 208, 337, 355
   scholarly publication (research), 81, 176
Schoolmasters (teachers, pedagogues), 226, 229, 244, 253–4, 395
   in Goldsmith's *Deserted Village*, 230
   mapping as sideline, 248, 256 n.10, 257 n.41
   National, 257 n.41
   rural, 254
   schoolboys, 418
   schoolmaster-labourers, 254
   stewards (principals), 269, 289 n.38, 360 n.67
   surveyor-teachers, 229
Schoolmasters (teachers), of
   arithmetic, 228
   art, 282
   English, writing, drawing, 257 n.34
   land surveying, 130
   mathematics, 22, 96, 230, 271, 314, 425, 427
   navigation, 229–30, 269
   valuing, 250
   writing, 248
Schools, 110, 228, 269, 365
   Agricultural, 258
   boarders and day pupils, 271

Catholic, 230–31
Charter, 258 n.46
Erasmus Smith, 267, 287 n.7
Figure and ornament drawing, 291 n. 67
Foundation, 258 n.46
'ordinary', 170, 230
Marine, 324 n.22
'Mathematical, Drawing and Writing', 182 n.61, 229–30, 271, 274–5, 289 n.35
National, 257 n.41
Protestant, 230–31
Vocational, 403 n.26
'Schools' of land surveyors (cartography), 159, 172
   Civil engineering, 263
   'French', 167, 184 nn.82,94, 185 n.100, 276, 347, 377, 441
   'Irish', 353, 389
   Rocque's, 15, 164, 166, 344
   regional, 232
   topographical, 164
'Scotch',
   firs, 203
   perches, 139 n.60
   quarters, 155
Scottish,
   plantations (influence), 53, 122
   surveyors (cartographers), 227, 256 n.15, 285, 253
Scots, 226, *see also* Old English, New British (English), Gaelic
Scripts, *see also* Manuscripts, Transcripts,
   on maps, 229
Scriveners, 397, *see also* Draughtsmen, Engravers
Seals, 5, 56
Sea, *see also* Maritime features,
   coasts (charting of), 214, 338
   distances, 298
   sea-crossings, 17, 132, 224
   incursions, 200
   seaports, 229
   seaside, 178
   seaweed, 119
   soundings, 65
Seasonal distribution (of surveying), 249
Seats,
   country, 346

INDEX OF SUBJECTS   515

gentlemen's, 336, 338, 362 n.100
  of ancient local families, 176
Second, *see also* First, Third,
  career, 244, 277
  hoeing, 407
  landmark, 305
  line, 302
  second-best (rank, rate, choice), 39,
    99, 190, 270, 287, 308, 373
  series, 86
  survey, 32, 40, 126–7, 214, 427
  thoughts, 19
Secondary
  measurements, 311
  motives (roles, reasons), 68, 268, 313
  roads, 280
Secrecy, 64, 99, 132, 230, *see also*
  Conspiracy,
  stones (boundary) being secretly
    buried, 118
  trees (boundary) cut down at night, 118
Secretaries, *see also* Clerks,
  Chief Secretary's office, 386
  'secretary' (compared with 'clerk',
    'surveyor'), 253
  Secretary of the Irish Linen Board, 277
  secretary hand, 248
  Under-secretary of Ireland, 386
Sections or profiles, 200-1, 288, 398, *see also*
  Mapping
Seed, *see also* Fertility,
  corn, 8
  measures (bushels, barrels), 408
  mixing, 202
  plough, 408
  sowing, 408
Seeds,
  grass, 408–09
  grey pea, 409
  hay, 408
  red turnip, 407
Seignories, 28, 29, 31, 32, 39, 40, 42
Selions (plough strips), 13, 121, 209, *see also*
  Metes and Bounds
Selling, *see under* Sale
Semi-circles, 35, 305, *see also* Circles,
  Instruments
Sergeants,
  Ordnance Survey, 394
  on native estates (rent-gatherers,
    bailiffs), 18

Servants,
  menial, 244
  of noblemen and gentlemen (upper),
    38, 253
  public, 55
Sessiaghs, 8, *see also* Carucates, Ploughlands
Setting (land, farms), 129, 184 n.93
  down (documenting), 42
  forth (mapping) 54
  out (foundations, towns, areas,
    boundaries), 192, 193, 206, 312,
    328 n.79
  up (landmarks), 38
Settings (backgrounds, context)s, 110, 252
Settlement, Act of, 90, 94, 97
Shading, of, *see also* Colouring,
  capital letters, 379
  density of surveyors, 233
  hills (slopes, relief), 198, 285, 380, 392
  land-use, 166, 392, 166
Shambles (rundale system), 208
Shape, 20, *see also* Size,
  better, 91
  exact, 1
  identically-shaped rectangles, 13
Shape, of,
  British Ordnance Survey, 265
  ideal farm, 203
  Ireland, 332
  lay-outs (square, linear, cruciform,
    T-shaped, crescent), 191
  parishes, 373
  plots of land (rectangular, square), 208,
    212, 311
  Trustees Survey, 96
Sharing (shared) shares, of, 107n.83, *see also*
  Equality,
  advantages and disadvantages (town
    plans), 396
  ambivalence (lack of commitment) of
    cartographers, 166, 192
  baronial populations, 240
  burden of cess, 363
  credit, 355
  houses, 277
  names, 69
  soil types (qualities of land), 208, 214
  spatial information (through maps), 42
  success, 281
  status, 273–4
  trademarks, 283

towns, 164
world-markets, 232
work-sharing, 193, 291 n.66
Sheet-lines, 396, see also Lines
Sheets (OS), 7, 121, 148, 173, 380, 389 see also Mapping,
connecting, 179 n.9
index, 396
multi-sheet, 146, 340, 347, 362 n.100, 377, 390
single (separate), 144, 149, 166, 335
printed, 128
sheet-size, 149, 159, 166, 179 n.12, 320
survival rates of, 178 n.2
unbroken, 166
undated, 323 n.2
working, 104
Sheep, 112, 407, 409–10, see also Animals
Shepherds, 410
Shops,
blacksmiths', 208
book-shops, 320
druggists', 261 n.92
instrument-makers', 270
print-shops, 355
workshops (map engravers'), 282
Shopkeepers, 270
Shop-keeping 244
Shovel, 406, see also Spade
Sickle-smiths, 244
Siege and battle maps, 332, see also Mapping
Signing (signatures) 61, 83, 266, 282, 365
countersigning, 194
certificates, 273, 374
covenants, 128
deeds, 5
leases, 132
maps (on oath), 54–5, 69, 86, 114, 188, 270, 326 n.44, 418, 422–3, 426
testamonials, 98
unsigned maps, 49 n.59, 84, 188
Signs, 99, 115, 116, 202, 234, 352, see also Images, Pictures, Symbols,
on maps, 131, 340
plus and minus, 327 n.78
Similarities, between, see also Metaphors, Resemblances, Differences,
mapmakers, 28, 41, 51, 66, 67, 74 n.8, 96, 204, 388
surveyors and teachers, 229

Similarities in,
appointment, 347
approximation, 14
argument, 80, 365, 395
character, 78 n.58, 254
coffee rooms, 113
decision, 200
design, 161, 392
documents, 4, 74, 107 n.88
land transfers (plantations), 3
maps, 176, 189, 286, 340, 352, 389, 396
Similarities, of
idea, 168, 385 n.68
irregularity, 364
pattern, 307
problem, 120
quality, 20
quantity, 240, 440
rarity, 176
technique, 47 n.30, 58, 203, 250, 270, 345, 397, 400
terminology, 13, 57, 140 nn.71,72, 288 n.26
title (book), 289, 383 n.15
transmission, 140
treatment, 191
Simplified,
reductions (of maps), 57
versions (of 'in-field' maps), 164
Simplified (on maps),
borders, 160
details (topographical), 379, 396
marks of distinction, 168
Simplifying, see also Oversimplifying, Diversifying,
arithmetic (surveyor's), 299
calculations (using tables), 318
Size, 8, 20, see also Shape,
as 'area', 12, 14–15, 31, 146, 247, 306, 312
ascertain (determine) area, 1–2
farm-size, 32, 42, 199, 208, 210, 230, 232, 234
field-size, 407
sheet-size (maps), 159, 164, 356 n.1, 389, 396, 439
Sizes, of,
baronies, 365
demesnes, 190

INDEX OF SUBJECTS 517

enclosures, 118
estates, 112, 234
land surveying practices, 249
seignories, 40
tenements, 112, 159
townlands, 10, 310, 369
vocabulary, 246
Skeletal (style of plantation maps), 155, *see also* Patterning, Structure
Skeletalism (of ordinary estate index), 335
Skeleton,
  base-skeleton (of local roads), 150
  of traverse survey, 313
  skeleton-maps, 354, 357 n.13
  trigonometrical, 345
Sketches, 121, 183 n.71, 188, 218 n.55, 307, *see also* Maps ('true'),
  boundary sketch-maps, 30, 116
  copying of, 188
  diagrammatic, 56
  farm sketch-maps, 121
  field, 34, 139 n.56
  military, 28
Sketch-maps, 126, 139 n.56, 315, 371
  sketch-surveys (military), 170, 197
Sketching, 1, 183 n.71, 218 n.55
  background, 282
  diagrammatically, 30
  interior points, 36
Sketchy,
  to a fault, 271
  coverage of basic geographical features, 336
  representations, 70, 271,
  trace enlargements, 358 n.36
Skinners' Company, 180 n.35, 356 n.1
Slope,
  as influence, 202, 439
  measuring (chaining), 298, 320
  shading, 285, 379
Social,
  ambiguity, 33
  classes (planes, levels), 112, 135, 148, 174, 253
  climate, 265
  commentators, 254
  concerns (topics), 176
  context, 2
  handicaps, 346
  history, 23 n. 15
  ladder, 253

motives, 154
scientists (modern), 224
status, 230
Society,
  agrarian, 2, 11
  surveyors' place in, 253
  'stratigraphical column' of, 253
Societies (officially recognised, incorporated, professional), 265, 376, 413, *see also* Institutions,
  Dublin Society (of Artists), 27, 140 n.67, 203, 229, 265, 272, 274–5, 282, 289, 298, 300, 333, 433, 436
  Dublin Philosophical Society, 258 n.46
  Dublin Physico-Historical Society, 335–6, 337, 344, 347
  Geological Society of Dublin, 403 n.29
  Incorporated Society of Solicitors and Attorneys, 104 n. 40
  Irish Society for Archives, Dublin, 186 n.113
  Royal Dublin Society, 219 n. 69, 288 n. 26, 329 n.101
  Royal Society of London, 90
  Social Inquiry Society of Ireland, 405 n.57
  Society of Antiquaries, 336
  Society of Friends Historical Library, 138 n.42
  Society of King's Inns, 116, 137 n.27
  The Honourable the Irish Society, 138 n. 51, 216 n.33
Soil, 168, 170, 200, 394, 401, *see also* Manuring, Rocks, Stones,
  boundaries, 214, 313
  types, 208, 391, 393, 406
Soldiers, 45, 55, 206, *see also* Adventurers,
  English, 28
  foot-soldiers, 68
  provisions for, 60, 62, 79 n.77, 93
  subdivision of lands of, 106
Soldiers'
  claims, 60, 88
  maps, 352
  surveys, 62, 77 n.52, 92
Solutions, *see also* Problems,
  additional staff, 46, 277
  annexing maps to new leases, 115
  appointment of commissioners (court), 200, 397

county maps, 382
invention of isopleth, 70
land confiscation, 28
municipality resolutions, 115
partnership, 378
photographing fragile maps, 86
sub-contracting, 234
survey revision, 147
surveying without measuring angles, 315
terminological simplification, 6
town maps, 120
two-part data collection, 60
tracing Petty lines out on the ground, 90
Sources, 224
   accessible, 367
   alternative, 66, 103 n.28
   badly-documented, 193, 372
   cadastral, 44
   estate surveys as, 332
   inaccessible (obscure) to posterity, 82, 191, 332
   latent, 400
   local, 375
   pre-medieval (medieval, early modern, nineteenth-century) 4, 13, 193
   primary (authentic historical, contemporary), 63, 208, 258 n. 49
   quest for, 54
Sources, of
   error (inaccuracy, weakness), 297, 315, 390
   ideas, 71, 174, 283, 310
   information, 62, 87, 94, 99, 342, 366, 369
   revenue (income), 82, 369
   supply, 83, 230
   variation, 312
Spade, 65, 138 n. 43, 406, 410, *see also* Shovel,
   ridges, 13
Spear-throwing, 6, 8, *see also* Boundary marks
Specialisation (increasing), 338, 387
   county cartography, 353
   county surveys, 347
   map-making, 338
   narrow (mapping estates), 68, 247
   specialities, 199
Specialised,
   measuring apparatus, 1
   occupations, 187
Specialists, 58, 69–70
   draughtsmen, 247
   instrument-makers, 288 n.30
   military engineers, 58
   non-specialists, 396
Spheres of influence (surveyors'), 238, 239, 241, 243, 245, 247
Sports, *see also* Recreation,
   spectator, 246
   sporting venues, 355
Spots,
   beauty-spots, 355
   'on the spot' (residents, proprietors, custodians), 8, 56, 93, 113, 168
   spot-heights, 63, 215 n. 8, 285, 392, 433
Square,
   diagrams, 31
   edges, 32
   grids, 86
   lay-outs, 191
   perches, 13, 406–7
Squares,
   method of (Petty), 316
   optical, 311
   printed, 64, 72, 133
'Squaring and Striping' (programmes), 31, 212, 214, 390, *see also* Triangulation
Squatters, 128–9
Squatting, 112, 114, 131, *see also* Migration
Stables, 155, 409, *see also* Horses
Standing stones, 120, *see also* Antiquities
Stangs, 13, *see also* Roods
State Papers, 52, 219 n.78, 220 n.81, *see also* Papers (collections of),
   calendars of, 11
   Chancery of Ireland, 22, 108 n.104
   Chief Secretary's office, 386 n.76
Stations (survey, surveyors'), 66, 299, 301, 310, 312, 314, 315, 384, 396
Statute measure, 126, 297. *See also* English measure, Perch
'Stepping out' ('pacing'), 133, 217 n.39, 364, *see also* Proctor
Stewards, 129, 187–8, 230, *see also* Agents
   duties of, 268–9
Stippling, 37, 340, *see also* Drawing
Stone, *see also* Geology, Rocks, Soils

limestone-gravel, 128, 203
walls, 155
Stones,
boundary, 118, 208, 377
great, 65
mearing, 399
milestones, 164, 194
tombstones, 302
Stratigraphy, 253, *see also* Metaphors, Society
Strafford Survey of Connaught (1636–40), 52, 59–60, 73, 83, 332, *see also* Down Survey,
coverage, 60, 63–4, 76 n.36, 88
instructions, 59
joint-care of, 55, 59, 63, 136 n.15
maps, 64, 66–7, 83, 102 n.16
reference books (loss of), 82–4, 104 n.44
surveyors, 59, 63, 69
transcripts, 61, 82
use of, 87, 106 n.67, 364, 368
Streams, *see also* Rivers,
boundary, 40, 66, 119, 121
courses of, (alteration, straightening, damming, road crossings), 176, 189, 198, 390
mainstream, 168, 188
mapping of, 189, 311, 390
network density of, 203
Streets, 187, 208, 278, *see also* Lanes, Roads
laying (staking) out of, 155, 191–92, 277, 283
main, 176, 191
street-cleaning, 338
street-indexes, 138 n. 47
street-maps, 396
street-names, 120
street-patterns (networks), 275, 314
wide, 113, 190–93, 277, 323 n. 9
Strip,
definition of, 118
fields (medieval-type), 121
maps (single road, Post Office), 139 n.53, 196, 354
Stripes,
depopulated (amalgamation of), 214
fashion for, 214
for former rundale tenants, 212, 214
Strips (of land), 13
consolidated, 398

curved, 212
narrow, 398
parallel, 316
plough, 208
scattered, 120
Striping, *see also* Squaring,
more common than squaring, 212
programmes, 31
sustaining demand (for surveying expertise), 214
striped farms, 390
Stripers, 212
Structure, *see also* Patterning, Skeleton,
command structure, 73
communal infrastructure, 187
hierarchy of, 29
inquisitorial, 22
occupational, 244, 266, 398, 440
of single-storey thatched dwelling houses, 10
territorial, 32
tier, 5
Styles (of maps), 87, 127, 144, 149, 156, 168, 377, *see also* Decorations, Tastes,
Armstrong, 380
Bath, 350
diocesan (17th century), 335
Down Survey, 66, 365
'French', 167–70, 347
frontier-style surveying technique 120
Gibson and Stokes, 272–3
Hood-McCool, 171–2
Irish (traditional), 391
lettering, 174, 283
Moland, 156
'naive', 186
naturalistic landscaping, 189
of drapery, furniture, monumental masonry, 151
old/modern (new), 4, 21, 159, 305
plain (neutered), 86
plantation survey maps (skeletal), 36, 155, 190
Rocque-Scalé, 160–61, 162, 165–6, 185 n.100, 280, 344
soldier's map, 352
'topographical', 161, 169, 277, 341
Vallencey, 353
Williamson style, 283
Subletting, 112, 128, *see also* Leases
Sub poenas, 395

Subtleties, of, *see also* Hints,
  colour, 166
  offsetting, 313
  shading (of land-use, hills), 166, 380, 399
Suburban, *see also* Rural, Urban,
  housing estates, 400
  inner-suburban portions (of estates), 179 n.9
  properties, 185, 240, 278, 282
'Succession' maps, 148, *see also* Maps
Summits, 66, 401, *see also* Hills
Supervision, 17, *see also* Custodianship, Overseeing
Supervision, of
  estates, 112
  partible inheritance, 206
  surveys, 59, 62, 103, 375, 378, 379
  salaried, 240
Supervisor General, 74 n. 6
Supervisors (of county roads), 252
'Surrounds', 59, 65, 307–08, *see also* Instruments
Survey, *see also* Courts of, Commissions of,
  'benefit of', 131
  costs of, 131, 142 n.103
  maps, 3
Survey and Distribution, Books of, 22, 25 n.36, 26 n.53, 102 n.16, 106 n.67
Surveying, 1–4, *see also* Land surveying, Mapping, Plotting, Protracting
  activity (distribution of), 233, 236–9, 241–5, *see also* seasonal activity
  agencies, 377
  appliances, 295
  art of, 232, 422, 425–6, 428
  as 'spectator sport', 246
  books on, 320, *see also* Literature
  business, 232
  chain, 258 n.41, 315, 430
  charges, 234
  combined surveying and levelling instruments, 305
  community, 227, 232, 336, 377
  comparative, 38, 40, 78 n.62, 92, 105 n.49, 128
  devices, 300
  estate surveying, 286, 345, 353, 377
  exact surveying, 340
  expertise in, 214
  fraternity of, 222
  geodetic, 252, 376
  hills, 298
  history of, 300
  hydrographic, 23 n.2
  industry, 232
  in winter, 244
  instruments, 150, 260 n.85
  Irish, 398
  knowledge, reservoir of, 395
  land, *see under* Land surveying
  literature, 190, 224, 226, 310
  frontier-style, 35, 120
  medium-scale, 202
  methods, 14, 29–30, 35, 62, 64, 90–91, 93–5, 108 n.100, 116, 118, 124, 172, 364
  'old' English, 43, 69
  ordinary, 192–4
  practice of, 64–5
  process of, 68
  profession, 42, 59, 222, 230–31, 265, 269
  public, 273
  purpose of, 30, 73
  resurveying, 62, 84, 308
  seasonal activity, 248
  shift in methods, 20
  styles, 277
  surveying partnerships (firms), 280, 346
  surveying and valuation, 250, 275, 280, 361 n.93, 381, 393
  system of, 430
  'taking a survey', 307
  teaching, 229–31
  techniques, 35, 38, 306
  textbooks, 19, 69, 115, 132, 168, 271, 331
  traditions, 227, 277, 377
  treatises, 277, 430–38
  topographical, 277
  trigonometrical, 252, 376
  uneven ground, 298
  utility of, 278, 304
  woods and forests, 304
Surveyor-General, 19, 41, 46, 72, 98, 370
  certificates, 232, 265
  duties, 95, 98, 99, 100, 274, 417, 419
  fees, 102 n.12

INDEX OF SUBJECTS 521

maps, 86–7, 95
office, 55, 57, 63, 83–6, 96, 98, 99, 226, 367
office holders, 29, 54, 55, 56, 61–2, 74 n.9, 79 n.85, 82, 85, 86, 95, 102 n.21, 273
salary, 26 n.56
Surveyor-General, Deputy, 49 n.58, 54, 83, 85–6, 96, 98, 102 n.14, 107 n.88, 271
Surveyors, 1–2, 6, 8, 10–11, 13, 19, 29, 38, 187–90, 202, 210, 222, *see also* Land surveyors,
American, 255 n.5
archaeologically-minded, 118
autometric, 260 n.78
average, 312, *see also* ordinary
bog-surveyors, 251
certified (registered, chartered), 99, 108 n.107, 140 n.77, 228, 235
chain surveyors, 313
City Surveyors, 99, 137 n.36, 146 182 n.57, 192, 240, 266, 268, 274–5, 295, 303, 338, 419
classification of, 224, 244
commission's surveyors, 278
common, 251–3, 378
compass-surveyors, 305
'country surveyors, 210, 254, 346, 352, *see also* local, regional
'county surveyors', 252
conversant with Irish language, 120
Cork surveyors, 352
Dublin surveyors, 340
definition of, 17, 253, 267
demand for, 227
dynasties of, 228
engineer-surveyors, 137 n.27
English, 39, 43, 172, 183 n.75, 227, 244, 316, 320
estate, 81, 155, 161, 176, 196, 200, 202, 209, 247, 284, 302, 337, 344, 353, 373, 393
farm, 302, 373
fashionable, 346
freelance, 395
French, 247
gardener-surveyors, 189
general, 46, 146–7
'gentlemen' surveyors, 251, 283, 378, 401
graduate, 401

highway, 17
Irish, 170, 176, 227–8, 230, 238, 244, 246, 252, 265–6, 269, 273, 276, 278, 282, 286, 295, 299, 305, 314–16, 318, 320, 323, 324 n.16, 331, 346, 354, 387, 394, 398
immigrant, 223–4
itinerant, 234
land, *see under* Land surveyors
lease, 115
Linen Board, 219 n.69
local, 60, 93, 128, 155, 172, 199, 254, 268, 282, 336, 342, 344, 346, 352
middle-rank, 280
military, 320, 332
'Mr Wiseacre', 295
network of, 232
non-surveyors, 230, 322
official (government, state), 73, 81, 95, 144
ordinary, 64, 73, 202, 331, 337, 388
part-time, 223
permanent, 240
plantation, 43, 55, 73, 81, 87, 101, 190
Post Office, 17, 197, 199, 379
practical, 300
private (independent), 58, 62, 82, 94, 100–01, 116, 152, 234, 240, 242, 271, 273, 308, 320, 373, 390, 397
professional, 63, 130, 204, 212, 250, 322, 335, 371, 373, 397
provenance of, 227
provincial, 337
railway, 218 n.61
regional ('country'), 236, 247–8, 332
resident, 170
revenue, 17, 20
road, 353
sailor-surveyors, 305
Scottish, 227, 256 n.15
subordinate, 200
surveyor-diarists, 91
'surveyor and hydrographer', 272
surveyor-map-sellers, 355
surveyor-philomaths, 185 n.107
surveyor-publishers, 340
surveyor-teachers, 229
tide, 18
town, 81, 192
town-dwelling surveyors, 283
typical surveyors, 253

Ulster surveyors, 282–3
unconnected groups of, 54
Surveyors, of
building and public works, 17
canals, 196
manors, 19, 137 n.37
roads, 121, 198, 216 n.37
'the Crown lands', 283, 442
'the natives', 230
Surveyors', *see also* Surveying,
achievements, 206
'acreages', 19
advertisements, 149, 225, 228–9, 235, 249, 252, 257 n.34, 392
advice to farmers, 406
affidavits, 203
apprentices, 228, 249
art (craft), 54, 58, 68, 76 n.27, 98
careers, 242, 253, 282
chains, 297, 302
charges, 250, 270, 280, 439–43
compass needles, 304
cross, 311
deaths, of, 60, 107 n.89, 127
disagreements (controversies), 132, 249, 254, 411
documents, 52, 101, 132
duties, 204
fees, 130–31, 247, 249, 266, 268–9, 278, 304, 336, 395, 397, 439
field books, 122, 298, 311, 314
field notes, 299, 310, 431
field work, 248
forestaff, 269
Institute, 400, 404
instructions, 59, 66, 69–70, 72, 90, 301
manuals, 318
maps, 113, 232, 313, 321
names (family, surnames), 151, 191. 223, 228, 231, 242, 258 n.49, 274, 276, 289 n.38, 302, 336
oaths, 370
other occupations, 242
pictures of, 302
records, 41, 113, 254
retirement, 244
routines, 133, 345
services, 135
skills, 126, 130, 226, 395
tombstones, 302
training, 224, 252
travel-time, 234
virtues, 255
visits, 40–41
workloads, 234, 238, 242
Surveys, 4, 14, 19, 26 n.61, 363
'ancient', 127, 141 n.82
'balance', 206
barony, 354, 365
bay, 270
bogs, 202, 263 n.120, 378
'book surveys', 366
cadastral, 139 n.57, 369
canal, 196–7, 262 n.105, 335
cartographic, 369
centrally-directed surveys, 372
chain, 299, 315
city, 342
coast, 335
commissions of, 32, 49 n.60
commons, 219 n.80, 220 n.81
compass, 302–03
comprehensive, 147, 373
conflicting (counter, disputed, controverted), 128, 132, 307, 310, 313, 428
control surveys, 334
costs, 206
county, 286, 342, 344–5, 347, 349–51, 353–4, 431
directors of, 55, 72
ecclesiastical, 369
errors in, 40, 92, 130
estate (landowners'), 73, 87, 112, 125, 131, 144–5, 155–6, 158, 161, 174, 247, 268, 273, 276, 284, 306, 332, 342, 347, 350, 389, 391
exact and perfect, 54, 354, 423, 428
examiners, 73
extensive, 148
false, 417
farm, 144, 147, 178 n.5, 199, 238, 244, 246, 271, 314, 316, 322, 364, 379, 395, 398
fortifications, 431
geological, 394
general, 52, 372
glebe terrier survey, 369
government (official, state), 44, 68, 81–2, 86, 114, 370, 391
harbour, 270, 342, 431
'in-farms', 159–60

INDEX OF SUBJECTS 523

'in-fields', 159–60
initial, 31
'joint', 142 n.100, 277
lease, 166
local, 273
manor, 431
military (sketch), 170, 197, 353
measured, 42
national survey and valuation, 286, 377–8, 402 n.11
nation-wide, 52, 71, 375–6
'new', 132, 286, 367, 371, 378
official, 286, 370, 375
of peripheral denominations, 149
of tenements, 149
ordnance, *see under* Ordnance Survey
Post Office (post-road), 353–4
pre-lease, 137 n.26
private, 43, 87, 132, 366, 369, 372
proctor surveys, 364
property, 286, 394
public, 87, 369
regional, 332
revisions, 249, 335
road, 336, 353, 379, 389, 395
sales, for, 112
second, third (re-surveys), 126–30, 244, 344, 354, 372, 392, 400, 427
small, 234
soldiers', 62
statistical, 140 n.67, 209, 306
superimposing surveys, 303
survey-areas, 310, 312, 314, 431
survey lines, 312
survey-polygons, 307
survey stations, 308
timing of, 34
topographical, 28, 271, 314
town, 334, 342
townland, 48 n.49, 77 n.44, 80 n.90, 93, 314, 322, 364, 393, 395
transcripts of, 82
traverse, 296, 310, 313, 315, 439
triangulated, 36
trigonometrical, 285, 403 n.15, 425
urban properties, 120
witnesses, of, 114, 125
Surveys (Named), *see also* People and Place Indexes,
    Adventurers', 62, 70–71, 77 n.51, 92, 222

Armstrong's, 379–80, 382
Ballahanaskadan (Limerick), 76 n.27, 107 n.90
Barker's, 140 n.72
Bodley's (Ulster), 55–6, 58, 82, 87
Boundary (Griffith), 362 n.103
'Civil Survey', 16, 25 n.46, 27 n.65, 60, 68, 366
Clandeboyes 55, 74 n.9
Cromwellian surveys, 56, 60
Cuttle's, 195, 220 n.83
Desmond, 25 n.47
Down Survey (Petty's), 27 n.65, 52, 59, 63–4, 66–73, 82–94, 96, 98, 100, 116, 118, 120, 127, 144, 149, 161, 164, 230, 298–300, 302, 304, 313, 318, 335, 365–6, 369–71, 375, 390–91, 399, 440
Elizabethan (Munster), 70
General, 9, 52, 146–7, 372, 382 n.2
'Gross', 60, 62, 65, 77 n.44
Jobson's, 43, 49 n.62
Johnson's 385 n.55
Mason's 105 n.44, 384 n.38
Midland surveys, 55
Molahiffe (Kerry), 40
Moland's, 126, 267
Munster surveys, 39, 41, 55
North Wexford (Bodley), 55
Offaly, 20
Ordnance, *see under* Ordnance Survey
Pattison's, 173
Plantation surveys, 35–6, 52, 56, 58, 63, 82, 145, 149, 228, 232, 266, 295, 308, 332
Plunkett and McDermott's, 181 n.51
Pynner's, 55, 59
Raven's, 58, 75 n.24, 139 n.60, 149, 154–5, 306
Robins's, 34, 41–2
Rocque's, 163, 184 n.90, 192, 279, 358 n.41
Scalé's, 128, 136 n.12, 162, 167, 179 n.15, 181 n.47, 184 n.93, 290 n.57, 342
Sherrard and Brassington's, 137 n.33, 169, 179 n.22, 201
Smith's, 142 n.94
Stokes's, 117, 271, 337
Strafford's (Connaught), 52, 55, 59–61, 63–4, 66–7, 73,

524 PLANTATION ACRES: THE IRISH LAND SURVEYOR AND HIS MAPS

76 nn.36,40, 78 n.58, 83, 87–8,
102 n.16, 104 n.44, 106 n.67,
136 n.15, 332, 364, 368
Travers', 185 n.105
Trustees' (1700–03), 72–3, 80 n.90,
83–4, 87, 96, 104 n.35, 152, 229,
269, 273, 295, 316
Ulster (1609), *see* Bodley's
Vallancey's, 101 n.7, 353
West Riding (Yorks), 26 n.49
White Knight's country, 43, 49 n.58
Wicklow, 55, 243, 364, *see also* Pynner's
Worsley's, 56, 440, *see also* Cromwellian
Wren's, 344
Young's, 204
Symbolic (human figures), 151
Symbolising (connection between
geographical and cadastral maps), 161
Symbolism,
dislike of written explanations, 162,
'getting it right' (on maps), 170
Symbols, 23 n.8, 131, *see also* Images,
Pictures, Signs,
arable, 162
address, 243
block-plan (planiform), 155, 172, 285,
348–9
boundary junction-symbols, 116, 152,
168
furrow, 164, 172, 285
green herringbone, 162
hill, 339–40
house-symbols, 151, 183 n.75
minor, 392
paling, 154
profile (hill), 164
tree, 154
Systems of,
cartography, 167
certification, 99, 265
classification (cartography), 68
inheritance (gavelkind), 6
land assessment (valuation), 373, 377
landscape organisation ('townland',
rundale, open-field), 23 n.10, 112,
120, 208–10, 212, 231, 399
land surveying (non-arbitrary acreages,
discredited, setbacks, scope,
prevailing, 5, 14, 62, 69, 73, 84, 93,
95, 226, 314–15, 318, 395, 430, 436

lease maps, 158
manors (manorial), 146
mensuration (modern), 125
'middlemen', 133
Ordnance Survey (rectangular maps),
146
parishes (parochial), 364
premiums (Dublin Society), 203
recording (surveyors' work), 41
roads, 121
systematic anticipation of demand, 86
tithes, 369
transcripts (Petty), 82
tenurial systems, 143 n. 112, 231

Tacheometry, 302
Talent,
and heredity, 227
and pay, 251, 253
cartographic, 28, 334
gardening, 190
Talents,
combined, 202, 230, 271, 347, 376
in question, 372
Taste, *see also* Distaste, Styles,
foretaste of future, 19, 249
lads of, 228
matters of, 174
of advertisers, 283
present, 248
reasons of, 151
Tasteful (lettering styles), 283
Tates (land measure), 5, 12, 125, 363
Taverns, 254, *see also* Inns
Tax, 363, 365, *see also* Cess, County cess,
Tithes
assessment, 322, 364
burden, 367
levels of, 4, 102 n.15
local, 9
payment, 110
Taxpayers, 209
Teachers, *see under* Schoolmasters
Teaching, *see also* Schools,
about Elizabethan mapmaking, 43
land surveying as an art, 23 n.2
of brethren of official land surveyors in
private sector, 73
profession, 230
self-teaching, 188, 222

INDEX OF SUBJECTS   525

Teachings (about surveying without
  measuring angles), 315
Telescopes (telescopic sights), 269, 306
Tenement,
  maps, 156, 159, 398
  survey, 146, 149
  valuation, 394
Tenements, 19, 21, 25 n. 43, 112, 154
  colouring of, 137 n. 28, 152, 166
  omission of, 167
  sizes of, 159
Tenure, 19, 158. 376, *see also* Proprietorship,
  change of, 208
  con acre (corn acre), 138 n.43
  territorial extent of, 373
  systems of, 143 n. 112, 231
Tenurial,
  acreages, 390
  arrangements, 45
  bargains, 166
  boundaries, 390
  circumstances, 45
  data, 150
  features, 172
Terminology,
  clarification of, 1
  of medieval boundary descriptions, 3
  of surveyors, 312, 317
  modern (international), 315, 399
Terrain,
  forfeited, 29
  'open-field', 172
  quality (character) of , 51, 121, 238
  quantity of, 40
  terra Incognita, 145
Terriers,
  glebe terriers, 369, 372, 383 n.36
  terriers accompanying maps (leases, conveyances), 66, 89, 115, 157
  'terrier-charts' (ter-chart, terre chart), 113, 136 n.9, 373
  terrier definition, 384 n. 40
Territorial,
  blocks, 51
  boundaries, 15, 64, 66, 83, 217 n.39, 310, 368, 388
  boundary changes, 72
  considerations, 285
  disputes, 116, 369
  divisions, 5, 12, 115, 380

  extent, 133, 144, 238, 373
  hierarchies, 5, 144, 368, 377
  inscriptions, 37
  names, 37
  organisation, 25 n.35
  range, 236, 236
  scope, 280
  settlements, 52
  structure (native), 32
  units, 6, 73, 89, 146, 367
Territories, *see also* Catrons, Ploughlands,
  Perambulation,
  allotted to (Boards of Poor Law
    Guardians), 375
  assigned to (surveyors), 75 n.24
  common denominators of, 11, 15
  compact, 236
  Irish, 16
  larger, 5, 347
  lists of, 11, 37
  maps of, 79 n.72
  middle of, 36
  network of, 4, 62
  overlapping, 64
  under survey, 15
  un-Irish, 16
  variation of (qualitative), 10, 75 n.25
Textbooks (surveying), 35, 57, 250, 306,
  320, *see also* Books, Surveying,
  English, 18, 33, 132, 226, 289 n.43
  Irish, 69, 90, 115, 130, 151, 272, 296,
    299, 305, 310, 319, 331, 429–38
Theodelitus, 34, *see also* Instruments
Theodolite, 272, 285, 303, 307-8, 313, 348,
  356, 357, 398
Theoreticians (theorists), 322
  Evans, Eyre, 1
  Harding, Thomas, 304
  Petty, William, 52, 29, 318
  Wood, Dr R., 318
Theories (of), 2, 15, 32, 52, 59, 70, 89,
  435–6
  ancient Irish, 158
  cartographic evolution, 121, 156, 159
  checking fragmentary evidence against
    tithe applotment books, 371
  comparative acreage, 322
  enclosure 206
  estate and farm surveys, 247
  ideal farm shapes, 203

land-reclamation, 204
land-surveying, 98, 222, 240, 310, 312, 433
link between cess and plantation, 363
road design, 197
rundale, 208
Third, *see also* First, Second,
admeasurements, 391
dimension, 274
maps, 391
surveys, 128, 392, 427
surveyors, 142 n.100
'Threads' (of property boundaries), 400
Tidal (phenomena), 272, *see also* Sea
Tide surveyors, 18, 200, *see also* Land, surveyors, Marine features
Tie lines, 122, *see also* Lines
Tillage, 128, 152, 162, 172, 391 *see also* Grass, Meadows, Pasture,
enlargement of, 383 n.28
fit for, 138 n.43
in, 408
profitable, 128
spread of, 208
under, 364
Time (Future, Past, Present), 10, 35, 125, 130, 138 n.45, 196, 146, 298, 364, 387
Future (foretaste of, leap into, forecast), 19, 168, 318
change, 248
conquest or reconquest (of townlands), 149
date, 191
demand, 86
experts (researchers, research), 12, 188, 256 n.15, 366
landscape changes, 130
livelihood (employment), 32, 346
map-users, 84
Ordnance Survey maps, 394
output, 146
partners, 276
patronage
plans, 407
prices, 442
reference, 344
rent-levels (predicting), 70
resolutions, 115
sales, 397
surveys (chaining), 129, 131, 423
mapping the future, 187

Past
break with the, 272, 376
common in the, 298
debt to the, 388
justified in the, 364
outgrowing the, 174
landscape changes, 130
output, 146
practice, 138 n.45
pre-cartographic past, 8
survey methods of the, 30
'unremembered past recaptured', 215 n.17
Present,
at, 10, 12, 114, 172, 174, 188, 212, 236, 278, 286, 386, 430, 434
context, 10, 196, 387, 396
generation, 52, 387
mapping the, 187
present-day (maps, cartographic meaning, capital city, streets), 41, 161, 275, 278
practice, 138 n.45
purposes, 4, 20, 303
state of scholarship, 35
state of the adventurers, 77 n.49
state of the county, 355
systems, 218 n.55
taste, 248
the present book, 2
the present essay, 15, 81, 125
the present purpose, 20, 303
the present study, 23 n.2
the present writer, 78 n.64
the present work, 257, 32
time, 218 n.55
year, 287 n.6
Tithe, proctors, 133, 364
Tithes, 95, 364, 369–71, 373, 375, 444, *see also* Tax
Topographical,
criticism, 70
data (information), 121, 166, 238
dictionary, 280
description, 4
draughtsmen (artists), 153, 166
engineers, 251–2, 280, 286, 354, 376, 378
features (details, entities), 71, 117, 144, 152, 396

guidance, 39
history, 6
interests, 2, 161
knowledge, 196
literature, 4
manner (method, school, style, treatment), 162–3, 164–5, 169, 277, 314, 338, 341, 379–80, 431, 434
maps, 1, 35, 148, 162, 284, 335, 344, 352, 366, 389, 400
portraits, 391
prints, 402 n.28
surveys, 28, 271, 314
Topographers, 161, 164, 166–8, 170, 191, 267
Topography (subordination to proprietorship, 119
Tourist resorts, 332
Towers (church), 120, 202
ivory-tower assumption (about misclosures), 308
Townlands, 5–6
atlas of, 392
bisection (subdiving) of, 156, 200, 368
boundaries of, 66, 116, 159, 166, 170, 198, 311–14, 321, 380, 386 n.72
comparison with 'townships' (Scotland), 285
'diagrammatic', 379
disputed areas of, 268
exchanges of land in, 220 n.83
index maps of, 7, 184 n.96, 356 n. 1
mapping of, 164, 361 n.83
measures of, 57, 268, 368
names of, 120, 365
networks (meshes) of, 6, 150, 202
official delimitation of, 387
problems with in towns, 120
Protestant, 366
relations of (to roads), 354
surveys of, 48 n. 48, 286, 364, 389, 393, 395, 440
system of, 23 n.10
valuations of, 262 n.109, 387
Towns, 30, 65, 101 n.2, 113, 115, 150, 181 n.40, 193, 241, 336
amenities, 244
cartographers, 155
clerk's office, 113
east-coast, 115
estate, 190

fortified, 180, 332
improvements (extensions), 192
lands, 115
maps, 161, 183 n.75, 267, 287 n.7, 332, 336, 340, 352
market, 236, 338
new, 75 n.24, 190–91, 215 n.14, 283
Ordnance maps, 7
owners of, 120, 154, 164
plans, 28, 138, 155, 164–5, 176, 190–91, 293 n.97, 328 n.92, 337, 340, 342–3, 356 n.1, 396, 402 n.11, 403 n.26
property in, 108 n.106, 135 n.6, 282
provincial, 247, 261 n.92, 392, 395
roads, 119
schools, 229
shops, 244
sites, 113
small-town characters, 192, 238, 247
streets, 193
surveyors, 81, 155, 192, 247, 259 n.70, 283, 346–7
surveys, 120, 297, 306, 334
town-dwellers, 60, 247
townlands in, 120
Townships, 3, 115, 285
Traces (of evidence), 8, 97, 112, 227, 315, 352
Tracing,
boundaries, 40, 57, 83, 90, 95, 98, 104 n.35, 276, 358,
cartographic influences, 167–8, 172, 279
map, 78, 87, 104 n.41, 137 n.38
method, 91, 103 n.26, 392, 431
survey lines, 90–91, 358. 64
survival of land units (enclosures), 125, 155
Trade,
in derivative estate maps, 392 397
mechanical, 253
retail, 277
stock-in-trade, 90
tricks of the trade, 295
trademarks, 168, 283
Tradesmen, 68
jacks-of-all-trades, 192
trading on reputation, 272
Transcripts (system of), 82, *see also* Manuscripts, Mis-transcription

Transcripts, of,
    county books, 382 n.5
    family diaries, 404 n.31
    maps, 82, 349
    surveys, 25 n.47, 61, 82
Transit of Mercury, 352
Transition,
    career, 81
    land quality, 162
Transitional (figures), 251, 354
Translation, of
    acreage and linear distance, 194
    (confiscated) ploughlands, 3, 367
    Gaelic names
    medieval documents, 4
    reasoning into practical terms, 236, 371, see also Theories
Trapeziums, 316–17
Traverse,
    lines, 66, 313–14
    stations, 64, 312
    surveys, 296, 310, 313–14, 439
    tables, 316, 432–3
Traverses, see also Triangulation,
    boundary, 35–6, 41, 57, 308
    closed, 35–6, 316
    method of, 59, 271, 308, 310, 313–15, 317–18, 320, 345, 388, 424
    road, 198, 335, 354
Trees, 8, 65–6, 138
    as boundary markers, 116, 118, 203
    'remarkable' (old), 137 n.30, 345
    tree-plantations, 189, 250, 395
    tree symbols, 154, 162
    whitethorn, 176
Triads (church, inn, blacksmith's shop), 208, see also Trios, Clusters
Triangles, 31, 314, 329 n.102, 403 n.15, see also Squares
    chain, 388
    'fat' and 'thin', 176
    networks (meshes) of, 35, 66, 314
    use of, 64, 133, 154, 314, 316–17, 422
Triangulation, 35, see also Squaring, Traversing,
    accuracy of, 285
    chain, 328 n.94
    diagrams, 284, 349–50
    general (of Ireland), 286

of farms, 252
'simple', 314
triangulated surveys, 36, 315, 336, 348
Trigonometrical,
    calculation (calculators), 418, 423, 425, 428
    control (basis, skeleton, foundations), 73, 202, 345, 353–4, 378, 388
    data, 350
    maps, 354
    operations (functions), 202, 318
    stations, 380, 392
    surveying (surveys), 252, 285, 376, 437–8
    surveyors, 280
Trigonometry, 229, 286, 433, 436, see also Geometry
Trios, see also Triads,
    three (of dots), 166
    unique (Scalé, Sherrard, Brownrigg), 276
Trips (road, boat), 268, 353
Trouble, 369, 390, 414, 431–2, 435, see also Conflict,
    chain of, 415
    taking (saving, causing), 35, 52, 85, 120, 133, 156, 206, 253, 280, 306–07, 316, 393, 430
    trouble-shooters (cartographic), 55
    troublesome methods (states, problems), 14, 18, 93, 367, 441
    troubling, 423
Troubles (dangers), 38, 45, 127, 131, 144, 254, 370
Trousers (surveyors'), 253
Trustees' Survey, 72, 83, 88, 96, 152, see also Surveys (Named),
    maps, 83–4, 86–7, 104, 269
    methods, 72–3, 80 nn.90,91, 295, 316
    personnel, 73, 81, 229, 266–7, 269, 271, 273, 289 n.35
    plans, 72
Tumbrels (tumbrel boxes, cars), 408, 410
Turnpike,
    gates, 164
    legislation, 197
    roads, 198, 217 n.43
    trusts, 187,
Turf, 6, see also Bogs,
    'breast' (face) dividing cut from uncut, 133

INDEX OF SUBJECTS 529

salaried supervision of, 240
turf soil, 406–08
Typical, 266, *see also* Individual, Untypical,
   appeal to money as ultimate criterion,
     298
   atlas (18th century), 150
   dependence (on word-of-mouth
     communication), 113
   document (13th century), 11
   estate, 110
   estate (lease) map, 152, 158, 285
   estate office, 389
   imprecision (18th century), 197
   Irish bipartisanship, 370
   Irish county map-maker, 346
   Irish features (of Rocque's career), 227
   manner, 40
   map (Down and Strafford Surveys),
     66, 98, 339
   of genre, 411
   Protestant Irish landlord (18th century),
     110
   rundale features, 209
   school (mathematical) curriculum, 229
   style (Down Survey, 18th century),
     171, 365
   surveyor, 190, 253, 302
   townland, 120
   versatility (of new immigrant
     generation), 226

Uncultivated lands (tracts), 6, 112, 125,
   233, 238, *see also* Waste, Cultivation
'Undisposed lands', 96
Unemployment ('frictional'), 238, *see also*
   Employment
Uniform,
   application of colours, 152
   base map, 167
   practice, 415
   principles, 372
   speed of change, 326 n.44
   standards (homogeneity), 54, 232, 377
   survey of Ireland, 375
   textures, 174
   vagueness about 'acres', 12
Uniformity (nameless), 390, *see also*
   Diversity

Units, 12, 147, *see also* Acres, Content,
   Quarters, Cartrons, Perches, Ploughlands,
   Size, Townlands,
   ancient (medieval, historic), 6, 14–15,
     89, 125, 363
   choice of (appropriate, unsuitable), 45,
     297, 338
   difficulty of distinguishing
     (reconciling), 12, 16, 58, 124, 194
   English, 58
   Irish, 17, 20
   large (larger, largest), 236, 377
   normal, 208
   original acre-units, 13
   per unit-area (unit cost), 100, 124,
     368, 439
   seventeenth-century, 25 n.36
   small (smaller, smallest, lowest), 10,
     13–14, 73, 144, 234, 236, 238,
     323
   supposedly less inconstant (vague,
     variable), 15, 29
   territorial, 6, 146, 367
Units, of
   cattle capacity, 125
   land reckoning, 9, 118, 122
   land measurement, 10, 15, 17, 61,
     108 n.100, 123, 139 n.60
   selling and letting, 112
'Unite' (surveys), 149, *see also* Integrate
Unity, of
   estates, 147–8, 234
   Irish map-making, 161
   surveying profession, 265
Unprecedented, *see also* Precedents,
   heavy wheat crop, 203
   large amount of mapping, 68
   lawyers preferring maps to words, 89
Untypical (educated in England), 43,
   see also Typical
Uplands, 72, 124, 209, *see also* Lowlands
Urban, *see also* Rural, *see also* Suburban,
   house-plots, 72
   lay-outs (designs), 190, 193
   street networks, 314
Urbanism (Irish Georgian), 192
Urbanity, 247

Validation, 77 n.53, 89, 302
Validity, 40, 84–5, 95, 120, 300
Valleys, 37, 65, 162, 245, 282, *see also* Ridges
Valuation, 9, 159, 251, 262 n.109, 394, *see also* Evaluation
   annual, 364
   appeal against, 370
   authenticity of, 370
   'casting up' (with maps), 395, 441
   Commissioners for Affairs of Ireland on the valuation of lands, 27 n.62, 405 n.62
   Commissioner of Valuation, 400
   of land and buildings (need for its own historian), 20, 387, 439
   methods (principles) of, 20, 158, 166, 403 n.30
   problems of, 373
   re-valuation, 405 n.60
   Select committee on the survey and valuation of Ireland, 360 n.75, 376
   survey and valuation, 102 n.13, 132, 170, 250, 277, 280, 286, 361 n.93, 379, 381, 443
   valuation and rent-fixing, 125
Valuation department (OS), 389
Valuation Office (government), 209, 359 n.65, 390–91, 394, 398
   farm maps, 402 n.11
Valuations,
   county, 375, 383n.25, 385 n.
   faulty (bad), 143 n.108, 372
   general v. of Ireland, 402 n.13
   independent, 250, 280
   local, 379
   parish (tithe), 372
   Poor Law Union, 375
   tenement, 394
   town, 403 n.26
   townland, 379
Valuators (land), 199, 226, 250–51, 393
   chief government valuator, 371
   government, 380, 385 n.67
   leading, 442
   nineteenth-century, 394
   talents of, 372, 394
   Ulster, 280
Vegetation (cover), 439
   representation (on maps), 162, 170
Vellum, 166, 261 n.92, *see also* Parchment

Vergers, 273, *see also* Churchwardens
Verge, of
   extinction (of rundale system), 210
   the topographical, 70
Vergers, 273, *see also* Church
Verges, 119, 189, *see also* Features (map)
Vernier scale, 304, 306, 436, *see also* Scale
Viewing, 19–22, 48 n.44, 49 n.58, 54, 74 n.12, 274, *see also* Estimation, Interviewing, Reviewing,
   exact and superficial, 52
   single comprehensive, 149, 162, 276, 432
   suitable, 82
Viewers, 170, 178 n.2, 282, 298, 316, 428, 439
Views, *see also* Prospects, Vistas,
   battle-views, 50 n.76
   best (of estates, houses, scenery), 148, 151, 160, 168, 182 n.53, 189
   broader (wider), 47 n.15, 161
   comparable (comparative), 137 n.37, 434
   contrary, 79 n.77
   endorsing, 224
   first and last (of the land surveyor), 4, 387, 406
   implicit, 144
   indulgent, 396
   local, 284
   long, 401
   marginal, 345, 396
   of non-Irish commentators, 127
   partial, 286
   pessimistic, 401
   points of (business), 346
   profile or half-profile (of houses), 155
   public, 413
   purview (of land surveyor), 396
   superficial (of evidence), 125
   support of views, 145
Villa-belts, 276, *see also* Suburban
Village (amenities), 244
Villages, *see also* Hamlets,
   centrally-placed, 150
   country, 229
   Deserted Village (Goldsmith), 230
   English village plan, 209
   manorial (landlord), 31, 112, 152, 154–5, 188
   mears of, 75 n.25

INDEX OF SUBJECTS 531

new, 191, 193
open-field (English Pale), 120, 208
rundale, 208
Vision,
   intellectual (narrowness of), 345
   of a general triangulation (of Ireland), 286
   panoramic (of Irish mapmaking), 286
Vistas, 154, 189, *see also* Ornamental features, Views
Visualisation, of
   areas (as rectangles), 13
   buildings (in context), 188
   maps (as books, not collections of sheets or rolls), 148
   'plotting' (as use of plane table), 34
   'qualities', 159
   topographical engineers (in agrarian settings), 252
Vocabulary, of
   Irish placenames, 71
   land management, 18
   surveyors, 246

Wages, *see also* Income, Salaries,
   application (claim) for increase of, 39, 135
   daily, 44
Walking, 72, 126, 189, 264 n.132, 294 n.115, 313, 364, 410, *see also* Perambulation, Riding
Walls, 6, 152, 162, 189, 298, 402 n. 12, *see also* Town walls,
   boundary, 65–6, 162
   church, 217 n. 39
   demesne, 187
   stable, 409
   stone-walled house, 155–6, 189
   walled-garden, 154
   wall-maps, 144, 154, 183 n.75
Wars, 20, 38, 331–2, *see also* Conflict, Calm, Quiet, Peace,
   American War of Independence, 360 n.79
   class war, 253
   Cromwell's wars, 60
   Elizabeth's war against Desmond, 28
   First World War, 400
   Irish civil war (1922), 86
   man-of-war, 388

   Napoleonic wars, 132, 187, 200, 206, 443
   Seven Years War, 85
   theatres of war, 28
   Tyrone wars, 44–5, 51, 55
   war of landlord *versus* tenant, 246
   Williamite wars, 72
Wartime, 1, *see also* Peacetime
Waste, 6, 33, 36, 38, 40, 48 n.44, 138 n.43, *see also* Bogs,
   reclamation, 112, 204, 370, 372
   surveying, 304
Water, *see also* Rivers, Lakes/Loughs, Ponds, Maritime,
   high water mark, 119
   water-cuts, 137 n.30
   waterfalls, 65
   water supply (pipes), 270, 337
Wattles, 409–10
Weapons, of
   armed guards for Down Survey, 304
   critics of Ordnance Survey, 199
Weather, *see also* Climate,
   fair, 34
   foul (bad, inclement), 33, 34, 238, 407, 426
   summer, 32
Weathering (hostile criticism), 342
Weirs, fish, 10, 168
Wheel,
   wheel-barrows, 410
   wheeled cars (tumbrels), 408
Wheels, (measuring instruments, odometers), 300, 324 nn.20, 21
Wide streets commission (Dublin), 113, 192, 277, 323 n.9, 328 n.78, *see also* Streets
'Woodland acre', 15, *see also* Acres
'Woodland perch', 142, *see also* Perches
Woods, mapping of, 36, 67, 147, 154, 164, 170, 380, 384
Woods and Forests, Office of, 88
'Workmen', 68, 226, 389
Work-room (of land surveyor), 161
Work-sharing, 193
World,
   all the, 88, 127, 161, 331
   atlas, 248
   cartography, 286
   coming down in the, 253
   first land measurer of the, 222

market, 332
old, 32
own, 33
parts of the, 15
War (First), 400
'Worlds', of
ancient and modern fiction-writers, 54
books, 355
farm and estate surveying, 202
mapmakers, 354
non-estate maps, 161
traditional Irish land survey, 162
Wretches, 268, 415
Writs, of, *see also* Law, Legal,
dower, 94
perambulation, 107 n. 82
Writing (on maps), 154, 178, 231, 251, 283, 285, 382, 395, *see also* Drawing

Yards (length),
combinations of (perches), 295
'correct to nearest', 197
five and a half (one perch), 122
fourteen (Pierce's leap), 345
seven (one perch), 122, 295
standard, 295
twenty-two (English), 297, 323 n. 7
twenty-eight (Irish), 297
Yards (space),
church, 203
dairy, 176
farm, 208, 410
house, 112

Zenith (cartographic), 334
Zincography, 79 n.83, 397

www.ingramcontent.com/pod-product-compliance
Lightning Source LLC
Chambersburg PA
CBHW020348080526
44584CB00014B/928